Newman on Worship, Reverence, and Ritual

A Selection of Texts

❧

JOHN HENRY NEWMAN

Newman on Worship, Reverence, and Ritual

A Selection of Texts

❧

edited by

Peter A. Kwasniewski

Os Justi Press

2019

This book collects excerpts from a variety of works written by
John Henry Newman (1801–1890).

ISBN 978-0-359-96995-1

Os Justi Press
www.peterkwasniewski.com/osjusti

Table of Contents

Editor's Note

NEWMAN'S life and thought were permeated with the ceremonies and hallowed texts of the Christian liturgy, which he performed daily for over six decades, starting as an Anglican deacon in 1824 and ending as a Cardinal of the Holy Roman Church. It is therefore no surprise that allusions to liturgical rites are ubiquitous in Newman's writings, principally in two contexts: first, when he is preaching on the reverent worship Christians owe to God, and second, when he is dilating upon the corruptions (real or imagined) of Roman Catholicism. The formal, public, solemn liturgy of the Church—the Anglican at first, and after his conversion, the Catholic—is taken as the model and best realization of the believer's trustful yielding of himself to his Maker and Redeemer.

It is a splendid challenge to select, from Newman's luxuriant wealth of writings, texts that best illustrate his thinking on worship, reverence, and ritual. Biographers of Newman have often remarked on the constancy and stability of his intellectual perspective across all of the phases of his life, in spite of an intense spiritual pilgrimage and momentous outward changes. Developments there are, to be sure, but they seem to be the elaborations of a single idea or a single cluster of ideas—making his own life a vivid example of the very thesis he was to argue concerning the Catholic Church in *An Essay on the Development of Christian Doctrine*. While the majority of writings contained herein are from Newman's Anglican period (particularly from the eight volumes of the incomparable *Parochial and Plain Sermons*), there is very little in their content that would even need to be rewritten, let alone retracted, by a Roman Catholic.

Newman's work is rooted in a deeply personal conviction of the infinite holiness of God, to which the only appropriate response is a profound reverence towards God in Himself and in all His works, natural and supernatural. This, I believe, accounts for the sober earnestness, filial fear, and restrained fervor that pervade his sermons, letters, diaries, novels, and poetry. He is a man who lives in the sight of God, whose presence is not merely a truth acknowledged by the intellect, but a reality felt in the heart: *cor ad cor loquitur*. He can speak so movingly about rites and ceremonies because in them he encounters Christ and His friends, the saints. The "ordinances" of the Church, her rich panoply of liturgies handed down across the ages and the manifold devotions that spontaneously arise in their midst, are, for Newman, doors or windows into the heavenly society for which we were created and to which God is calling us. We commune with Him above all in those moments when we come together for divine worship, in the company of our brethren, the great Mother of God and the holy angels, and all of our righteous forefathers singing the high praises of God in the court of heaven.

This volume has been compiled from texts available in the public domain, which, fortunately, are copious.[1] Generally, texts that illuminate the spiritual meaning and value of religious rites were preferred over texts that drill into remote historical issues, internal Anglican disputes, or the ins and outs of the breviary.[2] I include a few texts connected with the liturgical *cultus* of the Blessed Virgin Mary, but there is much more to Newman's Mariology, as can be seen in the secondary literature.[3] Again, a few passages touching on the veneration of saints will have to stand as examples of his hagiographical writing and his preaching occasioned by saints' feasts.

The contents are presented in chronological order of publication, to make it easy to distinguish which period of Newman's life one is in contact with: his Anglican period, his initial years as a Catholic convert, or his later career. Punctuation, spelling, and notes are those of the original editions.

From the time they were first published, Newman's writings have never ceased to benefit the Body of Christ on earth. I have no doubt that the eloquent, moving, incisive, wise reflections contained in this book will be a blessing for readers today who seek the Lord's face. Not abandoning us as orphans, Our Lord—already in this vale of shadows and images—shares the light of His countenance with us in the inherited rites and ceremonies of Holy Mother Church. As Newman says more than once, we are given our time on earth to begin to live, through personal prayer and corporate worship, the life of the blessed in heaven.

Peter A. Kwasniewski

September 14, 2019
Exaltation of the Holy Cross

---

[1] Thus we do not draw upon the volumes of private letters and diaries or the papers Newman left unpublished during his lifetime See, e.g., J. H. Newman, *Sermons 1824–1843, Volume I: Sermons on the Liturgy and Sacraments and on Christ the Mediator* (Oxford: Oxford University Press, 1992).

[2] See Donald Withey, *John Henry Newman: The Liturgy and the Breviary. Their Influence on His Life as an Anglican* (London: Sheed & Ward, 1992).

[3] See, e.g., Philip Boyce, ed., *Mary: The Virgin Mary in the Life and Writings of John Henry Newman* (Grand Rapids: Eerdmans, 2002); Nicholas L. Gregoris, *The Daughter of Eve Unfallen. Mary in the Theology and Spirituality of John Henry Newman* (Pine Beach, NJ: Newman House Press, 2017).

Newman in choir dress

Thoughts Respectfully Addressed to the Clergy
On Alterations in the Liturgy[†]

TTEMPTS are making to get the Liturgy altered. My dear Brethren, I
beseech you, consider with me, whether you ought not to resist the
alteration of even one jot or tittle of it. Though you would in your
own private judgments wish to have this or that phrase or arrangement
amended, is this a time to concede one tittle?

Why do I say this? because, though most of you would wish some immaterial points altered, yet not many of you agree in those points, and not many
of you agree what is and what is not immaterial. If all your respective emenda-
tions are taken, the alterations in the Services will be extensive; and though
each will gain something he wishes, he will lose more from those alterations
which he did not wish. Tell me, are the present imperfections (as they seem to
each) of such a nature, and so many, that their removal will compensate for
the recasting of much which each thinks to be no imperfection, or rather an
excellence?

There are persons who wish the Marriage Service emended; there are
others who would be indignant at the changes proposed. There are some who
wish the Consecration Prayer in the Holy Sacrament to be what it was in King
Edward's first book; there are others who think this would be an approach to
Popery. There are some who wish the imprecatory Psalms omitted; there are
others who would lament this omission as savouring of the shallow and detestable liberalism of the day. There are some who wish the Services shortened;
there are others who think we should have far more Services, and more frequent attendance at public worship than we have.

How few would be pleased by *any given* alterations; and how many
pained!

But once begin altering, and there will be no reason or justice in stopping, till the criticisms of all parties are satisfied. Thus, will not the Liturgy be
in the evil case described in the well-known story, of the picture subjected by
the artist to the observations of passers-by? And, even to speak at present of
comparatively immaterial alterations, I mean such as do not infringe upon the
doctrines of the Prayer Book, will not it even with these be a changed book,

---

† *Tracts for the Times*, Tract 3. First published in 1833.

and will not that new book be for certain an inconsistent one, the alterations being made, not on principle, but upon chance objections urged from various quarters?

But this is not all. A taste for criticism grows upon the mind. When we begin to examine and take to pieces, our judgment becomes perplexed, and our feelings unsettled. I do not know whether others feel this to the same extent, but for myself, I confess there are few parts of the Service that I could not disturb myself about, and feel fastidious at, if I allowed my mind in this abuse of reason. First, e.g. I might object to the opening sentences; "they are not evangelical enough; CHRIST is not mentioned in them; they are principally from the Old Testament." Then I should criticise the exhortation, as having too many words, and as antiquated in style. I might find it hard to speak against the Confession; but "the Absolution," it might be said, "is not strong enough; it is a mere declaration, not an announcement of pardon to those who have confessed." And so on.

Now I think this unsettling of the mind a frightful thing; both to ourselves, and more so to our flocks. They have long regarded the Prayer Book with reverence as the stay of their faith and devotion. The weaker sort it will make sceptical; the better it will offend and pain. Take, e.g. an alteration which some have offered in the Creed, to omit or otherwise word the clause, "He descended into *hell.*" Is it no comfort for mourners to be told that CHRIST Himself has been in that unseen state, or Paradise, which is the allotted place of sojourn for departed spirits? Is it not very easy to explain the ambiguous word, is it any great harm if it is misunderstood, and is it not very difficult to find any substitute for it in harmony with the composition of the Creed? I suspect we should find the best men in the number of those who would retain it as it is. On the other hand, will not the unstable learn from us a habit of criticising what they should never think of but as a divine voice supplied by the Church for their need?

But as regards ourselves, the Clergy, what will be the effect of this temper of innovation in us? We have the power to bring about changes in the Liturgy; shall we not exert it? have we any security, if we once begin, that we shall ever end? Shall not we pass from non-essentials to essentials? And then, on looking back after the mischief is done, what excuse shall we be able to make for ourselves for having encouraged such proceedings at first? Were there grievous errors in the Prayer Book, something might be said for beginning, but who can point out any? cannot we very well *bear* things as they are? does any part of it seriously disquiet us? no—we have before now freely given our testimony to its accordance with Scripture.

But it may be said that "we must conciliate an outcry which is made; that some alteration is demanded." By whom? no one can tell who cries, or who can be conciliated. Some of the laity, I suppose. Now consider this carefully. Who are these lay persons? Are they serious men, and are their consciences involuntarily hurt by the things they wish altered? Are they not rather the men you meet in company, worldly men, with little personal religion, of lax conversation and lax professed principles, who sometimes perhaps come to Church, and then are wearied and disgusted? Is it not so? You have been dining, perhaps, with a wealthy neighbour, or fall in with this great Statesman, or that noble Land-holder, who considers the Church two centuries behind the world, and expresses to you wonder that its enlightened members do nothing to improve it. And then you get ashamed, and are betrayed into admissions which sober reason disapproves. You consider, too, that it is a great pity so estimable or so influential a man should be disaffected to the Church; and you go away with a vague notion that something must be done to conciliate such persons. Is this to bear about you the solemn office of a GUIDE and TEACHER in Israel, or to *follow a lead*?

But consider what are the concessions which would conciliate such men. Would immaterial alterations? Do you really think they care one jot about the verbal or other changes which some recommend, and others are disposed to grant? whether "the unseen state" is substituted for "hell," "condemnation" for "damnation," or the order of Sunday Lessons is remodeled? No;—they dislike the *doctrine* of the Liturgy. These men of the world do not like the anathemas of the Athanasian Creed, and other such peculiarities of our Services. But even were the alterations, which would please them, small, are they the persons whom it is of use, whom it is becoming to conciliate by going out of our way?

I need not go on to speak against doctrinal alterations, because most thinking men are sufficiently averse to them. But, I earnestly beg you to consider whether we must not come to them if we once begin. For by altering immaterials, we merely *raise* without *gratifying* the desire of correcting; we excite the craving, but withhold the food. And it should be observed, that the changes called immaterial often contain in themselves the germ of some principle, of which they are thus the introduction:—e.g. If we were to leave out the imprecatory Psalms, we certainly countenance the notion of the day, that love and love only is in the Gospel the character of ALMIGHTY GOD and the duty of regenerate man; whereas that Gospel, rightly understood, shows His Infinite Holiness and Justice as well as His Infinite Love; and it enjoins on men the duties of zeal towards Him, hatred of sin, and separation from sinners, as well as that of kindness and charity.

To the above observations it may be answered, that changes have formerly been made in the Services without leading to the issue I am predicting now; and therefore they may be safely made again. But, waving all other remarks in answer to this argument, is not this enough, viz, that there *is* peril? No one will deny that the rage of the day is for concession. Have we not already granted (political) points, without stopping the course of innovation? This is a fact. Now, is it worth while even to risk fearful changes merely to gain petty improvements, allowing those which are proposed to be such?

We know not what is to come upon us; but the writer for one will try so to acquit himself now, that if any irremediable calamity befalls the Church, he may not have to vex himself with the recollections of silence on his part and indifference, when he might have been up and alive. There was a time when he, as well as others, might feel the wish, or rather the temptation, of steering a middle course between parties; but if so, a more close attention to passing events has cured his infirmity. In a day like this there are but two sides, zeal and persecution, the Church and the world; and those who attempt to occupy the ground between them, at best will lose their labour, but probably will be drawn back to the latter. Be practical, I respectfully urge you; do not attempt impossibilities; sail not as if in pleasure boats upon a troubled sea. Not a word falls to the ground, in a time like this. Speculations about ecclesiastical improvements which might be innocent at other times, have a strength of mischief now. They are realized before he who utters them understands that he has committed himself.

Be prepared then for petitioning against any alterations in the Prayer Book which may be proposed. And, should you see that our Fathers the Bishops seem to countenance them, petition still. Petition *them*. They will thank you for such a proceeding. *They do not wish these alterations*; but how can they resist them without the support of their Clergy? They consent to them, (if they do,) partly from the notion that they are thus pleasing you. Undeceive them. They will be rejoiced to hear that you are as unwilling to receive them as they are. However, if after all there be persons determined to allow some alterations, then let them quickly make up their minds *how far* they will go. They think it easier to draw the line elsewhere, than as things now exist. Let them point out the limit of their concessions now; and let them keep to it then; and, (if they can do this,) I will say that, though they are not as wise as they might have been, they are at least firm, and have at last come right.

WE hear many complaints about the Burial Service, as unsuitable for the use for which it was intended. It expresses a hope, that the person departed, over whom it is read, will be saved; and this is said to be dangerous when expressed about all who are called Christians, as leading the laity to low views of the spiritual attainments necessary for salvation; and distressing the Clergy who have to read it.

Now I do not deny, I frankly own, it is sometimes distressing to use the Service; but this it must ever be in the nature of things; wherever you draw the line. Do you pretend you can discriminate the wheat from the tares? of course not.

It is often distressing to use this Service, because it is often distressing to think of the dead at all; not that you are without hope, but because you have fear also.

How many are there whom you know well enough to dare to give any judgment about? Is a Clergyman only to express a hope where *he* has grounds for having it? Are not the feelings of relatives to be considered? And may there not be a difference of judgments? I may hope more, another less. If each is to use the precise words which suit his own judgment, then we can have no words at all.

But it may be said, "every thing of a *personal* nature may be left out from the Service." And do you really wish this? Is this the way in which your flock will wish their lost friends to be treated? a cold "edification," but no affectionate valediction to the departed? Why not pursue this course of (supposed) improvement, and advocate the omission of the Service altogether.

Are we to have no kind and religious thoughts over the good, lest we should include the bad?

But it will be said, that, at least we ought not to read the Service over the flagrantly wicked; over those who are a scandal to religion. But this is a very different position. I agree with it entirely. Of course we should not do so, and truly the Church never meant we should. She never wished we should profess our hope of the salvation of habitual drunkards and swearers, open sinners, blasphemers, and the like; not as daring to despair of their salvation, but thinking it unseemly to honour their memory. Though the Church is not endowed with a power of absolute judgment upon individuals, yet she is directed to decide according to external indications, in order to hold up the *rules* of GOD'S governance, and afford a type of it, and an assistance towards the realizing it. As she denies to the scandalously wicked the LORD'S Supper, so does she deprive them of her other privileges.

The Church, I say, does not bid us read the Service over open sinners. Hear her own words introducing the Service. "The office ensuing is not to be used for any that die unbaptized, or excommunicate, or have laid violent hands upon themselves." There is no room to doubt *whom* she meant to be excommunicated, open sinners. Those therefore who are pained at the general use of the Service, should rather strive to restore the practice of excommunication, than to alter the words used in the Service. Surely, if we do not this, we are clearly defrauding the religious, for the sake of keeping close to the wicked.

Here we see the common course of things in the world. We omit a duty. In consequence our services become inconsistent. Instead of retracing our steps we alter the Service. What is this but, as it were, to sin upon principle? While we keep to our principles, our sins are inconsistencies; at length, sensitive of the absurdity which inconsistency involves, we accommodate our professions to our practice. This is ever the way of the world; but it should not be the way of the church.

I will join heart and hand with any who will struggle for a restoration of that "godly discipline," the restoration of which our Church publicly professes she considers desirable; but GOD forbid any one should so depart from her spirit, as to mould her formularies to fit the case of deliberate sinners! And is not this what we are plainly doing, if we alter the Burial Service as proposed? we are recognizing the right of men to receive Christian Burial, about whom we do not like to express a hope. Why should they have Christian burial at all?

It will be said that the restoration of the practice of Excommunication is impracticable; and that therefore the other alternative must be taken, as the only one open to us. Of course it is impossible, if no one attempts to restore it; but if all willed it, how would it be impossible; and if no one stirs because he thinks no one else will, he is arguing in a circle.

But, after all, what have we to do with probabilities and prospects in matters of plain duty? Were a man the only member of the Church who felt it a duty to return to the Ancient Discipline, yet a duty is a duty, though he be alone. It is one of the great sins of our times to look to consequences in matters of plain duty. Is not this such a case? If not, prove that it is not; but do not argue from consequences.

In the mean while I offer the following texts in evidence of the duty: Matth. xviii. 15–17. Rom. xvi. 17. 1 Cor. v. 7–13. 2 Thess. iii. 6, 14, 15. 2 Tim. iii. 5. Tit. iii. 10, 11. 2 John 10, 11.

Testimony of St. Clement, the associate of St. Paul, [Phil. iv. 3.] to the Apostolical Succession. "The Apostles knew, through our LORD JESUS CHRIST, that strife would arise for the Episcopate. Wherefore having received an accurate foreknowledge, they appointed the men I before mentioned, and have given an orderly succession, that on their death other approved men might receive in turn their office." Ep. i. 44.

Testimony of St. Ignatius, the friend of St. Peter, to Episcopacy. "Your celebrated Presbytery, worthy of GOD, is as closely knit to the Bishop, as the strings to a harp, and so by means of your unanimity and concordant love JESUS CHRIST is sung." Eph. 4. "There are who profess to acknowledge a Bishop, but do every thing without him. Such men appear to lack a clear conscience." Magn. 4. "He for whom I am bound is my witness that I have not learned this doctrine from mortal man. The Spirit proclaimed to me these words: 'Without the Bishop do nothing.'" Phil. 7.

With these and other such strong passages in the Apostolical Fathers, how can we permit ourselves in our present *practical* disregard of the Episcopal Authority? Are not we apt to obey only so far as the law obliges us? Do we support the Bishop, and strive to move all together with him as our bond of union and head; or is not our every-day conduct as if, except with respect to certain periodical forms and customs, we were each independent in his own parish?

The Present Obligation of Primitive Practice†

WHEN WE LOOK around upon the present state of the Christian Church, and then turning to ecclesiastical history acquaint ourselves with its primitive form and condition, the difference between them so strongly acts upon the imagination, that we are tempted to think, that to base our conduct now on the principles acknowledged then, is but theoretical and idle. We seem to perceive, as clear as day, that as a Primitive Church had its own particular discipline and political character, so have we ours; and that to attempt to revive what is past, is as absurd as to seek to raise what is literally dead. Perhaps we even go on to maintain, that the constitution of the Church, as well as its actual course of acting, is different from what it was; that Episcopacy now is in no sense what it used to be; that our Bishops are the same as the Primitive Bishops only in name; and that the notion of an Apostolical Succession is "a fond thing." I do not wish to undervalue the temptation, which leads to this view of Church matters; it is the temptation of sight to overcome faith, and of course not a slight one.

But the following reflection on the history of the Jewish Church may perhaps be considered to throw light on our present duties.

1. Consider how exact are the injunctions of Moses to his people. He ends them thus: "These are the words of the covenant which the LORD commanded Moses to make with the children of Israel in the land of Moab, beside the covenant which He made with them in Horeb . . . Keep therefore the words of this covenant, and do them, that ye may prosper in all that ye do . . . Neither with you only do I make this covenant and this oath; but with him that standeth here this day before the LORD our GOD, and also with him that is not here with us this day." Deut. xxix.

2. Next, survey the history of the chosen people for the several first centuries after taking possession of Canaan. The exactness of Moses was unavailing. Can a greater contrast be conceived than the commands and promises of the Pentateuch, and the history of the Judges? "Every man did that which was right in his own eyes." Judges xvii. 6.

Samuel attempts a reformation on the basis of the Mosaic Law; but the effort ultimately fails, as being apparently against the stream of opinion and feeling then prevalent. The times do not allow of it. Again, contrast the opu-

---

† *Tracts for the Times*, Tract 6 (*Ad Populum*). First published in 1833.

lent and luxurious age of Solomon, though the covenant was then openly acknowledged and outwardly accepted more fully than at any other time, with the vision of simple piety and plain straightforward obedience, which is the scope of the Mosaic Law. Lastly, contemplate the state of the Jews after their return from the captivity; when their external political relations were so new, the internal principle of their government so secular, GOD'S arm apparently so far removed. This state of things went on for centuries. Who would suppose that the Jewish Law was binding in all its primitive strictness at the age when CHRIST appeared? Who would not say that length of time had destroyed the obligation of a projected system, which had as yet never been realized?

Consider, too, the impossible nature (so to say) of some of its injunctions. An infidel historian somewhere asks scoffingly, whether "the ruinous law which required all the males of the chosen people to go up to Jerusalem three times a year, was ever observed in its strictness." The same question may be asked concerning the observance of the Sabbatical year;—to which but a faint allusion, if that, is made in the books of Scripture subsequent to the Pentateuch.

3. And now, with these thoughts before us, reflect upon our SAVIOUR'S conduct. He set about to fulfil the Law in its strictness, just as if He had lived in the generation next to Moses. The practice of others, the course of the world, was nothing to Him; He received and He obeyed. It is not necessary to draw out the evidence of this in detail. Consider merely His emphatic words in the beginning of Matt. xxiii. concerning those, whom as individuals He was fearfully condemning. "The Scribes and Pharisees sit in Moses' seat: all therefore whatsoever they bid you observe, that observe and do."—Again, reflect upon the praise bestowed upon Zacharias and his wife, that "they were both righteous before GOD, walking in all the commandments and ordinances of the LORD blameless."—And upon the conduct of the Apostles.

Surely these remarkable facts impress upon us the necessity of going to the Apostles, and not to the teachers and oracles of the present world, for the knowledge of our duty, as individuals and as members of the Christian Church. It is no argument against a practice being right, that it is neglected; rather we are warned against going the broad way of the multitude of men.

Now is there any doubt in our minds, as to the feelings of the Primitive Church regarding the doctrine of the Apostolical Succession? Did not the Apostles observe, even in an age of miracles, the ceremony of Imposition of Hands? And are not we bound, not merely to acquiesce in, but zealously to maintain and inculcate the discipline which they established?

The only objection which can be made to this view of our duty, is, that the injunction to obey strictly is *not* precisely given to us, as it was in the instance of the Mosaic Law. But is not the real state of the case merely this; that the Gospel appeals rather to our love and faith, our divinely illuminated reason, and the free principle of obedience, than to the mere letter of its injunctions? And does not the conduct of the Jews just prove to us, that, *though* the commands of CHRIST were put before us ever so precisely, yet there would not be found in any extended course of history a more exact attention to them, than there is now; that the difficulty of resisting the influence, which the world's actual proceedings exert upon our imagination, would be just as great as we find it at present?

A SIN OF THE CHURCH

"Remember from whence thou art fallen, and repent, and do thy first works; or else I will come unto thee quickly, and will remove thy candlestick out of his place, except thou repent."

The following extract is from Bingham, *Antiq.* xv. 9. "In the primitive ages, it was both the rule and practice of all in general, both Clergy and Laity, to receive the Communion every LORD'S day . . . As often as they met together for Divine Service on the LORD'S day, they were obliged to receive the Eucharist under pain of Excommunication . . . And if we run over the whole history of the three first ages, we shall find this to have been the Church's constant practice . . . We are assured farther, that in some places they received the Communion every day."

Is there any one who will deny, that the Primitive Church is the best expounder in this matter of our SAVIOUR'S will as conveyed through His Apostles?

Can a learned Church, such as the English, plead ignorance of His will thus ascertained?

Do we fulfil it?

Is not the regret and concern of pious and learned writers among us, such as Bingham, at our neglect of it, upon record?

And is it not written, "THAT SERVANT WHICH KNEW HIS LORD'S WILL, AND PREPARED NOT HIMSELF, NEITHER DID ACCORDING TO HIS WILL, SHALL BE BEATEN WITH MANY STRIPES?"

And putting aside this disobedience, can we wonder, that faith and love wax cold, when we so seldom partake of the MEANS, mercifully vouchsafed to us, of communion with our LORD and SAVIOUR?

OXFORD, *Oct.* 29, 1833.

10

Holiness Necessary for Future Blessedness[†]

"Holiness, without which no man shall see the Lord."
Hebrews xii. 14

I N THIS TEXT it has seemed good to the Holy Spirit to convey a chief truth
of religion in a few words. It is this circumstance which makes it especially
impressive; for the truth itself is declared in one form or other in every
part of Scripture. It is told us again and again, that to make sinful creatures
holy was the great end which our Lord had in view in taking upon Him our
nature, and thus none but the holy will be accepted for His sake at the last
day. The whole history of redemption, the covenant of mercy in all its parts
and provisions, attests the necessity of holiness in order to salvation; as indeed
even our natural conscience bears witness also. But in the text what is elsewhere implied in history, and enjoined by precept, is stated doctrinally, as a
momentous and necessary fact, the result of some awful irreversible law in the
nature of things, and the inscrutable determination of the Divine Will.

Now some one may ask, "Why is it that holiness is a necessary qualification for our being received into heaven? why is it that the Bible enjoins upon
us so strictly to love, fear, and obey God, to be just, honest, meek, pure in
heart, forgiving, heavenly-minded, self-denying, humble, and resigned? Man is
confessedly weak and corrupt; *why* then is he enjoined to be so religious, so
unearthly? *why* is he required (in the strong language of Scripture) to become
'a new creature'? Since he is by nature what he is, would it not be an act of
greater mercy in God to save him altogether without this holiness, which it is
so difficult, yet (as it appears) so necessary for him to possess?"

Now we have no right to ask this question. Surely it is quite enough for a
sinner to know, that a way has been opened through God's grace for his salvation, without being informed why that way, and not another way, was chosen
by Divine Wisdom. Eternal life is "the *gift* of God." Undoubtedly He may
prescribe the terms on which He will give it; and if He has determined holiness to be the way of life, it is enough; it is not for us to inquire why He has so
determined.

Yet the question may be asked reverently, and with a view to enlarge our
insight into our own condition and prospects; and in that case the attempt to

---

[†] *Parochial & Plain Sermons*, vol. 1 (1834), Sermon 1.

answer it will be profitable, if it be made soberly. I proceed, therefore, to state one of the reasons, assigned in Scripture, why present holiness is necessary, as the text declares to us, for future happiness.

To be holy is, in our Church's words, to have "the true circumcision of the Spirit;" that is, to be separate from sin, to hate the works of the world, the flesh, and the devil; to take pleasure in keeping God's commandments; to do things as He would have us do them; to live habitually as in the sight of the world to come, as if we had broken the ties of this life, and were dead already. Why cannot we be saved without possessing such a frame and temper of mind?

I answer as follows: That, even supposing a man of unholy life were suffered to enter heaven, *he would not be happy there*; so that it would be no mercy to permit him to enter.

We are apt to deceive ourselves, and to consider heaven a place like this earth; I mean, a place where every one may choose and take his *own* pleasure. We see that in this world, active men have their own enjoyments, and domestic men have theirs; men of literature, of science, of political talent, have their respective pursuits and pleasures. Hence we are led to act as if it will be the same in another world. The only difference we put between this world and the next, is that *here*, (as we know well,) men are *not always sure*, but *there*, we suppose they *will be always sure*, of obtaining what they seek after. And accordingly we conclude, that *any man*, whatever his habits, tastes, or manner of life, if *once admitted* into heaven, would be happy there. Not that we altogether deny, that some preparation is necessary for the next world; but we do not estimate its real extent and importance. We think we can reconcile ourselves to God when we will; as if nothing were required in the case of men in general, but some temporary attention, more than ordinary, to our religious duties,— some strictness, during our last sickness, in the services of the Church, as men of business arrange their letters and papers on taking a journey or balancing an account. But an opinion like this, though commonly acted on, is refuted as soon as put into words. For heaven, it is plain from Scripture, is not a place where many different and discordant pursuits can be carried on at once, as is the case in this world. Here every man can do his *own* pleasure, but there he must do *God's* pleasure. It would be presumption to attempt to determine the employments of that eternal life which good men are to pass in God's presence, or to deny that that state which eye hath not seen, nor ear heard, nor mind conceived, may comprise an infinite variety of pursuits and occupations. Still so far we are distinctly told, that that future life will be spent in God's *presence*, in a sense which does not apply to our present life; so that it may be best described as an endless and uninterrupted worship of the Eternal Father,

Son, and Spirit. "They serve Him day and night in His temple, and He that sitteth on the throne shall dwell among them ... The Lamb which is in the midst of the throne shall feed them, and shall lead them unto living fountains of waters." Again, "The city had no need of the sun, neither of the moon to shine in it, for the glory of God did lighten it, and the Lamb is the light thereof. And the nations of them which are saved shall walk in the light of it, and the kings of the earth do bring their glory and honour into it." [Rev. vii. 15, 17; xxi. 23, 24.] These passages from St. John are sufficient to remind us of many others.

Heaven then is not like this world; I will say what it is much more like,—*a church*. For in a place of public worship no language of this world is heard; there are no schemes brought forward for temporal objects, great or small; no information how to strengthen our worldly interests, extend our influence, or establish our credit. These things indeed may be right in their way, so that we do not set our hearts upon them; still (I repeat), it is certain that we hear nothing of them in a church. Here we hear solely and entirely of *God*. We praise Him, worship Him, sing to Him, thank Him, confess to Him, give ourselves up to Him, and ask His blessing. And *therefore*, a church is like heaven; viz. because both in the one and the other, there is one single sovereign subject—religion—brought before us.

Supposing, then, instead of it being said that no irreligious man could serve and attend on God in heaven (or see Him, as the text expresses it), we were told that no irreligious man could worship, or spiritually see Him in church; should we not at once perceive the meaning of the doctrine? viz. that, were a man to come hither, who had suffered his mind to grow up in its own way, as nature or chance determined, without any deliberate habitual effort after truth and purity, he would find no real pleasure here, but would soon get weary of the place; because, in this house of God, he would hear only of that one subject which he cared little or nothing about, and nothing at all of those things which excited his hopes and fears, his sympathies and energies. If then a man without religion (supposing it possible) were admitted into heaven, doubtless he would sustain a great disappointment. Before, indeed, he fancied that he could be happy there; but when he arrived there, he would find no discourse but that which he had shunned on earth, no pursuits but those he had disliked or despised, nothing which bound him to aught *else* in the universe, and made him feel at home, nothing which he could enter into and rest upon. He would perceive himself to be an isolated being, cut away by Supreme Power from those objects which were still entwined around his heart. Nay, he would be in the presence of that Supreme Power, whom he never on earth could bring himself steadily to think upon, and whom now he regarded only as the destroyer of all that was precious and dear to him. Ah! he could not *bear* the face of the Living God; the Holy God would be no object of joy to him. "Let us alone! What have we to do with thee?" is the sole thought and desire of unclean souls, even while they acknowledge His majesty. None but the holy can look upon the Holy One; without holiness no man can endure to see the Lord.

When, then, we think to take part in the joys of heaven without holiness, we are as inconsiderate as if we supposed we could take an interest in the worship of Christians here below without possessing it in our measure. A careless, a sensual, an unbelieving mind, a mind destitute of the love and fear of God, with narrow views and earthly aims, a low standard of duty, and a benighted conscience, a mind contented with itself, and unresigned to God's will, would feel as little pleasure, at the last day, at the words, "Enter into the joy of thy Lord," as it does now at the words, "Let us pray." Nay, much less, because, while we are in a church, we may turn our thoughts to other subjects, and contrive to forget that God is looking on us; but that will not be possible in heaven.

We see, then, that holiness, or inward separation from the world, is necessary to our admission into heaven, because heaven is *not* heaven, is not a place of happiness *except* to the holy. There are bodily indispositions which affect the taste, so that the sweetest flavours become ungrateful to the palate; and indispositions which impair the sight, tinging the fair face of nature with some sickly hue. In like manner, there is a moral malady which disorders the inward sight and taste; and no man labouring under it is in a condition to enjoy what Scripture calls "the fulness of joy in God's presence, and pleasures at His right hand for evermore."

Nay, I will venture to say more than this;—it is fearful, but it is right to say it;—that if we wished to imagine a punishment for an unholy, reprobate soul, we perhaps could not fancy a greater than to *summon it to heaven.* Heaven would be hell to an irreligious man. We know how unhappy we are apt to feel at present, when alone in the midst of strangers, or of men of different tastes and habits from ourselves. How miserable, for example, would it be to have to live in a foreign land, among a people whose faces we never saw before, and whose language we could not learn. And this is but a faint illustration of the loneliness of a man of earthly dispositions and tastes, thrust into the society of saints and angels. How forlorn would he wander through the courts of heaven! He would find no one like himself; he would see in every direction the marks of God's holiness, and these would make him shudder. He would feel himself always in His presence. He could no longer turn his thoughts another way, as he does now, when conscience reproaches him. He would know that the Eternal Eye was ever upon him; and that Eye of holiness, which is joy and life to holy creatures, would seem to him an Eye of wrath and punishment. God cannot change His nature. Holy He must ever be. But while He is holy, no unholy soul can be happy in heaven. Fire does not inflame iron, but it inflames straw. It would cease to be fire if it did not. And so heaven itself would be fire to those, who would fain escape across the great gulf from the torments of hell. The finger of Lazarus would but increase their thirst. The very "heaven that is over their head" will be "brass" to them.

And now I have partly explained why it is that holiness is prescribed to us as the condition on our part for our admission into heaven. It seems to be necessary from the very nature of things. We do not see how it could be otherwise. Now then I will mention two important truths which seem to follow from what has been said.

1. If a certain character of mind, a certain state of the heart and affections, be necessary for entering heaven, our *actions* will avail for our salvation, chiefly as they tend to produce or evidence this frame of mind. Good works (as they are called) are required, not as if they had any thing of merit in them, not as if they could of themselves turn away God's anger for our sins, or purchase heaven for us, but because they are the means, under God's grace, of strengthening and showing forth that holy principle which God implants in the heart, and without which (as the text tells us) we cannot see Him. The more numerous are our acts of charity, self-denial, and forbearance, of course the more will our minds be schooled into a charitable, self-denying, and forbearing temper. The more frequent are our prayers, the more humble, patient, and religious are our daily deeds, this communion with God, these holy works, will be the means of making our hearts holy, and of preparing us for the future presence of God. Outward acts, done on principle, create inward habits. I repeat, the separate acts of obedience to the will of God, good works as they are called, are of service to us, as gradually severing us from this world of sense, and impressing our hearts with a heavenly character.

It is plain, then, what works are *not* of service to our salvation;—all those which either have no effect upon the heart to change it, or which have a bad effect. What then must be said of those who think it an easy thing to please God, and to recommend themselves to Him; who do a few scanty services, call these the walk of faith, and are satisfied with them? Such men, it is too evident, instead of being themselves profited by their acts, such as they are, of benevolence, honesty, or justice, may be (I might even say) injured by them. For these very acts, even though good in themselves, are made to foster in these persons a bad spirit, a corrupt state of heart; viz. self-love, self-conceit, self-reliance, instead of tending to turn them from this world to the Father of spir-

15

its. In like manner, the mere outward acts of coming to church, and saying prayers, which are, of course, duties imperative upon all of us, are really serviceable to those only who do them in a heavenward spirit. Because such men only use these good deeds to the improvement of the heart; whereas even the most exact outward devotion avails not a man, if it does not improve it.

2. But observe what follows from this. If holiness be not merely the doing a certain number of good actions, but is an inward character which follows, under God's grace, from doing them, how far distant from that holiness are the multitude of men! They are not yet even obedient in outward deeds, which is the first step towards possessing it. They have even to learn to practise good works, as the means of changing their hearts, which is the end. It follows at once, even though Scripture did not plainly tell us so, that no one is able to prepare himself for heaven, that is, make himself holy, in a short time;—at least we do not see how it is possible; and this, viewed merely as a deduction of the reason, is a serious thought. Yet, alas! as there are persons who think to be saved by a few scanty performances, so there are others who suppose they may be saved all at once by a sudden and easily acquired faith. Most men who are living in neglect of God, silence their consciences, when troublesome, with the promise of repenting some future day. How often are they thus led on till death surprises them! But we will suppose they *do* begin to repent when that future day comes. Nay, we will even suppose that Almighty God were to forgive them, and to admit them into His holy heaven. Well, but is nothing more requisite? are they in a fit state to *do Him service in heaven*? is not this the very point I have been so insisting on, that they are *not* in a fit state? has it not been shown that, even if admitted there without a change of heart, they would find no pleasure in heaven? and is a change of heart wrought in a day? Which of our tastes or likings can we change at our will in a moment? Not the most superficial. Can we then at a word change the whole frame and character of our minds? Is not holiness the result of many patient, repeated efforts after obedience, gradually working on us, and first modifying and then changing our hearts? We dare not, of course, set bounds to God's mercy and power in cases of repentance late in life, even where He has revealed to us the general rule of His moral governance; yet, surely, it is our duty ever to keep steadily before us, and act upon, those general truths which His Holy Word has declared. His Holy Word in various ways warns us, that, as no one will find happiness in heaven, who is not holy, so no one can learn to be so, in a short time, and when he will. It implies it in the text, which names a qualification, which we know in matter of fact does ordinarily take time to gain. It propounds it clearly, though in figure, in the parable of the wedding garment, in which inward sanctification is made a condition distinct from our acceptance of the proffer

16

of mercy, and not negligently to be passed over in our thoughts as if a necessary consequence of it; and in that of the ten virgins, which shows us that we must meet the bridegroom with the oil of holiness, and that it takes time to procure it. And it solemnly assures us in St. Paul's Epistles, that it is possible so to presume on Divine grace, as to let slip the accepted time, and be sealed even before the end of life to a reprobate mind.[4]

I wish to speak to you, my brethren, not as if aliens from God's mercies, but as partakers of His gracious covenant in Christ; and for this reason in especial peril, since those only can incur the sin of making void His covenant, who have the privilege of it. Yet neither on the other hand do I speak to you as wilful and obstinate sinners, exposed to the imminent risk of forfeiting, or the chance of having forfeited, your hope of heaven. But I fear there are those, who, if they dealt faithfully with their consciences, would be obliged to own that they had not made the service of God their first and great concern; that their obedience, so to call it, has been a matter of course, in which the heart has had no part; that they have acted uprightly in worldly matters chiefly for the sake of their worldly interest. I fear there are those, who, whatever be their sense of religion, still have such misgivings about themselves, as lead them to make resolve to obey God more exactly some future day, such misgivings as convict them of sin, though not enough to bring home to them its heinousness or its peril. Such men are trifling with the appointed season of mercy. To obtain the gift of holiness is the work of *a life*. No man will ever be perfect here, so sinful is our nature. Thus, in putting off the day of repentance, these men are reserving for a few chance years, when strength and vigour are gone, that work for which a *whole* life would not be enough. That work is great and arduous beyond expression. There is much of sin remaining even in the best of men, and "if the righteous scarcely be saved, where shall the ungodly and the sinner appear?" [1 Pet. iv. 18.] Their doom may be fixed any moment; and though this thought should not make a man despair today, yet it should ever make him tremble for tomorrow.

Perhaps, however, others may say:—"We know something of the power of religion—we love it in a measure—we have many right thoughts—we come to church to pray; this is a proof that we are prepared for heaven:—we are safe, and what has been said does not apply to us." But be not you, my brethren, in the number of these. One principal test of our being true servants of God is our wishing to serve Him better; and be quite sure that a man who is contented with his own proficiency in Christian holiness, is at best in a dark state, or rather in great peril. If we are really imbued with the grace of holiness, we shall abhor sin as something base, irrational, and polluting. Many men, it is true,

---

[4] Heb. vi. 4–6; x. 26–29. *Vide* also 2 Pet. ii. 20, 22.

are contented with partial and indistinct views of religion, and mixed motives. Be you content with nothing short of perfection; exert yourselves day by day to grow in knowledge and grace; that, if so be, you may at length attain to the presence of Almighty God.

Lastly; while we thus labour to mould our hearts after the pattern of the holiness of our Heavenly Father, it is our comfort to know, what I have already implied, that we are not left to ourselves, but that the Holy Ghost is graciously present with us, and enables us to triumph over, and to change our own minds. It is a comfort and encouragement, while it is an anxious and awful thing, to know that God works in and through us.[5] We are the instruments, but we are only the instruments, of our own salvation. Let no one say that I discourage him, and propose to him a task beyond his strength. All of us have the gifts of grace pledged to us from our youth up. We know this well; but we do not use our privilege. We form mean ideas of the difficulty, and in consequence never enter into the greatness of the gifts given us to meet it. Then afterwards, if perchance we gain a deeper insight into the work we have to do, we think God a hard master, who commands much from a sinful race. Narrow, indeed, is the way of life, but infinite is His love and power who is with the Church, in Christ's place, to guide us along it.

---

[5] Phil. ii. 12, 13.

Profession without Hypocrisy[†]

"As many of you as have been baptized into Christ have put on Christ."
Galatians iii. 27

IT IS SURELY most necessary to beware, as our Lord solemnly bids us, of the leaven of the Pharisees, which is hypocrisy. We may be infected with it, even though we are not conscious of our insincerity; for they did not *know* they were hypocrites. Nor need we have any definite bad object plainly before us, for they had none,—only the vague desire to be seen and honoured by the world, such as may influence us. So it would seem, that there are vast multitudes of Pharisaical hypocrites among baptized Christians; i.e. men professing without practising. Nay, so far we may be called hypocritical, one and all; for no Christian on earth altogether lives up to his profession.

But here some one may ask, whether in saying that hypocrisy is professing without practising, I am not, in fact, overthrowing all external religion from the foundation, since all creeds, and prayers, and ordinances, go beyond the real belief and frame of mind of even the best Christians. This is even the ground which some men actually take. They say that it is wrong to baptize, and call Christians, those who have not yet shown themselves to be really such. "As many as are baptized into Christ, put on Christ;" so says the text, and these men argue from it, that till we have actually put on Christ, that is, till we have given our heart to Christ's service, and in our degree become holy as He is holy, it can do no good to be baptized into His name. Rather it is a great evil, for it is to become hypocrites. Nay, really humble, well-intentioned men, feel this about themselves. They shrink from retaining the blessed titles and privileges which Christ gave them in infancy, as being unworthy of them; and they fear lest they are really hypocrites like the Pharisees, after all their better thoughts and exertions.

Now the obvious answer to this mistaken view of religion is to say, that, on the showing of such reasoners, *no* one at all ought to be baptized in any case, and called a Christian; for no one *acts up* to his baptismal profession; no one believes, worships, and obeys duly, the Father, Son, and Holy Ghost, whose servant he is made in baptism. And yet the Lord *did* say, "Go, baptize all nations;" clearly showing us, that a man may be a fit subject for baptism,

---

[†] *Parochial & Plain Sermons*, vol. 1 (1834), Sermon 11.

though he does not in fact practise every thing that he professes, and therefore, that any fears we may have, lest men should be in some sense like the Pharisees, must not keep us from making them Christians.

But I shall treat the subject more at length, in order that we may understand what kind of disobedience is really hypocrisy, and what is not, lest timid consciences should be frightened. Now men profess without feeling and doing, or are hypocrites, in nothing so much as in their prayers. This is plain. Prayer is the most directly religious of all our duties; and our falling short of our duty, is, then, most clearly displayed. Therefore I will enlarge upon the case of prayer, to explain what I do *not* mean by hypocrisy. We then use the most solemn words, either without attending to what we are saying, or (even if we do attend) without worthily entering into its meaning. Thus we seem to resemble the Pharisees; a question in consequence arises, whether, this being the case, we should go on repeating prayers which evidently do not suit us. The men I just now spoke of, affirm that we ought to leave them off. Accordingly, such persons in their own case first give up the Church prayers, and take to others which they think will suit them better. Next, when these disappoint them, they have recourse to what is called extempore prayer; and afterwards perhaps, discontented in turn with this mode of addressing Almighty God, and as unable to fix their thoughts as they were before, they come to the conclusion that they ought not to pray, except when specially moved to prayer by the influence of the Holy Spirit.

Now, in answer to such a manner of reasoning and acting, I would maintain that no one is to be reckoned a Pharisee or hypocrite in his prayers who *tries* not to be one,—who aims at knowing and correcting himself,—and who is accustomed to pray, though not perfectly, yet not indolently or in a self-satisfied way; however lamentable his actual wanderings of mind may be, or, again, however poorly he enters into the meaning of his prayers, even when he attends to them.

1. First take the case of not being *attentive* to the prayers. Men, it seems, are tempted to leave off prayers because they cannot follow them, because they find their thoughts wander when they repeat them. I answer, that to pray attentively is a *habit*. This must ever be kept in mind. No one *begins* with having his heart thoroughly in them; but by trying, he is enabled to attend more and more, and at length, after many trials and a long schooling of himself, to fix his mind steadily on them. No one (I repeat) *begins* with being attentive. Novelty in prayers is the cause of persons being attentive in the outset, and novelty is out of the question in the Church prayers, for we have heard them from childhood, and knew them by heart long before we could understand them. No one, then, when he first turns his thoughts to religion, finds it easy to pray;

20

he is irregular in his religious feelings; he prays more earnestly at some times than at others; his devotional seasons come by fits and starts; he cannot account for his state of mind, or reckon upon himself; he frequently finds that he is more disposed for prayer at any time and place than those set apart for the purpose. All this is to be expected; for no habit is formed at once; and before the flame of religion in the heart is purified and strengthened by long practice and experience, of course it will be capricious in its motions, it will flare about (so to say) and flicker, and at times seem almost to go out.

However, impatient men do not well consider this; they overlook or are offended at the necessity of humble, tedious practice to enable them to pray attentively, and they account for their coldness and wanderings of thought in any way but the true one. Sometimes they attribute this inequality in their religious feelings to the arbitrary coming and going of God's Holy Spirit; a most irreverent and presumptuous judgment, which I should not mention, except that men *do* form it, and therefore it is necessary to state in order to condemn it. Again, sometimes they think that they shall make themselves attentive all at once by bringing before their minds the more sacred doctrines of the Gospel, and thus rousing and constraining their souls. This does for a time; but when the novelty is over, they find themselves relapsing into their former inattention, without apparently having made any advance. And others, again, when discontented with their wanderings during prayer, lay the fault on the prayers themselves as being too long. This is a common excuse, and I wish to call your attention to it.

If any one alleges the *length* of the Church prayers as a reason for his not keeping his mind fixed upon them, I would beg him to ask his conscience whether he sincerely believes this to be at bottom the real cause of his inattention? Does he think he should attend *better* if the prayers were shorter? This is the question he has to consider. If he answers that he believes he *should* attend more closely in that case, then I go on to ask, whether he attends more closely (as it *is*) to the first part of the service than to the last; whether his mind is his own, regularly fixed on what he is engaged in, for any time in any part of the service? Now, if he is obliged to own that this is not the case, that his thoughts are wandering in all parts of the service, and that even during the Confession, or the Lord's Prayer, which come first, they are not his own, it is quite clear that it is not the *length* of the service which is the real cause of his inattention, but his being deficient *in the habit* of being attentive. If, on the other hand, he answers that he *can* fix his thoughts for a time, and during the early part of the service, I would have him reflect that even this degree of attention was not always his own, that *it* has been the work of time and practice; and, if by trying he has got so far, by trying he may go on and learn to attend for a still longer time, till at length he is able to keep up his attention through the whole service.

However, I wish chiefly to speak to such as are dissatisfied with themselves, and despair of attending properly. Let a man once set his heart upon learning to pray, and strive to learn, and no failures he may continue to make in his manner of praying are sufficient to cast him from God's favour. Let him but persevere, not discouraged at his wanderings, not frightened into a notion he is a hypocrite, not shrinking from the honourable titles which God puts on him. Doubtless he should be humbled at his own weakness, indolence, and carelessness; and he should feel (he cannot feel too much) the guilt, alas! which he is ever contracting in his prayers by the irreverence of his inattention. Still he must not leave off his prayers, but go on looking towards Christ his Saviour. Let him but be in earnest, striving to master his thoughts, and to be serious, and all the guilt of his incidental failings will be washed away in his Lord's blood. Only let him not be contented with himself; only let him not neglect to *attempt* to obey. What a simple rule it is, to *try* to be attentive in order to be so! and yet it is continually overlooked; that is, we do not *systematically* try, we do not make a point of attempting and attempting over and over again in spite of bad success; we attempt only now and then, and our best devotion is merely when our hearts are excited by some accident which may or may not happen again.

So much on inattention to our prayers, which, I say, should not surprise or frighten us, which does not prove us to be hypocrites unless we acquiesce in it; or oblige us to leave them off, but rather to learn to attend to them.

2. I proceed, secondly, to remark on the difficulty of *entering into* the meaning of them, when we *do* attend to them.

Here a tender conscience will ask, "How is it possible I *can* rightly use the solemn words which occur in the prayers?" A tender conscience *alone* speaks thus. Those confident objectors whom I spoke of just now, who maintain that set prayer is necessarily a mere formal service in the generality of instances, a service in which the heart has no part, they are silent here. They do not feel *this* difficulty, which is the real one; they use the most serious and awful words lightly and without remorse, as if they really entered into the meaning of what is, in truth, beyond the intelligence of Angels. But the humble and contrite believer, coming to Christ for pardon and help, perceives the great strait he is in, in having to address the God of heaven. This perplexity of mind it was which led convinced sinners in former times to seek refuge in beings short of God; not as denying God's supremacy, or shunning Him, but discerning the vast distance between themselves and Him, and seeking some resting places by the way, some Zoar, some little city near to flee unto, [Gen. xix.

20.] because of the height of God's mountain, up which the way of escape lay. And then gradually becoming devoted to those whom they trusted, Saints, Angels, or good men living, and copying them, their faith had a fall, and their virtue trailed upon the ground, for want of props to rear it heavenward. We Christians, sinners though we be like other men, are not allowed thus to debase our nature, or to defraud ourselves of God's mercy; and though it be very terrible to speak to the living God, yet speak we must, or die; tell our sorrows we must, or there is no hope; for created mediators and patrons are forbidden us, and to trust in an arm of flesh is made a sin.

Therefore let a man reflect, whoever from tenderness of conscience shuns the Church as above him (whether he shuns her services, or her sacraments), that, awful as it is to approach Christ, to speak to Him, to "eat His flesh and drink His blood," and to live in Him, *to whom shall he go*? See what it comes to. Christ is the only way of salvation open to sinners. Truly we *are* children, and cannot suitably feel the words which the Church teaches us, though we say them after her, nor feel duly reverent at God's presence! Yet let us but know our own ignorance and weakness, and we are safe. God accepts those who thus come in faith, bringing nothing as their offering, but a confession of sin. And this is the highest excellence to which we ordinarily attain; to understand our own hypocrisy, insincerity, and shallowness of mind,—to own, while we pray, that we cannot pray aright,—to repent of our repentings,—and to submit ourselves wholly to His judgment, who could indeed be extreme with us, but has already shown His loving-kindness in bidding us to pray. And, while we thus conduct ourselves, we must learn to feel that God knows all this before we say it, and far better than we do. He does not need to be informed of our extreme worthlessness. We must pray in the spirit and the temper of the extremest abasement, but we need not search for adequate words to express this, for in truth no words are bad enough for our case. Some men are dissatisfied with the confessions of sin we make in Church, as not being strong enough; but none *can* be strong enough; let us be satisfied with sober words, which have been ever in use; it will be a great thing if we enter into *them*. No need of searching for impassioned words to express our repentance, when we do not rightly enter even into the most ordinary expressions.

Therefore, when we pray let us not be as the hypocrites, making a show; nor use vain repetitions with the heathen; let us compose ourselves, and kneel down quietly as to a work far above us, preparing our minds for our own imperfection in prayer, meekly repeating the wonderful words of the Church our Teacher, and desiring with the Angels to look into them. When we call God our Father Almighty, or own ourselves miserable offenders, and beg Him to spare us, let us recollect that, though we are using a strange language, yet

Christ is pleading for us in the same words with full understanding of them, and availing power; and that, though we know not what we should pray for as we ought, yet the Spirit itself maketh intercession for us with plaints unutterable. Thus feeling God to be around us and in us, and therefore keeping ourselves still and collected, we shall serve Him acceptably, with reverence and godly fear; and we shall take back with us to our common employments the assurance that He is still gracious to us, in spite of our sins, not willing we should perish, desirous of our perfection, and ready to form us day by day after the fashion of that divine image which in baptism was outwardly stamped upon us.

I have spoken only of our prayers, and but referred to our general profession of Christianity. It is plain, however, what has been said about praying, may be applied to all we do and say as Christians. It is true that we profess to be saints, to be guided by the highest principles, and to be ruled by the Spirit of God. We have long ago promised to believe and obey. It is also true that we cannot do these things aright; nay, even with God's help (such is our sinful weakness), still we fall short of our duty. Nevertheless we must not cease to profess. We must not put off from us the wedding garment which Christ gave us in baptism. We may still rejoice in Him without being hypocrites, that is, if we labour day by day to make that wedding garment our own; to fix it on us and so incorporate it with our very selves, that death, which strips us of all things, may be unable to tear it from us, though as yet it be in great measure but an outward garb, covering our own nakedness.

I conclude by reminding you, how great God's mercy is in thus allowing us to clothe ourselves in the glory of Christ from the first, even before we are worthy of it [Matt. xxii. 8; Col. i. 10.]. I suppose there is nothing so distressing to a true Christian as to have to *prove himself* such to others; both as being conscious of his own numberless failings, and from his dislike of display. Now Christ has anticipated the difficulties of his modesty. He does not allow such an one to speak for himself; He speaks for him. He introduces each of us to his brethren, not as we are in ourselves, fit to be despised and rejected on account of "the temptations which are in our flesh," but "as messengers of God, even as Christ Jesus." It is our happiness that we need bring nothing in proof of our fellowship with Christians, besides our baptism. This is what a great many persons do not understand; they think that none are to be accounted fellow-Christians but those who evidence themselves to be such to their fallible understandings; and hence they encourage others, who wish for their praise, to practise all kinds of display, as a seal of their regeneration. Who can tell the harm this does to the true modesty of the Christian spirit? Instead of using the words of the Church, and speaking to God, men are led to use their own words, and make man their judge and justifier. [1 Cor. iv. 3–5.] They think it necessary to tell out their secret feelings, and to enlarge on what God has done to their own souls in particular. And thus making themselves really answerable for all the words they use, which are altogether their own, they do in this case become hypocrites; they do say more than they can in reality feel. Of course a religious man will naturally, and unawares, out of the very fulness of his heart, show his deep feeling and his conscientiousness to his near friends; but when to do so is made a matter of *necessity*, an *object* to be aimed at, and is an *intentional* act, then it is that hypocrisy must, more or less, sully our faith. "As many of you as have been baptized into Christ, have put on Christ;" this is the Apostle's decision. "There is neither Jew nor Greek, there is neither bond nor free, there is neither male nor female; for ye are all one in Christ Jesus." The Church follows this rule, and bidding us keep quiet, speaks for us; robes us from head to foot in the garments of righteousness, and exhorts us to live henceforth to God. But the disputer of this world reverses this procedure; he strips off all our privileges, bids us renounce our dependence on the Mother of saints, tells us we must each be a Church to himself, and must show himself to the world to be by himself and in himself the elect of God, in order to prove his right to the privileges of a Christian.

Far be it from us thus to fight against God's gracious purposes to man, and to make the weak brother perish, for whom Christ died! [1 Cor. viii. 11.] Let us acknowledge all to be Christians, who have not by open word or deed renounced their fellowship with us, and let us try to lead them on into all truth. And for ourselves, let us endeavour to enter more and more fully into the meaning of our own prayers and professions; let us humble ourselves for the very little we do, and the poor advance we make; let us avoid unnecessary display of religion; let us do our duty in that state of life to which God has called us. Thus proceeding, we shall, through God's grace, form within us the glorious mind of Christ. Whether rich or poor, learned or unlearned, walking by this rule, we shall become, at length, true saints, sons of God. We shall be upright and perfect, lights in the world, the image of Him who died that we might be conformed to His likeness.

Religious Emotion[†]

"But he spake the more vehemently, If I should die with Thee,
I will not deny Thee in any wise."
Mark xiv. 31

IT IS NOT my intention to make St. Peter's fall the direct subject of our consideration today, though I have taken this text; but to suggest to you an important truth, which that fall, together with other events at the same season, especially enforces; viz. that violent impulse is not the same as a firm *determination*,—that men may have their religious feelings roused, without being on that account at all the more likely to obey God in practice, rather the less likely. This important truth is in various ways brought before our minds at the season sacred to the memory of Christ's betrayal and death. The contrast displayed in the Gospels between His behaviour on the one hand, as the time of His crucifixion drew near, and that both of His disciples and of the Jewish populace on the other, is full of instruction, if we will receive it; *He* steadily fixing His face to endure those sufferings which were the atonement for our sins, yet without aught of mental excitement or agitation; His disciples and the Jewish multitude first protesting their devotion to Him in vehement language, then, the one deserting Him, the other even clamouring for His crucifixion. He entered Jerusalem in triumph; the multitude cutting down branches of palm-trees, and strewing them in the way, as in honour of a king and conqueror [Matt. xxi. 8., John xii. 13.]. He had lately raised Lazarus from the dead; and so great a miracle had given Him great temporary favour with the populace. Multitudes flocked to Bethany to see Him and Lazarus [John xii. 1–18.]; and when He set out for Jerusalem where He was to suffer, they, little thinking that they would soon cry "Crucify Him," went out to meet Him with the palm-branches, and hailing Him as their Messiah, led Him on into the holy city. Here was an instance of a *popular* excitement. The next instance of excited feeling is found in that melancholy self-confidence of St. Peter, contained in the text. When our Saviour foretold Peter's trial and fall, Peter at length "spake the more vehemently, If I should die with Thee, I will not deny Thee in any wise." Yet in a little while both the people and the Apostle abandoned their Messiah; the ardour of their devotion had run its course.

[†] *Parochial & Plain Sermons*, vol. 1 (1834), Sermon 14.

26

Now it may, perhaps, appear, as if the circumstance I am pointing out, remarkable as it is, still is one on which it is of little use to dwell, in addressing a mixed congregation, on the ground that most men feel too *little* about religion. And it may be thence argued, that the aim of Christian teaching, rather should be to rouse them from insensibility, than to warn them against excess of religious feeling. I answer, that to mistake mere transient emotion, or mere good thoughts, for obedience, is a far commoner deceit than at first sight appears. How many a man is there, who, when his conscience upbraids him for neglect of duty, comforts himself with the reflection that he has never treated the subject of religion with open scorn,—that he has from time to time had serious thoughts,—that on certain solemn occasions he has been affected and awed,—that he has at times been moved to earnest prayer to God,—that he has had accidentally some serious conversation with a friend! This, I say, is a case of frequent occurrence among men called Christian. Again, there is a further reason for insisting upon this subject. No one (it is plain) can be religious without having his heart in his religion; his affections must be actively engaged in it; and it is the aim of all Christian instruction to promote this. But if so, doubtless there is great danger lest a perverse use should be made of the affections. In proportion as a religious duty is difficult, so is it open to abuse. For the very reason, then, that I desire to make you earnest in religion, must I also warn you against a counterfeit earnestness, which often misleads men from the plain path of obedience, and which most men are apt to fall into just on their first awakening to a serious consideration of their duty. It is not enough to bid you to serve Christ in faith, fear, love, and gratitude; care must be taken that it is the faith, fear, love, and gratitude of a sound mind. That vehement tumult of zeal which St. Peter felt before his trial failed him under it. That open-mouthed admiration of the populace at our Saviour's miracle was suddenly changed to blasphemy. This may happen now as then; and it often happens in a way distressing to the Christian teacher. He finds it is far easier to interest men in the subject of religion (hard though this be), than to rule the spirit which he has excited. His hearers, when their attention is gained, soon begin to think he does not go far enough; then they seek means which he will not supply, of encouraging and indulging their mere feelings to the neglect of humble practical efforts to serve God. After a time, like the multitude, they suddenly turn round to the world, abjuring Christ altogether, or denying Him with Peter, or gradually sinking into a mere form of obedience, while they still think themselves true Christians, and secure of the favour of Almighty God.

For these reasons I think it is as important to warn men against impetuous feelings in religion, as to urge them to give their heart to it. I proceed therefore to explain more fully what is the connexion between strong emotions and sound Christian principle, and how far they are consistent with it.

Now that perfect state of mind at which we must aim, and which the Holy Spirit imparts, is a deliberate preference of God's service to every thing else, a determined resolution to give up all for Him; and a love for Him, not tumultuous and passionate, but such love as a child bears towards his parents, calm, full, reverent, contemplative, obedient. Here, however, it may be objected, that this is not always possible: that we cannot help feeling emotion at times; that even to take the case of parents and children, a man is at certain times thrown out of that quiet affection which he bears towards his father and mother, and is agitated by various feelings; again, that zeal, for instance, though a Christian virtue, is almost inseparable from ardour and passion. To this I reply, that I am not describing the state of mind to which any one of us has *attained*, when I say it is altogether calm and meditative, but that which is the *perfect* state, that which we should aim at. I know it *is* often impossible, for various reasons, to avoid being agitated and excited; but the question before us is, whether we should *think highly* of violent emotion, whether we should encourage it. Doubtless it is no sin to feel at times passionately on the subject of religion; it is natural in some men, and under certain circumstances it is praiseworthy in others. But these are accidents. As a general rule, the more religious men become, the calmer they become; and at all times the religious principle, viewed by itself, is calm, sober, and deliberate.

Let us review some of the accidental circumstances I speak of.

1. The natural tempers of men vary very much. Some men have ardent imaginations and strong feelings; and adopt, as a matter of course, a vehement mode of expressing themselves. No doubt it is impossible to make all men think and feel alike. Such men of course may possess deep-rooted principle. All I would maintain is, that their ardour does not of itself make their faith deeper and more genuine; that they must not think themselves better than others on account of it; that they must be aware of considering it a proof of their real earnestness, instead of narrowly searching into their conduct for the satisfactory *fruits* of faith.

2. Next, there are, besides, particular occasions on which excited feeling is natural, and even commendable; but not for its own sake, but *on account* of the peculiar circumstances under which it occurs. For instance, it is natural for a man to feel especial remorse at his sins when he first begins to think of religion; he *ought* to feel bitter sorrow and keen repentance. But all such emotion evidently is not the highest state of a Christian's mind; it is but the first stirring of grace in him. A sinner, indeed, can do no better; but in proportion as he learns more of the power of true religion, such agitation will wear away.

What is this but saying, that change of mind is only the inchoate state of a Christian? Who doubts that sinners are bound to repent and turn to God? yet the Angels have no repentance; and who denies their peacefulness of soul to be a higher excellence than ours? The woman who had been a sinner, when she came behind our Lord wept much, and washed His feet with tears. [Luke vii. 38.] It was well done in her; she did what she could; and was honoured with our Saviour's praise. Yet it is clear this was not a permanent state of mind. It was but the first step in religion, and would doubtless wear away. It was but the accident of a season. Had her faith no deeper root than this emotion, it would soon have come to an end, as Peter's zeal.

In like manner, whenever we fall into sin, (and how often is this the case!) the truer our faith is, the more we shall for the time be distressed, perhaps agitated. No doubt; yet it would be a strange procedure to make much of this disquietude. Though it is a bad sign if we do not feel it (according to our mental temperament), yet if we do, what then? It argues no high Christian excellence; I repeat it, it is but the virtue of a very imperfect state. Bad is the best offering we can offer to God after sinning. On the other hand, the more consistent our habitual obedience, the less we shall be subject to such feelings.

3. And further, the accidents of life will occasionally agitate us:—affliction and pain; bad news; though here, too, the Psalmist describes the higher excellence of the mind, viz. the calm confidence of the believer, who "will not be afraid of any evil tidings, *for* his heart standeth fast, and believeth in the Lord." [Ps. cxii. 7.] Times of persecution will agitate the mind; circumstances of especial interest in the fortunes of the Church will cause anxiety and fear. We see the influence of some of these causes in various parts of St. Paul's Epistles. Such emotion, however, is not the essence of true faith, though it accidentally accompanies it. In times of distress religious men will speak more openly on the subject of religion, and lay bare their feelings; at other times they will conceal them. They are neither better nor worse for so doing.

Now all this may be illustrated from Scripture. We find the same prayers offered, and the same resolutions expressed by good men, sometimes in a calm way, sometimes with more ardour. How quietly and simply does Agur offer his prayer to God! "Two things have I required of Thee; deny me them not before I die. Remove far from me vanity and lies; give me neither poverty nor riches; feed me with food convenient for me." St. Paul, on the other hand, with greater fervency, because he was in more distressing circumstances, but with not more acceptableness on that account in God's sight, says, "I have learned in whatsoever state I am, therewith to be content. I know both how to be abased, and I know how to abound;" and so he proceeds. Again, Joshua says, simply but firmly, "As for me and my house, we will serve the Lord." St.

Paul says as firmly, but with more emotion, when his friends besought him to keep away from Jerusalem:—"What mean ye to weep and to break mine heart? for I am ready not to be bound only, but also to die at Jerusalem for the name of the Lord Jesus." Observe how calm Job is in his resignation: "The Lord gave, and the Lord hath taken away; blessed be the name of the Lord." And on the other hand, how calmly that same Apostle expresses his assurance of salvation at the close of his life, who, during the struggle, was accidentally agitated:—"I am now ready to be offered . . . I have kept the faith. Henceforth there is laid up for me a crown of righteousness." [Prov. xxx. 7, 8. Phil. iv. 11, 12. Josh. xxiv. 15. Acts xxi. 13. Job i. 21. 2 Tim. iv. 6–8.]

These remarks may suffice to show the relation which excited feelings bear to true religious principle. They are sometimes natural, sometimes suitable; but they are not religion itself. They come and go. They are not to be counted on, or encouraged; for, as in St. Peter's case, they may supplant true faith, and lead to self-deception. They will gradually lose their place within us as our obedience becomes confirmed;—partly because those men are kept in perfect peace, and sheltered from all agitating feelings, whose minds are stayed on God [Isa. xxvi. 8.];—partly because these feelings themselves are fixed into habits by the power of faith, and instead of coming and going, and agitating the mind from their suddenness, they are permanently retained so far as there is any thing good in them, and give a deeper colour and a more energetic expression to the Christian character.

Now, it will be observed, that in these remarks I have taken for granted, as not needing proof, that the highest Christian temper is free from all vehement and tumultuous feeling. But, if we wish some evidence of this, let us turn to our Great Pattern, Jesus Christ, and examine what was the character of that perfect holiness which He alone of all men ever displayed.

And can we find any where such calmness and simplicity as marked His devotion and His obedience? When does He ever speak with fervour or vehemence? Or, if there be one or two words of His in His mysterious agony and death, characterized by an energy which we do not comprehend, and which sinners must silently adore, still how conspicuous and undeniable is His composure in the general tenour of His words and conduct! Consider the prayer He gave us; and this is the more to the purpose, for the very reason that He has given it as a model for our worship. How plain and unadorned is it! How few are the words of it! How grave and solemn the petitions! What an entire absence of tumult and feverish emotion! Surely our own feelings tell us, it could not be otherwise. To suppose it otherwise were an irreverence towards Him.—At another time when He is said to have "rejoiced in spirit," His thanksgiving is marked with the same undisturbed tranquility. "I thank Thee,

O Father, Lord of heaven and earth, that Thou hast hid these things from the wise and prudent, and hast revealed them unto babes. Even so, Father, for so it seemed good in Thy sight."—Again, think of His prayer in the garden. He then was in distress of mind beyond our understanding. Something there was, we know not what, which weighed heavy upon Him. He prayed He might be spared the extreme bitterness of His trial. Yet how subdued and how concise is His petition! "Abba, Father, all things are possible unto Thee: take away this cup from Me; nevertheless, not what I will, but what Thou wilt." [Luke x. 21. Mark xiv. 36.] And this is but one instance, though a chief one, of that deep tranquility of mind, which is conspicuous throughout the solemn history of the Atonement. Read the thirteenth chapter of St. John, in which He is described as washing His disciples' feet, Peter's in particular. Reflect upon His serious words addressed at several times to Judas who betrayed Him; and His conduct when seized by His enemies, when brought before Pilate, and lastly, when suffering on the cross. When does He set us an example of passionate devotion, of enthusiastic wishes, or of intemperate words?

Such is the lesson our Saviour's conduct teaches us. Now let me remind you how diligently we are taught the same by our own Church. Christ gave us a prayer to guide us in praying to the Father; and upon this model our own Liturgy is strictly formed. You will look in vain in the Prayer Book for long or vehement Prayers; for it is only upon occasions that agitation of mind is right, but there is ever a call upon us for seriousness, gravity, simplicity, deliberate trust, deep-seated humility. Many persons, doubtless, think the Church prayers, for this very reason, cold and formal. They do not discern their high perfection, and they think they could easily write better prayers. When such opinions are advanced, it is quite sufficient to turn our thoughts to our Saviour's precept and example. It cannot be denied that those who thus speak, ought to consider our Lord's prayer defective; and sometimes they are profane enough to think so, and to confess they think so. But I pass this by. Granting for argument's sake His *precepts* were intentionally defective, as delivered before the Holy Ghost descended, yet what will they say to His *example*? Can even the fullest light of the Gospel revealed after His resurrection, bring us His followers into the remotest resemblance to our Blessed Lord's holiness? yet how calm was He, who was perfect man, in His own obedience!

To conclude:—Let us take warning from St. Peter's fall. Let us not promise much; let us not talk much of ourselves; let us not be high-minded, nor encourage ourselves in impetuous bold language in religion. Let us take warning, too, from that fickle multitude who cried, first Hosanna, then Crucify. A miracle startled them into a sudden adoration of their Saviour;—its effect upon them soon died away. And thus the especial mercies of God sometimes

31

excite us for a season. We feel Christ speaking to us through our consciences and hearts; and we fancy He is assuring us we are His true servants, when He is but calling on us to receive Him. Let us not be content with saying "Lord, Lord," without "doing the thing which He says." The husbandman's son who said, "I go, sir," yet went not to the vineyard, gained nothing by his fair words. One secret act of self-denial, one sacrifice of inclination to duty, is worth all the mere good thoughts, warm feelings, passionate prayers, in which idle people indulge themselves. It will give us more comfort on our deathbed to reflect on one deed of self-denying mercy, purity, or humility, than to recollect the shedding of many tears, and the recurrence of frequent transports, and much spiritual exultation. These latter feelings come and go; they may or may not accompany hearty obedience; they are never tests of it; but good actions are the fruits of faith, and assure us that we are Christ's; they comfort us as an evidence of the Spirit working in us. By them we shall be judged at the last day; and though they have no worth in themselves, by reason of that infection of sin which gives its character to every thing we do, yet they will be accepted for His sake, who bore the agony in the garden, and suffered as a sinner on the cross.

Times of Private Prayer[†]

"Thou, when thou prayest, enter into thy closet,
and when thou hast shut thy door, pray to thy Father which is in secret;
and thy Father which seeth in secret shall reward thee openly."
Matt. vi. 6

HERE is our Saviour's own sanction and blessing vouchsafed to private prayer, in simple, clear, and most gracious words. The Pharisees were in the practice, when they prayed by themselves, of praying in *public*, in the corners of the streets; a strange inconsistency according to our notions, since in our language prayer by oneself is even called *private* prayer. Public private prayer, this was their self-contradictory practice. Warning, then, His disciples against the particular form of hypocrisy in which the self-conceit of human nature at that day showed itself, our Lord promises in the text His Father's blessing on such humble supplications as were really addressed to Him, and not made to gain the praise of men. Those who seek the unseen God (He seems to say), seek Him in their hearts and hidden thoughts, not in loud words, as if He were far off from them. Such men would retire from the world into places where no human eye saw them, there to meet Him humbly and in faith, who is "about their path, and about their bed, and spieth out all their ways." And He, the Searcher of hearts, would reward them openly. Prayers uttered in secret, according to God's will, are treasured up in God's Book of Life. They seem, perhaps, to have sought an answer here, and to have failed. Their memory perishes even in the mind of the petitioner, and the world never knew of them. But God is ever mindful, and in the last day, when the books are opened, they shall be disclosed and rewarded before the whole world.

Such is Christ's gracious promise in the text, acknowledging and blessing, in His condescension, those devotional exercises which were a duty even before Scripture enjoined them; and changing into a privilege that work of faith, which, though bidden by conscience, and authorized by reason, yet before He revealed His mercy, is laden, in every man's case who attempts it, with guilt, remorse, and fear. It is the Christian's unspeakable privilege, and his alone, that he has at all times free access to the throne of grace through the mediation of his Lord and Saviour.

But, in what I shall now say concerning prayer, I shall not consider it as a

---

[†] *Parochial & Plain Sermons*, vol. 1 (1834), Sermon 19.

privilege, but as a duty; for till we have some experience of the duties of religion, we are incapable of entering duly into the privileges; and it is too much the fashion of the day to view prayer chiefly as a mere privilege, such a privilege as it is inconsiderate indeed to neglect, but only inconsiderate, not sinful; and optional to use.

Now, we know well enough that we are bound to be in one sense in prayer and meditation all the day long. The question then arises, are we to pray in any other way? Is it enough to keep our minds fixed upon God through the day, and to commune with Him in our hearts, or is it necessary, over and above this habitual faith, to set apart particular times for the more systematic and earnest exercise of it? Need we pray at certain times of the day in a set manner? *Public* worship, indeed, from its very nature, requires *places*, *times*, and even set *forms*. But *private* prayer does not necessarily require set *times*, because we have no one to consult but ourselves, and we are always with ourselves; nor *forms*, for there is no one else whose thoughts are to keep pace with ours. Still, though set times and forms of prayer are not absolutely *necessary* in private prayer, yet they are highly expedient; or rather, times are actually commanded us by our Lord in the text, "Thou, *when* thou prayest, enter into thy closet, and when thou hast shut thy door, pray to thy Father which is in secret; and thy Father which seeth in secret shall reward thee openly."

In these words certain *times* for private prayer, over and above the secret thought of God which must ever be alive in us, are clearly enjoined; and the practice of good men in Scripture gives us an example in confirmation of the command. Even our Saviour had His peculiar seasons of communing with God. *His* thoughts indeed were one continued sacred service offered up to His Father; nevertheless, we read of His going up "into a mountain apart to pray," and again, of His "continuing all night in prayer to God." [Matt. xiv. 23. Luke vi. 12.] Doubtless, you well recollect that solitary prayer of His, before His passion, thrice repeated, "that the cup might pass from Him." St. Peter too, as in the narrative of the conversion of Cornelius, the Roman centurion, in the tenth chapter of the Acts, went up upon the house-top to pray about the sixth hour; then God visited him. And Nathanael seems to have been in prayer under the fig-tree, at the time our Saviour saw him, and Philip called him. [John i. 48.] I might multiply instances from Scripture of such "Israelites without guile;" which are of course to us, because, though they were under a Divine government in many respects different from the Christian, yet *personal* religion is the same at all times; "the just" in every dispensation "shall live by faith," and whatever reasons there were then for faith to display and maintain itself by stated prayer, remain substantially the same now. Let two passages suffice. The Psalmist says, "*Seven* times a day do I praise Thee, because of Thy righteous judgments." [Ps. cxix. 164.] And Daniel's practice is told us on a memorable occasion: "Now when Daniel knew that the writing was signed (the impious decree, forbidding prayer to any but king Darius for thirty days), he went into his house, and his windows being open in his chamber toward Jerusalem, he kneeled upon his knees *three times* a day, and prayed, and gave thanks before his God, *as he did aforetime.*" [Dan. vi. 10.]

It is plain, then, besides the devotional temper in which we should pass the day, more solemn and direct acts of worship, nay, *regular and periodical,* are required of us by the precept of Christ, and His own example, and that of His Apostles and Prophets under both covenants.

Now it is necessary to insist upon this duty of observing private prayer at stated times, because amid the cares and hurry of life men are very apt to neglect it: and it is a much more important duty than it is generally considered, even by those who perform it.

It is important for the two reasons which follow.

1. It brings religious subjects before the mind in regular course. Prayer *through* the day, is indeed the characteristic of a Christian spirit, but we may be sure that, in most cases, those who do not pray at stated times in a more solemn and direct manner, will never pray well at other times. We know in the common engagements of life, the importance of collecting and arranging our thoughts calmly and accurately before proceeding to any important business, in order to the right performance of it; and so in that one really needful occupation, the care of our eternal interests, if we would have our minds composed, our desires subdued, and our tempers heavenly through the day, we must, before commencing the day's employment, stand still awhile to look into ourselves, and commune with our hearts, by way of preparing ourselves for the trials and duties on which we are entering. A like reason may be assigned for evening prayer, viz. as affording us a time of looking back on the day past, and summing up (as it were) that account, which, if *we* do not reckon, at least God has reckoned, and written down in that book which will be produced at the Judgment; a time of confessing sin, and of praying for forgiveness, of giving thanks for what we have done well, and for mercies received, of making good resolutions in reliance on the help of God, and of sealing up and setting sure the day past, at least as a stepping-stone of good for the morrow. The precise times indeed of private prayer are no where commanded us in Scripture; the most obvious are those I have mentioned, morning and evening. In the texts just now read to you, you heard of praying three times a day, or seven times. All this depends of course on the opportunities of each individual. Some men have not leisure for this; but for morning and evening prayer all men can and should *make* leisure.

35

Stated times of private prayer, then, are useful as impulses (so to say) to the continuous devotion of the day. They instruct us and engage us in what is ever our duty. It is commonly said, that what is every one's business is practically no one's; this applies here. I repeat it, if we leave religion as a subject of thought for all hours of the day equally, it will be thought of in none. In all things it is by small beginnings and appointed channels that an advance is made to extensive works. Stated times of prayer put us in that posture (as I may call it) in which we ought ever to be; they urge us forward in a heavenly direction, and then the stream carries us on. For the same reason it is expedient, if possible, to be solemn in the forms of our private worship, in order to impress our minds. Our Saviour *kneeled* down, fell on His face, and prayed,[6]—so did His Apostles;[7] and so did the Saints of the Old Testament. Hence many persons are accustomed (such as have the opportunity) to set apart a particular place for their private devotions; still for the same reason, to compose their mind,—as Christ tells us in the text, to enter into our closet.

2. I now come to the second reason for stated private prayer. Besides its tending to produce in us lasting religious impressions, which I have already enlarged upon, it is also a more direct means of gaining from God an answer to our requests. He has so sanctioned it in the text:—"Shut thy door, and pray to thy Father which seeth in secret, and He shall reward thee openly." We do not know *how* it is that prayer receives an answer from God at all. It is strange, indeed, that weak man should have strength to move God; but it is our privilege to know that we *can* do so. The whole system of this world is a history of man's interfering with Divine decrees; and if we have the melancholy power of baffling His good-will, to our own ruin (an awful, an incomprehensible truth!), if, when He designs our eternal salvation, we can yet annul our heavenly election, and accomplish our eternal destruction, much more have we the power to move Him (blessed be His name!) when He, the Searcher of hearts, discerns in us the mind of that Holy Spirit, which "maketh intercession for the saints according to His will." And, as He has thus promised an answer to our poor prayers, so it is not more strange that prayers offered up at particular times, and in a particular way, should have especially prevailing power with Him. And the reason of it may be as follows. It is faith that is the appointed means of gaining all blessings from God. "All things are possible to him that believeth." [Mark ix. 23.] Now, at stated times, when we gather up our thoughts to pray, and draw out our petitions in an orderly and clear manner, the act of faith is likely to be stronger and more earnest; then we realize more perfectly the presence of that God whom we do not see, and Him on whom

---

[6] Matt. xxvi. 39. Luke xxii. 41.
[7] Acts xx. 36; xxi. 5. Eph. iii. 14.

once all our sins were laid, who bore the weight of our infirmities and sickness once for all, that in all our troubles we might seek Him, and find grace in time of need. Then this world is more out of sight, and we more simply appropriate those blessings, which we have but to claim humbly and they are really ours.

Stated times of prayer, then, are necessary; first, as a means of making the mind sober, and the general temper more religious; secondly, as a means of exercising earnest faith, and thereby of receiving a more certain blessing in answer, than we should otherwise obtain.

Other reasons, doubtless, may be given; but these are enough, not only as containing subject for thought which may be useful to us, but besides, as serving to show how wise and merciful those Divine provisions really are, which our vain minds are so apt to question. All God's commands, indeed, ought to be received at once upon faith, though we saw no reason for them. It is no excuse for a man's disobeying them, even if he thinks he sees reasons against them; for God knows better than we do. But in great condescension He has allowed us to see here and there His reasons for what He does and enjoins; and we should treasure up these occasional notices as memorials against the time of temptation, that when doubt and unbelief assail us, and we are perplexed at His revealed word, we may call to mind those former instances in our own experience, where what at first seemed strange and hard, on closer consideration was found to have a wise end.

Now the duty of having stated times of private prayer is one of those observances, concerning which we are apt to entertain the unbelieving thoughts I have been describing. It seems to us to be a form, or at least a light matter, to observe or omit; whereas in truth, such creatures are we, there is the most close and remarkable connexion between small observances and the permanence of our chief habits and practices. It is easy to see why it is irksome; because it presses upon us and is inconvenient. It is a duty which claims our attention continually, and its irksomeness leads our hearts to rebel; and then we proceed to search for reasons to justify our own dislike of it. Nothing is more difficult than to be disciplined and regular in our religion. It is very easy to be religious by fits and starts, and to keep up our feelings by artificial stimulants; but regularity seems to trammel us, and we become impatient. This is especially the case with those to whom the world is as yet new, and who can do as they please. Religion is the chief subject which meets them, which enjoins regularity; and they bear it only so far as they can make it like things of this world, something curious, or changeable, or exciting. Satan knows his advantage here. He perceives well enough that stated private prayer is the very emblem and safeguard of true devotion to God, as impressing on us and keeping up in us a rule of conduct. He who gives up regularity in prayer has lost a principal means of reminding himself that spiritual life is obedience to a Lawgiver, not a mere feeling or a taste. Hence it is that so many persons, especially in the polished ranks of society, who are out of the way of temptation to gross vice, fall away into a mere luxurious self-indulgent devotion, which they take for religion; they reject every thing which implies self-denial, and regular prayer especially. Hence it is that others run into all kinds of enthusiastic fancies; because, by giving up set private prayer in written forms, they have lost the chief rule of their hearts. Accordingly, you will hear them exclaim against regular prayer (which is the very medicine suited to their disease) as a formal service, and maintain that times and places and fixed words are beneath the attention of a spiritual Christian. And others, who are exposed to the seductions of sin, altogether fall away from the same omission. Be sure, my brethren, whoever of you is persuaded to disuse his morning and evening prayers, is giving up the armour which is to secure him against the wiles of the Devil. If you have left off the observance of them, you may fall any day;—and you will fall without notice. For a time you will go on, seeming to yourselves to be the same as before; but the Israelites might as well hope to lay in a stock of manna as you of grace. You pray God for your daily bread, your bread day by day; and if you have not prayed for it this morning, it will profit you little that you prayed for it yesterday. You did then pray and you obtained,—but not a supply for two days. When you have given over the practice of stated prayer, you gradually become weaker without knowing it. Samson did not know he had lost his strength till the Philistines came upon him; you will think yourselves the men you used to be, till suddenly your adversary will come furiously upon you, and you will as suddenly fall. You will be able to make little or no resistance. This is the path which leads to death. Men first leave off private prayer; then they neglect the due observance of the Lord's day (which is a stated service of the same kind); then they gradually let slip from their minds the very idea of obedience to a fixed eternal law; then they actually allow themselves in things which their conscience condemns; then they lose the direction of their conscience, which being ill used, at length refuses to direct them. And thus, being left by their true inward guide, they are obliged to take another guide, their reason, which by itself knows little or nothing about religion; then, this their blind reason forms a system of right or wrong for them, as well as it can, flattering to their own desires, and presumptuous where it is not actually corrupt. No wonder such a scheme contradicts Scripture, which it is soon found to do; not that they are certain to perceive this themselves; they often do not know it, and think themselves still believers in the Gospel, while they maintain doctrines which the Gospel condemns. But sometimes they perceive that their system is contrary to Scripture; and then, instead of giving it up, they give up

Scripture, and profess themselves unbelievers. Such is the course of disobedience, beginning in (apparently) slight omissions, and ending in open unbelief; and all men who walk in the broad way which leads to destruction are but at different stages of it, one more advanced than another, but all in one way. And I have spoken of it here, in order to remind you how intimately it is connected with the neglect of set private prayer; whereas, he who is strict in the observance of prayer morning and evening, praying with his heart as well as his lips, can hardly go astray, for every morning and evening brings him a monitor to draw him back and restore him.

Beware then of the subtilty of your Enemy, who would fain rob you of your defence. Do not yield to his bad reasonings. Be on your guard especially, when you get into novel situations or circumstances which interest and delight you, lest they throw you out of your regularity in prayer. Any thing new or unexpected is dangerous to you. Going much into mixed society, and seeing many strange persons, taking share in any pleasant amusements, reading interesting books, entering into a new line of life, forming some new acquaintance, the sudden prospect of any worldly advantage, travelling; all these things and such like, innocent as they are in themselves, and capable of a religious use, become means of temptation if we are not on our guard. See that you are not *unsettled* by them; this is the danger; fear becoming *unsettled*. Consider that stability of mind is the chief of virtues, for it is Faith. "Thou wilt keep him in perfect peace, whose mind is stayed on Thee, because he trusteth in Thee;" [Isa. xxvi. 3.] this is the promise. But "the wicked are like the troubled sea when it cannot rest, whose waters cast up mire and dirt; there is no peace, saith my God, to the wicked." [Isa. lvii. 20, 21.] Nor to the wicked only, in our common sense of the word "wicked," but to none is there rest, who in any way leave their God, and rove after the goods of this world. Do not indulge visions of earthly good, fix your hearts on higher things, let your morning and evening thoughts be points of rest for your mind's eye, and let those thoughts be upon the narrow way, and the blessedness of heaven, and the glory and power of Christ your Saviour. Thus will you be kept from unseemly risings and fallings, and steadied in an equable way. Men in general will know nothing of this; they witness not your private prayers, and they will confuse you with the multitude they fall in with. But your friends and acquaintance will gain a light and a comfort from your example; they will see your good works, and be led to trace them to their true secret source, the influences of the Holy Ghost sought and obtained by prayer. Thus they will glorify your heavenly Father, and in imitation of you will seek Him; and He who seeth in secret, shall at length reward you openly.

Forms of Private Prayer[†]

"Lord, teach us to pray, as John also taught his disciples."
Luke xi. 1

THESE WORDS express the natural feelings of the awakened mind, perceiving its great need of God's help, yet not understanding well what its particular wants are, or how they are to be relieved. The disciples of John the Baptist, and the disciples of Christ, waited on their respective Masters for instruction *how to pray*. It was in vain that the duty of repentance was preached to the one, and of faith to the other; in vain that God's mercies and His judgments were set before them, and their own duties; they seemed to have all that was necessary for making prayers for themselves, yet they could not; their hearts were full, but they remained dumb; they could offer no petition except to *be taught* to pray; they knew the Truth, but they could not use it. So different a thing is it to be instructed in religion, and to have so mastered it in practice that it is altogether our own.

Their need has been the need of Christians ever since. All of us in childhood, and most men ever after, require direction how to pray; and hence the use of *Forms of prayer*, which have always obtained in the Church. John taught his disciples; Christ gave the Apostles the prayer which is distinguished by the name of the *Lord's Prayer*; and after He had ascended on high, the Holy Spirit has given us excellent services of devotion by the mouth of those blessed Saints, whom from time to time He has raised up to be overseers in the Church. In the words of St. Paul, "We know not what we should pray for as we ought;" [Rom. viii. 26.] but "the Spirit helpeth our infirmities;" and that, not only by guiding our thoughts, but by directing our words.

This, I say, is the origin of *Forms of prayer*, of which I mean to speak to-day; viz. these two undeniable truths, first, that all men have the same spiritual wants, and, secondly, that they cannot of themselves express them.

Now it has so happened, that in these latter times self-wise reasoners have arisen who have questioned the use of Forms of prayer, and have thought it better to pray out of their own thoughts at random, using words which come into their minds at the time they pray. It may be right, then, that we should have some reason at hand for our use of those Forms, which we have

---

[†] *Parochial & Plain Sermons*, vol. 1 (1834), Sermon 20.

adopted because they were handed down to us. Not, as if it were not quite a *sufficient* reason for using them, that we have received them, and (in St. Paul's words) that "neither we nor the Churches of God have known any other custom," [1 Cor. xi. 16.] and that the best of Christians have ever used them; for this *is* an abundantly satisfactory reason;—nor again, as if we could hope by reasons ever so good, to persuade those who inquire of us, which most likely we shall not be able to do; for a man is far gone in extravagance who deliberately denies the use of Forms, and is likely to find our reasons as difficult to receive as the practice we are defending;—so that we can only say of such men, after St. Paul's manner, "if any man be ignorant, let him be ignorant," there is no help for it. But it may be useful to show you *how* reasonable the practice is, in order that you yourselves may turn it to better account; for when we know why we do a thing, we are likely (the same circumstances being supposed) to do it more comfortably than when we obey ignorantly.

Now, I suppose no one is in any difficulty about the use of Forms of prayer in *public* worship; for common sense almost will tell us, that when many are to pray together *as one* man, if their thoughts are to go together, they *must* agree beforehand what is to be the subject of their prayers, nay, what the *words* of their prayers, if there is to be any certainty, composure, ease, and regularity, in their united devotions. To be present at extempore prayer, is to *hear prayers*. Nay, it might happen, or rather often would happen, that we did not understand what was said; and then the person praying is scarcely praying "in a tongue understanded of the people" (as our Article expresses it); he is rather interceding *for* the people, than praying *with* them, and leading their worship. In the case, then, of *public* prayer the need of Forms is evident; but it is not at first sight *so* obvious that in *private* prayer also we need use written Forms, instead of praying *extempore* (as it is called); so I proceed to show the use of them.

1. Let us bear in mind the precept of the wise man. "Be not rash with thy mouth, and let not thine heart be hasty to utter any thing before God; for God is in heaven, and thou upon earth; therefore let thy words be few." [Eccles. v. 2.] Prayers framed at the moment are likely to become *irreverent*. Let us consider for a few moments before we pray, into whose presence we are entering,—the presence of God. What need have we of humble, sober, and subdued thoughts! as becomes *creatures*, sustained hourly by His bounty;—as becomes *lost sinners* who have no right to speak at all, but must submit in silence to Him who is holy;—and still more, as grateful *servants of Him* who bought us from ruin at the price of His own blood; meekly sitting at His feet like Mary to learn and to do His will, and like the penitent at the great man's feast, quietly adoring Him, and doing Him service without disturbance, wash-

41

ing His feet (as it were) with our tears, and anointing them with precious ointment, as having sinned much and needing a large forgiveness. Therefore, to avoid the irreverence of many or unfit words and rude half-religious thoughts, it is necessary to pray from book or memory, and not at random.

It may be objected, that this reason for using Forms proves too much; viz. that it would be wrong ever to do without them; which is an over-rigorous bond upon Christian liberty. But I reply, that reverence in our prayers will be sufficiently secured, if at our stated seasons for prayer we make use of Forms. For thus a tone and character will be imparted to our devotion throughout the day; nay, even the very petitions and ejaculations will be supplied, which we need. And much more will our souls be influenced by the power of them, at the very time we are using them; so that, should the occasion require, we shall find ourselves able to go forward naturally and soberly into such additional supplications, as are of too particular or private a nature, to admit of being written down in set words.

2. In the next place, Forms of prayer are necessary to guard us against the irreverence of *wandering* thoughts. If we pray without set words (read or remembered), our minds will stray from the subject; other thoughts will cross us, and we shall pursue them; we shall lose sight of His presence whom we are addressing. This wandering of mind is in good measure prevented, under God's blessing, by Forms of prayer. Thus a chief use of them is that of *fixing the attention*.

3. Next, they are useful in securing us from the irreverence of *excited thoughts*. And here there is room for saying much; for, it so happens, Forms of prayer are censured for the very circumstance about them which is their excellence. They are accused of impeding the current of devotion, when, in fact, that (so called) current is in itself faulty, and ought to be checked. And those persons (as might be expected) are most eager in their opposition to them, who require more than others the restraint of them. They sometimes throw their objection into the following form, which it may be worth while to consider. They say, "If a man is in earnest, he will soon find words; there is no need of a set Form of prayer. And if he is not in earnest, a Form can do him no good." Now that a man who is in earnest will soon find words, is true or not true, according to what is meant by being in earnest. It is true that at certain times of strong emotion, grief or joy, remorse or fear, our religious feelings outrun and leave behind them any Form of words. In such cases, not only is there no *need* of Forms of prayer, but it is perhaps impossible to write *Forms* of prayer for Christians agitated by such feelings. For each man feels in his own way,—perhaps no two men exactly alike;—and we can no more write down *how* men ought to pray at such times, than we can give rules how they

should weep or be merry. The better men they are, of course the better they will pray in such a trying time; but you cannot make them better; they must be left to themselves. And, though good men have before now set down in writing Forms of prayer for persons so circumstanced, these were doubtless meant rather as patterns and helps, or as admonitions and (if so be) quietings of the agitated mind, than as prayers which it was expected would be used literally and entirely in their detail. As a general rule, Forms of prayer should not be written in strong and impassioned language; but should be calm, composed, and short. Our Saviour's own prayer is our model in this respect. How few are its petitions! how soberly expressed! how reverently! and at the same time how deep are they, and how comprehensive!—I readily grant, then, that there *are* times when the heart outruns any written words; as the jailor cried out, "What shall I do to be saved?" Nay, rather I would maintain that set words should not attempt to imitate the impetuous workings to which all minds are subject at times in this world of change (and therefore religious minds in the number), lest one should seem to encourage them.

Still the question is not at all settled; granting there *are* times when a thankful or a wounded heart bursts through all Forms of prayer, yet these are not *frequent*. To be excited is not the *ordinary* state of the mind, but the extraordinary, the now and then state. Nay, more than this, it *ought not* to be the common state of the mind; and if we are encouraging within us this excitement, this unceasing rush and alternation of feelings, and think that this, and this only, is being in earnest in religion, we are harming our minds, and (in one sense) I may even say grieving the peaceful Spirit of God, who would silently and tranquilly work His Divine work in our hearts. This, then, is an especial *use* of Forms of prayer, *when* we are in earnest, as we ought always to be; viz. to keep us from self-willed earnestness, to still emotion, to calm us, to remind us what and where we are, to lead us to a purer and serener temper, and to that deep unruffled love of God and man, which is really the fulfilling of the law, and the perfection of human nature.

Then, again, as to the usefulness of Forms, if we are *not* in earnest,—this also is true or not, as we may take it. For there are degrees of earnestness. Let us recollect, the power of praying, being a habit, must be acquired, like all other habits, by practice. In order at length to pray well, we must begin by praying ill, since ill is all we can do. Is not this plain? Who, in the case of any other work, would wait till he could do it perfectly, before he tried it? The idea is absurd. Yet those who object to Forms of prayer on the ground just mentioned, fall into this strange error. If, indeed, we could pray and praise God like the Angels, we might have no need of Forms of prayer; but Forms are to teach those who pray poorly to pray better. They are helps to our devotion, as teaching us what to pray for and how, as St. John and our Lord taught their disciples; and, doubtless, even the *best* of us prays *but* poorly, and *needs* the help of them. However, the persons I speak of, think that prayer is nothing else but the bursting forth of strong feeling, not the action of a habit, but an emotion, and, therefore, *of course* to such men the very notion of *learning* to pray seems absurd. But this indulgence of emotion is in truth founded on a mistake, as I have already said.

4. Further, Forms are useful to *help our memory*, and to set before us at once, completely, and in order, what we have to pray for. It does not follow, that when the heart is really full of the thought of God, and alive to the reality of things unseen, then it is easiest to pray. Rather, the deeper insight we have into His Majesty and our innumerable wants, the less we shall be able to draw out our thoughts into words. The publican could only say, "God be merciful to me a sinner;" this was enough for his *acceptance*; but to offer such a scanty service was not to exercise the *gift* of prayer, the privilege of a ransomed and exalted son of God. He whom Christ has illuminated with His grace, is heir of all things. He has an interest in the world's multitude of matters. He has a boundless sphere of duties within and without him. He has a glorious prospect before him. The saints shall hereafter judge the world; and shall they not *here* take cognizance of its doings? are they not in one sense counsellors and confidential servants of their Lord, intercessors at the throne of grace, the secret agents by and for whom He guides His high Providence, and carries on the nations to their doom? And in their own persons is forgiveness merely and acceptance (extreme blessings as these are) the scope of their desires? else might they be content with the publican's prayer. Are they not rather bidden to go on to perfection, to use the spirit given them, to enlarge and purify their own hearts, and to draw out the nature of man into the fulness of its capabilities after the image of the Son of God? And for the thought of all these objects at once, who is sufficient? Whose mind is not overpowered by the view of its own immense privilege, so as eagerly to seek for words of prayer and intercession, carefully composed according to the number and the nature of the various petitions it has to offer? so that he who prays without plan, is in fact losing a great part of the privilege with which his Baptism has gifted him.

5. And further, the use of a Form as a help to the memory is still more obvious, when we take into account the engagements of this world with which most men are surrounded. The cares and businesses of life press upon us with a reality which we cannot overlook. Shall we trust the matters of the next world to the chance thoughts of our own minds, which come this moment, and go the next, and may not be at hand when the time of employing them arrives, like unreal visions, having no substance and no permanence? This

world is Satan's efficacious Form, it is the instrument through which he spreads out in order and attractiveness his many snares; and these doubtless will engross us, unless we also give Form to the spiritual objects towards which we pray and labour. How short are the seasons which most men have to give to prayer? Before they can collect their memories and minds, their leisure is almost over, even if they have the power to dismiss the thoughts of this world, which just before engaged them. Now Forms of prayer do this *for* them. They keep the ground occupied, that Satan may not encroach upon the seasons of devotion. They are a standing memorial, to which we can recur as to a temple of God, finding every thing in order for our worship as soon as we go into it, though the time allotted us at morning and evening be ever so circumscribed.

6. And this use of Forms in prayer becomes great beyond power of estimating, in the case of those multitudes of men, who, after going on well for a while, fall into sin. If even conscientious men require continual aids to be reminded of the next world, how extreme is the need of those who try to forget it! It cannot be denied, fearful as it is to reflect upon it, that far the greater number of those who come to manhood, for a while (at least) desert the God who has redeemed them; and, then, if in their earlier years they have learned and used no prayers or psalms by which to worship Him, what is to keep them from blotting altogether from their minds the thought of religion? But here it is that the Forms of the Church have ever served her children, both to restrain them in their career of sin, and to supply them with ready utterance on their repentance. Chance words and phrases of her services adhere to their memories, rising up in moments of temptation or of trouble, to check or to recover them. And hence it happens, that in the most irreligious companies a distinction is said to be observable between those who have had the opportunity of using our public Forms in their youth, and those whose religious impressions have not been thus happily fortified; so that, amid their most reckless mirth, and most daring pretence of profligacy, a sort of secret reverence has attended the wanderers, restraining them from that impiety and profaneness in which the others have tried to conceal from themselves the guilt and peril of their doings.

And again on their repentance (should they be favoured with so high a grace), what friends do they seem to find amid their gloom in the words they learned in their boyhood,—a kindly voice, aiding them to say what they otherwise would not know how to say, guiding and composing their minds upon those objects of faith which they ought to look to, but cannot find of themselves, and so (as it were) interceding for them with the power of the blessed Spirit, while nature can but groan and travail in pain! Sinners as they are by their own voluntary misdeeds, and with a prospect of punishment before them, enlightened by but few and faint gleams of hope, what shall keep them from feverish restlessness, and all the extravagance of fear, what shall soothe them into a fixed, resigned waiting for their Judge, and such lowly efforts to obey Him, however poorly, as become a penitent, but those words, long buried in their minds, and now rising again as if with the life of their uncorrupted boyhood? It requires no great experience of sick beds to verify the truth of this statement. Blessed, indeed, is the power of those formularies, which thus succeed in throwing a sinner for a while out of himself, and in bringing before him the scenes of his youth, his guardian friends now long departed, their ways and their teaching, their pious services, and their peaceful end; and though all this is an excitement, and lasts but for a season, yet, if improved by him, it may be converted into an habitual contemplation of persons and deeds which now live to God, though removed hence,—if improved by his acting upon it, it will become an abiding motive to seek the world to come, an abiding persuasion, winning him from the works of darkness, and raising him to the humble hope of future acceptance with his Saviour and Judge.

7. Such is the force of association in undoing the evil of past years, and recalling us to the innocence of children. Nor is this all we may gain from the prayers we use, nor are penitent sinners the only persons who can profit by it. Let us recollect for how long a period our prayers have been the standard Forms of devotion in the Church of Christ, and we shall gain a fresh reason for loving them, and a fresh source of comfort in using them. I know different persons will feel differently here, according to their different turn of mind; yet surely there are few of us, if we dwelt on the thought, but would feel it a privilege to use, as we do (for instance, in the Lord's Prayer), the very petitions which Christ spoke. He gave the prayer and used it. His Apostles used it; all the Saints ever since have used it. When we use it we seem to join company with them. Who does not think himself brought nearer to any celebrated man in history, by seeing his house, or his furniture, or his handwriting, or the very books that were his? Thus does the Lord's Prayer bring us near to Christ, and to His disciples in every age. No wonder, then, that in past times good men thought this Form of prayer so sacred, that it seemed to them impossible to say it too often, as if some especial grace went with the use of it. Nor *can* we use it too often; it contains in itself a sort of plea for Christ's listening to us; we cannot, so that we keep our thoughts fixed on its petitions, and use our minds as well as our lips when we repeat it. And what is true of the Lord's Prayer, is in its measure true of most of those prayers which our Church teaches us to use. It is true of the Psalms also, and of the Creeds; all of which have become sacred, from the memory of saints departed who have used them, and whom we hope one day to meet in heaven.

One caution I give in conclusion as to using these thoughts. Beware lest your religion be one of sentiment merely, not of practice. Men may speak in a high imaginative way of the ancient Saints and the Holy Apostolic Church, without making the fervour or refinement of their devotion bear upon their conduct. Many a man likes to be religious in graceful language; he loves religious tales and hymns, yet is never the better Christian for all this. The works of every day, these are the tests of our glorious contemplations, whether or not they shall be available to our salvation; and he who does one deed of obedience for Christ's sake, let him have no imagination and no fine feeling, is a better man, and returns to his home justified rather than the most eloquent speaker, and the most sensitive hearer, of the glory of the Gospel, if such men do not practise up to their knowledge.

Christian Reverence[†]

"Serve the Lord with fear, and rejoice with trembling."
Psalm ii. 11

WHY DID Christ show Himself to so few witnesses after He rose from the dead? Because *He was a King*, a King exalted upon God's "Holy hill of Zion;" as the Psalm says which contains the text. Kings do not court the multitude, or show themselves as a spectacle at the will of others. They are the rulers of their people, and have their state as such, and are reverently waited on by their great men: and when they show themselves, they do so out of their condescension. They act by means of their servants, and must be *sought* by those who would gain favours from them.

Christ, in like manner, when exalted as the Only-begotten Son of God, did not mix with the Jewish people, as in the days of His humiliation. He rose from the grave in secret, and taught in secret for forty days, because "the government was upon His shoulder." He was no longer a servant washing His disciples' feet, and dependent on the wayward will of the multitude. He was the acknowledged Heir of all things. His throne was established by a Divine decree; and those who desired His salvation, were bound to *seek* His face. Yet not even by those who sought was He at once found. He did not permit the world to approach Him rashly, or curiously to gaze on Him. Those only did He call beside Him who had been His friends, who loved Him. Those only He bade "ascend the hill of the Lord," who had "clean hands and a pure heart, who had not worshipped vanity nor sworn deceitfully." These drew near, and "saw the Lord God of Israel," and so were fitted to bear the news of Him to the people at large. *He* remained "in His holy temple;" *they* from Him proclaimed the tidings of His resurrection, and of His mercy, His free pardon offered to all men, and the promises of grace and glory which His death had procured for all who believe.

Thus are we taught to serve our risen Lord with fear, and rejoice with trembling. Let us pursue the subject thus opened upon us.—Christ's second sojourn on earth (after His resurrection) was *in secret*. The time had been when He "preached openly in the synagogues," and in the public ways; and openly wrought miracles such as man never did. Was there to be no end of

---

[†] *Parochial & Plain Sermons*, vol. 1 (1834), Sermon 23.

His labours in our behalf? His *death* "finished" them; afterwards He taught His *followers* only. Who shall complain of His withdrawing Himself at last from the world, when it was of His own spontaneous loving-kindness that He ever showed Himself at all?

Yet it must be borne in mind, that even before He entered into His glory, Christ spoke and acted as a King. It must not be supposed that, even in the days of His flesh, He could forget who He was, or "behave Himself unseemly" by any weak submission to the will of the Jewish people. Even in the lowest acts of His self-abasement, still He showed His greatness. Consider His conduct when He washed St. Peter's feet, and see if it were not calculated (assuredly it was) to humble, to awe, and subdue the very person to whom He ministered. When He taught, warned, pitied, prayed for, His ignorant hearers, He never allowed them to relax their reverence or to overlook His condescension. Nay, He did not allow them to praise Him aloud, and publish His acts of grace; as if what is called popularity would be a dishonour to His holy name, and the applause of men would imply their right to censure. The world's praise is akin to contempt. Our Lord delights in the tribute of the secret heart. Such was His conduct in the days of His flesh. Does it not interpret His dealings with us after His resurrection? He who was so reserved in His communications of Himself, even when He came to minister, much more would withdraw Himself from the eyes of men when He was exalted over all things.

I have said, that even when a servant, Christ spoke with the authority of a king; and have given you some proof of it. But it may be well to dwell upon this. Observe then, the difference between His promises, stated doctrinally and generally, and His mode of addressing those who came actually before Him. While He announced God's willingness to forgive *all* repentant sinners, in all the fulness of loving-kindness and tender mercy, yet He did not use supplication to these persons or those, whatever their number or their rank might be. He spoke as one who knew He had great favours to confer, and had nothing to gain from those who received them. Far from urging them to accept His bounty, He showed Himself even backward to confer it, inquired into their knowledge and motives, and cautioned them against entering His service without counting the cost of it. Thus sometimes He even repelled men from Him.

For instance: When there went "great multitudes with Him . . . He turned and said unto them, If any man come to Me, and hate not his father and mother, and wife and children, and brothers and sisters, yea, and his own life also, he cannot be My disciple." These were not the words of one who courted popularity. He proceeds;—"Which of you intending to build a tower, sitteth not down first, and counteth the cost, whether he have sufficient to finish it? . . . So likewise, whosoever he be of you, that forsaketh not all that he hath, he cannot be My disciple." [Luke xiv. 25–33.] On the other hand, observe His conduct to the powerful men, and the learned Scribes and Pharisees. There are persons who look up to human power, and who are pleased to associate their names with the accomplished and cultivated of this world. Our blessed Lord was as inflexible towards these, as towards the crowds which followed Him. They asked for a sign; He named them "an evil and adulterous generation," who refused to profit by what they had already received [Matt. xii. 39; xxi. 23–27.]. They asked Him, whether He did not confess Himself to be One with God; but He, rather than tell such proud disputers, seemed even to abandon His own real claim, and made His former clear words ambiguous. [John x. 30–37.] Such was the King of Israel in the eyes both of the multitude and of their rulers; a "hard saying," a "rock of offence even to the disobedient," who came to Him "with their lips, while their hearts were far from Him." Continue this survey to the case of individuals, and it will still appear, that, loving and merciful as He was most abundantly, yet still He showed both His power and His grace with reserve, even to them, as well as to the fickle many, or the unbelieving Pharisees.

One instance is preserved to us of a person addressing Him, with some notions, indeed, of His greatness, but in a light and careless tone. The narrative is instructive from the mixture of good and bad which the inquirer's character displays.[8] He was young, and wealthy, and is called "a ruler;" yet was anxious for Christ's favour. So far was well. Nay, he "came running and kneeling to Him." And he *seemed* to address Him in what would generally be considered as respectful terms: "Good Master," he said. Yet our Saviour saw in his conduct a deficiency;—"One thing thou lackest:" viz. *devotion* in the true sense of the word,—a giving himself up to Christ. This young man seems to have considered religion as an easy work, and thought he could live as the world, and yet serve God acceptably. In consequence, we may suppose, he had little right notion of the dignity of a Messenger from God. He did not associate the Ministers of religion with awful prospects beyond the grave, in which he was interested; nor *reverence* them accordingly, though he was not without some kind of *respect* for them. Doubtless he thought he was *honouring* our Lord when he had called Him "*Good Master*," and would have been surprised to hear his attachment to sacred subjects and appointments called in question. Yet our Saviour rejected such half homage, and rebuked what even seemed piously offered.—"*Why* callest thou Me good?" He asked; "There is none good but One, that is, God:" as if He said, "Observest thou *what* words thou art using as if words of course? '*Good Master*'—am I accounted by thee as a teach-

---

[8] Matt. xix. 16–22. Mark x. 17–22. Luke xviii. 18–23.

er of man's creation, and over whom man has power, and to be accosted by a form of honour, which, through length of time, has lost its meaning; or am I acknowledged to come and have authority from Him who is the only source of goodness?" Nor did our Lord relax His severity even after this reproof. Expressly as it is told us, "*He loved him*," and spoke to him therefore in great compassion and mercy, yet He strictly charged him to sell all he had and give it away, if he would show he was in earnest, and He sent him away "sorrowful."

You may recollect, too, our Lord's frequent inquiry into *the faith* of those who came to Him. This arose, doubtless, from the same rule,—a regard to His own Majesty as a King. "If thou canst believe, all things are possible to him that believeth." [Mark ix. 23.] He did not work miracles as a mere display of power; or allow the world profanely to look on as at some exhibition of art. In this respect, as in others, even Moses and Elias stand in contrast with Him. Moses wrought miracles before Pharaoh to rival the magicians of Egypt. Elijah challenged the prophets of Baal to bring down fire from heaven. The Son of God deigned not to exert His power before Herod, after Moses' pattern; nor to be judged by the multitude, as Elijah. He subdued the power of Satan at His own appointed seasons; but when the Devil tempted Him and demanded a miracle in proof of His Divinity, He would do none.

Further, even when an inquirer showed earnestness, still He did not try to gain him over by smooth representations of His doctrine. He declared, indeed, the general characteristic of His doctrine, "My yoke easy;" but "He made Himself strange and spake roughly" to those who came to Him. Nicodemus was another ruler of the Jews, who sought Him, and he professed his belief in His miracles and Divine mission. Our Saviour answered in these severe words;—"Verily, verily, I say unto thee, Except a man be born again, he cannot see the kingdom of God."

Such was our Saviour's conduct even during the period of His ministry; much more might we expect it to be such, when He had risen from His state of servitude, and such we find it.

No man saw Him rise from the grave. His Angels indeed beheld it; but His earthly followers were away, and the heathen soldiers were not worthy. They saw, indeed, the great Angel, who rolled away the stone from the opening of the tomb. This was Christ's servant; but Him they saw not. *He* was on His way to see His own faithful and mourning followers. To these He had revealed His doctrine during His humiliation, and called them "His friends." [Matt. xiii. 11. John xv. 15.] First of all, He appeared to Mary Magdalene in the garden itself where He had been buried; then to the other women who ministered unto Him; then to the two disciples travelling to Emmaus; then to all the Apostles separately; besides, to Peter and to James; and to Thomas in the presence of them all. Yet not even these, His friends, had free access to Him. He said to Mary, "Touch Me not." He came and left them according to His own pleasure. When they saw Him, they felt an awe which they had not felt during His ministry. While they doubted if it were He, "None of them," St. John says, "durst ask Him, Who art Thou? believing that it was the Lord." [John xxi. 12.] However, as kings have their days of state, on which they show themselves publicly to their subjects, so our Lord appointed a meeting of His disciples, when they might see Him. He had determined this even before His crucifixion; and the Angels reminded them of it. "He goeth before you into Galilee; there shall ye see Him, as He said unto you." [Mark xvi. 7.] The place of meeting was a mountain; the same (it is supposed) as that on which He had been transfigured; and the number who saw Him there was five hundred at once, if we join St. Paul's account to that in the Gospels. At length, after forty days, He was taken from them; He ascended up, "and a cloud received Him out of their sight."

Are *we* to feel less humble veneration for Him now, than His Apostles then? Though He is our Savior, and has removed all slavish fear of death and judgment, are we, therefore, to make light of the prospect before us, as if we were sure of that reward which He bids us struggle for? Assuredly, we are still to "serve the Lord with fear, and rejoice with reverence,"—to "kiss the Son, lest He be angry, and so we perish from the right way, if His wrath be kindled, yea but a little." In a Christian's course, *fear and love must go together*. And this is the lesson to be deduced from our Saviour's withdrawing from the world after His resurrection. He showed His love for men by dying for them, and rising again. He maintained His honour and great glory by retiring from them when His merciful purpose was attained, that they might seek Him if they would find Him. He ascended to His Father out of our sight. Sinners would be ill company for the exalted King of Saints. When we have been duly prepared to see Him, we shall be given to approach Him.

In heaven, love will absorb fear; but in this world, *fear and love must go together*. No one can love God aright without fearing Him; though many fear Him, and yet do not love Him. Self-confident men, who do not know their own hearts, or the reasons they have for being dissatisfied with themselves, do not fear God, and they think this bold freedom is to love Him. Deliberate sinners fear but cannot love Him. But devotion to Him consists in love and fear, as we may understand from our ordinary attachment to each other. No one really loves another, who does not feel a certain reverence towards him. When friends transgress this sobriety of affection, they may indeed continue associates for a time, but they have broken the bond of union. It is mutual

52

respect which makes friendship lasting. So again, in the feelings of inferiors towards superiors. Fear must go before love. Till he who has authority shows he has it and can use it, his forbearance will not be valued duly; his kindness will look like weakness. We learn to contemn what we do not fear; and we cannot love what we contemn. So in religion also. We cannot understand Christ's mercies till we understand His power, His glory, His unspeakable holiness, and our demerits; that is, until we first fear Him. Not that fear comes first, and then love; for the most part they will proceed together. Fear is allayed by the love of Him, and our love sobered by our fear of Him. Thus He draws us on with encouraging voice amid the terrors of His threatenings. As in the young ruler's case, He loves us, yet speaks harshly to us that we may learn to cherish mixed feelings towards Him. He hides Himself from us, and yet calls us on, that we may hear His voice as Samuel did, and, believing, approach Him with trembling. This may seem strange to those who do not study the Scriptures, and to those who do not know what it is earnestly to seek after God. But in proportion as the state of mind is strange, so is there in it, therefore, untold and surpassing pleasure to those who partake it. The bitter and the sweet, strangely tempered, thus leave upon the mind the lasting taste of Divine truth, and satisfy it; not so harsh as to be loathed; nor of that insipid sweetness which attends enthusiastic feelings, and is wearisome when it becomes familiar. Such is the feeling of conscience too, God's original gift; how painful! yet who would lose it? "I opened my mouth and panted, for I longed for Thy commandments." [Ps. cxix. 131.] This is David's account of it. Ezekiel describes something of the same feeling when the Spirit lifted him up and took him away, "and he went in bitterness, in the heat of his spirit," "the hand of the Lord" being "strong upon him." [Ezek. iii. 14.]

Now how does this apply to us here assembled? Are we in danger of speaking or thinking of Christ irreverently? I do not think we are in any immediate danger of deliberate profaneness; but we are in great danger of this, viz. first, of allowing ourselves to appear profane, and secondly, of gradually becoming irreverent, while we are pretending to be so. Men do not begin by *intending* to dishonour God; but they are afraid of the ridicule of others: they are ashamed of appearing religious; and thus are led to pretend that they are worse than they really are. They say things which they do not mean; and, by a miserable weakness, allow actions and habits to be imputed to them which they dare not really indulge in. Hence, they affect a liberty of speech which only befits the companions of evil spirits. They take God's name in vain, to show that they can do what devils do, and they invoke the evil spirit, or speak familiarly of all that pertains to him, and deal about curses wantonly, as though they were not fire-brands,—as if acknowledging the Author of Evil to be their great master and lord. Yes! he *is* a master who allows himself to be served without trembling. It is his very art to lead men to be at ease with him, to think lightly of him, and to trifle with him. He will submit to their ridicule, take (as it were) their blows, and pretend to be their slave, that he may ensnare them. *He* has no dignity to maintain, and he waits his time when his malice shall be gratified. So it has ever been all over the earth. Among all nations it has been his aim to make men laugh at him; going to and fro upon the earth, and walking up and down in it, hearing and rejoicing in that light perpetual talk about him which is his *worship*.

Now, it is not to be supposed that all this careless language can be continued without its affecting a man's heart at last; and this is the second danger I spoke of. Through a false shame, we disown religion with our lips, and next our words affect our thoughts. Men at last become the cold, indifferent, profane characters they professed themselves to be. They think contemptuously of God's Ministers, Sacraments, and Worship; they slight His Word, rarely looking into it, and never studying it. They undervalue all religious profession, and judging of others by themselves, impute the conscientious conduct they witness to bad motives. Thus they are in heart infidels; though they may not formally be such, and may attempt to disguise their own unbelief under pretence of objecting to one or other of the doctrines or ordinances of religion. And should a time of temptation come, when it would be *safe* to show themselves as they really are, they will (almost unawares) throw off their profession of Christianity, and join themselves to the scoffing world.

And how must Christians, on the other hand, treat such heartless men? They have our Lord's example to imitate. Not that they dare precisely follow the conduct of Him who had no sin. They dare not assume to themselves any honour on their own account; and they are bound, especially if they are His Ministers, to humble themselves as the Apostles did, and "going out to the highways and hedges (as it were) compel" men to be saved. [Luke xiv. 23.] Yet, while they use greater earnestness of entreaty than their Lord, they must not forget His dignity the while, who sends them. He manifested His love towards us, "in deed and in truth," and we, His Ministers, declare it in word; yet for the very reason that it is so abundant, we must in very gratitude learn reverence towards Him. We must not take advantage (so to say) of His goodness; or misuse the powers committed to us. Never must we solicitously press the truth upon those who do not profit by what they already possess. It dishonours Christ, while it does the scorner harm, not good. It is casting pearls before swine. We must wait for all opportunities of being useful to men, but beware of attempting too much at once. We must impart the Scripture doctrines, in measure and season, as they can bear them; not being eager to re-

54

count them all, rather, hiding them from the world. Seldom must we engage in controversy or dispute; for it lowers the sacred truths to make them a subject for ordinary debate. Common propriety suggests rules like these at once. Who would speak freely about some revered friend in the presence of those who did not value him? or who would think he could with a few words overcome their indifference towards him? or who would hastily dispute about him when his hearers had no desire to be made love him?

Rather, shunning all intemperate words, let us show our light before men by our *works*. Here we must be safe. In doing justice, showing mercy, speaking the truth, resisting sin, obeying the Church,—in thus glorifying God, there can be no irreverence. And, above all, let us look at home, check all bad thoughts, presumptuous imaginings, vain desires, discontented murmurings, self-complacent reflections, and so in our hearts ever honour Him in secret, whom we reverence by open profession.

May God guide us in a dangerous world; and deliver us from evil. And may He rouse to serious thought, by the power of His Spirit, all who are living in profaneness or unconcern!

The Religion of the Day[†]

"Let us have grace, whereby we may serve God acceptably
with reverence and godly fear. For our God is a consuming fire."
Heb. xii. 28, 29

IN EVERY AGE of Christianity, since it was first preached, there has been what may be called a *religion of the world*, which so far imitates the one true religion, as to deceive the unstable and unwary. The world does not oppose religion *as such*. I may say, it never has opposed it. In particular, it has, in all ages, acknowledged in one sense or other the Gospel of Christ, fastened on one or other of its characteristics, and professed to embody this in its practice; while by neglecting the other parts of the holy doctrine, it has, in fact, distorted and corrupted even that portion of it which it has exclusively put forward, and so has contrived to explain away the whole;—for he who cultivates only one precept of the Gospel to the exclusion of the rest, in reality attends to no part at all. Our duties *balance* each other; and though we are too sinful to perform them all perfectly, yet we may in some measure be performing them all, and preserving the balance on the whole; whereas, to give ourselves only to this or that commandment, is to incline our minds in a wrong direction, and at length to pull them down to the earth, which is the aim of our adversary, the Devil.

It is his *aim* to break our strength; to force us down to the earth,—to bind us there. The world is his instrument for this purpose; but he is too wise to set it in open opposition to the Word of God. No! he affects to be a prophet like the prophets of God. He calls his servants also prophets; and they mix with the scattered remnant of the true Church, with the solitary Micaiahs who are left upon the earth, and speak in the name of the Lord. And in one sense they speak the truth; but it is not the whole truth; and we know, even from the common experience of life, that half the truth is often the most gross and mischievous of falsehoods.

Even in the first age of the Church, while persecution still raged, he set up a counter religion among the philosophers of the day, partly like Christianity, but in truth a bitter foe to it; and it deceived and made shipwreck of the faith of those who had not the love of God in their hearts.

[†] *Parochial & Plain Sermons*, vol. 1 (1834), Sermon 24.

Time went on, and he devised a second idol of the true Christ, and it remained in the temple of God for many a year. The age was rude and fierce. Satan took the darker side of the Gospel: its awful mysteriousness, its fearful glory, its sovereign inflexible justice; and here *his* picture of the truth ended, "God is a consuming fire;" so declares the text, and we know it. But we know more, viz. that God is love also; but Satan did not add this to his religion, which became one of *fear*. The religion of the world was then a fearful religion. Superstitions abounded, and cruelties. The noble firmness, the graceful austerity of the true Christian were superseded by forbidding spectres, harsh of eye, and haughty of brow; and these were the patterns or the tyrants of a beguiled people.

What is Satan's device in this day? a far different one; but perhaps a more pernicious. I will attempt to expose it, or rather to suggest some remarks towards its exposure, by those who think it worth while to attempt it; for the subject is too great and too difficult for an occasion such as the present, and, after all, no one can detect falsehood for another;—every man must do it for himself; we can but *help* each other.

What is the world's religion now? It has taken the brighter side of the Gospel,—its tidings of comfort, its precepts of love; all darker, deeper views of man's condition and prospects being comparatively forgotten. This is the religion *natural* to a civilized age, and well has Satan dressed and completed it into an idol of the Truth. As the reason is cultivated, the taste formed, the affections and sentiments refined, a general decency and grace will of course spread over the face of society, quite independently of the influence of Revelation. That beauty and delicacy of thought, which is so attractive in books, then extends to the conduct of life, to all we have, all we do, all we are. Our manners are courteous; we avoid giving pain or offence; our words become correct; our relative duties are carefully performed. Our sense of propriety shows itself even in our domestic arrangements, in the embellishments of our houses, in our amusements, and so also in our religions profession. Vice now becomes unseemly and hideous to the imagination, or, as it is sometimes familiarly said, "out of taste." Thus elegance is gradually made the test and standard of virtue, which is no longer thought to possess an intrinsic claim on our hearts, or to exist, *further than* it leads to the quiet and comfort of others. Conscience is no longer recognized as an independent arbiter of actions, its authority is explained away; partly it is superseded in the minds of men by the so-called moral sense, which is regarded merely as the love of the beautiful; partly by the rule of expediency, which is forthwith substituted for it in the details of conduct. Now conscience is a stern, gloomy principle; it tells us of guilt and of prospective punishment. Accordingly, when its terrors disappear, then disappear also, in the creed of the day, those fearful images of Divine wrath with which the Scriptures abound. They are explained away. Every thing is bright and cheerful. Religion is pleasant and easy; benevolence is the chief virtue; intolerance, bigotry, excess of zeal, are the first of sins. Austerity is an absurdity;—even firmness is looked on with an unfriendly, suspicious eye. On the other hand, all open profligacy is discountenanced; drunkenness is accounted a disgrace; cursing and swearing are vulgarities. Moreover, to a cultivated mind, which recreates itself in the varieties of literature and knowledge, and is interested in the ever-accumulating discoveries of science, and the ever-fresh accessions of information, political or otherwise, from foreign countries, religion will commonly seem to be dull, from want of novelty. Hence excitements are eagerly sought out and rewarded. New objects in religion, new systems and plans, new doctrines, new preachers, are necessary to satisfy that craving which the so-called spread of knowledge has created. The mind becomes morbidly sensitive and fastidious; dissatisfied with things as they are, desirous of a change *as such*, as if alteration must of itself be a relief.

Now I would have you put Christianity for an instant out of your thoughts; and consider whether such a state of refinement as I have attempted to describe, is not that to which men might be brought, quite independent of religion, by the mere influence of education and civilization; and then again, whether, nevertheless, this mere refinement of mind is not more or less all that is called religion at this day. In other words, is it not the case, that Satan has so composed and dressed out what is the mere natural produce of the human heart under certain circumstances, as to serve his purposes as the counterfeit of the Truth? I do not at all deny that this spirit of the world uses words, and makes professions, which it would not adopt except for the suggestions of Scripture; nor do I deny that it takes a general colouring from Christianity, so as really to be modified by it, nay, in a measure enlightened and exalted by it. Again, I fully grant that many persons in whom this bad spirit shows itself, are but partially infected by it, and at bottom, good Christians, though imperfect. Still, after all, here is an existing teaching, only partially evangelical, built upon worldly principle, yet pretending to be the Gospel, dropping one whole side of the Gospel, its austere character, and considering it enough to be benevolent, courteous, candid, correct in conduct, delicate,—though it includes no true fear of God, no fervent zeal for His honour, no deep hatred of sin, no horror at the sight of sinners, no indignation and compassion at the blasphemies of heretics, no jealous adherence to doctrinal truth, no especial sensitiveness about the particular means of gaining ends, provided the ends be good, no loyalty to the Holy Apostolic Church, of which the Creed speaks, no sense of the authority of religion as external to the mind: in a word, no seriousness,—

and therefore is neither hot nor cold, but (in Scripture language) *lukewarm.* Thus the present age is the very contrary to what are commonly called the dark ages; and together with the faults of those ages we have lost their virtues. I say their virtues; for even the errors then prevalent, a persecuting spirit, for instance, fear of religious inquiry, bigotry, these were, after all, but perversions and excesses of *real virtues,* such as zeal and reverence; and we, instead of limiting and purifying them, have taken them away root and branch. Why? because we have not acted from a love of the Truth, but from the influence of the Age. The old generation has passed, and its character with it; a new order of things has arisen. Human society has a new framework, and fosters and developes a new character of mind; and this new character is made by the enemy of our souls, to resemble the Christian's obedience as near as it may, its likeness all the time being but accidental. Meanwhile, the Holy Church of God, as from the beginning, continues her course heavenward; despised by the world, yet influencing it, partly correcting it, partly restraining it, and in some happy cases reclaiming its victims, and fixing them firmly and for ever within the lines of the faithful host militant here on earth, which journeys towards the City of the Great King. God give us grace to search our hearts, lest we be blinded by the deceitfulness of sin! lest we serve Satan transformed into an Angel of light, while we think we are pursuing true knowledge; lest, overlooking and ill-treating the elect of Christ here, we have to ask that awful question at the last day, while the truth is bursting upon us, "Lord, *when* saw we Thee a stranger and a prisoner?" when saw we Thy sacred Word and Servants despised and oppressed, "and did not minister unto Thee?" [Matt. xxv. 44.]

Nothing shows more strikingly the power of the world's religion, as now described, than to consider the very different classes of men whom it influences. It will be found to extend its sway and its teaching both over the professedly religious and the irreligious.

1. Many religious men, rightly or not, have long been expecting a millennium of purity and peace for the Church. I will not say, whether or not with reason, for good men may well differ on such a subject. But, any how, in the case of those who have expected it, it has become a temptation to take up and recognize the world's religion as I have already delineated it. They have more or less identified their vision of Christ's kingdom with the elegance and refinement of mere human civilization; and have hailed every evidence of improved decency, every wholesome civil regulation, every beneficent and enlightened act of state policy, as signs of their coming Lord. Bent upon achieving their object, an extensive and glorious diffusion and profession of the Gospel, they have been little solicitous about the means employed. They have

countenanced and acted with men who openly professed unchristian principles. They have accepted and defended what they considered to be refor-
mations and ameliorations of the existing state of things, though injustice
must be perpetrated in order to effect them, or long cherished rules of conduct, indifferent perhaps in their origin but consecrated by long usage, must
be violated. They have sacrificed Truth to expedience. They have strangely
imagined that bad men are to be the immediate instruments of the approaching advent of Christ; and (like the deluded Jews not many years since in a foreign country) they have taken, if not for their Messiah (as the Jews did), at
least for their Elijah, their reforming Baptist, the Herald of the Christ, children of this world, and sons of Belial, on whom the anathema of the Apostle
lies from the beginning, declaring, "If any man love not the Lord Jesus Christ,
let him be Anathema Maran-atha." [1 Cor. xvi. 22.]

2. On the other hand, the form of doctrine, which I have called the religion of the day, is especially adapted to please men of sceptical minds, the opposite extreme to those just mentioned, who have never been careful to obey
their conscience, who cultivate the intellect without disciplining the heart, and
who allow themselves to speculate freely about what religion *ought to be*, without going to Scripture to discover what it really is. Some persons of this character almost consider religion itself to be an obstacle in the advance of our social and political well-being. But they know human nature requires it; therefore they select the most *rational* form of religion (so they call it) which they
can find. Others are far more seriously disposed, but are corrupted by bad example or other cause. But they *all* discard (what they call) gloomy views of
religion; they all trust themselves more than God's word, and thus may be
classed together; and are ready to embrace the pleasant consoling religion natural to a polished age. They lay much stress on works on *Natural Theology*,
and think that all religion is contained in these; whereas, in truth, there is no
greater fallacy than to suppose such works to be in themselves in any true sense
religious at all. Religion, it has been well observed, is something *relative to us*; a
system of commands and promises from God *towards* us. But how are we concerned with the sun, moon, and stars? or with the laws of the universe? how
will they teach us our *duty*? how will they speak to *sinners*? They do not speak
to sinners at all. They were created *before* Adam fell. They "declare the *glory* of
God," but not His *will*. They are all perfect, all harmonious; but that brightness and excellence which they exhibit in their own creation, and the Divine
benevolence therein seen, are of little moment to fallen man. We see nothing
there of God's *wrath*, of which the conscience of a sinner loudly speaks. So
that there cannot be a more dangerous (though a common) device of Satan,
than to carry us off from our own secret thoughts, to make us forget our own

hearts, which tell us of a God of justice and holiness, and to fix our attention merely on the God who made the heavens; who is *our* God indeed, but not God as manifested to us sinners, but as He shines forth to His Angels, and to His elect hereafter.

When a man has so far deceived himself as to trust his destiny to what the heavens tell him of it, instead of consulting and obeying his conscience, what is the consequence? that at once he misinterprets and perverts the whole tenor of Scripture. It cannot be denied that, pleasant as religious observances are declared in Scripture to be to the holy, yet to men in general they are said to be difficult and distasteful; to all men *naturally* impossible, and by few fulfilled even with the assistances of grace, on account of their wilful corruption. Religion is pronounced to be against nature, to be against our original will, to require God's aid to make us love and obey it, and to be commonly refused and opposed in spite of that aid. We are expressly told, that "strait is the gate and narrow the way that leads to life, and few there be that find it;" that we must "*strive*" or struggle "to enter in at the strait gate," for that "many shall *seek* to enter in," but that is not enough, they merely seek and therefore do not find; and further, that they who do not obtain everlasting life, "shall go into everlasting punishment" [Matt. vii. 14. Luke xiii. 24. Matt. xxv. 46.] This is the dark side of religion; and the men I have been describing cannot bear to think of it. They shrink from it as too terrible. They easily get themselves to believe that those strong declarations of Scripture do not belong to the present day, or that they are figurative. They have no language within their heart responding to them. Conscience has been silenced. The only information they have received concerning God has been from Natural Theology, and that speaks only of benevolence and harmony; so they will not credit the plain word of Scripture. They seize on such parts of Scripture as seem to countenance their own opinions; they insist on its being commanded us to "rejoice evermore;" and they argue that it is our duty to solace ourselves here (in moderation, of course) with the goods of this life,—that we have only to be thankful while we use them,—that we need not alarm ourselves,—that God is a merciful God,—that amendment is quite sufficient to atone for our offences,—that though we have been irregular in our youth, yet that is a thing gone by,—that we forget it, and therefore God forgets it,—that the world is, on the whole, very well disposed towards religion, —that we should avoid enthusiasm,—that we should not be over serious,—that we should have large views on the subject of human nature,—and that we should love all men. This indeed is the creed of shallow men, in *every* age, who reason a little, and feel not at all, and who think themselves enlightened and philosophical. Part of what they say is false, part is true, but misapplied; but why I have noticed it here, is to show how exactly it fits in with what I have already described as the peculiar religion of a civilized age; it fits in with it equally well as does that of the (so called) religious world, which is the opposite extreme.

One further remark I will make about these professedly rational Christians; who, be it observed, often go on to deny the mysteries of the Gospel. Let us take the text:—"Our God is a consuming fire." Now supposing these persons fell upon these words, or heard them urged as an argument against their own doctrine of the unmixed satisfactory character of our prospects in the world to come, and supposing they did not know what part of the Bible they occurred in, what would they say? Doubtless they would confidently say that they applied only to the Jews and not to Christians; that they only described the Divine Author of the Mosaic Law [Deut. iv. 24.]; that God formerly spoke in terrors to the Jews, because they were a gross and brutish people, but that civilization has made us quite other men; that our *reason*, not our *fears*, is appealed to, and that the Gospel is love. And yet, in spite of all this argument, the text occurs in the Epistle to the Hebrews, written by an Apostle of Christ.

I shall conclude with stating more fully what I mean by the dark side of religion; and what judgment ought to be passed on the superstitious and gloomy.

Here I will not shrink from uttering my firm conviction, that it would be a gain to this country, were it vastly more superstitious, more bigoted, more gloomy, more fierce in its religion, than at present it shows itself to be. Not, of course, that I think the tempers of mind herein implied desirable, which would be an evident absurdity; but I think them infinitely more desirable and more promising than a heathen obduracy, and a cold, self-sufficient, self-wise tranquillity. Doubtless, peace of mind, a quiet conscience, and a cheerful countenance are the gift of the Gospel, and the sign of a Christian; but the same effects (or, rather, what appear to be the same) may arise from very different causes. Jonah slept in the storm,—so did our Blessed Lord. The one slept in an evil security: the Other in the "peace of God which passeth all understanding." The two states cannot be confounded together, they are perfectly distinct; and as distinct is the calm of the man of the world from that of the Christian. Now take the case of the sailors on board the vessel; they cried to Jonah, "What meanest thou, O sleeper?"—so the Apostles said to Christ; "Lord, we perish." This is the case of the superstitious; they stand between the false peace of Jonah and the true peace of Christ; they are better than the one, though far below the Other. Applying this to the present religion of the educated world, full as it is of security and cheerfulness, and decorum, and benevolence, I observe that these appearances may arise either from a great deal of religion, or from the absence of it; they may be the fruits of shallowness of mind and a blinded conscience, or of that faith which has peace with God through our Lord Jesus Christ. And if this alternative be proposed, I might leave it to the common sense of men to decide (if they could get themselves to think seriously) to which of the two the temper of the age is to be referred. For myself I cannot doubt, seeing what I see of the world, that it arises from the sleep of Jonah; and it is therefore but a dream of religion, far inferior in worth to the well-grounded alarm of the superstitious, who are awakened and see their danger, though they do not attain so far in faith as to embrace the remedy of it.

Think of this, I beseech you, my brethren, and lay it to heart, as far as you go with me, as you will answer for having heard it at the last day. I would not willingly be harsh; but knowing "that the world lieth in wickedness," I think it highly probable that you, so far as you are in it (as you must be, and we all must be in our degree), are, most of you, partially infected with its existing error, that shallowness of religion, which is the result of a blinded conscience; and, therefore, I speak earnestly to you. Believing in the existence of a general plague in the land, I judge that you probably have your share in the sufferings, the voluntary sufferings, which it is spreading among us. The fear of God is the beginning of wisdom; till you see Him to be a consuming fire, and approach Him with reverence and godly fear, as being sinners, you are not even in sight of the strait gate. I do not wish you to be able to point to any particular time when you renounced the world (as it is called), and were converted; this is a deceit. Fear and love must go together; always fear, always love, to your dying day. Doubtless;—still you must know what it is to sow in tears here, if you would reap in joy hereafter. Till you know the weight of your sins, and that not in mere imagination, but in practice, not so as merely to confess it in a formal phrase of lamentation, but daily and in your heart in secret, you cannot embrace the offer of mercy held out to you in the Gospel, through the death of Christ. Till you know what it is to fear with the terrified sailors or the Apostles, you cannot sleep with Christ at your Heavenly Father's feet. Miserable as were the superstitions of the dark ages, revolting as are the tortures now in use among the heathen of the East, better, far better is it, to torture the body all one's days, and to make this life a hell upon earth, than to remain in a brief tranquillity here, till the pit at length opens under us, and awakens us to an eternal fruitless consciousness and remorse. Think of Christ's own words: "What shall a man give in exchange for his soul?" Again, He says, "Fear Him, who after He hath killed, hath power to cast into hell; yea, I say unto you, fear Him." Dare not to think you have got to the bottom of your hearts; you do not know what evil lies there. How long and earnestly must you pray, how many years must you pass in careful obedience, before you have any right to lay aside sorrow, and to rejoice in the Lord? In one sense, indeed, you may take comfort from the first; for, though you dare not yet anticipate you are in the number of Christ's true elect, yet from the first you know He desires your salvation, has died for you, has washed away your sins by baptism, and will ever help you; and this thought must cheer you while you go on to examine and review your lives, and to turn to God in self-denial. But, at the same time, you never can be sure of salvation, while you are here; and therefore you must always fear while you hope. Your knowledge of your sins increases with your view of God's mercy in Christ. And this is the true Christian state, and the nearest approach to Christ's calm and placid sleep in the tempest;—not per-fect joy and certainty in heaven, but a deep resignation to God's will, a sur-render of ourselves, soul and body, to Him; hoping indeed, that we shall be saved, but fixing our eyes more earnestly on Him than on ourselves; that is, acting for His glory, seeking to please Him, devoting ourselves to Him in all manly obedience and strenuous good works; and, when we do look within, thinking of ourselves with a certain abhorrence and contempt as being sinners, mortifying our flesh, scourging our appetites, and composedly awaiting that time when, if we be worthy, we shall be stripped of our present selves, and new made in the kingdom of Christ.

Mortification of the Flesh a Scripture Duty[†]

I F WE TAKE the example of the Holy men of Scripture as our guide, certainly bodily privation and chastisement are a very essential duty of all who wish to serve GOD, and prepare themselves for His presence.

1. First, we have the example of Moses. His recorded Fasts were miraculous; still they were Fasts, and the ordinance was recommended to the notice of all believers afterwards, by the honour put upon it. "I abode in the mount forty days and forty nights; I neither did eat bread nor drink water." Again; "I fell down before the LORD, as at the first, forty days and forty nights; I did neither eat bread nor drink water, because of all your sins." Deut. ix. 9, 18. Fasting is in the former instance subservient to divine contemplation, in the latter to humiliation and intercession for sinners.

Elijah. "He said unto him, What manner of man was he which came up to meet you, and told you these words? And they answered him, He was an hairy man, and girt with a girdle of leather about his loins. And he said, It is Elijah the Tishbite." 2 Kings i. 7, 8. It is indeed needless to show the ascetic character of him who was in fact the chief and type of those who "wandered about in sheepskins and goatskins," "in deserts, and in mountains, and in dens and caves of the earth." He too fasted by the power of GOD for forty days and nights; "He arose and did eat and drink, and went in the strength of that meat forty days and forty nights, unto Horeb the mount of GOD" 1 Kings xix. 8.

Daniel. "I set my face unto the LORD GOD, to seek by prayer and supplications, with fasting, and sackcloth, and ashes; and I prayed unto the LORD my GOD, and made my confession." Dan. ix. 3, 4. It must be observed, that Daniel was not bound by any vow, as Samson and Samuel. Moreover it would appear the gift of prophecy was given him in reward for his self-chastisements, as the following passage shows. "In those days I Daniel was mourning three full weeks; I ate no pleasant bread, neither came flesh nor wine in my mouth; neither did I anoint myself at all, till three whole weeks were fulfilled . . . And he said unto me, O Daniel, a man greatly beloved, understand the words that I speak unto thee, and stand upright; for unto thee am I now sent . . . Fear not, Daniel ; for *from the first day* that thou didst set thine heart to understand, and *to chasten thyself* before thy GOD, thy words were

---

[†] *Tracts for the Times*, Tract 21 (*Ad Populum*). First published in 1834.

heard, and I am come for thy words." Dan. x. 2, 3, 11, 12. Vide also Luke ii. 37. Acts x. 30.

2. Now here it will be objected, perhaps, that these instances are taken from the Old Testament, and belong to the Law of Moses, which is not binding on Christians.

I answer:

(1.) That in the above passages Fasting is connected with moral acts, humiliation, prayer, meditation, which are equally binding on us as on the Jews. Man is now what he was then; and if affliction of the flesh was good then, it is now.

(2.) In matter of fact, *private* Fasting, such as instanced in the passages above quoted, was no special duty of the Mosaic Law. Public Fasting, indeed, was on one occasion enjoined by Moses himself, and on others by subsequent rulers; but this was in part a ceremonial act, not a moral discipline, and was doubtless abolished with the other rites of the Law.

"Of Fasts," says Lewis, "there was no more than one appointed by the Law of Moses, called the Fast of Expiation . . . The great day of Expiation was a most severe Fast, kept every year upon the tenth day of the month Tizri, which answers to our September . . . This solemnity was observed with fasting and abstinence, not only from all meat and drink, but from all other pleasure whatsoever; insomuch that they did not wash their faces, much less anoint their heads, nor wear their shoes . . . nor, (if their Doctors say true,) read any portion of the law which would give them delight. They refrained likewise not only from pleasure, but from labour, nothing being to be done upon this day, but confessing of sins and repentance."[9]

Nay, it may rather be said, that the Jewish Law, as such, was rather opposed than otherwise to austerities. The Nazarites and Rechabites, being exceptions to the rule, are evidence of it. Vide, on the other hand, Deut. xii. Eccles. v. 18.[10]

Such then being the character of the Law in its formal letter, it tells just the contrary way to that which superficial reasoners might expect. For it is most remarkable, first, that the greatest prophets under it, such as Elijah and Daniel, were without express command singularly austere and self-afflicting men, in the midst of a people, who from the first went lusting after "the fish which they eat in Egypt freely; the cucumbers, and the melons, and the leeks, and the onions, and the garlick, and said, Who shall give us flesh to eat?" Next there is something of a very startling and admonitory nature in the *miraculous* fasts of Moses and Elijah, under this same imperfect dispensation. The miracle

---

[9] Lewis, *Hebrew Republic*, iv. 15.
[10] *Vide* Spencer, *de Regg. Hebræor.*, lib. 3. diss. 1. ii. 3. diss. 4. i. 5, &c.

evidently was for some purpose; yet it did not sanction, in any direct way, any injunction of the Law. Was it not an admonition to the Israelites, that there was a more excellent way of obedience than that which ALMIGHTY GOD as yet thought fit to promulgate by solemn enactment? Is it not an intimation serviceable for Christian practice, as much as Moses' announcement of the destined "Prophet like unto him" is intended for the comfort of Christian faith?

Surely the duty of bodily discipline might be rested on the answer to this plain question, *Why* did Daniel use austerities not enjoined by the Law?

3. Now turn to the New Testament, and observe what clear light is therein thrown upon the duty already recommended to us by the Old Testament Saints.

First, there is the instance of St. John the Baptist. "John came neither eating nor drinking," Matt. xi. 18: and his disciples fasted, Matt. ix. 14.

Our SAVIOUR did *not* statedly fast; but here also the exception proves the rule. He who did not fast statedly was the only one born of woman who was untainted by sinful flesh; which seems to imply, that all who are natural descendants of guilty Adam ought to fast.

He bade His disciples to fast. Consider his implied precept, which is an express command to those who obey the Law of Liberty. "When thou fastest, anoint thy head, and wash thy face, that thou appear not unto men to fast." Matt. vi. 17, 18.

Consider, moreover, the *general austere* character of Christian obedience, as enjoined by our LORD;—a circumstance much to be insisted on in an age like this, when what is really self-indulgence is thought to be a mere moderate and innocent use of this world's goods. I will but refer to a few, out of many texts, which I am persuaded are now forgotten by numbers of educated and amiable men who are fond of extolling what they call the mild, tolerant, enlightened spirit of the Gospel. Matt. v. 29, 30. vii. 13, 14. x. 37–39. Mark ix. 43–50. x. 25. Luke xiv. 12, 26–33.

And reflect, too, whether the spirit of texts such as the following will not move every true member of the Church Militant. "The ark, and Israel, and Judah abide in tents; and my lord Joab, and the servants of my lord, are encamped in the open fields; shall I then go into mine house, to eat and to drink? . . . as thou liveth, and as thy soul liveth, I will not do this thing." 2 Sam. xi. 11.

Now take the example of the Apostles. St. Peter was fasting, when he had the vision which sent him to Cornelius: Acts x. 10. The prophets and teachers at Antioch were fasting, when the HOLY GHOST revealed to them His purpose about Saul and Barnabas: Acts iii. 2, 3. Vide also Acts xiv. 23. 2 Cor. vi. 5. xi. 27.

Weigh well the following text, which I am persuaded many men would deny to be St. Paul's writing, had not a gracious Providence preserved to us the epistle containing it. "I keep under my body, and bring it into subjection; lest that by any means, when I have preached to others, I myself should be a cast-away." 1 Cor. ix. 27.

4. Lastly, Consider the practice of the Primitive Christians.

The following account of the early Christian Fasts, is from Bingham, Antiq. lib. xxi.

THE QUADRAGESIMAL OR LENT FAST.—"The Quadragesimal Fast before Easter," says Sozomen, "some observe six weeks, as the Illyrian and Western Churches, and all Libya, Egypt, and Palestine; others make it seven weeks, as the Constantinopolitans and neighbouring nations as far as Phœnicia; others fast three only of those six or seven weeks, by intervals; others the three weeks next immediately before Easter."

The manner of observing Lent among those that were piously disposed to observe it, was to abstain from all food till evening. For anciently a change of diet was not reckoned a fast: but it consisted in perfect abstinence from all sustenance for the whole day till evening.

THE FASTS OF THE FOUR SEASONS.—The next Anniversary fasting days were those which were called *Jejunia quatuor temporum*, the Fasts of the Four Seasons of the Year . . . These were at first designed . . . to beg a blessing of God upon the several seasons of the year, or to return thanks for the benefits received in each of them, or to exercise and purify both body and soul in a more particular manner, at the return of these certain terms of stricter discipline and more extraordinary devotion. [These afterwards became the Ember Fasts.]

MONTHLY FASTS.—In some places they had also Monthly Fasts throughout the year excepting in the two months of July and August . . . because of the sickness of the season.

WEEKLY FASTS.—Besides these they had their weekly Fasts or, Wednesday and Friday, called the Stationary Days, and Half-Fasts or Fasts of the Fourth and Sixth Days of the Week . . . These Fasts being of continual use every week throughout the Year, except in the Fifty Days between Easter and Pentecost, were not kept with that rigour and strictness which was observed in the time of Lent . . . [but] ordinarily held no longer than 9 o'clock, i.e. 3 in the afternoon.

OXFORD, *The Feast of the Circumcision*, 1834.

68

Rites and Customs of the Church[†]

*Ho men oun pistos, hōs chrē, kai errhōmenos oude deitai logou kai aitias,
huper ōn an epitachthēi, all' arkeitai tēi paradosei monēi.*

He who is duly strengthened in faith, does not go so far as to require argument and reason for what is enjoined, but is satisfied
with the tradition alone.

St John Chrysostom, in 1 Cor., Hom. 26

T HE READER of ecclesiastical history is sometimes surprised at finding
observances and customs generally received in the Church at an early
date, which have not express warrant in the Apostolic writings; *e.g.* the
use of the cross in baptism. The following pages will be directed to the consideration of this circumstance; with a view of suggesting from those writings
themselves, that a minute ritual was contemporaneous with them, that the
Apostles recognise it as existing anti binding, that it was founded on religious
principles, and tended to the inculcation of religious truth. Not that any formal
proof is attainable or conceivable, considering the brevity and subjects of the
inspired documents; but such fair evidence of the fact, as may recommend it
to the belief of the earnest and single-minded Christian. It is abundantly evident that the Epistles were not written to prescribe and enforce the Ritual of
religion; all then we can expect, if it existed in the days of the Apostles, is an
occasional allusion to it in their Epistles as existing, and a plain acquiescence
in it: and thus much we find.

Let us consider that remarkable passage, [1 Cor. xi. 2–16.] which, I am
persuaded, most readers pass over as if they could get little instruction from it.
St. Paul is therein blaming the Corinthians for not adhering to the *custom* of
the Church, which prescribed that men should wear their hair short, and that
women should have their head covered during divine service; a custom apparently most unimportant, if any one ever was, but in his view strictly binding
on Christians. He begins by implying that it is one out of many rules or traditions (*paradoseis*) which he had given them, and they were bound to keep. He
ends by refusing to argue with any one who obstinately cavils at it and rejects
it: "If any man seem to be contentious, we have no such custom, neither the

---

[†] *Tracts for the Times*, Tract 34 (*Ad Populum*). First published in 1834.

Churches of GOD." Here then at once a view is opened to us which is quite sufficient to remove the surprise we might otherwise feel at the multitude of rites, which were in use in the Primitive Church, but about which the New Testament is silent; and further, to command our obedience to such as come down to us from the first ages, and are agreeable to Scripture.

In accordance with this conclusion, is the clear and forcible command given by the Apostle, [2 Thess. ii. 15.] "Brethren, stand fast, and hold the traditions, which ye have been taught, whether *by word*, or our epistle."

To return. St. Paul goes on to give the reason of the usage, for the satisfaction of the weak brethren at Corinth. It was, he implied, a symbol or development (so to say) of the principle of the subordination of the woman to the man, and a memorial of the history of our creation; nay it was founded in "*nature*," *i.e.* natural reason. And lastly, it had a practical object: the woman ought to have her head covered "*because* of the angels." We need not stop to inquire *what* this reason was; but it was a reason of a practical nature which the Corinthians understood, though we may not. If it mean, as is probable, "because she is in the sight of the heavenly angels," [1 Tim. v. 21.] it gives a still greater importance to the ceremonies of worship, as connecting them with the unseen world.

It would seem indeed as if the very multiplicity of the details of the Church ritual made it plainly impossible for St. Paul to write them all down, or to do more than *remind* the Corinthians of his way of conducting religious discipline when he was among them. "Be ye *followers* of me;" he says, "I praise you that *ye remember me* in all things." It is evident there are ten thousand little points in the working of any large system, which a present instructor alone can settle. Hence it is customary at present, when a school is set up, or when any novel manufacture in trade, or extraordinary machinery, is to be brought into use, to set it going by sending a person fully skilled in its practical details. Such was St. Paul as regards the system of Christian discipline and worship; and when he could not go himself, he sent Timothy in his place. He says in the 4th chapter: "I beseech you, be ye followers of me. *For this cause* have I sent unto you Timotheus, who shall bring you into remembrance *of my ways which be in* CHRIST, *as I teach every where in every Church.*" Here there is a like reference to an uniform system of discipline,—whether as to Christian conduct, worship, or Church government.

Another important allusion appears to be contained in the 22d verse of the chapter above commented on. "What, have ye not houses to eat and drink in? or despise ye the *Church of* GOD?" This is remarkable as being a solitary allusion in Scripture to *houses* of prayer under the Christian System, which nevertheless we know from *ecclesiastical history* were used from the very first.

Here then is a most solemn ordinance of primitive Christianity, which barely escapes, if it escapes, omission in Scripture.

A passing allusion is made in another passage of the same Epistle, to the use of the word Amen at the conclusion of the Eucharistical prayer, as it is preserved after it and all other prayers to this day. Thus the ritual of the Apostles descended to minutiæ, and these so invariable in their use, as to allow of an appeal to them.

In the original institution of the Eucharist, as recorded in the Gospels, there is no mention of *consecrating* the cup; but in 1 Cor. x. 16, St. Paul calls it "the cup *of blessing which we bless.*" This incidental information, vouchsafed to us in Scripture, should lead us to be very cautious how we put aside other usages of the early Church concerning this Sacrament, which do not happen to be *clearly* mentioned in Scripture; as *e.g.* the solemn offering of the elements to GOD by way of pleading His mercy through CHRIST, which seems to have been universal in the early Church

As regards the same Sacrament, let us consider the use of the word [*leitourgountōn*], *ministering* [Acts xiii. 2.]; a word which, dropt (so to say) by accident, and interpreted, as is reasonable, by its use in the services of the Jewish Law, [Luke i. 23; Heb. x. 11.] remarkably coincides with the [*leitourgia*] of the Primitive Church, according to which the offering of the Altar was intercessory, as pleading CHRIST'S merits before the throne of grace.

Again, in 1 Cor. xv. 29, we incidentally discover the existence of persons who are styled "the baptized for the dead." Perhaps it is impossible to determine what is meant by this phrase, on which little light is thrown by early writers. However, any how it seems to refer to a *custom* of the Church, which was so usual as to admit of an appeal to it, which St. Paul approved, yet which he did not in the Epistle directly enforce, and but casually mentions.

In 1 Cor. i. 16, St. Paul happens to inform us that he baptized the *household* of Stephanas. It has pleased the HOLY SPIRIT to preserve to us this fact; by which is detected the existence of a rule of discipline for which the express doctrinal parts of Scripture afford but indirect warrant, viz. the custom of household baptism. (Vid. also Acts xvi. 15, 33.) This accidental disclosure accurately anticipates the after practice of the early Church, according to which families, infants included, were baptized, and that on a weighty doctrinal *reason*; viz. that all men were born in sin and in the wrath of GOD, and needed to be individually translated into that kingdom of grace, into which baptism is the initiation.

These instances, then, not to notice others of a like or a different kind, are surely sufficient to reconcile us to the complete ritual system which breaks upon us in the writings of the Fathers. If any parts of it indeed are contrary to

Scripture, that is of course a decisive reason at once for believing them to be additions and corruptions of the original ceremonial; but till this is shown, we are bound to venerate what is certainly primitive, and probably is apostolic.

It will be remarked, moreover, that many of the religious observances of the early Church are expressly built upon words of Scripture, and intended to be a visible memorial of them, after the manner of St. Paul's directions about the respective habits of men and women, which was just now noticed. Metaphorical or mystical descriptions were represented by a corresponding literal action. Our LORD Himself authorised this procedure when He took up the metaphor of the prophets concerning the fountain opened for our cleansing [Zech. xiii. 1.] and represented it in the visible rite of baptism. Accordingly, from the frequent mention of *oil* in Scripture as the emblem of spiritual gifts, [Is. lxi. 1–3, &c.] it was actually used in the Primitive Church in the ceremony of admitting catechumens, and in baptizing. And here again they had the precedent of the Apostles, who applied it in effecting their miraculous cures. [Mark vi. 13. James v. 14.] And so from the figurative mention in Scripture of *salt*, as the necessary preparation of every religious sacrifice, it was in use in the Western Church, in the ceremony of admitting converts into the rank of catechumens. So again from Phil. ii. 10, it was customary to bow the head at the name of JESUS. It were endless to multiply instances of a similar pious attention to the very words of Scripture, as their custom of continual public prayer from such passages as Luke xviii. 7; or of burying the bodies of martyrs under the altar, from Rev. vi. 9; or of the white vestments of the officiating ministers, from Rev. iv. 4.

Two passages on the subject from the Fathers shall now be laid before the reader, by way of further illustration, and first from Tertullian:

"Though this observance has not been determined by any Scripture, yet it is established by custom, which doubtless is derived from tradition. For how can an usage ever obtain, which has not first been given by tradition? But you say, even though tradition can be produced, still a written (Scripture) authority must be demanded. Let us examine, then, how far it is true, that a tradition itself, unless written in Scripture, is inadmissible. Now I will give up the point at once, if it is not already determined by instances of other observances, which are maintained without any Scripture proof, on the mere plea of tradition, and the sanction of consequent custom. To begin with baptism. Before we enter the water, we solemnly renounce the devil, his pomp, and his angels, in church in the presence of the Bishop. Then we are plunged in the water thrice, and answer certain questions over and above what the LORD has determined in the written gospel. After coming out of it, we taste a mixture of milk and honey; and for a whole week from that day we abstain from our daily bath. The sacrament of the Eucharist, though given by the LORD to all and at supper time, yet is celebrated in our meetings before day break, and only at the hand of our presiding ministers . . . We sign our forehead with the cross whenever we set out and walk, go in or out, dress, gird on our sandals, bathe, eat, light our lamps, sit or lie down to rest, whatever we do. If you demand a scripture rule for these and such like observances, we can give you none; all we say to you is, that tradition directs, usage sanctions, faith obeys. That reason justifies this tradition, usage, and faith, you will soon yourself see, or will easily learn from others; meanwhile you will do well to believe that there is a law to which obedience is due. I add one instance from the old dispensation. It is so usual among the Jewish females to veil their head, that they are even known by it. I ask where the law is to be found; the Apostle's decision of course is not to the point. Now if I no where find a law, it follows that tradition introduced the custom, which afterwards was confirmed by the Apostle when he explained the reason of it. These instances are enough to show that a tradition, even though not in Scripture, still binds our conduct, if a continuous usage be preserved as the witness of it."—Tertullian, *de Coron.* § 3.

Upon this passage it may be observed, that Tertullian, flourishing A.D. 200, is on the one hand a very early witness for the existence of the general doctrine which it contains, while on the other he gives no sanction to those later customs, which the Church of Rome upholds, but which cannot be clearly traced to primitive times.

St. Basil, whose work on the HOLY SPIRIT, § 66, shall next be cited, flourished in the middle of the fourth century, 150 years after Tertullian, and was of a very different school; yet he will be found to be in exact agreement with him on the subject before us, viz. that the ritual of the Church was derived from the Apostles, and was based on religious principles and doctrines. He adds a reason for its not being given us in Scripture, which we may receive or reject as our judgment leads us, viz. that the rites were memorials of doctrines not intended for publication except among baptized Christians, whereas the Scriptures were open to all men. This at least is clear, that the ritual could scarcely have been given in detail in Scripture, without imparting to the Gospel the character of a burdensome ceremonial, and withdrawing our attention from its doctrines and precepts.

"Of those articles of doctrine and preaching, which are in the custody of the Church, some come to us in Scripture itself, some are conveyed to us by a continuous tradition in mystical depositories. Both have equal claims on our devotion, and are received by all, at least by all who are in any respect Churchmen. For, should we attempt to supersede the usages which are not enjoined in Scripture as if unimportant, we should do most serious injury to

Evangelical truth: nay, reduce it to a bare name. To take an obvious instance; which Apostle has taught us in Scripture to sign believers with the cross? Where does Scripture teach us to turn to the east in prayer? Which of the saints has left us recorded in Scripture the words of invocation at the consecration of the bread of the Eucharist, and of the cup of blessing? Thus we are not content with what Apostle or Evangelist has left on record, but we add other rites before and after it, as important to the celebration of the mystery, receiving them from a teaching distinct from Scripture. Moreover, we bless the water of baptism, and the oil for anointing, and also the candidate for baptism himself . . . After the example of Moses, the Apostles and Fathers who modelled the Churches, were accustomed to lodge their sacred doctrine in mystic forms, as being secretly and silently conveyed . . . This is the reason why there is a tradition of observances independent of Scripture, lest doctrines, being exposed to the world, should be so familiar as to be despised . . . We stand instead of kneeling at prayer on the Sunday; but all of us do not know the reason of this . . . Again, every time we kneel down and rise up, we show by our outward action that sin has levelled us with the ground, and the loving mercy of our Creator has recalled us to heaven."

The conclusion to be drawn from all that has been said in these pages is this:—That rites and ordinances, far from being unmeaning, are in their nature capable of impressing our memories and imaginations with the great revealed verities; far from being superstitious, are expressly sanctioned in Scripture as to their principle, and delivered to the Church in their form by tradition. Further, that they varied in different countries, according to the respective founder of the Church in each. Thus *e.g.*, St. John and St. Philip are known to have adopted the Jewish rule for observing Easter-day; while other Apostles celebrated it always on a Sunday. Lastly, that, although the details of the early ritual varied in importance, and corrupt additions were made in the middle ages, yet that, as a whole, the Catholic ritual was a precious possession; and if we, who have rid ourselves of those corruptions, have lost not only the possession, but the sense of its value, it is a serious question whether we are not like men who recover from some grievous illness with the loss or injury of their sight or hearing;—whether we are not like the Jews returned from captivity, who could never find the rod of Aaron or the Ark of the Covenant, which, indeed, had ever been hid from the world, but then was removed from the Temple itself.

OXFORD, *The Feast of St. Philip and St. James*

Ceremonies of the Church[†]

"Suffer it to be so now: for thus it becometh us to fulfil all righteousness."
Matt. iii. 15

WHEN OUR LORD came to John to be baptized, He gave this reason for it, "Thus it becometh us to fulfil all righteousness;" which seems to mean,—"It is becoming in Me, the expected Christ, to conform in all respects to all the rites and ceremonies of Judaism, to everything hitherto accounted sacred and binding." Hence it was that He came to be baptized, to show that it was not His intention in any way to dishonour the Established Religion, but to fulfil it even in those parts of it (such as Baptism) which were later than the time of Moses; and especially to acknowledge thereby the mission of John the Baptist, His forerunner. And those ordinances which Moses himself was commissioned to appoint, had still greater claim to be respected and observed. It was on this account that He was circumcised, as we this day commemorate; in order, that is, to show that He did not renounce the religion of Abraham, to whom God gave circumcision, or of Moses, by whom it was embodied in the Jewish Law.

We have other instances in our Lord's history, besides those of His circumcision and baptism, to show the reverence with which He regarded the religion which He came to fulfil. St. Paul speaks of Him as "born of a woman, born under the Law," [Gal. iv. 4.] and it was His custom to observe that Law, like any other Jew. For instance, He went up for the feasts to Jerusalem; He sent the persons He had cured to the priests, to offer the sin-offering commanded by Moses; He paid the Temple-tax; and again, He attended as "a custom" the worship of the synagogue, though this had been introduced in an age long after Moses; and He even bade the multitudes obey the Scribes and Pharisees in all lawful things, as those who sat in Moses' place [Matt. xxiii. 2, 3.].

Such was our Saviour's dutiful attention to the religious system under which He was born; and that, not only so far as it was directly divine, but further, where it was the ordinance of uninspired though pious men, where it was but founded on ecclesiastical authority. His Apostles followed His pattern; and this is still more remarkable,—because after the Holy Spirit had descended, at

---

[†] *Parochial & Plain Sermons*, vol. 2 (1835), Sermon 7, preached on the Feast of the Circumcision of Our Lord.

first sight it would have appeared that all the Jewish ordinances ought at once to cease. But this was far from being the doctrine of the Apostles. They taught, indeed, that the Jewish rites were no longer of any use in obtaining God's favour; that Christ's death was now set forth as the full and sufficient Atonement for sin, by that Infinite Mercy who had hitherto appointed the blood of the sacrifices as in some sort means of propitiation: and, besides, that every convert who turned from Christ back to Moses, or who imposed the Jewish rites upon his brethren as necessary to salvation, was grievously erring against the Truth. But they neither abandoned the Jewish rites themselves, nor obliged any others to do so who were used to them. Custom was quite a sufficient reason for retaining them; every Christian was to remain in the state in which he was called; and in the case of the Jew, the practice of them did not necessarily interfere with a true and full trust in the Atonement which Christ had offered for sin.

St. Paul, we know, was the most strenuous opposer of those who would oblige the Gentiles to become Jews, as a previous step to their becoming Christians. Yet, decisive as he is against all attempts to force the Gentiles under the rites of Law, he never bids the Jews renounce them, rather he would have them retain them; leaving it for a fresh generation, who had not been born under them, to discontinue them, so that the use of them might gradually die away. Nay, he himself circumcised Timothy, when he chose him for his associate; in order that no offence might be given to the Jews [Acts xvi. 1–3.]. And how fully he adhered to the Law in his own person, we learn from the same inspired history; for instance, we hear of his shaving his head, as having been under a vow [Acts xviii. 18.], according to the Jewish custom.

Now from this obedience to the Jewish Law, enjoined and displayed by our Blessed Lord and His Apostles, we learn the great importance of retaining those religious forms to which we are accustomed, even though they are in themselves indifferent, or not of Divine origin; and, as this is a truth which is not well understood by the world at large, it may be of use to make some observations upon it.

We sometimes meet with men, who ask *why* we observe these or those ceremonies or practices; why, for example, we use Forms of prayer so cautiously and strictly? or why we persist in kneeling at the Sacrament of the Lord's Supper? why in bowing at the name of Jesus? or why in celebrating the public worship of God only in consecrated places? why we lay such stress upon these things? These, and many such questions may be asked, and all with this argument: "They are indifferent matters; we do not read of them in the Bible."

Now the direct answer to this objection is, that the Bible was never *intended* to enjoin us these things, but *matters of faith*; and that though it happens to mention our practical duties, and some points of form and discipline, still, that it does not set about telling us what to do, but chiefly what to believe; and that there are many duties and many crimes which are not mentioned in Scripture, and which we must find out by our own understanding, enlightened by God's Holy Spirit. For instance, there is no prohibition of suicide, duelling, gaming, in Scripture; yet we know them to be great sins; and it would be no excuse in a man to say that he does not find them forbidden in Scripture, because he may discover God's will in this matter independently of Scripture. And in like manner, various matters of form and discipline are binding, though Scripture says nothing about them; for we learn the duty in another way. No matter how we learn God's will, whether from Scripture, or Antiquity, or what St. Paul calls "Nature," so that we can be sure it *is* His will. Matters of faith, indeed, He reveals to us by inspiration, because they are supernatural: but matters of moral duty, through our own conscience and divinely-guided reason; and matters of form, by tradition and long usage, which bind us to the observance of them, though they are not enjoined in Scripture. This, I say, is the proper answer to the question, "Why do you observe rites and forms which are not enjoined in Scripture?" though, to speak the truth, our chief ordinances *are* to be found there, as the Sacraments, Public Worship, the Observance of the Lord's day, Ordination, Marriage, and the like. But I shall make another answer, which is suggested by the event commemorated this day, our Lord's conforming to the Jewish Law in the rite of circumcision; and my answer is this.

Scripture tells us what to believe, and what to aim at and maintain, but it does not tell us *how* to do it; and as we cannot do it at all unless we do it in this manner, or that, in fact we must add something to what Scripture tells us. For example, Scripture tells us to meet together for prayer, and has connected the grant of the Christian blessings on God's part, with the observance of *union* on ours; but since it does not tell us the times and places of prayer, the Church *must* complete that which Scripture has but enjoined generally. Our Lord has instituted two Sacraments, Baptism and the Lord's Supper; but has not told us, except generally, with what forms we are to administer them. Yet we *cannot* administer them without some sort of prayers; whether we use always the same, or not the same, or unpremeditated prayers. And so with many other solemn acts, such as Ordination, or Marriage, or Burial of the Dead, it is evidently pious, and becomes Christians to perform them decently and in faith; yet how is this to be done, unless the Church sanctions Forms of doing it?

The Bible then may be said to give us the *spirit* of religion; but the Church must provide the body in which that spirit is to be lodged. Religion must be realized in particular acts, in order to its continuing alive. Religionists, for example, who give up the Church rites, are forced to recall the strict Judaical Sabbath. There is no such thing as abstract religion. When persons attempt to worship in this (what they call) more spiritual manner, they end, in fact, in not worshipping at all. This frequently happens. Every one may know it from his own experience of himself. Youths, for instance (and perhaps those who should know better than they), sometimes argue with themselves, "What is the need of praying stately morning and evening? why use a form of words? why kneel? why cannot I pray in bed, or walking, or dressing?" they end in not praying at all. Again, what will the devotion of the country people be, if we strip religion of its external symbols, and bid them seek out and gaze upon the Invisible? Scripture gives the *spirit*, and the Church the *body*, to our worship; and we may as well expect that the spirits of men might be seen by us without the intervention of their bodies, as suppose that the Object of faith can be realized in a world of sense and excitement, without the instrumentality of an outward form to arrest and fix attention, to stimulate the careless, and to encourage the desponding. But observe what follows:—who would say our bodies are not part of ourselves? We may apply the illustration; for in like manner the forms of devotion are parts of devotion. Who can in practice separate his view of body and spirit? for example, what a friend would he be to us who should treat us ill, or deny us food, or imprison us; and say, after all, that it was our body he ill-treated, and not our soul? Even so, no one can really respect religion, and insult its forms. Granting that the forms are not immediately from God, still long use has made them divine *to us*; for the spirit of religion has so penetrated and quickened them, that to destroy them is, in respect to the multitude of men, to unsettle and dislodge the religious principle itself. In most minds usage has so identified them with the notion of religion, that the one cannot be extirpated without the other. Their faith will not bear transplanting. Till we have given some attention to the peculiarities of human nature, whether from watching our own hearts, or from experience of life, we can scarcely form a correct estimate how intimately great and little matters are connected together in all cases; how the circumstances and accidents (as they might seem) of our habits are almost conditions of those habits themselves. How common it is for men to have *seasons* of seriousness, how exact is their devotion during them, how suddenly they come to an end, how completely all traces of them vanish, yet how comparatively trifling is the cause of the relapse, a change of place or occupation, or a day's interruption of regularity in their religious course. Consider the sudden changes in opinion and profession, religious or secular, which occur in life, the proverbial fickleness of the multitude, the influence of watchwords and badges upon the fortunes of political parties, the surprising falls which sometimes overtake well-meaning and really respectable men, the inconsistencies of even the holiest and most perfect, and you will have some insight into the danger of practising on the externals of faith and devotion. Precious doctrines are strung, like jewels, upon slender threads.

Our Saviour and His Apostles sanction these remarks, in their treatment of those Jewish ceremonies, which have led me to make them. St. Paul calls them weak and unprofitable, weak and beggarly elements [Heb. vii. 18; Gal. iv. 9.]. So they were in themselves, but to those who were used to them, they were an edifying and living service. Else, why did the Apostles observe them? Why did they recommend them to the Jews whom they converted? Were they merely consulting for the prejudices of a reprobate nation? The Jewish rites were to disappear; yet no one was bid forcibly to separate himself from what he had long used, lest he lost his sense of religion also. Much more will this hold good with forms such as ours, which so far from being abrogated by the Apostles, were introduced by them or their immediate successors; and which, besides the influence they exert over us from long usage, are, many of them, witnesses and types of precious gospel truths; nay, much more, possess a sacramental nature, and are adapted and reasonably accounted to convey a gift, even where they are not formally sacraments by Christ's institution. Who, for instance, could be hard-hearted and perverse enough to ridicule the notion that a father's blessing may profit his children, even though Christ and His Apostles have not in so many words declared it?

Much might be said on this subject, which is a very important one. In these times especially, we should be on our guard against those who hope, by inducing us to lay aside our forms, at length to make us lay aside our Christian hope altogether. This is why the Church itself is attacked, because it is the living form, the visible body of religion; and shrewd men know that when it goes, religion will go too. This is why they rail at so many usages as superstitious; or propose alterations and changes, a measure especially calculated to shake the faith of the multitude. Recollect, then, that things indifferent in themselves become important to us when we are used to them. The services and ordinances of the Church are the outward form in which religion has been for ages represented to the world, and has ever been known to us. Places consecrated to God's honour, clergy carefully set apart for His service, the Lord's-day piously observed, the public forms of prayer, the decencies of worship, these things, viewed as a whole, are *sacred* relatively to us, even if they were not, as they are, divinely sanctioned. Rites which the Church has appointed, and with reason,—for the Church's authority is from Christ,—being long used, cannot be disused without harm to our souls. Confirmation, for instance, may be argued against, and undervalued; but surely no one who in the common run of men wilfully resists the Ordinance, but will thereby be *visibly* a worse Christian than he otherwise would have been. He will find (or rather others will find for him, for he will scarcely know it himself), that he has declined in faith, humility, devotional feeling, reverence, and sobriety. And so in the case of all other forms, even the least binding in themselves, it continually happens that a speculative improvement is a practical folly, and the wise are taken in their own craftiness.

Therefore, when profane persons scoff at our forms, let us argue with ourselves thus—and it is an argument which all men, learned or unlearned, can enter into: "These forms, even were they of mere human origin (which learned men say is *not* the case, but even if they were), are at least of as spiritual and edifying a character as the rites of Judaism. Yet Christ and His Apostles did not even suffer these latter to be irreverently treated or suddenly discarded. Much less may we suffer it in the case of our own; lest, stripping off from us the badges of our profession, we forget there is a faith for us to maintain, and a world of sinners to be eschewed."

The Christian Ministry[†]

"I say unto you, Among those that are born of women
there is not a greater prophet than John the Baptist;
but he that is least in the Kingdom of God is greater than he."
Luke vii. 28

S T. PETER'S DAY suitably follows the day of St. John the Baptist; for thus we have a striking memento, as the text suggests, of the especial dignity of the Christian Ministry over all previous Ministries which Almighty God has appointed. St. John was "much more than a Prophet;" he was as great as any messenger of God that had ever been born; yet the least in the Kingdom of heaven, the least of Christ's Ministers, is greater than he. And this, I observe, is a reflection especially fitted for this Festival, because the Apostle Peter is taken in various parts of the Gospel, as the appropriate type and representative of the Christian ministry.[11]

Now, let us consider in what the peculiar dignity of the Christian Minister consists. Evidently in this, that he is the representative of Christ; for, as Christ is infinitely above all other messengers from God, he who stands in His stead, must be superior, beyond compare, to all Ministers of religion, whether Prophets, Priests, Lawgivers, Judges, or Kings, whom Almighty God ever commissioned. Moses, Aaron, Samuel, and David, were shadows of the Saviour; but the Minister of the Gospel is His present substitute. As a type or prophecy of Grace is less than a pledge and means, as a Jewish sacrifice is less than a Gospel sacrament, so are Moses and Elias less by office than the representatives of Christ. This I consider to be evident, as soon as stated; the only question being, whether there is reason for thinking, that Christ *has*, in matter of fact, left representatives behind Him; and this, as I proceed to show, Scripture enables us to determine in the affirmative.

Now, in the first place, as we all know, Christ chose twelve out of His disciples, whom He called Apostles, to be His representatives even during His own ministry. And He gave them the power of doing the wonderful works which He did Himself. Of course I do not say He gave them equal power

[†] *Parochial & Plain Sermons*, vol. 2 (1835), Sermon 25, preached on the Feast of St. Peter the Apostle.
[11] *Vide* Matt. xvi. 18, 19. Luke xxii. 29, 30. John xxi. 15–17.

(God forbid!); but He gave them a certain sufficient portion of His power. "He gave them power," says St. Luke, "and authority over all devils, and to cure diseases; and He sent them to preach the Kingdom of God, and to heal the sick." [Luke ix. 1, 2.] And He expressly made them His substitutes to the world at large; so that to receive them was to receive Himself. "He that receiveth you, receiveth Me." [Matt. x. 40.] Such was their principal power before His passion, similar to that which He principally exercised, viz. the commission to preach and to perform bodily cures. But when He had wrought out the Atonement for human sin upon the Cross, and purchased for man the gift of the Holy Ghost, then He gave them a higher commission; and still, be it observed, parallel to that which He Himself then assumed. *"As My Father hath sent Me, even so send I you.* And when He had said this, He breathed on them, and saith unto them, Receive ye the Holy Ghost. Whose soever sins ye remit, they are remitted unto them; and whose soever sins ye retain, they are retained." [John xx. 21–23.] Here, then, the Apostles became Christ's representatives in the power of His Spirit, for the remission of sins, as before they were His representatives as regards miraculous cures, and preaching His Kingdom.

The following texts supply additional evidence that the Apostles were commissioned in Christ's stead, and inform us likewise in detail of some of the particular offices included in their commission. "Let a man so account of us, as of the *Ministers* of Christ, and *Stewards of the Mysteries* of God." "Ye received me as an *Angel*" or heavenly Messenger "of God, even *as Christ Jesus.*" "We *are Ambassadors* for Christ, as though God did beseech you by us; we pray you *in Christ's stead,* be ye reconciled to God." [1 Cor. iv. 1. Gal. iv. 14. 2 Cor. v. 20.]

The Apostles then, standing in Christ's place, were consequently exalted by office far above any divine Messengers before them. We come to the same conclusion from considering the sacred treasures committed to their custody, which (not to mention their miraculous powers, which is beside our present purpose) were those peculiar spiritual blessings which flow from Christ as a Saviour, as a Prophet, Priest, and King.

These blessings are commonly designated in Scripture as "the Spirit," or "the gift of the Holy Ghost." John the Baptist said of himself and Christ; "I indeed baptize you with water unto repentance; but He shall baptize you with the Holy Ghost, and with fire." [Matt. iii. 11.] In this respect, Christ's ministrations were above all that had ever been before Him, in bringing with them the gift of the Holy Ghost, that one gift, one, yet multiform, sevenfold in its operation, in which all spiritual blessedness is included. Accordingly, our Lord was solemnly anointed with the Holy Ghost Himself, as an initiation into His

Ministerial office. He was manifested as receiving, that He might be believed on as giving. He was thus commissioned, according to the Prophet, "to preach good tidings," "to heal the broken-hearted," "to give the oil of joy for mourning." Therefore, in like manner, the Apostles also were anointed with the same heavenly gift for the same Ministerial office. "He breathed on them, and saith unto them, Receive ye the Holy Ghost." Such as was the consecration of the Master, such was that of the Disciples; and such as His, were the offices to which they were thereby admitted.

Christ is a Prophet, as authoritatively revealing the will of God and the Gospel of Grace. So also were the Apostles; "He that heareth you, heareth Me; and he that despiseth you, despiseth Me; and he that despiseth Me, despiseth Him that sent Me;" "He that despiseth, despiseth not man, but God, who hath also given unto us His Holy Spirit." [Luke x. 16. 1 Thess. iv. 8.]

Christ is a Priest, as forgiving sin, and imparting other needful divine gifts. The Apostles, too, had this power; "Whose soever sins ye remit, they are remitted unto them; and whose soever sins ye retain, they are retained." "Let a man so account of us as . . . Stewards of the Mysteries of God."

Christ is a King, as ruling the Church; and the Apostles rule it in His stead. "I appoint unto you a Kingdom, as My Father hath appointed unto Me; that ye may eat and drink at My table in My Kingdom, and sit on thrones judging the twelve tribes of Israel." [Luke xxi. 29, 30.]

The gift, or office, cannot be named, which belongs to our Lord as the Christ, which He did not in its degree transfer to His Apostles by the communication of that Spirit, through which He Himself wrought; one of course excepted, the One great work, which none else in the whole world could sustain, of being the Atoning Sacrifice for all mankind. So far no one can take His place, and "His glory He does not give to another." His Death upon the Cross is the sole Meritorious Cause, the sole Source of spiritual blessing to our guilty race; but as to those offices and gifts which flow from this Atonement, preaching, teaching, reconciling, absolving, censuring, dispensing grace, ruling, ordaining, these all are included in the Apostolic Commission, which is instrumental and representative in His absence. "As My Father hath sent Me, so send I you." His gifts are not confined to Himself. "The whole house is filled with the odour of the ointment."

This being granted, however, as regards the Apostles themselves, some one may be disposed to inquire, whether their triple office has descended to Christian Ministers after them. I say their *triple* office, for few persons will deny that some portion of their commission still remains among us. The notion that there is no divine appointment of one man above another for Ministerial duties is not a common one, and we need not refute it. But it is very common for men to believe only as far as they can see and understand; and, because they are witnesses of the process and effects of instructing and ruling, and not of (what may be called) "the ministry of reconciliation," to accept Christ's Ministers as representatives of His Prophetic and Regal, not of His Priestly authority. Assuming then their claim to inherit two portions of His Anointing, I shall confine myself to the question of their possessing the third likewise: not however with a view of proving it, but rather of removing such antecedent difficulties as are likely to prejudice the mind against it.

By a Priest, in a Christian sense, is meant an appointed channel by which the peculiar Gospel blessings are conveyed to mankind, one who has power to apply to individuals those gifts which Christ has promised us generally as the fruit of His mediation. This power was possessed by the Apostles; I am now to show that it is possessed by their successors likewise.

1. Now, first, that there is a strong line of distinction between the Apostles and other Christian Ministers, I readily grant; nay, rather I would maintain it to be so clearly marked that there is no possibility of confusing together those respects in which they resemble with those in which they differ from their brethren. The Apostles were not only Ministers of Christ, but first founders of His Church; and their gifts and offices, so far forth as they had reference to this part of their commission, doubtless were but occasional and extraordinary, and ended with themselves. They were organs of Revelation, inspired Teachers, in some respects infallible, gifted with divers tongues, workers of miracles; and none but they are such. The duration of any gift depends upon the need which it supplies; that which has answered its purpose ends, that which is still necessary is graciously continued. Such at least seems to be the rule of a Merciful Providence. Therefore it is, that the Christian Ministry still includes in it the office of teaching, for education is necessary for every soul born into the world; and the office of governing, for "decency and order" are still necessary for the quiet and union of the Christian brotherhood. And, for the same reason, it is natural at first sight to suppose that the office of applying the gifts of grace should be continued also, while there is guilt to be washed away, sinners to be reconciled, believers to be strengthened, matured, comforted. What warrant have we from the nature of the case, for making any distinction between the ministry of teaching and the ministry of reconciliation? if one is still committed to us, why not the other also?

And it will be observed, that the only real antecedent difficulty which attaches to the doctrine of the Christian Priesthood, is obviated by Scripture itself. It might be thought that the power of remitting and retaining sins was too great to be given to sinful man over his fellows; but in matter of fact it was committed to the Apostles without restriction, though they were not infallible in what they did. "*Whose soever* sins ye remit they are remitted unto them; and *whose soever* sins ye retain, they are retained." The grant was in the very form of it unconditional, and left to their Christian discretion. What has once been given, may be continued. I consider this remark to be of weight in a case like the present, where the very nature of the professed gift is the only considerable reason against the fact of its bestowal.

2. But all this is on the bare antecedent view of the case. In fact, our Lord Himself has decided the question, by declaring that His presence, by means of His Apostles, *should* be with the Church to the end of the world. He promised this on the solemn occasion of His leaving them; He declared it when He bade them make converts, baptize, and teach. As well may we doubt whether it is our duty to preach and make proselytes, and prepare men for Heaven, as that His Apostolic Presence is with us, for those purposes. His words then at first sight even go to include *all* the gifts vouchsafed to His first Ministers; far from having a scanty grant of them, so large is the promise, that we are obliged to find out reasons to justify us in considering the Successors of the Apostles in any respects less favoured than themselves. Such reasons we know are to be found, and lead us to distinguish the extraordinary gifts from the ordinary, a distinction which the event justifies; but what is there either in Scripture or in Church History to make us place the commission of reconciliation among those which are extraordinary?

3. In the next place, it is deserving of notice that this distinction between ordinary and extraordinary gifts, is really made in Scripture itself, and that among the extraordinary there is no mention made of the sacerdotal power. No one can doubt, that on the day of Pentecost the formal inauguration of the Apostles took place into their high and singular office of building the Church of Christ. They were "wise Master-builders, according to the grace given them;" and that grace was extraordinary. However, among those gifts, "tongues and visions, prophecies and wonders," their priestly power is not enumerated. On the contrary, that power had been previously conferred, according to the passage already cited, when Christ breathed on them, and gave them, through the Holy Ghost, the authority to remit and retain sins.[12] And

---

[12] The following passage supplies a corroboration of the above argument, and carries it on to the doctrine of the Apostolical Succession:—"The very first act of the Apostles after Christ was gone out of their sight, was the ordination of Matthias in the room of the traitor Judas. That ordination is related very minutely. Every particular of it is full of instruction; but at present I wish to draw attention to one circumstance more especially: namely, the *time* when it occurred. It was contrived (if one may say so) exactly to fall within *the very short interval* which elapsed between the departure of our Lord, and the arrival of the Comforter in His place: on that 'little while,' during which the Church was comparatively left alone in the world. Then it was that St. Peter rose and declared with authority, that the time was come for supplying the vacancy which Judas

further, I would remind you, that this is certainly our Church's deliberate view of the subject: for she expressly puts into the Bishop's mouth at ordination the very words here used by our Saviour to His Apostles. "Receive the Holy Ghost;" "Whose soever sins ye remit, they are remitted to them; and whose soever sins ye retain, they are retained;" words, which it were inexpressibly profane for man to use to man, except by a plain divine commission to do so.

4: But again, has not the Gospel Sacraments? and have not Sacraments, as pledges and means of grace, a priestly nature? If so, the question of the existence of a Christian Priesthood is narrowed at once to the simple question whether it is or is not probable that so precious an ordinance as a channel of grace would be committed by Providence to the custody of certain guardians. The tendency of opinions at this day is to believe that nothing more is necessary for acceptance than faith in God's promise of mercy; whereas it is certain from Scripture, that the gift of reconciliation is not conveyed to individuals except through appointed ordinances. Christ has interposed something between Himself and the soul; and if it is not inconsistent with the liberty of the Gospel that a Sacrament should interfere, there is no antecedent inconsistency in a keeper of the Sacrament attending upon it. Moreover, the very circumstance that a standing Ministry has existed from the first, leads on to the inference that that Ministry was intended to take charge of the Sacraments; and thus the facts of the case suggest an interpretation of our Lord's memorable words, when He committed to St. Peter "the *keys* of the Kingdom of Heaven."

---

had made. 'One,' said he, 'must be ordained;' and without delay they proceeded to the ordination. Of course, St. Peter must have had from our Lord express authority for this step. Otherwise it would seem most natural to defer a transaction so important until the unerring Guide, the Holy Ghost, should have come among them, as they knew He would in a few days. On the other hand, since the Apostles were eminently Apostles of our Incarnate Lord, since their very being, *as* Apostles, depended entirely on their personal mission from Him (which is the reason why catalogues are given of them, with such scrupulous care, in many of the holy books): in that regard one should naturally have expected that He Himself before His departure would have supplied the vacancy by personal designation. But we see it was not His pleasure to do so. As the Apostles afterwards brought on the ordination sooner, so He had deferred it longer than might have been expected. Both ways it should seem as if there were a purpose of bringing the event within those ten days, *during which*, as I said, *the church was left to herself;* left to exercise her faith and hope, much as Christians are left now, without any *miraculous* aid or extraordinary illumination from above. Then, at that moment of the New Testament history in which the circumstances of believers corresponded most nearly to what they have been since miracles and inspiration ceased,—just at that time it pleased our Lord that a fresh Apostle should be consecrated, with authority and commission as ample as the former enjoyed. In a word, it was His will that the eleven Disciples alone, not Himself personally, should name the successor of Judas; and that they chose the right person, He gave testimony very soon after, by sending His Holy Spirit on St. Matthias, as richly as on St. John, St. James, or St. Peter."—*Tracts for the Times,* vol. ii, No. 52.

I would have this Scripture truth considered attentively; viz. that Sacraments are the channels of the peculiar Christian privileges, and not merely (as many men think, and as the rite of Confirmation really is) *seals* of the covenant. A man may object, indeed, that in St. Paul's Epistle to the Romans nothing is said about channels and instruments; that faith is represented as the sole medium of justification. But I will refer him, by way of reply, to the same Apostle's speech to Festus and Agrippa, where he describes Christ as saying to him on his miraculous conversion, "Rise and stand upon thy feet; for I have appeared unto thee for this purpose, to make thee a Minister and a Witness," sending him forth, as it might appear, to preach the Gospel, without instrumentality of Ordinance or Minister. Had we but this account of his conversion, who would not have supposed, that he who was "to open men's eyes, and turn them from darkness to light," had been pardoned and accepted at once upon his faith, without rite or form? Yet from other parts of the history, we learn what is here omitted, viz. that an especial revelation was made to Ananias, lest Saul should go without baptism; and that, so far from his being justified immediately on his faith, he was bid not to tarry, but "to arise and be baptized, and *to wash away his sins* calling on the name of the Lord." [Acts xxvi. 16–18; xxii. 16; ix. 17.[13]] So dangerous is it to attempt to prove a negative from insulated passages of Scripture.

Here then we have a clear instance in St. Paul's own case, that there are priestly Services between the soul and God, even under the Gospel; that though Christ has purchased inestimable blessings for our race, yet that it is still necessary ever to apply them to individuals by visible means; and if so, I confess, that to me at least it seems more likely antecedently, that such services should have, than that they should lack, an appropriate minister. But here again we are not left to mere conjecture, as I proceed to show.

5. You well know that the benefits of the Atonement are frequently represented in Scripture under the figure of spiritual food, bread from heaven, the water that never faileth, and in more sacred language, as the communion of the Body and Blood of the Divine Sacrifice. Now, this special Christian benefit is there connected, as on the one hand with an outward rite, so on the other with certain appointed Dispensers. So that the very context of Scripture leads us on from the notion of a priestly service to that of a priesthood.

"Who then is that faithful and wise *Steward*," says Christ, "whom his Lord shall make ruler over His household, to give them their *portion of food* in due season? Blessed is that servant, whom his Lord when He cometh shall find so doing." [Luke xii. 43.] Now, I infer from this passage; first, that there are, under the Gospel, especial Dispensers of the Christian's spiritual food, in oth-

---

13 *Vide* also Acts xiii. 2, 3.

er words (if the word "food" [*sitometoion*] may be interpreted from the parallel of the sixth chapter of St. John), Dispensers of invisible grace, or Priests;—next, that they are to continue to the Church in every age till the end, for it is said, "Blessed is he, whom his Lord, *when He cometh*, shall find so doing;"—further, that the Minister mentioned is also "Ruler over His household," as in the case of the Apostles, uniting the Regal with the Sacerdotal office;—lastly, the word "Steward," which incidentally occurs in the passage, a title applied by St. Paul to the Apostles, affords an additional reason for supposing that other like titles, such as "Ambassadors of Christ," given to the Apostles, do also belong in a true and sufficient sense to their Successors.

6. These considerations in favour of the existence of a Christian Priesthood, are strengthened by observing that the office of intercession, which though not a peculiarity, is ever characteristic of the Priestly Order, is spoken of in Scripture as a sort of prerogative of the Gospel Ministry. For instance, Isaiah, speaking of Christian times, says, "I have set watchmen upon thy walls, O Jerusalem, which shall never hold their peace day nor night. Ye that make mention of the Lord, keep not silence; and give Him no rest, till He establish, and till He make Jerusalem a praise in the earth." [Isa. lxii. 6, 7.] In the Acts of the Apostles, we find Christ's ministers engaged in this sacred service, according to the prophecy. "There were in the Church that was at Antioch certain prophets and teachers, as Barnabas, and Simeon called Niger, and Lucius of Cyrene, and Manaen, foster brother to Herod the Tetrarch, and Saul. As they *ministered* to the Lord, and fasted," [Acts xiii. 1, 2.] the Holy Ghost separated two of them for His work. This "ministering" to the Lord with fasting was surely some solemn intercessory service. And this agrees with a passage in St. James's Epistle, which seems to invest the Elders of the Church with this same privilege of the priesthood. "Is any sick among you? Let him call for the Elders of the Church, *and let them pray over him* (not pray *with* him merely), anointing him with oil in the name of the Lord; and *the prayer of faith* (not the oil merely) shall save the sick, and the Lord shall raise him up." In like manner St. Paul speaks of Epaphras as "our dear fellow-servant, who is *for* you," that is, for the Colossians to whom he is writing, "a faithful minister of Christ." Presently he explains what was the service which Epaphras did for them: "always *labouring fervently for you in prayer*, that ye may stand perfect and complete in all the will of God." [James v. 14, 15. Col. i. 7; iv. 12.].

7. We may end these remarks by recurring to the instances of St. Peter and St. John the Baptist; who, as types of God's ordained servants, before and after His Son's coming, may serve to explain the office of ordinary Christian Ministers. Even the lowest of them is "greater than John." Now what was it that he wanted? Was it the *knowledge of Gospel doctrine*? No, surely; no words

can be clearer than his concerning the New covenant. "Behold the Lamb of God, which taketh away the sin of the world." "He that cometh from above, is above all . . . He whom God hath sent speaketh the words of God, for God giveth not the Spirit by measure unto Him. The Father loveth the Son, and hath given all things into His hand. He that believeth on the Son hath everlasting life, and he that believeth not the Son shall not see life, but the wrath of God abideth on him." [John i. 29; iii. 31–36.] Therefore, the Baptist lacked not the full Christian *doctrine*; what he did lack was (as he says himself) the Baptism of *the Spirit*, conveying a commission from Christ the Saviour, in all His manifold gifts, ordinary and extraordinary, Regal and Sacerdotal. John was not inferior to us Gospel Ministers in knowledge, but in power.

On the other hand, if, as I have made appear, St. Peter's ministerial office continues as regards ordinary purposes, in the persons of those who come after him, we are bound to understand our Lord's blessing, pronounced in the first instance upon him, as descending in due measure on the least of us His ministers who "keep the faith," Peter being but the representative and type of them all. "Blessed art thou, Simon Barjona; for flesh and blood hath not revealed it unto thee, but My Father, which is in heaven. And I say also unto thee, that thou art Peter, and upon this rock I will build My Church, and the gates of hell shall not prevail against it. And I will give unto thee the keys of the Kingdom of Heaven; and whatsoever thou shalt bind on earth shall be bound in heaven, and whatsoever thou shalt loose on earth shall be loosed in heaven." August and glorious promise! Can it be, that it is all expended on St. Peter, how great soever that noble Apostle? Is it inserted in the "everlasting Gospel," to witness merely of one long since departed? Is it the practice of the inspired word to exalt individuals? Does not the very exuberance of the blessing resist any such niggardly use of it? Does it not flow over in spite of us, till our unbelief is vanquished by the graciousness of Him who spoke it? Is it, in short, anything but the prejudices of education, which prevent so many of us from receiving it in that fulness of grace in which it was poured out?

I say our *prejudices*,—for these surely are the cause of our inconsistency in faith; adopting, as we do, a rule of Scripture interpretation, which carries us a certain way, and stops short of the whole counsel of God, and should teach us nothing, or a great deal more. If the promises to Christ's Apostles are not fulfilled in the Church for ever after, why should the blessing attaching to the Sacraments extend after the first age? Why should the Lord's Supper be now the Communion of the Lord's Body and Blood? Why should Baptism convey spiritual privileges? Why should any part of Scripture afford permanent instruction? Why should the way of life be any longer narrow? Why should the burden of the Cross be necessary for every disciple of Christ? Why should the

Spirit of adoption any longer be promised us? Why should separation from the world be now a duty? Happy indeed it is for men that they *are* inconsistent; for then, though they lose some part of a Christian's faith, at least they keep a portion. This will happen in quiet times, and in the case of those who are of mature years, and whose minds have been long made up on the subject of religion. But should a time of controversy arise, then such inconsistencies become of fearful moment as regards the multitude called Christian, who have not any decided convictions to rest upon. Inconsistency of creed is sure to attract the notice of the intellect, unless habit has reconciled the heart to it. Therefore, in a speculative age, such as our own, a religious education which involves such inconsistency, is most dangerous to the unformed Christian, who will set straight his traditionary creed by unlearning the portion of truth it contains, rather than by adding that in which it is deficient. Hence, the lamentable spectacle, so commonly seen, of men who deny the Apostolic commission proceeding to degrade the Eucharist from a Sacrament to a bare commemorative rite; or to make Baptism such a mere outward form, and sign of profession, as it would be childish or fanciful to revere. And reasonably; for they who think it superstitious to believe that particular persons are channels of grace, are but consistent in denying virtue to particular ordinances. Nor do they stop even here; for denying the grace of baptism, they proceed to deny the doctrine of original sin, for which that grace is the remedy.[14] Further, denying the doctrine of original sin, they necessarily impair the doctrine of the Atonement, and so prepare a way for the denial of our Lord's Divinity. Again, denying the power of the Sacraments on the ground of its *mysteriousness*, demanding from the very text of Scripture the fullest proof of it conceivable, and thinking little of the blessedness of "not seeing, and yet believing," they naturally proceed to object to the doctrine of the Trinity as obstructing and obscuring the simplicity (as they consider it) of the Gospel, and but indirectly deducible from the extant documents of inspiration. Lastly, after they have thus divested the divine remedies of sin, and the treatment necessary for the sinner, of their solemnity and awe, having made the whole scheme of salvation of as intelligible and ordinary a character as the repair of any accident in the works of man, having robbed Faith of its mysteries, the Sacraments of their virtue, the Priesthood of its commission, no wonder that sin itself is soon considered a venial matter, moral evil as a mere imperfection, man as involved in no great peril or misery, his duties of no very arduous or anxious nature. In a word, religion, as such, is in the way to disappear from the mind altogether; and in its stead a

---

[14] *E.g.* A Dissenting Catechism has lately been published in the country for popular use, in which the doctrine of original sin is denied, by way of meeting the charge of cruelty towards children, as involved in the omission of infant baptism.

mere cold worldly morality, a decent regard to the claims of society, a cultivation of the benevolent affections, and a gentleness and polish of external deportment, will be supposed to constitute the entire duties of that being, who is conceived in sin, and the child of wrath, is redeemed by the precious blood of the Son of God, is born again and sustained by the Spirit through the invisible strength of Sacraments, and called, through self-denial and sanctification of the inward man, to the Eternal Presence of the Father, Son, and Holy Ghost.

Such is the course and issue of unbelief, though beginning in what the world calls trifles. Beware then, O my Brethren, of entering a way which leads to death. Fear to question what Scripture says of the Ministers of Christ, lest the same perverse spirit lead you on to question its doctrine about Himself and His Father. "Little children, it is the last time; and as ye have heard that Antichrist shall come, even now are there many Antichrists . . . They went out from us, but they were not of us." [1 John ii. 18, 19.] "Ye shall know them by their fruits." [Matt. vii. 16.] If any man come to you, bringing any scoff against the power of Christ's Ministers, ask him what he holds concerning the Sacraments, or concerning the Blessed Trinity; look narrowly after his belief as regards the Atonement, or Original Sin. Ascertain whether he holds with the Church's doctrine in these points; see to it whether at very best he does not try to evade the question, has recourse to explanations, or professes to have no opinion at all upon it. Look to these things, that you may see whither you are invited. Be not robbed of your faith blindfold. Do what you do with a clear understanding of the consequences. And if the arguments which he uses against you tend to show that your present set of opinions is in some measure inconsistent, and force you to see in Scripture more than you do at present, or else less, be not afraid to add to it, rather than to detract from it. Be quite sure that, go as far as you may, you will never, through God's grace, be led to see more in it than the early Christians saw; that, however you enlarge your creed, you will but carry yourselves on to Apostolic perfection, equally removed from the extremes of presumption and of unbelief, neither intruding into things not seen as yet, nor denying, on the other hand, what you cannot see.

Use of Saints' Days[†]

"Ye shall be Witnesses unto Me, both in Jerusalem, and in all Judea,
and in Samaria, and unto the uttermost part of the earth."

Acts i. 8

SO MANY were the wonderful works which our Saviour did on earth, that
not even the world itself could have contained the books recording
them. Nor have His marvels been less since He ascended on high;—
those works of higher grace and more abiding fruit, wrought in the souls of
men, from the first hour till now,—the captives of His power, the ransomed
heirs of His kingdom, whom He has called by His Spirit working in due season, and led on from strength to strength till they appear before His face in
Zion. Surely not even the world itself could contain the records of His love,
the history of those many Saints, that "cloud of Witnesses," whom we today
celebrate, His purchased possession in every age! We crowd these all up into
one day; we mingle together in the brief remembrance of an hour all the
choicest deeds, the holiest lives, the noblest labours, the most precious sufferings, which the sun ever saw. Even the least of those Saints were the contemplation of many days,—even the names of them, if read in our Service, would
outrun many settings and risings of the light,—even one passage in the life of
one of them were more than sufficient for a long discourse. "Who can count
the dust of Jacob, and the number of the fourth part of Israel?" [Numb. xxiii.
10.] Martyrs and Confessors, Rulers and Doctors of the Church, devoted
Ministers and Religious brethren, kings of the earth and all people, princes
and judges of the earth, young men and maidens, old men and children, the
first fruits of all ranks, ages, and callings, gathered each in his own time into
the paradise of God. This is the blessed company which today meets the
Christian pilgrim in the Services of the Church. We are like Jacob, when, on
his journey homewards, he was encouraged by a heavenly vision. "Jacob went
on his way, and the Angels of God met him; and when Jacob saw them, he
said, This is God's host: and he called the name of that place Mahanaim."
[Gen. xxxii. 1, 2.]

And such a host was also seen by the favoured Apostle, as described in
the chapter from which the Epistle of the day is taken. "I beheld, and lo, a

---

[†] *Parochial & Plain Sermons*, vol. 2 (1835), Sermon 32, preached on the Feast of All Saints.

great multitude, which no man could number, of all nations, and kindreds, and people, and tongues, stood before the Lamb, clothed with white robes, and palms in their hands . . . These are they which came out of great tribulation, and have washed their robes, and made them white in the blood of the Lamb." [Rev. vii. 9, 14.]

This great multitude, which no man could number, is gathered into this one day's commemoration, the goodly fellowship of the Prophets, the noble army of Martyrs, the Children of the Holy Church Universal, who have rested from their labours.

The reason of this disposition of things is as follows:—Some centuries ago there were too many Saints' days; and they became an excuse for idleness. Nay, worse still, by a great and almost incredible perverseness, instead of glorifying God in His Saints, Christians came to pay them an honour approaching to Divine worship. The consequence was, that it became necessary to take away their Festivals, and to commemorate them all at once in a summary way. Now men go into the contrary extreme. These Holydays, few though they be, are not duly observed. Such is the way of mankind, ever contriving to slip by their duty, and fall into one or other extreme of error. Idle or busy, they are in both cases wrong: idle, and so neglecting their duties towards man; busy, and so neglecting their duties towards God. We have little to do, however, with the faults of others;—let us then, passing by the error of idling time under pretence of observing many Holydays, rather speak of the fault of our own day, viz. of neglecting to observe them, and that, under pretence of being too busy.

Our Church abridged the number of Holydays, thinking it right to have but a few; but we account any as too much. For, taking us as a nation, we are bent on gain; and grudge any time which is spent without reference to our worldly business. We should seriously reflect whether this neglect of the appointments of religion be not a great national sin. As to individuals I can easily understand how it is that they pass them over. A considerable number of persons (for instance) have not their time at their own disposal. They are in service or business, and it is their duty to attend to the orders of their masters or employers,—which keep them from church. Or they have particular duties to keep them at home, though they are their own masters. Or, it even may be said, that the circumstances under which they find their calling, the mode in which it is exercised by others, may be a sort of reason for doing as others do. It may be such a worldly loss to them to leave their trade on a Saint's day and go to church, as to appear to them a reason in conscience for their not doing so? I do not wish to give an opinion upon this case or that, which is a matter for the individual immediately concerned. Still, I say, *on the whole*, that state of society must be defective, which renders it necessary for the Ordinances of religion to be neglected. There must be a fault *somewhere*; and it is the duty of every one of us to clear himself of his own portion of the fault, to avoid partaking in other men's sins, and to do his utmost that others may extricate themselves from the blame too.

I say this neglect of religious Ordinances is an especial fault of these latter ages. There was a time when men openly honoured the Gospel; and when, consequently, they had each of them more means of becoming religious. The institutions of the Church were impressed upon the face of society. Dates were reckoned not so much by months and seasons, as by sacred Festivals. The world kept pace with the Gospel; the arrangements of legal and commercial business were regulated by a Christian rule. Something of this still remains among us; but such customs are fast vanishing. Mere grounds of utility are considered sufficient for re-arranging the order of secular engagements. Men think it waste of time to wait upon the course of the Christian year; and they think they gain more by a business-like method, and the neatness, dispatch, and clearness in their worldly transactions consequent upon it (and this perhaps they really *do* gain, but they think they gain *more* by it), than they lose by dropping the Memorials of religion. These they really do lose; they lose those regulations which at stated times brought the concerns of another life before their minds; and, if the truth must be spoken, they often rejoice in losing what officiously interfered, as they consider, with their temporal schemes, and reminded them they were mortal.

Or view another part of the subject. It was once the custom for the churches to be open through the day, that at spare times Christians might enter them,—and be able to throw off for some minutes the cares of the world in religious exercises. Services were appointed for separate hours in the day, to allow of the attendance in whole or part of those who happened to be at hand. Those who could not come, still might keep their service-book with them; and at least repeat at times the prayers in private which were during the passing hour offered in church. Thus provision was made for the spiritual sustenance of Christians day by day; for that daily-needed bread which far exceeds "the bread that perisheth." All this is now at an end. We dare not open our churches, lest men should profane them instead of worshipping. As for an accurately arranged Ritual, too many of us have learned to despise it, and to consider it a form. Thus the world has encroached on the Church; the lean kine have eaten up the fat. We are threatened with years of spiritual famine, with the triumph of the enemies of the Truth, and with the stifling, or at least enfeebling of the Voice of Truth;—and why? All because we have neglected those religious observances through the year which the Church commands, which we are bound to observe; while, by neglecting them, we have provided a sort of argument for those who have wished to do them away altogether. No party of men can keep together without stated meetings; assemblings are, we know, the very life of political associations. Viewing, then, the institutions of the Church merely in a human point of view, how can we possess power as Christians, if we do *not*, and on the other hand, what great power we should have, if we *did*, flock to the Ordinances of religion, present a bold face to the world, and show that Christ has still servants true to Him? That we come to church on Sundays is a help this way, doubtless; but it would be a vastly more powerful evidence of our earnestness for the Truth, if we testified for Christ at some worldly inconvenience to ourselves, which would be the case with some of us on other Holydays. Can we devise a more powerful mode of preaching to men at large, and one in which the most unlearned and most timid among us might more easily partake, of preaching Christ as a warning and a remembrance, than if all who loved the Lord Jesus Christ in sincerity made it a practice to throng the churches on the weekday Festivals and various Holy Seasons, allowing less religious persons the while to make the miserable gains which greater keenness in the pursuit of this world certainly does secure?

I have not yet mentioned the peculiar benefit to be derived from the observance of Saints' days: which obviously lies in their setting before the mind patterns of excellence for us to follow. In directing us to these, the Church does but fulfil the design of Scripture. Consider how great a part of the Bible is historical; and how much of the history is merely the lives of those men who were God's instruments in their respective ages. Some of them are no patterns for us, others show marks of the corruption under which human nature universally lies:—yet the chief of them are specimens of especial faith and sanctity, and are set before us with the evident intention of exciting and guiding us in our religions course. Such are, above others, Abraham, Joseph, Job, Moses, Joshua, Samuel, David, Elijah, Jeremiah, Daniel, and the like; and in the New Testament the Apostles and Evangelists. First of all, and in His own incommunicable glory, our Blessed Lord Himself gives us an example; but His faithful servants lead us on towards Him, and confirm and diversify His pattern. Now it has been the aim of our Church in her Saints' days to maintain the principle, and set a pattern, of this peculiarly Scriptural teaching.

And we, at the present day, have particular need of the discipline of such commemorations as Saints' days to recall us to ourselves. It is a fault of these times (for we have nothing to do with the faults of other times) to despise the past in comparison of the present. We can scarce open any of the lighter or popular publications of the day without falling upon some panegyric on ourselves, on the illumination and humanity of the age, or upon some disparaging remarks on the wisdom and virtues of former times. Now it is a most salutary thing under this temptation to self-conceit to be reminded, that in all the highest qualifications of human excellence, we have been far outdone by men who lived centuries ago; that a standard of truth and holiness was then set up which we are not likely to reach, and that, as for thinking to become wiser and better, or more acceptable to God than they were, it is a mere dream. Here we are taught the true value and relative importance of the various gifts of the mind. The showy talents, in which the present age prides itself, fade away before the true metal of Prophets and Apostles. Its boasted "knowledge" is but a shadow of "power" before the vigorous strength of heart which they displayed, who could calmly work moral miracles, as well as speak with the lips of inspired wisdom. Would that St. Paul or St. John could rise from the dead! How would the minute philosophers who now consider intellect and enlightened virtue all their own, shrink into nothing before those well-tempered, sharp-edged weapons of the Lord! Are not we come to this, is it not our shame as a nation, that, if not the Apostles themselves, at least the Ecclesiastical System they devised, and the Order they founded, are viewed with coldness and disrespect? How few are there who look with reverent interest upon the Bishops of the Church as the Successors of the Apostles; honouring them, if they honour, merely because they like them as individuals, and not from any thought of the peculiar sacredness of their office! Well, let it be! the End must one time come. It cannot be that things should stand still thus. Christ's Church is indestructible; and, lasting on through all the vicissitudes of this world, she *must* rise again and flourish, when the poor creatures of a day who opposed Her, have crumbled into dust. "No weapon that is formed against her shall prosper." "Rejoice not against me, O mine enemy! when I fall, I shall arise; when I sit in darkness, the Lord shall be a light unto me." [Isa. liv. 17. Micah vii. 8.] In the meantime let us not forget our duty; which is, after the example of Saints, to take up our cross meekly, and pray for our enemies.

These are thoughts suitably to be impressed on us, on ending (as we do now) the yearly Festivals of the Church. Every year brings wonders. We know not any year, what wonders shall have happened before the circle of Festivals has run out again, from St. Andrew's to All Saints'. Our duty then is, to wait for the Lord's coming, to prepare His way before Him, to pray that when He comes we may be found watching; to pray for our country, for our King and all in authority under him, that God would vouchsafe to enlighten the understandings and change the hearts of men in power, and make them act in His faith and fear, for all orders and conditions of men, and especially for that branch of His Church which He has planted here. Let us not forget, in our lawful and fitting horror at evil men, that they have souls, and that they know not what they do, when they oppose the Truth. Let us not forget, that we are sons of sinful Adam as well as they, and have had advantages to aid our faith and obedience above other men. Let us not forget, that, as we are called to be Saints, so we are, by that very calling, called to suffer; and, if we suffer, must not think it strange concerning the fiery trial that is to try us, nor be puffed up by our privilege of suffering, nor bring suffering needlessly upon us, nor be eager to make out we have suffered for Christ, when we have but suffered for our faults, or not at all. May God give us grace to act upon these rules, as well as to adopt and admire them; and to say nothing for saying's sake, but to do much and say little!

Jeroboam†

"He cried against the altar in the word of the Lord, and said, O altar, altar, thus saith the Lord, Behold, a child shall be born unto
the house of David, Josiah by name; and upon thee shall he offer
the priests of the high places that burn incense upon thee, and
men's bones shall be burnt upon thee."   1 Kings xiii. 2

THESE WORDS are parts of a narrative which we hear read once a year
in the Sunday Service, but which can scarcely be understood without
some attention to the history which precedes it. It is a prophecy
against the form of worship set up in the kingdom of Israel; let us consider
what this kingdom and this worship were, and how this woe came to be uttered by a prophet of God.

When Solomon fell into idolatry, he broke what may be called his coro-
nation oath, and at once forfeited God's favour. The essential duty of a king of
the chosen people was to act as God's representative, to govern for Him. David was called a man after God's heart, because he was thus faithful; he fulfilled his trust. Solomon failed, failed in the very one duty which, as king of
Israel, he was bound to perform.

In consequence, a message came from Almighty God, revealing what the
punishment of his sin would be. He might be considered as having forfeited
his kingdom, for himself and his posterity. For David's sake, however, this
extreme sentence was not pronounced upon him. First, since the promise had
been made to David that his son should reign after him, though that son was
the very transgressor, yet *he* was spared the impending evil on account of the
promise. As an honour to David, Solomon's reign closed without any open
infliction of divine vengeance; only with the presage of it. "Forasmuch as this
is done of thee, I will surely rend the kingdom from thee, and will give it to
thy servant. Notwithstanding in thy days I will not do it, for David thy father's sake: but I will rend it out of the hand of thy son." [1 Kings xi. 11, 12.]
A still further mitigation of punishment was granted, still for David's sake. It
had been promised David, "I will set up thy seed after thee, and I will stablish
the throne of his kingdom for ever . . . If he commit iniquity, I will chasten
him with the rod of men; but My mercy shall not depart away from him, as I

---

† *Parochial & Plain Sermons*, vol. 3 (1836), Sermon 5.

took it from Saul, whom I put away before thee." [2 Sam. vii. 12–15.] Accordingly, when Solomon had sinned, and the kingdom was rent from him, still holy David's seed was not utterly put away before a new king, as the family of Saul had fallen before David; part of the kingdom was still left to the descendants of the faithful king. "Howbeit, I will not rend away *all* the kingdom; but will give one tribe to thy son," Solomon's son, "for *David My servant's sake.*" This one tribe was the tribe of Judah, David's own tribe; to which part of Benjamin was added, as being in the neighbourhood. And this kingdom, over which David's line reigned for four hundred years after him, is called the kingdom of Judah.—But with this kingdom of Judah we are not now concerned; but with that larger portion of the tribes, which was rent away from David's house, and forms what is called the kingdom of Israel.

These were the circumstances under which the division of the kingdom was made. Solomon seems to have allowed himself in tyrannical conduct towards his subjects, as well as in idolatry. On his death the people came to his son Rehoboam, at Shechem, and said, "Thy father made our yoke grievous; now therefore make thou the grievous service of thy father and his heavy yoke which he put upon us lighter, and we will serve thee." Rehoboam was rash enough to answer, after three days' deliberation, "My father made your yoke heavy, and I will add to your yoke; my father also chastised you with whips, but I will chastise you with scorpions." [1 Kings xii. 4, 14.] Now every one sees that Rehoboam here acted very wrongly, and Solomon too, as I have said, had sinned grievously before him. His oppression of the people was a *sin*; yet, you will observe, the people had no right to complain. They had brought this evil on themselves; they had obstinately courted and struggled after it. They would have "a king like the nations," a despotic king; and now they had one, they were discontented. Samuel had not only earnestly and solemnly protested against this measure, as an offence against their Almighty Governor, but had actually forewarned them of the evils which despotic power would introduce among them. "He will take your sons and appoint them for himself, for his chariots, and to be his horsemen; he will set them to ear [sic] his ground and to reap his harvest and to make his instruments of war. He will take your daughters to be confectionaries, and to be cooks, and to be bakers. And he will take your fields, and your vineyards, and your oliveyards, and give them to his servants." The warning ends thus: "And ye shall cry out in that day, *because of your king which ye shall have chosen you*, and the Lord will not hear you in that day." [1 Sam. viii. 11–18.] These were Samuel's words beforehand. Now all this had come upon them: as they had sown, so had they reaped. And, as matters stood, their best course would have been contentment, resignation; it was their duty to bear the punishment of their national self-will. But one sin was not enough for them. They proceeded, as men commonly do, to mend (as they considered) their first sin, by a fresh one;—they rebelled against their king. "What portion have we in David?" they said, "neither have we inheritance in the son of Jesse. To your tents, O Israel—now see to thine own house, David." [1 Kings xi. 16.] Ten tribes out of twelve revolted from their king in that day. Here they were quite inexcusable. Even putting it out of the question that they had brought the evil on themselves, still, independently of this, their king's tyranny did not justify their sudden, unhesitating, violent rebellion. He was acting against no engagement or stipulation. Because their king did not do his duty to them, this was no reason they should not do their duty to him. Say that he was cruel and rapacious, still they might have safely trusted the miraculous providence of God, to have restrained the king by His prophets, and to have brought them safely through. This would have been the way of *faith*; but they took the matter into their own hands, and got into further difficulty. And I wish you to observe, that all the evil arose from this original fault, worked out in its consequences through centuries, viz., their having a king at all.

So much, then, for their first sin, and their second sin. To continue further the history of their downward course, we must look to the man whom they made the leader of their rebellion. This was Jeroboam.

Jeroboam, the son of Nebat, had been, during Solomon's lifetime, appointed to collect the tribute from the tribe of Ephraim, the most powerful of the ten tribes; a situation which gave him influence and authority in that part of the country. The king appointed him, "seeing the young man that he was industrious." We are told, too, that he was "a mighty man of valour." [1 Kings xi. 28.] Thus honoured by Solomon, he abused his trust, even in the king's lifetime, by rebelling against him. "Jeroboam, Solomon's servant, even he lift up his hand against the king." When Solomon, in consequence, "sought to kill him," he fled to Egypt, when Shishak, the king, sheltered him. On Solomon's death he returned to his country, and at the invitation of the revolting tribes, headed their rebellion. "It came to pass when all Israel (*i.e.* the ten tribes) heard that Jeroboam was come again, that they sent and called him unto the congregation, and made him king over all Israel: there was none that followed the house of David, but the tribe of Judah only." [1 Kings xii. 20.]

Now, that Jeroboam was an instrument in God's hand to chastise Solomon's sin, is plain; and there is no difficulty in conceiving how a wicked man, without its being any excuse to him, still may bring about the Divine purposes. But in Jeroboam's particular case there *is* this difficulty at first sight; that Almighty God had seemed to sanction his act by *promising* him, in Solomon's lifetime, the kingdom of the ten tribes. The prophet Ahijah had met him, and delivered to him a message from "the Lord, the God of Israel." "I will rend the kingdom out of the hand of Solomon, and will give ten tribes *to thee*." And it was on account of this prophecy that Jeroboam "lifted up his hand against the king." On a little consideration, however, we shall find no difficulty here: for though Almighty God promised him the kingdom, He did not tell him to *gain it for himself*; and, if we must not do evil that good may come, surely we may not do evil that a promise may be fulfilled; and to "rebel against his lord" (in the words of Scripture) was a plain indisputable sin. God, who made the promise, could of course fulfil it in His own time. He did not require man's crime to bring it about. It was, of course, an insult to His holiness and power to suppose he did. Jeroboam ought to have waited patiently God's time; this would have been the part of true faith. But it had always been, as on this occasion, the sin of the Israelites, to outrun God's providence; and even when they chose to pursue His ends, to wish to work them out in their own way. They never would "be still and know that He was God," wait His word and follow His guidance. Thus, when they first took possession of the promised land, they were told to cast the nations out, and utterly destroy all that did not leave the country. They soon became weary of this, and thought they had found out a better way. They thought it wiser to spare their enemies, and form alliances with them, and put them under tribute. This brought them first into idolatry, then into captivity. When Samuel rescued them, and their hopes revived, their first act was to choose a king like the nations, contrary to God's will. And Jeroboam, in this instance, as a special emblem of the whole people in the rebellion itself, had not patience to wait, and faith to trust God, that "what He had promised He was able also to perform." That it was *a trial* to Jeroboam we need not deny; of course it was. He was tried and found wanting. Had he withstood the temptation, and refrained himself till lawfully called to reign, untold blessings might have been showered on him and on his people, who, in the actual history, were all cut off for their sins. He was not the first man who had thus been tried. David had been promised Saul's kingdom, and anointed thereunto by Samuel, years before he came into possession; yet, though he was persecuted by Saul, and had his life several times in his power, still he would not lift up his hand against his king. He had the faith of his forefather Abraham, who, though promised the land he dwelt in, wandered in it as a pilgrim, without daring to occupy it; wandered on with a band of trained servants at his command, who might have gained for him a territory had he desired it, as certainly as they smote Chedorlaomer and recovered Lot and his goods. David inherited this patient faith, and through it "obtained the promise," and founded a throne in righteousness and truth. Had Jeroboam followed it, he, too, might have been the father of a line of kings; he might have been the instrument and object of God's promised favour towards the house of Joseph; satisfying, in his own person, the prophecies which Jacob and Moses[15] had delivered, and Joshua, himself an Ephraimite, had begun to fulfil, and founding a dominion not inferior in glory to that of Judah and Jerusalem.

Jeroboam, then, is not excused, though Ahijah prophesied; but, next, let us inquire how did he act when at length seated on the throne? It is not surprising, after such a beginning, that he sinned further and more grievously. When a man begins to do wrong, he cannot answer for himself how far he may be carried on. He does not see beforehand, he cannot know where he shall find himself after the sin is committed. One false step forces him to another, for retreat is impossible. This, which occurs every day, is instanced, first, in the history of the whole people, and then, in the history of Jeroboam. For awhile, indeed, he seemed to prosper. Rehoboam, Solomon's son, had brought an extraordinary force of chosen men against him; but Almighty God, willing there should be no blood shed, designing to punish Solomon's idolatry, and intending to leave Jeroboam to himself, to work out the fruit of his rebellion, and then to judge and smite him with His own arm, would not allow the war. The prophet Shemaiah was sent to Rehoboam to put an end to it, and Rehoboam obeyed.

Thus Jeroboam seemed to have every thing his own way; but soon a difficulty arose which he had thought light of, if he thought of it at all. The Jewish nation was not only a kingdom, but a church, a religious as well as a political body; and Jeroboam found, before long, that in setting up a new kingdom in Israel, he must set up a new religion too.

It was ordered in the Law of Moses, that all the men throughout Israel should go up to Jerusalem to worship three times a year; but Jerusalem was, at this time, the capital of the kingdom of Judah, the rival kingdom; and Jeroboam clearly saw that if his new subjects were allowed to go up thither, they could not remain his subjects long, but would return to their former allegiance. Here, then, a second false step was necessary to complete the first; for a false step that must have been which, as it would seem, required for its protection a violation of the Law of Moses. He, doubtless, argued that he was obliged to do what he did, that he could not help himself. It is true;—sin *is* a hard master; once sold over to it, we cannot break our chain; one evil concession requires another.

"Jeroboam said in his heart, Now shall the kingdom return to the house of David: if this people go up to do sacrifice in the house of the Lord at Jerusalem, then shall the heart of this people turn again unto their lord, even unto Rehoboam, king of Judah, and they shall kill me, and go again to Rehoboam,

---

[15] Gen. xlix. 22–26. Deut. xxxiii. 13–17. cf. 1 Kings xi. 38.

king of Judah. Whereupon the king took counsel." [1 Kings xii. 26–28.] A melancholy counsel it was: he resolved to select places for religious worship in his own kingdom. This was against the Law, of course; but what he did was worse than this. He could not build a Temple like Solomon's, and yet he needed some visible sign of the presence of God. Almighty God had bid the Israelites take to themselves no sign of His presence, no likeness of him; but Jeroboam thought he could not do better than set up two figures of gold, one at each end of his country, not, indeed, as representations (he would argue), but as emblems and memorials of the true God, and as marking the established place of worship. It is probable that the age of Solomon, a season of peace, when the arts were cultivated and an intercourse opened with foreign nations, was a season also of a peculiar religious corruption, such as had never occurred before. All through their history, indeed, the Israelites had opposed God's will; but by this time they had learned to defend their disobedience by argument, and to transgress upon a system. Jeroboam's sins, in regard to religious worship, were not single, or inconsistent with each other, but depended on this principle—that there is no need to attend to the positive laws and the outward forms and ceremonies of religion, so that we attend to the substance. In setting up these figures of gold, it was far from his intention to oppose the worship of the One True God, the Maker of heaven and earth, the Saviour of Israel; the words he used on the occasion, and the course of the history, show this. He thought he was only altering the discipline of the Church, as we should now call it, and he might plausibly ask, What did that matter? he was but putting another emblem of God in the place of the Cherubim. He made merely such alterations as change of circumstances and the course of events rendered indispensable. He was in difficulties, and had to consider, not what was best, or what he himself should choose, had he to choose, but what was practicable.

The figure he adopted, as a memorial of Almighty God, was in the shape of an ox or calf, the same which the Israelites had set up in the wilderness. It is hardly known what is the meaning of the emblem, which, doubtless, came from Egypt. The ox is thought to be the emblem of life or strength; and, being set up as a religious monument, might be intended to signify God's creative power. But, however this might be, it was, at any rate, a direct and open transgression of the second Commandment. "The king took counsel, and made two calves of gold, and said unto the people, It is too much for you to go up to Jerusalem; behold thy gods, O Israel, which brought thee up out of the land of Egypt. And he set the one in Bethel, and the other put he in Dan."

Even this open idolatrous worship, not merely tolerated, but established, even this was not the last sin of this unhappy man, who had begun a course of

103

wickedness upon system, and then left it as an inheritance for others more abandoned than himself to perfect. The tribe of Levi, who were especially consecrated to religious purposes, had their possessions not in one place, but scattered up and down the country. It was not to be supposed that they, who executed judgment upon the sin of the calf in the wilderness, would tamely suffer this renewal of the ancient offence in a more heinous shape. They refused to countenance the idolatrous worship, and Jeroboam, led on by hard necessity, cast them out of the country, got possession of their cities and lands, and put in priests of his own making in their stead. "He made a house of high places," and "he and his sons cast off the Levites from executing the priest's office unto the Lord, and he ordained him priests for the high places, and for the devils, and for the calves which he had made; priests of the lowest of the people, which were not of the sons of Levi." [1 Kings xii. 31. 2 Chron. xi. 14, 15.] And he changed the solemn feast days, and dared to offer incense, himself intruding first, for example's sake, into the sacred office.

In consequence of these impious proceedings, not only "the priests and Levites, that were in all Israel," left his kingdom and retired to Judea, but also, "after them, out of all the" other "tribes, such as set their hearts to seek the Lord God of Israel, came to Jerusalem to sacrifice unto the Lord God of their fathers."

Truly this was an ill-omened commencement of his reign. He had made it impossible for pious Israelites to remain in the country. The irreligious alone held by him. Jeroboam ruled in a country given up, as it seemed, to evil spirits. So true is it, in a kindred sense to that in which the words were used by Samuel, that "rebellion is as the sin of witchcraft, and stubbornness is as iniquity and idolatry." [1 Sam. xv. 23.]

Now, then, we come to the concluding scene of this course of crime, perpetrated by one man—the transaction to which the text belongs.

It was on the new feast day "which he had devised of his own heart," and at Bethel where the idol was set up. The people were collected from all parts of the country, and the king "offered upon the altar and burnt incense." Such was the formal inauguration of the false religion in God's own hallowed country, answering to that sacred solemnity when Solomon offered the prayer of dedication in the Temple. The glory of God had come down on that chosen place in token of His favour, and now at Bethel, which He had once specially visited in an earlier age, He suffered not the heathen act to pass without an indication of His wrath. One of His prophets was sent from Judah to attend the festival; but, as if he were entering a country infected by the pestilence, he was bid go into no house, nor eat nor drink while he was in it, nay, he was not even to return to his home the same way by which he came, as if his feet must not touch the polluted earth twice.

When the prophet came, he uttered his message before the apostate king. It was a prophecy; a prophecy set up as a witness against the complicated sins of the people, the destiny of that rebellious and idolatrous kingdom stamped upon it in the day of its nativity. The man of God addressed the altar, as not deigning to speak to Jeroboam, and foretold its fate. He announced that, after no long time, the idolatrous power should be destroyed, and that very altar should last long enough to see its fall; for upon it, fragrant as it now was with incense, the impious priests should be sacrificed, and men's bones burned; moreover, that all this should be done by a prince of the house of Judah; thus intimating that David's royal line would outlive the revolting kingdom of Israel. "O altar, altar, thus saith the Lord, Behold, a child shall be born unto the house of David, Josiah by name; and upon thee shall he offer the priests of the high places that burn incense upon thee, and men's bones shall be burnt upon thee." To show his Divine commission, the prophet gave the word, and the altar was miraculously rent in twain, and the ashes of the sacrifice scattered on the ground. Nothing could be more public than a judgment like this, denounced from God Himself, after Rehoboam, Solomon's son, had not been allowed to take the matter into his own hands. And to make the occurrence still more impressive, two further signs were added. Jeroboam stretched forth his hand to seize the prophet; it was instantly shrivelled up, so that he could not pull it to him again. At the prophet's prayer, it was restored. The second miracle was still more awful. The prophet, wearied with his journey, was, on his return, persuaded by a bad man to eat and drink, against the express word of God declared to him. An immediate judgment followed. As he sat at table, his seducer was constrained to declare to him his punishment—that his body should not come into the sepulchre of his fathers; and as he went home, a lion, God's second instrument for its infliction, met and slew him, yet did not devour him, nor touch the ass he rode on, nor molest other passengers he met, but, fixed to the spot by miracle, he stood over the prophet's body, a sign, more truly than the idols at Dan and Bethel, of God's power, holiness, and severe justice, and suggesting, throughout all Israel, the fearful argument—"If God so punish his own children, what will be the final, though delayed, punishment of the wicked? If the righteous scarcely be saved, where shall the ungodly and the sinner appear?" [1 Pet. iv. 18.]

As for Jeroboam, in spite of all this, "after this thing he returned not from his evil way, but made again of the lowest of the people priests of the high places; whosoever would, he consecrated him, and he became one of the priests of the high places." [1 Kings xiii. 33.] Such was his life.

At the close of his reign, he lost even his earthly prosperity. "The Lord struck him, and he died." Such was his end.

His family was soon cut off from the throne; and after all his wise counsels and bold plans he has left but his name and title to posterity, "Jeroboam the son of Nebat who caused Israel to sin." Such is his memorial.

"Cursed be the man that trusteth in man, and maketh flesh his arm, and whose heart departeth from the Lord. For he shall be like the heath in the desert, and shall not see when good cometh, but shall inhabit the parched places in the wilderness, in a salt land, and not inhabited." [Jer. xvii. 5, 6.]

It requires but a very few words to show the application of this history to the circumstances in which we find ourselves. So strongly does it pourtray to us the existing disorders and schisms of the Christian Church—the profane and tyrannical usage which it meets with from the world—that the only question which can possibly arise in the mind is, whether it is allowable to apply it, and whether, as the events are alike, their respective character and their issue are like each other also. This, I say, is the only question, whether we may, without blame, judge of what we see by the light of what we read in the history of Israel; and I wish all readers would clearly understand that this is the only question. If the deeds of Israel and Jeroboam may be taken as types of what has been acted under the Gospel for centuries past, can we doubt that schism, innovation in doctrine, a counterfeit priesthood, sacrilege, and violence, are sins so heinous and crying, that there is no judgment too great for them, no woe which we may not expect will ultimately fall on the systems which have been born in them, and the lineage of their perpetrators? What other lesson can we draw from the history but this? but that we ought to draw a lesson, is plain from the repeated declaration of St. Paul:—"Whatsoever things were written aforetime, were written for our teaching." "All these things happened unto them as types, and they are written for our admonition, upon whom the ends of the world are come." "All Scripture is given by inspiration of God, and is profitable for teaching, for reproof, for correction, for instruction in righteousness." [Rom. xv. 4. 1 Cor. x. 11. 2 Tim. iii. 16.] St. Peter also and St. Jude expressly apply occurrences in the Old Testament to parallels under the Gospel.[16]

May God give us the will and the power to realize to our minds this most serious truth, and fairly to follow it out in its necessary consequences! And may He of His mercy have pity upon our poor distracted Church, rescue it from the dominion of the heathen, and grant that "the world's course may be so peaceably ordered by His governance, that" it and all branches of the One Church Catholic "may joyfully serve Him in all godly quietness!"

---

[16] 2 Pet. ii. 1–15; Jude 5–11.

Jewish Zeal, a Pattern for Christians[†]

"So let all thine enemies perish, O Lord; but let them that love Him,
be as the sun when he goeth forth in his might.
And the land had rest forty years."
Judges v. 31

WHAT A CONTRAST do these words present to the history which goes before them! "It came to pass," says the sacred writer, "when Israel was strong, that they put the Canaanites to tribute, and did not utterly drive them out. Neither did Ephraim drive out the Canaanites that dwelt in Gezer ... Neither did Zebulon drive out the inhabitants of Kitron ... Neither did Asher drive out the inhabitants of Accho ... Neither did Naphtali drive out the inhabitants of Bethshemesh." [Judges i. 28–32.] What was the consequence? "And the children of Israel did evil in the sight of the Lord and served Baalim ... they forsook the Lord and served Baal and Ashtaroth. And the anger of the Lord was hot against Israel, and He delivered them into the hands of spoilers that spoiled them, and He sold them into the hands of their enemies round about ... Whithersoever they went out, the hand of the Lord was against them for evil, as the Lord had said, and as the Lord had sworn unto them; and they were greatly distressed." [Judges ii. 11–15.] Here is the picture of indolence and unfaithfulness leading to cowardice, to apostasy, and to national ruin.

On the other hand, consider, by way of contrast, the narrative contained in the chapter which ends with the text. Ephraim and Benjamin, Machir and Zebulon, Issachar and Naphtali, rousing, uniting, assailing their enemies, and conquering; conquering in the strength of the Lord. Their long captivity was as nothing, through God's great mercy, when they turned to Him. In vain had their enemies trod them down to the ground; the Church of God had that power and grace within it, that whenever it could be persuaded to shake off its lassitude and rally, it smote as sharply and as effectively as though it had never been bound with the green withs and the new ropes of the Philistines. So it was now. "Awake, awake, Deborah: awake, awake, utter a song: arise, Barak, and lead thy captivity captive, thou son of Abinoam." Such was the inspired cry of war: and it was obeyed. In consequence the Canaanites were discomfit-

---

[†] *Parochial & Plain Sermons*, vol. 3 (1836), Sermon 13.

ed in battle and fled; "and the land had rest forty years." Here is a picture of manly obedience to God's will—a short trial of trouble and suffering—and then the reward, *peace*.

I propose now to make some remarks upon the lesson conveyed to us in this picture, which extends indeed through the greater part of the Old Testament—the lesson to us *as individuals*; for surely it is with reference to our own duties *as individuals*, that we should read every part of Scripture.

What the Old Testament especially teaches us is this:—that zeal is as essentially a duty of all God's rational creatures, as prayer and praise, faith and submission; and, surely, if so, especially of sinners whom He has redeemed; that zeal consists in a strict attention to His commands—a scrupulousness, vigilance, heartiness, and punctuality, which bears with no reasoning or questioning about them—an intense thirst for the advancement of His glory—a shrinking from the pollution of sin and sinners—an indignation, nay impatience, at witnessing His honour insulted—a quickness of feeling when His name is mentioned, and a jealousy how it is mentioned—a fulness of purpose, an heroic determination to yield Him service at whatever sacrifice of personal feeling—an energetic resolve to push through all difficulties, were they as mountains, when His eye or hand but gives the sign—a carelessness of obloquy, or reproach, or persecution, a forgetfulness of friend and relative, nay, a hatred (so to say) of all that is naturally dear to us, when He says, "Follow me." These are some of the characteristics of zeal. Such was the temper of Moses, Phinehas, Samuel, David, Elijah; it is the temper enjoined on all the Israelites, especially in their conduct towards the abandoned nations of Canaan. The text expresses that temper in the words of Deborah: "So let all thine enemies perish, O Lord; but let them that love Him be as the sun when he goeth forth in his might."

Now, it has sometimes been said that the commands of strenuous and stern service given to the Israelites—for instance, those relative to their taking and keeping possession of the promised land—do not apply to us Christians. There can be no doubt it is not our duty to take the sword and kill the enemies of God as the Jews were told to do; "Put up again thy sword into his place," [Matt. xxvi. 52.] are our Saviour's words to St. Peter. So far, then, if this is what is meant by saying that these commands do not apply to us, so far, doubtless, it is clear they do not apply to us. But it does not, hence, follow that the temper of mind which they pre-suppose and foster is not required of us; else, surely, the Jewish history is no longer profitable for doctrine, for reproof, for correction, for instruction in righteousness. St. Peter was blamed, not for his zeal, but for his use of the sword.

Man's duty, perfection, happiness, have always been one and the same. He is not a different being now from what he ever was; he has always been commanded the same duties. What was the holiness of an Israelite is still the holiness of a Christian, though the Christian has far higher privileges and aids for perfection. The Saints of God have ever lived by faith, and walked in the way of justice, mercy, truth, self-mastery, and love. It is impossible, then, that all these duties imposed on the Israelites of driving out their enemies, and taking and keeping possession of the promised land, should not in some sense or other apply to us; for it is clear they were not in their case mere accidents of obedience, but went to form a certain inward character, and as clear is it that our heart must be as the heart of Moses or David, if we would be saved through Christ.

This is quite evident, if we attentively examine the Jewish history, and the Divine commands which are the principles of it. For these commands, which some persons have said do not apply to us, are so many and varied, and repeated at so many and diverse times, that they certainly must have formed a peculiar character in the heart of the obedient Israelite, and were much more than an outward form and a sort of ceremonial service. They are so abundant throughout the Old Testament, that unless they in some way apply to us, it is difficult to see what is its direct use, at this day, in the way of precept; and this is the very conclusion which these same persons often go on to draw. They are willing to rid themselves of the Old Testament, and they say that Christians are not concerned in it, and that the Jews were almost barbarians; whereas St. Paul tells us, that the Jewish history is "written for our admonition and our learning." [1 Cor. x. 11; Rom. xv. 4.]

Let us consider some of the commands I have referred to, and the terms in which they are conveyed. For instance, that for the extirpation of the devoted nations from the land of Canaan. "When the Lord thy God shall bring thee into the land whither thou goest to possess it, . . . thou shalt smite" the nations that possess it, "and utterly destroy them; thou shalt make no covenant with them, nor show mercy unto them; neither shalt thou make marriages with them . . . Ye shall destroy their altars and break down their images, and cut down their groves, and burn down their graven images with fire . . . Thou shalt consume all the people which the Lord thy God shall deliver thee; thine eye shall have no pity upon them." [Deut. vii. 1–5, 16.]

Next observe, this merciless temper, as profane people would call it, but as well-instructed Christians say, this godly zeal, was enjoined upon them under far more distressing circumstances, viz., the transgressions of their own relations and friends. "If thy brother, the son of thy mother, or thy son, or thy daughter, or the wife of thy bosom, or thy friend which is as thine own soul, entice thee secretly, saying, Let us go and serve other gods, . . . Thou shalt not consent unto him, nor hearken unto him, neither shall thine eye pity him, neither shalt thou spare, neither shalt thou conceal him. But thou shalt surely kill him. Thine hand shall be first upon him to put him to death, and afterwards the hand of all the people." [Deut. xiii. 6–9.] Now, doubtless, we at this day are not to put men to death for idolatry; but, doubtless also, whatever temper of mind the fulfilment of this command implied in the Jew, such, essentially, must be our temper of mind, whatever else it may be also; for God cannot speak two laws, he cannot love two characters—good is good, and evil is evil, and the law He gave to the Jews was, in its substance, "perfect, converting the soul; the testimony of the Lord sure, making wise the simple; the statutes of the Lord right, rejoicing the heart; the commandment of the Lord pure, enlightening the eyes; . . . more to be desired than gold, yea than much fine gold; sweeter also than honey and the honeycomb. Moreover," as the Psalmist proceeds, "by them is thy servant taught, and in keeping of them there is great reward." [Ps. xix. 7, 8, 10, 11.]

A self-mastering fearless obedience was another part of this same religious temper enjoined on the Jews, and still incumbent, as I dare affirm, on us Christians. "Be ye very *courageous* to keep and to do all that is written in the book of the law of Moses." [Josh. xxiii. 6.] It required an exceeding moral courage in the Jews to enable them to go straight forward, seduced neither by their feelings nor their reason.

Nor was the severe temper under review a duty in the early ages of Judaism only. The book of Psalms was written at different times, between David's age and the captivity, yet it plainly breathes the same hatred of sin, and opposition to sinners. I will but cite one text from the hundred and thirty-ninth Psalm. "Do not I hate them, O Lord, that hate Thee? and am not I grieved with those that rise up against Thee? I hate them with perfect hatred; I count them mine enemies." And then the inspired writer proceeds to lay open his soul before God, as if conscious he had but expressed feelings which He would approve. "Search me, O God, and know my heart: try me, and know my thoughts, and see if there be any wicked way in me, and lead me in the way everlasting."

Further still, after the return from the captivity, after the Prophets had enlarged the compass of Divine Revelation, and purified and heightened the religious knowledge of the nation, still this rigid and austere zeal was enjoined and enforced in all its ancient vigour by Ezra. The Jews set about a reformation; and what was its most remarkable act? Let us attend to the words of Ezra: "The princes came to me, saying, The people of Israel, and the priests, and the Levites have not separated themselves from the people of the lands; for they have taken of their daughters for themselves and for their sons; so that the holy seed have mingled themselves with the people of those lands; yea, the hand of the princes and rulers hath been chief in this trespass." Now let me stop to ask what would most likely be the conduct of a temporizing Christian of this day, had he, in that day, been in Ezra's place? He would, doubtless, have said that such marriages were quite unjustifiable certainly, but now that they were made, there was no remedy for it; that they must be hindered in future; but in the existing instances, the evil being done could not be undone; and, besides, that great men were involved in the sin, whom it was impossible to interfere with. This he would have said, I think, though the prohibition of Moses seemed to make such marriages null and void from the first. Now, I do not say that every one ought to have done what Ezra did, for he was supernaturally directed; but would the course he adopted have ever entered into the mind of men of this day, or can they even understand or acquiesce in it, now that they know it? for what did he? "And when I heard this thing," he says, "I rent my garment and my mantle, and plucked off the hair of my head, and of my beard, and sat down astonied. Then were assembled unto me every one that trembled at the words of the God of Israel, because of the transgression of those that had been carried away, and I sat astonied until the evening sacrifice." [Ezra ix. 3, 4.] Then he offered a confession and intercession in behalf of the people; then at length he and the people came to a decision; which was no other than this—to command all persons who had married foreign wives to *put them away.* He undid the evil as well as hindered it in future. What an act of self-denying zeal was this in a multitude of people!

These are some, out of many instances, which might be brought from the Jewish history, in proof of the duty of strict and severe loyalty to God and His revealed will; and I here adduce them, first, to show that the commands involving it could not (their number and variety are so great), could not have related to a merely outward and ceremonial obedience, but must have wrought in the Jews a certain temper of mind, pleasing to God, and therefore necessary for us also to possess. Next, I deduce from that same circumstance of their number and variety, that they must be binding on us, else the Old Testament would be but a shadow of a revelation or law to the Christian.

I wish to insist on the lesson supplied merely by the Old Testament, and will not introduce into the argument the consideration of the Apostle's doctrine, which is quite in accordance with it. Yet it may be right, briefly, to refer to the sinless pattern of our Lord, and to what is told us of the holy inhabitants of heaven, in order to show that the temper of mind enjoined on the Jews belongs to those who are in a state of being superior to us, as well as to those who were living under a defective and temporary Dispensation. There was an occasion when our Lord is expressly said to have taken upon Him the zeal which consumed David. "Jesus went up to Jerusalem, and found in the Temple those that sold oxen, and sheep, and doves, and the changers of money, sitting; and when He had made a scourge of small cords, He drove them all out of the Temple, and the sheep, and the oxen; and poured out the changers' money, and overthrew the tables." Surely, unless we had this account given us by an inspired writer, we should not have believed it! Influenced by notions of our own devising, we should have said, this zealous action of our Lord's was quite inconsistent with his merciful, meek, and (what may be called) His majestic and serene temper of mind. To put aside form, to dispense with the ministry of His attendant Angels, to act before He had spoken His displeasure, to use His own hand, to hurry to and fro, to be a servant in the work of purification, surely this must have arisen from a fire of indignation at witnessing His Father's House insulted, which we sinners cannot understand. But any how, it is but the perfection of that temper which, as we have seen, was encouraged and exemplified in the Jewish Church. That energy, decision, and severity which Moses enjoined on his people, is manifested in Christ Himself, and is, therefore, undeniably a duty of man as such, whatever be his place or attainments in the scale of human nature.

Such is the pattern afforded us by our Lord; to which add the example of the Angels which surround him. Surely in Him is mingled "goodness and severity;" such, therefore, are all holy creatures, loving and severe. We read of their thoughts and desires in the Apocalypse, "Fear God, and give glory to Him, for the hour of His judgment is come." Again, "Thou art righteous, O Lord, which art, and wast, and shalt be, because Thou hast judged thus. For they have shed the blood of saints and prophets, and Thou hast given them blood to drink, for they are worthy." And again, "Even so, Lord God Almighty, true and righteous are Thy judgments." Once more, "Her sins have reached unto heaven, and God hath remembered her iniquities. Reward her even as she rewarded you, and double unto her double according to her works;" [Rev. xiv. 7; xvi. 5–7; xviii. 5, 6.]—all which passages imply a deep and solemn acquiescence in God's judgments.

Thus a certain fire of zeal, showing itself, not by force and blood, but as really and certainly as if it did—cutting through natural feelings, neglecting self, preferring God's glory to all things, firmly resisting sin, protesting against sinners, and steadily contemplating their punishment, is a duty belonging to all creatures of God, a duty of Christians, in the midst of all that excellent overflowing charity which is the highest Gospel grace, and the fulfilling of the second table of the Law.

And such, in fact, has ever been the temper of the Christian Church; in evidence of which I need but appeal to the impressive fact that the Jewish Psalter has been the standard book of Christian devotion from the first down to this day. I wish we thought more of this circumstance. Can any one doubt that, supposing that blessed manual of faith and love had never been in use among us, great numbers of the present generation would have clamoured against it as unsuitable to express *Christian* feelings, as deficient in charity and kindness? Nay, do we not know, though I dare say it may surprise many a sober Christian to hear that it is so, that there are men at this moment who (I hardly like to mention it) wish parts of the Psalms left out of the Service as ungentle and harsh? Alas! that men of this day should rashly put their own judgment in competition with that of all the Saints of every age hitherto since Christ came—should virtually say, "Either *they* have been wrong or *we* are," thus forcing us to decide between the two. Alas! that they should dare to criticise the words of inspiration! Alas! that they should follow the steps of the backsliding Israelites, and shrink from siding with the Truth in its struggle with the world, instead of saying with Deborah, "So let all Thine enemies perish, O Lord!"

Now I shall make a few observations in conclusion, with a view of showing how meekness and charity are compatible with this austere and valiant temper of the Christian soldier.

1. Of course it is absolutely sinful to have any private enmities. Not the bitterest personal assaults upon us should induce us to retaliate. We must do good for evil, "love those who hate, bless those who curse us, and pray for those who despitefully use us." It is only when it is impossible at once to be kind to them, and give glory to God, that we may cease to act kindly towards them. When David speaks of hating God's enemies, it was under circumstances when keeping friends with them would have been a desertion of the Truth. St. James says, "Know ye not that the friendship of the world is enmity with God?" [James iv. 4.] and so, on the other hand, devotion to God's cause is enmity with the world. But no personal feeling must intrude itself in any case. We hate sinners, by putting them out of our sight, as if they were not, by annihilating them, in our affections. And this we must do, even in the case of our friends and relations, if God requires it. But in no case are we to allow ourselves in resentment or malice.

2. Next, it is quite compatible with the most earnest zeal, to offer kind offices to God's enemies when in distress. I do not say that a denial of these offices may not be a duty ordinarily; for it is our duty, as St. John tells us in his second Epistle, not even to receive them into our houses. But the case is very different where men are brought into extremity. God "maketh His sun to

rise on the evil and on the good, and sendeth rain on the just and on the un-just." [Matt. v. 45.] We must go and do likewise, imitating the good Samari-tan; and as he thought nothing of difference of nations when a Jew was in dis-tress, in like manner we must not take account of wilful heresy, or profane-ness, in such circumstances.

3. And, further, the Christian keeps aloof from sinners in order to do them good. He does so in the truest and most enlarged charity. It is a narrow and weak feeling to please a man here, and to endanger his soul. A true friend is he who speaks out, and, when a man sins, shows him that he is displeased at the sin. He who sets up no witness against his friend's sin, is "partaker of his evil deeds." [2 John 11.] The Psalmist speaks in this spirit, when, after praying to God "to persecute" the ungodly "with His tempest," he adds, "fill their fac-es with shame, that they may seek Thy name, O Lord." [Ps. lxxxiii. 16.]

Accordingly, the more zealous a Christian is, therefore is he the more charitable. The Israelite, when he entered Canaan, was told to spare neither old nor young; the weak and the infirm were to be no exception in the list of victims whose blood was to be shed. "Of the cities of these people, which the Lord thy God doth give thee for an inheritance, thou shalt save alive nothing that breatheth." [Deut. xx. 16.] Accordingly, when the people fought against Sihon, they "took all his cities at that time, and utterly destroyed the men, and the women, and the little ones of every city," they "left none to remain." [Deut. ii. 34.] And when Jericho was taken, "they utterly destroyed all that was in the city, both man and woman, young and old, and ox, and sheep, and ass, with the edge of the sword." [Josh. vi. 21.] What an awful office was this, what an unutterably heart-piercing task, almost enough to make a man frantic, except as upheld by the power of him who gave the command! Yet Moses, thus severely-minded to do God's will, was the meekest of men. Samuel, too, who sent Saul to slay in Amalek "man and woman, infant and suckling, ox and sheep, camel and ass," was, from his youth up, the wise and heavenly-minded guide and prophet of Israel. David, who had a fiery zeal, so as even to consume him, was (as we see by his Psalms) most tender-hearted and gentle in his feelings and thoughts. Doubtless, while the servants of God executed His judgments, they still could bend in pity and in hope over the young and old whom they slew with the sword—merciful amid their severity—an unspeaka-ble trial, doubtless, of faith and self-mastery, and requiring a very exalted and refined spirit successfully to undergo. Doubtless, as they slew those who suf-fered for the sins of their fathers, their thoughts turned, first to the fall of Ad-am, next to that unseen state where all inequalities are righted, and they sur-rendered themselves as instruments unto the Lord, of mysteriously working out good through evil.

114

And shall *we* faint at our far lesser trials when they bore the greater? Spared the heavy necessity of piercing with the spear of Phinehas, and of hewing Agag in Gilgal—allowed to take instead of inflicting suffering and "to make a difference" instead of an indiscriminate severity—shall we, like cowards, shrink from bearing our lighter burdens, which our Lord commands, and in which He set us the pattern? Shall we be perversely persuaded by the appearance of amiableness or kindness in those whom God's word bids us depart from as heretics, or profligate livers, or troublers of the Church? Joseph could speak strangely to his brethren, and treat them as spies, put one of them in prison, and demand another from Canaan, while he hardly refrained himself in doing so, and his bowels yearned over them; and by turns he punished them, and wept for them. Oh, that there was in us this high temper of mingled austerity and love! Barely do we conceive of severity by itself, and of kindness by itself; but who unites them? We think we cannot be kind without ceasing to be severe. Who is there that walks through the world, wounding according to the rule of zeal, and scattering balm freely in the fulness of love; smiting as a duty, and healing as a privilege; loving most when he seems sternest, and embracing them most tenderly whom in semblance he treats roughly? What a state we are in, when any one who rehearses the plain threats of our Lord and His Apostles against sinners, or ventures to defend the anathemas of His Church, is thought unfeeling rather than merciful; when they who separate from the irreligious world are blamed as fanciful and extravagant, and those who confess the truth, as it is in Jesus, are said to be bitter, hot of head, and intemperate! Yet, with God's grace, with the history of the Old Testament before us, and the fearful recompense, to warn us, which came upon backsliding Israel, we, the Ministers of Christ, dare not keep silence amid this great error. In behalf of Christ, our Saviour and Lord, who yielded up His precious life for us, and now feeds us with His own blood, for the sake of the souls whom He has redeemed, and whom, by a false and cruel charity, the world would keep in ignorance and sin, we cannot refrain; and if His Holy Spirit be with us, as we trust He is, whatever betides, whatever is coming on this country, speak the truth we will, and overcome in our speaking we must; for He has given us to overcome!

The Visible Church an Encouragement to Faith†

"Wherefore seeing we also are compassed about with so great a cloud of witnesses, let us lay aside every weight, and the sin which doth so easily beset us, and let us run with patience the race that is set before us."

Heb. xii. 1

THE WARNING and consolation given by the Apostle to the Hebrews, amid their sufferings for the truth's sake, were as follows: they were to guard against unbelief, that easily-besetting sin under temptation, chiefly, and above all, by "looking unto Jesus, the Author and Finisher of faith;" but, besides this, a secondary stay was added. So glorious and holy is our Lord, though viewed in His human nature, so perfect when He was tempted, so heavenly even upon earth, that sinners, such as we are, cannot endure the sight of Him at first. Like the blessed Apostle in the book of Revelation, we "fall at His feet as dead." So, in mercy to us, without withdrawing His presence, He has included within it, His Saints and Angels, a great company of created beings, nay, of those who once were sinners, and subjects of His kingdom upon earth; that thus we may be encouraged by the example of others before us to look unto Him and live. St. Paul, in the foregoing chapter, enumerates many of the Ancient Saints who had run the course of faith; and then he says in the text, "Wherefore, let us also, being compassed about with so great a cloud of witnesses, lay aside every weight, and the sin which doth so easily beset us, and let us run with patience the race that is set before us." And presently he speaks in still more high and glowing language of the Christian Church, that august assemblage which Christ had formed of all that was holy in heaven and earth. "Ye are come unto Mount Sion, and unto the city of the living God, the heavenly Jerusalem, and to an innumerable company of Angels, to the general assembly and Church of the first-born, and to the spirits of the just made perfect, and to Jesus the Mediator of the New Covenant."

And much is needed, in every age, as a remedy against unbelief, that support which St. Paul suggested to the Hebrews in persecution, the vision of the Saints of God, and of the Kingdom of Heaven. Much is it needed, in every age, by those who have set their hearts to serve God, because they are few, and faint for company. We are told, expressly, "Broad is the way that leadeth to

---

† *Parochial & Plain Sermons*, vol. 3 (1836), Sermon 17.

116

destruction, and many there be which go in thereat." On the other hand, "Strait is the gate, and narrow is the way, which leadeth unto life, and few there be that find it." [Matt. vii. 13, 14.] Alas! is it not discouragement enough to walk in a path of self-denial, to combat with our natural lusts and high imaginations, to have the war of the flesh, that the war with the world must be added to it? Is it not enough to be pilgrims and soldiers all our days, but we must hear the mutual greetings, and exulting voices of those who choose the way of death, and must walk not only in pain but in solitude? Where is the blessing upon the righteous, where the joy of faith, the comfort of love, the triumph of self-mastery, in such dreariness and desolateness? Who are to sympathize with us in our joys and sorrows, who are to spur us on by the example of their own success? St. Paul answers us—the cloud of witnesses of former days. Let us then consider our need and its remedy.

1. Certainly it cannot be denied that, if we surrender our hearts to Christ and obey God, we shall be in the number of the few. So it has been in every age, so it will be to the end of time. It is hard, indeed, to find a man who gives himself up honestly to his Saviour. In spite of all the mercies poured upon us, yet in one way or other we are in danger of being betrayed by our own hearts, and taking up with a pretence of religion instead of the substance. Hence, in a country called Christian, the many live to the world. Nay, it would seem that as Christianity spreads, its fruit becomes less; or, at least, does not increase with its growth. It seems (some have said) as if a certain portion of truth were in the world, a certain number of the elect in the Church, and, as you increased its territory, you scattered this remnant to and fro, and made them seem fewer, and made them feel more desolate.

"Behold, I send you forth as sheep in the midst of wolves;" [Matt. x. 16.] what our Lord addressed to His Apostles is fulfilled to this day in all those who obey Him. They are sprinkled up and down the world; they are separated the one from the other, they are bid quit each other's dear society, and sent afar off to those who are differently minded. Their choice of profession and employment is not their own. Outward circumstances, over which they have no control, determine their line of life; accidents bring them to this place or that place, not knowing whither they go; not knowing the persons to whom they unite themselves, they find, almost blindly, their home and their company. And in this, moreover, differing from the Apostles, and very painfully; that the Apostles knew each other, and could communicate one with another, and could form, nay, were bound to form one body; but now, those honest and true hearts, in which the good seed has profitably fallen, do not even know each other; nay, even when they think they can single out their fellows, yet are they not allowed to form a separate society with them.

They do not know each other; they do not know themselves; they do not dare take to themselves the future titles of God's elect, though they be really reserved for them; and the nearer they are towards heaven, so much the more lowly do they think of themselves. "Lord, I am not worthy that Thou shouldest come under my roof," [Matt. viii. 8.] was the language of him who had greater faith than any in Israel. Doubtless, they do not know their own blessedness, nor can they single out those who are their fellows in blessedness. God alone sees the heart; now and then, as they walk their way, they see glimpses of God's work in others; they take hold of them awhile in the dark, but soon lose them; they hear their voices, but cannot find them. Some few, indeed, are revealed to them in a measure. Among those with whom their lot is cast, whom they see continually, one or two, perhaps, are given them to rejoice in, but not many even of these. For so it has pleased the Dresser of the Vineyard, who seems to have purposed that His own should not grow too thick together; and if they seem to do so, He prunes His vine, that, seeming to bear less, it may bear better. He plucks off some of the promise of the vintage; and they who are left, mourn over their brethren whom God has taken to Himself, not understanding that it is no strange providence, but the very rule of His government, to leave His servants few and solitary.

And, even when they know each other (as far as man can know man), still, as I have said, they may not form an exclusive communion together. Of course, every one will naturally live most with those whom he likes most; but it is one thing to have a preference, and quite another to draw a line of exclusion, and to form a select company within the Church. The Visible Church of God is that one only company which Christians know as yet; it was set up at Pentecost, with the Apostles for founders, their successors for rulers, and all professing Christian people for members. In this Visible Church the Church Invisible is gradually moulded and matured. It is formed slowly and variously by the Blessed Spirit of God, in the instance of this man and that, who belong to the general body. But all these blessed fulfilments of God's grace are as yet but parts of the Visible Church; they grow from it; they depend upon it; they do not hang upon each other; they do not form a body together; there is no Invisible Church yet formed; it is but a name as yet; a name given to those who are hidden, and known to God only, and as yet but half formed, the unripe and gradually ripening fruit which grows on the stem of the Church Visible. As well might we attempt to foretell the blossoms which will at length turn to account and ripen for the gathering, and then counting up all these and joining them together in our minds, call them by the name of a tree, as attempt now to associate in one the true elect of God. They are scattered about amid the leaves of that Mystical Vine which is seen, and receive their nurture from its trunk and branches. They live on its Sacraments and its Ministry; they gain light and salvation from its rites and ordinances; they communicate with each other through it; they obey its rulers; they walk together with its members; they do not dare to judge of this man or that man, on their right hand or their left, whether or not he is absolutely of the number of those who shall be saved; they accept all as their brethren in Christ, as partakers of the same general promises, who have not openly cast off Christ—as really brethren, till death comes, as those are who fulfil their calling most strictly.

Yet, at the same time, while in faith they love those, all around them, who are called by Christ's name, and forbear to judge about their real state in God's sight, they cannot but see much in many of them to hurt and offend them; they cannot but feel, most painfully, the presence of that worldly atmosphere which, however originating, encircles them; they feel the suffocation of those vapours in which the many are content to remain; and while they cannot trace the evil to its real authors individually, they are sure that it is an evil to be avoided and pointed out, and originating somewhere or other in the Church. Hence, in their spheres, whether high or low, the faithful few are witnesses; they are witnesses for God and Christ, in their lives, and by their protestations, without judging others, or exalting themselves. They are witnesses in various degrees, to various persons, more or less, as each needs it—differing from the multitude variously, as each of that multitude, before whom they witness, is better or worse, and as they themselves are more or less advanced in the truth; still, on the whole, they are witnesses, as light witnesses against darkness by the contrast;—giving good and receiving back evil; receiving back on themselves the contempt, the ridicule, and the opposition of the world, mixed, indeed, with some praise and reverence, reverence which does not last long, but soon becomes fear and hatred. And hence it is that religious men need some consolation to support them, which the Visible Church seems, at first sight, not to supply, when the overflowings of ungodliness make them afraid.

2. Now then, secondly, in such circumstances what shall we say? Are they but solitary witnesses, each in his place? Is the Church which they see really no consolation to them at all, except as contemplated by faith in respect of its invisible gifts? or does it, after all, really afford them some sensible stay, a vision of Heaven, of peace amid purity, antagonist to the world that now is, in spite of the evil which abounds in it, and overlays it? Through God's great mercy, it is actually, in no small degree, a present and a sensible consolation, as I proceed to show.

In truth, do what he will, Satan cannot quench or darken the light of the Church. He may incrust it with his own evil creations, but even opaque bodies transmit rays, and Truth shines with its own heavenly lustre, though "under a bushel." The Holy Spirit has vouchsafed to take up His abode in the Church, and the Church will ever bear, on its front, the visible signs of its hidden privilege. Viewed at a little distance, its whole surface will be illuminated, though the light really streams from apertures which might be numbered. The scattered witnesses thus become, in the language of the text, "a cloud," like the Milky Way in the heavens.

We have, in Scripture, the records of those who lived and died by faith in the old time, and nothing can deprive us of them. The strength of Satan lies in his being seen to have the many on his side; but, when we read the Bible, this argument loses its hold over us. There we find that we are not solitary; that others, before us, have been in our very condition, have had our feelings, undergone our trials, and laboured for the prize which we are seeking. Nothing more elevates the mind than the consciousness of being one of a great and victorious company. Does not the soldier exult in his commander, and consider his triumph as his own? He is but one, yet he identifies himself with the army, and the cause in which he serves, and dwells upon the thought of victories, and those who win them, more than on casual losses and defeats. Does not a native of a powerful country feel it a joy and boast to be so? Do we not hear men glory in being born Englishmen? And they go to and fro, gazing on the works of their own days, and the monuments of their forefathers, and say to themselves that their race is a noble one. Much more fully, much more reasonably is this the boast of a Christian, and without aught of arrogant or carnal feeling. He knows, from God's word, that he is "citizen of no mean city." He feels that his is no upstart line, but very ancient; Almighty God having purposed to bring many sons unto glory through His Son, and begetting them again, in their separate ages, to do Him service. He is one of a host, and all those blessed Saints he reads of are his brethren in the faith. He finds, in the history of the past, a peculiar kind of consolation, counteracting the influence of the world that is seen. He cannot tell who the Saints are now on earth; those yet unborn are known to God only; but the Saints of former times are sealed for heaven and are in their degree revealed to him. The spirits of the just made perfect encourage him to follow them. This is why it is a Christian's characteristic to look back on former times. The man of this world lives in the present, or speculates about the future; but faith rests upon the past and is content. It makes the past the mirror of the future. It recounts the list of faithful servants of God, to whom St. Paul refers in the text, and no longer feels sad as if it were alone. Abraham and the Patriarchs, Moses, Samuel, and the prophets, David and the kings who walked in his steps, these are the Christian's forefathers. By degrees he learns to have them as familiar images before his mind, to unite his cause with theirs, and, since their history comforts him, to defend them in his own day. Hence he feels jealous for their honour, and when they are attacked he answers eagerly, so as to surprise those who are contented with things as they are; but, truly, he is too grateful, too affectionate, too much interested in the matter, to be complimentary and generous towards their assailants. He had rather the present day should be proved captious, than a former day mistaken.

But to return: what a world of sympathy and comfort is thus opened to us in the Communion of Saints! The heathen, who sought truth most earnestly, fainted for want of companions; every one stood by himself. They were tempted to think that all their best feelings were but an empty name, and that it mattered not whether they served God or disobeyed Him. But Christ has "gathered together the children of God that were scattered abroad," and brought them near to each other in every time and place. Are we young, and in temptation or trial? we cannot be in worse circumstances than Joseph. Are we in sickness? Job will surpass us in sufferings as in patience. Are we in perplexities and anxieties, with conflicting duties and a bewildered mind, having to please unkind superiors, yet without offending God; so grievous a trial as David's we cannot have, when Saul persecuted him. Is it our duty to witness for the truth among sinners? No Christian can at this day be so hardly circumstanced as Jeremiah. Have we domestic trials? Job, Jacob, and David, were afflicted in their children. It is easy indeed to say all this, and many a man may hear it said, and not feel moved by it, and conceive it is a mere matter of words, easy and fitting indeed to say, but a cold consolation in actual suffering. And I will own that a man cannot profit by these considerations all at once. A man, who has never thought of the history of the Saints, will gain little benefit from it on first taking up the subject when he comes into trouble. He will turn from it disappointed. He may say, "My pain or my trial is not the less because another had it a thousand years since." But the consolation in question comes not in the way of argument but by habit. A tedious journey seems shorter when gone in company, yet, be the travellers many or few, each goes over the same ground.

Such is the Christian's feeling towards all Saints, but it is especially excited by the Church of Christ and by all that belong to it. For what is that Church but a pledge and proof of God's never-dying love and power from age to age? He set it up in mercy to mankind, and its presence among us is a proof that in spite of our sins He has not yet forsaken us;—"Hitherto hath the Lord helped us." He set it up on the foundation of His Twelve Apostles, and promised that the gates of hell should not prevail against it; and its presence among us is a proof of His power. He set it up to succeed to the four monster kingdoms which then were; and it lived to see those kingdoms of the earth crumble into dust and come to nought. It lived to see society new formed upon the model of the governments which last to this day. It lives still, and it is older than them all. Much and rightly as we reverence old lineage, noble birth, and illustrious ancestry, yet the royal dynasty of the Apostles is far older than all the kingly families which are now on the earth. Every Bishop of the Church whom we behold, is a lineal descendant of St. Peter and St. Paul after the order of a spiritual birth;—a noble thought, if we could realize it! True it is that at various times the Bishops have forgotten their high rank and acted unworthily of it. So have kings and princes, yet noble they were by blood in spite of their personal errors, and the line of their family is not broken or degraded thereby. And in like manner, true though it be that the descendants of the Apostles have before now lived to this world, have fancied themselves of this world, have thought their office secular and civil, or if religious, yet at least "of men and by man," not "by Jesus Christ," have judged it much to have riches, or to sit in high places, or to have rank and consideration, or to have the fame of letters, or to be king's counsellors, or to live in courts—yet, granting the utmost, for all this they are not the less inspiring an object to a believing mind, which sees in each of them the earnest of His promise, "I will never leave thee nor forsake thee." He said, He would be with His Church: He has continued it alive to this day. He has continued the line of His Apostles onwards through every age and all troubles and perils of the world. Here then, surely, is somewhat of encouragement for us amid our loneliness and weakness. The presence of every Bishop suggests a long history of conflicts and trials, sufferings and victories, hopes and fears, through many centuries. His presence at this day is the fruit of them all. He is the living monument of those who are dead. He is the promise of a bold fight and a good confession and a cheerful martyrdom now, if needful, as was instanced by those of old time. We see their figures on our walls, and their tombs are under our feet; and we trust, nay, we are sure, that God will be to us in our day what He was to them. In the words of the Psalmist, "The Lord hath been mindful of us; He will bless us; He will bless the house of Israel; He will bless the house of Aaron." [Psalm cxv. 12.]

And more especially does the sight of our living Apostles bring before our thoughts the more favoured of their line, who, at different times, have fought the good fight of faith valiantly and gloriously. Blessed be God, He has given us to know them as if we had lived in their day and enjoyed their pattern and instructions. Alas! in spite of the variety of books now circulated among all classes of the community, how little is known about the Saints of past times! How is this? has Christ's Church failed in any age? or have His witnesses betrayed their trust? are they not our bone and our flesh? Have they not partaken the same spiritual food as ourselves and the same spiritual drink, used the same prayers, and confessed the same creed? If a man merely looks into the Prayer-book, he will meet there with names, about which, perhaps, he knows and cares nothing at all. A prayer we read daily is called the prayer of St. Chrysostom; a creed is called the creed of St. Athanasius; another creed is called the Nicene Creed; in the Articles we read of St. Augustine and St. Jerome; in the Homilies of many other such besides. What do these names mean? Sad it is, you have no heart to inquire after or celebrate those who are fellow-citizens with you, and your great benefactors! Men of this world spread each other's fame—they vaunt loudly;—you see in every street the names and the statues of the children of men, you hear of their exploits in speeches and histories; yet you care not to know concerning those to whom you are indebted for the light of Gospel truth. Truly they were in their day men of God; they were rulers and teachers in the Church; they had received by succession of hands the power first given to the Apostles and now to us. They laboured and suffered and fainted not, and their writings remain to this day. Now a person who cultivates this thought, finds therein, through God's mercy, great encouragement. Say he is alone, his faith counted a dream, and his efforts to do good a folly, what then? He knows there have been times when his opinions were those of the revered and influential, and the opinions now in repute only not reprobated because they were not heard of. He knows that present opinions are the accident of the day, and that they will fall as they have risen. They will surely fall even though at a distant date! He labours for that time; he labours for five hundred years to come. He can bear in faith to wait five hundred years, to wait for an era long, long after he has mouldered into dust. The Apostles lived eighteen hundred years since; and as far as the Christian looks back, so far can he afford to look forward. There is one Lord, one faith, one baptism, one God and Father of all, from first to last.

I referred just now to our Sacred Services; these, again, may be made to furnish a support to our faith and hope. He who comes to Church to worship God, be he high or low, enters into that heavenly world of Saints of which I have been speaking. For in the Services of worship we elicit and realize the invisible. I know, indeed, that Christ is then especially present, and vouchsafes to bless us; but I am speaking all along of the help given to us by sensible objects, and, even in this lower view, doubtless much is done for us in the course of divine worship. We read from the Bible of the Saints who have gone before us, and we make mention of them in our prayers. We thank God for them, we praise God with them, we pray God to visit us in mercy as He visited them. And every earthly thought or principle is excluded. The world no longer rules as it does abroad; no longer teaches, praises, blames, scoffs, wonders, according to its own false standard. It is merely spoken of as one of the three great enemies whom we are sworn to resist; it holds its proper place; and its doom is confidently predicted, the final victory of the Church over it. And, further, it is much more impressive to hear and to see, than to read in a book. When we read the Bible and religious books in private, there is great comfort; but our minds are commonly more roused and encouraged in Church, when we see those great truths displayed and represented which Scripture speaks of. There we see "Jesus Christ, evidently set forth, crucified among us." The ordinances which we behold, force the unseen truth upon our senses. The very disposition of the building, the subdued light, the aisles, the Altar, with its pious adornments, are figures of things unseen, and stimulate our fainting faith. We seem to see the heavenly courts, with Angels chanting, and Apostles and Prophets listening, as we read their writings in due course. And thus, even attendance on a Sunday may, through God's mercy, avail even in the case of those who have not given themselves up to Him—not to their salvation (for no one can be saved by one or two observances merely, or without a life of faith), but so far as to break in upon their dream of sin, and give them thoughts and notions which may be the germ of future good. Even to those, I say, who live to the world, the mere Sunday attendance at Church is a continual memento on their conscience, giving them a glimpse of things unseen, and rescuing them in a measure from the servitude of Mammon or of Belial. And therefore it is, that Satan's first attempt, when he would ruin a soul, is to prevail upon him to desecrate the Lord's Day. And if such is the effect of coming to Church once a week, even to an undecided or carnal mind, how much more impressive and invigorating are the Services to serious men who come daily or frequently! Surely such attendance is a safeguard, such as amulets were said to be, a small thing to all appearance, but effectual. I say it with confidence, he who observes it, will grow in time a different man from what he was, God working in him. His heart will be more heavenly and aspiring; the world will lie under his feet; he will be proof against its opinions, threats, blandishments, ridicule. His very mode of viewing things, his very voice, his manner, gait, and countenance, will speak of Heaven to those who know him well, though the many see nothing in him.

The many understand him not, and even in St. Paul or St. John would see but ordinary men. Yet at times such a one will speak effectually even to the many. In seasons of unusual distress or alarm, when men's minds faint for fear, then he will have a natural power over the world, and will seem to speak, not as an individual, but as if in him was concentrated all the virtue and the grace of those many Saints who have been his life-long companions. He has lived with those who are dead, and he will seem to the world as one coming from the dead, speaking in the name of the dead, using the language of souls dead to things that are seen, revealing the mysteries of the heavenly world, and aweing and controlling those who are wedded to this. What slight account did the centurion and the crew make of St. Paul, till a tempest had long time "lain on them," and "all hope that they should be saved was then taken away!" But then, though he had done no miracle, "he stood forth in the midst," exhorted and encouraged them, bade them take meat, acted as their priest, giving thanks to God and breaking bread in the presence of them all, and so made them "of good cheer." Such is the gift, deeply lodged and displayed at times, of those who have ascended into the third heaven. One living Saint, though there be but one, is a pledge of the whole Church Invisible. Let this thought console us as it ought to do; let it have its full influence in us, and possess us. Let us "lift up our hearts," let us "lift them up unto the Lord!"

Regenerating Baptism[†]

"By one Spirit are we all baptized into one body."
1 Cor. xii. 13

A S THERE IS One Holy Ghost, so there is one only visible Body of
Christians which Almighty God "knows by name," and one Baptism
which admits men into it. This is implied in the text, which is nearly
parallel to St. Paul's words to the Ephesians: "there is one Body, and one Spirit, one Baptism." But more than this is taught us in it; not only that the Holy
Ghost is in the Church, and that Baptism admits into it, but that the Holy
Ghost admits by means of Baptism, that the Holy Ghost baptizes; in other
words, that each individual member receives the gift of the Holy Ghost as a
preliminary step, a condition, or means of his being incorporated into the
Church; or, in our Saviour's words, that no one can enter, except he be regenerated in order to enter it.

Now, this is much more than many men are willing to grant, their utmost concession being, that the Church has the presence of the Holy Spirit in
it, and therefore, to be in the Church is to be in that which has the presence of
the Holy Spirit; that is, to be in the *way* of the Spirit (so to speak), which cannot but be a state of favour and privilege; but, that the Holy Spirit is given to
infants, one by one, on their Baptism, this they will not admit. Yet, one would
think words could not be plainer than the text in proof of it; however, they do
not admit it.

This defective view of the Sacrament of Baptism, for so I must not
shrink from calling it, shall now be considered, and considered in its connection with a popular argument for the Baptism of infants, which, most true as it
is in its proper place, yet is scarcely profitable for these times, as seeming to
countenance the error in question. I mean, the assumed parallel between Baptism and Circumcision.

It is undeniable that Circumcision in some important respects resembles
Baptism, and may allowably, nay, usefully be referred to in illustration of it.
Circumcision was the entrance into the Jewish Covenant, and it typified the
renunciation of the flesh. In respects such as these it resembles Baptism; and
hence it has been of service in the argument for Infant Baptism, as having been

---

[†] *Parochial & Plain Sermons*, vol. 3 (1836), Sermon 19.

itself administered to infants. But, though it resembles Baptism in some respects, it is unlike it in others more important. When, then, it is found to be the chief and especially approved argument in favour of Infant Baptism among Christians, there is reason for some anxiety, lest this circumstance should betoken, or introduce, insufficient views of a Christian Sacrament. This remark, I fear, is applicable in the present day.

We baptize infants, in the first place, because the Church has ever done so; and, to say nothing of the duty of observing and transmitting what we have received, in the case of so great a privilege as Baptism, we should be ungrateful and insensible indeed if we did not give our children the benefit of the usage, even though Scripture said not a word on the subject, so that it said nothing the other way. But, besides, we consider we do find, in our Saviour's words, a command to bring children to Him, for His blessing. Again, He said they were to be members of His Kingdom; also, that Baptism is the only entrance, the new birth into it. We administer, then, Baptism to children as a sure *benefit* to their souls.

But, when men refuse to admit the doctrine of Baptismal Regeneration in the case of infants, then they look about how they may defend Infant Baptism, which, perhaps, from habit, good feeling, or other causes, they do not like to abandon. The ordinary and intelligible reason for the Baptism of infants, is the securing to them remission of sins, and the gift of the Holy Ghost—Regeneration; but if this sacred privilege is not given to them in Baptism, why, it may be asked, should Baptism be administered to them at all? Why not wait till they can understand the meaning of the rite, and can have faith and repentance themselves? Certainly it does seem a very intricate and unreasonable proceeding; first, to lay stress on the necessity of repentance and faith in persons to be baptized, and then to proceed to administer Baptism universally in such a way as to exclude the possibility of their having repentance and faith. I say, this would be strange and inconsistent, were not Baptism, in itself, so direct a blessing that, when parents demand it for their children, all abstract rules must, in very charity, necessarily give way. We administer it whenever we do not discover some actual obstacle in the recipient to hinder its efficacy, as we give medicine to the sick. Otherwise the objection holds; and, accordingly, clear-sighted men, who deny its regenerating power in the case of infants, often do come to the conclusion that to administer it to them is a needless and officious act, nay, a profanation of a sacred institution. It seems to them a mockery to baptize them; the waste of an edifying rite, not to say a Sacrament, upon those who cannot understand or use it; and, to speak the truth, they do appear reasonable and straightforward in their inference, granting their premises. It does seem as if those who deny the regeneration of infants ought, if they were consistent (which happily they are not), to refrain from baptizing them. Surely, if we go by Scripture, the question is decided at once; for no one can deny that there is much more said in Scripture in behalf of the connection between Baptism and Divine grace, than about the duty of Infant Baptism. The passage can scarcely be named, in the New Testament, where Baptism is referred to, without the mention, direct or indirect, of spiritual influences. What right have we to put asunder what God has united? especially since, on the other hand, the text cannot be found which plainly enjoins the Baptism of infants. If the doctrine and the practice are irreconcilable—Baptismal Regeneration and Infant Baptism—let the practice, which is not written in Scripture, yield to the doctrine which is; and let us (if we can bear to do so) defraud infants of Baptism, not Baptism of its supernatural virtue. Let us go counter to Tradition rather than to Scripture. This being the difficulty which comes upon those who deny the Regeneration, yet would retain the Baptism of infants, let us next see how they meet it.

We need not suppose that all I am drawing out passes through the mind of every one who denies that infants are regenerated in Baptism: but, surely, some such processes of thought are implied, which it may be useful to ourselves to trace out. This being understood, I observe that the partly assumed and partly real parallel of Circumcision comes, in fact, whether they know it or not, as a sort of refuge to those who have taken up this intermediate position between Catholic doctrine and heretical practice. They avail themselves of the instance of Circumcision as a proof that a divinely-appointed ordinance need not convey grace, even while it admits into a state of grace; and they argue from the analogy between Circumcision and Baptism, that what was the case with the Mosaic ordinance is the case with the Christian also. Circumcision admitted to certain privileges, to the means of grace, to teaching, and the like; Baptism, they consider, does the same and no more. It has also the same uses as Circumcision, in teaching the necessity of inward sanctification, and implying the original corrupt condition of our nature. In like manner, it ought to be administered to infants, since Circumcision was so administered under the Law.

I do not deny that this view is consistent with itself, and plausible. And it would be perfectly satisfactory, as a view, were it Scriptural. But the plain objection to it is, that Christ and His Apostles do attach a grace to the ordinance of Baptism, such as is not attached in the Old Testament to Circumcision—which is exactly that difference which makes the latter a mere rite, the former a Sacrament; and if this be so, it is nothing to the purpose to build up an argument on the assumption that the two ordinances are precisely the same.

Surely we have forgotten, in good measure, the difference between Jewish ordinances and Christian. It was said of old time, after St. Paul, "The Law has a shadow, the Gospel an image, Heaven the reality;" or, in other words, that of those heavenly blessings which the Jewish Dispensation prefigured, the Christian imparts a portion or earnest. This, then, is the distinction between our ritual and the Mosaic. The Jewish rites had no substance of blessing in them; they were but outward signs and types of spiritual privileges. They had in them no "grace and truth." When the Divine Antitype came, they were simply and merely in the way; they did but hide from the eye of faith the reality which they had been useful in introducing. They were as the forerunners in a procession, who, after announcing their Prince's coming, must themselves retire, or they crowd his path. Nor these alone, but all mere ceremonies were then for ever unseasonable, as mere obstacles intercepting the Divine light. Yet, while Christ abolished them, considered as means of expiation or mere badges of profession, or as prophetical types of what was no longer future, He introduced another class of ordinances in their stead; Mysteries, as they are sometimes called, among which are the Sacraments, viz., rites as valueless and powerless in themselves as the Jewish, but being, what the Jewish were not, instruments of the application of His merits to individual believers. Though He now sits on the right hand of God, He has, in one sense, never left the world since He first entered it; for, by the ministration of the Holy Ghost, He is really present with us in an unknown way, and ever imparts Himself to those who seek Him. Even when visibly on earth He, the Son of Man, was still "in heaven;" and now, though He is ascended on high, He is still on earth. And as He is still with us, for all that He is in heaven, so, again, is the hour of His cross and passion ever mystically present, though it be past these eighteen hundred years. Time and space have no portion in the spiritual Kingdom which He has founded; and the rites of His Church are as mysterious spells by which He annuls them both. They are not like the Jewish ordinances, long and laborious, expensive or irksome, with aught of value or merit in themselves: they are so simple, so brief, with so little of outward substance, that the mind is not detained for a moment from Him who works by means of them, but takes them for what they really are, only so far outward as to serve for a medium of the heavenly gift. Thus Christ shines through them, as through transparent bodies, without impediment. He is the Light and Life of the Church, acting through it, dispensing of His fulness, knitting and compacting together every part of it; and these its Mysteries are not mere outward signs, but (as it were) effluences of His grace developing themselves in external forms, as Angels might do when they appeared to men. He has touched them, and breathed upon them, when He ordained them; and thenceforth they have a virtue in them, which issues forth and encircles them round, till the eye of faith sees in them no element of matter at all. Once for all He hung upon the cross, and blood and water issued from His pierced side, but by the Spirit's ministration, the blood and water are ever flowing, as though His cross were really set up among us, and the baptismal water were but an outward image meeting our senses. Thus in a true sense that water is not what it was before, but is gifted with new and spiritual qualities. Not as if its material substance were changed, which our eyes see, or as if any new nature were imparted to it, but that the lifegiving Spirit, who could make bread of stones, and sustain animal life on dust and ashes, applies the blood of Christ through it; or according to the doctrine of the text, that He, and not man, is the baptizer.

St. Paul sets this great truth before us, among other places, in the second chapter of his Epistle to the Colossians. First, he says, "In Christ dwelleth all the fulness of the Godhead bodily, and ye have fulness in Him, who is the head of all principality and power." Here the most solemn and transporting doctrine of the Incarnation is disclosed to us, as the corner stone of the whole Church system; "the Word made flesh," being the divinely appointed Way whereby we are regenerated and saved. The Apostle then proceeds to describe the manner in which this divine fulness is imparted to us, and in so doing contrasts the Jewish ceremony of Circumcision with the spiritual Ordinance which has superseded it. "In whom also," in Christ, "ye are circumcised with a circumcision made without hands," heavenly, supernatural, invisible; "when ye strip yourselves of the body of the sins of the flesh, and receive" the true circumcision, "the circumcision of Christ, namely, buried with Him in Baptism." Thus Baptism is a spiritual Circumcision. He continues still more plainly. "Let no man *therefore* judge you in meat or in drink, or in respect of an holy day, or of the new moon, or of the Sabbath days; which are a shadow of things to come, but the body is of Christ." Now if Baptism were but an outward rite, like Circumcision, how strange a proof would it be of the Gospel's superseding *all* outward rites, to say that it enforced Baptism! He says, "Ye have Baptism, *therefore* do not think of *shadows*," as if Baptism took the place of shadows, as if it were certainly not a shadow but a substance. Again he says, "But the body is of Christ;" Circumcision is a shadow, but Baptism and the other Mysteries of the Church are "the *body*," and that because they are "of Christ." And lastly, he speaks of the duty of "holding to the Head," that is, to Christ, "from whom the whole body, being nourished and knit together by joints and bands, increaseth with a godly increase." What are these joints and bands but the Christian Ordinances and Ministrations, together with those who perform them? but observe, they are of such a nature as to subserve the "increase" of the Church.

Such is St. Paul's doctrine after Christ had died; St. John the Baptist teaches the same beforehand. "I indeed baptize you with water unto repentance, but He shall baptize you with the Holy Ghost and with fire." Doubtless there is an allusion here to the special descent of the Spirit at Pentecost; but, even taking it as such, the fulfilment of the Baptist's words then, becomes a pledge to us of the fulfilment of our Saviour's words to Nicodemus to the end of time. He who came by fire at Pentecost, will, as He has said, come by water now. But we may reasonably consider these very words of the Baptist as referring to ordinary Christian Baptism, as well as to the miraculous Baptism of the Apostles. As if he said, "Christ's Baptism shall not be mere water, as mine is. What you see of it indeed is water, but that is but the subordinate element of it; for it is water endued with high and supernatural qualities. Would it not surprise you if water burned like fire? Such, and more than such, is the mystery of that water which He shall pour out on you, having a searching and efficacious influence upon the soul itself."

Now, if any one says that such passages as this *need* not mean all I have supposed, I answer, that the question is not what they *must* mean, but what they *do* mean. I am not now engaged in proving, but in explaining the doctrine of Baptism, and in illustrating it from Scripture.

To return:—hence too the Baptismal Font is called "the washing *of regeneration*," not of mere water, "and renewing of the Holy Ghost which He hath poured out on us richly through Jesus Christ our Saviour;" and Christ is said to have "loved the Church and given Himself for it, that He might sanctify and cleanse it with the washing of water by the Word, that He might present it to Himself a glorious Church."

Further, let us consider the instances of the administration of Baptism in the Acts of the Apostles. If it be as serious a rite as I have represented, surely it must be there set forth as a great thing, and received with awe and thankfulness. Now we shall find these expectations altogether fulfilled. For instance, on the day of Pentecost, St. Peter said to the multitude, who asked what they must do, "Repent, and be baptized every one of you in the name of Jesus Christ for the remission of sins, and ye shall receive the gift of the Holy Ghost." Accordingly, "they that gladly received His word were baptized," in order to obtain these privileges; and, forthwith, we hear of their continuing "in gladness and singleness of heart, praising God." Again, when the Ethiopian Eunuch had been baptized by Philip, he "went on his way rejoicing." After St. Paul had been struck down by the Saviour whom he was persecuting, and sent to Damascus, he began to pray; but though in one sense a changed man already, he had not yet received the gift of regeneration, nor did he receive it except by the ministry of Ananias, who was sent to Him from Christ, expressly that he "might be filled with the Holy Ghost." Accordingly, Ananias said to him, "And now why tarriest thou? arise and be baptized, and wash away thy sins, calling on the name of the Lord." So again Cornelius, religious man as he was, and that doubtless by God's secret aid, yet was not received into Christ's family except by Baptism. Even the descent of the Holy Ghost upon him and his friends miraculously, while St. Peter was preaching to them, did not supersede the necessity of the Sacrament. And lastly, when the jailor at Philippi had been baptized, he "rejoiced, believing in God with all his house." [Acts ii. 38–47; viii. 39; ix. 17; xxii. 16; x. 44–48; xvi. 34.]

These and similar passages seem to prove clearly the superiority of Baptism to Circumcision, as being a Sacrament; but if they did not, what conclusion should we have arrived at? no other than this, that Baptism is like Circumcision, but a carnal ordinance (if the words may be spoken), not a spiritual possession. See what follows. Do you not recollect how much St. Paul says in depreciation of the rites of the Jewish Law, on the ground of their being rudiments of this world, carnal ordinances? Now if Baptism be altogether like Circumcision, can it, any more than they, have a place in the New Covenant? This was the very defect of the Mosaic Law, that it was but a form; this was one part of the bondage of the Jews, that they were put under forms, which contained in them no direct or intrinsic virtue, but had their spiritual use only as obeying for conscience' sake, and as means of prophetic instruction. Surely this cannot be our state under the Gospel: "We," says St. Paul, "when we were children," that is, Jews, "were in bondage under the elements of the world; but when the fulness of the time was come, God sent forth His Son, made of a woman . . . that we might receive the adoption of sons. And because ye are sons, God hath sent forth the Spirit of His Son into your hearts, crying, Abba, Father." Is it possible, then, now that the Spirit is come, we can be under dead rites and ordinances? It is plainly impossible. If Baptism then has no spiritual virtue in it, can it be intended for us Christians? If it has no regenerating power, surely they only are consistent who reject it altogether. I will boldly say it, we have nothing dead and earthly under the Gospel, and we act like the Judaizing Christians of old time if we submit to any thing such; therefore they only are consistent, who, denying the virtue of Baptism, also deny its authority as a permanent ordinance of the Gospel. Surely it was but intended for the infancy of the Church, ere men were weaned from their attachment to a ritual. Surely it was but an oriental custom, edifying to those who loved a symbolical worship, but needless, nay, harmful to us; harmful as impeding the prerogative of Christian liberty, obscuring our view of the one Christian Atonement, corrupting the simplicity of our faith and trust, and profaning the dispensation of the Spirit! I repeat it, either Baptism is an instrument of the Holy Ghost, or it has no place in Christianity. We indeed, who, in accordance with the teaching of the Church Universal, believe that it is an act of the Spirit, are under no difficulty in this matter. But let those who deny it look to themselves. They are on their own principles committing the sin of the Galatians, and severing themselves from Christ. Surely if their doctrine be right, they may consider themselves addressed by St. Paul in his language to those early Judaizers, "O senseless Galatians," he would have said to them, "who hath bewitched you? Are ye so foolish, having begun in the Spirit, are ye now made perfect by the flesh? Why burden yourselves with mere ceremonies, external washings, the rudiments of the world, shadows of good things, weak, beggarly, and unprofitable elements, whereunto ye desire to be in bondage? Stand fast in the liberty wherewith Christ hath made us free, and be not entangled with the yoke of bondage. Spiritual men are delivered from formal observances. If ye be baptized, Christ shall profit you nothing; for neither Baptism availeth anything nor want of Baptism, but faith which worketh by love. Neither Baptism availeth any thing nor want of Baptism, but a new creature; and as many as walk according to this rule, peace be on them and mercy, and upon the Israel of our God."

Such, doubtless, is the only consistent mode of regarding and treating this sacred ordinance, if it has no power or grace in it above a Jewish rite. We should discard it. And in whatever degree we think it thus unprofitable, so far we should discard it. If we think it but a figure in the case of children, though a Sacrament to grown men, we should keep from wasting upon children what would benefit them as men. And this holds good of all the ordinances of the Church; so far as they are but outward forms, let them be abolished as parts of dead Judaism. But, praised be God! they are none of them such. They all have life. Christ has lodged virtue in His Church, and she dispenses it forth from her in all her words and works. Why will you not believe this? What do you gain by so jealous and niggardly a spirit, such "slowness of heart," but the loss of thoughts full of comfort and of majesty? To view Christ as all but visibly revealed—to look upon His ordinances, not in themselves, but as signs of His presence and power, as the accents of His love, the very form and countenance of Him who ever beholds us, ever cherishes us—to see Him thus revealed in glory day by day—is not this to those who believe it an unspeakable privilege? Is it not so great that a man might well wish it true from the excellence of it, and count them happy who are able to receive it? And when this is all plainly revealed in Scripture, when we are expressly told that Christ washes us by Water to change us into a glorious Church, that the consecrated bread is His flesh, that He is present with His ministers, and is in the midst of His Church, why should we draw back, like Thomas doubting of our Lord's resurrection?

"Blessed are they that have not seen and yet have believed!" Surely, so it is; and however the world may scorn our faith, however those may despise us from whom we might expect better things, we will cheerfully bear what is a slight drawback indeed on our extreme blessedness. While they accuse us of trusting in ourselves, of trusting in our forms, and of ignorance of the Gospel, we will meekly say in our hearts, "'Thou God, seest me:' Thou knowest that we desire to love nothing but Thee, and to trust in nothing but the cross of Christ; and that we relinquish all self-reliance, and know ourselves in ourselves to have nothing but sin and misery, and esteem these ordinances of Thine not for their own sake, but as memorials of Thee and of Thy Son—memorials which He has appointed, which He has blessed, and in which, by faith, we see Him manifested, day by day, and through which we hope to receive the imputation of those merits, once for all wrought out on the Cross, and our only effectual help in the day of account."

The Daily Service[†]

"Not forsaking the assembling of ourselves together, as the manner of some is,
but exhorting one another; and so much the more,
as ye see the Day approaching."
Hebrews x. 25

THE FIRST CHRISTIANS set up the Church in continual prayer. "They persevering daily with one mind in the Temple, and breaking bread from house to house, did share their food with gladness and singleness of heart, praising God." [Acts ii. 46, 47.] St. Paul in his Epistles binds their example upon their successors for ever. Indeed, we could not have conceived, even if he and the other Apostles had been silent, that such a solemn opening of the Gospel, as that contained in the book of Acts, was only of a temporary nature, and not rather a specimen of what was to take place among the elect people in every age, and a shadow of that perfect service which will be their blessedness in heaven. However, St. Paul removes all doubt on this subject by expressly enjoining this united and unceasing prayer in various passages of his Epistles; as for instance, "I will . . . that men pray in every place, lifting up holy hands." [1 Tim. ii. 8.] "Persevere in prayer, and watch in the same with thanksgiving;" [Col. iv. 2.] and in the text.

But it will be said, "Times are altered; the rites and observances of the Church are local and occasional; what was a duty then, need not be a duty now, even though St. Paul happens to enjoin it on those whom he addresses. Such continual prayer was the particular form which the religion of the early Christians took, and ours has taken another form." Do not suppose, because I allow myself thus to word the objection, that I therefore, for an instant, allow that continual united prayer may religiously be considered a mere usage or fashion; but so it is treated—so, perhaps, some of us in our secret hearts have at times been tempted to imagine; that is, we have been disposed to think that public worship at intervals of a week has in it something of natural fitness and reasonableness which continual weekday worship has not. Still, supposing it— granting daily worship to be a mere observance, or an usage, while Sunday worship is not—calling it by any title the most slighting and disparaging—the question returns, was this observance or usage of continual united prayer in-

---

[†] *Parochial & Plain Sermons*, vol. 3 (1836), Sermon 21.

tended by the Apostles, for every age of the Church, or only for the early Christians? A precept may be but positive, not simply moral, and yet of perpetual obligation. Now, I answer confidently, that united prayer, unceasing prayer, is enjoined by St. Paul, in a passage just cited, from an Epistle which lays down rules for the government and due order of the Church to the end of time. More plausibly even might we desecrate Sunday, which he does not mention in it, than neglect continual prayer, which he does. Observe how explicitly he speaks, "I will therefore that men pray in *every place*;"—not only at Jerusalem, not only at Corinth, not only in Rome, but even in England; in England at this day, in our secluded villages, in our rich populous busy towns, whatever be the importance of those secular objects which absorb our thoughts and time.

Or, again, take the text, and consider whether it favours the notion of a change or relaxation of the primitive custom. "Not forsaking the assembling of ourselves together, as the manner of some is, but exhorting one another; and so *much the more*, as ye see the Day approaching." The increasing troubles of the world, the fury of Satan, and the madness of the people, the dismay of sun, moon, and stars, distress of nations with perplexity, men's hearts failing them for fear, the sea and the waves roaring, all these gathering tokens of God's wrath are but calls upon us for greater perseverance in united prayer. Let those men especially consider this, who say that we are but dreaming of centuries gone by, missing our mark and born out of time, when we insist on such duties and practices as are now merely out of fashion; those who point to the tumult and fever which agitates the whole nation, and say we must be busy and troubled too, in order to respond to it; who say that the tide of events has set in one way, and that we must give in to it, if we would be practical men; that it is idleness to attempt to stem a current, which it will be a great thing even to direct: that since the present age loves conversing and hearing about religion, and does not like silent thought, patient waiting, recurring prayers, severe exercises, that therefore we must obey it, and, dismissing rites and sacraments, convert the Gospel into a rational faith, so called, and a religion of the heart; let these men seriously consider St. Paul's exhortation, that we are to persevere in prayer—and that in every place—and the more, the more troubled and perplexed the affairs of this world become; not indeed omitting active exertions, but not, on that account, omitting prayer.

I have spoken of St. Paul, but, consider how this rule of "continuing in prayer" is exemplified in St. Peter's history also. He had learned from his Saviour's pattern not to think prayer a loss of time. Christ had taken him up with Him into the holy mount, though multitudes waited to be healed and taught below. Again, before His passion, He had taken him into the garden of Gethsemane; and while He prayed Himself, He called upon him likewise to "watch and pray lest he entered into temptation." In consequence, St. Peter warns us in his first Epistle, as St. Paul in the text, "The end of all things is at hand, be ye therefore sober, and watch unto prayer." [1 Pet. iv. 7.] And, in one memorable passage of his history, he received a revelation of a momentous and most gracious truth, when he was at his prayers. Who would not have said that he was wasting his time, when he retired to the house of Simon at Joppa, for many days, and went up upon the housetop to pray, about the sixth hour? Was that, it might be asked, the part of an Apostle, whose commission was to preach the Gospel? Was he thus burying his light, instead of meeting the exigencies of the time? Yet, there God met him, and put a word in his mouth. There he learned the comfortable truth that the Gentiles were no longer common or unclean, but admissible into the Covenant of Grace. And if continual prayer was the employment of an Apostle, much more was it observed by those Christians who were less prominently called to labour. Accordingly, when St. Peter was in prison, prayers were offered for him, "without ceasing," by the Church; and to those prayers he was granted. When miraculously released, and arrived at the house of Mary, the mother of Mark, he found "many gathered together praying." [Acts xii. 12.]

Stated and continual prayer, then, and especially united prayer, is plainly the duty of Christians. And if we ask how often we are to pray, I reply, that we ought to consider prayer as a plain privilege, directly we know that it is a duty, and therefore that the question is out of place. Surely, when we know we may approach the Mercy-seat, the only further question is, whether there be anything to forbid us coming often, anything implying that such frequent coming is presumptuous and irreverent. So great a mercy is it to be permitted to come, that a humble mind may well ask, "Is it a profane intrusion to come when I will?" If it be not, such a one will rejoice to come continually. Now, by way of removing these fears, Scripture contains most condescending intimations that we may come at all times. For instance, in the Lord's Prayer petition is made for *daily* bread for *this* day; therefore, our Saviour intended it should be used daily. Further, it is said, "give *us*," "forgive *us*;" therefore it may fairly be presumed to be given us as a social prayer. Thus in the Lord's Prayer itself there seems to be sanction for daily united prayer. Again, if we consider His words in the parable, twice a day at least seems permitted us, "Shall not God avenge His own elect, which cry day and night unto Him?" [Luke xviii. 7.] though this is to take the words according to a very restricted interpretation. And since Daniel prayed three times a day, and the Psalmist even seven, under the Law, we may infer, that Christians, certainly, are not irreverent, nor incur the blame of using vain repetitions, though they join in many Services.

Now, I do not see what can be said in answer to these arguments, imperfect as they are compared with the whole proof that might be adduced, except that some of the texts cited may, perhaps, refer to mere secret prayer almost without words, and some speak primarily of private prayer. Yet it is undeniable, on the other hand, that united prayer, not private or secret, is principally intended in those passages of the New Testament, which speak of prayer at all; and if so, the remainder may be left to apply indirectly or not, as we chance to decide, without interfering with a conclusion otherwise proved. If, however, it be said that family prayer is a fulfilment of the duty, without prayer in Church, I reply, that I am not at all speaking of it as a duty, but as a privilege; I do not tell men that they must come to Church, so much as declare the glad tidings that they may. This surely is enough for those who "hunger and thirst after righteousness," and humbly desire to see the face of God.

Now, I will say a few words on the manner in which the early Christians fulfilled this duty.

Quite at first, when the persecutions raged, they assembled when and where they could. At times they could but avail themselves of Christ's promise, that if two of His disciples "*agree* on earth, as touching anything that they shall ask, it shall be done for them of their Heavenly Father;" though, by small parties, and in the towns, they seem to have met together continually from the first. Gradually, as they grew stronger, or as they happened to be tolerated, they made full proof of their sacred privilege, and showed what was the desire of their hearts.

Their most solemn Service took place on the Lord's day, as might be expected, when the Holy Eucharist was celebrated.[17] Next to Sunday came Wednesday and Friday, when, also, assemblies for worship continued till three o'clock in the afternoon, and were observed with fasting; in some places with the Eucharist also. Saturday, too, was observed in certain branches of the Church with especial devotion, the Holy Mysteries being solemnized and other Services performed as on the Lord's day.

Next must be mentioned, the Festivals of the Martyrs, when, in addition to the sacred Services used on the Lord's day, there was read some account of the particular Martyr commemorated, with exhortations to follow his pattern.

These holydays, whether Sunday or Saint's day, were commonly ushered in by a Vigil or religious watching, as you find it noted down in the Calendar at the beginning of the Prayer Book. These lasted through the night.

Moreover, there were the sacred Seasons; such as the forty days of Lent for fasting, and the fifty days between Easter and Whitsuntide for rejoicing.

---

[17] Bingham's *Antiq.* xiii. 9.

Such was the course of special devotions in the early Church; but, be-sides, every day had its ordinary Services, viz., prayer morning and evening.

Besides these, might be mentioned the prayers at the canonical hours, which were originally used for private, but, at length, for united worship; viz., at the third hour, or nine in the morning, in commemoration of the Holy Ghost's descent at Pentecost at that hour; at the sixth, the time of St. Peter's vision at Joppa, in memory of our Saviour's crucifixion; and at the ninth, in memory of His death, which was the hour when St. Peter and St. John went up to the Temple and healed the lame man. It may be added, that in some places the Holy Eucharist was celebrated and partaken daily.

This is by no means a full enumeration of the sacred Services in the early Church; but it is abundantly sufficient for my purpose, which is to show how highly they valued the privilege of united prayer, and how literally they under-stood the words of Christ and His Apostles. I am by no means contending, that every point of discipline and order in this day must be precisely the same as it was then. Christians then had more time on their hands than many of us have; and certain peculiarities of the age and place might combine to allow them to do what we cannot do. Still, so far must be clear to every candid per-son who considers the state of the case, that they found some sort of pleasure in prayer which we do not; that they took delight in an exercise, which—(I am afraid I must say, though it seems profane even to say it)—which we should consider painfully long and tedious.

This too is worth observing of the primitive Christians, that they united social and private prayer in their Service. On holydays, for instance, when it was extended till three o'clock in the afternoon, they commenced with singing the Psalms, in the midst of which two Lessons were read, as is usual with us, commonly one from the Old and one from the New Testament. But in some places, instead of these Lessons, after every Psalm, a short space was allowed for private prayer to be made in silence, much in the way we say a short prayer on coming into and going out of Church. After the Psalms and Lessons came the Sermon, the more solemn prayers having not yet begun. Shortly after, fol-lowed the celebration of the Holy Communion, which again was introduced by a time of silence for private prayer, such as we at this day are allowed dur-ing the administration of the Sacred Elements to other communicants.

And in this way they lengthened out and varied their Services; principal-ly, that is, by means of private prayers and psalms: so that, when no regular course of service was proceeding, yet the Church might be full of people, pray-ing in secret and confessing their sins, or singing together psalms or hymns. Thus exactly did they fulfil the Scripture precepts—"Is any among you afflict-ed? let him pray; is any merry? let him sing psalms," and "Let the word of

Christ dwell in you richly in all wisdom; teaching and admonishing one another in psalms and hymns and spiritual songs, singing with grace in your hearts to the Lord." [James v. 13. Col. iii. 16.]

I have now said enough to let you into the reasons why I lately began Daily Service in this Church. I felt that we were very unlike the early Christians, if we went on without it; and that it was my business to give you an opportunity of observing it, else I was keeping a privilege from you. If you ask, why I did not commence it before? I will rather tell you why I began just at this time. It was, that the state of public affairs was so threatening, that I could not bear to wait longer; for there seemed quite a call upon all Christians to be earnest in prayer, so much the more, as they thought they saw the Day of vengeance approaching. Under these circumstances it seemed wrong to withhold from you a privilege, for as a privilege I would entirely consider it. I wish to view it rather as a privilege than as a duty, because then all those perplexed questions are removed at once, which otherwise beset the mind, whether a man should come or not. Considering it in the light of a privilege, I am not obliged to blame a man for not coming. I say to him, If you cannot come, then you have a great loss. Very likely you are right in not coming; you have duties connected with your temporal calling which have a claim on you; you must serve like Martha, you have not the leisure of Mary. Well, be it so; still you have a loss, as Martha had while Mary was at Jesus' feet. You have a loss; I do not say God cannot make it up to you; doubtless He will bless every one who continues in the path of duty. He blessed Peter in prison, and Paul on the sea, as well as the mother of Mark, or the daughters of Philip. Doubtless, even in your usual employments you can be glorifying your Saviour; you can be thinking of Him; you can be thinking of those who are met together in worship; you can be following in your heart, as far as may be, the prayers they offer. Doubtless: only try to realize to yourself that continual prayer and praise *is* a privilege; only feel in good earnest, what somehow the mass of Christians, after all, do not recognize, that "it is good to be here"—feel as the early Christians felt when persecution hindered them from meeting, or, as holy David, when he cried out, "My soul is athirst for God, yea, even for the Living God; when shall I come to appear before the presence of God?" [Ps. xlii. 2.] feel this, and I shall not be solicitous about your coming; you will come if you can.

With these thoughts in my mind, I determined to offer to God the Daily Service here myself, in order that all might have the opportunity of coming before Him who would come; to offer it, not waiting for a congregation, but independently of all men, as our Church sanctions; to set the example, and to save you the need of waiting for one another; and at least to give myself, with the early Christians, and St. Peter on the house-top, the benefit, if not of social, at least of private prayer, as becomes the Christian priesthood. It is quite plain that far the greater part of our Daily Service, though more fitted for a congregation than for an individual (as indeed is the Lord's Prayer itself), may yet be used, as the Lord's Prayer is used, by even one person. Such is our Common Prayer viewed in itself, and our Church has in the Introduction to it expressly directed this use of it. It is there said, "All priests and deacons are to say daily the morning and evening prayer, either privately or openly, not being let by sickness, or some other urgent cause." Again, "The curate that ministereth in every parish church or chapel, being at home, and not being otherwise reasonably hindered, shall say the same in the parish church or chapel where he ministereth, and shall cause a bell to be tolled thereunto a convenient time before he begin, that people may come to hear God's word and to pray with him." Now, doubtless, there are many reasons which may render the strict observances of these rules inexpedient in this or that place or time. The very disuse of them will be a reason for reviving them very cautiously and gradually; the paucity of clergy is another reason for suspending them. Still there they remain in the Prayer-Book—obsolete they cannot become, nay, even though torn from the book in some day of rebuke (to suppose what should hardly even be supposed), they still would have power, and live unto God. If prayers were right three centuries since, they are right now. If a Christian minister might suitably offer up common prayer by himself then, surely he may do so now. If he was then the spokesman of the saints far and near, gathering together their holy and concordant suffrages, and presenting them by virtue of his priesthood, he is so now. The revival of this usage is merely a matter of place and time; and though neither our Lord nor His Church would have us make sudden alterations, even though for the better, yet certainly we ought never to forget what is abstractedly our duty, what is in itself best, what it is we have to aim at and labour towards. If authority were needed, besides our Church's own, for the propriety of Christian Ministers praying even by themselves in places of worship, we have it in the life of our great pattern of Christian faith and wisdom, Hooker. "To what he persuaded others," says his biographer, "he added his own example of fasting and prayer; and did usually every Ember week take from the parish clerk the key of the church-door, into which place he retired every day, and locked himself up for many hours; and did the like most Fridays, and other days of fasting."

That holy man, in this instance, kept his prayers to himself. He was not offering up the Daily Service; but I adduce his instance to show that there is nothing strange or unseemly in a Christian minister praying in Church by himself; and if so, much less when he gives his people the opportunity of coming if they will. *This*, then, is what I felt and feel:—it is commonly said, when weekday prayers are spoken of, "You will not get a congregation, or you will get but a few;" but they whom Christ has brought near to Himself to be the Stewards of His Mysteries depend on no man; rather, after His pattern, they are to draw men after them. He prayed alone on the mountain; He prays alone (for who shall join with Him?) in his Father's presence. He is the one effectual Intercessor for sinners at the right hand of God. And what He is really, such are we in figure; what He is meritoriously, such are we instrumentally. Such are we by His grace; allowed to occupy His place visibly, however unworthily, in His absence, till He come; allowed to depend on Him, and not on our people; allowed to draw our commission from Him, not from them; allowed to be centres, about which the Church may grow, and about which it really exists, be it great or little.

Therefore, in beginning and continuing the Daily Service, I do not, will not measure the effect produced, by appearances. If we wait till all the world are worshippers, we must wait till the world is new made; but, if so, who shall draw the line, and say, how many are enough to pray together, when He has told us that His flock is little, and that where two or three are gathered together in His name, He is in the midst of them? So I account a few met together in prayer to be a type of His true Church; not actually His true Church (God forbid the presumption!) but as a token and type of it;—not *as being* His elect, one by one, for who can know whom He has chosen but He who chooses?— not *as* His elect for certain, for it often may be a man's duty to be away, as Martha was in her place when serving, and only faulty when she thought censoriously of Mary;—not as His complete flock, doubtless, for that were to exclude the old, and the sick, and the infirm, and little children;—not as His select and undefiled remnant, for Judas was one of the twelve—still as the earnest and promise of His Saints, the birth of Christ in its rudiments, and the dwelling-place of the Spirit; and precious, even though but one out of the whole number, small though it be, belong at present to God's hidden ones; nay, though, as is likely to be the case, in none of them there be more than the dawn of the True Light and the goings forth of the morning.—Some, too, will come at times, as accident guides them, giving promise that they may one day be settled and secured within the sacred fold. Some will come in times of grief or compunction, others in preparation for the Holy Communion.[18] Nor is it a service for those only who are present; all men know the time, and many mark

---

[18] It may be suggested here, that weekday services (with fasting) are the appropriate attendants on weekly communion, which has lately been advocated, especially in the impressive sermons of Mr. Dodsworth. When the one observance is used without the other, either the sacredness of the Lord's day is lost, from its wanting a peculiar Service, or the Eucharist is in danger of profanation, from its frequency leading us to remissness in preparing for it.

it, whose bodily presence is away. We have with us the hearts of many. Those who are conscious they are absent in the path of duty, will naturally turn their thoughts to the Church at the stated hour, and thence to God. They will recollect what prayers are then in course, and they will have fragments of them rising on their minds amid their worldly business. They will call to mind the day of the month, and the psalms used on it, and the chapters of Scripture then read out to the people. How pleasant to the wayfaring man, on his journey, to think of what is going on in his own Church! How soothing and consolatory to the old and infirm who cannot come, to follow in their thoughts, nay, with the prayers and psalms before them, what they do not hear! Shall not those prayers and holy meditations, separated though they be in place, ascend up together to the presence of God? Shall not they be with their minister in spirit, who are provoked unto prayer by his service? Shall not their prayers unite in one before the Mercy-seat, sprinkled with the Atoning Blood, as a pure offering of incense unto the Father, and an acceptable sacrifice both for the world of sinners and for His purchased Church? Who then will dare speak of loneliness and solitude, because in man's eyes there are few worshippers brought together in one place? or, who will urge it as a defect in our Service, even if that were the case? Who, moreover, will so speak, when even the Holy Angels are present when we pray, stand by us as guardians, sympathize in our need, and join us in our praises?

When thoughts such as these are set before the multitude of men, they appear to some of them strained and unnatural; to others, formal, severe, and tending to bondage. So must it be. Christ's commands will seem to be a servitude, and His privileges will be strange, till we act upon the one and embrace the other. To those who come in faith, to receive and to obey, who, instead of standing at a distance, reasoning, criticising, investigating, adjusting, hear His voice and follow Him, not knowing whither they go; who throw themselves, their hearts and wills, their opinions and conduct, into His Divine System with a noble boldness, and serve Him on a venture, without experience of results, or skill to defend their own confidence by argument: who, when He says "Pray," "Continue in prayer," take His words simply, and forthwith pray, and that instantly; these men, through His great mercy and the power of the Holy Ghost working in them, will at length find persevering prayer, praise, and intercession, neither a bondage nor a barrenness. But it is in the nature of things that Christ's word must be a law *while* it is good tidings. That very message of good tidings, that Christ saves sinners, is no good tidings to those who have not a heart to abandon sin; and as no one, by nature, has this good heart, and, even under grace, no one obtains it except gradually, there must ever be a degree of bondage in the Gospel, till, by obeying the Law and creating within us a love of God and holiness, we, by little and little, enter into the meaning of His promises.

May He lead us on evermore in the narrow way, who is the One Aid of all that need, the Helper of all that flee to Him for succour, the Life of them that believe, and the Resurrection of the dead!

The Good Part of Mary[†]

"Martha, Martha, thou art careful and troubled about many things;
but one thing is needful: and Mary hath chosen that good part
which shall not be taken away from her."
Luke x. 41, 42

EVERY WORD of Christ is good; it has its mission and its purpose, and does not fall to the ground.[19] It cannot be that He should ever speak transitory words, who is Himself the very Word of God, uttering, at His good pleasure, the deep counsels and the holy will of Him who is invisible. Every word of Christ is good; and did we receive a record of His sayings even from ordinary men, yet we might be sure as to whatever was thus preserved, whether spoken to disciple or enemy, whether by way of warning, advice, rebuke, comfort, argument, or condemnation, that nothing had a merely occasional meaning, a partial scope and confined range, nothing regarded merely the moment, or the accident, or the audience; but all His sacred speeches, though clothed in a temporary garb, and serving an immediate end, and difficult, in consequence, to disengage from what is temporary in them and immediate, yet all have their force in every age, abiding in the Church on earth, "enduring for ever in heaven," and running on into eternity. They are our rule, "holy, just, and good," "the lantern of our feet and the light of our paths," in this very day as fully and as intimately as when they were first pronounced.

And if this had been so, though mere human diligence had gathered up the crumbs from His table, much more sure are we of the value of what is recorded of Him, receiving it, as we do, not from man, but from God. The Holy Ghost, who came to glorify Christ, and inspired the Evangelists to write, did not trace out for us a barren Gospel; but doubtless, praised be His name, selected and saved for us those words which were to have an especial usefulness in after times, those words which might be the Church's law, in faith, conduct, and discipline; not a law written in tables of stone, but a law of faith and love, of the spirit, not of the letter; a law for willing hearts, which could bear to "live by every word," however faint and low, "which proceeded from His

---

[†] *Parochial & Plain Sermons*, vol. 3 (1836), Sermon 22.
[19] Basil, *Const. Mon.* 1.

mouth," and who out of the seeds which the Heavenly Sower scattered, could foster into life a Paradise of Divine Truth. Let us then humbly try with this thought before us, and the help of His grace, to gain some benefit from the text.

Martha and Mary were the sisters of Lazarus, who was afterwards raised from the dead. All three lived together, but Martha was mistress of the house. St. Luke mentions, in a verse preceding the text, that Christ came to a certain village, "and a certain woman, named Martha, received Him into her house." Being then at the head of a family, she had duties which necessarily engaged her time and thoughts. And on the present occasion she was especially busy, from a wish to do honour to her Lord. "Martha was cumbered about much serving." On the other hand, her sister was free from the necessity of worldly business, by being the younger. "She had a sister called Mary, which also sat at Jesus' feet, and heard His word." The same distinction, at once of duty and character, appears in the narrative of Lazarus' death and restoration, as contained in St. John's Gospel. "Then Martha, as soon as she heard that Jesus was coming, went and met Him; but Mary sat still in the house." [John xi. 20.] Afterwards Martha "went her way and called Mary her sister secretly, saying, The Master is come, and calleth for thee." Again, in the beginning of the following chapter, "There they made Him a supper; and Martha served . . . Then took Mary a pound of ointment of spikenard, very costly, and anointed the feet of Jesus, and wiped His feet with her hair." [John xii. 2, 3.] In these passages the same general difference between the sisters presents itself, though in a different respect;—Martha still directs and acts, while Mary is the retired and modest servant of Christ, who, at liberty from worldly duties, loves to sit at His feet and hear His voice, and silently honours Him with her best, without obtruding herself upon His sacred presence.

To return:—"Martha was cumbered about much serving, and came to Him, and said, Lord, dost Thou not care that my sister hath left me to serve alone? bid her therefore that she help me. And Jesus answered and said unto her," in the words of the text, "Martha, Martha, thou art careful and troubled about many things; but one thing is needful: and Mary hath chosen that good part which shall not be taken from her."

I shall draw two observations from this incident, and our Saviour's comment on it.

1. First, it would appear from hence, on His own authority, that there are two ways of serving Him—by active business, and by quiet adoration. Not, of course, that He speaks of those who call themselves His servants and are not; who counterfeit the one or the other manner of life; either those who are "choked with the cares of this world," or those who lie idle and useless as the

hard way-side, and "bring no fruit to perfection." Nor, again, as if His words implied that any Christians were called to nothing but religious worship, or any to nothing but active employment. There are busy men and men of leisure, who have no part in Him; there are others, who are not without fault, as altogether sacrificing leisure to business, or business to leisure. But putting aside the thought of the untrue and of the extravagant, still after all there remain two classes of Christians;—those who are like Martha, those like Mary; and both of them glorify Him in their own line, whether of labour or of quiet, in either case proving themselves to be not their own, but bought with a price, set on obeying, and constant in obeying His will. If they labour, it is for His sake; and if they adore, it is still from love of Him.

And further, these two classes of His disciples do not choose for themselves their course of service, but are allotted it by Him. Martha might be the elder, Mary the younger. I do not say that it is never left to a Christian to choose his own path, whether He will minister with the Angels or adore with the Seraphim; often it is: and well may he bless God if he has it in his power freely to choose that good portion which our Saviour especially praises. But, for the most part, each has his own place marked out for him, if he will take it, in the course of His providence; at least there can be no doubt *who* are intended for worldly cares. The necessity of getting a livelihood, the calls of a family, the duties of station and office, these are God's tokens, tracing out Martha's path for the many. Let me, then, dismiss the consideration of the many, and rather mention who they are who may be considered as called to the more favoured portion of Mary; and in doing so I shall more clearly show what that portion is.

First, I instance the Old, as is natural, whose season of business is past, and who seem to be thereby reminded to serve God by prayer and contemplation. Such was Anna; "she was of a great age . . . and was a widow of about fourscore and four years, which departed not from the Temple, but served God with fastings and prayers night and day." [Luke ii. 36, 37.] Here we see both the description of person called, and the occupation itself. Further, observe, it was the promises stored in Christ the Saviour, which were the object, towards which her service had respect. When He was brought into the Temple, she "gave thanks to the Lord, and spake of Him to all them that looked for redemption in Jerusalem." Again, the same description of person, certainly the same office, is set before us in the parable of the importunate widow. "He spake a parable unto them to this end, that we ought always to pray and not to faint." [Luke xviii. 1.] The widow said, "Avenge me of mine adversary." "And shall not God avenge His own elect," our Lord asks, "which cry day and night unto Him, though He bear long with them?" Add to these St. Paul's description: "Now she that is a widow indeed, and desolate, trusteth in God, and continueth in supplications and prayers night and day." [1 Tim. v. 5.]

Next those, who minister at the Altar, are included in Mary's portion. "Blessed is the man whom thou choosest and causest to approach unto Thee," says the Psalmist, "that he may dwell in Thy courts." [Ps. lxv. 4.] According to the Apostles' rule, the Deacons were to minister the worldly matters of the Church, the Evangelists were to go among the heathen, the Bishops were to govern; but the Elders were to remain, more or less, in the very bosom of the Lord's people, in the courts of his house, in the services of His worship, "executing the priest's office," as we read in the book of Acts [Acts xiii. 2.], offering up the Sacrifice of praise and thanksgiving, teaching, catechising, but not busy or troubled with the world. I do not mean that these distinct offices were never united in one person, but that they were in themselves distinct, and that the tendency of the Apostles' discipline was to separate off from the multitude of Christian Ministers certain who should serve God and the Church by giving thanks, and intercession.

And next, I may mention Children as in some respects partakers of Mary's portion. Till they go out into the world, whether into its trades or its professions, their school-time should be, in some sort, a contemplation of their Lord and Saviour. Doubtless they cannot enter into sacred subjects as steadily as is possible afterwards; they must not be unnaturally compelled to serve, and they are to be exercised in active habits of obedience, and in a needful discipline for the future; still, after all, we must not forget that He, who is the pattern of children as well as grown men, was, at twelve years old, found in His Father's House; and that afterwards, when He came thither before His passion, the children welcomed him with the words, "Hosanna to the Son of David," and fulfilled a prophecy, and gained His praise, in so doing.

Further, we are told, on St. Paul's authority (if that be necessary on so obvious a point), that Mary's portion is allotted, more or less, to the unmarried. I say more or less, for Martha herself, though unmarried, yet as mistress of a household, was in a measure an exception; and because servants of God, as St. Paul, may remain unmarried, not to labour less, but to labour more directly for the Lord. St. Paul's words, some have observed, almost appear to refer to the language used in the text, when read in the original Greek; which is the more likely, as St. Luke was an attendant on the Apostle, and his Gospel seems to be cited elsewhere by him. As if he said, "The unmarried careth for the things of the Lord, so as to be holy both in body and in spirit. And this I speak for your own profit, that ye may sit at the Lord's feet without being cumbered."

And further still, there are vast numbers of Christians, in Mary's case, who are placed in various circumstances, and of whom no description can well be given; rich men having leisure, or active men during seasons of leisure, as when they leave their ordinary work for recreation's sake. Certainly our Lord meant that some or other of His servants should be ever worshipping Him in every place, and that not in their hearts merely, but with the ceremonial of devotion. St. Paul says, "I will therefore that men," even that sex whose especial punishment it was that they should "eat bread in the sweat of their face," "that men pray every where, *lifting up holy hands*," in common and public worship, "without wrath and doubting." [1 Tim. ii. 8.] And we find, accordingly, that even a Roman Centurion, Cornelius, had found time, amid his military duties, to serve God continually, before he became a Christian, and was rewarded with the knowledge of the Gospel in consequence. "He prayed to God alway," we are told, and his "prayers and alms came up for a memorial before God." [Acts x. 4.]

And last of all, in Mary's portion, doubtless, are included the souls of those who have lived and died in the faith and fear of Christ. Scripture tells us that they "rest from their labours;" [Rev. xiv. 13.] and in the same sacred book, that their employment is prayer and praise. While God's servants below cry to Him day and night in every place; these "serve Him day and night in His temple" above, and from their resting-place beneath the altar intercede, with loud voice, for those holy interests which they have left behind them. "How long, O Lord, holy and true, dost Thou not judge and avenge our blood on them that dwell on the earth?" "We give Thee thanks, because Thou hast taken to Thee Thy great power, and hast reigned." [Rev. vi. 10; xi. 17.]

This then is the company of those who stand in Mary's lot;—the Aged and the Children—the Unmarried and the Priests of God—and the spirits of the just made perfect, all with one accord, like Moses on the Mount, lifting up holy hands to God, while their brethren fight, or meditating on the promises, or hearing their Saviour's teaching, or adorning and beautifying His worship.

2. Such being the two-fold character of Christian obedience, I observe, secondly, that Mary's portion is the better of the two. Our Lord does not expressly say so, but He clearly implies it: "Martha, Martha, thou art careful and troubled about many things; but one thing is needful: and Mary hath chosen that good part, which shall not be taken away from her." If His words be taken literally, they might, indeed, even mean that Martha's heart was not right with Him, which, it is plain from other parts of the history, they do not mean. Therefore, what He intimated surely was, that Martha's portion was full of snares, as being one of worldly labour, but that Mary could not easily go wrong in hers; that we may be busy in a wrong way, we cannot well adore

Him except in a right one; that to serve God by prayer and praise continually, when we can do so consistently with other duties, is the pursuit of the "one thing needful," and emphatically "that good part which shall not be taken away from us."

It is impossible to read St. Paul's Epistles carefully without perceiving how faithfully they comment on this rule of our Lord's. Is it doubtful to any one, that they speak much and often of the duties of worship, meditation, thanksgiving, prayer, praise, and intercession; and in such a way as to lead the Christian, so far as other duties will allow him, to make them the ordinary employment of his life? not, indeed, to neglect his lawful calling, nor even to be content without some active efforts to do good, whether in the way of the education of the young, attendance on the sick and needy, pastoral occupation, study, or other toil, yet to devote himself to a life at Jesus' feet, and a continual hearing of His word? And is it not plainly a privilege, above other privileges, if we really love Him, to be called to this unearthly life? Consider the following passages, in addition to those already quoted, and see if they can possibly be completely realized in the life of the common run of Christians, though all, doubtless, must cultivate inwardly, and in due measure bring into outward act, the spirit which they enjoin. See if they be not illustrations of that more blessed portion with which Mary was favoured. "Continue in prayer, watching in it with thanksgiving." [Col. iv. 2.] "Let the word of Christ dwell in you richly in all wisdom; teaching and admonishing one another in psalms, and hymns, and spiritual songs, singing with grace in your hearts to the Lord." [Col. iii. 16.] "Rejoice evermore, pray without ceasing, in every thing give thanks, . . . quench not the Spirit, despise not prophesyings." [1 Thess. v. 16–20.] "I will that men pray every where, lifting up holy hands." [1 Tim. ii. 8.] "Be not drunk with wine, wherein is excess, but be filled with the Spirit, speaking to each other in psalms, and hymns, and spiritual songs, singing and making melody in your heart to the Lord; giving thanks always, for all things, unto God our Father in the name of our Lord Jesus Christ." [Eph. v. 18–20.] "Stand therefore, having your loins girt about with truth, . . . taking the shield of faith, . . . and the sword of the Spirit, which is the word of God, praying always with all prayer and supplication in the Spirit, and watching thereunto with all perseverance and supplication for all the saints." [Eph. vi. 14–18.] Thus St. Paul speaks: in like manner St. Peter, "casting all your care" (such as Martha's) "upon Him, for He is concerned for you." [1 Pet. v. 7.] "Abstain from wine, that you may pray;" [1 Pet. iv. 7.] and St. James, "Is any among you afflicted? let him pray. Is any merry? let him sing psalms." [James v. 13.]

These are the injunctions of the Apostles; next, observe how they were fulfilled in the early Church. Before the Comforter came down, they "all (the Apostles) *continued*," St. Paul's very word in the passages above cited, they persevered steadily, they endured, "with one accord, in prayer and supplication, with the women, and Mary the mother of Jesus, and with His brethren." And so, after Pentecost; "They *continuing*,"—the same word—steadfastly enduring, "daily with one accord, in the Temple, and breaking bread from house to house, did eat their meat with gladness and singleness of heart, praising God." [Acts i. 14; ii. 46.] That early privilege, we know, was soon taken from them as a body. Persecution arose, and they were "scattered" [Acts viii. 1.] to and fro, over the earth. Henceforth Martha's portion befell them. They were full of labours, whether pleasant or painful;—pleasant, for they had to preach the Gospel over the earth—but painful as losing, not only earthly comforts, but, in some sort, spiritual quietness. They were separated from the Ordinances of Divine grace, as wanderers in a wilderness. Here and there, as they journeyed, they met a few of their brethren, "prophets and teachers, ministering to the Lord" at Antioch; or Philip's daughters, "virgins, which did prophesy" [Acts xiii. 2; xxi. 9.] at Cæsarea. They met for worship in secret, fearing their enemies; and in course of time, when the fire of persecution became fiercer, they fled to the deserts, and there set up houses for God's service. Thus Mary's portion was withheld from the Church for many years, while it laboured and suffered. St. Paul himself, that great Apostle, though he had his seasons of privilege, when he was caught up into the third heaven, and heard the hymns of Angels, yet he, too, was a man of contention and toil. He fought for the Truth, and so laid the foundations of the Temple. He was "sent to preach, not to baptize." He was not allowed to build the House of God, for He was, in figure, like David, a "man of blood." He did but bring together into one the materials for the Sacred Building. The Order of the Ministry, the Succession of Apostles, the Services of Worship, the Rule of Discipline, all that is calm, beautiful, and soothing in our Holy Religion, was brought forth piecemeal, out of his writings, by his friends and fellow-disciples, in his own day, and in the time after him, as the state of the Church admitted.

Accordingly, as peace was in any measure enjoyed, so the building was carried on, here and there, at this time and that, in the cavern, or the desert, or the mountain, where God's stray servants lived; till a time of peace came, and by the end of three hundred years the work was accomplished. From that time onwards to the present day, Mary's lot has been offered to vast multitudes of Christians, if they could receive it. If they knew their blessedness, there are numbers now, in various ranks of society, who might enjoy the privilege of continual praise and prayer, and a seat at Jesus' feet. Doubtless they are, after all, but the few: for the great body of Christians have but the Lord's day, as a day of rest, and would be deserting their duty if they lived on other days as on it. But what is not granted to some, is granted to others, to serve God in His Temple, and be at rest. Who these favoured persons are, has already been said generally; which is all that can be said in a matter in which every one must decide for himself, according to his best light and his own peculiar case. Yet surely, without attempting to pronounce upon individuals, so far at least we may say, that if there be an age when Mary's portion is altogether let alone and decried, that age is necessarily so far a stranger to the spirit of the Gospel.

Let me then, in conclusion, ask, for our edification, whether perchance this is not such an age? I say "perchance;" because in matters of this kind, men show their motives and principles less openly than in other matters, as being of a nature more immediately lying between themselves and God. Yet, taking account of this, at least is not this an age in which few persons are in a condition, from the very state of society, to "give themselves continually to prayer" and other direct religious services? Has not the desire of wealth so eaten into our hearts, that we think poverty the worst of ills, that we think the security of property the first of blessings, that we measure all things by mammon, that we not only labour for it ourselves, but so involve in our own evil earnestness all around us, that they cannot keep from the pursuit of it though they would? Does not the frame-work of society move forward on such a plan as to enlist into the service of the world all its members, almost whether they will or no? Would not a man be thought unaspiring and unproductive, who cared not to push forward in pursuit of that which Scripture calls "the root of all evil," the love of which it calls "covetousness which is idolatry," and the possession of which it solemnly declares all but excludes a man from the kingdom of Heaven? Alas! can this be denied? And therefore, of course, the entire system of tranquil devotion, holy meditation, freedom from worldly cares, which our Saviour praises in the case of Mary, is cast aside, misunderstood, or rather missed altogether, as much as the glorious sunshine by a blind man, slandered and ridiculed as something contemptible and vain. Surely, no one, who is candid, can doubt, that, were Mary now living, did she choose on principle that state of life in which Christ found her, were she content to remain at Jesus' feet hearing His word and disengaged from this troublesome world, she would be blamed and pitied. Careless men would gaze strangely, and wise men compassionately, on such an one, as wasting her life, and choosing a melancholy, cheerless portion. Long ago was this the case. Even in holy Martha, zealous as she was and true-hearted, even in her instance we are reminded of the impatience and disdain with which those who are far different from her, the children of this world, regard such as dedicate themselves to God. Long ago, even in her, we seem to witness, as in type, the rash, unchristian way in which this age disparages devotional services. Do we never hear it said, that the daily Service of the Church is unnecessary? Is it never hinted that it is scarcely worth while to keep it up unless we get numbers to attend it, as if one single soul, if but one, were not precious enough for Christ's love and His Church's rearing? Is it never objected, that a partially-filled Church is a discouraging sight, as if, after all, our Lord Jesus had chosen the many and not the few to be His true disciples? Is it never maintained, that a Christian minister is off his post unless he is for ever labouring for the heartless many, instead of ministering to the more religious few? Alas! there must be something wrong among us; when our defenders recommend the Church on the mere plea of its activity, its popularity, and its visible usefulness, and would scarcely scruple to give us up, had we *not* the many on our side! If our ground of boasting be, that rich men, and mighty men, and many men love us, it never can be a religious boast, and may be our condemnation. Christ made His feast for "the poor, the maimed, the lame, and the blind." It is the widow and the fatherless, the infirm, the helpless, the devoted, bound together in prayer, who are the strength of the Church. It is their prayers, be they many or few, the prayers of Mary and such as Mary, who are the safety, under Christ, of those who with Paul and Barnabas fight the Lord's battles. "It is but lost labour to rise up early, to sit up late, to eat the bread of sorrows," if prayers are discontinued. It is mere infatuation, if we think to resist the enemies who at this moment are at our doors, if our Churches remain shut, and we give up to prayer but a few minutes in the day.

Blessed indeed are they whom Christ calls near to Him to be His own peculiar attendants and familiar friends; more blessed if they obey and fulfil their calling! Blessed even if they are allowed to seize intervals of such service towards Him; but favoured and honoured beyond thought, if they can, without breach of duty, put aside worldly things with full purpose of heart, renounce the pursuit of wealth, keep clear of family cares, and present themselves as a holy offering, without spot or blemish, to Him who died for them.[20] These are they who "follow Him whithersoever He goeth," and to them He more especially addresses those lessons of faith and resignation which are recorded in His Gospel. "Take heed," He says, "and beware of covetousness; for

---

[20] The life here advocated is one of which Prayer, Praise, Intercession, and other devotional services, are made the object and business, in the same sense in which a certain profession or trade is the object and business of life to the mass of men: one in which devotion is *the* end to which everything else gives way. This explanation will answer the question, *how much* of each day it supposes set aside for devotion. Callings of this world do not necessarily occupy the whole, or half, or a third of our time, but they *rule* and *dispose* of the whole of it.

153

man's life consisteth not in the overabundance of the things which he possesseth. Take no care for your life, what ye shall eat, neither for the body, what ye shall put on. Consider the lilies how they grow, they toil not, they spin not. Seek not ye what ye shall eat or what ye shall drink, neither be ye unsettled; for all these things do the nations of the world seek after, and your Father knoweth that ye have need of these things. Fear not, little flock, for it is your Father's good pleasure to give you the Kingdom. Sell that ye have, and give alms; provide yourselves bags which wax not old, where no thief approacheth, neither moth corrupteth. Let your loins be girded about, and your lights burning; and ye yourselves like unto men that wait for their Lord, when He will return from the wedding. Blessed are those servants, whom the Lord, when He cometh, shall find watching. Verily I say unto you, that He will gird Himself,"—He who on earth has let them sit at His feet hearing His word, or let them anoint His feet with ointment, kissing them, He in turn, as He did before His passion, by an inexpressible condescension, "will gird Himself; and make them to sit down to meat, and will come forth and serve them. And if He shall come in the second watch, or come in the third watch, and find them so, blessed are those servants. Be ye therefore ready also; for the Son of man cometh at an hour when ye think not." [Luke xii. 15–40.]

Religious Worship a Remedy for Excitements[†]

"Is any among you afflicted? let him pray. Is any merry? let him sing psalms."
James v. 13

S T. JAMES seems to imply in these words that there is that in religious worship which supplies all our spiritual need, which suits every mood of mind and every variety of circumstances, over and above the heavenly and supernatural assistance which we are allowed to expect from it. Prayer and praise seem in his view to be an universal remedy, a panacea, as it is called, which ought to be used at once, whatever it be that affects us. And, as is implied in ascribing to them this universal virtue, they produce very opposite effects, according to our need; allaying or carrying off the fever of the mind, as the case may be. The Apostle is not speaking of *sin* in the text; he speaks of the *emotions* of the mind, whether joyful or sorrowful, of good and bad spirits; and for these and all other such disturbances, prayer and praise are a medicine. Sin indeed has its appropriate remedies too, and more serious ones; penitence, self-abasement, self-revenge, mortification, and the like. But the text supposes the case of a Christian, not of a mere penitent—not of scandalous wickedness, but of emotion, agitation of mind, regret, longing, despondency, mirthfulness, transport, or rapture; and in case of such ailments it says, prayer and praise is the remedy.

Indisposition of body shows itself in a *pain* somewhere or other;—a distress, which draws our thoughts to it, centres them upon it, impedes our ordinary way of going on, and throws the mind off its balance. Such too is indisposition of the soul, of whatever sort, be it passion or affection, hope or fear, joy or grief. It takes us off from the clear contemplation of the next world, ruffles us, and makes us restless. In a word, it is what we call an excitement of mind. Excitements are the indisposition of the mind; and of these excitements in different ways the services of divine worship are the proper antidotes. How they are so, shall now be considered.

1. Excitements are of two kinds, secular and religious: First, let us consider secular excitements. Such is the pursuit of gain, or of power, or of distinction. Amusements are excitements; the applause of a crowd, emulations, hopes, risks, quarrels, contests, disappointments, successes. In such cases the

---

† *Parochial & Plain Sermons*, vol. 3 (1836), Sermon 23.

object pursued naturally absorbs the mind, and excludes all thoughts but those relating to itself. Thus a man is sold over into bondage to this world. He has one idea, and one only before him, which becomes his idol. Day by day he is engrossed by this one thing, to which his heart pays worship. It may attract him through the imagination, or through the reason; it may appeal to his heart, or to his self-interest, or to his pride; still, whether we be young or old, rich or poor, each age, each fortune is liable to its own peculiar excitement, which has power to fascinate the eye of our minds, to enervate and destroy us. Not all at once (God forbid!), but by a gradual process, till every thought of religion is lost before the contemplation of this nearer good.

The most ordinary of these excitements, at least in this country, is the pursuit of gain. A man may live from week to week in the fever of a decent covetousness, to which he gives some more specious name (for instance, desire of doing his duty by his family), till the heart of religion is eaten out of him. He may live and die in his farm or in his merchandise. Or he may be labouring for some distinction, which depends on his acquitting himself well on certain trying occasions, and requires a laborious preparation beforehand. Or he may be idly carried away by some light object of sense, which fills his mind with empty dreams and pains which profit not. Or he may be engaged in the general business of life; be full of schemes and projects, of political manœuvres and efforts, of hate, or jealousy, or resentment, or triumph. He may be busy in managing, persuading, outwitting, resisting other men. Again, he may be in one or other of these states, not for a life, but for a season; and this is the more general case. Anyhow, *while* he is so circumstanced, whether for a longer or a shorter season, this will hold good—viz., the thought of religion is excluded by the force of the excitement which is on him.

Now, then, observe what is the remedy. "Is any afflicted? let him pray. Is any merry? let him sing psalms." Here we see one very momentous use of prayer and praise to all of us; it breaks the current of worldly thoughts. And this is the singular benefit of stated worship, that it statedly interferes with the urgency of worldly excitements. Our daily prayer, morning and evening, suspends our occupations of time and sense. And especially the daily prayers of the Church do this. I say especially, because a man, amid the business of life, is often tempted to defraud himself of his private devotions by the pressure of engagements. He has not many minutes to give to them; and if by accident they are broken in upon, the season is gone and lost. But the public Service is of a certain length, and cannot be interrupted; and it is long enough to calm and steady the mind. Scripture must be read, psalms must be sung, prayers must be offered; every thing comes in course. I say, it is impossible (under God's blessing) for any one to attend the Daily Service of the Church "with reverence and godly fear," and a wish and effort to give his thoughts to it, and not find himself thereby sobered and brought to recollection. What kinder office is there, when a man is agitated, than for a friend to put his hand upon him by way of warning, to startle and recall him? It often has the effect of saving us from angry words, or extravagant talking, or inconsiderate jesting, or rash resolves. And such is the blessed effect of the sacred Services on Christians busied about many things; reminding them of the one thing needful, and keeping them from being drawn into the great whirlpool of time and sense.

This, let it be observed, is one important benefit arising from the institution of the Lord's day. Over and above the privilege of being allowed one day in seven for religious festivity, the Christian may accept it as a merciful break in upon his usual employments, lest they should engross him. Most men, indeed, perceive this; they will feel wearied with the dust of this world when Saturday comes, and understand it to be a mercy that they are not obliged to go on toiling without cessation. But still, there are many who, if it were not an express ordinance of religion, would feel tempted, or think it their duty, to continue their secular labours, even though the custom of society allowed them to rest. Many, as it is, are so tempted; that is, at times, when they have some pressing object in view, and think they cannot afford to lose a day: and many always—such, for instance, as are in certain professions, which are not regulated (as trade is, more or less) by times and places. And great numbers, it is to be feared, yield to the temptation; and the evil effect of it shows itself in various miserable ways, even in the overthrow of their health and reason. In all these cases, then, the weekly Services of prayer and praise come to us as a gracious relief, a pause from the world, a glimpse of the third heaven, lest the world should rob us of our hope, and enslave us to that hard master who is plotting our eternal destruction.

You see, then, how secular excitements are remedied by religious worship; viz., by breaking them up, and disabling them.

2. Next, let us consider how religious excitements are set right by the same Divine medicine.

If we had always continued in the way of light and truth, obeying God from childhood, doubtless we should know little of those swellings and tumults of the soul which are so common among us. Men who have grown up in the faith and fear of God, have a calm and equable piety; so much so, that they are often charged on that very account with being dull, cold, formal, insensible, dead to the next world. Now, it stands to reason, that a man who has always lived in the contemplation and improvement of his Gospel privileges, will not feel that agitating surprise and vehemence of joy, which he would feel, and ought to feel, if he had never known anything of them before. The jailor, who for the first time heard the news of salvation through Christ, gave evident signs of transport. This certainly is natural and right; still it is a state of excitement, and, if I might say it, all states of excitement have dangerous tendencies. Hence one never can be sure of a new convert; for, in that elevated state of mind in which he is at first, the affections have much more sway than the reason or conscience; and unless he takes care, they may hurry him away, just as a wind might do, in a wrong direction. He is balanced on a single point, on the summit of an excited mind, and he may easily fall. However, though this danger would not exist, or, at least, not commonly or seriously, did men turn to God from early youth, yet, alas! in matter of fact they do not so turn; in matter of fact they are open to the influence of excitement, when they begin to seek God; and the question is, what is then to be done with them?

Now this advice is often given:—"Indulge the excitement; when you flag, seek for another; live upon the thought of God; go about doing good; let your light shine before men; tell them what God has done for your soul;"—by all which is meant, when we go into particulars, that they ought to fancy that they have something above all other men; ought to neglect their worldly calling, or at best only bear it as a cross; to join themselves to some particular set of religionists; take part in this or that religious society; go to hear strange preachers, and obtrude their new feelings and new opinions upon others, at times proper and improper. I am speaking now of the temper, not of those who profess adherence to the Church, but of such as detach themselves, more or less, from its discipline; and the reason I allude to them is this. It is often said, that schism and dissent are but accidents of a religious temper; that they who fall into them, if pious, are the same in heart as Churchmen, only are divided by some outward difference of forms and circumstances. Not so; the mind of dissent, viewed in itself, is far other than the mind of Christ and His Holy Church Catholic; in whatever proportion it may or may not be realized in individuals. It is full of self-importance, irreverence, censoriousness, display, and tumult. It is right, therefore, ever to insist that it is different, lest men should be seduced into it, by being assured that it is not different.

That it is different from the mind and spirit of the early Christians at least, is quite plain from history. If there was a time, when those particular irregularities, which now are so common, were likely to abound, it was in the primitive Church. Men, who had lived all their lives in the pollutions of sin unspeakable, who had been involved in the darkness of heathenism, were suddenly brought to the light of Christian truth. Their sins were all freely forgiven them, clean washed away in the waters of Baptism. A new world of ideas was opened upon them; and the most astonishing objects presented to their faith. What a state of transport must have been theirs! We know it was so, by the account of such men in the book of Acts. The jailor *"rejoiced,* believing in God, with all his house." And what an excited and critical state was theirs! Critical and dangerous in proportion to its real blessedness; for, in proportion to the privileges we enjoy, ever will be our risk of misusing them. In spite, then, of their blessedness, they were in a state of risk, and that from the excitement of their minds. How then did they escape that enthusiasm which now prevails, that irreverence, immodesty, and rudeness? I say, if in any age that feverish spirit was likely to have prevailed, which now prevails, the early times of the Gospel was such; how is it we do not read generally of what happened in a measure and for a season in the Corinthian Church, of Christians disobeying their Rulers, saying that their own hearts were the best judges in religious matters, censuring those about them, taking teachers for themselves, and so breaking up the Church of Christ into ten thousand parts? If at any time the outward frame-work of Christianity was in jeopardy, surely it was then. How was it the ungovernable elements within it did not burst forth and shiver to pieces the vessel which contained them? How was it, that for fifteen hundred years the Church was preserved from those peculiar affections of mind and irregularities of feeling and conduct, which now torment it like an ague?

Now certainly, looking at external and second causes, the miracles had much to do in securing this blessed sobriety in the early Christians. These kept them from wilfulness and extravagance, and tempered them to the spirit of godly fear. Thus St. Paul, when converted, was not let go by himself, so to speak. His merciful Lord kept His hand upon him, and directed his every step, lest he should start aside and go astray. Thus He would not tell him all at once what to do, though St. Paul wished it; but bade him "arise, and go into the city," and there it was to be told him what he was to do. He was *led by the hand* (a fit emblem of his spiritual condition), and brought to Damascus. Then he was three days without sight, and without meat and drink. During this time he was still kept in suspense and ignorance what was to happen, and was employed in praying. Such desolateness—his darkness, fasting, and suspense—had a sobering influence. Then Ananias was sent to him to baptize him. Forthwith he began to preach Christ at Damascus, but was soon checked, thwarted, sent into Arabia out of the way, for three years. Then he returned to Damascus, and again, preaching Christ, was in no long time obliged to flee for his life. He came to Jerusalem, and began again to preach. Here first he had a difficulty in getting acknowledged by the Apostles, who were for a time afraid of him; then the Jews laid a plot to kill him. As he was praying in the Temple, Christ appeared to him, and bade him depart from Jerusalem. The brethren brought him down to Cæsarea; thence he went to

Tarsus. Now, who does not see in this history how the Apostle was repressed and brought under by the plain commands and providences of God, hurrying him to and fro, without saying why? After all this, many years passed before he was employed to preach to the heathen, and then only after a solemn ordination.

Thus, God's miraculous providence, awing and controlling the heart, would seem to be one especial means by which the early Christians were kept from enthusiasm; and the persecutions of the Church became another. But the more ordinary means was one which we may enjoy at this day, if we choose: the course of religious Services, the round of prayer and praise, which, indeed, was also part of St. Paul's discipline, as we have seen, and which has a most gracious effect upon the restless and excited mind, giving it an outlet, yet withal calming, soothing, directing, purifying it.

To go into details. It often happens that in a family who have been brought up together, one suddenly takes what is called a religious turn. Such a person wishes to be more religious than the rest, wishes to do something more than ordinary, but does not know exactly what to do. You will find, generally, that he joins himself to some dissenting party, mainly for this reason, to evidence to himself greater strictness. His mind is under excitement; he seems to say with St. Paul, "Lord, what wilt Thou have me to do?" This is the cause, again and again, of persons falling from the Church. And hence, a notion has got abroad that dissenting bodies have more of true religion within them than the Church; I say, for this reason, because earnest men, awaking to a sense of religion, wish to do something more than usual, and join sects and heresies as a relief to their minds, by way of ridding themselves of strong feelings, which, pent up within them, distress them. And I cannot deny, that in this way these bodies do gain, and the Church does lose, earnestly religious people, or rather those who would have been such in time; for it is, I fear, too true that, while the sects in question are in this way recruited and improved from the Church, the persons themselves, who join them, are injured. They lose the greater part of that religious light and warmth which hung about them, even though they have been hitherto careless, and but partially availed themselves of it. It is as if a living hand were to touch cold iron; the iron is somewhat warmed, but the hand is chilled. And thus the blossom of truth, the promise of real religion, is lost to the Church. Men begin well, but being seduced by their own waywardness fall away.

Here, then, if we knew how to employ them, the Services of the Church come in to soothe and guide the agitated mind. "Is any afflicted? let him pray: is any merry? let him sing psalms." Is any in a perturbed state of mind? he need not go off to strange preachers and meetings, in order to relieve himself

160

of his uneasiness. We can give him a stricter rule of life, and a safer one. Did not our Lord make a distinction between the life of Martha and that of Mary, and without disclaiming Martha, who was troubled for His sake with the toils of life, yet praise Mary the rather, who sat at His feet? Does not St. Paul make a distinction between the duties *necessary* for a Christian, and those which are *comely and of good report*? Let restless persons attend upon the worship of the Church, which will attune their minds in harmony with Christ's law, while it unburdens them. Did not St. Paul "pray" during his three days of blindness? Afterwards he was praying in the Temple, when Christ appeared to him. Let this be well considered. We may build Houses of God without number, up and down the land, as indeed our duty is; we may multiply resident ministers; we may (with a less commendable zeal) do our utmost to please the many or the wealthy; but all this will not deprive Dissenting bodies of their virtue and charm, such as it is. Their strength is their semblance of a strictness beyond members of the Church. Till we act up to our professed principles more exactly; till we have in deed and actual practice more frequent Services of praise and prayer, more truly Catholic plans for honouring God and benefiting man; till we exhibit the nobler and more beautiful forms of Christian devotedness for the admiration and guidance of the better sort, we have, in a manner, done nothing. Surely we want something more than the material walls, we want the "spirit and truth" of the Heavenly Jerusalem, the worshippers "with one accord continuing in the Temple, with gladness and singleness of heart, praising God," persevering and prevailing in prayer, and thus, without seeking it, "having favour with all the people."

Is any one then desirous of gaining comfort to his soul, of bringing Christ's presence home to his very heart, and of doing the highest and most glorious things for the whole world? I have told him how to proceed. Let him praise God; let holy David's Psalter be as familiar words in his mouth, his daily service, ever repeated, yet ever new and ever sacred. Let him pray; especially let him intercede. Doubt not the power of faith and prayer to effect all things with God. However you try, you cannot do works to compare with those which faith and prayer accomplish in the name of Christ. Did you give your body to be burned, and all your goods to feed the poor, you could not do so much as by continual intercession. Few are rich, few can suffer for Christ; all may pray. Were you an Apostle of the Church, or a Prophet, you could not do more than you can do by the power of prayer. Go not then astray to find out new modes of serving God and benefiting man. I show you "a more excellent way." Come to our Services; come to our Litanies; throw yourself out of your own selfish heart; pour yourself out upon the thought of sin and sinners, upon the contemplation of God's Throne, of Jesus the Mediator between God and man, and of that glorious Church to which the dispensation of His merits is committed. Aspire to be what Christ would make you, His friend; having power with Him and prevailing. Other men will not pray for themselves. You may pray for them and for the general Church; and while you pray, you will find enough in the defects of your praying to remind you of your own nothingness, and to keep you from pride while you aim at perfection.

But I must draw to an end. Thus, in both ways, whether our excitements arise from objects of this world or the next, praise and prayer will be, through God's mercy, our remedy; keeping the mind from running to waste; calming, soothing, sobering, steadying it; attuning it to the will of God and the mind of the Spirit, teaching it to love all men, to be cheerful and thankful, and to be resigned in all the dispensations of Providence towards us.

Oh that we knew our own true bliss, now that Christ is come, instead of being, as we still are, for the most part, like the heathen, as sheep without a shepherd! May the good Lord fulfil His purpose towards us in His own time! Amen.

On the Abuse of Private Judgment[†]

F IRST, there are texts which bid us ask wisdom of God, and promise that it will be granted.[21] It is true; but this does not show that the *private* reading of *Scripture* is the *one* essential requisite for gaining it. If such texts are taken by themselves, they would rather prove that *no* external means at all is necessary, not even Scripture, for Scripture is not mentioned. To be consistent, we ought to call the Scripture an outward form as well as the Church, and to say that "asking," in other words, prayer, is alone necessary. If then one external means of gaining light is admitted as intervening between the Holy Ghost and the soul, though it is not mentioned, why not another? When Christ says, "Seek, and ye shall find," He does not specify the *mode* of seeking; He means, as we may suppose, by all methods which are vouchsafed to us, and are otherwise specified. He includes the Church, which is called by St. Paul "the pillar and ground of the Truth." Our Service applies our Lord's promise to seeking God in Baptism, and as He may include the use of the Sacraments in seeking, so may He include the use of Catholic teaching.

Again, no Christian can doubt that without divine grace we cannot discern the sense of Scripture profitably; but it does not follow from this that with it we can gain everything from Scripture, or that the "wisdom unto salvation," which we thence gain, is theological knowledge. The grace of God seems to be promised us chiefly for practical purposes, for enabling us to receive what we receive, whatever it is, doctrine or precept, or from whatever quarter, profitably, with a lively faith, with love and zeal. If it supersedes Creeds, why should it not supersede Sacraments? it acts through Sacraments, and in like manner it acts through Creeds. Sacraments, without the presence of the Holy Ghost, would sink into mere Jewish rites; and Creeds, without a similar presence, are but a dead letter. The appointment of Sacraments is in Scripture, and so is the proof of the Creed; yet Scripture is no more a Creed, than it is a Sacrament,—no more does the work of a Creed, than it does the work of a Sacrament. By continuous Tradition we have received the Sacraments embodied in a certain definite form; and by a like Tradition we have received the doctrines also; Scripture may justify both the one and the other, when given, without being sufficient to enable individuals to put into shape

---

[†] Excerpt from *Lectures on the Prophetical Office of the Church* (1837), Lecture 6.
[21] Matt. vii. 7. James i. 5.

163

whether doctrines or Sacraments, apart from oral teaching and tradition. Besides, if the Holy Spirit illuminates the word of God for the use of the individual in all things, then of course as regards unfulfilled prophecy also; which we know is not the case. As then, for all that the Spirit is given us, the event is necessary in order to interpret prophecy, so in like manner a similar external fact may be necessary for understanding doctrine. True then though it be that "the natural man discerneth not the things of the Spirit of God;" it does not therefore follow that the spiritual man discerneth spiritual things through Scripture only, not through Creeds.

Lastly: there are texts which recite the various purposes for which Scripture is useful; but it does not follow thence that no medium is necessary for its becoming useful to individuals. Scripture may be profitable for doctrine, instruction, and correction, that the man of God may be perfect, without thereby determining at all whether or not there are instruments for preparing, dispensing, and ministering the word for this or that purpose which it is to effect. Certainly Christ says, "Search the Scriptures," but He is speaking to the Jews about their Scriptures, and about definite prophecies; how does it follow that because it was the duty of the Jews to examine such documents as prophecies, which profess to be prophecies, that therefore we are meant to gather our doctrines from documents which do not profess to be doctrinal? Besides, when Christ told them to search the Scriptures for notices of Himself, He had vouchsafed already to present Himself before them; He was a living comment on those Scriptures to which He referred.[22] What He was to be, was *not* understood before He appeared. The case is the same with Christian doctrine now. The Creed confronts Scripture, and seems to say to us, "Search the Scriptures, for they testify of Me." But if we attempt to gain the truth of doctrine without the Creed, perhaps we shall not be more successful in our search than the Jews were in seeking Christ before He came,—yet under circumstances different from theirs, in that in our case knowledge is necessary to salvation, and error is a sin.

---

[22] *Vide* Acts viii. 30–35; xvii. 11.

On Ecclesiastical Hymns†

O F THE THREE kinds of poetical composition which, in accordance
with the Apostle's direction, have ever been in use in the Church,
"Psalms and Hymns and Spiritual Songs," two are supplied by inspiration. We have no need, through God's bounty, to turn our thoughts to the
composition of Psalms or Songs; and, to judge from the attempts which have
been made, doubtless we are unequal to it. And the unapproachable excellence
of the two which have been supplied serves to suggest the difficulties which
beset the composition of the third which has not been supplied. Indeed, it is
hardly too strong to say that to write Hymns is as much beyond us as to origi-
nate Psalmody. The peculiarity of the Psalms is their coming nearer than any
other kind of devotion to a converse with the powers of the unseen world.
They are longer and freer than Prayers; and, as being so, are less a direct address to the Throne of Grace than a sort of intercourse, first with oneself, then
with one's brethren, then with Saints and Angels, nay, even the world and all
creatures. They consist mainly of the praises of God; and the very nature of
praise involves a certain abstinence from intimate approaches to Him, and the
introduction of other beings into our thoughts, through whom our offering
may come round to Him. For as He, and He only, is the direct object of prayer, so it is more becoming not to regard Him as directly addressed in praise,
which would imply passing a judgment on Him who is above all scrutiny and
all standards. The Seraphim cried *one to another*, "Holy, Holy, Holy," veiling
their faces; neither looking nor speaking to Him. The Psalms, then, as being
praises, and thanksgivings, are the language, the ordinary converse, as is may
be called, of Saints and Angels in heaven; and, being such, could not be written except by men who had heard the "unspeakable things" which there are
uttered. In this light they are more difficult than Prayers. Beggars can express
their wants to a prince; they cannot converse like his courtiers.

Much the same remark may be made about the Songs or Canticles of the
Church, which are also inspired, and are a kind of Psalms written for particular occasions, chiefly occasions of thanksgiving. Such are the two Songs of Moses, the Song of Hannah, those in Isaiah, the Song of Hezekiah, of Habakkuk,
of the Three Children, of Zacharias, of the Blessed Virgin, and of Simeon;

---

† From Newman's Preface (1838) to *Hymni Ecclesiæ*, Pars I: *E Breviario Parisiensi*, published in
London by Alexander Macmillan. The title of this selection is editorial.

165

most of which are in the Breviary, and the last four are retained in our own Reformed Prayer Book.

Yet though Hymns, as being of a measured length, and restrained metrically, are so far safer to attempt than Psalms or Songs, they have their own peculiar difficulties. They are direct addresses to Almighty God, which ever must be most difficult to the serious mind, whatever be the difficulty of other devotions. This, in the instance of Prayers, has led to the use of Sentences, such as occur in our own Services; which, besides the advantage of extreme brevity, for the most part admit of being taken from Scripture. It has led also to the repetition of the Lord's Prayer, and of the *Kyrie Eleison*; and, again, to the use of Collects, which lessen the difficulty of addressing God by subjecting it to fixed rules. Hence our best Family Prayers are what may be called a succession of Sentences strung together, the simple and concise expression of our humiliation, fear, hope, and desire for ourselves and others. Long Public Prayers, to make a general assertion which of course admits of exceptions, are arrogant and irreverent; hence the Pharisees made them. Hence, too, the unchastised effusions which abound in the present day among those who have left the Church or lost her spirit. The great Eucharistic Prayer is nearly the only long prayer in the Catholic Church; and there is every reason to suppose that in its substance it proceeds from inspired authorities. In our own Service it has been separated by our Reformers into three distinct portions.

Hymns, however, being of the nature of praises, cannot be altogether brought down to that grave and severe character which, as being direct addresses to God, they seem to require; and this is their peculiar difficulty. To praise God specially for Redemption, to contemplate the mysteries of the Divine Nature, to enlarge upon the details of the Economy of Grace and yet not to offend, to invoke with awe, to express affection with a pure heart, to be subdued and sober while we rejoice, and to make professions without display, and all this not under the veil of figurative language, as in the Psalms, but plainly, and (as it were) abruptly, surely requires to have had one's lips touched with a "coal from the Altar," to have caught from heaven that "new song" "which no man could learn, but the hundred and forty and four thousand which were redeemed from the earth"—the virgin followers of the Lamb.

Our Church, with the remarkable caution which she displays so often, has not attempted it. She has received the Psalms and Songs from Scripture; and, rejecting the Roman Hymns, has substituted in their stead, not others, but a metrical version of the Psalms. This abstinence has led on one hand to some of her members on their own responsibility supplying the deficiency, and has incurred the complaint of others, who argued that she ought to have taken on herself what, being right in itself, will certainly be done by private hands, if not by the fitting authority. But, in truth, when it was necessary for her to abandon those she had received, nothing was left to her but to wait till she should receive others, as in the course of ages she had already received, by little and little.

The Roman Hymns, whether good or bad, were the work of no one generation, much less the outpourings of one mind. They were not the contents of one collection, published all new in a day according to the will of man. They were the gradual accumulations of centuries, bearing in old and new upon one treasure-house. When there was a call to reject them, there was nothing to be done but begin again. We could not be young and old at once. It was a stern necessity alone which could compel us to change from what we were; but being changed, so far we were not what we were, and must be what the primitive Church was in these respects, poor and ill-furnished. We began the world again. This is the proper answer to inconsiderate complaints and impatient interference. There have before now been divines who could write a Liturgy in thirty-six hours. Such is not our Church's way. She is not the empiric to make things to order, and to profess and to anticipate the course of nature, which, under grace, as under Providence, is slow. She waits for that majestic course to perfect in its own good time, what she cannot extort from it; for the gradual drifting of precious things upon her shore, now one and now another, out of which she may complete her rosary and enrich her beads,—beads and rosary more pure and true than those which at the command of duty she flung away.

As far as we know, the public Hymns of the early Church were not much more than the following. First, starting from Scripture, she adopted the repetition of the *Hallelujah*, which is described by St. John, in the Revelations, to be the chant of the blessed inhabitants of heaven. Next may be mentioned the *Gloria Patri*, pretty much as we now use it. Thirdly, the *Trisagion*, or "Holy, Holy, Holy," from Isaiah vi.; or, as it was also used, and now is, in the Roman Church, "Sanctus Deus, Sanctus Fortis, Sanctus Immortalis." Besides these, there was the Morning or Angelic Hymn, beginning with the words used by the Angels at the nativity; and for the evening the Hymn beginning "Hail gladdening Light," preserved by St. Basil. These are not metrical, as they were afterwards; nor are two others of a later date, which we still retain, the *Te Deum* and the *Athanasian Creed*. They are both of Gallican origin, though the former has been ascribed to St. Ambrose. Others, however, now extant, are certainly his; others are the compositions of St. Hilary, Prudentius, St. Gregory, and later saints. It is not too much to say then that, judging by what we know of the Hymns of the primitive Church, we should not be dissatisfied with the paucity of those which custom has, with a sort of tacit authority, introduced among us in the course of several centuries.

More, doubtless, might be selected from the writings of our sacred Poets; but since, from unhappy circumstances, such a work does not seem likely at the present day, thoughtful minds naturally revert to the discarded collections of the ante-reform era, discarded because of associations with which they were then viewed, and of the interpolations by which they were disfigured; but which, when purified from these, are far more profitable to the Christian than the light and wanton effusions which are their present substitute among us. Nay, even such as the Parisian, which are here first presented to the reader, which have no equal claims to antiquity, breathe an ancient spirit; and even where they are the work of one pen, are the joint and invisible contribution of many ancient minds. Moreover, the ancient language used has a tendency to throw the reader out of every-day thoughts and familiar associations, and to make him fervent without ceasing to be mortified. Many a man could bear to read the Canticles in a foreign language who is unequal to it in his own.

It only remains to say, that the following selection of Hymns, from the Paris Breviary, has been confined to such holy days and seasons as are recognized by our Church, or to special events or things recorded in Scripture; those Hymns, however, being omitted which contained invocations to the Saints of such a nature as to be, even in the largest judgment of charity, not mere apostrophes, but supplications.

J. H. N.
February 21, 1838.

Righteousness the Fruit of our Lord's Resurrection[†]

THESE CONSIDERATIONS will serve to throw some light on a difficult passage in the end of St. John's Gospel, where our Lord says to St. Mary Magdalen—"Touch Me not, for I am not yet ascended to My Father." [John xx. 17.] The question arises here, *Why* might not our Lord be touched *before* His ascension, and how *could* He be touched *after* it? But Christ speaks, it would seem, thus (if, as before, we might venture to paraphrase His sacred words)—"Hitherto you have only known Me after the flesh. I have lived among you as a man. You have been permitted to approach Me sensibly, to kiss and embrace My feet, to pour ointment upon My head. But all this is at an end, now that I have died and risen again in the power of the Spirit. A glorified state of existence is begun in Me, and will soon be perfected. At present, though I bid you at one moment handle Me as possessed of flesh and bones, I vanish like a spirit at another; though I let one follower embrace My feet, and say, 'Fear not,' I repel another with the words, 'Touch Me not.' Touch Me not, for I am fast passing for your great benefit from earth to heaven, from flesh and blood into glory, from a natural body to a spiritual body. When I am ascended, then the change will be completed. To pass hence to the Father in My bodily presence, is to descend from the Father to you in spirit. When I am thus changed, when I am thus present to you, more really present than now though invisibly, then you may touch Me,[23]—may touch Me, more really though invisibly, by faith, in reverence, through such outward approaches as I shall assign. Now you but see Me from time to time; when you see most of Me I am at best but 'going in and out among you.' Thou hast seen Me, Mary, but couldst not hold Me; thou hast approached Me, but only to embrace My feet, or to be touched by My hand; and thou sayest, 'O that I knew where I might find Him, that I might come even to His seat! O that I might hold Him and not let Him go!' Henceforth this shall be; when I am ascended, thou shalt see nothing, thou shalt have everything. Thou shalt 'sit down under My shadow with great delight, and My fruit shall be sweet to thy taste.' Thou shalt have Me whole and entire. I will be near thee, I will be in thee; I will come into thy heart a whole Saviour, a whole Christ,—in all My fulness as God and man,—in the awful virtue of that Body and Blood, which

---

[†] Excerpt from *Lectures on the Doctrine of Justification* (1838), Lecture 9, sections 8 & 9.

[23] *Vid.* Leon. *Serm.* 74, c. 4, ed. Ballerin. Vigil. Taps. *contr. Eutych.* iv. *sub fin.*

has been taken into the Divine Person of the Word, and is indivisible from it, and has atoned for the sins of the world,—not by external contact, not by partial possession, not by momentary approaches, not by a barren manifestation, but inward in presence, and intimate in fruition, a principle of life and a seed of immortality, that thou mayest 'bring forth fruit unto God.'"

⚘

THIS LEADS ME to offer a suggestion as to the sense of another text, which has no great obscurity on the face of it, yet seems to mean more than cursory readers are apt to consider. I mean St. Paul's words to the Colossians,—"your life is hid with Christ in God." [Col. iii. 3.]

Now, when we come to consider these words, are they not harsh and strange, if they mean nothing more than what is contained in the popular view of them taken in our day? If life means, what men at present are content that it should mean, the life of religion and devotion, spiritual-mindedness (as it is sometimes called), is it not a very violent phrase to say, "it is hid in God?" Is it not irreverent, taken literally? Can it be made reverent without explaining away its wording? If, however, the foregoing remarks be admitted as true, we are able to take this and similar statements of Scripture literally. For it would seem that, in truth, the principle of our spiritual existence is divine, is an ineffable presence of God. Christ, who promised to make all his disciples one in God with Him, who promised that we should be in God and God in us, has made us so,—has in some mysterious way accomplished for us this great work, this stupendous privilege. It would seem, moreover, as I have said, that He has done so by ascending to the Father; that His ascent bodily is His descent spiritually; that His taking our nature up to God, is the descent of God into us; that He has truly, though in an unknown sense, taken us to God, or brought down God to us, according as we view it.[24] Thus, when St. Paul says that our life is hid with Him in God, we may suppose him to intimate that our principle of existence is no longer a mortal, earthly principle, such as Adam's after his fall, but that we are baptized and hidden anew in God's glory, in that Shekinah of light and purity which we lost when Adam fell,—that we are new-created, transformed, spiritualized, glorified in the Divine Nature,—that through the participation of Christ, we receive, as through a channel, the true Presence of God within and without us, imbuing us with sanctity and immortality. *This*, I repeat, is our justification, our ascent through Christ to God, or God's descent through Christ to us; we may call it either of the two; we ascend into Him, He descends into us; we are in Him, He in us; Christ being the

---

[24] On this subject, *vid.* the Author's *Via Media*, vol. ii., edit. 1884, pp. 235, &c.

170

One Mediator, the way, the truth, and the life, joining earth with heaven. And this is our true Righteousness,—not the mere name of righteousness, not only forgiveness or favour as an act of the Divine Mind, not only sanctification within (great indeed as these blessings would be, yet it is somewhat more),—it implies the one, it involves the other, it is the indwelling of our glorified Lord. This is the one great gift of God purchased by the Atonement, which is light instead of darkness and the shadow of death, power instead of weakness, bondage and suffering, spirit instead of the flesh, which is the token of our acceptance with God, the propitiation of our sins in His sight, and the seed and element of renovation.

Witnesses to the Christian Altar[†]

YOU WRITE as follows:—"The term Altar, as synonymous with the Lord's Table, *does not appear to have been adopted till about the end of the second century*; and then merely in a figurative sense, and *out of a spirit of accommodation*, as it should seem, to the *prejudices* of Jews and Pagans, who habitually reproached the Christians as having neither Altar nor Sacrifice," pp. 18, 19. You are of opinion that the word Altar was not used for the Lord's Table "till *about* the end of the second century." On the contrary I read it in as many as *four* out of the seven brief Epistles of St. Ignatius, at the end of the *first*. If you are right, even this glorious Saint and Martyr, the immediate companion of Apostles, acted in a "spirit of accommodation" to the "prejudices of Jews and Pagans." Do my eyes play me false in reading Ignatius, or in reading your "Revival of Popery"?

First he uses it in his Epistle to the Ephesians:—"For if I in so short a season formed such an intimacy with your Bishop, not a human but a spiritual, how much more do I call you fortunate, who are so united to him, as the Church to Jesus Christ, and Jesus Christ to the Father, that all things may be concordant in unity? Let no one err; unless a man be *within the Altar* (*entos tou thusiastēriou*) he comes short of the bread of God. For if the prayer of one and a second has such power, how much more that of the Bishop and all the Church?" §. 5.

Next, in that to the Magnesians:—"Let there be one prayer, one supplication, one mind, one hope, in love, in that joy which is irreprovable. There is one Jesus Christ to whom nought is preferable; all of you then run together as to one Temple, as *for one Altar* (*epi en thusiastērion*), as for One Jesus Christ, who is come forth from One Father, and returned again to One." §. 7.

Thirdly, in that to the Trallians:—"Guard against such [sectarians,] and this will be if we are not puffed up, nor separated from Jesus Christ our God, and the Bishop, and the ordinances of the Apostles. He who is within *the Altar* (*entos thusiastēriou*) is clean; that is, he who does any thing without Bishop, and Presbytery, and Deacons, such a one is not clean in conscience." §. 7.

Lastly, in that to the Philadelphians:—"Be careful to use one Eucharist; for the Flesh of our Lord Jesus Christ is one, and one Cup for the uniting of

---

[†] From *Letter to the Margaret Professor of Divinity on Mr. R. H. Froude's Statements on the Holy Eucharist*, in *Via Media*, vol. 2 (1838). The title of this excerpt is editorial.

His blood; *one Altar* (*en thusiastērion*), as one Bishop, together with the Presbytery, and Deacons my fellow-servants; that whatever ye do, ye may do after God." §. 4.

And while the list of ecclesiastical witnesses to the use of the word Altar for the Lord's Table begins as early as it can after the Apostles and Evangelists, (who use it also as I would contend, in Matt. v. 23. Heb. xiii. 10, but who are not at present under review,) it proceeds downwards, not only in an uninterrupted series, but with a sort of prerogative of usage; for it is very remarkable that, excepting one passage in a letter of St. Dionysius of Alexandria, no ecclesiastical writer at all is found to use the word "Table" till St. Athanasius in the fourth century; and what is also remarkable, when St. Athanasius uses it, he does so with the explanation, "that is, the Holy Altar;" as if he were not using a word commonly adopted. On the contrary, the word Altar is used after St. Ignatius by St. Irenæus, Tertullian, St. Cyprian, Origen, Eusebius, St. Athanasius, St. Ambrose, St. Gregory Nazianzen, St. Optatus, St. Jerome, St. Chrysostom, and St. Austin [Augustine].[25]

LET ME REFER to two statements in Mr. Froude's Volumes, on which you dwell, to the effect that our present Communion Service is "a judgment on the Church," and that there would be advantage in "replacing it by a good translation of the Liturgy of St. Peter." The state of the case is this; the original Eucharistic form is with good reason assigned to the Apostles and Evangelists themselves. It exists to this day under four different rites, which seem to have come from four different Apostles and Evangelists. These rites differ in some points, agree in others; among the points in which they agree, are of course those in which the Essence of the Sacrament consists. At the time of the Reformation we in common with all the West possessed the rite of the Roman Church, or St. Peter's Liturgy. This formulary is called the Canon of the Mass, and except a very few words, appears, even as now used in the Roman Church, to be free from interpolation, and thus is distinguished from the Ordinary of the Mass, which is the additional and corrupt service prefixed to it, and peculiar to Rome.[26] This sacred and most precious monument, then, of the Apostles, our Reformers received whole and entire from their predecessors; and they mutilated the tradition of 1500 years. Well was it for us that they did not discard it, that they did not touch any vital part; for through God's good provi-

---

[25] Vid. Johnson, *Unbl. Sacr.* vol. i. pp. 306–9.
[26] Newman was later to add the note: "What can this mean? The Ordinary consists of Gloria in excelsis, Collects, Epistle, Gospel, Creed, Offertory."

dence, though they broke it up and cut away portions, they did not touch life; and thus we have it at this day, a violently treated, but a holy and dear possession, more dear perhaps and precious than if it were in its full vigour and beauty, as sickness or infirmity endears to us our friends and relatives. Now the first feeling which comes upon an ardent mind, on mastering these facts, is one of indignation and impatient grief; the second, is the more becoming thought, that, as he deserves nothing at all at God's hand, and is blessed with Christian privileges only at His mere bounty, it is nothing strange that he does not enjoy every privilege which was given through the Apostles; and his third, that we are mysteriously bound up with our forefathers and bear their sin, or in other words, that our present condition is a judgment on us for what they did.

These, I conceive, to be the feelings which dictated to Mr. Froude the sentences on which you animadvert; the earlier is more ardent, the latter is more subdued. In the one he says of a friend, "I verily believe he would now gladly consent to see our Communion Service replaced by a good translation of the Liturgy of St. Peter, a name which I advise you to substitute in your notes to Hooker for the obnoxious phrase 'Mass Book.'" vol. i. p. 287. Lest any misconception of the author's meaning should arise from the use of the word "replaced," I would observe, that such "replacing" would not remove one prayer, one portion of our present Service; it would consist but of addition and re-arrangement, of a return to the original Canon.

Reliance on Religious Observances[†]

"When ye shall have done all those things which are commanded you, say,
We are unprofitable servants; we have done that which was our duty to do."
Luke xvii. 10

I F, WHEN we have done all, we are unprofitable, what are we when we
have but a part? and then again, what are we, if that part itself be defective, and defiled with evil? There is no sort of question then, that if *reason*
is to be judge, there can be no boasting towards God even on the part of His
most matured saints and exactest servants. There can, I say, be no boasting,
because whatever we do is the fruit of His grace, and because we do very little,
and because, in spite of His grace, what we do is infected with sin, and because
even if we did all, we should be doing no more than we are bound to do. I
cannot conceive any one who fairly gave his mind to consider the matter,
whatever weight he might give to this or that consideration in particular, however disposed he might be to exalt his natural powers, or his actual services,
not coming after all to this conclusion,—to this conclusion in the judgment of
reason.

And yet, it will be said, there are many persons in the world who are well
pleased with what they are and what they do, who are well satisfied with themselves, who think themselves in so fair a way for attaining heaven, that they
need not give themselves any extraordinary trouble about it; who are what is
commonly called self-righteous. Now I do not allow that those *are* self-
righteous necessarily who are *called* so, because there is among us much unfair
and harsh judging of the feelings and motives of others; but still after all there
is a state of mind which is self-righteous,—I mean a state of mind in which a
person has no serious fears of future judgment, and is well satisfied with himself. Certainly; but this is no objection to what I have been saying, for you will
find this to arise from persons *not* thinking of God. What I said just now was,
that no one who thinks seriously of Almighty God and himself, can pride
himself on his services; but this is what men in general cannot bring themselves steadily to do. Self-righteous men are men who live to the world, and do
not think of God. They do not think of judgment as sure to come one day or
another. They have no fears for the future, because they have no prospect

---

[†] *Parochial & Plain Sermons*, vol. 4 (1839), Sermon 5.

about the future. They are contented with the present, and with themselves, because they live in what is visible and tangible, and do not measure themselves by what is unseen and spiritual. "They, measuring themselves by themselves, and comparing themselves among themselves, are not wise . . . for not he that commendeth himself is approved, but whom the Lord commendeth." [2 Cor. x. 12, 18.] Worldly men are self-righteous men.

Another class of self-righteous men are they who do not believe in the Divinity and Atonement of Christ. These men, again, do not really measure themselves by a heavenly standard and by God's judgment; they measure themselves merely by their own conscience, and their conscience is dark and blind. They have low and narrow views of duty.

Once more, men who fasten their minds on any particular object of religion short of God, become self-righteous, for they narrow the field of duty, and make this object the measure of it. Hence, whether men make benevolent schemes and exertions to be the whole of their religion, or ceremonial observances, or maintenance of true doctrine, or obedience to any other portion of God's law, they are insensibly led to be satisfied with their own doings, both because of the vivid consciousness which this prominent object creates in them, that religion is their chief employment, and because of the persuasion which readily comes on them that they duly act up to it. Such was the case of the Pharisee in the parable. And if this is true in the case of objects and observances good in themselves, much more will it happen when men place their religion in such things as are not so;—the main fault in all cases being this, that the persons in question, instead of thinking anxiously of God and His law, think only of a portion of it, which they have of themselves set apart, and make it a sort of idol. On the whole, then, what I have said is true, that in spite of the existence of self-righteous men in fact, no one can really think himself meritorious in God's sight, who comes seriously to consider himself and God, apparent exceptions being those cases in which persons do not think duly of either.

This I consider to be the real state of the case; however, the popular view of spiritual pride or self-righteousness is this, that those men are self-righteous, or in great danger of being so, who come often to Church, and are diligent in their moral duties. Now this is the point on which I consider that there is a great deal of unfair and uncharitable judgment among us, persons being said to be satisfied with themselves who are really not so. However, our business is, when the world blames and slanders us, not to be vexed at it, but rather to consider whether there is any foundation for it, any truth at bottom, though there be exaggeration and mistake. I conceive a person may always gain good to his own soul, gain instruction and useful suggestions, by the mistakes of the world about him. Now then let us consider, from this hint given us by ignorant and prejudiced men, whether we, who are blessed so frequently as we are with the ordinances of the Gospel, with the privilege of Prayer and Holy Communion, are or are not in any special danger of spiritual pride, or as of late years it has been called, self-righteousness.

Now of course there *is* a danger of persons becoming self-satisfied, in being regular and exemplary in devotional exercises; there is danger, which others have not, of their so attending to them as to forget that they have other duties to attend to. I mean the danger, of which I was just now speaking, of having their attention drawn off from other duties by their very attention to this duty in particular. And what is still most likely of all, persons who are regular in their devotions may be visited with passing thoughts every now and then, that they are thereby better than other people; and these occasional thoughts may secretly tend to make them self-satisfied, without their being aware of it, till they have a latent habit of self-conceit and contempt of others. Such cases certainly are possible or probable; in none of them do persons actually rely on their merit, or boastfully plead their services in God's sight; but still those services do seem to be a snare to them, leading some of them to forget how far they are from perfection on the whole, and how much they sin; leading others to forget that they have other duties also to do; and encouraging others again in a quiet, unobtrusive self-complacency, while they still acknowledge themselves to be sinners. What is done statedly forces itself upon the mind, impresses the memory and imagination, and seems to be a *substitute* for other duties; and what is contained in definite outward acts has a completeness and tangible form about it, which is likely to *satisfy* the mind. I do not deny then there is some danger, lest persons who are frequent in devotional services should be as the Pharisees,—do nothing else, and be well contented that they do so much. Accordingly you may hear ill-natured persons, or scoffers, say severe things against those who are strict in their religious observances, as if in other respects they were *worse* than others, or were hypocritical. All this is but the language of the world, and not to be believed; still I do not deny that persons who are frequent in prayers and other religious exercises should be jealous over themselves, and not take for granted they are going on right, particularly since their very strictness is a call on them for a more exact observance of their other duties. But all this is quite a different matter, from such danger being an *objection* to observing devotional duties. If there is a danger, let it be watched and prevented, but let not the observance be omitted: there are few things which are not dangerous. All things may be perverted and abused. The great lesson set before us in the Gospel is to use the world without abusing it, and in like manner to use *God's mercies* without abusing them.

If frequent attendance at the Lord's Table or at prayers leads, unless we are watchful, to spiritual pride, our duty is *to be* watchful, not to omit attendance.

However, I do not think, after all, that there *is* any very great danger to a serious mind in the frequent use of these great privileges. Indeed, it were a strange thing to say that the simple performance of what God has told us to do *can* do harm to any but those who have not the love of God in their hearts, and to such persons all things are harmful; *they* pervert every thing into evil. It is impossible (praised be God!) that earnest and humble minds should derive any thing from Christ's ordinances but those high and ineffable blessings which are lodged in them. Christ's gifts are not snares, but mercies. Let us then see how this danger, which I have allowed to exist in devotional observances, is counteracted in the case of serious minds.

1. Now, first, the evil in question (supposing it to exist) is singularly adapted to be its own corrective. It can only do us injury when we do not know its existence. When a man knows and feels the intrusion of self-satisfied and self-complacent thoughts, here is something at once to humble him and destroy that complacency. To know of a weakness is always humbling; now humility is the very grace needed here. To know we are passionate, or slothful, or severe, is indeed the first step towards removing such defects, but does not directly tend to remove them. Knowledge of our indolence does not encourage us to exertion, but induces despondence; but to know we are self-satisfied is a direct blow to self-satisfaction. There is no satisfaction in perceiving that we are self-satisfied. No one can be self-righteous who knows and laments his proud thoughts; but a person may be slothful who knows and laments that he is slothful. Here then is one great safeguard against our priding ourselves on our observances. Evil thoughts do us no harm, if recognized, if repelled, if protested against by the indignation and self-reproach of the mind. It is when we do not discern them, when we admit them, when we cherish them, that they ripen into principles. And if this is true of all bad thoughts, much more is it of those now spoken of, which humble us on their detection as much as they elate us on their first entrance. I do not deny that the intrusion of such vain and foolish thoughts takes off from the comfort of our devotion, when they occur; but that is another matter. The question is not about comfort, but about mischief. It is no good reason for giving over devotional exercises, that we have not all the comfort from them which we might have.

2. But again, if religious persons are troubled with proud thoughts about their own excellence and strictness, I think it is only when they are young in their religion, and that the trial will wear off; and that for many reasons. I would not indeed speak with undue decision on such a point,—every one has his particular temptations; yet one should hardly think that any but minds

very young in the faith, minds to whom religion was a new thing, would pride themselves on their performances or rest upon them,—I mean, would even have the temptation to do so; for surely it does not require much keenness of spiritual sight to see how very far our best is from what it should be. Satisfaction with our own doings, as I have said, arises from fixing the mind on some *one part* of our duty, instead of attempting the whole of it. In proportion as we narrow the field of our duties, we become able to compass them. Men who pursue only this duty or only that duty, are in danger of self-righteousness;— zealots, bigots, devotees, men of the world, sectarians, are for this reason self-righteous. For the same reason, persons beginning a religious course are self-righteous, though they often think themselves just the reverse. They consider, perhaps, all religion to lie in confessing themselves sinners, and having warm feelings concerning their redemption and justification, in having what they consider faith; and, as all this is fulfilled in them, they come to think they have attained and are sure of heaven; and all because they have so very contracted a notion of the range of God's commandments, of the rounds of that ladder which reaches from earth to heaven. And in the same way, I admit that religious persons who for one reason or another are led to begin a greater strictness than hitherto in their devotional observances, in attending prayers or the Lord's Supper, or in fasting, or in almsgiving, are, on beginning, in some danger of becoming self-satisfied; for the same reason,—as fixing their minds on one certain portion of their duty and becoming excited about *it*; and this the more, inasmuch as the observances in question are something definite and precise, and on the other hand are evidently neglected by others.

But the remedy of the evil is obvious, and one which, since it will surely be applied by every religious person, because he *is* religious, will, under God's grace, effect in no long time a cure. Try to do your *whole* duty, and you will soon cease to be well-pleased with your religious state. If you are in earnest, you will try to add to your faith virtue; and the more you effect, the less will you seem to yourself to do. On the other hand, attend prayer and the Holy Eucharist without corresponding strictness in other matters; and it is plain what will follow, from the nature of the human mind, without going to more solemn considerations. The more you neglect your daily, domestic, relative, temporal, duties, the more you will prize yourself on your (I cannot call them religious, your) formal, ceremonial observances. Thus it is plain that self-satisfaction is the feeling either of a beginner, or of a very defective and negligent Christian.

3. But this is not all. Certainly this objection, that devotional practices, such as prayer, fasting, and communicating, tend to self-righteousness, is the objection of those, or at least is just what the objection of those would be, who

never attempted them. Men speak as if it was the easiest thing in the world to fast and pray, and do austerities, and as if such courses were the most seductive, easiest, pleasantest, methods of attaining heaven. I do not deny that there are certain states of society, certain ages and countries, in which they are much easier than in others; but this is true of all duties. We, for instance, of this day, find *manliness* and *candour* as easy as some eastern nations might find fasting and meditation. But that is not the question. We are what we are,—Englishmen; and for us who are active in our habits and social in our tempers, fasting and meditation have no such great attractions, and are of no such easy observance. When then an objector fears lest such observances should make him self-righteous, were he to attempt them, I do think he is over-anxious, over-confident in his own power to fulfil them; he trusts too much in his own strength already, and, depend on it, to attempt them would make him less self-righteous, not more so. He need not be so very fearful of being too good; he may assure himself that the smallest of his Lord's commandments are to a spiritual mind solemn, arduous, and inexhaustible. Is it an easy thing to pray? It *is* easy to wait for a rush of feelings, and then to let our petitions be borne upon them; and never to attempt the duty till then; but it is not at all easy to be in the habit day after day and hour after hour, in all frames of mind, and under all outward circumstances, to bring before God a calm, collected, awakened soul. It is not at all easy to keep the mind from wandering in prayer, to keep out all intrusive thoughts about other things. It is not at all easy to realize what we are about, who is before us, what we are seeking, and what our state is. It is not at all easy to throw off the world and to understand that God and Christ hear us, that Saints and Angels are standing by us, and the devil desiring to have us. What indeed *is* after all meant, by asserting that regular and stated prayers are dangerous to a sensitive and serious mind? They are dangerous to the blind and formal; but so all things are; but where is the really serious mind that will say it is easy to take delight in stated prayer, to attend to it duly? Is not at the best our delight in it transient, and our attention irregular? Is all this satisfactory and elating?

And so again of austerities; there may be persons so constituted by nature as to take pleasure in mortifications for their own sake, and to be able to practise them adequately; and *they* certainly *are* in danger of practising them for their own sakes, not through faith, and of becoming spiritually proud in consequence: but surely it is idle to speak of this as an ordinary danger.

And so again a religious mind has a perpetual source of humiliation from *this* consciousness also, viz., how far his *actual conduct in the world* falls short of the profession which his devotional observances involve. It is not a pleasant, not an inspiring, not an elating reflection, to think that you are making a profession which you must in some measure dishonour by your daily imperfections. There is nothing flattering and soothing in the thought that you are inviting the world to criticise you, and preparing it to expect more than it will find; to say nothing of the more bitter feelings which the professions and the vows of obedience, made in Church and broken in the world, cost you when thought of in God's sight. Alas! is it at all a comfort to add to the catalogue of those sins which we must answer for in the Last Day? yet this we must do, or at least run the risk of it, if we attempt those services which some persons would persuade us necessarily tend to self-righteousness.

4. But, after all, what is this shrinking from responsibility, which fears to be obedient lest it should fail, but cowardice and ingratitude? What is it but the very conduct of the Israelites, who, when Almighty God bade them encounter their enemies and so gain Canaan, feared the sons of Anak, because they were giants? To fear to do our duty lest we should become self-righteous in doing it, is to be wiser than God; it is to distrust Him; it is to do and to feel like the unprofitable servant who hid his Lord's talent, and then laid the charge of his sloth on his Lord, as being a hard and austere man. At best we are unprofitable servants when we have done all; but if we are but unprofitable when we do our best to be profitable, what are we, when we fear to do our best, but unworthy to be His servants at all? No! to *fear* the *consequences* of obedience is to be worldly-wise, and to go by reason when we are bid go by faith. Let us dare to do His commandments, leaving to Him to bring us through, who has imposed them. Let us risk dangers which cannot in truth be realized, however they threaten, since He has bid us risk them, and will protect us in them. Let us bear, what probably will befall us, the assaults of Satan, the sins of infirmity, the remains of the old Adam, involuntary mistakes, the smarting of our wounds, and the dejection and desolateness ensuing, if it be His will. He has promised to lead us safely heavenward, in spite of all things being against us; He will keep us from all wilful sin: but the infirmities which beset us, our ignorances, waywardnesses, weaknesses, and misconceptions, these He still ordains should try us and humble us, should move in us vexation of spirit and self-abasement, and should bring us day by day to the foot of His Cross for pardon. Let us then compose ourselves, and bear a firm and courageous heart. Let us steel ourselves, not against self-reproach and self-hatred, but against unmanly fear. Let us feel what we really are,—sinners attempting great things, and succeeding at best only so far as to show that we do attempt them. Let us simply obey God's will, whatever may befall; whether it tend to elate us or to depress us, what is that to us? He can turn all things to our eternal good. He can bless and sanctify even our infirmities. He can lovingly chastise us, if we be puffed up, and He can cheer us when we despond. He can and

will exalt us the more we afflict ourselves; and we shall afflict ourselves the more, in true humbleness of mind, the more we really obey Him. Blessed are they who in any matter do His will; and they are thrice blessed who, in what they are doing, are also interesting themselves, as in the case which has been under our consideration, in His special sacramental promises. Blessed indeed are they, who, while obeying God, are seeking Christ; who, while they do a duty, receive a privilege; who commemorate His death because He bids them, and while they do so gain the virtue of it in the very commemoration; who live in Him, both in the thought of Him and the possession of Him; who glory in Him who died for them, and was buried, and rose again, and now lives in their hearts; who are willing to take their part with Him, in suffering as in joy; who willingly associate themselves in that Mysterious Communion which He offers them, and which, though it brings glory in the end, brings suffering and affliction at present,—which makes them at present in a special way heirs of tears and pain and disappointment and reproach, heirs of special trials which may come upon them though they live in the most peaceful times, which may come without the world perceiving that they differ in their lot from other men, trials which work for them a far more exceeding and eternal weight of glory, and which in the present world are recompensed by the faith, humility, patience, and gentleness resulting from them.

Christe Hidden from the World[†]

"The light shineth in darkness, and the darkness comprehended it not."
John i. 5

OF ALL THE THOUGHTS which rise in the mind when contemplating the sojourn of our Lord Jesus Christ upon earth, none perhaps is more affecting and subduing than the obscurity which attended it. I do not mean His obscure condition, in the sense of its being humble; but the obscurity in which He was shrouded, and the secrecy which He observed. This characteristic of His first Advent is referred to very frequently in Scripture, as in the text, "The light shineth in darkness, and the darkness comprehended it not;" and is in contrast with what is foretold about His second Advent. Then "every eye shall see Him;" which implies that all shall recognize Him; whereas, when He came for the first time, though many saw Him, few indeed discerned Him. It had been prophesied, "When we shall see Him there is no beauty that we should desire Him;" and at the very end of his ministry, He said to one of His twelve chosen friends, "Have I been so long time with you, and yet hast thou not known Me, Philip?" [Isai. liii. 2. John xiv. 9.]

I propose to set before you one or two thoughts which arise from this very solemn circumstance, and which may, through God's blessing, be profitable.

1. And first, let us review some of the circumstances which marked His sojourn when on earth.

His condescension in coming down from heaven, in leaving His Father's glory and taking flesh, is so far beyond power of words or thought, that one might consider at first sight that it mattered little whether He came as a prince or a beggar. And yet after all, it *is* much more wonderful that He came in low estate, for this reason; because it might have been thought beforehand, that, though He condescended to come on earth, yet He would not submit to be overlooked and despised: now the rich are not despised by the world, and the poor are. If He had come as a great prince or noble, the world without knowing a whit more that He was God, yet would at least have looked up to Him and honoured Him, as being a prince; but when He came in a low estate, He

---

[†] *Parochial & Plain Sermons*, vol. 4 (1839), Sermon 16, preached on Christmas Day.

took upon him one additional humiliation, *contempt,*—being contemned, scorned, rudely passed by, roughly profaned by His creatures.

What were the actual circumstances of His coming? His Mother is a poor woman; she comes to Bethlehem to be taxed, travelling, when her choice would have been to remain at home. She finds there is no room in the inn; she is obliged to betake herself to a stable; she brings forth her firstborn Son, and lays Him in a manger. That little babe, so born, so placed, is none other than the Creator of heaven and earth, the Eternal Son of God.

Well; He was born of a poor woman, laid in a manger, brought up to a lowly trade, that of a carpenter; and when He began to preach the Gospel He had not a place to lay His head: lastly, He was put to death, to an infamous and odious death, the death which criminals then suffered.

For the three last years of His life, He preached the Gospel, I say, as we read in Scripture; but He did not begin to do so till He was thirty years old. For the first thirty years of His life, He seems to have lived, just as a poor man would live now. Day after day, season after season, winter and summer, one year and then another, passed on, as might happen to any of us. He passed from being a babe in arms to being a child, and then He became a boy, and so He grew up "like a tender plant," increasing in wisdom and stature; and then He seems to have followed the trade of Joseph, His reputed father; going on in an ordinary way without any great occurrence, till He was thirty years old. How very wonderful is all this! that He should live here, doing nothing great, so long; living here, as if for the sake of living; not preaching, or collecting disciples, or apparently in any way furthering the cause which brought Him down from heaven. Doubtless there were deep and wise reasons in God's counsels for His going on so long in obscurity; I only mean, that *we* do not know them.

And it is remarkable that those who were about Him, seem to have treated Him as one of their equals. His brethren, that is, His near relations, His cousins, did not believe in him. And it is very observable, too, that when He began to preach and a multitude collected, we are told, "When His friends heard of it they went out to lay hold on Him; for they said, He is beside himself." [Mark iii. 21.] They treated Him as we might be disposed, and rightly, to treat any ordinary person now, who began to preach in the streets. I say "rightly," because such persons generally preach a *new* Gospel, and therefore must be wrong. Also, they preach without being sent, and against authority; all which is wrong too. Accordingly we are often tempted to say that such people are "beside themselves," or mad, and not unjustly. It is often charitable to say so, for it is better to be mad than to be disobedient. Well, what we should say of such persons, this is what our Lord's friends said of Him. They had lived so long with Him, and yet did not know Him; did not understand what He was. They saw nothing to mark a difference between Him and them. He was dressed as others, He ate and drank as others, He came in and went out, and spoke, and walked, and slept, as others. He was in all respects a man, except that He did not sin; and this great difference the many would not detect, because none of us understands those who are much better than himself: so that Christ, the sinless Son of God, might be living close to us, and we not discover it.

2. I say that Christ, the sinless Son of God, might be living now in the world as our next door neighbour, and perhaps we not find it out. And this is a thought that should be dwelt on. I do not mean to say that there are not a number of persons, who we could be sure were not Christ; of course, no persons who lead bad and irreligious lives. But there are a number of persons who are in no sense irreligious, or open to serious blame, who are very much like each other at first sight, yet in God's eyes are very different. I mean the great mass of what are called respectable men, who vary very much: some are merely decent and outwardly correct persons, and have no great sense of religion, do not deny themselves, have no ardent love of God, but love the world; and, whereas their interest lies in being regular and orderly, or they have no strong passions, or have early got into the way of being regular, and their habits are formed accordingly, they are what they are, decent and correct, but very little more. But there are others who look just the same to the world, who in their hearts are very different; they make no great show, they go on in the same quiet ordinary way as the others, but really they are training to be saints in Heaven. They do all they can to change themselves, to become like God, to obey God, to discipline themselves, to renounce the world; but they do it in secret, both because God tells them so to do, and because they do not like it to be known. Moreover, there are a number of others between these two with more or less of worldliness and more or less of faith. Yet they all look about the same, to common eyes, because true religion is a hidden life in the heart; and though it cannot exist without deeds, yet these are for the most part secret deeds, secret charities, secret prayers, secret self-denials, secret struggles, secret victories.

Of course in proportion as persons are brought out into public life, they will be seen and scrutinized, and (in a certain sense) known more; but I am talking of the ordinary condition of people in private life, such as our Saviour was for thirty years; and these look very like each other. And there are so many of them, that unless we get very near them, we cannot see any distinction between one and another; we have no means to do so, and it is no business of ours. And yet, though we have no right to judge others, but must leave this to

God, it is very certain that a really holy man, a true saint, though he looks like other men, still has a sort of secret power in him to attract others to him who are like-minded, and to influence all who have any thing in them like him. And thus it often becomes a test, whether we are like-minded with the Saints of God, whether they have influence over us. And though we have no means of knowing at the time who are God's own Saints, yet after all is over we have; and then on looking back on what is past, perhaps after they are dead and gone, if we knew them, we may ask ourselves what power they had over us, whether they attracted us, influenced us, humbled us, whether they made our hearts burn within us. Alas! too often we shall find that we were close to them for a long time, had means of knowing them, and knew them not; and that is a heavy condemnation on us, indeed. Now this was singularly exemplified in our Saviour's history, by how much He was so very holy. The holier a man is, the less he is understood by men of the world. All who have any spark of living faith will understand him in a measure, and the holier he is, they will, for the most part, be attracted the more; but those who serve the world will be blind to him, or scorn and dislike him, the holier he is. This, I say, happened to our Lord. He was All-holy, but "the light shined in darkness, and the darkness comprehended it not." His near relations did not believe in Him. And if this was really so, and for the reason I have said, it surely becomes a question whether we should have understood Him better than they: whether though he had been our next door neighbour, or one of our family, we should have distinguished Him from any one else, who was correct and quiet in his deportment; or rather, whether we should not, though we respected Him, (alas, what a word! what language towards the Most High God!) yet even if we went as far as this, whether we should not have thought Him strange, eccentric, extravagant, and fanciful. Much less should we have detected any sparks of that glory which He had with the Father before the world was, and which was merely hidden not quenched by His earthly tabernacle. This, truly, is a very awful thought; because if He were near us for any long time, and we did not see any thing wonderful in Him, we might take it as a clear proof that we were not His, for "His sheep know His voice, and follow Him;" we might take it as a clear proof that we should not know Him, or admire His greatness, or adore His glory, or love His excellency, if we were admitted to His presence in heaven.

3. And here we are brought to another most serious thought, which I will touch upon. We are very apt to wish we had been born in the days of Christ, and in this way we excuse our misconduct, when conscience reproaches us. We say, that had we had the advantage of being with Christ, we should have had stronger motives, stronger restraints against sin. I answer, that so far

from our sinful habits being reformed by the presence of Christ, the chance is, that those same habits would have hindered us from recognizing Him. We should not have known He was present; and if He had even told us who He was, we should not have believed Him. Nay, had we seen His miracles (incredible as it may seem), even they would not have made any lasting impression on us. Without going into this subject, consider only the possibility of Christ being close to us, even though He did no miracle, and our not knowing it; yet I believe this literally would have been the case with most men. But enough on this subject. What I am coming to is this: I wish you to observe what a fearful light this casts upon our prospects in the next world. We think heaven must be a place of happiness to us, if we do but get there; but the great probability is, if we can judge by what goes on here below, that a bad man, if brought to heaven, would not know He was in heaven;—I do not go to the further question, whether, on the contrary, the very fact of his being in heaven with all his unholiness upon him, would not be a literal torment to him, and light up the fires of hell within him. This indeed would be a most dreadful way of finding out where he was. But let us suppose a lighter case: let us suppose he could remain in heaven unblasted, yet it would seem that at least he would not know that he was there. He would see nothing wonderful there. Could men come nearer to God than when they seized Him, struck Him, spit on Him, hurried Him along, stripped him, stretched out His limbs upon the cross, nailed Him to it, raised it up, stood gazing on Him, jeered Him, gave Him vinegar, looked close whether He was dead, and then pierced Him with a spear? O dreadful thought, that the nearest approaches man has made to God upon earth have been in blasphemy! Whether of the two came closer to Him, St. Thomas, who was allowed to reach forth his hand and reverently touch His wounds, and St. John, who rested on His bosom, or the brutal soldiers who profaned Him limb by limb, and tortured Him nerve by nerve? His Blessed Mother, indeed, came closer still to Him; and we, if we be true believers, still closer, who have Him really, though spiritually, within us; but this is another, an inward sort of approach. Of those who approached Him externally, they came nearest, who knew nothing about it. So it is with sinners: they would walk close to the throne of God; they would stupidly gaze at it; they would touch it; they would meddle with the holiest things; they would go on intruding and prying, not meaning any thing wrong by it, but with a sort of brute curiosity, till the avenging lightnings destroyed them;—all because they have no *senses* to guide them in the matter. Our bodily senses tell us of the approach of good or evil on earth. By sound, by scent, by feeling we know what is happening to us. We know when we are exposing ourselves to the weather, when we are exerting ourselves too much. We have warnings, and feel we must not neglect them.

187

Now, sinners have no spiritual senses; they can presage nothing; they do not know what is going to happen the next moment to them. So they go fearlessly further and further among precipices, till on a sudden they fall, or are smitten and perish. Miserable beings! and this is what sin does for immortal souls; that they should be like the cattle which are slaughtered at the shambles, yet touch and smell the very weapons which are to destroy them!

4. But you may say, how does this concern us? Christ is not here; *we* cannot thus or in any less way insult His Majesty. Are we so sure of this? Certainly we cannot commit such open blasphemy; but it is another matter whether we cannot commit as great. For often sins are greater which are less startling; insults more bitter, which are not so loud; and evils deeper, which are more subtle. Do we not recollect a very awful passage? "Whosoever speaketh a word against the Son of man, it shall be forgiven him; but whosoever speaketh against the Holy Ghost, it shall not be forgiven him." [Matt. xii. 32.] Now, I am not deciding whether or not this denunciation can be fulfilled in the case of Christians now, though when we recollect that we *are* at present under the ministration of that very Spirit of whom our Saviour speaks, this is a very serious question; but I quote it to show that there may be sins greater even than insult and injury offered to Christ's Person, though we should think that impossible, and though they could not be so flagrant or open. With this thought let it be considered:—

First, that Christ is still on earth. He said expressly that He would come again. The Holy Ghost's coming is so really His coming, that we might as well say that He was not here in the days of His flesh, when He was visibly in this world, as deny that He is here now, when He is here by His Divine Spirit. This indeed is a mystery, how God the Son and God the Holy Ghost, two Persons, can be one, how He can be in the Spirit and the Spirit in Him; but so it is.

Next, if He is still on earth, yet is not visible (which cannot be denied), it is plain that He keeps Himself still in the condition which He chose in the days of His flesh. I mean, He is a hidden Saviour, and may be approached (unless we are careful) without due reverence and fear. I say, wherever He is (for that is a further question), still He is here, and again He is secret; and whatever be the tokens of His Presence, still they must be of a nature to admit of persons doubting where it is; and if they will argue, and be sharpwitted and subtle, they may perplex themselves and others, as the Jews did even in the days of His flesh, till He seems to them nowhere present on earth now. And when they come to think him far away, of course they *feel* it to be impossible so to insult Him as the Jews did of old; and if nevertheless He *is* here, they *are* perchance approaching and insulting Him, though they so feel. And this was just the case of the Jews, for they too were ignorant what they were doing. It is probable, then, that we can now commit at least as great blasphemy towards Him as the Jews did first, because we are under the dispensation of that Holy Spirit, against whom even more heinous sins *can* be committed; next, because His presence now as little witnesses of itself, or is impressive to the many, as His bodily presence formerly.

We see a further reason for this apprehension, when we consider what the tokens of His presence now are; for they will be found to be of a nature easily to lead men into irreverence, unless they be humble and watchful. For instance, the Church is called "His Body:" what His material Body was when He was visible on earth, such is the Church now. It is the instrument of His Divine power; it is that which we must approach, to gain good from Him; it is that which by insulting we awaken His anger. Now, what is the Church but, as it were, a body of humiliation, almost provoking insult and profaneness, when men do not live by faith? an earthen vessel, far more so even than His body of flesh, for that was at least pure from all sin, and the Church is defiled in all her members. We know that her ministers at best are but imperfect and erring, and of like passions with their brethren; yet of them He has said, speaking not to the Apostles merely but to all the seventy disciples (to whom Christian ministers are in office surely equal), "He that heareth you, heareth Me, and he that despiseth you, despiseth Me, and he that despiseth Me, despiseth Him that sent Me."

Again: He has made the poor, weak, and afflicted, tokens and instruments of His Presence; and here again, as is plain, the same temptation meets us to neglect or profane it. What He was, such are His chosen followers in this world; and as His obscure and defenceless state led men to insult and ill-treat Him, so the like peculiarities, in the tokens of His Presence, lead men to insult Him now. That such are His tokens is plain from many passages of Scripture: for instance, He says of children, "Whoso shall receive one such little child in My Name, receiveth Me." Again: He said to Saul, who was persecuting His followers, "Why persecutest thou Me?" And He forewarns us, that at the Last Day He will say to the righteous, "I was an hungered, and ye gave Me meat; I was thirsty, and ye gave Me drink; I was a stranger, and ye took Me in; naked, and ye clothed Me; I was sick, and ye visited Me; I was in prison, and ye came unto Me." And He adds, "Inasmuch as ye have done it unto the least of these My brethren, ye have done it unto Me." [Matt. xviii. 5. Acts ix. 4. Matt. xxv. 35–40.] He observes the same connexion between Himself and His followers in His words to the wicked. What makes this passage the more awful and apposite, is this, which has been before now remarked,[27] that neither righteous

---

[27] *Vide* Pascal's Thoughts [*Pensées*].

nor wicked *knew* what they had done; even the righteous are represented as unaware that they had approached Christ. They say, "Lord, *when* saw we Thee an hungered, and fed Thee, or thirsty, and gave Thee drink?" In every age, then, Christ is both in the world, and yet not publicly so more than in the days of His flesh.

And a similar remark applies to His Ordinances, which are at once most simple, yet most intimately connected with Him. St. Paul, in his First Epistle to the Corinthians, shows both how easy and how fearful it is to profane the Lord's Supper, while he states how great the excess of the Corinthians had been, yet also that it was a want of "*discerning* the Lord's Body." When He was born into the world, the world knew it not. He was laid in a rude manger, among the cattle, but "all the Angels of God worshipped Him." Now too He is present upon a table, homely perhaps in make, and dishonoured in its circumstances; and faith adores, but the world passes by.

Let us then pray Him ever to enlighten the eyes of our understanding, that we may belong to the Heavenly Host, not to this world. As the carnal-minded would not perceive Him even in Heaven, so the spiritual heart may approach Him, possess Him, see Him, even upon earth.

The Gainsaying of Korah[†]

"Woe unto them; for they have gone in the way of Cain,
and ran greedily after the error of Balaam for reward,
and perished in the gainsaying of Core."
Jude 11

THERE ARE two special sins which trouble the Church, and are denounced in Scripture, ambition and avarice, the sin of Korah and the sin of Balaam; both of which are spoken of in the text. The sin of Balaam is denounced again and again by St. Paul, in his Epistles to Timothy and Titus; as where he says, "A Bishop must be . . . not greedy of filthy lucre . . . not covetous;" "the Deacons must be . . . not greedy of filthy lucre;" noticing the while that some supposed that "gain was godliness," and "taught things which they ought not for filthy lucre's sake." [1 Tim. iii. 8; vi. 5. Tit. i. 7, 11.] And the sin of Korah, or ambition, is condemned by our Lord, when He commands, Whosoever will be great among you, let him be your minister; by St. James, when he says, "Be not many masters, knowing that we shall receive the greater condemnation;" and by St. Paul, when he directs that a Bishop should not be a "novice, lest being lifted up with pride he fall into the condemnation of the devil." [Matt. xx. 26. James iii. 1. 1 Tim. iii. 6.] And both sins together are spoken of by St. Peter, in his exhortation to the Elders to "feed the flock of God . . . not for filthy lucre, but of a ready mind; neither as being lords over God's heritage, but being ensamples to the flock." [1 Pet. v. 2, 3.]

Accordingly, these are the two sins brought before us by our Church in the first lessons of the first Sunday after Easter, which is, as it were, the festival in commemoration of the Ministerial Commission. After celebrating the resurrection of Christ, when He became "a Priest for ever after the order of Melchizedek," we proceed to make mention of the means which He has instituted for exercising His Priesthood on earth continually,—for commemorating and applying in the Spirit, among His elect people, again and again, day after day, to the end of the world, that atoning death and glorious resurrection, which He wrought out once for all in His own person on Calvary. He Himself instituted that means on the very day that He rose from the dead, ordaining man,

---

[†] *Parochial & Plain Sermons*, vol. 4 (1839), Sermon 18.

frail and fallible as he is, to be the vessel of His gifts, and to represent Him. When He was risen, He did not first show Himself to His enemies, nor manifest the Spirit, nor unfold His new law, nor destroy the Temple; but He consecrated His Ministers: "As My Father hath sent Me," He said to His Apostles, "even so send I you." And, as if after His pattern, we too, even at this day, follow up the celebration of His "taking to Himself His great power," with that of His delegating it to His Church, as the Gospel selected for the same Sunday shows.

Of such high importance then, in our Church's judgment, is the subject of the Christian Ministry; so intimately connected with the Divine scheme of mercy, so full of reverence and awe. This will be best seen by proceeding, as I shall now do, to consider the lesson derived from the rebellion of Korah, Dathan, and Abiram, which, though properly belonging to the Old Covenant, our Church certainly considers applicable to us Christians.

The history in question contains an account, not only of the ambition of Korah himself, who was a Levite or minister, but of the rebellion of Dathan and Abiram, who were not ministers, but, as we now speak, laymen.

In considering it, I shall confine myself to this point, viz. to determine the feelings and circumstances under which these wicked men rebelled against Moses and Aaron, and that, with a view of warning those who speak lightly of schism, separation, and dissent, in this day. For I think it will be seen that they are feelings and circumstances which prevail very widely now as well as then, and, if they do prevail, are as evil now as they were then; St. Jude, in the text plainly intimating that such gainsaying as Korah's is a sin in a Christian, as well as formerly in the Jews, and that those who commit it are in the way to perish. This, then, is a very serious thought; considering, as I have said, how men in these days make light of it.

The outline of the history of Korah, Dathan, and Abiram is this: they rebelled against Moses and Aaron, and in consequence Dathan and Abiram were swallowed up by an earthquake, and Korah's company was burnt with fire. Now, then let us proceed to the remarks proposed.

1. First, then, let the number and dignity of the offenders be observed. They seem to have been some of the most eminent and considerable persons in Israel. Dathan and Abiram's party are said more than once, with some emphasis, to have been "famous in the congregation, men of renown." [Numb. xvi. 2; xxvi. 9.] Moreover there were among them as many as two hundred and fifty *princes*, or as we should now say, noblemen. A very great and formidable opposition to Moses and Aaron was it, when so great a number of eminent persons rebelled against, or (in modern language) became dissenters from the Church. Nor was this all,—a portion of God's appointed ministers joined

them. The Levites, as we all know, were the especially holy tribe: a portion of them, viz. the family of Aaron, were priests; but all of them were ministers. Such was Korah; but, dissatisfied with being merely what God had made him, he aspired to be something more, to have the priesthood. And it appears that just as many of his brethren joined him in his rebellion as there were princes who joined Dathan and Abiram. Two hundred and fifty Levites, or ministers, were banded together in this opposition to Moses, forming, from their rank and number a body (to use once more modern language) of very high respectability, to say the least, that is, respectability in the eyes of men.

2. Next, let us observe how confident they were that they were right. They seemed to have entertained no kind of doubt or hesitation. When Moses denounced Dathan and Abiram, and bade all those who wished to escape their curse, to "depart" at once "from the tents of those wicked men," "Dathan and Abiram came out, and stood in the door of their tents, and their wives, and their sons, and their little children." You see they had no misgivings, no fears, no perplexity; they saw their way clear; they were sure they were in the right; and they came out, to stand any test, any sentence of wrath which Moses might attempt, as thinking that nothing could come of it. Nor was Korah's confidence less. Moses challenged him and the rest to appear before God, to perform the priest's office, and so to stand the test whether or not He would accept them; and they promptly accepted the proposal. They were to "take their censers, and put fire therein, and put incense in them before the Lord," "and it shall be, that the man whom the Lord doth choose, he shall be holy." Korah and his company accordingly "stood in the door of the tabernacle of the congregation with Moses and Aaron;" nay, in that sacred and awful place, where was the glory of the Lord visibly displayed, did Korah endure to "gather all *the congregation*" against Moses and Aaron. Sceptics, were there such standing by, might have made the remark, that both parties were equally sincere, equally confident; and therefore neither was more pleasing to God than the other.

Such was the confidence of Korah, Dathan, and Abiram, of the two hundred and fifty princes or nobles, and the two hundred and fifty ministers of God. And we, who believe that in spite of their confidence Almighty God was against them, are perhaps at first sight tempted to attribute it to some extraordinary infatuation, judicial blindness, special hard-heartedness, or the like,—something quite out of the way, peculiar perhaps to the Jews,—something which cannot happen now. We cannot comprehend how their confidence could possibly be based on *reason*—I do not say on correct reason, but on even *apparent* reason. We do not consider that perhaps they *thought* they had good reasons for what they did, as we often think in our own case, when we really have not. Rather we attribute their conduct to something irrational, to pride, obstinacy, or hatred of the truth, as indeed it was in its origin; but I mean, to some such evil principle operating on the soul *at once*, and not operating on it *through* the pretence of reason, not so operating as to be hidden whether from themselves or others. And thus we lose the lesson which this solemn history is calculated to convey to us at this day; because, since the opposition made to God's Church in these days is professedly based upon reason, not upon mere prejudice, passion, or wilfulness, persons think that the confidence with which they oppose themselves to it, is a very different sort of confidence from that of Korah, Dathan, and Abiram, whereas it is really very much the same.

3. What, then, were the reasons or arguments which made Korah, Dathan, and Abiram so confident they were in the right,—so confident, that they even ventured to appeal to God, and to rise up against Moses and Aaron as if in the Name of the Lord? Their ground was this: they accused Moses and Aaron of what is now called *priestcraft*. Let us pay attention to this circumstance.

Now, let it be observed, that there were many rebellions of the people, founded on open and professed *unbelief*. This was not the character of the particular sin under review: it was not a disbelief in God, but in Moses. Distrust in Moses, indeed, was mixed up in all their rebellions; but generally their rebellion was more strictly directed against Almighty God. Thus, when the spies returned, and spread about an evil report of the good land, and the people believed them, this implied a disbelief in the Divine Arm altogether, as manifested in their deliverance and protection. Thus they complained of the manna; and thus they went out on the seventh day to gather it. But it is remarkable, that in the rebellion before us, there is no hint of the promoters of it disbelieving in the power or providence of God over the chosen people; only they accuse Moses of altering or (as we should say) corrupting the divine system. Dathan and Abiram were sons of Reuben, the first-born of the tribes: they might consider that Moses was interfering with their prerogative by birth to lead and govern the people. But, any how, they seem to have relied on their rank and eminence; they and their companions were "famous in the congregation, men of renown," and they could not bring themselves to submit to God's appointment, by which the nation was formed into a Church, and Levi was chosen, at God's inscrutable will, to be the priest instead of Reuben. Accordingly, far from denying that God was with the nation, they maintained it; they only said that He was not specially with Moses and Aaron; they only claimed an equality of honour and power with Moses and Aaron; they only denounced Moses and Aaron as usurpers, tyrants, and hypocrites. Far from

194

showing any scoffing or lightness of mind, or profaneness, such as Esau's who rejected the blessing, they so esteemed it as to claim it as their own, in all its fulness; nay, they claimed it for the whole people. They were only opposed to what is now called *exclusiveness*; they were champions of the rights of the people against what they called the encroachments, the arrogant pretensions, the priestcraft of Moses their Lawgiver, and Aaron the Saint of the Lord. They said, "Ye take too much upon you, seeing *all* the congregation are holy, *every one of them*; and the Lord is among them; wherefore then lift ye up yourselves *above* the congregation of the Lord?" Their objection was, that Moses was interposing himself as a mediator between God and them,—limiting the mercies of God, restraining the freedom, obscuring the glory of His grace, and robbing them of their covenanted privileges; that he had instituted an order of priests, whereas they were *all* priests, every one, and needed no human assistance, no voice or advice, or direction, or performance, from fallible man, from men of like passions and imperfections with themselves, in order to approach God withal, and serve Him acceptably. "*All* the congregation are holy," say they, "every one of them; and the Lord is among them." "The Lord is not far off; He is not in the clouds only, He is not on Sinai, He is not on the mercy-seat, He is not with Aaron; but He is among us, in the congregation, as near one man as another, as near to all of us as He is to Moses." Their partisans affect the same tone even after God's judgment has fallen on the rebels. The people say to Moses and Aaron, "Ye have killed the people of the Lord." Yes; they call those separatists and schismatists "the Lord's people," and they accuse Moses and Aaron forsooth of having, by some device of juggling priests, some strange and diabolical stratagem, some secret of magic or science, compassed the death of their enemies, while they pretended to refer it to a miraculous judgment; and they seem as if to pride themselves on their discernment, on the clearness of intellectual vision by which they saw through the fraud, and brought it home to the impostors.

Awful guilt indeed in these self-wise men, if this representation be true! yet it is apparently true, as the words show with which the rebels themselves answer the summons of Moses to come to him. "Wilt thou," say they, "put out the eyes of these men? we will not come up." No; we have eyes; we are not mere dull, brutish, superstitious bigots, to crouch before a priest, and submit to his yoke of bondage; we can reason, we can argue, we are resolved to exercise our free unfettered private judgment, and to determine (candidly indeed and dispassionately), but still to determine for ourselves before we act. We will indeed give a fair hearing to what is told us; we will listen with a becoming deference and with all patience, nay with a sort of consideration and prepossession to what you, O Moses and Aaron, say to us; but still we will not have

195

our eyes put out. No, seeing is believing; we will not go by instinctive feeling, by conscience, by mere probabilities; but everything shall be examined in a rational and enlightened way, everything searched, and sifted, and scrutinized, and rigidly tested, before it is admitted. The burden of proof lies with you; till you have proved to us your claims, we will not go up, we will not obey. To tell the truth, we are suspicious of you. We are "jealous with a godly jealousy" (alas! for men do so speak!) of any encroachments on our spiritual liberty, any assumption of superior holiness, superior acceptableness in one of us over another. We are all brethren, we are all equal, all independent. "Wilt thou make thyself altogether a prince over us?" "Moreover," they continue, "thou hast not brought us into a land that floweth with milk and honey, or given us inheritance of fields and vineyards;" or as men now speak, The present system does not work well; there are many abuses, abundant need of reform, much still undone which should be done, much idleness, much inefficiency, many defects in the Church. We see it quite plainly. Do not seek to defend yourselves. "Wilt thou put out the eyes of these men? we will not come up."

Something of the same kind of spirit had already shown itself in the sin of the golden calf, though that sin was open idolatry. Then also the people thought that they had found a better religion than Moses had taught them. They were far from denying God's miraculous providences; but they said that Moses had taken to himself what belonged to the nation; he had taught them in his own way, and they had a right to choose for themselves. "Up," they said, "make us gods, which shall go before us; for as for this Moses, the man that brought us up out of the land of Egypt, we wot not what is become of him." [Exod. xxxii. 1.] And where was Moses? He was with God in prayer and vision. They did not know, or at least understand this. So they said, "What a time for a ruler to be absent! in what a crisis! how much is there that wants doing!—forty days are gone, and he is still away. Is he lost? has he left us here to ourselves? is he feigning any communication from heaven? any how, what binds us to *him*? We are bound indeed to the God who has brought us out of Egypt, but not to the rule of Moses or the line of Aaron." Moses was away; and where was Aaron?—where? the people could not ask, for they were partakers in his sin, rather, they had forced him into their sin, the sin of the golden calf. Aaron was receiving their gold ornaments, and was moulding them into an idol. Alas! the people could not accuse him, who had seduced him into the sin. But there *were* those who might, who did complain; and who they were, since I have been led to the subject, it will be found to our present purpose to inquire.

They were the Levites. While Aaron sinned, they, the inferior ministers, stood silent, but wondering and distressed. These had no part in the sin; and when Moses came down from the mount and said, "Who is on the Lord's side?" [Exod. xxii. 26.] then they, and they only, answered the call. "All the sons of Levi gathered themselves together unto him;" and when he ordered them, they promptly "put every man his sword by his side, and went in and out from gate to gate throughout the camp, and slew every man his brother, and every man his companion, and every man his neighbour;" and "there fell of the people that day about three thousand men." This is considered in Scripture [Exod. xxxii. 29] the act of consecration by which the Levites became the sacred tribe; so that their advancement to the ministerial office is historically coincident with Aaron's temporary defection from his more sacred duties in it. All this had happened, as some suppose shortly before, as others think as much as twenty years before, the occurrence which has been under our immediate review; but whether or not the one occurrence, as has been reasonably conjectured, led to the other, whether or not Korah's stouthearted rebellion was the result[28] of ambitious views in the Levites, which their advancement to the sacred ministry had occasioned, still certain it is that at this time "it seemed but a small thing unto them" (in Moses' words) "that the God of Israel had separated them from the congregation of Israel, to bring them near to Himself to do the service of the tabernacle of the Lord, and to stand before the congregation to minister unto them;" and "they sought the priesthood also," Aaron's portion, on whom they were appointed to attend. [Numb. iii. 10.] And the circumstance that Aaron had failed on that trying occasion when they were rewarded, might dispose them to contemn him at this time, not recollecting that God's will made the difference between man and man, and that He who gave them His covenanted blessings through bulls and calves, might also vouchsafe them, did it please Him, through frail and erring men; and might dispense with inward perfection, and take up with mere earthen vessels, and be content with faith instead of consistent obedience, as He dispensed with eloquence, or wisdom, or strength. Such then were the circumstances under which the Levites rebelled, being elated by their existing privileges, as the Reubenites were stimulated by jealousy.

The parties then concerned in this formidable conspiracy were not besotted idolaters; they were not infidels; they were not obstinate, prejudiced, unreasoning zealots; they were not the victims of unscrupulous and desperate ambition; but though ambitious, proud, head-strong, obstinate, unbelieving, they veiled all these bad principles, even from their own conscience, under a show of reason, of clear, simple, straightforward, enlightened reason, under a plain argument open to the meanest capacity: "*All* the congregation," they said, "were holy, *every one*." God had signified no exception or exclusion; all

---

[28] Vid. Patrick on Numb. xvi. 2.

had been baptized in the Red Sea, all had been at Sinai. Moses, however, thus they might speak, had added to this simple and primitive religion a system of his own, a system of priestcraft. The especial favours which God had shown Moses were done twenty years before, and could be denied without much chance of contradiction; or if the rebellion took place (as others say) shortly after the Exodus, then it came close upon Aaron's sin in the matter of the golden calf. Any how, an excuse was easily found for explaining away the authority of Moses and Aaron, for denying the priesthood, and accusing it of being a corruption; and for professing to be the champions of a pure and enlightened, and uncorrupt worship,—a worship which would be quite clear of the idolatrous acts of Aaron, because in it Aaron's prerogative would be destroyed altogether.

Such is the history of the Church in the wilderness, in which we see as in a type the history of the Gospel. And how did it end? I stated in the commencement. The earth opened, and swallowed up Dathan, and covered the congregation of Abiram, their houses, their families, their possessions, and all that belonged to them. Fire went out from the Lord, and consumed the two hundred and fifty men who offered incense.

A very few words will suffice to suggest the lesson to be derived from this awful history; it is this:—If the Old Testament is still our rule of duty, except in such details as imply a local religion and a material sanctuary; if it is our rule of duty in its principles, its doctrines, its precepts; if the Gospel is but the fulfilment and development of the Law: if the parts in both are the same, only the circumstances without and the Spirit within new; if though Circumcision is abolished, yet there is Baptism instead of it; the Passover abolished, yet Holy Communion instead; the Sabbath abolished, yet instead of it the Lord's Day; if the two tables of stone which contained the Law are destroyed, yet the Sermon on the Mount takes their place; if though Moses is gone, Christ is come; and if in like manner, though Aaron is gone and his priestly line, another order of priests is come instead; (and unless this is so, the Old Testament is in a great measure but a dead letter to Christians; and if there be but a chance that it is so, and if it has always been taken to be so, it is a most serious matter to act as if it were not so;) how great must be the sin of resisting the ministers of Christ, or of intruding into their office! How great the sin of presuming to administer the rites of the Church, to baptize, to celebrate the Holy Communion, or to ordain, or to bless, without a commission! Korah's sin was kept in remembrance for ever on the covering of the Altar, "to be a memorial," says the inspired writer, "that no stranger which is not of the seed of Aaron, come near to offer incense before the Lord, that he be not as Korah and his company;" in other words (as the warning is to be interpreted now), "that no one, who is not descended from the Apostles by laying on of hands, come near to perform the ministerial office before the Lord, that he be not such as Korah and his company." Many, you will say, intrude into it in this day in ignorance. True, it is so. Therefore, for them let us pray in our Lord's words, "Father, forgive them, for they know not what they do."

Keeping Fast and Festival[†]

"A time to weep, and a time to laugh: a time to mourn, and a time to dance."
Eccles. iii. 4

A T CHRISTMAS we joy with the natural, unmixed joy of children, but at
Easter our joy is highly wrought and refined in its character. It is not
the spontaneous and inartificial outbreak which the news of Redemption might occasion, but it is thoughtful; it has a long history before it, and
has run through a long course of feelings before it becomes what it is. It is a
last feeling and not a first. St. Paul describes its nature and its formation, when
he says, "Tribulation worketh patience, and patience experience, and experience hope; and hope maketh not ashamed, because the love of God is shed
abroad in our hearts by the Holy Ghost which is given unto us." [Rom. v. 3–
5.] And the prophet Isaiah, when he says, "They joy before Thee according to
the joy in harvest, and as men rejoice when they divide the spoil." [Isa. ix. 3.]
Or as it was fulfilled in the case of our Lord Himself, who, as being the Cap-
tain of our salvation, was made perfect through sufferings. Accordingly,
Christmas Day is ushered in with a time of awful expectation only, but Easter
Day with the long fast of Lent, and the rigours of the Holy Week just past:
and it springs out and (as it were) is born of Good Friday.

On such a day, then, from the very intensity of joy which Christians
ought to feel, and the trial which they have gone through, they will often be
disposed to say little. Rather, like sick people convalescent, when the crisis is
past, the illness over, but strength not yet come, they will go forth to the light
of day and the freshness of the air, and silently sit down with great delight under the shadow of that Tree, whose fruit is sweet to their taste. They are disposed rather to muse and be at peace, than to use many words; for their joy
has been so much the child of sorrow, is of so transmuted and complex a nature, so bound up with painful memories and sad associations, that though it
is a joy only the greater from the contrast, it is not, cannot be, as if it had never been sorrow.

And in this too the feeling at Easter is not unlike the revulsion of mind
on a recovery from sickness, that in sickness also there is much happens to us
that is strange, much that we must feebly comprehend and vaguely follow af-

---

[†] *Parochial & Plain Sermons*, vol. 4 (1839), Sermon 23, preached on Easter Day.

ter. For in sickness the mind wanders from things that are seen into the unknown world, it turns back into itself, and is in company with mysteries; it is brought into contact with objects which it cannot describe, which it cannot ascertain. It sees the skirts of powers and providences beyond this world, and is at least more alive, if not more exposed to the invisible influences, bad and good, which are its portion in this state of trial. And afterwards it has recollections which are painful, recollections of distress, of which it cannot recall the reasons, of pursuits without an object, and gleams of relief without continuance. And what is all this but a parallel feeling to that, with which the Christian has gone through the contemplations put before his faith in the week just passed, which is to him as a fearful harrowing dream, of which the spell is now broken? The subjects, indeed, which have been brought before him are no dream, but a reality,—his Saviour's sufferings, his own misery and sin. But, alas! to him at best they are but a dream, because, from lack of faith and of spiritual discernment, he understands them so imperfectly. They have been to him a dream, because only at moments his heart has caught a vivid glimpse of what was continually before his reason,—because the impression it made upon him was irregular, shifting, and transitory,—because even when he contemplated steadily his Saviour's sufferings, he did not, could not understand the deep reasons of them, or the meaning of His Saviour's words,—because what most forcibly affected him came through his irrational nature, was not of the mind but of the flesh, not of the scenes of sorrow which the Lessons and Gospels record, but of his own discomfort of body, which he has been bound, as far as health allows, to make sympathize with the history of those sufferings which are his salvation. And thus I say his disquiet during the week has been like that of a bad dream, restless and dreary; he has felt he ought to be very sorry, and could not say why,—could not master his grief, could not realize his fears, but was as children are, who wonder, weep, and are silent, when they see their parents in sorrow, from a feeling that there is something wrong, though they cannot say what.

And therefore now, though it is over, he cannot so shake off at once what has been, as to enter fully into what is. Christ indeed, though He suffered and died, yet rose again vigorously on the third day, having loosed the pains of death; but we cannot accomplish in our contemplation of Him, what He accomplished really; for He was the Holy One, and we are sinners. We have the languor and oppression of our old selves upon us, though we be new; and therefore we must beg Him who is the Prince of Life, the Life itself, to carry us forth into His new world, for we cannot walk thither, and seat us down whence, like Moses, we may see the land, and meditate upon its beauty!

And yet, though the long season of sorrow which ushers in this Blessed Day, in some sense sobers and quells the keenness of our enjoyment, yet without such preparatory season, let us be sure we shall not rejoice at all. None rejoice in Easter-tide less than those who have not grieved in Lent. This is what is seen in the world at large. To them, one season is the same as another, and they take no account of any. Feast-day and fast-day, holy tide and other tide, are one and the same to them. Hence they do not realize the next world at all. To them the Gospels are but like another history; a course of events which took place eighteen hundred years since. They do not make our Saviour's life and death present to them: they do not transport themselves back to the time of His sojourn on earth. They do not act over again, and celebrate His history, in their own observance; and the consequence is, that they feel no interest in it. They have neither faith nor love towards it; it has no hold on them. They do not form their estimate of things upon it; they do not hold it as a sort of practical principle in their heart. This is the case not only with the world at large, but too often with men who have the Name of Christ in their mouths. They think they believe in Him, yet when trial comes, or in the daily conduct of life, they are unable to act upon the principles which they profess: and why? because they have thought to dispense with the religious Ordinances, the course of Service, and the round of Sacred Seasons of the Church, and have considered it a simpler and more spiritual religion, not to act religiously except when called to it by extraordinary trial or temptation; because they have thought that, since it is the Christian's duty to rejoice evermore, they would rejoice better if they never sorrowed and never travailed with righteousness. On the contrary, let us be sure that, as previous humiliation sobers our joy, it alone secures it to us. Our Saviour says, "Blessed are they that mourn, for they shall he comforted;" and what is true hereafter, is true here. Unless we have mourned, in the weeks that are gone, we shall not rejoice in the season now commencing. It is often said, and truly, that providential affliction brings a man nearer to God. What is the observance of Holy Seasons but such a means of grace?

This too must be said concerning the connexion of Fasts and Feasts in our religious service, viz., that that sobriety in feasting which previous fasting causes, is itself much to be prized, and especially worth securing. For in this does Christian mirth differ from worldly, that it is subdued; and how shall it be subdued except that the past keeps its hold upon us, and while it warns and sobers us, actually indisposes and tames our flesh against indulgence? In the world feasting comes first and fasting afterwards; men first glut themselves, and then loathe their excesses; they take their fill of good, and then suffer; they are rich that they may be poor; they laugh that they may weep; they rise that

202

they may fall. But in the Church of God it is reversed; the poor *shall* be rich, the lowly shall be exalted, those that sow in tears shall reap in joy, those that mourn shall be comforted, those that suffer with Christ shall reign with Him; even as Christ (in our Church's words) "went not up to joy, but first He suffered pain. He entered not into His glory before He was crucified. So truly our way to eternal joy is to suffer here with Christ, and our door to enter into eternal life is gladly to die with Christ, that we may rise again from death, and dwell with him in everlasting life."[29] And what is true of the general course of our redemption is, I say, fulfilled also in the yearly and other commemorations of it. Our Festivals are preceded by humiliation, that we may keep them duly; not boisterously or fanatically, but in a refined, subdued, chastised spirit, which is the true rejoicing in the Lord.

In such a spirit let us endeavour to celebrate this most holy of all Festivals, this continued festal Season, which lasts for fifty days, whereas Lent is forty, as if to show that where sin abounded, there much more has grace abounded. Such indeed seems the tone of mind which took possession of the Apostles when certified of the Resurrection; and while they waited for, or when they had the sight of their risen Lord. If we consider, we shall find the accounts of that season in the Gospels, marked with much of pensiveness and tender and joyful melancholy; the sweet and pleasant frame of those who have gone through pain, and out of pain receive pleasure. Whether we read the account of St. Mary Magdalen weeping at the sepulchre, seeing Jesus and knowing Him not, recognizing His voice, attempting to embrace His feet, and then sinking into silent awe and delight, till she rose and hastened to tell the perplexed Apostles;—or turn to that solemn meeting, which was the third, when He stood on the shore and addressed His disciples, and Peter plunged into the water, and then with the rest was awed into silence and durst not speak, but only obeyed His command, and ate of the fish in silence, and so remained in the presence of One in whom they joyed, whom they loved, as He knew, more than all things, till He broke silence by asking Peter if he loved Him:—or lastly, consider the time when He appeared unto a great number of disciples on the mountain in Galilee, and all worshipped Him, but some doubted:—who does not see that their Festival was such as I have been describing it, a holy, tender, reverent, manly joy, not *so* manly as to be rude, not *so* tender as to be effeminate, but (as if) an Angel's mood, the mingled offering of all that is best and highest in man's and woman's nature brought together,—St. Mary Magdalen and St. Peter blended into St. John? And here perhaps we learn a lesson from the deep silence which Scripture observes concerning the Blessed

---

[29] Visitation of the Sick.

Virgin[30] after the Resurrection; as if she, who was too pure and holy a flower to be more than seen here on earth, even during the season of her Son's humiliation, was altogether drawn by the Angels within the veil on His Resurrection, and had her joy in Paradise with Gabriel who had been the first to honour her, and with those elder Saints who arose after the Resurrection, appeared in the Holy City, and then vanished away.

May we partake in such calm and heavenly joy; and, while we pray for it, recollecting the while that we are still on earth, and our duties in this world, let us never forget that, while our love must be silent, our faith must be vigorous and lively. Let us never forget that in proportion as our love is "rooted and grounded" in the next world, our faith must branch forth like a fruitful tree into this. The calmer our hearts, the more active be our lives; the more tranquil we are, the more busy; the more resigned, the more zealous; the more unruffled, the more fervent. This is one of the many paradoxes in the world's judgment of him, which the Christian realizes in himself. Christ is risen; He is risen from the dead. We may well cry out, "Alleluia, the Lord Omnipotent reigneth." He has crushed all the power of the enemy under His feet. He has gone upon the lion and the adder. He has stopped the lion's mouth for us His people, and has bruised the serpent's head. There is nothing impossible to us now, if we do but enter into the fulness of our privileges, the wondrous power of our gifts. The thing cannot be named in heaven or earth within the limits of truth and obedience which we cannot do through Christ; the petition cannot be named which may not be accorded to us for His Name's sake. For, we who have risen with Him from the grave, stand in His might, and are allowed to use His weapons. His infinite influence with the Father is ours,—not always to use, for perhaps in this or that effort we make, or petition we prefer, it would not be good for us; but so far ours, so fully ours, that when we ask and do things according to His will, we are really possessed of a power with God, and do prevail:—so that little as we may know when and when not, we are continually possessed of heavenly weapons, we are continually touching the springs of the most wonderful providences in heaven and earth; and by the Name, and the Sign, and the Blood of the Son of God, we are able to make devils tremble and Saints rejoice. Such are the arms which faith uses, small in appearance, yet "not carnal, but mighty through God to the pulling down of strongholds;" [2 Cor. x. 4.] despised by the world, what seems a mere word, or a mere symbol, or mere bread and wine; but God has chosen the weak things of the world to confound the mighty, and foolish things of the world to confound the wise; and as all things spring from small beginnings, from seeds and elements invisible or insignificant, so when God would renew the race of man, and reverse

---

[30] *Vide* Christian Year. Fourth Sunday in Lent.

the course of human life and earthly affairs, He chose cheap things for the rudiments of His work, and bade us believe that He *could* work through them, and He would do so. As then we Christians discern in Him, when He came on earth, not the carpenter's son, but the Eternal Word Incarnate, as we see beauty in Him in whom the world saw no form or comeliness, as we discern in that death an Atonement for sin in which the world saw nothing but a malefactor's sentence; so let us believe with full persuasion that all that He has bequeathed to us has power from Him. Let us accept His Ordinances, and His Creed, and His precepts; and let us stand upright with an undaunted faith, resolute, with faces like flint, to serve Him in and through them; to inflict them upon the world without misgiving, without wavering, without anxiety; being sure that He who saved us from hell through a Body of flesh which the world insulted, tortured, and triumphed over, much more can now apply the benefits of His passion through Ordinances which the world has lacerated and now mocks.

This then, my brethren, be our spirit on this day. God rested from His labours on the seventh day, yet He worketh evermore. Christ entered into His rest, yet He too ever works. We too, if it may be said, in adoring and lowly imitation of what is infinite, while we rest in Christ and rejoice in His shadow, let us too beware of sloth and cowardice, but serve Him with steadfast eyes yet active hands; that we may be truly His in our hearts, as we were made His by Baptism,—as we are made His continually, by the recurring celebration of His purifying Fasts and holy Feasts.

Worship, a Preparation for Christ's Coming[†]

"Thine eyes shall see the King in his beauty:
they shall behold the land that is very far off."
Isaiah xxxiii. 17

YEAR AFTER YEAR, as it passes, brings us the same warnings again and again, and none perhaps more impressive than those with which it comes to us at this season. The very frost and cold, rain and gloom, which now befall us, forebode the last dreary days of the world, and in religious hearts raise the thought of them. The year is worn out: spring, summer, autumn, each in turn, have brought their gifts and done their utmost; but they are over, and the end is come. All is past and gone, all has failed, all has sated; we are tired of the past; we would not have the seasons longer; and the austere weather which succeeds, though ungrateful to the body, is in tone with our feelings, and acceptable. Such is the frame of mind which befits the end of the year; and such the frame of mind which comes alike on good and bad at the end of life. The days have come in which they have no pleasure; yet they would hardly be young again, could they be so by wishing it. Life is well enough in its way; but it does not satisfy. Thus the soul is cast forward upon the future, and in proportion as its conscience is clear and its perception keen and true, does it rejoice solemnly that "the night is far spent, the day is at hand," that there are "new heavens and a new earth" to come, though the former are failing; nay, rather that, because they are failing, it will "soon see the King in His beauty," and "behold the land which is very far off." These are feelings for holy men in winter and in age, waiting, in some dejection perhaps, but with comfort on the whole, and calmly though earnestly, for the Advent of Christ.

And such, too, are the feelings with which we now come before Him in prayer day by day. The season is chill and dark, and the breath of the morning is damp, and worshippers are few, but all this befits those who are by profession penitents and mourners, watchers and pilgrims. More dear to them that loneliness, more cheerful that severity, and more bright that gloom, than all those aids and appliances of luxury by which men nowadays attempt to make prayer less disagreeable to them. True faith does not covet comforts. It only

---

[†] *Parochial & Plain Sermons*, vol. 5 (1840), Sermon 1, preached in Advent.

complains when it is forbidden to kneel, when it reclines upon cushions, is protected by curtains, and encompassed by warmth. Its only hardship is to be hindered, or to be ridiculed, when it would place itself as a sinner before its Judge. They who realize that awful Day when they shall see Him face to face, whose eyes are as a flame of fire, will as little bargain to pray pleasantly now, as they will think of doing so then.

One year goes and then another, but the same warnings recur. The frost or the rain comes again; the earth is stripped of its brightness; there is nothing to rejoice in. And then, amid this unprofitableness of earth and sky, the well-known words return; the Prophet Isaiah is read; the same Epistle and Gospel, bidding us "awake out of sleep," and welcome Him "that cometh in the Name of the Lord;" the same Collects, beseeching Him to prepare us for judgment. O blessed they who obey these warning voices, and look out for Him whom they have not seen, because they "love His appearing!"

We cannot have fitter reflections at this Season than those which I have entered upon. What may be the destiny of other orders of beings we know not;—but this we know to be our own fearful lot, that before us lies a time when we must have the sight of our Maker and Lord face to face. We know not what is reserved for other beings; there may be some, which, knowing nothing of their Maker, are never to be brought before Him. For what we can tell, this may be the case with the brute creation. It may be the law of their nature that they should live and die, or live on an indefinite period, upon the very outskirts of His government, sustained by Him, but never permitted to know or approach Him. But this is not our case. We are destined to come before Him; nay, and to come before Him in judgment; and that on our first meeting; and that suddenly. We are not merely to be rewarded or punished, we are to be judged. Recompense is to come upon our actions, not by a mere general provision or course of nature, as it does at present, but from the Lawgiver Himself in person. We have to stand before His righteous Presence, and that one by one. One by one we shall have to endure His holy and searching eye. At present we are in a world of shadows. What we see is not substantial. Suddenly it will be rent in twain and vanish away, and our Maker will appear. And then, I say, that first appearance will be nothing less than a personal intercourse between the Creator and every creature. He will look on us, while we look on Him.

I need hardly quote any of the numerous passages of Scripture which tell us this, by way of proof; but it may impress the truth of it upon our hearts to do so. We are told then expressly, that good and bad shall see God. On the one hand holy Job says, "Though after my skin worms destroy this body, yet in my flesh shall I see God: whom I shall see for myself, and mine eyes shall behold, and not another." On the other hand unrighteous Balaam says, "I shall see Him, but not now; I shall behold Him, but not nigh; there shall come a Star out of Jacob, and a Sceptre shall rise out of Israel." Christ says to His disciples, "Look up, and lift up your heads, for your redemption draweth nigh;" and to His enemies, "Hereafter ye shall see the Son of man sitting on the right hand of power, and coming in the clouds of heaven." And it is said generally of all men, on the one hand, "Behold He cometh with clouds; and every eye shall see Him, and they also which pierced Him; and all kindreds of the earth shall wail because of Him." And on the other, "When He shall appear, we shall be like Him; for we shall see Him as He is." Again, "Now we see through a glass, darkly; but then face to face:" and again, "They shall see His face; and His Name shall be in their foreheads." [Job xix. 26, 27. Numb. xxiv. 17. Luke xxi. 28. Matt. xxvi. 64. Rev. i. 7. 1 John iii. 2. 1 Cor. xiii. 12. Rev. xxii. 4.]

And, as they see Him, so will He see them, for His coming will be to judge them. "We must all appear before the judgment-seat of Christ," says St. Paul. Again, "We shall all stand before the judgment-seat of Christ. For it is written, As I live, saith the Lord, every knee shall bow to Me, and every tongue shall confess to God. So then every one of us shall give account of himself to God." And again, "When the Son of man shall come in His glory, and all the holy Angels with Him, then shall He sit upon the throne of His glory. And before Him shall be gathered all nations; and He shall separate them one from another, as a shepherd divideth his sheep from the goats." [2 Cor. v. 10. Rom. xiv. 10–12. Matt. xxv. 31, 32.]

Such is our first meeting with our God; and, I say, it will be as sudden as it is intimate. "Yourselves know perfectly," says St. Paul, "that the day of the Lord so cometh as a thief in the night. For when they shall say, Peace and safety, then sudden destruction cometh upon them." This is said of the wicked,— elsewhere He is said to surprise good as well as bad. "While the Bridegroom tarried," the wise and foolish virgins "all slumbered and slept. And at midnight there was a cry made, Behold, the Bridegroom cometh; go ye out to meet Him." [1 Thess. v. 2, 3. Matt. xxv. 5, 6.]

Now, when this state of the case, the prospect which lies before us, is brought home to our thoughts, surely it is one which will lead us anxiously to ask, Is this all that we are told, all that is allowed to us, or done for us? Do we know only this, that all is dark now, and all will be light then; that now God is hidden, and one day will be revealed? that we are in a world of sense, and are to be in a world of spirits? For surely it is our plain wisdom, our bounden duty, to prepare for this great change;—and if so, are any directions, hints, or rules given us *how* we are to prepare? "Prepare to meet thy God," "Go ye out to meet Him," is the dictate of natural reason, as well as of inspiration. But *how* is this to be?

Now observe, that it is scarcely a sufficient answer to this question to say that we must strive to obey Him, and so to approve ourselves to Him. This indeed might be enough, were reward and punishment to follow in the mere way of nature, as they do in this world. But, when we come steadily to consider the matter, appearing before God, and dwelling in His presence, is a very different thing from being merely subjected to a system of moral laws, and would seem to require another preparation, a special preparation of thought and affection, such as will enable us to endure His countenance, and to hold communion with Him as we ought. Nay, and, it may be, a preparation of the soul itself for His presence, just as the bodily eye must be exercised in order to bear the full light of day, or the bodily frame in order to bear exposure to the air.

But, whether or not this be safe reasoning, Scripture precludes the necessity of it, by telling us that the Gospel Covenant is intended, among its other purposes, to prepare us for this future glorious and wonderful destiny, the sight of God,—a destiny which, if not most glorious, will be most terrible. And in the worship and service of Almighty God, which Christ and His Apostles have left to us, we are vouchsafed means, both moral and mystical, of approaching God, and gradually learning to bear the sight of Him.

This indeed is the most momentous reason for religious worship, as far as we have grounds for considering it a true one. Men sometimes ask, Why need they *profess* religion? Why need they go to church? Why need they observe certain rites and ceremonies? Why need they watch, pray, fast, and meditate? Why is it not enough to be just, honest, sober, benevolent, and otherwise virtuous? Is not this the true and real worship of God? Is not activity in mind and conduct the most acceptable way of approaching Him? How can they please Him by submitting to certain religious forms, and taking part in certain religious acts? Or if they must do so, why may they not choose their own? Why must they come to church for them? Why must they be partakers in what the Church calls Sacraments? I answer, they must do so, first of all and especially, because God tells them so to do. But besides this, I observe that we see this plain reason why, that they are one day to change their state of being. They are not to be here for ever. Direct intercourse with God on their part now, prayer and the like, may be necessary to their meeting Him suitably hereafter: and direct intercourse on His part with them, or what we call sacramental communion, may be necessary in some incomprehensible way, even for preparing their very nature to bear the sight of Him.

Let us then take this view of religious service; it is "going out to meet the Bridegroom," who, if not seen "in His beauty," will appear in consuming fire. Besides its other momentous reasons, it is a preparation for an awful event, which shall one day be. What it would be to meet Christ at once without preparation, we may learn from what happened even to the Apostles when His glory was suddenly manifested to them. St. Peter said, "Depart from me, for I am a sinful man, O Lord." And St. John, "when he saw Him, fell at His feet as dead." [Luke v. 8. Rev. i. 17.]

This being the case, it is certainly most merciful in God to vouchsafe to us the means of preparation, and such means as He has actually appointed. When Moses came down from the Mount, and the people were dazzled at his countenance, he put a veil over it. That veil is so far removed in the Gospel, that we are in a state of preparation for its being altogether removed. We are with Moses in the Mount so far, that we have a sight of God; we are with the people beneath it so far, that Christ does not visibly show Himself. He has put a veil on, and He sits among us silently and secretly. When we approach Him, we know it only by faith; and when He manifests Himself to us, it is without our being able to realize to ourselves that manifestation.

Such then is the spirit in which we should come to all His ordinances, considering them as anticipations and first-fruits of that sight of Him which one day must be. When we kneel down in prayer in private, let us think to ourselves, Thus shall I one day kneel down before His very footstool, in this flesh and this blood of mine; and He will be seated over against me, in flesh and blood also, though divine. I come, with the thought of that awful hour before me, I come to confess my sin to Him now, that He may pardon it then, and I say, "O Lord, Holy God, Holy and Strong, Holy and Immortal, in the hour of death and in the day of judgment, deliver us, O Lord!"

Again, when we come to church, then let us say:—The day will be when I shall see Christ surrounded by His Holy Angels. I shall be brought into that blessed company, in which all will be pure, all bright. I come then to learn to endure the sight of the Holy One and His Servants; to nerve myself for a vision which is fearful before it is ecstatic, and which they only enjoy whom it does not consume. When men in this world have to undergo any great thing, they prepare themselves beforehand, by thinking often of it, and they call this making up their mind. Any unusual trial they thus make familiar to them. Courage is a necessary step in gaining certain goods, and courage is gained by steady thought. Children are scared, and close their eyes, at the vision of some mighty warrior or glorious king. And when Daniel saw the Angel, like St. John, "his comeliness was turned in him into corruption, and he retained no strength." [Dan. x. 8.] I come then to church, because I am an heir of heaven.

It is my desire and hope one day to take possession of my inheritance: and I come to make myself ready for it, and I would not see heaven yet, for I could not bear to see it. I am allowed to be in it without seeing it, that I may learn to see it. And by psalm and sacred song, by confession and by praise, I learn my part.

And what is true of the ordinary services of religion, public and private, holds in a still higher or rather in a special way, as regards the sacramental ordinances of the Church. In these is manifested in greater or less degree, according to the measure of each, that Incarnate Saviour, who is one day to be our Judge, and who is enabling us to bear His presence then, by imparting it to us in measure now. A thick black veil is spread between this world and the next. We mortal men range up and down it, to and fro, and see nothing. There is no access through it into the next world. In the Gospel this veil is not removed; it remains, but every now and then marvellous disclosures are made to us of what is behind it. At times we seem to catch a glimpse of a Form which we shall hereafter see face to face. We approach, and in spite of the darkness, our hands, or our head, or our brow, or our lips become, as it were, sensible of the contact of something more than earthly. We know not where we are, but we have been bathing in water, and a voice tells us that it is blood. Or we have a mark signed upon our foreheads, and it spake of Calvary. Or we recollect a hand laid upon our heads, and surely it had the print of nails in it, and resembled His who with a touch gave sight to the blind and raised the dead. Or we have been eating and drinking; and it was not a dream surely, that One fed us from His wounded side, and renewed our nature by the heavenly meat He gave. Thus in many ways He, who is Judge to us, prepares us to be judged,—He, who is to glorify us, prepares us to be glorified, that He may not take us unawares; but that when the voice of the Archangel sounds, and we are called to meet the Bridegroom, we may be ready.

Now consider what light these reflections throw upon some remarkable texts in the Epistle to the Hebrews. If we have in the Gospel this supernatural approach to God and to the next world, no wonder that St. Paul calls it an "enlightening," "a tasting of the heavenly gift," a being "made partaker of the Holy Ghost," a "tasting of the good word of God, and the powers of the world to come." No wonder, too, that utter apostasy after receiving it should be so utterly hopeless; and that in consequence, any profanation of it, any sinning against it, should be so perilous in proportion to its degree. If He, who is to be our Judge, condescend here to manifest Himself to us, surely if that privilege does not fit us for His future glory, it does but prepare us for His wrath.

And what I have said concerning Ordinances, applies still more fully to Holy Seasons, which include in them the celebration of many Ordinances.

They are times when we may humbly expect a larger grace, because they invite us especially to the means of grace. This in particular is a time for purification of every kind. When Almighty God was to descend upon Mount Sinai, Moses was told to "sanctify the people," and bid them "wash their clothes," and to "set bounds to them round about:" much more is this a season for "cleansing ourselves from all defilement of the flesh and spirit, perfecting holiness in the fear of God;" [Exod. xix. 10–12. 2 Cor. xii. 1.] a season for chastened hearts and religious eyes; for severe thoughts, and austere resolves, and charitable deeds; a season for remembering what we are and what we shall be. Let us go out to meet Him with contrite and expectant hearts; and though He delays His coming, let us watch for Him in the cold and dreariness which must one day have an end. Attend His summons we must, at any rate, when He strips us of the body; let us anticipate, by a voluntary act, what will one day come on us of necessity. Let us wait for Him solemnly, fearfully, hopefully, patiently, obediently; let us be resigned to His will, while active in good works. Let us pray Him ever, to "remember us when He cometh in His kingdom;" to remember all our friends; to remember our enemies; and to visit us according to His mercy here, that He may reward us according to His righteousness hereafter.

Reverence, a Belief in God's Presence[†]

"Thine eyes shall see the King in his beauty:
they shall behold the land that is very far off."
Isaiah xxxiii. 17

THOUGH MOSES was not permitted to enter the land of promise, he was vouchsafed a sight of it from a distance. We too, though as yet we are not admitted to heavenly glory, yet are given to see much, in preparation for seeing more. Christ dwells among us in His Church really though invisibly, and through its Ordinances fulfils towards us, in a true and sufficient sense, the promise of the text. We are even now permitted to "see the King in His beauty," to "behold the land that is very far off." The words of the Prophet relate to our present state as well as to the state of saints hereafter. Of the future glory it is said by St. John, "They shall see His face, and His name shall be in their foreheads." [Rev. xxii. 4.] And of the present, Isaiah himself speaks in passages which may be taken in explanation of the text: "The glory of the Lord shall be revealed, and all flesh shall see it together;" and again, "They shall see the glory of the Lord, and the excellency of our God." [Isa. xl. 5; xxxv. 2.] We do not see God face to face under the Gospel, but still, for all that, it is true that "we know in part;" we see, though it be "through a glass darkly;" which is far more than any but Christians are enabled to do. Baptism, by which we become Christians, is an illumination; and Christ, who is the Object of our worship, is withal a Light to worship by.

Such a view is strange to most men; they do not realize the presence of Christ, nor admit the duty of realizing it. Even those who are not without habits of seriousness, have almost or quite forgotten the duty. This is plain at once: for, unless they had, they would not be so very deficient in reverence as they are. It is scarcely too much to say that awe and fear are at the present day all but discarded from religion. Whole societies called Christian make it almost a first principle to disown the duty of reverence; and we ourselves, to whom as children of the Church reverence is as a special inheritance, have very little of it, and do not feel the want of it. Those who, in spite of themselves, are influenced by God's holy fear, too often are ashamed of it, consider it even as a mark of weakness of mind, hide their feeling as much as they can, and,

---

[†] *Parochial & Plain Sermons*, vol. 5 (1840), Sermon 2, preached in Advent.

when ridiculed or censured for it, cannot defend it to themselves on intelligible grounds. They wish indeed to maintain reverence in their mode of speaking and acting, in relation to sacred things, but they are at a loss how to answer objections, or how to resist received customs and fashions; and at length they begin to be suspicious and afraid of their own instinctive feelings. Let us then take occasion from the promise in the text both to describe the religious defect to which I have alluded, and to state the remedy for it.

There are two classes of men who are deficient in awe and fear, and, lamentable to say, taken together, they go far to make up the religious portion of the community. This is lamentable indeed, if so it is: it is not wonderful that sinners should live without the fear of God; but what shall we say of an age or country, in which even the more serious classes, those who live on principle, and claim to have a judgment in religious matters, who look forward to the future, and think that their account stands fair, and that they are in God's favour, when even such persons maintain, or at least act as if they maintained, that "the spirit of God's holy fear" is no part of religion? "If the light that is in us be darkness, how great is that darkness!"

These are the two classes of men who are deficient in this respect: first, those who think that they never were greatly under God's displeasure; next, those who think that, though they once were, they are not at all now for all sin has been forgiven them;—those on the one hand who consider that sin is no great evil in itself, those on the other who consider that it is no great evil in them, because their persons are accepted in Christ for their faith's sake.

Now it must be observed that the existence of fear in religion does not depend on the circumstance of our being sinners; it is short of that. Were we pure as the Angels, yet in His sight, one should think, we could not but fear, before whom the heavens are not clean, nor the Angels free from folly. The Seraphim themselves veiled their faces while they cried, Glory! Even then were it true that sin was not a great evil, or was no great evil in us, nevertheless the mere circumstance that God is infinite and all-perfect is an overwhelming thought to creatures and mortal men, and ought to lead all persons who profess religion to profess also religious fear, however natural it is for irreligious men to disclaim the feeling.

And next let it be observed, it is no dispute about terms. For at first sight we may be tempted to think that the only question is whether the word "fear" is a good or bad word;—that one man makes it all one with slavish dread, and another with godly awe and reverence;—and that therefore the two seem to oppose each other, when they do not,—as if both parties agreed that reverence is right and selfish terror wrong, and the only point between them were, whether by the word fear was meant terror or reverence. This is not the case: it is a question not of words but of things; for these persons whom I am describing plainly consider that state of mind wrong, which the Church Catholic has ever prescribed and her Saints have ever exemplified.

To show that this is so, I will in a few words state what the two sets of opinion are to which I allude; and what that fault is, which, widely as they differ in opinion from each other, they have in common.

The one class of persons consists of those who think the Catholic Creed too strict,—who hold that no certain doctrines need be believed in order to salvation, or at least question the necessity; who say that it matters not what a man believes, so that his conduct is respectable and orderly,—who think that all rites and ceremonies are mere niceties (as they speak) and trifles, and that a man pleases God equally by observing them or not,—who perhaps go on to doubt whether Christ's death is strictly speaking an atonement for the sin of man,—who, when pressed, do not allow that He is strictly speaking and literally God,—and who deny that the punishment of the wicked is eternal. Such are the tenets, more or less clearly apprehended and confessed, which mark the former of the two classes of which I speak.

The other class of men are in their formal doctrines widely different from the former. They consider that, though they were by nature children of wrath, they are now by God's grace so fully in His favour, that, were they to die at once, they would be certain of heaven,—they consider that God so absolutely forgives them day by day their trespasses, that they have nothing to answer for, nothing to be tried upon at the Last Day,—that they have been visited by God's grace in a manner quite distinct from all around them, and are His children in a sense in which others are not, and have an assurance of their saving state peculiar to themselves, and an interest in the promises such as Baptism does not impart;—they profess to be thus beyond the reach of doubt and anxiety, and they say that they should be miserable without such a privilege.

I have alluded to these schools of religion, to show how widely a feeling must be spread which such contrary classes of men have in common. Now, what they agree in is this: in considering God as simply a God of love, not of awe and reverence also,—the one meaning by love *benevolence*, and the other *mercy*; and in consequence neither the one nor the other regard Almighty God with *fear*; and the signs of want of fear in both the one and the other, which I proposed to point out, are such as the following.

For instance:—they have no scruple or misgiving in speaking freely of Almighty God. They will use His Name as familiarly and lightly, as if they were open sinners. The one class adopts a set of words to denote Almighty God, which remove the idea of His personality, speaking of Him as the "Deity," or the "Divine Being;" which, as they use them, are of all others most cal-culated to remove from the mind the thought of a living and intelligent Gov-ernor, their Saviour and their Judge. The other class of men, going into the other extreme, but with the same result, use freely that incommunicable Name by which He has vouchsafed to denote to us His perfections. When He ap-peared to Moses, He disclosed His Name; and that Name has appeared so sa-cred to our translators of Scripture, that they have scrupled to use it, though it occurs continually in the Old Testament, substituting the word "Lord" out of reverence. Now, the persons in question delight in a familiar use, in prayers and hymns and conversation, of that Name by which they designate Him be-fore whom Angels tremble. Not even our fellow-men do we freely call by their own names, unless we are at our ease with them; yet sinners can bear to be familiar with the Name by which they know the Most High has distinguished Himself from all creatures.

Another instance of want of fear, is the bold and unscrupulous way in which men speak of the Holy Trinity and the Mystery of the Divine Nature. They use sacred terms and phrases, should occasion occur, in a rude and ab-rupt way, and discuss points of doctrine concerning the All-holy and Eternal, even (if I may without irreverence state it) over their cups, perhaps arguing against them, as if He were such a one as themselves.

Another instance of this want of fear is found in the peremptory manner in which men lay down what Almighty God must do, what He cannot but do, as if they were masters of the whole scheme of salvation, and might anticipate His high providence and will.

And another is the confidence with which they often speak of their hav-ing been converted, pardoned, and sanctified, as if they knew their own state as well as God knows it.

Another is the unwillingness so commonly felt, to bow at the Name of Jesus, nay the impatience exhibited towards those who do; as if there were nothing awful in the idea of the Eternal God being made man, and as if we did not suitably express our wonder and awe at it by practising what St. Paul has in very word prescribed.

Another instance is the careless mode in which men speak of our Lord's earthly doings and sayings, just as if He were a mere man. He was man indeed, but He was more than man: and He did what man does, but then those deeds of His were the deeds of God,—and we can as little separate the deed from the Doer as our arm from our body. But, in spite of this, numbers are apt to use rude, familiar, profane language, concerning their God's childhood, and youth, and ministry, though He is their God.

And another is the familiarity with which many persons address our Lord in prayer, applying epithets to Him and adopting a strain of language which does not beseem creatures, not to say sinners.

And another is their general mode of prayer; I mean, in diffuse and free language, with emphatic and striking words, in a sort of coloured or rich style, with pomp of manner, and an oratorical tone, as if praying were preaching, and as if its object were not to address Almighty God, but to impress and affect those who heard them.

And another instance of this want of reverence is the introduction, in speaking or writing, of serious and solemn words, for the sake of effect, to round, or to give dignity to, a sentence.

And another instance is irreverence in church, sitting instead of kneeling in prayer, or pretending to kneel but really sitting, or lounging or indulging in other unseemly attitudes; and, much more, looking about when prayers are going on, and observing what others are doing.

These are some out of a number of peculiarities which mark the religion of the day, and are instanced some in one class of men, some in another; but all by one or other;—and they are specimens of what I mean when I say that the religion of this day is destitute of *fear*.

Many other instances might be mentioned of very various kinds. For instance, the freedom with which men propose to alter God's ordinances, to suit their own convenience, or to meet the age; their reliance on their private and antecedent notions about sacred subjects; their want of interest and caution in inquiring what God's probable will is; their contempt for any view of the Sacraments which exceeds the evidence of their senses; and their confidence in settling the order of importance in which the distinct articles of Christian faith stand;—all which shows that it is no question of words whether men have fear or not, but that there is a something they really have not, whatever name we give it.

So far I consider to be plain:—the only point which can be debated is this, whether the feelings which I have been describing are necessary; for each of the two classes which I have named contends that they are unnecessary; the one decides them inconsistent with reason, the other with the Gospel; the one calls them superstitious, and the other legal or Jewish. Let us then consider, are these feelings of fear and awe Christian feelings or not? A very few words will surely be sufficient to decide the question.

I say this, then, which I think no one can reasonably dispute. They are the class of feelings we *should* have,—yes, have in an intense degree—if we literally had the sight of Almighty God; therefore they are the class of feelings which we shall have, *if* we realize His presence. In proportion as we believe that He is present, we shall have them; and not to have them, is not to realize, not to believe that He is present. If then it is a duty to feel as though we saw Him, or to have faith, it is a duty to have these feelings; and if it is a sin to be destitute of faith, it is a sin to be without them. Let us consider this awhile.

Who then is there to deny, that if we saw God, we should fear? Take the most cold and secular of all those who explain away the Gospel; or take the most heated and fanatic of those who consider it peculiarly their own; take those who think that Christ has brought us nothing great, or those who think He has brought it all to themselves,—I say, would either party keep from fearing greatly if they saw God? Surely it is quite a truism to say that any creature would fear. But why would he fear? would it be merely because he saw God, or because he knew that God was present? If he shut his eyes, he would still fear, for his eyes had conveyed to him this solemn truth; to *have* seen would be enough. But if so, does it not follow at once, that, if men do not fear, it is because they do not act as they would act if they saw Him, that is,—they do not feel that He is present? Is it not quite certain that men would not use Almighty God's Name so freely, if they thought He was really in hearing,—nay, close beside them when they spoke? And so of those other instances of want of godly fear, which I mentioned, they one and all come from deadness to the presence of God. If a man believes Him present, he will shrink from addressing Him familiarly, or using before Him unreal words, or peremptorily and on his own judgment deciding what God's will is, or claiming His confidence, or addressing Him in a familiar posture of body. I say, take the man who is most confident that he has nothing to fear from the presence of God, and that Almighty God is at peace with him, and place him actually before the throne of God; and would he have no misgivings? and will he dare to say that those misgivings are a weakness, a mere irrational perturbation, which he ought not to feel?

This will be seen more clearly, by considering how differently we feel towards and speak of our friends as present or absent. Their presence is a check upon us; it acts as an external law, compelling us to do or not do what we should not do or do otherwise, or should do but for it. This is just what most men lack in their religion at present,—such an external restraint arising from the consciousness of God's presence. Consider, I say, how differently we speak of a friend, however intimate, when present or absent; consider how we feel, should it so happen that we have begun to speak of him as if he were not present, on finding suddenly that he is; and that, though we are conscious of nothing but what is loving and open towards him. There is a tone of voice and a manner of speaking about persons absent, which we should consider disrespectful, or at least inconsiderate, if they were present. When that is the case, we are ever thinking more or less, even though unconsciously to ourselves, how they will take what we say, how it will affect them, what they will say to us or think of us in turn. When a person is absent, we are tempted perhaps confidently to say what his opinion is on certain points;—but should he be present, we qualify our words; we hardly like to speak at all, from the vivid consciousness that we may be wrong, and that he is present to tell us so. We are very cautious of pronouncing what his feelings are on the matter in hand, or how he is disposed towards ourselves; and in all things we observe a deference and delicacy in our conduct towards him. Now, if we feel this towards our fellows, what shall we feel in the presence of an Angel? and if so, what in the presence of the All-knowing, All-searching Judge of men? What is respect and consideration in the case of our fellows, becomes godly fear as regards Almighty God; and they who do not fear Him, in one word, do not believe that He sees and hears them. If they did, they would cease to boast so confidently of His favourable thoughts of them, to foretell His dealings, to pronounce upon His revelations, to make free with His Name, and to address Him familiarly.

Now, in what has been said, no account has been taken, as I have already observed, of our being sinners, a corrupt, polluted race at the best, while He is the All-holy God,—which must surely increase our fear and awe greatly, and not at all the less because we have been so wonderfully redeemed. Nor, again, has account been taken of another point, on which I will add two or three words.

There is a peculiar feeling with which we regard the dead. What does this arise from?—that he is absent? No; for we do not feel the same towards one who is merely distant, though he be at the other end of the earth. Is it because in this life we shall never see him again? No, surely not; because we may be perfectly certain we shall never see him when he goes abroad, we may know he is to die abroad, and perhaps he does die abroad; but will any one say that, when the news of his death comes, our feeling when we think of him is not quite changed? Surely it is the passing into another state which impresses itself upon us, and makes us speak of him as we do,—I mean, with a sort of awe. We cannot tell what he is now,—what his relations to us,—what he knows of us. We do not understand him,—we do not see him. He is passed into the land "that is very far off," but it is not at all certain that he has not some mysterious hold over us. Thus his not being seen with our bodily eyes, while perchance he is present, makes the thought of him more awful. Apply this to the subject before us, and you will perceive that there is a sense, and a true sense, in which the *invisible* presence of God is more awful and overpowering than if we saw it. And so again, the presence of Christ, now that it is invisible, brings with it a host of high and mysterious feelings, such as nothing else can inspire. The thought of our Saviour, absent yet present, is like that of a friend taken from us, but, as it were, in dream returned to us, though in this case not in dream, but in reality and truth. When He was going away, He said to His disciples, "I will see you again, and your heart shall rejoice." Yet He had at another time said, "The days will come when the Bridegroom shall be taken from them, and then shall they fast in those days." See what an apparent contradiction, such as attends the putting any high feeling into human language! they were to joy because Christ was come, and yet weep because He was away; that is, to have a feeling so refined, so strange and new, that nothing could be said of it, but that it combined in one all that was sweet and soothing in contrary human feelings, as commonly experienced. As some precious fruits of the earth are said to taste like all others at once, not as not being really distinct from all others, but as being thus best described, when we would come as near the truth as we can, so the state of mind which they are in who believe that the Son of God is here, yet away,—is at the right hand of God, yet in His very flesh and blood among us,—is present, though invisible,—is one of both joy and pain, or rather one far above either; a feeling of awe, wonder, and praise, which cannot be more suitably expressed than by the Scripture word *fear*, or by holy Job's words, though he spoke in grief, and not as being possessed of a blessing. "Behold, I go forward, but He is not there; and backward, but I cannot perceive Him: on the left hand, where He doth work, but I cannot behold Him: He hideth Himself on the right hand, that I cannot see Him. Therefore am I troubled at His presence; when I consider, I am afraid of Him." [Job xxiii. 8, 9, 15.]

To conclude. Enough has been said now to show that godly fear must be a duty, if to live as in God's [presence] is a duty,—must be a privilege of the Gospel, if the spiritual sight of "the King in His beauty" be one of its privileges. Fear follows from faith necessarily, as would be plain, even though there were not a text in the Bible saying so. But in fact, as it is scarcely needful to say, Scripture abounds in precepts to fear God. Such are the words of the Wise Man: "The fear of the Lord is the beginning of knowledge." Such again is the third commandment, in which we are solemnly bidden not to take God's Name in vain. Such the declaration of the prophet Habakkuk, who beginning by declaring "The just shall live by his faith," ends by saying, "The Lord is in His Holy Temple; let the whole earth keep silence before Him." Such is St. Paul's, who, in like manner, after having discoursed at length upon faith as "the realizing of things hoped for, the evidence of things not seen," adds: "Let us have grace, whereby we may serve God acceptably with reverence and godly fear." Such St. Luke's account of the Church militant on earth, that "walking in the fear of the Lord and in the comfort of the Holy Ghost," it was "multiplied." Such St. John's account of the Church triumphant in heaven, "Who shall not fear Thee," they say, "O Lord, and glorify Thy Name; for Thou only art Holy?" Such the feeling recorded of the three Apostles on the Mount of Transfiguration, who, when they heard God's voice, "fell on their face, and were sore afraid." [Prov. i. 7. Hab. ii. 4, 20. Heb. xii. 28. Acts ix. 31. Rev. xv. 4. Matt. xvii. 6.] And now, if this be so, can anything be clearer than that the *want* of fear is nothing else but *want* of faith, and that in consequence we in this age are approaching in religious temper that evil day of which it is said, "When the Son of Man cometh, shall He find faith on the earth?" [Luke xviii. 8.] Is it wonderful that we have no fear in our words and mutual intercourse, when we exercise no *acts* of faith? What, you will ask, are acts of faith? Such as these,—to come often to prayer, is an act of faith; to kneel down instead of sitting, is an act of faith; to strive to attend to your prayers, is an act of faith; to behave in God's House otherwise than you would in a common room, is an act of faith; to come to it on weekdays as well as Sundays, is an act of faith; to come often to the most Holy Sacrament, is an act of faith; and to be still and reverent during that sacred service, is an act of faith. These are all acts of faith, because they all are acts such as we should perform, if we saw and heard Him who *is* present, though with our bodily eyes we see and hear Him *not*. But, "blessed are they who have not seen, and yet have believed;" for, be sure, if we thus act, we shall, through God's grace, be gradually endued with the spirit of His holy fear. We shall in time, in our mode of talking and acting, in our religious services and our daily conduct, manifest, not with constraint and effort, but spontaneously and naturally, that we fear Him while we love him.

The New Works of the Gospel[†]

> "If any man be in Christ, he is a new creature: old things are passed away;
> behold, all things are become new."
> 2 Cor. v. 17

NOTHING is more clearly stated, or more strongly insisted on, by St. Paul, than the new creation, or second beginning, or regeneration, of the world, which has been vouchsafed in Christ. It had been announced in prophecy. "Behold, I create *new* heavens and a *new* earth; and the former shall not be remembered, nor, come into mind." Again: "Behold, the days come, saith the Lord, that I will make a *new* covenant with the house of Israel and with the house of Judah . . . I will put My law in their inward parts, and write it in their hearts; and will be their God, and they shall be My people." And again: "A *new* heart will I give you, and a *new* spirit will I put within you; and I will take away the stony heart out of your flesh, and I will give you an heart of flesh. And I will put My Spirit within you, and cause you to walk in My statutes, and ye shall keep My judgments and do them." [Isa. lxv. 17. Jer. xxxi. 31, 33. Ez. xxxvi. 26, 27.] In the text, St. Paul declares the fulfilment of these promises in the Gospel. "If any man be in Christ, he is a *new* creature; *old things are passed away,*" as the heavens and earth shall pass away, at the end of the world; "behold, all things are become *new*." And hence he calls Christ, not only "the Image of the Invisible God," but also "the *first-born* of every creature;" or, as He calls Himself in the book of Revelation, "the *beginning* of the creation of God." [Col. i. 15. Rev. iii. 14.] St. Paul also speaks of "the *new* and living way which He hath consecrated for us through His flesh;" of Christians having "put off the old man with his deeds," and having "put on the *new* man, which is renewed in knowledge, after the Image of Him that created him;" of "*newness* of life," and "*newness* of spirit;" of "ministers of the *New* Testament, not of the letter, but of the Spirit;" and of our being God's "workmanship, *created* in Christ Jesus unto good works." [Heb. x. 20. Col. iii. 9, 10. Rom. vi. 4; vii. 6. 2 Cor. iii. 6. Eph. ii. 10.] Elsewhere he says, that true and availing "circumcision is that of the heart, in the Spirit and not in the letter, whose praise is not of men, but of God;" and that "circumcision is noth-

---

[†] *Parochial & Plain Sermons*, vol. 5 (1840), Sermon 12, preached for Epiphany.

ing, and uncircumcision is nothing, but the keeping the commandments of God." [Rom. ii. 29. 1 Cor. vii. 19.]

Now it may be asked, Is there not some contrariety in these statements? The Gospel is said to be a *new* covenant, and yet, after all, it is to consist in "walking in God's statutes" and "doing His judgments," and "keeping His commandments," and being "created unto good works." Now these were but the terms of the old covenant: "Fear God and keep His commandments;" "If thou wilt enter into life, keep the commandments;" "The man that doeth those things shall live by them." [Eccles. xii. 13. Rom. x. 5.] If the new Covenant be of works too, how is the Gospel other than the Law? how can it justly be called new? If the way of salvation be now what it ever has been, how are we gainers? What privilege is there in being brought under the Gospel? What has Christ done for us? Hence some persons have concluded that salvation under the Gospel is *not* of works; and in confirmation of this they urge, that St. Paul elsewhere speaks expressly of salvation as being not of works but of faith; and they allege that faith *is* a new way of salvation, though works of obedience are not and cannot be.

Now there can be no doubt at all that salvation is by faith, and that its being by faith is one of those special circumstances which make the Gospel a new covenant; but still it may be by works also; for, to use a familiar illustration, obedience is the *road* to heaven, and faith the *gate*. Those who attempt to be saved simply without works, are like persons who should attempt to travel to a place, not along the road, but across the fields. If we wish to get to our journey's end, we shall keep to the road; but even then we may go the *wrong* road. This was the case with the Jews. They professed to go along the road of works,—they did not wander into the fields,—so far well: but they took the wrong road. That particular road of which faith is the gate, that particular obedience, those particular works, which commence in faith, these are the only right and sure road to heaven. It is wrong to leave the road for the open country; again, it is wrong to go along the wrong road;—but it is not wrong to go along the right road. And in like manner it is sinful to attempt no obedience whatever; it is blind perversity to attempt obedience by the Jewish law or the law of nature; but it is not sinful, it is not perverse, it is nothing else than wisdom, nothing else than true godliness, to follow after that obedience which is of faith.

The illustration may be pursued further. A road may want repairing,—it may get worse and worse as we go on, till it ceases to be a road: it may fall off from a road into a lane, from a lane to a path, or a wild heath, or a marsh; or it may be cut off by high impassable mountains; so that a person who attempts that way will never arrive at his journey's end. This was case with the works of the Law by which the Jews thought to gain heaven,—this is the case with all works done in our natural strength: they are like a road over fens or precipices, which is sure to fail us. At first we might seem to go on well, but we should find at length that we made no progress. We should never get to our journey's end. Our best obedience in our own strength is worth nothing; it is altogether unsound, it is ever failing, it never grows firmer, it never can be reckoned on, it does nothing well, it has nothing in it pleasing or acceptable to God:—and not only so, it is the obedience of souls born and living under God's wrath, for a state of nature is a state of wrath. On the other hand, obedience which is done in faith is done with the aid of the Holy Spirit; it is holy and acceptable in God's sight; it grows habitual and consistent; it tends to possess the soul wholly; and it leads straight onward to heaven. This was the very promise of the Gospel as the prophet Isaiah announces it. "An highway shall be there and a way, and it shall be called the *way of holiness*: the unclean shall not pass over it . . . the wayfaring men, though fools, shall not err therein." [Isa. xxxv. 8.] This being understood, we shall have no difficulty in understanding St. Paul's language. The way of salvation is by works, as under the Law, but it is by "works which spring out of faith," and which come of "the inspiration of the Spirit." It is because works are living and spiritual, from the heart, and by faith, that the Gospel is a new covenant. Hence in the passages above quoted we are told again and again of "the law *in our inward parts*;" "a new *heart*;" "a new *spirit*;" the Holy "*Spirit within us*;" "newness of *life*," and "circumcision of the *heart* in the Spirit." And hence St. Paul says, that though we have not been "saved by works," yet we are "*created* unto *good* works;" and that "the blood of Christ purges the conscience from *dead* works to *serve* the *living* God." Salvation then is not by dead works, but by living works. The Jews could but do dead works; but Christians can do good and spiritual works. The Gospel Covenant, then, is both a new way and not a new way. It is not a new way, seeing it is *in* works: it is a new way, in that it is *by* faith. It is, as St. Paul words it, the "obedience of faith;"—new because of faith, old because of obedience.

And thus there is no opposition between St. Paul and St. James. St. James says, that justification is by works, and St. Paul that it is by faith: but, observe, St. James does not say that it is by dead or Jewish works; he mentions expressly *both* faith *and* works; he only says, "not faith *only* but works also:"— and St. Paul is far from denying it is by works, he only says that it is by faith and denies that it is by *dead* works. And what proves this, among other circumstances, is, that he never calls those works, which he condemns and puts aside, *good* works, but simply works: whenever he speaks of good works in his Epistles, he speaks of Christian works; not of Jewish. On the whole, then, salvation is both by faith and by works. St. James says, not *dead* faith, and St.

Paul, not *dead* works. St. James, "not by faith *only*," for that *would* be dead faith: St Paul, "not by works only," for such *would* be dead works. Faith alone can make works living; works alone can make faith living. Take away either, and you take away both;—he alone has faith who has works,—he alone has works who has faith.

It is not at all wonderful, then, that though the way of salvation under the Gospel is new, still in certain respects it is still what the Jews, nay, and what the heathen thought it to be. The way of justification has in all religions been by means of works; so it is under the Gospel; but in the Gospel alone it is by the means of good works.

However, this statement, simple and obvious as it is, is a hard saying to many persons, who think that the way of salvation should be altogether new under the Gospel, altogether different from what is prescribed under other religions; whereas they think little has been gained for us by Christ, if after all He has left us, as before, to be saved by obedience. This is a difficulty with them. They think Christianity is made Jewish, or almost heathen, if salvation is attained by what is the old way; and this being the case, I shall make some remarks, with the hope of reconciling the mind to it.

I observe, then, that whether it came from Noah after the flood or not, so it is, that all religions, the various heathen religions as well as the Mosaic religion, have many things in them which are very much the same. They seem to come from one common origin, and so far have the traces of truth upon them. They are all branches, though they are corruptions and perversions, of that patriarchal religion which came from God. And of course the Jewish religion came entirely and immediately from God. Now God's works are like each other, not different; if, then, the Gospel is from God, and the Jewish religion was from God, and the various heathen religions in their first origin were from God, it is not wonderful, rather it is natural, that they should have in many ways a resemblance one with another. And, accordingly, that the Gospel is in certain points like the religions which preceded it, is but an argument that "God is One, and that there is none other but He;"—the difference between them being that the heathen religions are a true religion corrupted; the Jewish, a true religion dead; and Christianity, the true religion living and perfect. The heathen thought to be saved by works, so did the Jews, so do Christians; but the heathen took the works of darkness for good works, the Jews thought cold, formal and scanty works to be good works, and Christians believe that works done in the Spirit of grace, the fruit of faith, and offered up under the meritorious intercession of Christ, that these only are good works, but that these really *are* good:—so that while the heathen thinks to be saved by sin, and the Jew by self, the Christian relies on the Spirit of Him who died on the Cross for him. Thus they differ; but they all agree in thinking that works are the means of salvation; they differ in respect to the quality of these works.

Let us take some parallel instances in religious doctrine and worship, for they abound.

1. For example: Religion, considered in itself, cannot but have much which is the same in all systems, true and false. It is the worship of God. This involves saying prayers, postures of devotion, and the like, whatever the particular worship be; nor is the Gospel less a new covenant, because it retains these old usages, unless it ceases to be new, because it retains religion. While man is man, it could not be otherwise. These observances are right when performed well, evil when performed ill; evil as performed by the heathen, right as performed by Christians. The heathen worship devils, as St. Paul tells us. As is their god, such is their service. The Gospel came to destroy the worship of devils, not to destroy worship; we do not cease to have a new worship, because we worship, not devils, but Almighty God.

2. Again, meetings for worship have been in all religions from the first. But it does not follow from this that "old things" have not been made to pass till coming to church is denounced as a sin. On the contrary, St. Paul expressly tells us *not* to forsake the assembling of ourselves together, though "all things have become new." What had been done of old time for bad purposes or in a bad way, is to be done for a holy purpose and in a heavenly way under the Gospel. A new life is infused into what once was evil, or at least profitless; so that, whereas of old time men came together to worship as "dry bones," in consequence of the creative power of Christ, "the dead bones live."

3. Again, religion has ever existed in a large organized body, with orders and officers, with ministers and people. It has always exercised an influence over the State, and it has ever been what is called established, or had rank and property. Now there is abundant evidence that this was intended to be the condition of religion under the Gospel, in spite of its being a new religion. Ranks existed from the first,—Apostles, Evangelists, Prophets, Bishops, and Deacons, as we read in Scripture. And property was held by the Church, for the rich gave up their wealth, and laid it at the Apostles' feet. And St. Paul used his privilege as a citizen of Rome. Here again, then, though salvation be of faith, and religion be spiritual, and old things be passed away, and all things have become new, yet the old framework remains as far as this, that there are men set apart to preach the Gospel, and that they "live by the Gospel."

4. Again, all religions, before the Gospel came, had their mysteries; I mean alleged disclosures of Truth, which could not be fully understood all at once, if at all, and which were open to some more than to others. The Gospel, though it be light and liberty, has not materially altered things here. It has

mysteries as we all know; such as the doctrines of the Holy Trinity, and the Incarnation. And these mysteries cannot be equally entered into by all, but in proportion as men are humble and holy, and intellectually gifted, and blessed with leisure. St. Paul speaks of "the hidden wisdom;" and declares that "the natural man receiveth not the things of the Spirit of God, for they are foolishness unto him; neither can he know them, because they are spiritually discerned." And elsewhere he declines to speak to the Hebrews about Melchizedec, "of whom" he had "many things to say, and hard to be uttered, seeing" they were "dull of hearing." [1 Cor. ii. 14. Heb. v. 11.]

5. Again, religions before Christ came ever had holy days and festivals, both among heathen and Jews. The Gospel has not done away with holy days, only it has changed them, and made them more truly holy. For instance, it has not destroyed the Feast of one day in seven, or the Lord's day; not to mention other instances. This is the more remarkable, because St. Paul's words are at first sight very strong against the observance, under the Gospel, of any days above others, as a matter of religion. He finds fault with the Galatians, because they observe "days, and months, and times, and years." And he bids the Colossians not to let any man "judge them in meat or in drink, or in respect of an holy day, or of the new moon, or of the Sabbath days, which are a shadow of things to come, but the body is of Christ." [Gal. iv. 10. Col. ii. 16, 17.] Who would not, at first sight, suppose from these words, that all holy days, all holy seasons, were to be done away, under the Gospel, as mere shadows,—Sunday, Christmas-day, Easter-tide, Lent, and all the rest? Yet it is not so. The Apostles in the Acts, and St. John in the Revelation, observe and recognise the Lord's day as a Gospel festival. Jewish days *are* shadows, but Christian are not; just as Jewish works, or works of the Law, avail not, but Christian works avail. The weekly festival is not one of the "old things" which have "passed away" in Christ, neither have righteous works. The Sabbath has "become new" by becoming the Lord's day; works become new, by becoming spiritual.

6. Again, washing with water was a heathen rite of purification, and also a Jewish rite. Yet it remains under the Gospel; and with the same change. The "divers washings" of the Jews were "carnal ordinances;" [Heb. ix. 10.] but Baptism, our washing, is a washing of the Spirit; and because the former are annulled, it does not follow that the latter should be. On the contrary, our Lord distinctly commanded His Apostles, "Go ye and teach all nations, baptizing them." [Matt. xxviii. 19.]

7. Once more. The heathen had temples; the Jews had a temple; and our Lord said to the Samaritan woman, that the hour was coming when the true worshippers should worship, not in the temple at Jerusalem, but "in spirit and in truth." But this did not mean that there were to be no Christian temples, or

churches, as we call them; at least it has never been taken so to mean. All it would seem to mean is, that the Jewish temple is not like a Christian temple, but differs in some essential points.

I have said enough to explain St. Paul's statement in the text, that "old things are passed away," and "all things new" under the Gospel. By all things being "*new*" is meant that they are *renewed*; by "old things *passing away*" is meant that they are *changed*. The substance remains; the form, mode, quality, and circumstances are different and more excellent. Religion has still forms, ordinances, precepts, mysteries, duties, assemblies, festivals, and temples as of old time; but, whereas all these were dead and carnal before, now, since Christ came, they have a life in them. He has brought life to the world; He has given life to religion; He has made everything spiritual and true by His touch, full of virtue, full of grace, full of power: so that ordinances, works, forms, which before were unprofitable, now, by the inward meritorious influence of His blood imparted to them, avail for our salvation.

This one point, in addition, is clear from what has been said; that if all Christian worship is "in spirit and in truth," nothing has a place under the Gospel which is *not* spiritual. It is very inconsistent then, to say, as some people do say, that Baptism should be observed, and yet that it does not convey Divine grace, and is a mere outward ordinance; for if so, it is nothing better than a Jewish rite, and instead of being observed, it ought to be abolished altogether. And again, unless the Church itself, and the ministerial order attached to it, be a means of grace and the instrument of the Holy Ghost, they are no better than the Jewish temple and the Jewish priests, which have come to nought, and have no part in the spiritual system of the Gospel. And so, in like manner, works of obedience also, if they are no better than "the works of the Law," which cannot justify; if they are not pleasing to God, if they be filthy rags, as some persons say, and as the works of nature *are*; if so, then I do not see that they need be attempted at all; for all works of the Law are done away. Everything is done away in the Gospel but what is spirit and truth; and our works, our ordinances, our discipline, are spirit and truth, or they are done away.

And, lastly, hereby we see why justification must be of faith: because, as Christ, by means of His Spirit, makes a new beginning in us, so faith, on our part, receives that new beginning, and cooperates with Him. And it is the only principle which can do this: for as things spiritual are unseen, so faith is in its very nature that which apprehends and uses things unseen. We renounce our old unprofitable righteousness, which is from Adam, and accept, through faith, that new righteousness which is imparted by the Spirit; or, in St. Paul's words, "we, through the Spirit, wait for the hope of righteousness by faith."

To conclude. Let us think much, and make much, of the grace of God; let us beware of receiving it in vain; let us pray God to prosper it in our hearts, that we may bring forth much fruit. We see how grace wrought in St. Paul: it made him labour, suffer, and work righteousness almost above man's nature. This was not his own doing; it was not through his own power. He says himself, "Yet not I, but the grace of God which was in me." God's grace was "sufficient for him." It was its triumph in him, that it made him quite another man from what he was before. May God's grace be efficacious in us also. Let us aim at doing nothing in a dead way; let us beware of dead works, dead forms, dead professions. Let us pray to be filled with the spirit of love. Let us come to Church joyfully; let us partake the Holy Communion adoringly; let us pray sincerely; let us work cheerfully; let us suffer thankfully; let us throw our heart into all we think, say, and do; and may it be a spiritual heart! This is to be a new creature in Christ; this is to walk by faith.

The Cross of Christ the Measure of the World[†]

"And I, if I be lifted up from the earth, will draw all men unto Me."
John xii. 32

A GREAT NUMBER of men live and die without reflecting at all upon the state of things in which they find themselves. They take things as they come, and follow their inclinations as far as they have the opportunity. They are guided mainly by pleasure and pain, not by reason, principle, or conscience; and they do not attempt to *interpret* this world, to determine what it means, or to reduce what they see and feel to system. But when persons, either from thoughtfulness of mind, or from intellectual activity, begin to contemplate the visible state of things into which they are born, then forthwith they find it a maze and a perplexity. It is a riddle which they cannot solve. It seems full of contradictions and without a drift. Why it is, and what it is to issue in, and how it is what it is, and how we come to be introduced into it, and what is our destiny, are all mysteries.

In this difficulty, some have formed one philosophy of life, and others another. Men have thought they had found the key, by means of which they might read what is so obscure. Ten thousand things come before us one after another in the course of life, and what are we to think of them? what colour are we to give them? Are we to look at all things in a gay and mirthful way? or in a melancholy way? in a desponding or a hopeful way? Are we to make light of life altogether, or to treat the whole subject seriously? Are we to make greatest things of little consequence, or least things of great consequence? Are we to keep in mind what is past and gone, or are we to look on to the future, or are we to be absorbed in what is present? *How* are we to look at things? this is the question which all persons of observation ask themselves, and answer each in his own way. They wish to think by rule; by something within them, which may harmonize and adjust what is without them. Such is the need felt by reflective minds. Now, let me ask, what *is* the real key, what is the Christian interpretation of this world? What is given us by revelation to estimate and measure this world by? The event of this season,—the Crucifixion of the Son of God.

[†] *Parochial & Plain Sermons*, vol. 6 (1842), Sermon 7, preached on the Sixth Sunday in Lent.

It is the death of the Eternal Word of God made flesh, which is our great lesson how to think and how to speak of this world. His Cross has put its due value upon every thing which we see, upon all fortunes, all advantages, all ranks, all dignities, all pleasures; upon the lust of the flesh, and the lust of the eyes, and the pride of life. It has set a price upon the excitements, the rivalries, the hopes, the fears, the desires, the efforts, the triumphs of mortal man. It has given a meaning to the various, shifting course, the trials, the temptations, the sufferings, of his earthly state. It has brought together and made consistent all that seemed discordant and aimless. It has taught us how to live, how to use this world, what to expect, what to desire, what to hope. It is the tone into which all the strains of this world's music are ultimately to be resolved.

Look around, and see what the world presents of high and low. Go to the court of princes. See the treasure and skill of all nations brought together to honour a child of man. Observe the prostration of the many before the few. Consider the form and ceremonial, the pomp, the state, the circumstance; and the vainglory. Do you wish to know the worth of it all? look at the Cross of Christ.

Go to the political world: see nation jealous of nation, trade rivalling trade, armies and fleets matched against each other. Survey the various ranks of the community, its parties and their contests, the strivings of the ambitious, the intrigues of the crafty. What is the end of all this turmoil? the grave. What is the measure? the Cross.

Go, again, to the world of intellect and science: consider the wonderful discoveries which the human mind is making, the variety of arts to which its discoveries give rise, the all but miracles by which it shows its power; and next, the pride and confidence of reason, and the absorbing devotion of thought to transitory objects, which is the consequence. Would you form a right judgment of all this? look at the Cross.

Again: look at misery, look at poverty and destitution, look at oppression and captivity; go where food is scanty, and lodging unhealthy. Consider pain and suffering, diseases long or violent, all that is frightful and revolting. Would you know how to rate all these? gaze upon the Cross.

Thus in the Cross, and Him who hung upon it, all things meet; all things subserve it, all things need it. It is their centre and their interpretation. For He was lifted up upon it, that He might draw all men and all things unto Him.

But it will be said, that the view which the Cross of Christ imparts to us of human life and of the world, is not that which we should take, if left to ourselves; that it is not an obvious view; that if we look at things on their surface, they are far more bright and sunny than they appear when viewed in the light which this season casts upon them. The world seems made for the enjoyment of just such a being as man, and man is put into it. He has the *capacity* of enjoyment, and the world supplies the *means*. How natural this, what a simple as well as pleasant philosophy, yet how different from that of the Cross! The doctrine of the Cross, it may be said, disarranges two parts of a system which seem made for each other; it severs the fruit from the eater, the enjoyment from the enjoyer. How does this solve a problem? does it not rather itself create one?

I answer, first, that whatever force this objection may have, surely it is merely a repetition of that which Eve felt and Satan urged in Eden; for did not the woman see that the forbidden tree was "good for food," and "a tree to be *desired*"? Well, then, is it wonderful that we too, the descendants of the first pair, should still be in a world where there is a forbidden fruit, and that our trials should lie in being within reach of it, and our happiness in abstaining from it? The world, at first sight, appears *made* for pleasure, and the vision of Christ's Cross is a solemn and sorrowful sight interfering with this appearance. Be it so; but why may it not be our duty to abstain from enjoyment notwithstanding, if it was a duty even in Eden?

But again; it is but a superficial view of things to say that this life is made for pleasure and happiness. To those who look under the surface, it tells a very different tale. The doctrine of the Cross does but teach, though infinitely more forcibly, still after all it does but teach the very same lesson which this world teaches to those who live long in it, who have much experience in it, who know it. The world is sweet to the lips, but bitter to the taste. It pleases at first, but not at last. It looks gay on the outside, but evil and misery lie concealed within. When a man has passed a certain number of years in it, he cries out with the Preacher, "Vanity of vanities, all is vanity." Nay, if he has not religion for his guide, he will be forced to go further, and say, "All is vanity and vexation of spirit;" all is disappointment; all is sorrow; all is pain. The sore judgments of God upon sin are concealed within it, and force a man to grieve whether he will or no. Therefore the doctrine of the Cross of Christ does but anticipate for us our experience of the world. It is true, it bids us grieve for our sins in the midst of all that smiles and glitters around us; but if we will not heed it, we shall at length be forced to grieve for them from undergoing their fearful punishment. If we will not acknowledge that this world has been made miserable by sin, from the sight of Him on whom our sins were laid, we shall experience it to be miserable by the recoil of those sins upon ourselves.

It may be granted, then, that the doctrine of the Cross is not on the surface of the world. The surface of things is bright only, and the Cross is sorrowful; it is a hidden doctrine; it lies under a veil; it at first sight startles us, and we are tempted to revolt from it. Like St. Peter, we cry out, "Be it far from Thee,

Lord; this shall not be unto Thee." [Matt. xvi. 22.] And yet it is a true doctrine; for truth is not on the surface of things, but in the depths.

And as the doctrine of the Cross, though it be the true interpretation of this world, is not prominently manifested in it, upon its surface, but is concealed; so again, when received into the faithful heart, there it abides as a living principle, but deep, and hidden from observation. Religious men, in the words of Scripture, "live by the faith of the Son of God, who loved them and gave Himself for them:" [Gal. ii. 20.] but they do not tell this to all men; they leave others to find it out as they may. Our Lord's own command to His disciples was, that when they fast, they should "anoint their head and wash their face." [Matt. vi. 17.] Thus they are bound not to make a display, but ever to be content to look outwardly different from what they are really inwardly. They are to carry a cheerful countenance with them, and to control and regulate their feelings, that those feelings, by not being expended on the surface, may retire deep into their hearts and there live. And thus "Jesus Christ and He crucified" is, as the Apostle tells us, "a hidden wisdom;"—hidden in the world, which seems at first sight to speak a far other doctrine,—and hidden in the faithful soul, which to persons at a distance, or to chance beholders, seems to be living but an ordinary life, while really it is in secret holding communion with Him who was "manifested in the flesh," "crucified through weakness," "justified in the Spirit, seen of angels, and received up into glory."

This being the case, the great and awful doctrine of the Cross of Christ, which we now commemorate, may fitly be called, in the language of figure, the *heart* of religion. The heart may be considered as the seat of life; it is the principle of motion, heat, and activity; from it the blood goes to and fro to the extreme parts of the body. It sustains the man in his powers and faculties; it enables the brain to think; and when it is touched, man dies. And in like manner the sacred doctrine of Christ's Atoning Sacrifice is the vital principle on which the Christian lives, and without which Christianity is not. Without it no other doctrine is held profitably; to believe in Christ's divinity, or in His manhood, or in the Holy Trinity, or in a judgment to come, or in the resurrection of the dead, is an untrue belief, not Christian faith, unless we receive also the doctrine of Christ's sacrifice. On the other hand, to receive it presupposes the reception of other high truths of the Gospel besides; it involves the belief in Christ's true divinity, in His true incarnation, and in man's sinful state by nature; and it prepares the way to belief in the sacred Eucharistic feast, in which He who was once crucified is ever given to our souls and bodies, verily and indeed, in His Body and in His Blood. But again, the heart is hidden from view; it is carefully and securely guarded; it is not like the eye set in the forehead, commanding all, and seen of all: and so in like manner the sacred doctrine of the Atoning Sacrifice is not one to be talked of, but to be lived upon; not to be put forth irreverently, but to be adored secretly; not to be used as a necessary instrument in the conversion of the ungodly, or for the satisfaction of reasoners of this world, but to be unfolded to the docile and obedient; to young children, whom the world has not corrupted; to the sorrowful, who need comfort; to the sincere and earnest, who need a rule of life; to the innocent, who need warning; and to the established, who have earned the knowledge of it.

One more remark I shall make, and then conclude. It must not be supposed, because the doctrine of the Cross makes us sad, that therefore the Gospel is a sad religion. The Psalmist says, "They that sow in tears shall reap in joy;" and our Lord says, "They that mourn shall be comforted." Let no one go away with the impression that the Gospel makes us take a gloomy view of the world and of life. It hinders us indeed from taking a superficial view, and finding a vain transitory joy in what we see; but it forbids our immediate enjoyment, only to grant enjoyment in truth and fulness afterwards. It only forbids us to *begin* with enjoyment. It only says, If you begin with pleasure, you will end with pain. It bids us begin with the Cross of Christ, and in that Cross we shall at first find sorrow, but in a while peace and comfort will rise out of that sorrow. That Cross will lead us to mourning, repentance, humiliation, prayer, fasting; we shall sorrow for our sins, we shall sorrow with Christ's sufferings; but all this sorrow will only issue, nay, will be undergone in a happiness far greater than the enjoyment which the world gives,—though careless worldly minds indeed will not believe this, ridicule the notion of it, because they never have tasted it, and consider it a mere matter of words, which religious persons think it decent and proper to use, and try to believe themselves, and to get others to believe, but which no one really feels. This is what they think; but our Saviour said to His disciples, "Ye now therefore have sorrow, but I will see you again, and your heart shall rejoice, and your joy no man taketh from you." . . . "Peace I leave with you; My peace I give unto you; not as the world giveth, give I unto you." [John xvi. 22; xiv. 27.] And St. Paul says, "The natural man receiveth not the things of the Spirit of God; for they are foolishness unto him; neither can he know them, because they are spiritually discerned." "Eye hath not seen, nor ear heard, neither have entered into the heart of man, the things which God hath prepared for them that love Him." [1 Cor. ii. 9, 14.] And thus the Cross of Christ, as telling us of our redemption as well as of His sufferings, wounds us indeed, but so wounds as to heal also.

And thus, too, all that is bright and beautiful, even on the surface of this world, though it has no substance, and may not suitably be enjoyed for its own sake, yet is a figure and promise of that true joy which issues out of the

Atonement. It is a promise beforehand of what is to be: it is a shadow, raising hope because the substance is to follow, but not to be rashly taken instead of the substance. And it is God's usual mode of dealing with us, in mercy to send the shadow before the substance, that we may take comfort in what is to be, before it comes. Thus our Lord before His Passion rode into Jerusalem in triumph, with the multitudes crying Hosanna, and strewing His road with palm branches and their garments. This was but a vain and hollow pageant, nor did our Lord take pleasure in it. It was a shadow which stayed not, but flitted away. It could not be more than a shadow, for the Passion had not been undergone by which His true triumph was wrought out. He could not enter into His glory before He had first suffered. He could not take pleasure in this semblance of it, knowing that it was unreal. Yet that first shadowy triumph was the omen and presage of the true victory to come, when He had overcome the sharpness of death. And we commemorate this figurative triumph on the last Sunday in Lent, to cheer us in the sorrow of the week that follows, and to remind us of the true joy which comes with Easter-Day.

And so, too, as regards this world, with all its enjoyments, yet disappointments. Let us not trust it; let us not give our hearts to it; let us not begin with it. Let us begin with faith; let us begin with Christ; let us begin with His Cross and the humiliation to which it leads. Let us first be drawn to Him who is lifted up, that so He may, with Himself, freely give us all things. Let us "seek first the kingdom of God and His righteousness," and then all those things of this world "will be added to us." They alone are able truly to enjoy this world, who begin with the world unseen. They alone enjoy it, who have first abstained from it. They alone can truly feast, who have first fasted; they alone are able to use the world, who have learned not to abuse it; they alone inherit it, who take it as a shadow of the world to come, and who for that world to come relinquish it.

The Gospel Palaces[†]

"He built His sanctuary like high palaces,
like the earth which He hath established for ever."
Psalm lxxviii. 69

THERE WAS one occasion when our Saviour said, "The hour cometh, when ye shall neither in this mountain, nor yet at Jerusalem, worship the Father. The hour cometh, when the true worshippers shall worship the Father in spirit and in truth." [John iv. 21, 23.] Did we take these words by themselves, we might consider they implied, that, under the Gospel, there would be no outward tokens of religion, no rites and ordinances at all, no public services, no assemblings of ourselves together, and, especially, no sacred buildings. Such an inference, however, would be a great error, if it were only for this reason, that it has never been received, never acted on in any age of the Church; so far from it, that I suppose there are few indeed but would shrink from the very mention of it, and none at all who could be found to testify that they had adopted it in their own case, yet had not suffered from it in point of inward devotion to God's service. That cannot be the true sense of Scripture, which never has been fulfilled, which ever has been contradicted and disobeyed; for God's word shall not return unto Him void, but shall accomplish His pleasure and prosper in His purpose. Our Saviour did *not* say to the Samaritan woman that there should be no places and buildings for worship under the Gospel, *because* He has *not* brought it to pass, *because* such ever have been, at all times and in all countries, and amid all differences of faith. And the same reasons which lead us to believe that religious edifices are a Christian ordinance, though so very little is said about them in Scripture, will also show that it is right and pious to make them enduring, and stately, and magnificent, and ornamental; so that our Saviour's declaration, when He foretold the destruction of the Temple at Jerusalem, was not that there should never be any other house built to His honour, but rather that there should be many houses; that they should be built, not merely at Jerusalem, or at Gerizim, but every where; what was under the Law a local ordinance, being henceforth a Catholic privilege, allowed not here and there, but wherever was the Spirit and the Truth. The glory of the Gospel is not the *abolition* of rites, but

---

[†] *Parochial & Plain Sermons*, vol. 6 (1842), Sermon 19, preached on Whitsuntide (Pentecost).

236

their *dissemination*; not their absence, but their living and efficacious presence through the grace of Christ. Accordingly, such passages as the text, though spoken in the times of the Law, are fulfilled even at this day, and, as we trust, among ourselves. The Jewish Temple, indeed, of which the Psalmist spoke in the first instance, has come to nought; but he has a meaning still, and a noble one, as signifying the Christian institution of Churches.

"He built His sanctuary like high palaces, like the earth which He hath established for ever." How much more strikingly and fully is this accomplished in our times than in those of the Law! Rich and "exceeding magnifical" as was Solomon's Temple, and built at the immediate command of God, it is not presumptuous surely to say that Christian Temples have as far surpassed it in size, beauty, and costliness, as in divine gifts and privileges, as in spirit and in truth. "He built His sanctuary like high palaces;" look through this very country,—compare its palaces with its Cathedrals and Churches, even in their present state of disadvantage, and say whether these words are not more than accomplished; so that the palaces of England should rather, by way of honour, be compared to the Cathedrals, than the Cathedrals to the palaces. And rightly so; for our first duty is towards our Lord and His Church, and our second towards our earthly Sovereign. And still more strikingly has the promise of permanence been fulfilled to us. For what were the years of Solomon's Temple? Four hundred. What of the second Temple? Six hundred. These were long periods, certainly; yet is it plain that the Church of Christ can more than equal them, and that in a great number of cases. Nay, there are Christian Temples in some parts of the world, which have lasted as much as fourteen hundred years. Surely, then, when Christ multiplied His sacred palaces, He also gave them an extended age, bringing back under the Gospel the days of the Antediluvian patriarchs. The times are reversed, and a more vigorous life has been infused among us than at the first, and the reign of Christ and His saints has begun long since, and the Apostles fill their thrones in His Temples. "He hath built His sanctuary like high palaces, like the earth which He hath established for ever.

Stability and permanence are, perhaps, the especial ideas which a Church brings before the mind. It represents, indeed, the beauty, the loftiness, the calmness, the mystery, and the sanctity of religion also, and that in many ways; still, I will say, more than all these, it represents to us its eternity. It is the witness of Him who is the beginning and the ending, the first and the last; it is the token and emblem of "Jesus Christ, the same yesterday, today, and for ever;" it is the pledge of One, who has said, "I will never leave thee nor forsake thee," but "even to your old age I am He, and even to hoar hairs I will carry you." All ye who take part in the building of a Church, know that you have been admitted to the truest symbol of God's eternity. You have built what may be destined to have no end but in Christ's coming. Cast your thoughts back on the time when our ancient buildings were first reared. Consider the Churches all around us; how many generations have past since stone was put upon stone till the whole edifice was finished! The first movers and instruments of its erection, the minds that planned it, and the limbs that wrought at it, the pious hands that contributed to it, and the holy lips that consecrated it, have long, long ago, been taken away; yet we benefit by their good deed. Does it not seem a very strange thing that *we* should be fed, and lodged, and clothed in spiritual things, by persons we never saw or heard of, and who never saw us, or could think of us, hundreds of years ago? Does it not seem strange that men should be able, not merely by acting on others, not by a continued influence carried on through many minds in a long succession, but by one simple and direct act, to come into contact with us, and as if with their own hand to benefit us, who live centuries later? What a visible, palpable specimen this, of the communion of saints! What a privilege thus to be immediately interested in the deeds of our forefathers! and what a call on us, in like manner, to reach out our own hands towards our posterity! Freely we have received; let us freely give. Let us not be slack to do what our fathers have done; to do a work, the fruits of which we cannot see, because they are too vast to be seen. If it were told us, that a word of ours, uttered by the mouth, should take, as it were, consistence, and float and continue in the air, and impart advice or comfort to men who were to live five hundred years to come, it would be an inspiring thought; and what but this is our very privilege, in the leave granted us to multiply the One Temple of God all over the earth, unto all time? It is to make our deeds live; it is to hold fellowship with the future.

See what a noble principle faith is. Faith alone lengthens a man's existence, and makes him, in his own feelings, live in the future and in the past. Men of this world are full of plans of the day. Even in religion they are ever coveting immediate results, and will do nothing at all, unless they can do every thing,—can have their own way, choose their methods, and see the end. But the Christian throws himself fearlessly upon the future, because he believes in Him which is, and which was, and which is to come. He can endure to be one of an everlasting company while in this world, as well as in the next. He is content to begin, and break off; to do his part, and no more; to set about what others must accomplish; to sow where others must reap. None has finished his work, and cut it short in righteousness but He who is One. We, His members, who have but a portion of His fulness, execute but a part of His purpose. One lays the foundation, and another builds thereupon; one levels the mountain, and another "brings forth the headstone with shoutings." Thus were our

Churches raised. One age would build a Chancel, and another a Nave, and a third would add a Chapel, and a fourth a Shrine, and a fifth a Spire. By little and little the work of grace went forward; and they could afford to take time about it, and be at pains to do it best, who had a promise that the gates of hell should not prevail against it. Powers of the earth rise and fall; revolutions come in course; great families appear, and are swept away; wise men are in high places, and walk amid the sparks which they have kindled. They *feel* that they are short-lived, and they determine to make the most of their time. They grasp and push forwards, they are busy and feverish, not only from the feebleness and waywardness of their nature, but from the conviction of their reason, that they have but a short time. "Our time is short," say they; "let us buy and sell, and plant and build, and marry wives, and give in marriage, and eat and drink, for tomorrow we die." Poor worms of the earth, it is too true of them! Their aims and desires, their instruments, their goods, their bodies, their souls, are all perishable. In the words of the wise man, "as soon as they are born, they *begin* to draw to an end," [Wisdom v. 13.] they begin to die. Their growth and progress, their successes, are but the first stages of corruption and dissolution. Poor children of time, what are they? They triumph over religion in their day; they insult its ordinances and its ministers; they tyrannize in its Temples, showing themselves that they are gods. They carry away its massive stones to their own houses, and trick themselves out with its jewels. They build up their families by rapine and sacrilege; they are wanton when they are not covetous; and, when satiated with pillage, they mutilate and defile what they do not destroy. But, after all, how speaks the Psalmist? "I have said, Ye are gods, and ye are all the children of the Most Highest. But ye shall die like men, and fall like one of the princes." "The proud have robbed, they have slept their sleep, and all the men whose hands were mighty have found nothing." "Fret not thyself because of the ungodly; neither be thou envious against the evil-doers; for they shall soon be cut down like the grass, and be withered even as the green herb. I myself have seen the ungodly in great power, and flourishing like a green bay tree; I went by, and lo, he was gone; I sought him, but his place could no where be found." [Ps. lxxxii. 6, 7; lxxvi. 5; xxxvii. 1, 2, 36, 37.] We rise in the morning, and, behold, they are all dead corpses. The storm has passed, the morning has broken, the Egyptians are cast on the seashore, God's Tabernacle is still standing. As though no violence had been in the night, no assaults of Satan and Antichrist, no arm of force, no envious or covetous eye, they remain, those holy places, where they were; for the Church abides for evermore, and her Temples, in their deep foundations, and their arching heights, are her image and manifestation.

I have said that the sacred edifices which we see around us, and in which we worship, remind us of their builders, though they lived so long ago; but in truth they remind us of a time far earlier even than theirs. Do we suppose that the very builders of these shrines were all in all in their building? Could any men whatever, did they but will it, at any time, build what they have built? is a Cathedral the offspring of a random thought, a thing to will and to accomplish at our pleasure? or rather, were not those builders merely the successors and the children of others long before them, who made them what they were, and enabled them, under God, to do works, which it was not given to every one to do, but only to the sons of such fathers? Surely the Churches which we inherit are not the purchase of wealth nor the creation of genius, they are the fruits of martyrdom. They come of high deeds and sufferings, as long before their very building as we are after it. Their foundations are laid very deep, even in the preaching of Apostles, and the confession of Saints, and the first victories of the Gospel in our land. All that is so noble in their architecture, all that captivates the eye and makes its way to the heart, is not a human imagination, but a divine gift, a moral result, a spiritual work. The Cross is ever planted in hazard and suffering, and is watered with tears and blood. No where does it take root and bear fruit, except its preaching be with self-denial. It is easy, indeed, for the ruling powers to make a decree, and set religion on high, and extend its range, and herald its name; but they cannot plant it, they can but impose it. The Church alone can plant the Church. The Church alone can found her sees, and inclose herself within walls. None but saintly men, mortified men, preachers of righteousness, and confessors for the truth, can create a home for the truth in any land. Thus the Temples of God are withal the monuments of His Saints, and we call them by their names while we consecrate them to His glory. Their simplicity, grandeur, solidity, elevation, grace, and exuberance of ornament, do but bring to remembrance the patience and purity, the courage, meekness, and great charity, the heavenly affections, the activity in well-doing, the faith and resignation, of men who themselves did but worship in mountains, and in deserts, and in caves and dens of the earth. They laboured, but not in vain, for other men entered into their labours; and, as if by natural consequence, at length their word prospered after them, and made itself a home, even these sacred palaces in which it has so long dwelt, and which are still vouchsafed to us, in token, as we trust, that they too are still with us who spoke that word, and, with them, His Presence, who gave them grace to speak it.

O happy they, who, in a sorrowful time, avail themselves of this bond of communion with the Saints of old and with the Universal Church! O wise and dutiful, who, when the world has robbed them of so much, set the more account upon what remains! We have not lost all, while we have the dwelling-places of our forefathers; while we can repair those which are broken down, and build upon the old foundations, and propagate them upon new sites! Happy they, who when they enter within their holy limits, enter in heart into the court of heaven! And most unhappy, who, while they have eyes to admire, admire them only for their beauty's sake, and the skill they exhibit; who regard them as works of art, not fruits of grace; bow down before their material forms, instead of worshipping "in spirit and in truth;" count their stones, and measure their spaces, but discern in them no tokens of the invisible, no canons of truth, no lessons of wisdom, to guide them forward in the way heavenward!

In heaven is the substance, of which here below we are vouchsafed the image; and thither, if we be worthy, we shall at length attain. There is the holy Jerusalem, whose light is like unto a stone most precious, even like a jasper stone, clear as crystal; and whose wall is great and high, with twelve gates, and an Angel at each;—whose glory is the Lord God Almighty, and the Lamb is the light thereof.

The Visible Temple[†]

"Whether is greater, the gold, or the Temple that sanctifieth the gold?"
Mark xxiii. 17

A TEMPLE there has been upon earth, a spiritual Temple, made up of living stones, a Temple, as I may say, composed of souls; a Temple with God for its Light, and Christ for the High Priest, with wings of Angels for its arches, with Saints and Teachers for its pillars, and with worshippers for its pavement; such a Temple has been on earth ever since the Gospel was first preached. This unseen, secret, mysterious, spiritual Temple exists every where, throughout the kingdom of Christ, in all places, as perfect in one place as if it were not in another. Wherever there is faith and love, this Temple is; faith and love, with the Name of Christ, are as heavenly charms and spells, to make present to us this Divine Temple, in every part of Christ's kingdom. This Temple is invisible, but it is perfect and real because it is invisible, and gains nothing in perfection by possessing visible tokens. There needs no outward building to meet the eye, in order to make it more of a Temple than it already is in itself. God, and Christ, and Angels, and souls, are not these a heavenly court, all perfect, to which this world can add nothing? Though faithful Christians worship without splendour, without show, in a homely and rude way, still their worship is as acceptable to God, as excellent, as holy, as though they worshipped in the public view of men, and with all the glory and riches of the world.

Such was the Church in its beginnings; "built upon the foundation of Apostles and Prophets, Jesus Christ Himself being the chief cornerstone," "builded together for an habitation of God through the Spirit." In the Apostles' lifetime it was poor and persecuted, and the holy Temple was all but invisible. There were no edifying rites, no various ceremonies, no rich music, no high Cathedrals, no mystic vestments, no solemn altars, no stone, or marble, or metals, or jewels, or woods of cost, or fine linen, to signify outwardly, and to honour duly, the heavenly Temple in which we stand and serve. The place where our Lord and Saviour first celebrated the holy Sacrament of the Eucharist, was the upper room of a house, hired too or used for the occasion [Mark xiv. 15.]; that in which the Apostles and the holy women waited for the prom-

---

[†] *Parochial & Plain Sermons*, vol. 6 (1842), Sermon 20, preached on Whitsuntide (Pentecost).

ised coming of the Comforter, was also "an upper room;" [Acts i. 13.] and that also in which St. Paul preached at Troas, was an "upper chamber, where they were gathered together." [Acts xx. 8.] What other places of worship do we hear of? The water side, out in the open air; as at Philippi, where, we are told, "on the Sabbath," St. Paul and his companions "went out of the city by a river side, where prayer was wont to be made." [Acts xvi. 13.] And the sea shore; "They all brought us on our way with wives and children, till we were out of the city; and we kneeled down on the shore and prayed." [Acts xxi. 5.] And St. Peter was in prayer on the house-top; and St. Paul and St. Silas sang their hymns and psalms in prison with their feet in the stocks; and St. Philip baptized the Ethiopian eunuch in the desert. Yet, wherever they were, whether in prison, or on the house-top, or in the wilderness, or by the river side, or on the sea shore, or in a private room, God and Christ were with them. The Spirit of Grace was there, the Temple of God was around them. They were come unto the mystical Sion, and to the heavenly Jerusalem, and to an innumerable company of Angels, and to the spirits of the Just. There needed not gold, nor jewels, nor costly array for those, who had, what according to the text was greater, who had the Temple. It might be right and fitting, if possible, to have these precious things also, but it was not necessary; for which was the greater? Such things did not make the temple more holy, but became themselves holy by being used for the Temple; the gold did not sanctify the Temple, but the Temple was greater, and sanctified the gold. Gold is a thing of nought without Christ's presence; and with His Presence, as in the days of His earthly ministry, it might be dispensed with.

The case is the same as regards the immediate successors of the Apostles, who were in still more forlorn circumstances, as regards worship, than the Apostles themselves. The Christians who came after them, were obliged to worship in graves and tombs to save their lives from the persecutor. In the eastern and southern parts, where the Apostles and the first converts lived, before the glad sound of the Gospel had reached these northern and distant countries, they were accustomed to bury in caves dug out of the rock. Long galleries there are still remaining, in some places for miles underground, on each side of which the dead were placed. There the poor persecuted Christians met for worship, and that by night. Or the great people of the time built for themselves high and stately tombs above ground, as large as houses for the living; here too, in the darkness and solitude of night, did the Saints worship. Or in the depth of some wood, perhaps, where no one was likely to discover them. Such were the places in which the Invisible Temple manifested itself in times of heathenism; and who shall say that it wanted aught of outward show to make it perfect?

This is true and ever to be borne in mind; and yet no one can deny, on the other hand, that a great object of Christ's coming was to subdue this world, to claim it as His own, to assert His rights as its Master, to destroy the usurped dominion of the enemy, to show Himself to all men, and to take possession. He is that Mustard-tree which was destined silently to spread and overshadow all lands; He is that Leaven which was secretly to make its way through the mass of human opinion and institutions till the whole was leavened. Heaven and earth had hitherto been separate. His gracious purpose was to make them one, and that by making earth like heaven. He was in the world from the beginning, and man worshipped other gods; He came into the world in the flesh, and the world knew Him not; He came unto His own, and His own received Him not. But He came in order to *make* them receive Him, know Him, worship Him. He came to absorb this world into Himself; that, as He was light, so it might be light also. When He came, He had not a place to lay His head; but He came to make Himself a place, to make Himself a home, to make Himself houses, to fashion for Himself a glorious dwelling out of this whole world, which the powers of evil had taken captive. He came in the dark, in the dark night was He born, in a cave underground; in a cave where cattle were stabled, there was He housed; in a rude manger was He laid. There first He laid His head; but He meant not, blessed be His Name! He meant not there to remain for ever. He did not resign Himself to that obscurity; He came into that cave to leave it. The King of the Jews was born to claim the kingdom;—yea, rather, the Hope of all nations and the King of the whole earth, the King of kings and Lord of lords; and He gave not "sleep to His eyes or slumber to His eyelids," till He had changed His manger for a royal throne, and His grot for high palaces. Lift up your eyes, my brethren, and look around, for it is fulfilled at this day; yea, long ago, for many ages, and in many countries. "Wisdom hath builded her house, she hath hewn out her seven pillars." Where is the grot? where the stall for cattle? where the manger? where the grass and straw? where the unseemly furniture of that despised place? Is it possible that the Eternal Son should have been born in a hole of the earth? was the great miracle there wrought, whereby a pure and spotless Virgin brought forth God? Strange condescension undergone to secure a strange triumph! He purposed to change the earth, and He began "in the lowest pit, in a place of darkness, and in the deep." All was to be by Him renewed, and He availed Himself of nothing that was, that out of nothing He might make all things. He was not born in the Temple of Jerusalem; He abhorred the palace of David; He laid Himself on the damp earth in the cold night, a light shining in a dark place, till by the virtue that went out of Him, He should create a Temple worthy of His Name.

And lo, in omen of the future, even in His cradle, the rich and wise of the earth seek Him with gold, and frankincense, and myrrh, as an offering. And He puts aside the swaddling clothes, and takes instead "a coat without seam, woven from the top throughout." And He changes water into wine; and Levi feasts Him; and Zacchaeus receives Him; and Mary anoints His head. Pass a few generations, and the whole face of things is changed; the earth is covered with His Temples; as it has been for ages. Go where you will, you find the eternal mountains hewn and fashioned into shrines where He may dwell, who was an outcast in the days of His flesh. Rivers and mines pay tribute of their richest jewels; forests are searched for their choicest woods; the skill of man is put to task to use what nature furnishes. Go through the countries where His name is known, and you will find all that is rarest and most wonderful in nature or art has been consecrated to Him. King's palaces are poor, whether in architecture or in decoration, compared with the shrines which have been reared to Him. The Invisible Temple has become visible. As on a misty day, the gloom gradually melts and the sun brightens, so have the glories of the spiritual world lit up this world below. The dull and cold earth is penetrated by the rays. All around we see glimpses or reflections of those heavenly things, which the elect of God shall one day see face to face. The kingdoms of this world are become the kingdoms of our Lord and of His Christ; "the Temple has sanctified the gold," and the prophecies made to the Church have been fulfilled to the letter. "The glory of Lebanon" has been "given unto it, the excellency of Carmel and Sharon." "The glory of Lebanon, the fir-tree, the pine-tree, and the box together, to beautify the place of His sanctuary, and to make the place of His feet glorious. The multitude of camels have covered it, the dromedaries of Midian and Ephah; all they from Sheba have come; they have brought gold and incense, and shown forth the praises of the Lord." "The labour of Egypt, and merchandize of Ethiopia, and of the Sabeans, men of stature, have come over to it, in chains have they come over; they have fallen down, they have made supplication." [Isa. xxxv. 2; lx. 6, 13; xlv. 14.]

And He has made Him a Temple, not only out of inanimate things, but of men also as parts of it. Not gold and silver, jewels and fine linen, and skill of man to use them, make the House of God, but worshippers, the souls and bodies of men, whom He has redeemed. Not souls alone, He takes possession of the whole man, body as well as soul; for St. Paul says, "I beseech you, therefore, brethren, by the mercies of God, that ye present your *bodies* a living sacrifice, holy, acceptable unto God, which is your reasonable service." [Rom. xii. 1.] And He claims us as His own, not one by one, but altogether, as one great company; for St. Peter says, that we "as living stones, are built up a spiritual house, an holy priesthood, to offer up spiritual sacrifices, acceptable to God by

Jesus Christ." [1 Pet. ii. 5.] All of us, and every one, and every part of every one, must go to make up His mystical body; for the Psalmist says, "O God, my heart is ready; I will sing and give praise with the best member that I have. Awake thou, lute and harp, I myself will awake right early. I will give thanks unto Thee, O Lord, among the people; I will sing praises unto Thee among the nations." [Psa. cviii. 1–3.] Our tongues must preach Him, and our voices sing of Him, and our knees adore Him, and our hands supplicate Him, and our heads bow before Him, and our countenances beam of Him, and our gait herald Him. And hence arise joint worship, forms of prayer, ceremonies of devotion, the course of services, orders of ministers, holy vestments, solemn music, and other things of a like nature; all which are, as it were, the incoming into this world of the Invisible Kingdom of Christ, the fruit of its influence, the sample of its power, the earnest of its victories, the means of its manifestation.

Things temporal have their visible establishment. Kings' courts and palaces, councils and armies, have dazzled the multitude, and blinded them, till they worshipped them as idols. Such is our nature, we must have something to look up to. We cannot help admiring *something*; and if there is nothing good to admire, we admire what is bad. When then men see proud Babel set up on high with all her show and pomp, when they see or hear of great cities, with their stately mansions, the streets swarming with chariots and horses innumerable, and the shops filled with splendid wares, and great men and women richly dressed, with many attendants, and men crying, Bow the knee, and soldiers in bright array, with the sound of the trumpet, and other military music, and other things which one could mention, were it reverent to be particular,—simple men are tempted to look up to all this as the summit of perfection and blessedness, nay, as I have said, to worship what seems to them, though they do not so express it, the presence of the Unseen. Hence come in servility, coveting, jealousy, ambition; men wish to be great in this world, and try to be great; they aim at riches, or they lie in wait for promotion. Christ, then, in order to counteract this evil, has mercifully set up His own court and His own polity, that men might have something to fix their eyes upon of a more Divine and holy character than the world can supply; that poverty might at least divide men's admiration with riches; that meekness might be set up on high as well as pride, and sanctity become our ambition as well as luxury. Saintly bishops with their clergy, officials of all kinds, religious bodies, austere Nazarites, prayer and praise without ceasing,—all this hath Christ mercifully set up, to outshine the fascinations of the world. So ran the promise: "I have set watchmen upon thy walls, O Jerusalem, which shall never hold their peace day nor night." "Sing unto the Lord a new song, and His praise from the end of the earth; ye that go down to the sea, and all that is therein . . . Let the wilderness and the cities thereof lift up their voice, the villages that Kedar doth inhabit; let the inhabitants of the rock sing; let them shout from the top of the mountains. Let them give glory unto the Lord, and declare His praise in the islands." [Isa. lxii. 6; xlii. 10–12.] And these words began to have their fulfilment even from the time that Christ came; for, as I said when I began, St. Paul and St. Silas *sang* in the prison; and when he and his party left Tyre, the men, women, and children, who accompanied them out, *kneeled down* on the shore with them, and prayed. Such were the forms of worship in the beginning; till, as time went on, the Church, like some fair tree, put out her branches and foliage, and stood complete in all manner of holy symbols and spiritual ordinances, an outward sign of that unseen Temple in which Christ had dwelt from the first.

And now, in conclusion, let me observe, that such a view as has been taken of the connexion of the ritual of religion with its spiritual and invisible power, will enable us to form a right estimate of things external, and keep us both from a curious and superstitions use, and an arrogant neglect of them. The Temple is greater than the gold; therefore care not though the gold be away:—it sanctifies it; therefore cherish the gold while it is present. Christ is with us, though there be no outward show; suppose all the comely appendages of our worship stripped off, yet where two or three are gathered together in His Name, He is in the midst of them. Be it a cottage, or the open fields, or even a prison or a dungeon, Christ can be there, and will be there, if His servants are there. You will ask whether this does not countenance persons who hold meetings apart from the Church, or who preach in the streets? No, it does not; because, in such cases, men do not meet together "in the Name of Christ." He says, "Where two or three are gathered together in My Name." Now, it does not follow that men *are* met in His Name because they say or think they are; for He warns us, "Many shall come in My Name, saying, I am Christ, and shall deceive many." Many a man *thinks* he is speaking in Christ's Name, when he is preaching his own doctrine. Christ did not send such men, yet they have run; and He owns them not, though they even worship in Church. In Church, or in the fields, would be the same in this matter. Stone walls do not make a Church. Though they were in the vastest, noblest, richest building on earth, still Christ would not be with those who preach another gospel than that which He delivered once for all. This is the very point I am insisting on. It is the Temple which sanctifieth the gold; it is nothing but the invisible and heavenly Presence which sanctifieth any place or any thing. Magnificent or mean, costly or common, it alone sanctifies either worshippers or building. As it avails not to have sumptuous Churches without the Spirit of

Christ, so it is but a mockery to have large congregations, eloquent preachers, and much excitement, if that gracious Spirit is away. But where He really places His *Name*, there, be the spot a palace or a cottage, it is sacred and glorious. He who once lay in a manger, will still condescend to manifest Himself any where, as He did in primitive times. No indignities can he done to Him who inhabiteth eternity. "Heaven is His throne, and earth His footstool;" "the very heaven of heavens cannot contain Him;" much less any house which we can build. High or low is alike to Him.

This is an obvious and very comfortable reflection, when we think of the great irreverences and profanations which sometimes take place in Church. Men come in lightly and thoughtlessly; they care not to uncover their heads; they talk, and laugh, and even sing, as if they were in a common building; or, when there is any needful work to be done in it, and tools and other implements are brought in, they seem to think as if, all of a sudden, it were turned into an unconsecrated place, because it is necessary to exercise a trade in it. Or, perhaps, if it so happen, they turn aside into it at other times, and think that God is not there, because man is not there to see them. And so again, when we go into certain Churches, and see the neglected state in which they are left, the font cast aside, or, if not, used as a place to keep any sort of litter in; and the Holy Table mean and unsightly, with a miserable covering, and the pavement defiled and broken, and the whole building in a state of neglect, of which any neat person would be ashamed even in his own cottage (to say nothing what wealthy people would feel, if their rooms were left in such a condition); I say, when these and such like sights meet us, perhaps, for an instant, we are tempted to say, Can Christ be here? Can the Holy Spirit design to sanctify water for the washing away of sins, brought in, as it is, with such irreverence of manner, and in so mean a vessel? Or, can the life-giving Presence and the sacrificial power of Christ be upon that Altar? nay, can it *be* an Altar, which is so wretched to look upon? But, I ask, or rather, any one will ask himself, on second thoughts, Could Christ be in a manger? Doubtless then He, whom the Angels of God worshipped as the Only-begotten, when brought into the world in a place for cattle, can be manifested, can be worshipped, in the most neglected Church. No; our distress must not be at all for *Him*; such would be superstitious and carnal; our distress must be for the insult offered Him, and so far as there is insult. If the state of neglect I am speaking of is no one's fault, then distress there must be none. But if there be blame, then we may and must feel distress, that our Lord should be insulted by His own servants; and yet more on their account, that they should insult Him. They who profane His Presence, who treat its resting-place as a common house, and make free with it, these men do not hurt Christ, but they hurt themselves. The Temple is greater than the gold.

And, while He is displeased with the profane, He accepts such offerings as are made in faith, whether they be greater or less. He accepts our gold and our silver, not to honour Himself thereby, but in mercy to us. When Mary poured the ointment upon His head, it was her advantage, not His: He praised her, and said, "She hath done what she could." Every one must do his best; he must pray his best, he must sing his best, he must attend his best. If we did all, it would be little, not worthy of Him; if we do little, it may suffice to show our faith, and He in His mercy will accept whatever we can offer. He will accept, what we prefer giving to Him to giving to ourselves. When, instead of spending money on our own homes, we spend it on His house, when we prefer that He should have the gold and silver to our having it, we do not make our worship more spiritual, but we bring Christ nearer to us; we show that we are in earnest, we evidence our faith. It requires very little of true faith and love, to feel an unwillingness to spend money on one's self. Fine dresses, fine houses, fine furniture, fine establishments, are painful to a true Christian; they create misgivings in his mind whether his portion is with the Saints or with the world. Rather he will feel it suitable to lay out his money in God's service, to feed the hungry, to clothe the naked, to educate the young, to spread the knowledge of the truth; and, among other pious objects, to build and to decorate the visible House of God.

"Remember me, O my God, concerning this, and wipe not out my good deeds that I have done for the house of my God, and for the offices thereof." [Neh. xiii. 14.] Such was Nehemiah's prayer, when he had been stirred up to cleanse the sanctuary. May God remember us also, if in any measure His grace has moved us to similar acts of zeal for His glory! And, O may He in His mercy grant that our outward show does not outstrip our inward progress; that whatever gift, rare or beautiful, we introduce here, may be but a figure of inward beauty and unseen sanctity ornamenting our hearts! Hearts are the true shrine wherein Christ must dwell. "The King's daughter is all-glorious within;" and when we are repenting of past sin, and cleansing ourselves from all defilement of flesh and spirit, and perfecting holiness in the fear of the Lord, then, and then only, may we safely employ ourselves in brightening, embellishing, and making glorious the dwelling-place of His invisible Presence, doing it with that severity, gravity, and awe, which a chastened heart and sober thoughts will teach us.

Offerings for the Sanctuary[†]

"The glory of Lebanon shall come unto thee, the fir-tree, the pine-tree
and the box together, to beautify the place of My Sanctuary;
and I will make the place of My feet glorious."
Isaiah lx. 13

EVERY ATTENTIVE READER of Scripture must be aware what stress is
there laid upon the duty of costliness and magnificence in the public
service of God. Even in the first rudiments of the Church, Jacob, an
outcast and wanderer, after the vision of the Ladder of Angels, thought it not
enough to bow down before the Unseen Presence, but parted with, or, as the
world would say, wasted a portion of the provisions he had with him for the
way, in an act of worship. Like David, he did not "offer unto the Lord of that
which cost him nothing;" but like that religious woman at the opening of a
more gracious Covenant, though he had not "an alabaster box of ointment of
spikenard very precious," yet he did "what he could;" making a sacrifice less
than hers in its costliness, greater in his own destitute condition, for he "took
the stone that he had put for his pillows, and set it up for a pillar, and poured
oil upon the top of it." [Gen. xxviii. 18.]

What Jacob did as a solitary pilgrim, David as a wealthy king, Mary as a
private woman, is pressed upon us both in sacred history and in prophecy, as
fulfilled under the Law, as foretold of the Gospel. The Book of Exodus shows
what cost was lavished upon the Tabernacle even in the wilderness; the Books
of Kings and Chronicles set before us the devotion of heart, the sedulous zeal,
the carelessness of expense or toil, with which the first Temple was reared upon Mount Sion, in the commencement of the monarchy of Israel. "Now have
I prepared," says David, "*with all my might* for the house of my God, the gold
. . . and the silver . . . and the brass . . . the iron . . . and wood . . . onyx stones,
and stones to be set, glistering stones, and of divers colours, and all manner of
precious stones, and marble stones in abundance. Moreover, because I *have set
my affection* to the house of my God, I have *of my own proper good*, of gold and
silver, which I have given to the house of my God, over and above all that I
have prepared for the Holy House." And he "rejoiced with great joy," and
"blessed the Lord," because the people also "*offered willingly*, because *with per-*

[†] *Parochial & Plain Sermons*, vol. 6 (1842), Sermon 21, preached on Whitsuntide (Pentecost).

fect heart they offered willingly to the Lord." And Solomon, when he came to use these costly offerings, sent to another country for "a cunning man," "skilful to work in gold, and in silver, in brass, in iron, in stone, and in timber, in purple, in blue, and in fine linen and in crimson; also to grave any manner of graving, and to find out every device which should be put to him, with the cunning men in Judah and in Jerusalem." [1 Chron. xxix. 2, 3, 9, 10. 2 Chron. ii. 7, 14.] Such was the outward splendour of the Jewish Sanctuary; nor were the glories of the Christian to be less outward and visible, though they were to be more spiritual also. The words of the Prophet in the text are but one instance out of several, of the promise of temporal magnificence made to that Covenant which was to be eternal. "The glory of Lebanon," says Isaiah, addressing the Gospel Church, "shall come unto thee, the fir-tree, the pine-tree, and the box together, to beautify the place of My Sanctuary; and I will make the place of My feet glorious." Again; "For brass I will bring gold, and for iron I will bring silver, and for wood brass, and for stones iron; thou shalt call thy walls Salvation, and thy gates Praise." And again; "O thou afflicted, tossed with tempest, and not comforted, behold, I will lay thy stones with fair colours, and lay thy foundations with sapphires. And I will make thy windows of agates, and thy gates of carbuncles, and all thy borders of pleasant stones." [Isa. lx. 17, 18; liv. 11, 12.] Now if it be said that some of these expressions are figurative, this may be true; but still the very fact that such figures are used in the prophecy, would seem to show that the materials literally denoted may be suitably used in its fulfilment, unless, indeed, such use is actually forbidden. They do not cease to be figures because they are actually present as well as spoken of. Real gold is as much a figure in the Church, as the mention of it is such in Scripture; and it is surely in itself dutiful and pleasant thus to make much of the words of inspired truth; and moreover, the mere circumstance that, when the Gospel came, Christians did thus proceed, and sanctified the precious things of this world to religious uses, looks like the fulfilment of the prophecy, and is of the nature of an authoritative command.

However, it may be objected that every attentive reader of Scripture will be familiar with this circumstance also, that such outward splendour in the worship of God is spoken of in terms of censure or jealousy by our Lord and Saviour. Thus He says, when enumerating the offences of the Pharisees, "Woe unto you, Scribes and Pharisees, hypocrites! for ye make clean the *outside* of the cup and of the platter, but within they are full of extortion and excess." And again, "Ye are like unto whited sepulchres, which indeed appear beautiful outward, but are within full of dead men's bones, and of all uncleanness." And when His disciples pointed out to our Lord the great size of the stones of which the Temple was built,—a Temple, let it be noted, thus ornamented by the impious Herod,—He answered abruptly, "There shall not be left here one stone upon another, that shall not be thrown down." [Matt. xxiii. 25, 27; xxiv. 2.]

These passages certainly should be taken into account; but what do they mean? did our Saviour say that magnificence in worshipping God, magnificence in His house, in its furniture, and in its decorations, is wrong, wrong since He has come into the world? Does He discourage us from building handsome Churches, or beautifying the ceremonial of religion? Did He exhort us to niggardness? did He put a slight on architectural skill? did He imply we should please Him the more, the less study and trouble we gave to the externals of worship? In rejecting the offering of Herod, did He forbid the devotion of Christians?

This is what many persons think. I do not exaggerate when I say, that they think the more homely and familiar their worship is, the more spiritual it becomes. And they argue, that to aim at external beauty in the service of the Sanctuary, is to be like the Pharisees, to be fair without and hollow within; that whereas the Pharisees pretended a sanctity and religiousness outside which they had not inside, therefore, every one who aims at outward religion sacrifices to it inward.

This is a consideration worth dwelling on; not indeed for its own weight, but because it weighs with so many people. The objection is this; because the hollow Pharisees were outwardly holy, therefore every one who shows any outward holiness is, or is in danger of becoming, a Pharisee.

Now, to take a parallel instance, most of us perhaps have heard a proverb, that "cleanliness is next to godliness;" which means, that the habit spoken of is of a moral nature, at least accidentally, and is a moral excellence, and that those who are deficient in it are commonly deficient also in other and more religious excellences also. Who among us will not admit that nothing is more unwelcome, nay, under circumstances, nothing raises more serious and anxious thoughts, than the absence of neatness and what is called tidiness, in appearance and dress? We can often tell at once how young persons are conducting themselves by the first glance at them. Alas! we read what is painful in their history; we read of a change in their religions state in the disorder of their look and the negligence of their gait. Or enter a village school: are we not at once pleased with a neat and bright-faced child? and do we not at once take a dislike to such as are not so?

But, now, suppose any one were to come to us and say, "This is all outside; what God requires is a clean heart, not a neat appearance:" would this seem a pertinent objection? We should answer surely, that what our duty requires of us is cleanness of heart *and* decency of attire also; that the one point

252

of duty does not interfere with the other; nay, on the contrary, that inward exactness and sanctity are likely to *show* themselves in this very way,—in propriety of appearance; and that if persons who are exact in their lives are, notwithstanding, negligent in their persons, this ought not to be so, and we wish it were otherwise.

But supposing the objector went on to say that those who were neat and respectable in their persons and homes had often very bad tempers, were ever making a *point* of being neat, and what is called "particular," and quarrelled with every one who interfered with their own habits and ways. We should answer, that if so, it was to be lamented; but still, in spite of this, it was a right thing to be neat, and a wrong thing to be slovenly; that exactness within best showed itself in exactness without, and that cleanliness was the natural and most appropriate attendant on godliness.

And again; supposing the objector in question said that propriety in dress became love of finery; that those who attended to their persons became vain; that it was impossible to be neat and respectable without going on to dress gaily, and making a show to attract the attention of others. We should answer that all this ought not to be, and was very wrong; that vanity was a great sin; that those who studied their dress disobeyed our Lord's command not to think about raiment, and were exposing themselves to temptations, and were going forth they knew not whither, going the way of death, going the way to become reckless, as about greater matters, so about dress itself. This we should say; but we should add, that such considerations did not prove that neatness and decency were not praiseworthy, but that love of finery was perilous, and vanity sinful.

But supposing the objector supported what he said by Scripture: supposing he said, for instance, that our Lord blamed persons who washed their hands before eating bread, and that this proves that washing the hands before a meal is wrong. I am taking no fictitious case; such objections really have been made before now: yet the answer surely is easy, namely, that our Saviour objected, not to the mere washing of the hands, but to the making too much of such an observance; to our thinking it religion, thinking that it would stand in the stead of inward religion, and would make up for sins of the heart. This is what He condemned, the show of great attention to outward things, *while* inward things, which were more important, were neglected. This, He says Himself, in His denunciation of the Pharisees, "These ought ye to have done," He says, "*and not* to leave the other," the inward, "*undone.*" He says expressly they ought to do the outward, but they ought to do more. They did the one and not the other; they ought to have done both the one and the other.

Now, apply this to the case of beautifying Churches:—as is neatness and decency in an individual, such is decoration in a Church; and as we should be offended at slovenliness in an individual, so ought we to be offended at disorder and neglect in our Churches. It is quite true, men *are* so perverse (as the Pharisees were) that they sometimes attend only to the outward forms, and neglect the inward spirit; they may offer to Him costly furniture and goodly stones, while they are cruel or bigoted;—just as persons may be neat in their own persons and houses, and yet be ill-tempered and quarrelsome. Or, again, they may carry their attention to the outward forms of religion too far, and become superstitious; just as persons may carry on a love of neatness into love of finery. And, moreover, Scripture speaks against the hypocrisy of those who are religious outwardly, while they live in sin,—just as it speaks against those who wash their hands, while their heart is defiled. But still, in spite of all this, propriety in appearance and dress is a virtue,—is next to godliness; and, in like manner, decency and reverence are to be observed in the worship of God, and are next to devotion, in spite of its being true that not all are holy who are grave and severe, not all devout who are munificent.

What Scripture reproves is the *inconsistency*, or what it more solemnly called the *hypocrisy* of being fair without and foul within; of being religious in appearance, not in truth. It was one offence not to be religious, it was a second offence to pretend to be religious. "Ye fools," says our Lord, "did not He that made that which is without, make that which is within also?" Such as a man is outwardly, such should he be inwardly. "How can ye, being evil, speak good things? for out of the abundance of the heart the mouth speaketh. A good man, out of the good treasure of the heart, bringeth forth good things; and an evil man, out of the evil treasure, bringeth forth evil things." [Luke xi. 40. Matt. xii. 34, 35.] The light of Divine truth, when in the heart, ought to beam forth outwardly; and when a man is dark within, well were it that he should show himself outwardly what he is. Such as a man is inside, such should be his outside. Well; but do you not see that such a view of doctrine condemns not only those who affect outward religion without inward, but those also who affect inward without outward? For, if it is an inconsistency to pretend to religion outwardly, while we neglect it inwardly, it is also an inconsistency, surely, to neglect it outwardly while we pretend to it inwardly. It is wrong, surely, to believe and not to profess; wrong to put our light under a bushel. St. Paul says expressly, "If thou shalt *confess with thy mouth* the Lord Jesus, and shalt believe in thine heart that God had raised Him from the dead, thou shalt be saved." [Rom. x. 9.] Belief is not enough; we must confess. Nor must we confess with our mouth only; but by word and by deed, by speech and by silence, by doing and by not doing, by walk and conversation, when in company and when alone, in time and in place, when we labour and when we rest, when we lie down and when we rise up, in youth and in age, in life and in death,—and, in like manner, in the world and in Church. Now, to adorn the worship of God our Saviour, to make the beauty of holiness visible, to bring offerings to the Sanctuary, to be curious in architecture, and reverent in ceremonies,—all this external religion is a sort of profession and confession; it is nothing but what is natural, nothing but what is consistent, in those who are cultivating the life of religion within. It is most unbecoming, most offensive, in those who are not religious; but most becoming, most necessary, in those who are so.

Persons who put aside gravity and comeliness in the worship of God, that they may pray more spiritually, forget that God is a Maker of *all* things, *visible* as well as invisible; that He is the Lord of our bodies as well as of our souls; that He is to be worshipped in public as well as in secret. The Creator of this world is none other than the Father of our Lord Jesus Christ; there are not two Gods, one of matter, one of spirit; one of the Law, and one of the Gospel. There is one God, and He is Lord of all we are, and all we have; and, therefore, all we do must be stamped with His seal and signature. We must begin, indeed, with the heart; for out of the heart proceed all good and evil; but while we begin with the heart, we must not end with the heart. We must not give up this visible world, as if it came of the evil one. It is our duty to change it into the kingdom of heaven. We must manifest the kingdom of heaven upon earth. The light of Divine truth must proceed *from* our hearts, and shine out *upon* every thing we are, and every thing we do. It must bring the *whole* man, soul and body, into captivity to Christ. They who are holy in spirit, are holy in body. They who submit their wills to Christ, bow their bodies; they who offer the heart, bow the knee; they who have faith in His Name, bow the head; they who honour His cross inwardly, are not ashamed of it before men. They who rejoice *with* their brethren in their common salvation, and desire to worship together, *build a place* to worship in, and they build it as the *expression* of their feelings, of their mutual love, of their common reverence. They build a building which will, as it were, speak; which will profess and confess Christ their Saviour; which will herald forth His death and passion at first sight; which will remind all who enter that we are saved by His cross, and must bear our Cross after Him. They will build what may tell out their deepest and most sacred thoughts, which they dare not utter in word: not a misshapen building, not a sordid building, but a noble dwelling, a palace all-glorious within; unfit, indeed, for God's high Majesty, whom even the heaven of heavens cannot contain, but fit to express the feelings of the builders,—a monument which may stand and (as it were) preach to all the world while the world lasts; which may show how they desire to praise, bless, and glorify their eternal Benefactor; how they desire to get others to praise Him also; a Temple which may cry out to all passers by, "Oh, magnify the Lord our God, and fall down before His footstool, for He is Holy! Oh, magnify the Lord our God, and worship Him upon His holy hill, for the Lord our God is Holy!" [Ps. xcix. 5, 9.]

This, then, is the real state of the case; and when our Lord blamed the Pharisees as hypocrites, it was not for attending to the outside of the cup, but for not attending to the inside also.

Now, in answer to the parallel I have been drawing out, it may be objected, that "if the decoration of God's public service be like the personal duty of propriety in dress and demeanour, then decoration is wrong when it is intentional and studied. Those who are anxious how they look, and what others think of them, are in the way to be vain, if they are not so already; decorum should be the *spontaneous* result of inward exactness; grace in manner and apparel should be the mere outward image of harmony and purity of soul. Therefore, holy persons attire themselves with simplicity, speak with modesty, behave with gravity. Their ease, and their amiableness, and their gentleness, and their composure, and their majesty, are as little known to themselves as the features of their countenance. If, then, the parallel holds, external religion becomes excessive as soon as it is made an object; and this, of course, becomes practically an argument against all consecration of wealth and of art to the worship of God." One single remark, however, is sufficient to invalidate this objection; for, let it be observed, in making much of our own appearance, we are contemplating ourselves; but in making much of the ceremonial of religion, we are contemplating another, and Him our Maker and Redeemer. This is so obvious and decisive a distinction, that I should not care to notice the objection to which it is an answer, except that it will open upon us a further consideration connected with our subject. For it so happens that, at present, far from acknowledging its force, it is the way of the world to be most sensitively jealous of over-embellishment in the worship of God, while it has no scruples or misgivings whatever at an excess of splendour and magnificence in its own apparel, houses, furniture, equipages, and establishments.

I say it is the way with us Englishmen, who are the richest people upon earth, to lay out our wealth upon ourselves; and when the thought crosses our minds, if it ever does, that such an application of God's bounties is unworthy those who are named after Him who was born in a stable, and died upon the Cross, we quiet them by asking, "What is the use of all the precious things which God has given us, if we may not enjoy them? The earth overflows with beauty and richness, and man is gifted with skill to improve and perfect what he finds in it. What delicate and costly things do the streets of any rich town present to our eyes! what bales of merchandize! what fine linen! what silks from afar! what precious metals! what jewels! what choice marbles! and what exquisite workmanship, making what is in itself excellent, of double worth! What," it is inquired, "*can* be done with all this bounty of Providence? has He not poured it all lavishly into our hands? was it given, except to be used? And what is true of the more precious things, is true of the less precious; it is true of such things as come in the way of ordinary persons; the luxuries of opulence are, in their degree, offered to all of us, as if we were opulent, for we partake in the common opulence of our country; why, then, may we not enjoy the gifts of nature and art, which God has given?"

I have already suggested the true answer to this difficulty. The earth is full of God's wonderful works, do you say, and what are we to do with them? what to do with marbles and precious stones, gold and silver, and fine linen? Give them to God. Render them to Him from whom, and through whom, and to whom are all things. This is their proper destination. Is it a better thing to dress up our sinful bodies in silk and jewels, or to ornament therewith God's House and God's ritual? Does any one doubt what all these excellent things are meant for? or, at least, can he doubt what they are *not* meant for? not meant, surely, for sinners to make themselves fine withal. What presumption would that be, what senselessness! Does not the whole world speak in praise of God? Does not every star in the sky, every tree and flower upon earth, all that grows, all that endures, the leafy woods, the everlasting mountains, speak of God? Do not the pearls in the sea, and the jewels in the rocks, and the metals in the mine, and the marbles in the quarry,—do not all rich and beautiful substances every where witness of Him who made them? Are they not His work, His token, His glory? Are they not a portion of a vast natural Temple, the heavens, earth, and sea,—a vast Cathedral for the Bishop of our souls, the All-sufficient Priest, who first created all things, and then again, became, by purchase, their Possessor? Does it not strike you, then, as extreme presumption, and a sort of sacrilege, to consecrate them to any one's glory but God's? If we saw things aright, could there be a more frightful spectacle, an instance of more complete self-worship, a more detestable idolatry, than men and women making themselves fine that others might admire them? keeping all these things for self, denying them to the rightful Owner? viewing them as if mere works of "nature," as they are sometimes called, and incapable of any religious purpose? Recollect Herod; he was smitten by the Angel and eaten of worms, because he gave not God the glory; and *how* did he withhold it? By arraying himself in royal apparel, making an oration, and being patient of the cry, "It is the voice of a god and not of a man." The royal apparel was imputed to him as a sin, because he used it, not to remind himself that he was God's minister, but to impress upon the people that he was a god. And every one, high and low, who is in the practice of dressing ostentatiously, whether in silk or in cotton, that is, every one who dresses to be looked at and admired, is using God's gifts for an idol's service, and offering them up to self.

No; let us master this great and simple truth, that all rich materials and productions of this world, being God's property, are intended for God's service; and sin only, nothing but sin, turns them to a different purpose. All things are His; He in His bounty has allowed us to take freely of all that is in the world, for food, clothing, and lodging; He allows us a large range, He afflicts us not by harsh restrictions; He gives us a discretionary use, for which we are answerable to Him alone. Still, after all permission, on the whole we must not take what we do not need. We may take for life, for comfort, for enjoyment; not for luxury, not for pride. Let us give Him of His own, as David speaks; let us honour Him, and not ourselves. Let the house of God be richly adorned, for it is His dwelling-place; priests, for they represent Him; kings, magistrates, judges, heads of families, for they are His ministers. These are called gods in Scripture, and "all that is called God or that is worshipped," may receive of His gifts whose Name they bear. Nothing, however rich, is sinful, which has a religious meaning; which reminds us of God,—or of the absent, whom we revere or love,—or of relations or friends departed; or which is a gift, and not a purchase. In proportion as we disengage it from the thought of self, and associate it with piety towards others, do we succeed in sanctifying it.

Hence it is that while Abraham sent jewels to Rebekah, and Jacob made Joseph a coat of many colours, St. Paul gives his judgment "that women adorn themselves with shamefacedness and sobriety, *not* with broidered hair, or gold, or pearls, or costly array;" and St. Peter, that their "adorning" should not be "that outward adorning of plaiting the hair, and of wearing of gold, or of putting on of apparel, but the hidden man of the heart." [1 Tim. ii. 9. 1 Pet. iii. 3, 4.] Or again; compare the Book of Ezekiel with the Apocalypse, and you will see the right and the wrong use of earthly magnificence instanced in the city of Antichrist and Holy Jerusalem. God's judgments are denounced upon Tyre by the Prophet, for being proud of her wealth and spending it on herself. "Thou hast been in Eden, the garden of God; every precious stone was thy covering; the sardius, topaz, and the diamond, the beryl, the onyx, and the jasper; the sapphire, the carbuncle, and gold." And what followed or was involved in this? "Thine heart was lifted up because of thy beauty; thou hast corrupted thy wisdom by reason of thy brightness; I will cast thee to the ground." On the other hand, of new Jerusalem we read also, that the foundations of her wall "were garnished with all manner of precious stones. The first foundation was jasper, the second sapphire, the third a chalcedony, the fourth an emerald, the fifth sardonyx, the sixth sardius, the seventh chrysolite, the eighth beryl, the ninth a topaz, the tenth a chrysoprasus, the eleventh a jacinth, the twelfth an amethyst. And the twelve gates were twelve pearls; every several gate was of one pearl, and the street of the city was pure gold as it were transparent glass." And all this suitably; for it was God's city, "and the glory of God did lighten it, and the Lamb was the light thereof." [Ezek. xxviii. 13, 17. Rev. xxi. 19–23.]

Let us then, from what has been said, on the whole, learn this lesson:— to be at least as exact and as decent in the service of God, as we are in our own persons and our own homes; and if we are in possession of precious things besides, let us rather devote them to God than keep them for ourselves. And let us never forget that all we can give, though of His creation, is worthless in comparison of the more precious gifts which He bestows on us in the Gospel. Though our Font and Altar were of costly marbles, though our communion vessels were of gold and jewels, though our walls were covered with rich tapestries, what is all this compared to Christ, the Son of God and Son of man, present here, but unseen! Let us use visible things not to hide, but to remind us of things invisible; and let us pray Him, that while we cleanse the outside of the cup and of the platter, He will give us the Living Bread from heaven, and the Wine, which is His Blood.

The Season of Epiphany[†]

"This beginning of miracles did Jesus in Cana of Galilee,
and manifested forth His glory; and His disciples believed on Him."
John ii. 11

THE EPIPHANY is a season especially set apart for adoring the glory of Christ. The word may be taken to mean the manifestation of His glory, and leads us to the contemplation of Him as a King upon His throne in the midst of His court, with His servants around Him, and His guards in attendance. At Christmas we commemorate His grace; and in Lent His temptation; and on Good Friday His sufferings and death; and on Easter Day His victory; and on Holy Thursday His return to the Father; and in Advent we anticipate His second coming. And in all of these seasons He does something, or suffers something: but in the Epiphany and the weeks after it, we celebrate Him, not as on His field of battle, or in His solitary retreat, but as an august and glorious King; we view Him as the Object of our worship. Then only, during His whole earthly history, did He fulfil the type of Solomon, and held (as I may say) a court, and received the homage of His subjects; viz. when He was an infant. His throne was His undefiled Mother's arms; His chamber of state was a cottage or a cave; the worshippers were the wise men of the East, and they brought presents, gold, frankincense, and myrrh. All around and about Him seemed of earth, except to the eye of faith; one note alone had He of Divinity. As great men of this world are often plainly dressed, and look like other men, all but as having some one costly ornament on their breast or on their brow; so the Son of Mary in His lowly dwelling, and in an infant's form, was declared to be the Son of God Most High, the Father of Ages, and the Prince of Peace, by His star; a wonderful appearance which had guided the wise men all the way from the East, even unto Bethlehem.

This being the character of this Sacred Season, our services throughout it, as far as they are proper to it, are full of the image of a king in his royal court, of a sovereign surrounded by subjects, of a glorious prince upon a throne. There is no thought of war, or of strife, or of suffering, or of triumph, or of vengeance connected with the Epiphany, but of august majesty, of power, of prosperity, of splendour, of serenity, of benignity. Now, if at any time, it

---

[†] *Parochial & Plain Sermons*, vol. 7 (1842), Sermon 6.

is fit to say, "The Lord is in His holy temple, let all the earth keep silence before Him." [Hab. ii. 20.] "The Lord sitteth above the waterflood, and the Lord remaineth a king for ever." "The Lord of Hosts is with us; the God of Jacob is our refuge." "O come, let us worship, and fall down, and kneel before the Lord our Maker." "O magnify the Lord our God, and fall down before His footstool, for He is Holy." "O worship the Lord in the beauty of holiness; bring presents, and come into His courts."

I said that at this time of year the portions of our services which are proper to the season are of a character to remind us of a king on his throne, receiving the devotion of his subjects. Such is the narrative itself, already referred to, of the coming of the wise men, who sought Him with their gifts from a place afar off, and fell down and worshipped Him. Such too, is the account of His baptism, which forms the Second Lesson of the feast of the Epiphany, when the Holy Ghost descended on Him, and a Voice from heaven acknowledged Him to be the Son of God. And if we look at the Gospels read throughout the season, we shall find them all containing some kingly action of Christ, the Mediator between God and man. Thus in the Gospel for the First Sunday, He manifests His glory in the temple at the age of twelve years, sitting among the doctors, and astonishing them with His wisdom. In the Gospel for the Second Sunday He manifests His glory at the wedding feast, when He turned the water into wine, a miracle not of necessity or urgency, but especially an august and bountiful act—the act of a King, who out of His abundance gave a gift to His own, therewith to make merry with their friends. In the Third Sunday, the leper worships Christ, who thereupon heals him; the centurion, again, reminds Him of His Angels and ministers, and He speaks the word, and his servant is restored forthwith. In the Fourth, a storm arises on the lake, while He is peacefully sleeping, without care or sorrow, on a pillow; then He rises and rebukes the winds and the sea, and a calm follows, deep as that of His own soul, and the beholders worship Him. And next He casts out Legion, after the man possessed with it had also "run and worshipped Him." [Mark v. 6.] In the Fifth, we hear of His kingdom on earth, and of the enemy sowing tares amid the good seed. And in the Sixth, of His second Epiphany from heaven, "with power and great glory."

Such is the series of manifestations which the Sundays after the Epiphany bring before us. When He is with the doctors in the temple, He is manifested as a prophet—in turning the water into wine, as a priest—in His miracles of healing, as a bounteous Lord, giving out of His abundance—in His rebuking the sea, as a Sovereign, whose word is law—in the parable of the wheat and tares, as a guardian and ruler—in His second coming, as a lawgiver and judge.

And as in these Gospels we hear of our Saviour's greatness, so in the Epistles and First Lessons we hear of the privileges and the duties of the new people, whom He has formed to show forth His praise. Christians are at once the temple of Christ, and His worshippers and ministers *in* the temple; they are the Bride of the Lamb taken collectively, and taken individually, they are the friends of the Bridegroom and the guests at the marriage feast. In these various points of view are they presented to us in the Services during these weeks. In the Lessons from the prophet Isaiah we read of the gifts and privileges, the characteristics, the power, the fortunes of the Church—how widely spreading, even throughout all the Gentiles; how awful and high, how miraculously endowed, how revered, how powerful upon earth, how rich in temporal goods, how holy, how pure in doctrine, how full of the Spirit. And in the Epistles for the successive Sundays, we hear of the duties and distinguishing marks of her true members, principally as laid down in the twelfth and thirteenth chapters of St. Paul to the Romans; then as the same Apostle enjoins them upon the Colossians; and then in St. John's exhortations in his General Epistle.

The Collects are of the same character, as befit the supplications of subjects coming before their King. The first is for knowledge and power, the second is for peace, the third is for strength in our infirmities, the fourth is for help in temptation, the fifth is for protection, and the sixth is for preparation and purification against Christ's second coming. There is none which would suit a season of trial, or of repentance, or of waiting, or of exultation—they befit a season of peace, thanksgiving, and adoration, when Christ is not manifested in pain, conflict, or victory, but in the tranquil possession of His kingdom.

It will be sufficient to make one reflection, which suggests itself from what I have been saying.

You will observe, then, that the only display of royal greatness, the only season of majesty, homage, and glory, which our Lord had on earth, was in His infancy and youth. Gabriel's message to Mary was in its style and manner such as befitted an Angel speaking to Christ's Mother. Elisabeth, too, saluted Mary, and the future Baptist his hidden Lord, in the same honourable way. Angels announced His birth, and the shepherds worshipped. A star appeared, and the wise men rose from the East and made Him offerings. He was brought to the temple, and Simeon took Him in His arms, and returned thanks for Him. He grew to twelve years old, and again He appeared in the temple, and took His seat in the midst of the doctors. But here His earthly majesty had its end, or if seen afterwards, it was but now and then, by glimpses and by sudden gleams, but with no steady sustained light, and no diffused radiance. We are told at the close of the last-mentioned narrative, "And He went down with His parents, and came to Nazareth, *and was subjected unto them.*" [Luke ii. 51.] His subjection and servitude now began in fact. He had come in the form of a servant, and now He took on Him a servant's office. How much is contained in the idea of His subjection! and it began, and His time of glory ended, when He was twelve years old.

Solomon, the great type of the Prince of Peace, reigned forty years, and his name and greatness was known far and wide through the East. Joseph, the much-loved son of Jacob, who in an earlier age of the Church, was a type of Christ in His kingdom, was in power and favour eighty years, twice as long as Solomon. But Christ, the true Revealer of secrets, and the Dispenser of the bread of life, the true wisdom and majesty of the Father, manifested His glory but in His early years, and then the Sun of Righteousness was clouded. For He was not to reign really, till He left the world. He has reigned ever since; nay, reigned *in* the world, though He is not in sensible presence in it—the invisible King of a visible kingdom—for He came on earth but to show what His reign would be, after He had left it, and to submit to suffering and dishonour, that He *might* reign.

It often happens, that when persons are in serious illnesses, and in delirium in consequence, or other disturbance of mind, they have some few minutes of respite in the midst of it, when they are even more than themselves, as if to show us what they really are, and to interpret for us what else would be dreary. And again, some have thought that the minds of children have on them traces of something more than earthly, which fade away as life goes on, but are the promise of what is intended for them hereafter. And somewhat in this way, if we may dare compare ourselves with our gracious Lord, in a parallel though higher way, Christ descends to the shadows of this world, with the transitory tokens on Him of that future glory into which He could not enter till He had suffered. The star burned brightly over Him for awhile, though it then faded away.

We see the same law, as it may be called, of Divine Providence in other cases also. Consider, for instance, how the prospect of our Lord's passion opens upon the Apostles in the sacred history. Where did they hear of it? "Moses and Elias on the mountain appeared with Him in glory, and spake of His decease, which He should accomplish at Jerusalem." [Luke ix. 30, 31.] That is, the season of His bitter trial was preceded by a short gleam of the glory which was to be, when He was suddenly transfigured, "and the fashion of His countenance was altered, and His raiment was white and glistering." [Luke ix. 29.] And with this glory in prospect, our Lord abhorred not to die: as it is written,

"Who for the joy that was set before Him, endured the Cross, despising the shame."

Again, He forewarned His Apostles that they in like manner should be persecuted for righteousness' sake, and be afflicted and delivered up, and hated and killed. Such was to be their life in this world, "that if in this world only they had had hope in Christ, they had been of all men most miserable." [1 Cor. xv. 19.] Well then, observe, their trial too was preceded by a season of peace and pleasantness, in anticipation of their future reward; for before the day of Pentecost, for forty days Christ was with them, soothing, comforting, confirming them, "and speaking of the things pertaining unto the kingdom of God." [Acts i. 3.] As Moses stood on the mount and saw the promised land and all its riches, and yet Joshua had to fight many battles before he got possession, so did the Apostles, before descending into the valley of the shadow of death, whence nought of heaven was to be seen, stand upon the heights, and look over that valley, which they had to cross, to the city of the living God beyond it.

And so again, St. Paul, after many years of toil, refers back to a time when he had a celestial vision, anticipatory of what was to be his blessedness in the end. "I knew a man in Christ," he says, meaning himself, "about fourteen years ago, caught up to the third heaven . . . And I knew such a man . . . how that he was caught up into Paradise, and heard unspeakable words, which it is not lawful for a man to utter." [2 Cor. xii. 3, 4.] St. Paul then, as the twelve Apostles, and as our Lord before him, had his brief season of repose and consolation before the battle.

And lastly: the whole Church also may be said to have had a similar mercy vouchsafed to it at first, in anticipation of what is to be in the end. We know, alas, too well, that, according to our Lord's account of it, tares are to be with the wheat, fish of every kind in the net, all through its sojourning on earth. But in the end, "the saints shall stand before the throne of God, and serve Him day and night in His temple: and the Lamb shall feed them, and shall lead them unto living fountains of waters," and there shall be no more "sorrow nor pain, nor any thing that defileth or worketh abomination," "for without are dogs, and sorcerers, and whore-mongers, and murderers, and idolaters, and whosoever loveth and maketh a lie." Now was not this future glory shadowed forth in that infancy of the Church, when before the seal of the new dispensation was opened and trial began, "there was silence in heaven for half an hour;" and "the disciples continued daily with one accord in the temple, and in prayers, breaking bread from house to house, being of one heart, and of one soul, eating their meat with gladness and singleness of heart, praising God, and having favour with all the people;" [Acts ii. 46, 47.] while hypocrites and "liars," like Ananias and Sapphira, were struck dead, and "sorcerers," like Simon, were detected and denounced?

To conclude; let us thankfully cherish all seasons of peace and joy which are vouchsafed us here below. Let us beware of abusing them, and of resting in them, of forgetting that they *are* special privileges, of neglecting to look out for trouble and trial, as our due and our portion. Trial is our portion here—we must not think it strange when trial comes after peace. Still God mercifully does grant a respite now and then; and perhaps He grants it to us the more, the more careful we are not to abuse it. For all seasons we must thank Him, for time of sorrow and time of joy, time of warfare and time of peace. And the more we thank Him for the one, the more we shall be drawn to thank Him for the other. Each has its own proper fruit, and its own peculiar blessedness. Yet our mortal flesh shrinks from the one, and of itself prefers the other;—it prefers rest to toil, peace to war, joy to sorrow, health to pain and sickness. When then Christ gives us what is pleasant, let us take it as a refreshment by the way, that we may, when God calls, go in the strength of that meat forty days and forty nights unto Horeb, the mount of God. Let us rejoice in Epiphany with trembling, that at Septuagesima we may go into the vineyard with the labourers with cheerfulness, and may sorrow in Lent with thankfulness; let us rejoice now, not as if we have attained, but in hope of attaining. Let us take our present happiness, not as our true rest, but, as what the land of Canaan was to the Israelites,—a type and shadow of it. If we now enjoy God's ordinances, let us not cease to pray that they may prepare us for His presence hereafter. If we enjoy the presence of friends, let them remind us of the communion of saints before His throne. Let us trust in nothing here, yet draw hope from every thing—that at length the Lord may be our everlasting light, and the days of our mourning may be ended.

Attendance on Holy Communion[†]

"Ye will not come to Me, that ye might have life."
John v. 40

S T. JOHN tells us in today's Epistle that "God hath given unto us eternal life, and this life is in His Son. He that hath the Son hath life, and he that hath not the Son hath not life." Yet in the text the Son Himself, our Saviour, sorrowfully and solemnly expostulates with His own brethren, "Ye will not come to Me, that ye might have life." "He came unto His own, and His own received Him not." We know from history, as a matter of fact, that they did not receive Him, that they did not come to Him when He came to them; but He says in the text that they would not come, that they did not wish to come, implying that they, and none else but they, were the cause of their not coming.

Does it not seem a plain natural instinct that every one should seek his own good? What then is meant by this unwillingness to come for the greatest of goods, life; an unwillingness, which, guided by the light of Scripture and by experience, we can confidently affirm to prevail at this day as widely and as fully as in the age in which Christ said it?

Here is no question of a comparison of good with good. We cannot account for this unconcern about Christ's gift, by alleging that we have a sufficient treasure in our hands already, and therefore are not interested by the news of a greater. Far from it; for is not the world continually taking away its own gifts, whatever they are? and does it not thereby bring home to us, does it not importunately press upon us, and weary us with the lesson of its own nothingness? Do we not confess that eternal life is the best of all conceivable gifts, before which none other deserve to be mentioned? yet we live to the world.

Nay, and sin also warns us not to trust to its allurements; like the old prophet of Bethel, sin is forced to bear witness against itself, and in the name of the Lord to denounce the Lord's judgments upon us. While it seduces us, it stings us with remorse; and even when the sense of guilt is overcome, still the misery of sinning is inflicted on us in the inward disappointments and the

---

[†] *Parochial & Plain Sermons*, vol. 7 (1842), Sermon 11, preached on the First Sunday after Easter.

temporal punishments which commonly follow upon transgression. Yet we will not come unto Christ that we may have life.

Further, it is not that God treats us as servants or slaves; He does not put a burden on us above our strength: He does not repel us from His Presence till we have prepared some offering to bring before Him, or have made some good progress in the way of life. No; He has begun His dealings with us with special, spontaneous acts of mercy. He has, by an inconceivable goodness, sent His Son to be our life. Far from asking any gift at our hands in the first instance, He has from our infancy taken us in charge, and freely given us "all things that pertain unto life and godliness." He has been urgent with us in the very morning of our days, and by the fulness of His grace has anticipated the first stirrings of pride and lust, while as yet sin slept within us. Is it not so? What more could have been done for us? Yet, in spite of all this, men will not come unto Him that they may have life.

So strange is this, that thoughtful persons are sometimes tempted to suppose that the mass of mankind do not sufficiently know what their duty is; that they need teaching, else they would be obedient. And others fancy that if the doctrines of the Gospel were set before them in a forcible or persuasive manner, this would serve as a means of rousing them to an habitual sense of their true state. But ignorance is not the true cause why men will not come to Christ.

Who are these willing outcasts from Christ's favour, of whom I speak? Do not think I say a strong thing, my brethren, when I tell you that I am speaking of some of those who now hear me. Not that I dare draw the line any where, or imagine that I can give any rule for knowing for certain, just who come to Him in heart and spirit, and who do not; but I am quite sure that many, who would shrink from giving up their interest in the Gospel, and who profess to cast their lot with Christ, and to trust in His death for their salvation, nevertheless, do not really seek Him that they may have life, in spite of their fair speeches. This I say I am too well enabled to know, because in fact so it is, that He has shown us *how* to come to Him, and I see that men do *not* come to Him in that way which He has pointed out. He has shown us, that to come to Him for life is a literal bodily action; not a mere figure, not a mere movement of the heart towards Him, but an action of the visible limbs; not a mere secret faith, but a coming to church, a passing on along the aisle to His holy table, a kneeling down there before Him, and a receiving of the gift of eternal life in the form of bread and wine. There can be no mistaking His own appointment. He said indeed, "He that cometh to Me shall never hunger;" but then He explained what this coming was, by adding, "He that eateth Me, even he shall live by Me." If then a man does not seek Him where He is, there is no profit in seeking Him where He is not. What is the good of sitting at home seeking Him, when His Presence is in the holy Eucharist? Such perverseness is like the sin of the Israelites who went to seek for the manna at a time when it was not given. May not He who gives the gift, prescribe the place and mode of giving it?

Observe how plain and cogent is the proof of what I have been saying. Our Lord declares, "Except ye eat the flesh of the Son of Man, and drink His blood, ye have no life in you:" no life, life being the gift He offers in the text; also He says of the bread which He had broken, "*This* is My Body;" and of the cup, "*This* is My Blood;" is it not very plain, then, that if we refuse to eat that Bread, and drink that Cup, we are refusing to come unto Him that we may have life?

The true reason why people will not come to this Holy Communion is this,—they do not wish to lead religious lives; they do not like to promise to lead religious lives; and they think that that blessed Sacrament does bind them to do so, bind them to live very much more strictly and thoughtfully than they do at present. Allow as much as we will for proper distrust of themselves, reasonable awe, the burden of past sin, imperfect knowledge, and other causes, still after all there is in most cases a reluctance to bear, or at least to pledge themselves to bear, Christ's yoke; a reluctance to give up the service of sin once for all; a lingering love of their own ease, of their own will, of indolence, of carnal habits, of the good opinion of men whom they do not respect; a distrust of their perseverance in holy resolves, grounded on a misgiving about their present sincerity. This is why men will not come to Christ for life; they know that He will not impart Himself to them, unless they consent to devote themselves to Him.

In what way does He offer Himself to them in Holy Communion? through the commands and sanctions of the Law. First, we are warned against secret sin, and called to self-examination; a week's preparation follows; then, when the time of celebration is come, we hear the Commandments read, we are solemnly exhorted to put off every thing which may offend God; we confess our sins and our deep sorrow for them; lastly, after being admitted to the Sacrament, we expressly bind ourselves to the service of our Lord and Saviour. Doubtless *this* it is which the unrenewed heart cannot bear, the very notion of giving up sin altogether and once for all. And thus, though a gracious voice cry ever so distinctly from the altar, "Come unto Me, and I will refresh you;" and though it be ever so true that this refreshment is nothing short of life, eternal life, yet we recollect the words which follow, "Take My yoke upon you, and learn of Me," and we forthwith murmur and complain, as if the gift were most ungracious, laden with conditions, and hardly purchased, merely because it is offered in that way in which alone a righteous Lord could offer it,—the way of righteousness.

Men had rather give up the promise than implicate themselves in the threats which surround it. Bright and attractive as is the treasure presented to us in the Gospel, still the pearl of great price lies in its native depths, at the bottom of the ocean. We see it indeed, and know its worth; but not many dare plunge in to bring it thence. What reward offered to the diver shall overcome the imminent peril of a frightful death? and those who love sin, and whose very life consists in habits and practices short of religious, what promised prize can reconcile them to the certain destruction of what they delight in, the necessary annihilation of all their most favourite indulgences and enjoyments which are contrary to the rule of the Gospel? Let us not suppose that any exhortations will induce such men to change their conduct; they confess the worth of the soul, their obligation to obey, and their peril if they do not; yet, for all this, the present sacrifice required of them is too much for them. They may be told of their Lord's love for them, His self-denying mercy when on earth, His free gifts, and His long-suffering since; they will not be influenced; and why? because the fault is in their heart; they do not like God's service. *They* know full well what they would have, if they might choose. Christ is said to have done all things for us; "Far from it," say they, "He is not a Mediator suited to our case. Give life, give holiness, give truth, give a Saviour to deliver from sin; this is not enough: no, *we* want a Saviour to deliver *in* sin. This is our need. It is a small thing to offer us life, if it be in the way of God's commandments; it is a mockery of our hopes to call that a free gift, which is, in fact, a heavy yoke. We want to do nothing at all, and then the gift will be free indeed. If our hearts *must* be changed to fit us for heaven, let them be changed, only let us have no trouble in the work ourselves. Let the change be part of the work done for us; let us literally be clay in the hands of the potter; let us sleep, and dream, and wake in the morning new men; let us have no fear and trembling, no working out salvation, no self-denial. Let Christ suffer, but be it ours to rejoice only. What we wish is, to be at ease; we wish to have every thing our own way; we wish to enjoy both this world and the next; we wish to be happy all at once. If the Gospel promises this, we accept it; but if not, it is but a bondage, it has no persuasiveness, it will receive no acceptance from us." Such is the language of men's hearts, though their tongues do not utter it; language most unthankful, most profane, most sinful.

These reflections I recommend to the serious attention of those who live in neglect of Holy Communion; but, alas! I must not quit the subject without addressing some cautions to those who are in the observance of it. I would that none of us had need of cautions; but the best of us is in warfare, and on his trial, and none of us can be the worse for them. I need not remind you, my brethren, that there is a peril attached to the unworthy reception; for this is the very excuse which many plead for not receiving; but it often happens, as in other matters also, that men have fears when they should not fear, and do not fear when they should fear. A slight consideration will show this; for what is the danger in communicating? that of coming to it, as St. Paul implies, *without* fear. It is evident then, that, in spite of what was just now said, when persons are in danger of receiving it unworthily, they commonly do not really feel their danger; for their very danger consists in their not fearing. If they did truly and religiously fear the blessed Sacrament, so far they would not be in danger of an unworthy reception.

Now it is plain when it is that persons are in danger of receiving it fearlessly and thoughtlessly; not when they receive it for the first time, but when they have often received it, when they are in the habit of receiving it. This is the dangerous time.

When a Christian first comes to Holy Communion, he comes with awe and anxiety. At least, I will not suppose the case of a person so little in earnest about his soul, and so profane, as to despise the ordinance when he first attends it. Perhaps he has no clear doctrinal notion of the sacred rite, but the very title of it, as the Sacrament of his Lord's Body and Blood, suffices to make him serious. Let us believe that he examines himself, and prays for grace to receive the gift worthily; and he feels at the time of celebration and afterwards, that, having bound himself more strictly to a religious life, and received Divine influences, he has more to answer for. But after he has repeated his attendance several times, this fear and reverence wear away with the novelty. As he begins to be familiar with the words of the prayers, and the order of the Service, so does he both hear and receive with less emotion and solemnity. It is not that he is a worse man than he was at first, but he is exposed to a greater temptation to be profane. He had no deeper religious principle when he first communicated than he has now (probably not so deep), but his want of acquaintance with the Service kept him from irreverence, indifference, and wandering thoughts: but now this accidental safeguard is removed, and as he has not succeeded in acquiring any habitual reverence from former seasons of communicating, and has no clear knowledge of the nature of the Sacrament to warn and check him, he is exposed to his own ordinary hardness of heart and unbelief, in circumstances much more perilous than those in which they are ordinarily displayed. If it is a sin to neglect God in the world, it is a greater sin to neglect Him in church. Now is the time when he is in danger of not discerning the Lord's Body, of receiving the gift of life as a thing of course, without awe, gratitude, and self-abasement. And the more constant he is in his attendance at the sacred rite, the greater will be his risk; his *risk*, I say; that is, if he neglects to be jealous over himself, to watch himself narrowly, and to condemn and hate in himself the faintest risings of coldness and irreverence; for, of course, if he so acts, the less will be his risk, and the greater will be his security that his heart will not betray him. But I speak of those who are not sufficiently aware of their danger, and these are many.

Here, too, let me mention another sin of a similar character into which communicants are apt to fall; *viz.* a forgetfulness, after communicating, that they have communicated. Even when we resist the coldness which frequent communion may occasion, and strive to possess our minds in as profound a seriousness as we felt when the rite was new to us, even then there is often a painful difference between our feelings before we have attended it, and after. We are diligent in preparation, we are careless in retrospect; we dismiss from our memory what we cherished in our expectations; we forget that we ever hoped and feared. But consider; when we have solemn thoughts about Holy Communion only till we have come to it, what does this imply, but that we imagine that we have received the benefit of it once for all, as a thing done and over, and that there is nothing more to seek? This is but a formal way of worshipping; as if we had wiped off a writing which was against us, and there was an end of the matter. But blessed are those servants who are ever expecting Him, who is ever coming to them; whether He come "at even, or at midnight, or at cock-crowing, or in the morning;" whereas those who first come to Him for the gift of grace, and then neglect to wait for its progressive accomplishment in their hearts, how profanely they act! it is as if to receive the blessing in mockery, and then to cast it away. Surely, after so great a privilege, we ought to behave ourselves as if we had partaken some Divine food and medicine (if great things may be compared to ordinary), which, in its own inscrutable way, and in its own good time, will "prosper in the thing whereunto God sends it"—the fruit of the tree of life which Adam forfeited, which had that virtue in it, that it was put out of his reach in haste, lest he should take and eat, and live for ever. How earnest, then, should be our care lest this gracious treasure which we carry within us should be lost by our own fault, by the unhealthy excitements, or the listless indolence, to which our nature invites us! "Quench not the Spirit," says the Apostle; surely our privilege is a burden heavy to bear, before it turn to a principle of life and strength, till Christ be formed in us perfectly; and we the while, what cause have we to watch, and pray, and fulfil all righteousness, till the day dawn, and the daystar arise in our hearts!

Nor let us suppose that by once or twice seeking God in this gracious ordinance, we can secure the gift for ever: "Seek the Lord and His strength, seek His face evermore." The bread which comes down from heaven is like the manna, "*daily* bread," and that "till He come," till His "kingdom come." In His coming at the end of the world, all our wishes and prayers rest and are accomplished; and in His present communion we have a stay and consolation meanwhile, joining together the past and future, reminding us that He has come once, and promising us that He will come again. Who can live any time in the world, pleasant as it may seem on first entering it, without discovering that it is a weariness, and that if this life is worth any thing, it is because it is the passage to another? It needs no great religion to feel this; it is a self-evident truth to those who have much experience of the world. The only reason why all do not feel it is, that they have not lived long enough to feel it; and those who feel it more than others, have but been thrown into circumstances to feel it more. But while the times wax old, and the colours of earth fade, and the voice of song is brought low, and all kindreds of the earth can but wail and lament, the sons of God lift up their heads, for their salvation draweth nigh. Nature fails, the sun shines not, and the moon is dim, the stars fall from heaven, and the foundations of the round world shake; but the Altar's light burns ever brighter; there are sights there which the many cannot see, and all above the tumults of earth the command is heard to show forth the Lord's death, and the promise that the Lord is coming.

"Happy are the people that are in such a case!" who, when wearied of the things seen, can turn with good hope to the things unseen; yea, "blessed are the people who have the Lord for their God!" "Come unto Me," He says, "all ye that labour and are heavy laden, and I will give you rest." Rest is better than toil; peace satisfies, and quietness disappoints not. These are sure goods. Such is the calm of the heavenly Jerusalem, which is the mother of us all; and such is their calm worship, the foretaste of heaven, who for a season shut themselves out from the world, and seek Him in invisible Presence, whom they shall hereafter see face to face.

The Gospel Feast[†]

"When Jesus then lifted up His eyes, and saw a great company come unto Him,
He saith unto Philip, Whence shall we buy bread that these may eat?"
John vi. 5

AFTER THESE WORDS the Evangelist adds, "And this He said to prove him, for He Himself knew what He would do." Thus, you see, our Lord had secret meanings when He spoke, and did not bring forth openly all His divine sense at once. He knew what He was about to do from the first, but He wished to lead forward His disciples, and to arrest and open their minds, before He instructed them: for all cannot receive His words, and on the blind and deaf the most sacred truths fall without profit.

And thus, throughout the course of His gracious dispensations from the beginning, it may be said that the Author and Finisher of our faith has hid things from us in mercy, and listened to our questionings, while He Himself knew what He was about to do. He has hid, in order afterwards to reveal, that then, on looking back on what He said and did before, we may see in it what at the time we did not see, and thereby see it to more profit. Thus He hid Himself from the disciples as He walked with them to Emmaus: thus Joseph, too, under different and yet similar circumstances, hid himself from his brethren.

With this thought in our minds, surely we seem to see a new and further meaning still, in the narrative before us. Christ spoke of buying bread, when He intended to create or make bread; but did He not, in that bread which He made, intend further that Heavenly bread which is the salvation of our souls?—for He goes on to say, "Labour not for the meat" or food "which perisheth, but for that food which endureth unto everlasting life, which the Son of man shall give unto you." Yes, surely the wilderness is the world, and the Apostles are His priests, and the multitudes are His people; and that feast, so suddenly, so unexpectedly provided, is the Holy Communion. He alone is the same, He the provider of the loaves then, of the heavenly manna now. All other things change, but He remaineth.

And what is that Heavenly Feast which we now are vouchsafed, but in its own turn the earnest and pledge of that future feast in His Father's kingdom,

---

[†] *Parochial & Plain Sermons*, vol. 7 (1842), Sermon 12.

when "the marriage of the Lamb shall come, and His wife hath made herself ready," and "holy Jerusalem cometh down from God out of heaven," and "blessed shall they be who shall eat bread in the kingdom of God"?

And further, since to that Feast above we do lift up our eyes, though it will not come till the end; and as we do not make remembrance of it once only, but continually, in the sacred rite which foreshadows it; therefore, in like manner, not in the miracle of the loaves only, though in that especially, but in all parts of Scripture, in history, and in precept, and in promise, and in prophecy, is it given us to see the Gospel Feast typified and prefigured, and that immortal and never-failing Supper in the visible presence of the Lamb which will follow upon it at the end. And if they are blessed who shall eat and drink of that table in the kingdom, so too blessed are they who meditate upon it, and hope for it now,—who read Scripture with it in their thoughts, and endeavour to look beneath the veil of the literal text, and to catch a sight of the gleams of heavenly light which are behind it. "Blessed are your eyes, for they see; and your ears, for they hear; for verily I say unto you, that many prophets and righteous men have desired to see those things which ye see, but have not seen them; and to hear those things which ye hear, and have not heard them." "Blessed are they which have not seen, and yet have believed." Blessed they who see in and by believing, and who have, because they doubt not.

Let us, then, at this time of year,[31] as is fitting, follow the train of thought thus opened upon us, and, looking back into the Sacred Volume, trace the intimations and promises there given of that sacred and blessed Feast of Christ's Body and Blood which it is our privilege now to enjoy till the end come.

Now the Old Testament, as we know, is full of figures and types of the Gospel; types various, and, in their literal wording, contrary to each other, but all meeting and harmoniously filled in Christ and His Church. Thus the histories of the Israelites in the wilderness, and of the Israelites when settled in Canaan, alike are ours, representing our present state as Christians. Our Christian life is a state of faith and trial; it is also a state of enjoyment. It has the richness of the promised land; it has the marvellousness of the desert. It is a "good land, a land of brooks of water, of fountains and depths that spring out of vallies and hills; a land of wheat and barley, and vines, and fig-trees, and pomegranates; a land of oil olive, and honey; a land wherein thou shalt eat bread without scarceness; thou shalt not lack any thing in it; a land whose stones are iron, and out of whose hills thou mayest dig brass." And, on the other hand, it is still a land which to the natural man seems a wilderness, a "great and terrible wilderness, wherein are fiery serpents, and scorpions, and

---

[31] Easter.

drought, where there is no water;" where faith is still necessary, and where, still more forcibly than in the case of Israel, the maxim holds, that "man doth not live by bread only, but by every word that proceedeth out of the mouth of the Lord doth man live."

This is the state in which we are,—a state of faith and of possession. In the desert the Israelites lived by the signs of things, without the realities: manna was to stand for the corn, oil, and honey, of the good land promised; water, for the wine and milk. It was a time for faith to exercise itself; and when they came into the promised land, then was the time of possession. That was the land of milk and honey; they needed not any divinely provided compensations or expedients. Manna was not needed, nor the pillar of the cloud, nor the water from the rock. But we Christians, on the contrary, are at once in the wilderness and in the promised land. In the wilderness, because we live amid wonders; in the promised land, because we are in a state of enjoyment. That we are in the state of enjoyment is surely certain, unless all the prophecies have failed; and that we are in a state in which faith alone has that enjoyment, is plain from the fact that God's great blessings are not seen, and in that the Apostle says, "We walk by faith, not by sight." In a word, we are in a supernatural state,—a word which implies both its greatness and its secretness: for what is above nature, is at once not seen, and is more precious than what is seen; "the things which are seen are temporal, the things which are not seen are eternal."

And if our state altogether is parallel to that of the Israelites, as an antitype to its type, it is natural to think that so great a gift as Holy Communion would not be without its appropriate figures and symbols in the Old Testament. All that our Saviour has done is again and again shadowed out in the Old Testament; and this, therefore, it is natural to think, as well as other things: His miraculous birth, His life, His teaching, His death, His priesthood, His sacrifice, His resurrection, His glorification, His kingdom, are again and again prefigured: it is not reasonable to suppose that if this so great gift is really given us, it should be omitted. He who died for us, is He who feeds us; and as His death is mentioned, so we may beforehand expect will be mentioned the feast He gives us. Not openly indeed, for neither is His death nor His priesthood taught openly, but covertly, under the types of David or Aaron, or other favoured servants of God; and in like manner we might expect, and we shall find, the like reverent allusions to His most gracious Feast,—allusions which we should not know to *be* allusions but for the event; just as we should not know that Solomon, Aaron, or Samuel, stood for Christ at all, except that the event explains the figure. When Abraham said to Isaac, "God will provide Himself a lamb for a burnt offering," who can doubt this is a prophecy concerning Christ?—yet we are nowhere told it in Scripture. The case is the same as regards the Sacrament of Baptism. Now that it is given, we cannot doubt that the purifications of the Jews, Naaman's bathing, and the prophecy of a fountain being opened for sin and all uncleanness, have reference to it, as being the visible fulfilment of the great spiritual cleansing: and St. Peter expressly affirms this of the Deluge, and St. Paul of the passage of the Red Sea. And in like manner passages in the Bible, which speak prophetically of the Gospel Feast, cannot but refer (if I may so speak) to the Holy Sacrament of the Lord's Supper, as being, in fact, the Feast given us under the Gospel.

And let it be observed, directly we know that we have this great gift, and that the Old Testament history prefigures it, we have a light thrown upon what otherwise is a difficulty; for, it may be asked with some speciousness, whether the Jews were not in a higher state of privilege than we Christians, until we take this gift into account. It may be objected that our blessings are all future or distant,—the hope of eternal life, which is to be fulfilled hereafter, God's forgiveness, who is in heaven: what do we gain now and here above the Jews? God loved the Jews, and He *gave* them something; He gave them present gifts; the Old Testament is full of the description of them; He gave them "the precious things of heaven, and the dew, and the deep that coucheth beneath, and precious things brought forth by the sun, and by the moon, and the chief things of the ancient mountains, and the precious things of the lasting hills, and the precious things of the earth, and the fulness thereof," "honey out of the rock, and oil out of the flinty rock, butter of kine, and milk of sheep, with fat of lambs, and rams of the breed of Bashan, and goats, with the fat of kidneys of wheat, and the pure blood of the grape." [Deut. xxxii. 13; xxxiii. 13–15.] These were present real blessings. What has He given *us*?— *nothing* in possession? *all* in promise? This, I say, is in itself not likely; it is not likely that He should so reverse His system, and make the Gospel inferior to the Law. But the knowledge of the great gift under consideration clears up this perplexity; for every passage in the Old Testament which speaks of the temporal blessings given by God to His ancient people, instead of conveying to us a painful sense of destitution, and exciting our jealousy, reminds us of our greater blessedness; for every passage which belongs to them is fulfilled now in a higher sense to us. We have no need to envy them. God did not take away their blessings, without giving us greater. The Law was not so much taken away, as the Gospel given. The Gospel supplanted the Law. The Law went out by the Gospel's coming in. Only our blessings are not seen; *therefore* they are higher, *because* they are unseen. Higher blessings could not be visible. How could spiritual blessings be visible ones? If Christ now feeds us, not with milk and honey, but "with the spiritual food of His most precious Body and

Blood;" if "our sinful bodies are made clean by His Body, and our souls washed through His most precious Blood," truly we are not without our precious things, any more than Israel was: but they are unseen, because so much greater, so spiritual; they are given only under the veil of what is seen: and thus we Christians are both with the Church in the wilderness as regards faith, and in the Church in Canaan as regards enjoyment; having the fulfilment of the words spoken by Moses, repeated by our Lord, to which I just now referred, "Man shall not live by bread only, but by every word which proceedeth out of the mouth of God."

Now, then, I will refer to some passages of both the Old Testament and the New, which both illustrate and are illustrated by this great doctrine of the Gospel.

1. And, first, let it be observed, from the beginning, the greatest rite of religion has been a feast; the partaking of God's bounties, in the way of nature, has been consecrated to a more immediate communion with God Himself. For instance, when Isaac was weaned, Abraham "made a great feast," [Gen. xxi. 10.] and then it was that Sarah prophesied; "Cast out this bondwoman and her son," she said, prophesying the introduction of the spirit, grace, and truth, which the Gospel contains, instead of the bondage of the outward forms of the Law. Again, it was at a feast of savoury meat that the spirit of prophecy came upon Isaac, and he blessed Jacob. In like manner the first beginning of our Lord's miracles was at a marriage feast, when He changed water into wine; and when St. Matthew was converted he entertained our Lord at a feast. At a feast, too, our Lord allowed the penitent woman to wash with tears and anoint His feet, and pronounced her forgiveness; and at a feast, before His passion, He allowed Mary to anoint them with costly ointment, and to wipe them with her hair. Thus with our Lord, and with the Patriarchs, a feast was a time of grace; so much so, that He was said by the Pharisees to come eating and drinking, to be "a winebibber and gluttonous, a friend of publicans and sinners." [Matt. xi. 19. Luke vii. 34.]

And next, in order to make this feasting still more solemn, it had been usual at all times to precede it by a direct act of religion,—by a prayer, or blessing, or sacrifice, or by the presence of a priest, which implied it. Thus, when Melchizedek came out to meet Abraham, and *bless* him, "he brought forth bread and wine;" [Gen. xiv. 18.] to which it is added, "and he was the priest of the Most High God." Such, too, was the lamb of the Passover, which was eaten roast with fire, and with unleavened bread, and bitter herbs, with girded loins and shoes on, and staff in hand; as the Lord's Passover, being a solemn religious feast, even if not a sacrifice. And such seems to have been the common notion of communion with God all the world over, however it was gained; *viz.* that we arrived at the possession of His invisible gifts by participation in His visible; that there was some mysterious connexion between the seen and the unseen; and that, by setting aside the choicest of His earthly bounties, as a specimen and representative of the whole, presenting it to Him for His blessing, and then taking, eating, and appropriating it, we had the best hope of gaining those unknown and indefinite gifts which human nature needs. This the heathen practised towards their idols also; and St. Paul seems to acknowledge that in that way they did communicate, though most miserably and fearfully, with those idols, and with the evil spirits which they represented. "The things which the Gentiles sacrifice, they sacrifice to devils, and not to God; and I would not that ye should hold communion with devils." [1 Cor. x. 20.] Here, as before, a feast is spoken of as the means of communicating with the unseen world, though, when the feast was idolatrous, it was the fellowship of evil spirits.

3. And next let this be observed, that the descriptions in the Old Testament of the perfect state of religious privilege, *viz.* that under the Gospel which was then to come, are continually made under the image of a feast, a feast of some special and choice goods of this world, corn, wine, and the like; goods of this world chosen from the mass as a specimen of all, as types and means of seeking, and means of obtaining, the unknown spiritual blessings, which "eye hath not seen nor ear heard." And these special goods of nature, so set apart, are more frequently than any thing else, corn or bread, and wine, as the figures of what was greater, though others are mentioned also. Now the first of these of which we read is the fruit of the tree of life, the leaves of which are also mentioned in the prophets. The tree of life was that tree in the garden of Eden, the eating of which would have made Adam immortal; a divine gift lay hid in an outward form. The prophet Ezekiel speaks of it afterwards in the following words, showing that a similar blessing was in store for the redeemed:—"By the river, upon the bank thereof, on this side, and on that side, shall grow all trees for meat, whose leaf shall not fade, neither shall the fruit thereof be consumed. It shall bring forth new fruits according to his months, because their waters they issued out of the sanctuary; and the fruit thereof shall be for meat, and the leaf thereof for medicine." [Ezek. xlvii. 12.] Like to which is St. John's account of the tree of life, "which bare twelve manner of fruits, and yielded her fruit every month; and the leaves of the tree were for the healing of the nations." [Rev. xxii. 2.] And hence we read in the Canticles of the apple-tree, and of sitting down under its shadow, and its fruit being sweet to the taste. Here then in type is signified the sacred gift of which I am speaking; and yet it has not seemed good to the gracious Giver literally to select fruit or leaves as the means of His invisible blessings. He might have spiritually fed us

with such, had He pleased—for man liveth not by bread only, but by the word of His mouth. His Word might have made the fruit of the tree His Sacrament, but He has willed otherwise.

The next selection of gifts of the earth which we find in Scripture, is the very one which He at length fixed on, bread and wine, as in the history of Melchizedek; and there the record stands as a prophecy of what was to be: for who is Melchizedek but our Lord and Saviour, and what is the Bread and Wine but the very feast which He has ordained?

Next the great gift was shadowed out in the description of the promised land, which was said to flow with milk and honey, and in all those other precious things of nature which I have already recounted as belonging to the promised land, oil, butter, corn, wine, and the like. These all may be considered to refer to the Gospel feast typically, because they were the rarest and most exquisite of the blessings given to the Jews, as the Gospel Feast is the most choice and most sacred of all the blessings given to us Christians; and what is most precious under the one Dispensation is signified by what is most precious under the other.

Now let us proceed to the Prophets, and we shall find the like anticipation of the Gospel Feast.

For instance, you recollect, the prophet Hosea says: "It shall come to pass in that day, I will hear, saith the Lord, I will hear the heavens, and they shall hear the earth, and the earth shall hear the corn, and the wine, and the oil, and they shall hear Jezreel. And I will sow her unto Me in the earth." [Hos. ii. 21–23.] By Jezreel is meant the Christian Church; and the Prophet declares in God's name, that the time was to come when the Church would call upon the corn, wine, and oil, and they would call on the earth, and the earth on the heavens, and the heavens on God; and God should answer the heavens, and the heavens should answer the earth, and the earth should answer the corn, wine, and oil, and they should answer to the wants of the Church. Now, doubtless, this may be fulfilled only in a general way; but considering Almighty God has appointed corn or bread, and wine, to be the special instruments of His ineffable grace,—He, who sees the end from the beginning, and who views all things in all their relations at once,—He, when He spoke of corn and wine, knew that the word would be fulfilled, not generally only, but even literally in the Gospel.

Again: the prophet Joel says, "It shall come to pass in that day that the mountains shall drop down new wine, and the hills shall flow with milk, and all the rivers of Judah shall flow with waters, and a fountain shall come forth of the house of the Lord, and shall water the valley of Shittim." [Joel iii. 18.]

How strikingly is this fulfilled, if we take it to apply to what God has given us in the Gospel, in the feast of the Holy Communion!

Again: the prophet Amos says: "Behold, the days come, saith the Lord, when the plowman shall overtake the reaper, and the treader of grapes him that soweth seed; and the mountains shall drop sweet wine, and all the hills shall melt;" [Amos ix. 13.] that is, with God's marvellous grace, whereby He gives us gifts new and wonderful.

And the prophet Isaiah: "In this mountain shall the Lord of Hosts make unto all people a feast of fat things, a feast of wines on the lees; of fat things full of marrow, of wines on the lees well refined." And again: "Surely I will no more give thy corn to be meat for thine enemies, and the sons of the stranger shall not drink thy wine, for the which thou hast laboured; but they that have gathered it shall eat it, and praise the Lord, and they that have brought it together shall drink it in the courts of My holiness." And again: "Behold My servants shall eat, but ye shall be hungry; behold My servants shall drink, but ye shall be thirsty." [Isa. xxv. 6; lxii. 8, 9; lxv. 13.]

Again: the prophet Jeremiah says: "They shall come and sing in the height of Zion, and shall flow together to the goodness of the Lord, for wheat, and for wine, and for oil, and for the young of the flock and of the herd; and their soul shall be as a watered garden, and they shall not sorrow any more at all . . . And I will satiate the soul of the priests with fatness, and My people shall be satisfied with My goodness, saith the Lord." [Jer. xxxi. 12–14.]

And the prophet Zechariah: "How great is His goodness, and how great is His beauty! corn shall make the young men cheerful, and new wine the maids." [Zech. ix. 17.]

And under a different image, but with the same general sense, the prophet Malachi: "From the rising of the sun even unto the going down of the same, My Name shall be great among the Gentiles; and in every place incense shall be offered unto My Name, and a pure offering, for My Name shall be great among the heathen, saith the Lord of Hosts." [Mal. i. 11.]

Further, if the Psalms are intended for Christian worship, as surely they are, the Prophetic Spirit, who inspired them, saw that they too would in various places describe that sacred Christian feast, which we feel they do describe; and surely we may rightly call this coincidence between the ordinance in the Christian Church and the form of words in the Psalms, a mark of design. For instance: "Thou shalt prepare a Table before me against them that trouble me. Thou hast anointed my head with oil, and my Cup shall be full." "I will wash my hands in innocency, O Lord, and so will I go to Thine Altar." "O send out Thy light and Thy truth, that they may lead me, and bring me unto Thy holy hill, and to Thy dwelling; and that I may go unto the Altar of God, even unto the God of my joy and gladness." "The children of men shall put their trust under the shadow of Thy wings. They shall be satisfied with the plenteousness of Thy house, and Thou shalt give them drink of Thy pleasures as out of the river. For with Thee is the well of life, and in Thy light shall we see light." "Blessed is the man whom Thou choosest and receivest unto Thee; he shall dwell in Thy court, and shall be satisfied with the pleasures of Thy house, even of Thy Holy Temple." "My soul shall be satisfied, even as it were with marrow and fatness, when my mouth praiseth Thee with joyful lips . . . because Thou hast been my helper, therefore under the shadow of Thy wings will I rejoice." [Ps. xxiii. 5; xxvi. 6; xxxvi. 7–9; xliii. 3, 4; lxv. 4; lxiii. 6–8.]

The same wonderful feast is put before us in the book of Proverbs, where Wisdom stands for Christ. "Wisdom hath builded her house," that is, Christ has built His Church; "she hath hewn out her seven pillars, she hath killed her beasts, she hath mingled her wine (that is, Christ has prepared His Supper), she hath also furnished her table (that is, the Lord's Table), she hath sent forth her maidens (that is, the priests of the Lord), she crieth upon the highest plac-es of the city, Whoso is simple, let him turn in hither; as for him that wanteth understanding, she saith to him, Come, eat of My Bread and drink of the Wine which I have mingled," [Prov. ix. 1–5.]—which is like saying, "Come unto Me all ye that labour and are heavy laden and I will refresh you." Like which are the prophet Isaiah's words: "Ho, every one that thirsteth, come ye to the waters, and he that hath no money, come ye buy and eat; yea, come, buy wine and milk without money and without price." [Isa. lv. 1.] And such too is the description in the book of Canticles: "The fig tree putteth forth her green figs, and the vines with the tender grapes give a good smell" . . . "Until the day break and the shadows flee away, I will get me to the mountain of myrrh, and to the hill of frankincense" . . . "I have gathered My myrrh with My spice, I have eaten My honeycomb with My honey, I have drunk My wine with My milk; eat, O friends, drink, yea drink abundantly, O beloved!" [Cant. ii. 13; iv. 6; v. 1.] In connexion with such passages as these should be observed St. Paul's words, which seem from the antithesis to be an allusion to the same most sacred Ordinance: "Be not drunk with wine, wherein is excess, but be filled with the Spirit," with that new wine which God the Holy Spirit minis-ters in the Supper of the Great King. God grant that we may be able ever to come to this Blessed Sacrament with feelings suitable to the passages which I have read concerning it! May we not regard it in a cold, heartless way, and keep at a distance from fear, when we should rejoice! May the spirit of the un-profitable servant never be ours, who looked at his lord as a hard master in-stead of a gracious benefactor! May we not be in the number of those who go on year after year, and never approach Him at all! May we not be of those who went, one to his farm, another to his merchandise, when they were called to the wedding! Nor let us be of those, who come in a formal, mechanical way, as a mere matter of obligation, without reverence, without awe, without wonder, without love. Nor let us fall into the sin of those who complained that they have nothing to gather but the manna, wearying of God's gifts.

But let us come in faith and hope, and let us say to ourselves, May this be the beginning to us of everlasting bliss! May these be the first-fruits of that banquet which is to last for ever and ever; ever new, ever transporting, inexhaustible, in the city of our God!

Love of Religion, a New Nature[†]

"If we be dead with Christ, we believe that we shall also live with Him."
Romans vi. 8

TO BE DEAD with Christ, is to hate and turn from sin; and to live with Him, is to have our hearts and minds turned towards God and Heaven. To be dead to sin, is to feel a disgust at it. We know what is meant by disgust. Take, for instance, the case of a sick man, when food of a certain kind is presented to him,—and there is no doubt what is meant by disgust. Consider how certain scents, which are too sweet or too strong, or certain tastes, affect certain persons under certain circumstances, or always,—and you will be at no loss to determine what is meant by disgust at sin, or deadness to sin. On the other hand, consider how pleasant a meal is to the hungry, or some enlivening odour to the faint; how refreshing the air is to the languid, or the brook to the weary and thirsty;—and you will understand the sort of feeling which is implied in being alive with Christ, alive to religion, alive to the thought of heaven. Our animal powers cannot exist in all atmospheres; certain airs are poisonous, others life-giving. So is it with spirits and souls: an unrenewed spirit could not live in heaven, he would die; an Angel could not live in hell. The natural man cannot live in heavenly company, and the angelic soul would pine and waste away in the company of sinners, unless God's sacred presence were continued to it. To be dead to sin, is to be so minded, that the atmosphere of sin (if I may so speak) oppresses, distresses, and stifles us,— that it is painful and unnatural to us to remain in it. To be alive with Christ, is to be so minded, that the atmosphere of heaven refreshes, enlivens, stimulates, invigorates us. To be alive, is not merely to bear the thought of religion, to assent to the truth of religion, to wish to be religious; but to be drawn towards it, to love it, to delight in it, to obey it. Now I suppose most persons called Christians do not go farther than this,—to wish to be religious, and to think it right to be religious, and to feel a respect for religious men; they do not get so far as to have any sort of love for religion.

So far, however, they do go; not, indeed, to do their duty and to love it, but to have a sort of wish that they did. I suppose there are few persons but, at the very least, now and then feel the wish to be holy and religious. They bear

---

[†] *Parochial & Plain Sermons*, vol. 7 (1842), Sermon 13.

witness to the excellence of virtuous and holy living, they consent to all that their teachers tell them, what they hear in church, and read in religious books; but all this is a very different thing from acting according to their knowledge. They confess one thing, they do another.

Nay, they confess one thing *while* they do another. Even sinners,—wilful, abandoned sinners,—if they would be honest enough to speak as they really in their hearts feel, would own, while they are indulging in the pleasures of sin, while they idle away the Lord's Day, or while they keep bad company, or while they lie or cheat, or while they drink to excess, or do any other bad thing,—they would confess, I say, did they speak their minds, that it is a far happier thing, even at present, to live in obedience to God, than in obedience to Satan. Not that sin has not its pleasures, such as they are; I do not mean, of course, to deny that,—I do not deny that Satan is able to give us something in exchange for future and eternal happiness; I do not say that irreligious men do not gain pleasures, which religious men are obliged to lose. I know they do; if they did not, there would be nothing to tempt and try us. But, after all, the pleasures which the servants of Satan enjoy, though pleasant, are always attended with pain too; with a bitterness, which, though it does not destroy the pleasure, yet is by itself sufficient to make it far less pleasant, even while it lasts, than such pleasures as are without such bitterness, viz. the pleasures of religion. This, then, alas! is the state of multitudes; not to be dead to sin and alive to God, but, while they are alive to sin and the world, to have just so much sense of heaven, as not to be able to enjoy either.

I say, when any one, man or woman, young or old, is conscious that he or she is going wrong, whether in greater matter or less, whether in not coming to church when there is no good excuse, neglecting private prayer, living carelessly, or indulging in known sin,—this bad conscience is from time to time a torment to such persons. For a little while, perhaps, they do not feel it, but then the pain comes on again. It is a keen, harassing, disquieting, hateful pain, which hinders sinners from being happy. They *may* have pleasures, but they cannot be *happy*. They know that God is angry with them; and they know that, at some time or other, He will visit, He will judge, He will punish. They try to get this out of their minds, but the arrow sticks fast there; it keeps its hold. They try to laugh it off, or to be bold and daring, or to be angry and violent. They are loud or unkind in their answers to those, who remind them of it either in set words, or by their example. But it keeps its hold. And so it is, that all men who are not very abandoned, bad men as well as good, wish that they were holy as God is holy, pure as Christ was pure, even though they do not try to be, or pray to God to make them, holy and pure; not that they *like* religion, but that they know, they are convinced in their reason, they feel sure, that religion alone is happiness.

Oh, what a dreadful state, to have our desires one way, and our knowledge and conscience another; to have our life, our breath and food, upon the earth, and our eyes upon Him who died once and now liveth; to look upon Him who once was pierced, yet not to rise with Him and live with Him; to feel that a holy life is our only happiness, yet to have no heart to pursue it; to be certain that the wages of sin is death, yet to practise sin; to confess that the Angels alone are perfectly happy, for they do God's will perfectly, yet to prepare ourselves for nothing else but the company of devils; to acknowledge that Christ is our only hope, yet deliberately to let that hope go! O miserable state! miserable they, if any there are who now hear me, who are thus circumstanced!

At first sight, it might seem impossible that any such persons could be found in church. At first sight, one might be tempted to say, "All who come to church, at least, are in earnest, and have given up sin; they are imperfect indeed, as all Christians are at best, but they do not fall into wilful sin." I should be very glad, my Brethren, to believe this were the case, but I cannot indulge so pleasant a hope. No; I think it quite certain that some persons at least, I do not say how many, to whom I am speaking, have not made up their minds fully to lead a religious life. They come to church because they think it right, or from other cause. It is very right that they should come; I am glad they do. This is good, as far as it goes; but it is not all. They are not so far advanced in the kingdom of God, as to resist the devil, or to flee from him. They cannot command themselves. They act rightly one day, and wrongly the next. They are afraid of being laughed at. They are attracted by bad company. They put off religion to a future day. They think a religious life dull and unpleasant. Yet they have a certain sense of religion; and they come to church in order to satisfy this sense. Now, I say it is right to come to church; but, O that they could be persuaded of the simple truth of St. Paul's words, "He is not a Jew which is one outwardly; but he is a Jew which is one inwardly; and circumcision is that of the heart in the spirit, and not in the letter, whose praise is not of men, but of God;" [Rom. ii. 28, 29.] which may be taken to mean:—He is not a Christian who is one outwardly, who merely comes to church, and professes to desire to be saved by Christ. It is very right that he should do so, but it is not enough. He is not a Christian who merely has not cast off religion; but he is the true Christian, who, while he is a Christian outwardly, is one inwardly also; who lives to God; whose secret life is hid with Christ in God; whose heart is religious; who not only knows and feels that a religious life is true happiness, but loves religion, wishes, tries, prays to be religious, begs God Almighty to give him the will and the power to be religious; and, as time goes on, grows more and more religious, more fit for heaven.

We can do nothing right, unless God gives us the will and the power; we cannot please Him without the aid of His Holy Spirit. If any one does not deeply feel this as a first truth in religion, he is preparing for himself a dreadful fall. He will attempt, and he will fail signally, utterly. His own miserable experience will make him sure of it, if he will not believe it, as Scripture declares it. But it is not unlikely that some persons, perhaps some who now hear me, may fall into an opposite mistake. They may attempt to excuse their lukewarmness and sinfulness, on the plea that God does not inwardly move them; and they may argue that those holy men whom they so much admire, those saints who are to sit on Christ's right and left, are of different nature from themselves, sanctified from their mother's womb, visited, guarded, renewed, strengthened, enlightened in a peculiar way, so as to make it no wonder that they *are* saints, and no fault that they themselves are not. But this is not so; let us not thus miserably deceive ourselves. St. Paul says expressly of himself and the other Apostles, that they were "men of like passions" with the poor ignorant heathen to whom they preached. And does not his history show this? Do you not recollect what he was before his conversion? Did he not rage like a beast of prey against the disciples of Christ? and how was he converted? by the vision of our Lord? Yes, in one sense, but not by it alone; hear his own words, "Whereupon, O King Agrippa, I was not *disobedient* unto the heavenly vision." His obedience was necessary for his conversion; he could not obey without grace; but he would have received grace in vain, had he not obeyed. And, afterwards, was he at once perfect? No; for he says expressly, "not as though I had already attained, either were already perfect;" and elsewhere he tells us that he had a "thorn in the flesh, the messenger of Satan to buffet him;" and he was obliged to "bruise his body and bring it into subjection, lest, after he had preached to others, he should be himself a castaway." St. Paul conquered, as any one of us must conquer, by "striving," struggling, "to enter in at the strait gate;" he "wrought out his salvation with fear and trembling," as we must do.

This is a point which must be insisted on for the encouragement of the fearful, the confutation of the hypocritical, and the abasement of the holy. In this world, even the best of men, though they are dead to sin, and have put sin to death, yet have that dead and corrupt thing within them, though they live to God; they have still an enemy of God remaining in their hearts, though they keep it in subjection. This, indeed, is what all men now have in common, a root of evil in them, a principle of sin, or what may become such;—what they differ in is this, not that one man has it, another not; but that one lives in and to it, another not; one subdues it, another not. A holy man is by nature subject to sin equally with others; but he is holy because he subdues, tramples on, chains up, imprisons, puts out of the way this law of sin, and is ruled by religious and spiritual motives. Of Christ alone can it be said that He "did no sin, neither was guile found in His mouth." The prince of this world came and found nothing in Him. He had no root of sin in His heart; He was not born in Adam's sin. Far different are we. He was thus pure, because He was the Son of God, and born of a Virgin. But we are conceived in sin and shapen in iniquity. And since that which is born of the flesh, is flesh, we are sinful and corrupt because we are sinfully begotten of sinners. Even those then who in the end turn out to be saints and attain to life eternal, yet are not born saints, but have with God's regenerating and renewing grace to make themselves saints. It is nothing but the Cross of Christ, without us and within us, which changes any one of us from being (as I may say) a devil, into an Angel. We are all by birth children of wrath. We are at best like good olive trees, which have become good by being grafted on a good tree. By nature we are like wild trees, bearing sour and bitter fruit, and so we should remain, were we not grafted upon Christ, the good olive tree, made members of Christ, the righteous and holy and well-beloved Son of God. Hence it is that there is such a change in a saint of God from what he was at the first. Consider what a different man St. Paul was after his conversion and before,—raging, as I just now said, like some wild beast, with persecuting fury against the Church, before Christ appeared to him, and meekly suffering persecution and glorying in it afterwards. Think of St. Peter denying Christ before the resurrection, and confessing, suffering, and dying for Him afterwards. And so now many an aged saint, who has good hope of heaven, may recollect things of himself when young, which fill him with dismay. I do not speak as if God's saints led vicious and immoral lives when young; but I mean that their lower and evil nature was not subdued, and perhaps from time to time broke out and betrayed them into deeds and words so very different from what is seen in them at present, that did their friends know of them what they themselves know, they would not think them the same persons, and would be quite overpowered with astonishment. We never can guess what a man is by nature, by seeing what self-discipline has made him. Yet if we do become thereby changed and prepared for heaven, it is no praise or merit to us. It is God's doing—glory be to Him, who has wrought so wonderfully with us! Yet in this life, even to the end, there will be enough evil in us to humble us; even to the end, the holiest men have remains and stains of sin which they would fain get rid of, if they could, and which keep this life from being to them, for all God's grace, a heaven upon earth. No, the Christian life is but a shadow of heaven. Its festal and holy days are but shadows of eternity. But hereafter it will be otherwise. In heaven, sin will be utterly destroyed in every elect soul. We shall have no earthly wishes, no tendencies to disobedience or irreligion, no love of the world or the flesh, to draw us off from supreme devotion to God. We shall have our Saviour's holiness fulfilled in us, and be able to love God without drawback or infirmity.

That indeed will be a full reward of all our longings here, to praise and serve God eternally with a single and perfect heart in the midst of His Temple. What a time will that be, when all will be perfected in us which at present is but feebly begun! Then we shall see how the Angels worship God. We shall see the calmness, the intenseness, the purity, of their worship. We shall see that awful sight, the Throne of God, and the Seraphim before and around it, crying, "Holy!" We attempt now to imitate in church what there is performed, as in the beginning, and ever shall be. In the Te Deum, day by day we say, "Holy, Holy, Holy, Lord God of Sabaoth." In the Creed, we recount God's mercies to us sinners. And we say and sing Psalms and Hymns, to come as near heaven as we can. May these attempts of ours be blest by Almighty God, to prepare us for Him! may they be, not dead forms, but living services, living with life from God the Holy Ghost, in those who are dead to sin and who live with Christ! I dare say some of you have heard persons, who dissent from the Church, say (at any rate, they do say), that our Prayers and Services, and Holy days, are only forms, dead forms, which can do us no good. Yes, they are dead forms to those who are dead, but they are living forms to those who are living. If you come here in a dead way, not in faith, not coming for a blessing, without your hearts being in the service, you will get no benefit from it. But if you come in a living way, in faith, and hope, and reverence, and with holy expectant hearts, then all that takes place will be a living service and full of heaven.

Make use, then, of this Holy Easter Season, which lasts forty to fifty days, to become more like Him who died for you, and who now liveth for evermore. He promises us, "Because I live, ye shall live also." He, by dying on the Cross, opened the Kingdom of Heaven to all believers. He first died, and then He opened heaven. We, therefore, first commemorate His death, and then, for some weeks in succession, we commemorate and show forth the joys of heaven. They who do not rejoice in the weeks after Easter, would not rejoice in heaven itself. These weeks are a sort of beginning of heaven. Pray God to enable you to rejoice; to enable you to keep the Feast duly. Pray God to make you better Christians. This world is a dream,—you will get no good from it. Perhaps you find this difficult to believe; but be sure so it is. Depend upon it, at the last, you will confess it. Young people expect good from the world, and people of middle age devote themselves to it, and even old people do not like to give it up. But the world is your enemy, and the flesh is your enemy. Come to God, and beg of Him grace to devote yourselves to Him. Beg of Him the will to follow Him; beg of Him the power to obey Him. O how comfortable, pleasant, sweet, soothing, and satisfying is it to lead a holy life,— the life of Angels! It is difficult at first; but with God's grace, all things are possible. O how pleasant to have done with sin! how good and joyful to flee temptation and to resist evil! how meet, and worthy, and fitting, and right, to die unto sin, and to live unto righteousness!

Steadfastness in Old Paths[†]

"Thus saith the Lord, Stand ye in the ways, and see, and ask for the old paths, where is the good way, and walk therein, and ye shall find rest for your souls."
Jer. vi. 16

REVERENCE for the old paths is a chief Christian duty. We look to the future indeed with hope; yet this need not stand in the way of our dwelling on the past days of the Church with affection and deference. This is the feeling of our own Church, as continually expressed in the Prayer Book;—not to slight what has gone before, not to seek after some new thing, not to attempt discoveries in religion, but to keep what has once for all been committed to her keeping, and to be at rest.

Now it may be asked, "Why should we for ever be looking back at past times? were men perfect then? is it not possible to improve on the knowledge then possessed?" Let us examine this question.

In what respect should we follow old times? Now here there is this obvious maxim—what God has given us from heaven cannot be improved, what man discovers for himself does admit of improvement: we follow old times then *so far* as God has spoken in them; but in those respects in which God has not spoken in them, we are not bound to follow them. Now what is the knowledge which God has *not* thought fit to reveal to us? *knowledge connected merely with this present world.* All this we have been left to acquire for ourselves. Whatever may have been told to Adam in paradise, or to Noah, about which we know nothing, still at least since that time no divinely authenticated directions (it would appear) have been given to the world at large, on subjects relating merely to this our temporal state of being. How we may till our lands and increase our crops; how we may build our houses, and buy and sell and get gain; how we may cross the sea in ships; how we may make "fine linen for the merchant," or, like Tubal-Cain, be artificers in brass and iron: as to these objects of this world, necessary indeed for the time, not everlastingly important, God has given us no clear instruction. He has not set His sanction here upon any rule of art, and told us what is best. They have been found out by man (as far as we know), and improved by man; and the first essays, as might be expected, were the rudest and least successful. Here then we have no

[†] *Parochial & Plain Sermons*, vol. 7 (1842), Sermon 18.

need to follow the old ways. Besides, in many of these arts and pursuits, there is really neither right nor wrong at all; but the good varies with times and places. Each country has its own way, which is best for itself, and bad for others.

Again, God has given us no authority in questions of science. The heavens above, and the earth under our feet, are full of wonders, and have within them their own vast history. But the knowledge of the secrets they contain, the tale of their past revolutions, is not given us from Divine revelation; but left to man to attain by himself. And here again, since discovery is difficult, the old knowledge is generally less sure and complete than the modern knowledge. If we wish to boast about little matters, *we* know more about the motions of the heavenly bodies than Abraham, whose seed was in number as the stars; we can measure the earth, and fathom the sea, and weigh the air, more accurately than Moses, the inspired historian of the creation; and we can discuss the varied inhabitants of this globe better than Solomon, though "he spake of trees, from the cedar that is in Lebanon, even unto the hyssop that springeth out of the wall . . . and of beasts, and of fowl, and of creeping things, and of fishes." [1 Kings iv. 33.] The world is more learned in these things than of old, probably will learn more still; a vast prospect is open to it, and an intoxicating one. Like the children of Cain, before the flood came and destroyed them all, men may increase and abound in such curious or merely useful knowledge; nay, there is no limit to the progress of the human mind here; we may build us a city and a tower, whose top may reach almost to the very heavens.

Such is the knowledge which time has perfected, and in which the old paths are commonly the least direct and safe. But let us turn to that knowledge which God has given, and which therefore does not admit of improvement by lapse of time; this is *religious knowledge.* Here, whether a man might or might not have found out the truth for himself, or how far he was able without Divine assistance, waiving this question, which is nothing to the purpose, as a fact it has been from the beginning given him by revelation. God taught Adam how to please Him, and Noah, and Abraham, and Job. He has taught every nation all over the earth sufficiently for the moral training of every individual. In all these cases, the world's part of the work has been to pervert the truth, not to disengage it from obscurity. The new ways are the crooked ones. The nearer we mount up to the time of Adam, or Noah, or Abraham, or Job, the purer light of truth we gain; as we recede from it we meet with superstitions, fanatical excesses, idolatries, and immoralities. So again in the case of the Jewish Church, since God expressly gave the Jews a precise law, it is clear man could not improve upon it; he could but add the "traditions of men." Nothing was to be looked for from the cultivation of the human mind. "To the law and to the testimony" was the appeal; and any deviation from it was, not a sign of increasing illumination, but "because there was no light" in the authors of innovation. Lastly, in the Christian Church, we cannot add or take away, as regards the doctrines that are contained in the inspired volume, as regards the faith once delivered to the saints. "Other foundation can no man lay than that is laid, which is Jesus Christ." [1 Cor. iii. 11.]

But it may be said that, though the word of God is an infallible rule of faith, yet it requires interpreting, and why, as time goes on, should we not discover in it more than we at present know on the subject of religion and morals?

But this is hardly a question of practical importance to us as individuals; for in truth a very little knowledge is enough for teaching a man his duty: and, since Scripture is intended to teach us our duty, surely it was never intended as a storehouse of mere knowledge. Discoveries then in the details of morals and religion, by means of the inspired volume, whether possible or not, must not be looked out for, as the expectation may unsettle the mind, and take it off from matters of duty. Certainly all curious questions at least are forbidden us by Scripture, even though Scripture may be found adequate to answer them.

This should be insisted on. Do we think to become better men by knowing more? Little knowledge is required for religious obedience. The poor and rich, the learned and unlearned, are here on a level. We have all of us the means of doing our duty; we have not the *will*, and this no knowledge can give. We have need to subdue our own minds, and this no other person *can* do for us. The case is different in matters of learning and science. There others can and do labour for us; *we* can make use of *their* labours; we begin where they ended; thus things progress, and each successive age knows more than the preceding. But in religion each must begin, go on, and end, for himself. The religious history of each individual is as solitary and complete as the history of the world. Each man will, of course, gain more knowledge as he studies Scripture more, and prays and meditates more; but he cannot make another man wise or holy by his own advance in wisdom or holiness. When children cease to be born children, because they are born late in the world's history, when we can reckon the world's past centuries for the age of this generation, then only can the world increase in real excellence and truth as it grows older. The character will always require forming, evil will ever need rooting out of each heart; the grace to go before and to aid us in our moral discipline must ever come fresh and immediate from the Holy Spirit. So the world ever remains in its infancy, as regards the cultivation of moral truth; for the knowledge required for practice is little, and admits of little increase, except in the case of individuals, and then to them alone; and it cannot be handed on to another. "As it was in the beginning, is now, and ever shall be," such is the general history of man's moral discipline, running parallel to the unchanging glory of that All-Perfect God, who is its Author and Finisher.

Practical religious knowledge, then, is a personal gift, and, further, a gift from God; and, therefore, as experience has hitherto shown, more likely to be obscured than advanced by the lapse of time. But further, we know of the existence of an evil principle in the world, corrupting and resisting the truth in its measure, according to the truth's clearness and purity. Whether it be from the sinfulness of our nature, or from the malignity of Satan, striving with peculiar enmity against Divine truth, certain it is that the best gifts of God have been the most woefully corrupted. It was prophesied from the beginning, that the serpent should bruise the heel of Him who was ultimately to triumph over him; and so it has ever been. Our Saviour, who was the Truth itself, was the most spitefully entreated of all by the world. It has been the case with His followers too. He was crucified with thieves; *they* have been united and blended against their will with the worst and basest of mankind. The purer and more precious the gift which God bestows on us, far from this being a security for its abiding and increasing, rather the more grievously has that gift been abused. St. John even seems to make the greater wickedness in the world the clear consequence and evidence of our Lord's having made His appearing. "Little children, it is the last time" (i.e. the time of the Christian Dispensation): "and as ye have heard that Antichrist shall come, even now are there many Antichrists, *whereby we know* that it is the last time." [1 John ii. 18.] St. Paul drew the same picture. So far from anticipating brighter times in store for the Church before the end, he portends evil only. "This know" (he says to Timothy), "that in the last days perilous times will come . . . Evil men and seducers shall wax worse and worse, deceiving and being deceived." [2 Tim. iii. 13.] In these and other passages surely there is no encouragement to look out for a more enlightened, peaceful, and pure state of the Church than it enjoys at present: rather, there is a call on us to consider the old and original way as the best, and all deviations from it, though they seem to promise an easier, safer, and shorter road, yet as really either tending another way, or leading to the right object with much hazard and many obstacles.

Such is the case as regards the knowledge of our duty,—that kind of knowledge which alone is really worth earnest seeking. And there is an important reason why we should acquiesce in it;—because the conviction that things are so has no slight influence in forming our minds into that perfection of the religious character, at which it is our duty ever to be aiming. While we think it possible to make some great and important improvements in the subject of religion, we shall be unsettled, restless, impatient; we shall be drawn from the consideration of improving ourselves, and from using the day while it is given us, by the visions of a deceitful hope, which promises to make rich but tendeth to penury. On the other hand, if we feel that the way is altogether closed against discoveries in religion, as being neither practicable nor desirable, it is likely we shall be drawn more entirely and seriously to our own personal advancement in holiness; our eyes, being withdrawn from external prospects, will look more at home. We shall think less of circumstances, and more of our duties under them, whatever they are. In proportion as we cease to be theorists we shall become practical men; we shall have less of self-confidence and arrogance, more of inward humility and diffidence; we shall be less likely to despise others, and shall think of our own intellectual powers with less complacency.

It is one great peculiarity of the Christian character to be dependent. Men of the world, indeed, in proportion as they are active and enterprising, boast of their independence, and are proud of having obligations to no one. But it is the Christian's excellence to be diligent and watchful, to work and persevere, and yet to be in spirit *dependent*; to be willing to serve, and to rejoice in the permission to do so; to be content to view himself in a subordinate place; to love to sit in the dust. Though in the Church a son of God, he takes pleasure in considering himself Christ's "servant" and "slave;" he feels glad whenever he can put himself to shame. So it is the natural bent of his mind freely and affectionately to visit and trace the footsteps of the saints, to sound the praises of the great men of old who have wrought wonders in the Church and whose words still live; being jealous of their honour, and feeling it to be even too great a privilege for such as he is to be put in trust with the faith once delivered to them, and following them strictly in the narrow way, even as they have followed Christ. To the ears of such persons the words of the text are as sweet music: "Thus saith the Lord, Stand ye in the ways, and see, and ask for the old paths, where is the good way, and walk therein, and ye shall find rest for your souls."

The history of the Old Dispensation affords us a remarkable confirmation of what I have been arguing from these words; for in the time of the Law there was an increase of religious knowledge by fresh revelations. From the time of Samuel especially to the time of Malachi, the Church was bid look forward for a growing illumination, which, though not necessary for religious obedience, subserved the establishment of religious comfort. Now, I wish you to observe how careful the inspired prophets of Israel are to prevent any kind of disrespect being shown to the memory of former times, on account of that increase of religious knowledge with which the later ages were favoured; and if such reverence for the past were a duty among the Jews when the Saviour was still to come, much more is it the duty of Christians, who expect no new revelation, and who, though they look forward in hope, yet see the future only in the mirror of times and persons past, who (in the Angel's words) "wait for that same Jesus: . . . so to come in like manner as they saw Him go into heaven."

Now, as to the reverence enjoined and taught the Jews towards persons and times past, we may notice first the commandment given them to honour and obey their parents and elders. This, indeed, is a natural law. But that very circumstance surely gives force to the express and repeated injunctions given them to observe it, sanctioned too (as it was) with a special promise. Natural affection might have taught it; but it was rested by the Law on a higher sanction. Next, this duty of reverently regarding past times was taught by such general injunctions (more or less express) as the text. It is remarkable, too, when Micah would tell the Jews that the legal sacrifices appointed in time past were inferior to the moral duties, he states it not as a new truth, but refers to its announcement by a prophet in Moses' age,—to the answer of Balaam to Balak, king of Moab.

But, further, to bind them to the observance of this duty, the past was made the pledge of the future, hope was grounded upon memory; all prayer for favour sent them back to the old mercies of God. "The Lord *hath been* mindful of us, He *will* bless us;" [Ps. cxv. 12.] this was the form of their humble expectation. The favour vouchsafed to Abraham and Israel, and the deliverance from Egypt, were the objects on which hope dwelt, and were made the types of blessings in prospect. For instance, out of the many passages which might be cited, Isaiah says, "Awake . . . O arm of the Lord, *as in the ancient days, in the generations of old.*" [Isa. li. 9.] Micah, "Feed thy people with thy rod, the flock of thine heritage, which dwell solitary in the wood, in the midst of Carmel; let them feed in Bashan and Gilead, *as in the days of old*; according to the days of thy coming out of Egypt will I show unto him marvellous things." [Micah vii. 14, 15.] The Psalms abound with like references to past mercies, as pledges and types of future. Prophesying of the reign of Christ, David says, "The Lord said, I will bring again from Bashan, I will bring My people again from the depths of the sea," and Moses too, speaking to the Israelites—"*Remember the days of old*, consider the years of many generations; ask thy father and he will show thee; thy elders, and they will tell thee." [Deut. xxxii. 7.] Accordingly, while a coming Saviour was predicted, still the claims of past times on Jewish piety were maintained, by His being represented by the prophets under the name and character of David, or in the dress and office of Aaron; so that, the clearer the revelation of the glory in prospect, in the same degree greater honour was put upon the former Jewish saints who typified it. In like manner the blessings promised to the Christian Church are granted to it in the character of Israel, or of Jerusalem, or of Sion.

Lastly, as Moses directed the eyes of his people towards the line of prophets which the Lord their God was to raise up from among them, ending in the Messiah, they in turn dutifully exalt Moses, whose system they were superseding. Samuel, David, Isaiah, Micah, Jeremiah, Daniel, Ezra, Nehemiah, each in succession, bear testimony to Moses. Malachi, the last of the prophets, while predicting the coming of John the Baptist, still gives this charge, "*Remember ye the law of Moses*, My servant, which I commanded unto him in Horeb for all Israel, with the statutes and judgments." [Mal. iv. 4.] In like manner in the New Testament the last of the prophets and apostles describes the saints as singing "the song of Moses, the servant of God" (this is his honourable title, as elsewhere), "*and* the song of the Lamb." [Rev. xv. 3.] Above all, our blessed Lord Himself sums up the whole subject we have been reviewing, both the doctrine and Jewish illustration of it, in His own authoritative words,—"If they hear not Moses and the prophets, neither will they be persuaded, though one rose from the dead." [Luke xvi. 31.] After this sanction, it is needless to refer to the reverence with which St. Paul regards the law of Moses, and to the commemoration he has made of the Old Testament saints in the eleventh chapter of his Epistle to the Hebrews.

Oh that we had duly drunk into this spirit of reverence and godly fear! Doubtless we are far above the Jews in our privileges; we are favoured with the news of redemption; we know doctrines, which righteous men of old time earnestly desired to be told, and were not. To us is revealed the Eternal Son, the Only-begotten of the Father, full of grace and truth. We are branches of the True Vine, which is sprung out of the earth and spread abroad. We have been granted Apostles, Prophets, Evangelists, pastors, and teachers. We celebrate those true Festivals which the Jews possessed only in shadow. For us Christ has died; on us the Spirit has descended. In these respects we are honoured and privileged, oh how far above all ages before He came! Yet our honours are our shame, when we contrast the glory given us with our love of the world, our fear of men, our lightness of mind, our sensuality, our gloomy tempers. What need have we to look with wonder and reverence at those saints of the Old Covenant, who with less advantages yet so far surpassed us; and still more at those of the Christian Church, who both had higher gifts of grace and profited by them! What need have we to humble ourselves; to pray God not to leave us, though we have left Him; to pray Him to give us back what we have lost, to receive a repentant people, to renew in us a right heart and give us a religious will, and to enable us to follow Him perseveringly in His narrow and humbling way.

Wilfulness, the Sin of Saul[†]

> "It repenteth Me that I have set up Saul to be king; for he is turned back
> from following Me, and hath not performed My commandments."
>
> 1 Sam. xv. 11

THE THREE chief religious patterns and divine instruments under the first Covenant, have each his complement in the Sacred History, that we may have a warning as well as an instruction. The distinguishing virtue, moral and political, of Abraham, Moses, and David, was their faith; by which I mean an implicit reliance in God's command and promise, and a zeal for His honour; a surrender and devotion of themselves, and all they had, to Him. At His word they each relinquished the dearest wish of their hearts, Isaac, Canaan, and the Temple; the Temple was not to be built, the land of promise not to be entered, the child of promise not to be retained. All three were tried by the anxieties and discomforts of exile and wandering; all three, and especially Moses and David, were very zealous for the Lord God of Hosts.

2. The faith of Abraham is illustrated in the luke-warmness of Lot, who, though a true servant of God, and a righteous man, chose for his dwelling-place the fertile country of a guilty people. To Moses, who was faithful in all God's house, is confronted the untrue prophet Balaam, who, gifted from the same Divine Master, and abounding in all knowledge and spiritual discernment, mistook words for works, and fell through love of lucre. The noble self-consuming zeal of David, who was at once ruler of the chosen people, and type of the Messiah, is contrasted with a still more conspicuous and hateful specimen of unbelief, as disclosed to us in the history of Saul. To this history it is proposed now to draw your attention, not indeed with the purpose of surveying it as a whole, but with hope of gaining thence some such indirect illustration, in the way of contrast, of the nature of religious Faith, as it is adapted to supply.

3. It cannot be denied that the designs of Providence towards Saul and David are, at first sight, of a perplexing nature, as implying distinctions in the moral character of the two men, which their history does not clearly warrant. Accordingly, it is usual, with a view of meeting the difficulty, to treat them as mere instruments in the Divine Governance of the Israelites, and to determine

---

[†] *Oxford University Sermons* (1843), Sermon 9, preached in 1832.

their respective virtues and defects, not by a moral, but by a political standard. For instance, the honourable title by which David is distinguished, as "a man after God's own heart," is interpreted with reference merely to his activity and success in enforcing the principles of the Mosaic system, no account being taken of the motives which influenced him, or of his general character, or of his conduct in other respects. Now, it is by no means intended here to dispute the truth of such representations, or to deny that the Church, in its political relations, must even treat men with a certain reference to their professions and outward acts, such as it withdraws in its private dealings with them; yet, to consider the difference between Saul and David to be of a moral nature, is more consistent with the practical objects with which we believe Scripture to have been written, and more reverent, moreover, to the memory of one whose lineage the Saviour almost gloried in claiming, and whose devotional writings have edified the Church even to this day. Let us then drop, for the present, the political view of the history which it is here proposed to consider, and attempt to discover the moral lesson intended to be conveyed to us in the character of Saul, the contrast of the zealous David.

4. The unbelief of Balaam discovers itself in a love of secular distinction, and was attended by self-deception. Saul seems to have had no base ends in view; he was not self-deceived; his temptation and his fall consisted in a certain perverseness of mind, founded on some obscure feelings of self-importance, very commonly observable in human nature, and sometimes called pride,—a perverseness which shows itself in a reluctance absolutely to relinquish its own independence of action, in cases where dependence is a duty, and which interferes a little, and alters a little, as if with a view of satisfying its own fancied dignity, though it is afraid altogether to oppose itself to the voice of God. Should this seem, at first sight, to be a trifling fault, it is the more worth while to trace its operation in the history of Saul. If a tree is known by its fruit, it is a great sin.

5. Saul's character is marked by much that is considered to be the highest moral excellence,—generosity, magnanimity, calmness, energy, and decision. He is introduced to us as "a choice young man, and a goodly," and as possessed of a striking personal presence, and as a member of a wealthy and powerful family.[32]

6. The first announcement of his elevation came upon him suddenly, but apparently without unsettling him. He kept it secret, leaving it to Samuel, who had made it to him, to publish it. "Saul said unto his uncle, He (that is, Samuel) told us plainly that the asses were found. But of the matter of the

---

[32] Some sentences which follow have already been inserted in *Parochial & Plain Sermons*, vol. 3, sermon 3 (not included in this collection).—*JHN*

kingdom, whereof Samuel spake, he told him not." Nay, it would even seem as if he were averse to the dignity intended for him; for when the Divine lot fell upon him, he had hid himself, and was not discovered by the people without Divine assistance.

7. The appointment was at first unpopular. "The children of Belial said, How shall this man save us?" Here again his high-mindedness is discovered, and his remarkable force and energy of character. He showed no signs of resentment at the insult. "They despised him, and brought him no presents. But he held his peace." Soon the Ammonites invaded the country beyond Jordan, with the avowed intention of reducing its inhabitants to slavery. They, almost in despair, sent to Saul for relief; and the panic spread in the interior, as well as among those whose country was immediately threatened. The conduct of their new king brings to mind the celebrated Roman story. "Behold, Saul came after the herd out of the field and Saul said, What aileth the people, that they weep? And they told him the tidings of the men of Jabesh. And the Spirit of God came upon Saul, and his anger was kindled greatly." His order for an immediate gathering throughout Israel was obeyed with the alacrity with which, in times of alarm, the many yield themselves up to the will of the strong-minded. A decisive victory over the enemy followed. Then the popular cry became, "Who is he that said, Shall Saul reign over us? Bring the men, that we may put them to death. And Saul said, There shall not a man be put to death this day: for today the Lord hath wrought salvation in Israel."

8. We seem here to find noble traits of character; at the same time it must not be forgotten that sometimes such exhibitions are also the concomitants of a certain strangeness and eccentricity of mind, which are very perplexing to those who study it, and very unamiable. Reserve, sullenness, headstrong self-confidence, pride, caprice, sourness of temper, scorn of others, a scoffing at natural feeling and religious principle; all those characters of mind which, though distinct from mental aberration, are temptations to it, frequently take the form, and have in some degree the nature, of magnanimity. It is probable, from the sequel of Saul's history, that the apparent nobleness of his first actions was connected with some such miserable principles and feelings, which then existed only in their seeds, but which afterwards sprang up and ripened to his destruction; and this in consequence of that one fatal defect of mind which has been already noticed, as corrupting the integrity of his faith.

9. The world prevailed over the faith of Balaam; a more subtle, though not a rare temptation, overcame the faith of Saul; wilfulness, the unaccountable desire of acting short of simple obedience to God's will, a repugnance of unreserved self-surrender and submission to Him. This, it will at once be seen, was one characteristic of the Jewish nation; so that the king was but a type of

the people; nor, indeed, was it likely to be otherwise, born as he was in the original sin of that very perverseness which led them to choose a king, instead of God. It is scarcely necessary to refer to the details of their history for instances of a like wilfulness,—such as their leaving the manna till the morning, their going out to gather it on the seventh day, Nadab and Abihu's offering strange fire, their obstinate transgression of the Second Commandment, their presumptuous determination to fight with the Canaanites, though Moses foretold their defeat, and, when possessed of the promised land, their putting under tribute the idolaters whom they were bid exterminate. The same was the sin of Jeroboam, who is almost by title the Apostate; when God had promised him the kingdom of Israel, he refused to wait God's time, but impatiently forced a crisis, which ought to have been left to Him who promised it.

10. On the other hand, Abraham and David, with arms in their hands, waited upon Him for the fulfilment of the temporal promise in His good time. It is on this that the distinction turns, so much insisted on in the Books of Kings, of serving God with a "perfect," or not with a perfect, heart. "Ahaz went to Damascus to meet Tiglath-pileser, King of Assyria, and saw an altar that was at Damascus; and King Ahaz sent to Urijah the priest the fashion of the altar, . . . and Urijah . . . built an altar according to all that king Ahaz had sent from Damascus." Here was a wanton innovation on received usages, which had been appointed by Almighty God. The same evil temper is protested against in Hezekiah's proclamation to the remnant of the Israelites: "Be ye not like your fathers, and like your brethren, which trespassed against the Lord God of their fathers, who therefore gave them up to desolation, as ye see. Now be ye not stiff-necked, as your fathers were, but yield yourselves unto the Lord, and enter into His sanctuary." It is indirectly condemned, also, in the precept given to the Israelites, before their final deliverance from Pharaoh. When they were on the Red Sea shore, Moses said, "Fear ye not, stand still, and see the salvation of the Lord . . . The Lord shall fight for you, and ye shall hold your peace." Again, in the Book of Psalms, "Be still, and know that I am God. I will be exalted among the heathen, I will be exalted in the earth;" the very trial of the people consisting in their doing nothing out of their place, but implicitly following when the Almighty took the lead.

11. The trial and the sin of the Israelites were continued to the end of their history. They fell from their election on Christ's coming, in consequence of this very wilfulness; refusing to receive the terms of the New Covenant, *as* they were vouchsafed to them, and attempting to incorporate them into their own ceremonial system. "They being ignorant of God's righteousness and going about to establish their own righteousness, have not submitted themselves unto the righteousness of God."

12. Such was one distinguishing sin of the Israelites as a nation; and, as it proved the cause of their rejection, so had it also, ages before, corrupted the faith, and forfeited the privileges, of their first king. The signs of wilfulness run through his history from first to last: but his formal trial took place at two distinct times, and in both cases terminated in his deliberate fall. Of these, the latter is more directly to our purpose. When sent to inflict a Divine judgment upon the Amalekites, he spared those whom he was bid slay; their king Agag, the best of the sheep and cattle, and all that was good. We are not concerned with the general state of mind and opinion which led him to this particular display of wilfulness. Much might be said of that profaneness, which, as in the case of Esau, was a distinguishing trait in his character. Indeed, we might even conjecture that from the first he was an unbeliever in heart; that is, that he did not recognize the exclusive divinity of the Mosaic theology, compared with those of the surrounding nations, and that he had by this time learned to regard the pomp and splendour of the neighbouring monarchies with an interest which made him ashamed of the seeming illiberality and the singularity of the institutions of Israel. A perverse will easily collects together a system of notions to justify itself in its obliquity. The real state of the case was this, that he preferred his own way to that which God had determined. When directed by the Divine Hand towards the mark for which he was chosen, he started aside like a broken bow. He obeyed, but with a reserve, yet distinctly professing to Samuel that he had performed the commandment of the Lord, because the sheep and cattle were reserved for a pious purpose, a sacrifice to the Lord. The Prophet, in his reply, explained the real moral character of this limited and discretionary obedience, in words which are a warning to all who are within the hearing of Revealed Religion to the end of time: "Hath the Lord as great delight in burnt offerings and sacrifices, as in obeying the voice of the Lord? Behold, to obey is better than sacrifice; and to hearken, than the fat of rams. For rebellion is as the sin of witchcraft, and stubbornness is as iniquity and idolatry."

13. The moral of Saul's history is forced upon us by the events which followed this deliberate offence. By wilful resistance to God's will, he opened the door to those evil passions which till then, at the utmost, only served to make his character unamiable, without stamping it with guilt. The reserve and mysteriousness, which, when subordinate to such magnanimity as he possessed, were even calculated to increase his influence as a ruler, ended in an overthrow of his mind, when they were allowed full scope by the removal of true religious principle, and the withdrawal of the Spirit of God. Derangement was the consequence of disobedience. The wilfulness which first resisted God, next preyed upon himself, as a natural principle of disorder; his moods and

changes, his compunctions and relapses, what were they but the convulsions of the spirit, when the governing power was lost? At length the proud heart, which thought it much to obey its Maker, was humbled to seek comfort in a witch's cavern; essaying, by means which he had formerly denounced, to obtain advice from that Prophet when dead, whom in his lifetime he had dishonoured.

14. In contemplating this miserable termination of a history which promised well in the beginning, it should be observed, how clearly the failure of the divine purpose which takes place in it is attributable to man. Almighty God chose an instrument adapted, as far as external qualifications were concerned, to fulfil His purpose; adapted in all those respects which He reserved in His own hands, when He created a free agent; in character and gifts, in all respects except in that in which all men are, on the whole, on a level,—in will. No one could be selected in talents or conduct more suitable for maintaining political power at home than the reserved mysterious monarch whom God gave to His people; none more suitable for striking terror into the surrounding nations than a commander gifted with his coolness and promptitude in action. But he fell from his election, because of unbelief,—because he would take another part, and not the very part which was actually assigned him in the decrees of the Most High.

15. And again, considering his character according to the standard of moral excellence, here also it was one not without great promise. It is from such stern materials that the highest and noblest specimens of our kind are formed. The pliant and amiable by nature, generally speaking, are not the subjects of great purposes. They are hardly capable of extraordinary discipline; they yield or they sink beneath the pressure of those sanctifying processes which do but mature the champions of holy Church. "Unstable as water, thou shalt not excel," is a representation true in its degree in the case of many, who nevertheless serve God acceptably in their generation, and whose real place in the ranks of the unseen world we have no means of ascertaining. But those minds, which naturally most resemble the aboriginal chaos, contain within them the elements of a marvellous creation of light and beauty, if they but open their hearts to the effectual power of the Holy Spirit. Pride and sullenness, obstinacy and impetuosity, then become transformed into the zeal, firmness, and high-mindedness of religious Faith. It depended on Saul himself whether or not he became the rival of that exalted saint, who, being once a fierce avenger of his brethren, at length became "the meekest of men," yet not losing thereby, but gaining, moral strength and resoluteness.

16. Or again, a comparison of him in this respect with the Apostle who originally bore his name, is not perhaps so fanciful as it may appear at first

sight. St. Paul was distinguished by a furiousness and vindictiveness equally incongruous as Saul's pride, with the obedience of Faith. In the first persecution against the Christians, he is described by the sacred writer as ravening like a beast of prey. And he was exposed to the temptation of a wilfulness similar to that of Saul—the wilfulness of running counter to God's purposes, and interfering in the course of Dispensations which he should have humbly received. He indeed was called miraculously, but scarcely more so than Saul, who, when he least expected it, was called by Samuel, and was, at his express prediction, suddenly filled by the Spirit of God, and made to prophesy. But, while Saul profited not by the privilege thus vouchsafed to him, St. Paul was "not disobedient to the heavenly vision," and matured in his afterlife in those exalted qualities of mind which Saul forfeited. Every attentive reader of his Epistles must be struck with the frequency and force of the Apostle's declarations concerning unreserved submission to the Divine will, or rather of his exulting confidence in it. But the wretched king of Israel, what is his ultimate state, but the most forlorn of which human nature is capable? "How are the mighty fallen!" was the lament over him of the loyal though injured friend who succeeded to his power. He, who might have been canonized in the catalogue of the eleventh of Hebrews, is but the prototype of that vision of obduracy and self-inflicted destitution, which none but unbelieving poets of these latter ages have ever thought worthy of aught but the condemnation and abhorrence of mankind.

17. Two questions must be answered before we can apply the lesson of Saul's history to our own circumstances. It is common to contrast Christianity with Judaism, as if the latter were chiefly a system of positive commands, and the former addressed itself to the Reason and natural Conscience; and accordingly, it will perhaps be questioned whether Christians can be exposed to the temptation of wilfulness, that is, disobedience to the external word of God, in any way practically parallel to Saul's trial. And secondly, granting it possible, the warning against wilfulness, contained in his history and that of his nation, may be met by the objection that the Jews were a peculiarly carnal and gross-minded people, so that nothing can be argued concerning our danger at this day, from their being exposed and yielding to the temptation of perversity and presumption.

18. (1.) But such an assumption evidences a great want of fairness towards the ancient people of God, in those who make it, and is evidently perilous in proportion as it is proved to be unfounded. All men, not the Jews only, have a strange propensity, such as Eve evidenced in the beginning, to do what they are told not to do. It is plainly visible in children, and in the common people; and in them we are able to judge what we all are, before education and

habit lay restraints upon us. Need we even do more than appeal to the events of the past year, to the conduct of the lower classes when under that fearful visitation, from which we are now, as we trust, recovering, in order to detect the workings of that innate spirit of scepticism and obduracy which was the enemy of Jewish faith? Of course, all places did not afford the same evidence of it; but on the whole there was enough for my present allusion to it. A suspicion of the most benevolent exertions in their favour, a jealousy of the interference of those who knew more than themselves, a perverse rejection of their services, and a counteraction of their plans and advice, an unthankful credulity in receiving all the idle tales told in disparagement of their knowledge and prudence; these were admonitions before our eyes, not to trust those specious theories which are built on the supposition, that the actual condition of the human mind is better now than it was among the Jews. This is not said without regard to the difference of guilt in disobeying a Divine and a human command; nor, again, in complaint of the poorer classes, of whom we are especially bound to be tender, and who are not the worse merely because they are less disguised in the expression of their feelings; but as pointing out for our own instruction the present existence of a perversity in our common nature, like that which appears in the history of Israel. Nor, perhaps, can any one doubt, who examines himself, that he has within him an unaccountable and instinctive feeling to resist authority as such, which conscience or the sense of interest is alone able to overcome.

19. Or, again, to take the case of young persons who have not yet taken their place in the serious business of life; consider the false shame they feel at being supposed to be obedient to God or man; their endeavours to be more irreligious than they really can be; their affected indifference to domestic feelings, and the sanctity and the authority of relationship; their adoption of ridicule as an instrument of retaliation on the constraints of duty or necessity. What does all this show us, but that our nature likes its own way, not as thinking it better or safer, but simply because it is its own? In other words, that the principle of Faith is resisted, not only by our attachment to objects of sense and sight, but by an innate rebellious principle, which disobeys as if for the sake of disobedience.

20. (2.) Now if wilfulness be a characteristic of human nature, it is idle to make any such distinction of Dispensations, as will deprive us of the profitableness of the history of Saul; which was the other question just now raised concerning it. Under any circumstances it must be a duty to subdue that which is in itself vicious; and it is no excuse for wilfulness to say that we are not under a positive system of commands, such as the Mosaic, and that there is no room for the sin in Christianity. Rather, it will be our duty to regard

ourselves in all our existing religious relations, and not merely according to some abstract views of the Gospel Covenant, and to apply the principles of right and wrong, exemplified in the Jewish history, to our changed circumstances on the whole.

21. But, to speak plainly, it may be doubted whether there be any such great difference between the Jewish system and our own, in respect of positive institutions and commandments. Revealed Religion, as such, is of the nature of a positive rule, implying, as it does, an addition, greater or less, to the religion of nature, and the disclosure of facts, which are thus disclosed, because otherwise not discoverable. Accordingly, the difference between the state of Jews and Christians is one simply of degree. We have to practise submission as they had, and we can run counter to the will of God in the very same way as they did, and under the same temptations which overcame them. For instance, the reception of the Catholic faith is a submission to a positive command, as really as was that of the Israelites to the Second Commandment. And the belief in the necessity of such reception, in order to salvation, is an additional instance of submission. Adherence to the Canon of Scripture is a further instance of this obedience of Faith; and St. John marks it as such in the words with which the Canon itself closes, which contain an anathema parallel to that which we use in the Creed. Moreover, the duty of Ecclesiastical Unity is clearly one of positive institution; it is a sort of ceremonial observance, and as such, is the tenure on which the evangelical privileges are chartered to us. The Sacraments, too, are of the same positive character.

22. If these remarks be well founded, it is plain that instead of our being very differently situated from the Jews, all persons who are subjects of Revealed Religion, coincide in differing from all who are left under the Dispensation of Nature. Revelation puts us on a trial which exists but obscurely in Natural Religion; the trial of obeying for obedience-sake, or on Faith. Deference to the law of Conscience, indeed, is of the nature of Faith; but it is easily perverted into a kind of self-confidence, namely, a deference to our own judgment. Here, then, Revelation provides us with an important instrument for chastening and moulding our moral character, over and above the matter of its disclosures. Christians as well as Jews must submit as little children. This being considered, how strange are the notions of the present day concerning the liberty and irresponsibility of the Christian! If the Gospel be a message, as it is, it ever must be more or less what the multitude of self-wise reasoners declare it shall not be,—a law; it must be of the nature of what they call a form, and a bondage; it must, in its degree, bring darkness, instead of flattering them with the promise of immediate illumination; and must enlighten them only in proportion as they first submit to be darkened. This, then, if they knew their

meaning, is the wish of the so-called philosophical Christians, and men of no party, of the present day; namely, that they should be rid altogether of the shackles of a Revelation: and to this assuredly their efforts are tending and will tend,—to identify the Christian doctrine with their own individual convictions, to sink its supernatural character, and to constitute themselves the prophets, not the recipients, of Divine Truth; creeds and discipline being already in their minds severed from its substance, and being gradually shaken off by them in fact, as the circumstances of the times will allow.

23. Let us, then, reflect that, whatever be the trial of those who have not a Revelation, the trial of those who have is one of Faith in opposition to self-will. Those very self-appointed ordinances which are praiseworthy in a heathen, and the appropriate evidence of his earnestness and piety, are inexcusable in those to whom God has spoken. Things indifferent become sins when they are forbidden, and duties when commanded. The emblems of the Deity might be invented by Egyptian faith, but were adopted by Jewish unbelief. The trial of Abraham, when called on to kill his son, as of Saul when bid slay the Amalekites, was the duty of quitting the ordinary rules which He prescribes to our obedience, upon a positive commandment distinctly conveyed to them by revelation.

24. And so strong is this tendency of Revealed Religion to erect positive institutions and laws, that it absorbs into its province even those temporal ordinances which are, strictly speaking, exterior to it. It gives to the laws of man the nature of a divine authority, and where they exist makes obedience to them a duty. This is evident in the case of civil government, the forms and officers of which, when once established, are to be received for conscience-sake by those who find themselves under them. The same principle is applied in a more remarkable manner to sanction customs originally indifferent, in the case of the Rechabites; who were rewarded with a promise of continuance as a family, on the ground of their observance of certain discomforts and austerities, imposed on them by the simple authority of an ancestor.

25. With these principles fresh in the memory, a number of reflections crowd upon the mind in surveying the face of society, as at present constituted. The present open resistance to constituted power, and (what is more to the purpose) the indulgent toleration of it, the irreverence towards Antiquity, the unscrupulous and wanton violation of the commands and usages of our forefathers, the undoing of their benefactions, the profanation of the Church, the bold transgression of the duty of Ecclesiastical Unity, the avowed disdain of what is called party religion (though Christ undeniably made a party the vehicle of His doctrine, and did not cast it at random on the world, as men would now have it), the growing indifference to the Catholic Creed, the sceptical

objections to portions of its doctrine, the arguings and discussings and comparings and correctings and rejectings, and all the train of presumptuous exercises, to which its sacred articles are subjected, the numberless discordant criticisms on the Liturgy, which have shot up on all sides of us; the general irritable state of mind, which is every where to be witnessed, and craving for change in all things; what do all these symptoms show, but that the spirit of Saul still lives?—that wilfulness, which is the antagonist principle to the zeal of David, the principle of cleaving and breaking down all divine ordinances, instead of building up. And with Saul's sin, Saul's portion awaits his followers,—distraction, aberration; the hiding of God's countenance; imbecility, rashness, and changeableness in their counsels; judicial blindness, fear of the multitude; alienation from good men and faithful friends; subserviency to their worst foes, the kings of Amalek and the wizards of Endor. So was it with the Jews, who rejected their Messiah only to follow impostors; so is it with infidels, who become the slaves of superstition; and such is ever the righteous doom of those who trust their own wills more than God's word, in one way or other to be led eventually into a servile submission to usurped authority. As the Apostle says of the Roman Christians, they were but slaves of sin, while they were emancipated from righteousness. "What fruit," he asks, "had ye then in those things whereof ye are now ashamed?"

26. These remarks may at first sight seem irrelevant in the case of those who, like ourselves, are bound by affection and express promises to the cause of Christ's Church; yet it should be recollected that very rarely have its members escaped the infection of the age in which they lived: and there certainly is the danger of our considering ourselves safe, merely because we do not go the lengths of others, and protest against the extreme principles or measures to which they are committed.

Reverence in Worship†

"Samuel ministered before the Lord, being a child, girded with a linen ephod."
1 Samuel ii. 18

SAMUEL, viewed in his place in sacred history, that is, in the course of events which connect Moses with Christ, appears as a great ruler and teacher of his people; this is his prominent character. He was the first of the prophets; yet, when we read the sacred narrative itself, in which his life is set before us, I suppose those passages are the more striking and impressive which represent him, in the office which belonged to him by birth, as a Levite, or minister of God. He was taken into God's special service from the first; he lived in His Temple; nay, while yet a child, he was honoured with the apparel of a sacred function, as the text tells us, "he ministered before the Lord, being a child, girded with a linen ephod."

His mother had "given him unto the Lord all the days of his life," [1 Sam. i. 11.] by a solemn vow before his birth; and in him, if in any one, were fulfilled the words of the Psalmist, "Blessed are they that dwell in Thy house, they will be always praising Thee." [Ps. lxxxiv. 4.]

Such a constant abode in God's house would make common minds only familiar with holy things, and irreverent; but where God's grace is present in the heart, the effect is the reverse; which we might be sure would happen in the case of Samuel. "The Lord was with him," we are told; and therefore the more the outward signs of that Lord met his eye, the more reverent he became, not the more presuming. The more he acquainted himself with God, the greater would be his awe and holy fear.

Thus the first notice we have of his ministering before the Lord, reminds us of the decency and gravity necessary at all times, and in all persons, in approaching Him. "He ministered before the Lord, being a child, girded with a linen ephod." His mother had made him yearly a little coat for his common use, but in Divine Service he wore, not this, but a garment which would both express, and impress upon him, reverence.

And, in like manner, in his old age, when Saul sent to seek David at Naioth, where Samuel was, his messengers found Samuel and the prophets under him all in decent order. "They saw the company of prophets prophesy-

† *Parochial & Plain Sermons*, vol. 8 (1843), Sermon 1.

ing, and Samuel over them." And this was so impressive a sight, that it became an instrument of God's supernatural power towards them, and they prophesied also.

On the other hand, if we would have an example of the want of this reverence, we have it in Saul himself, the reprobate king, who, when he was on his way to Naioth, and was visited by God's Holy Spirit, did not thereupon receive the garment of salvation, nor was clothed in righteousness, but behaved himself in an unseemly wild way, as one whose destitution and shame were but detected by the visitation. He stript off his clothes and prophesied before Samuel, and lay down in that state all that day and all that night.

This difference we see even at this day:—of persons professing religion, some are like Samuel, some like Saul; some (as it were) cast off their garments and prophesy in disorder and extravagance; others minister before the Lord, "girded with a linen ephod," with "their loins girt and their lamps burning," like men awfully expecting the coming of their great and glorious Judge. By the latter, I mean the true children of the Holy Catholic Church; by the former, I mean heretics and schismatics.

There have ever been from the first these two kinds or Christians—those who belonged to the Church, and those who did not. There never was a time since the Apostles' day, when the Church was not; and there never was a time but men were to be found who preferred some other way of worship to the Church's way. These two kinds of professed Christians ever have been—Church Christians, and Christians not of the Church; and it is remarkable, I say, that while, on the one hand, reverence for sacred things has been a characteristic of Church Christians on the whole, so, want of reverence has been the characteristic on the whole of Christians not of the Church. The one have prophesied after the figure of Samuel, the other after the figure of Saul.

Of course there are many exceptions to this remark in the case of individuals. Of course I am not speaking of inconsistent persons and exceptional cases, in the Church, or out of it; but of those who act up to what they profess. I mean that zealous, earnest, and faithful members of the Church have generally been reverent; and zealous, earnest, and faithful members of other religious bodies have generally been irreverent. Again, after all, there will be real exceptions in the case of individuals which we cannot account for; but I mean that, *on the whole*, it will be found that reverence is one of the marks or notes of the Church; true though it may be that some particular individuals, who have kept apart from it, have not been without a reverential spirit notwithstanding.

Indeed so natural is the connexion between a reverential spirit in worshipping God, and faith in God, that the wonder only is, how any one can for a moment imagine he has faith in God, and yet allow himself to be irreverent towards Him. To believe in God, is to believe the being and presence of One who is All-holy, and All-powerful, and All-gracious; how can a man really believe thus of Him, and yet make free with Him? it is almost a contradiction in terms. Hence even heathen religions have ever considered faith and reverence identical. To believe, and not to revere, to worship familiarly, and at one's ease, is an anomaly and a prodigy unknown even to false religions, to say nothing of the true one. Not only the Jewish and Christian religions, which are directly from God, inculcate the spirit of "reverence and godly fear," but those other religions which have existed, or exist, whether in the East or the South, inculcate the same. Worship, forms of worship—such as bowing the knee, taking off the shoes, keeping silence, a prescribed dress, and the like—are considered as necessary for a due approach to God. The whole world, differing about so many things, differing in creed and rule of life, yet agree in this—that God being our Creator, a certain self-abasement of the whole man is the duty of the creature; that He is in heaven, we upon earth; that He is All-glorious, and we worms of the earth and insects of a day.

But those who have separated from the Church of Christ have in this respect fallen into greater than pagan error. They may be said to form an exception to the concordant voice of a whole world, always and every where; they break in upon the unanimous suffrage of mankind, and determine, at least by their conduct, that reverence and awe are not primary religious duties. They have considered that in some way or other, either by God's favour or by their own illumination, they are brought so near to God that they have no need to fear at all, or to put any restraint upon their words or thoughts when addressing Him. They have considered awe to be superstition, and reverence to be slavery. They have learnt to be familiar and free with sacred things, as it were, on principle. I think this is really borne out by facts, and will approve itself to inquirers as true in substance, however one man will differ from another in the words in which he would express the fact itself.

Samuel was a little child who had never fallen away from God, but by His grace had ever served Him. Let us take a very different instance, the instance of a penitent sinner as set before us in the parable of the Publican and Pharisee. I need hardly say which of the two was the most pleasing to God—the Publican; whereas the Pharisee was not accepted by Him. Now what did the Pharisee do? He did not even go so far as to behave in an unseemly, extravagant way: he was grave and solemn, and yet what he did was enough to displease God, because he took too much upon himself, and made too much of himself. Though grave and solemn, he was not reverent; he spoke in a haughty, proud way, and made a long sentence, thanking God that he was not as other men are, and despising the Publican. Such was the behaviour of the Pharisee; but the Publican behaved very differently. Observe how he came to worship God; "he stood afar off; he lift not up so much as his eyes unto heaven, but smote upon his breast, saying, God be merciful to me a sinner." [Luke xviii. 13.] You see his words were few, and almost broken, and his whole conduct humble and reverent; he felt that God was in heaven, he upon earth, God All-holy and Almighty, and he a poor sinner.

Now all of us are sinners, all of us have need to come to God as the Publican did; every one, if he does but search his heart, and watch his conduct, and try to do his duty, will find himself to be full of sins which provoke God's wrath. I do not mean to say that all men are equally sinners; some are wilful sinners, and of them there is no hope, till they repent; others sin, but they try to avoid sinning, pray to God to make them better, and come to Church to be made better; but all men are quite sinners enough to make it their duty to behave as the Publican. Every one ought to come into Church as the Publican did, to say in his heart, "Lord, I am not worthy to enter this sacred place; my only plea for coming is the merits of Jesus Christ my Saviour." When, then, a man enters Church, as many do, carelessly and familiarly, thinking of himself, not of God, sits down coldly and at his ease, either does not say a prayer at all, or merely hides his face for form's sake, sitting all the while, not standing or kneeling; then looks about to see who is in the Church, and who is not, and makes himself easy and comfortable in his seat, and uses the kneeler for no other purpose than to put his feet upon; in short, comes to Church as a place, not of meeting God and His holy Angels, but of seeing what is to be seen with the bodily eyes, and hearing what is to be heard with the bodily ears, and then goes and gives his judgment about the sermon freely, and says, "I do not like this or that," or "This is a good argument, but that is a bad one," or "I do not like this person so much as that," and so on; I mean when a man acts in all respects as if he was at home, and not in God's House,—all I can say is, that he ventures to do in God's presence what neither Cherubim nor Seraphim venture to do, for they veil their faces, and, as if not daring to address God, praise Him to each other, in few words, and those continually repeated, saying, Holy, holy, holy, Lord God of Sabaoth.

What I have said has been enough to suggest what it is to serve God acceptably, viz. "with reverence and godly fear," as St. Paul says. We must not aim at forms for their own sake, but we must keep in mind where we are, and then forms will come into our service naturally. We must in all respects act as if we saw God; that is, if we believe that God is here, we shall keep silence; we shall not laugh, or talk, or whisper during the Service, as many young persons do; we shall not gaze about us. We shall follow the example set us by the

Church itself. I mean, as the words in which we pray in Church are not our own, neither will our looks, or our postures, or our thoughts, be our own. We shall, in the prophet's words, not "do our own ways" there, nor "find our own pleasure," nor "speak our own words;" in imitation of all Saints before us, including the Holy Apostles, who never spoke their own words in solemn worship, but either those which Christ taught them, or which the Holy Ghost taught them, or which the Old Testament taught them. This is the reason why we always pray from a book in Church; the Apostles said to Christ, "Lord, teach us to pray," and our Lord graciously gave them the prayer called the Lord's Prayer. For the same reason we too use the Lord's Prayer, and we use the Psalms of David and of other holy men, and hymns which are given us in Scripture, thinking it better to use the words of inspired Prophets than our own. And for the same reason we use a number of short petitions, such as "Lord, have mercy upon us," "O Lord, save the Queen," "O Lord, open Thou our lips," and the like, not using many words, or rounding our sentences, or allowing ourselves to enlarge in prayer.

Thus all we do in Church is done on a principle of *reverence*; it is done with the thought that we are in God's presence. But irreverent persons, not understanding this, when they come into Church, and find nothing there of a striking kind, when they find every thing is read from a book, and in a calm, quiet way, and still more, when they come a second and a third time, and find every thing just the same, over and over again, they are offended and tired. "There is nothing," they say, "to rouse or interest them." They think God's service dull and tiresome, if I may use such words; for they do not come to Church to honour God, but to please themselves. They want something new. They think the prayers are long, and wish that there was more preaching, and that in a striking oratorical way, with loud voice and florid style. And when they observe that the worshippers in Church are serious and subdued in their manner, and will not look, and speak, and move as much at their ease as out of doors, or in their own houses, then (if they are very profane) they ridicule them, as weak and superstitious. Now is it not plain that those who are thus tired, and wearied, and made impatient by our sacred services below, would most certainly get tired and wearied with heaven above? because there the Cherubim and Seraphim "rest not day and night," saying, "Holy, holy, holy, Lord God Almighty." Such as this, too, will be the way of the Saints in glory, for we are told that there will be a great voice of much people saying, Alleluia; and again they said Alleluia; and the four-and-twenty elders said Alleluia; and a voice of many waters and of mighty thunderings said Alleluia. Such, too, was our Lord's way, when in His agony He three times repeated the same words, "Thy will, not Mine, be done." It is the delight of all holy beings, who stand around the Throne, to use one and the same form of worship; they are not tired, it is ever new pleasure to them to say the words anew. They are never tired; but surely all those persons would be soon tired of hearing them, instead of taking part in their glorious chant, who are wearied of Church now, and seek for something more attractive and rousing.

Let all persons, then, know for certain, and be assured beforehand, that if they come to Church to have their hearts put into strange and new forms, and their feelings moved and agitated, they come for what they will not find. We wish them to join Saints and Angels in worshipping God; to say with the Seraphim, "Holy Lord God of Sabaoth;" to say with the Angels, "Glory to God in the highest, and in earth peace, goodwill towards men;" to say after our Lord and Saviour, "Our Father, which art in heaven," and what follows; to say with St. Mary, "My soul doth magnify the Lord;" with St. Simeon, "Lord, now lettest Thou Thy servant depart in Peace;" with the Three Children who were cast into the fiery furnace, "O all ye works of the Lord, bless ye the Lord, praise Him, and magnify Him for ever;" with the Apostles, "I believe in God the Father Almighty, Maker of heaven and earth; and in Jesus Christ His only Son our Lord; and in the Holy Ghost." We wish to read to them words of inspired Scripture, and to explain its doctrine to them soberly after its pattern. This is what we wish them to say, again and again: "Lord, have mercy;" "We beseech Thee to hear us, O Lord;" "Good Lord, deliver us;" "Glory be to the Father, and to the Son, and to the Holy Ghost." All holy creatures are praising God continually—we hear them not, still they are praising Him and praying to Him. All the Angels, the glorious company of the Apostles, the goodly fellowship of the Prophets, the noble army of Martyrs, the Holy Church universal, all good men all over the earth, all the spirits and souls of the righteous, all our friends who have died in God's faith and fear, all are praising and praying to God: we come to Church to join them; our voices are very feeble, our hearts are very earthly, our faith is very weak. We do not deserve to come, surely not;—consider what a great favour it is to be allowed to join in the praises and prayers of the City of the Living God, we being such sinners;—we should not be allowed to come at all but for the merits of our Lord and Saviour. Let us firmly look at the Cross, that is the token of our salvation. Let us ever remember the sacred Name of Jesus, in which devils were cast out of old time. These are the thoughts with which we should come to Church; and if we come a little before the Service begins, and want something to think about, we may look, not at who are coming in and when, but at the building itself, which will remind us of many good things; or we may look into the Prayer Book for such passages as the 84th Psalm, which runs thus: "O how amiable are Thy dwellings, Thou Lord of hosts! my soul hath a desire and longing to enter into the Courts of the Lord: my heart and my flesh rejoice in the Living God."

Such will be our conduct and our thoughts in Church, if we be true Christians; and I have been giving this description of them, not only for the sake of those who are not reverent, but for the sake of those who try to be so,—for the sake of all of us who try to come to Church soberly and quietly, that we may know why we do so, and may have an answer if any one asks us. Such will be our conduct even when we are out of Church. I mean, those who come to Church again and again, in this humble and heavenly way, will find the effect of it, through God's mercy, in their daily walk. When Moses came down from Mount Sinai, where he had been forty days and forty nights, his face quite shone and dazzled the people, so that he was obliged to put a veil over it. Such is the effect of God's grace on those who come to Church in faith and love; their mode of acting and talking, their very manner and behaviour, show they have been in God's presence. They are ever sober, cheerful, modest, serious, and earnest. They do not disgrace their profession, they do not take God's Name in vain, they do not use passionate language, they do not lie, they do not jest in an unseemly way, they do not use shameful words, they keep their mouth; they have kept their mouth in Church, and avoided rashness, so they are enabled to keep it at home. They have bright, smiling, pleasant faces. They do not wear a mock gravity, and, like the hypocrites whom Christ speaks of, make themselves sad countenances, but they are easy and natural, and without meaning it cannot help showing in their look, and voice, and manner, that they are God's dear children, and have His grace within them. They are civil and obliging, kind and friendly; not envious or jealous, not quarrelsome, not spiteful or resentful, not selfish, not covetous, not niggardly, not lovers of the world, not afraid of the world, not afraid of what man can do against them.

Such are they who worship God in spirit and in truth in Church; they love Him and they fear Him. And, besides those who profess to love without fearing, there are two sorts of persons who fall short; first, and worst, those who neither fear nor love God; and, secondly, those who fear Him, but do not love Him. There are, every where, alas! some bold, proud, discontented persons, who, as far as they dare, speak against religion altogether; they do not come to Church, or if they come, come to see about what is going on, not to worship. These are those who neither love nor fear; but the more common sort of persons are they who have a sort of fear of God without the love of Him, who feel and know that some things are right, and others wrong, yet do not adhere to the right; who are conscious they sin from time to time, and that wilfully, who have an uneasy conscience, who fear to die; who have, indeed, a

314

sort of serious feeling about sacred things, who reverence the Church and its Ordinances, who would be shocked at open impiety, who do not make a mock at Baptism, much less at the Holy Communion, but, still, who have not the heart to love and obey God. This, I fear, my brethren, may be the state of some of you. See to it, that you are clear from the sin of knowing and confessing what is your duty, and yet not doing it. If you be such, and make no effort to become better; if you do not come to Church honestly, for God's grace to make you better, and seriously strive to be better and to do your duty more thoroughly, it will profit you nothing to be ever so reverent in your manner, and ever so regular in coming to Church. God hates the worship of the mere lips; He requires the worship of the heart. A person may bow, and kneel, and look religious, but he is not at all the nearer heaven, unless he tries to obey God in all things, and to do his duty. But if he does honestly strive to obey God, then his outward manner will be reverent also; decent forms will become natural to him; holy ordinances, though coming to him from the Church, will at the same time come (as it were) from his heart; they will be part of himself, and he will as little think of dispensing with them as he would dispense with his ordinary apparel, nay, as he could dispense with tongue or hand in speaking or doing. This is the true way of doing devotional service; not to have feelings without acts, or acts without feelings; but both to do and to feel;—to see that our hearts and bodies are both sanctified together, and become one; the heart ruling our limbs, and making the whole man serve Him, who has redeemed the whole man, body as well as soul.

Miracles no Remedy for Unbelief†

"And the Lord said unto Moses, How long will this people provoke Me?
and how long will it be ere they believe Me, for all the signs
which I have showed among them?"
Numbers xiv. 11

NOTHING, I suppose, is more surprising to us at first reading, than the history of God's chosen people; nay, on second and third reading, and on every reading, till we learn to view it as God views it. It seems strange, indeed, to most persons, that the Israelites should have acted as they did, age after age, in spite of the miracles which were vouchsafed to them. The laws of nature were suspended again and again before their eyes; the most marvellous signs were wrought at the word of God's prophets, and for their deliverance; yet they did not obey their great Benefactor at all better than men now-a-days who have not these advantages, as we commonly consider them. Age after age God visited them by Angels, by inspired messengers; age after age they sinned. At last He sent His well-beloved Son; and He wrought miracles before them still more abundant, wonderful, and beneficent than any before Him. What was the effect upon them of His coming? St. John tells us, "Then gathered the Chief Priests and the Pharisees a council, and said, What do we? for this Man doeth many miracles . . . Then from that day forth they took counsel together for to put Him to death." [John xi. 47, 53.]

In matter of fact, then, whatever be the reason, nothing is gained by miracles, nothing comes of miracles, as regards our religious views, principles, and habits. Hard as it is to believe, miracles certainly do not make men better; the history of Israel proves it. And the only mode of escaping this conclusion, to which some persons feel a great repugnance, is to fancy that the Israelites were much worse than other nations, which accordingly has been maintained. It has often been said, that they were stiff-necked and hard-hearted beyond the rest of the world. Now, even supposing, for argument's sake, I should grant that they were so, this would not sufficiently account for the strange circumstance under consideration; for this people was not moved at all. It is not a question of more or less: surely they must have been altogether distinct from other men, destitute of the feelings and opinions of other men, nay, hardly partakers of

† *Parochial & Plain Sermons*, vol. 8 (1843), Sermon 6.

human nature, if other men would, as a matter of course, have been moved by those miracles which had no influence whatever upon them. That there *are*, indeed, men in the world who would have been moved, and would have obeyed in consequence, I do not deny; such were to be found among the Israelites also; but I am speaking of men in general; and I say, that if the Israelites had a common nature with us, surely that insensibility which they exhibited on the whole, must be just what we should exhibit on the whole under the same circumstances.

It confirms this view of the subject to observe, that the children of Israel *are* like other men in all points of their conduct, save this insensibility, which other men have not had the opportunity to show as they had. There is no difference between their conduct and ours in point of *fact*; the difference is entirely in the external discipline to which God subjected them. Whether or not miracles ought to have influenced them in a way in which God's dealings in Providence do not influence us, so far is clear, that looking into their modes of living and of thought, we find a nature just like our own, not better indeed, but in no respect worse. Those evil tempers which the people displayed in the desert, their greediness, selfishness, murmuring, caprice, waywardness, fickleness, ingratitude, jealousy, suspiciousness, obstinacy, unbelief, all these are seen in the uneducated multitude now-a-days, according to its opportunity of displaying them.

The pride of Dathan and the presumption of Korah are still instanced in our higher ranks and among educated persons. Saul, Ahithophel, Joab, and Absalom, have had their parallels all over the world. I say there is nothing unlike the rest of mankind in the character or conduct of the chosen people; the difference solely is in God's dealings with them. They *act* as other men; it is their religion which is not as other men; it is miraculous; and the question is, how it comes to pass, their religion being different, their conduct is the same? and there are two ways of answering it; either by saying that they were worse than other men, and were not influenced by miracles when others would have been influenced (as many persons are apt to think), or (what I conceive to be the true reason) that, after all, the difference between miracle and no miracle is not so great in any case, in the case of any people, as to secure the success or account for the failure of religious truth. It was not that the Israelites were much more hard-hearted than other people, but that a miraculous religion is not much more influential than other religions.

For I repeat, though it be granted that the Israelites were much worse than others, still that will not account for the fact that miracles made no impression whatever upon them. However sensual and obstinate they may be supposed to have been in natural character, yet if it be true that a miracle has a necessary effect upon the human mind, it must be considered to have had some effect on their conduct for good or bad; if it had not a good effect, at least it must have had a bad; whereas their miracles left them very much the same in outward appearance as men are now-a-days, who neglect such warnings as are now sent them, neither much more lawless and corrupt than they, nor the reverse. The point is, that while they were so hardened, as it appears to us, in their conduct towards their Lord and Governor, they were not much worse than other men in social life and personal behaviour. It is a rule that if men are extravagantly irreligious, profane, blasphemous, infidel, they are equally excessive and monstrous in other respects; whereas the Jews were like the Eastern nations around them, with this one peculiarity, that they had rejected direct and clear miraculous evidence, and the others had not. It seems, then, I say, to follow, that, guilty as were the Jews in disobeying Almighty God, and blind as they became from shutting their eyes to the light, they were not much more guilty than others may be in disobeying Him; that it is almost as great a sin to reject His service in the case of those who do not see miracles, as in the case of those who do; that the sight of miracles is not the way in which men come to believe and obey, nor the absence of them an excuse for not believing and obeying.

Now let me say something in explanation of this, at first sight, startling truth, that miracles on the whole would not make men in general more obedient or holy than they are, though they were generally displayed. It has sometimes been said by unbelievers, "If the Gospel were written on the Sun, I would believe it." Unbelievers have said so by way of excusing themselves for not believing it, as it actually comes to them; and I dare say some of us, my brethren, have before now uttered the same sentiment in our hearts, either in moments of temptation, or when under the upbraidings of conscience for sin committed. Now let us consider, why do we think so?

I ask, why should the sight of a miracle make you better than you are? Do you doubt at all the being and power of God? No. Do you doubt what you ought to *do*? No. Do you doubt at all that the rain, for instance, and sunshine, come from Him? or that the fresh life of each year, as it comes, is His work, and that all nature bursts into beauty and richness at His bidding? You do not doubt it at all. Nor do you doubt, on the other hand, that it is your duty to obey Him who made the world and who made you. And yet, with the knowledge of all this, you find you cannot prevail upon yourselves to do what you know you should do. Knowledge is not what you want to make you obedient. You have knowledge enough already. Now what truth would a miracle convey to you which you do not learn from the works of God around you?

What would it teach you concerning God which you do not already believe without having seen it?

But, you will say, a miracle would startle you; true: but would not the startling pass away? could you be startled for ever? And what sort of a religion is that which consists in a state of fright and disturbance? Are you not continually startled by the accidents of life? You see, you hear things suddenly, which bring before your minds the thoughts of God and judgment; calamities befall you which for the time sober you. Startling is not conversion, any more than knowledge is practice.

But you urge, that perhaps that startling might issue in amendment of life; that it might be the beginning of a new course, though it passed away itself; that a miracle would not indeed convert you, but it would be the first step towards thorough conversion; that it would be the turning point in your life, and would suddenly force your path into the right direction, and that in this way shocks and startlings, and all the agitation of the passions and affections, are really the means of conversion, though conversion be something more than they. This is very true: sudden emotions—fear, hope, gratitude, and the like, all do produce such effects sometimes; but why is a miracle necessary to produce such effects? Other things startle us besides miracles: we have a number of accidents sent us by God to startle us. He has not left us without warnings, though He has not given us miracles; and if we are not moved and converted by those which come upon us, the probability is, that, like the Jews, we should not be converted by miracles.

Yes, you say; but if one came from the dead, if you saw the spirit of some departed friend you knew on earth: what then? What would it tell you that you do not know now? Do you now in your sober reason doubt the reality of the unseen world? not at all; only you cannot get yourself to act as if it *were* real. Would such a sight produce this effect? you think it would. Now I will grant this on one supposition. Do the startling accidents which happen to you now, produce *any* lasting effect upon you? Do they lead you to any *habits* of religion? If they do produce some effect, then I will grant to you that such a strange visitation, as you have supposed, would produce a greater effect; but if the events of life which now happen to you produce *no* lasting effect on you, and this I fear is the case, then too sure I am, that a miracle too would produce no lasting effect on you, though of course it would startle you more at the time. I say, I fear that what happens to you, as it is, produces no lasting effect on you. I mean, that the warnings which you really have, do not bring you to any habitual and regular religiousness; they may make you a little more afraid of this or that sin, or of this or that particular indulgence of it; but they do not tend at all to make you break with the world, and convert you to God. If they did make you take up religion in earnest, though in ever so poor a way, then I will grant that miracles would make you *more* in earnest. If God's *ordinary* warnings moved you, His extraordinary would move you more. It is quite true, that a serious mind would be made more serious by seeing a miracle, but this gives no ground for saying, that minds which are *not* serious, careless, worldly, self-indulgent persons, who are made not at all better by the warnings which *are* given them, would be made serious by those miraculous warnings which are not given.

Of course it might so happen in this or that particular case,—just as the same person is moved by one warning, not by another; not moved by a warning today, moved by a warning tomorrow; but I am sure, taking men as we find them, miracles would leave them, as far as their conduct is concerned, very much as they are. They would be very much startled and impressed at first, but the impression would wear away. And thus our Saviour's words would come true of all those multitudes who have the Bible to read, and know what they ought to do, but do it not:—"If they hear not Moses and the Prophets," He says, "neither will they be persuaded though one rose from the dead." Do we never recollect times when we have said, "We shall never forget this; it will be a warning all through our lives"? have we never implored God's forgiveness with the most eager promises of amendment? have we never felt as if we were brought quite into a new world, in gratitude and joy? Yet was the result what we had expected? We cannot anticipate more from miracles, than before now we have anticipated from warnings, which came to nought.

And now, what *is* the real reason why we do not seek God with all our hearts, and devote ourselves to His service, if the absence of miracles be not the reason, as most assuredly it is not? What was it that made the Israelites disobedient, who *had* miracles? St. Paul informs us, and exhorts *us* in consequence. "Harden not your hearts, *as* in the provocation, in the day of temptation in the wilderness . . . take heed . . . lest there be in any of *you*" (as there was among the Jews) "an evil heart of unbelief in departing from the Living God." Moses had been commissioned to say the same thing at the very time; "Oh that there were such a heart in them, that they would fear Me, and keep My Commandments always!" We cannot serve God, because we want the will and the heart to serve Him. We like any thing better than religion, as the Jews before us. The Jews liked this world; they liked mirth and feasting. "The people sat down to eat and to drink, and rose up to play;" so do we. They liked glitter and show, and the world's fashions. "Give us a king like the nations," they said to Samuel; so do we. They wished to be let alone; they liked ease; they liked their own way; they disliked to make war against the natural impulses and leanings of their own minds; they disliked to attend to the state of their souls, to have to treat themselves as spiritually sick and infirm, to watch, and rule, and chasten, and refrain, and change themselves; and so do we. They disliked to think of God, and to observe and attend His ordinances, and to reverence Him; they called it a weariness to frequent His courts; and they found this or that false worship more pleasant, satisfactory, congenial to their feelings, than the service of the Judge of quick and dead; and so do we: and therefore we disobey God as they did,—not that we have not miracles; for they actually had them, and it made no difference. We act as they did, though they had miracles, and we have not; because there is one cause of it *common* both to them and us—heartlessness in religious matters, an evil heart of unbelief; both they and we disobey and disbelieve, because we do not love.

But this is not all; in another respect we are really far more favoured than they were; they had outward miracles; we too have miracles, but they are not outward but inward. Ours are not miracles of evidence, but of power and influence. They are secret, and more wonderful and efficacious because secret. Their miracles were wrought upon external nature; the sun stood still, and the sea parted. Ours are invisible, and are exercised upon the soul. They consist in the sacraments, and they just do that very thing which the Jewish miracles did not. They really touch the heart, though we so often resist their influence. If then we sin, as, alas! we do, if we do not love God more than the Jews did, if we have no heart for those "good things which pass men's understanding," we are not more excusable than they, but less so. For the supernatural works which God showed to them were wrought outwardly, not inwardly, and did not influence the will; they did but convey warnings; but the supernatural works which He does towards us are in the heart, and impart grace; and if we disobey, we are not disobeying His command only, but resisting His presence.

This is our state; and perhaps so it is that, as the Israelites for forty years hardened their hearts in the wilderness, in spite of the manna and the quails, and the water from the rock, so we for a course of years have been hardening ours in spite of the spiritual gifts which are the portion of Christians. Instead of listening to the voice of conscience, instead of availing ourselves of the aid of heavenly grace, we have gone on year after year with the vain dream of turning to God some future day. Childhood and boyhood are past; youth, perhaps middle age, perhaps old age is come; and now we find that we cannot "love the thing which God commandeth, and desire that which He doth promise;" and then, instead of laying the blame where it is due, on ourselves, for having hardened ourselves against the influences of grace, we complain that enough has not been done for us; we complain we have not enough light, enough help, enough inducements; we complain we have not seen miracles. Alas! how exactly are God's words fulfilled in us, which He deigned to speak to His former people. O inhabitants of Jerusalem, and men of Judah, judge, I pray you, betwixt Me and My vineyard. What could have been done more to My vineyard that I have not done in it? wherefore, when I looked that it should bring forth grapes, brought it forth wild grapes?" [Isa. v. 3, 4.]

Let us then put aside vain excuses; and, instead of looking for outward events to change our course of life, be sure of this, that if our course of life is to be changed, it must be from within. God's grace moves us from within, so does our own will. External circumstances have no real power over us. If we do not love God, it is because we have not wished to love Him, tried to love Him, prayed to love Him. We have not borne the idea and the wish in our mind day by day, we have not had it before us in the little matters of the day, we have not lamented that we loved Him not, we have been too indolent, sluggish, carnal, to attempt to love Him in little things, and begin at the beginning; we have shrunk from the effort of moving from within; we have been like persons who cannot get themselves to rise in the morning; and we have desired and waited for a thing impossible,—to be changed once and for all, all at once, by some great excitement from without, or some great event, or some special season; something or other we go on expecting, which is to change us without our having the trouble to change ourselves. We covet some miraculous warning, or we complain that we are not in happier circumstances, that we have so many cares, or so few religious privileges; or we look forward for a time when religion will come easy to us as a matter of course. This we used to look out for as boys; we used to think there was time enough yet to think of religion, and that it was a natural thing, that it came without trouble or effort, for men to be religious as life went on; we fancied that all old persons must be religious; and now even, as grown men, we have not put off this deceit; but, instead of giving our hearts to God, we are waiting, with Felix, for a convenient season.

Let us rouse ourselves, and act as reasonable men, before it is too late; let us understand, as a first truth in religion, that *love* of heaven is the only *way* to heaven. Sight will not move us; else why did Judas persist in covetousness in the very presence of Christ? why did Balaam, whose eyes were opened, remain with a closed heart? why did Satan fall, when he was a bright Archangel? Nor will reason subdue us; else why was the Gospel, in the beginning, "to the Greeks foolishness"? Nor will excited feelings convert us; for there is one who "heareth the word, and anon with joy receiveth it;" yet "hath no root in himself," and "dureth" only "for a while." Nor will self-interest prevail with us; or the rich man would have been more prudent, whose "ground brought forth plentifully," and would have recollected that "that night his soul" might be "required of him." Let us understand that nothing but the love of God can

322

make us believe in Him or obey Him; and let us pray Him, who has "prepared for them that love Him, such good things as pass man's understanding, to pour into our hearts such love towards Him, that we, loving Him above all things, may obtain His promises, which exceed all that we can desire."

Indulgence in Religious Privileges[†]

"These are spots in your feasts of charity, when they feast with you,
feeding themselves without fear."
Jude 12

T
HE FALSE BRETHREN, spoken of by St. Jude in this passage, were stained with such heinous guilt, both in life and doctrine, that it may seem to promise little profit to us to take any part of it as a text. Their sin has passed with the early age, and let it pass from our thoughts. So it may be said, and in one sense both rightly and truly said; for it is true that the enormities which once were, are not now, and it is right surely to turn away from evil and hide it, when it is a thing past, not present. And yet, without recurring to those instances of fearful depravity and corruption, which insinuated themselves even into the Apostolic Church, according to the prophecy that the kingdom of heaven is like a net which gathers of every kind, good and bad, I think we may gain a lesson in matters which concern ourselves from the words in question, which have occurred in the Service, and are not unsuitable to this season of the year.

The first thought which the text suggests to us, when it speaks of religious feasting, obviously relates to the temper of mind in which we are accustomed to come to the most Holy Sacrament of the Lord's Supper. The feasts indeed spoken of by St. Jude were of a different kind; they were an institution which soon came to an end, in consequence of the abuses to which they led; but still Holy Communion is especially "a feast of charity," and the fault which the Apostle imputes to certain apostate Christians of his day, may, in its degree (though God grant but in a very slight degree!), adhere to us. He says, that they were "spots in the feast," a disfigurement, and a disgrace, because they "feasted with" their brethren "without fear." They did in no sense recognize and realize that Holy Presence, before whom even St. John fell down as dead, till He laid His hand on him and said, "Fear not." [Rev. i. 17.] He says to all His servants "Fear not," *when* they fear; but till then, He says on the contrary, very emphatically, "Fear." For instance, "Serve the Lord with fear, and rejoice with trembling." [Ps. ii. 11.] "Let us have grace, whereby we may serve God acceptably, with reverence and godly fear." "Work out your own

---

[†] *Sermons on Subjects of the Day* (1843), Sermon 9, preached on Rogation Sunday, 1842.

324

salvation with fear and trembling, for it is God which worketh in you, both to will and to do of His good pleasure." [Heb. xii. 28. Phil. ii. 12, 13.]

We must come to God with fear. Yet we are told to "come boldly unto the throne of grace." [Heb. iv. 16.] Are not these precepts incompatible with each other? No, surely, not in themselves, but *we* are very likely to find them incompatible, when we attempt them. We are very likely to find it difficult to fulfil two opposite duties, which are nevertheless both possible, and which *are* duties, *because* they are so opposite, *because* they are so difficult; for no one can suppose that easy matters are our duty, but difficult matters. We are very likely from our Lord's great condescension, from His gracious invitations, so free, so repeated, so unwearied, to forget His Majesty, and to become familiar with Him; and then we "feast without fear." And it stands to reason, the more frequently we accept His invitation, and seek Him in His sacred ordinance, the greater is our danger of this irreverence, unless we be on our guard.

Now in saying this, my brethren, I am not addressing myself to those of us who are in the practice of availing themselves in this church of our Lord's invitation to seek His Presence once a week. I have no reason for saying, I humbly trust I may with truth deny, that they are wanting in "reverence and godly fear;" though, of course, all of us, any one of us, might have far deeper and more solemn thoughts than we have at present, and (it is to be hoped) shall have, as year after year passes away; and though we, as others, are in danger of irreverence, unless we are on our guard. But I am not speaking of ourselves; I am thinking of the Church generally; I am thinking of the age. There is at this moment a growing perception of the beauty of religion, a growing reverence for, and insight into the privileges of the Gospel. Persons begin to understand far more than they did, that Christianity is not a mere law, a Jewish yoke, but a new law, a service of freedom, a rule of spirit and truth, which wins us as well as commands, and influences us while it threatens. Hitherto, it has seemed as if all sense of the privileges and pleasures of religion were possessed by those who had but erroneous views of doctrine, and who, however well-intentioned and respectable in themselves, came more or less of an heretical stock; while men of more correct and more orthodox views seemed to be of a cold and forbidding school—nay, the less fervent, the less spiritual for their very exactness: but all this is gone by. A more primitive, Catholic, devout, ardent spirit, is abroad among the holders of orthodox truth. The piercing, and thrilling, and kindling, and enrapturing glories of the kingdom of Christ are felt in their degree by many. Men are beginning to understand that influence, which in the beginning made the philosopher leave his school, and the soldier beat his spear into a pruning-hook. They are beginning to understand that the Gospel is not a mere scheme or doctrine, but a reality and a life; not a subject for books only, for private use, for individuals, but for public profession, for combined action, for outward manifestation. Hence there is an increasing cultivation of all that is external, from a feeling that external religion is the great development and triumph of the inward principle. For instance, much curiosity is directed towards the science of ecclesiastical architecture, and much appreciation shown of architectural proprieties. Attention, too, is paid to the internal arrangement and embellishment of sacred buildings. Devotional books also of an imaginative cast, religious music, painting, poetry, and the like are in request. Churches are more frequently attended on weekdays, and continual service is felt to be a privilege, not a task. And two services are felt to be short of that measure of devotion which the religious mind desires to pay to its God and Saviour.

Now no one can suspect me of meaning to imply that such signs of the times are not in themselves hopeful ones. They are so; but, O my brethren, be jealous of these things, excellent as they are in themselves, lest they be not accompanied with godly fear. I grieve to say, that the spirit of penitence does not keep pace with the spirit of joy. With all this outward promise of piety, we are suspicious of that which alone is its inward soul and life; we are very jealous indeed of personal strictness and austerity. We are alarmed at any call to national or personal humiliation and amendment; we like to be told of the excellence of our institutions, we do not like to hear of their defects; we like to abandon ourselves to the satisfactions of religion, we do not like to hear of its severities. We do not like to hear of our past sins, and the necessity of undoing them; and thus, however gay our blossoms may be in this our spring, we have a fault within which will show itself ere our fruits are gathered in the autumn. "The sun is no sooner risen with a burning heat, but it withereth the grass, and the flower thereof falleth, and the grace of the fashion of it perisheth." We are cherishing a shallow religion, a hollow religion, which will not profit us in the day of trouble. We are taking words for things; we are led captive by an unreality. This is no new language on my part; I have said it[33] before men took that interest which now they take in the Catholic doctrine: I say so now. I said then, as now, that the age, whatever be its peculiar excellences, has this serious defect, it loves an exclusively cheerful religion. It is determined to make religion bright and sunny and joyous, whatever be the form of it which it adopts. And it will handle the Catholic doctrine in this spirit; it will skim over it; it will draw it out in mere buckets-full; it will substitute its human cistern for the well of truth; it will be afraid of the deep well, the abyss of God's judgments and God's mercies.

---

[33] See "The Religion of the Day," above, p. 56.

Alas! . . . Surely we are pretending allegiance to the Church to no purpose, or rather to our own serious injury, if we select her doctrines and precepts at our pleasure; choose this, reject that; take what is beautiful and attractive, shrink from what is stern and painful. I fear a number of persons, a growing number, in various parts of the country, are likely to abandon themselves to what may be called the luxuries of religion—nay, I will even call them the luxuries of devotion; and the consequence of this it is very distressing to contemplate. They are tending to "feast without fear." For this reason I should even look with jealousy on any considerable revival of weekly Communions. We are not fit for them; I am sure, men in general, such as we are, even religious persons, are not fit for them. We need a much deeper religion, a more consistent creed, a keener faith, a clearer insight into things unseen, a more real understanding of what sin is, and the consequences of sin, a more practical and self-denying rule of conduct, before such a blessed usage will be safely extended among our congregations. I really do trust, as I have already said, that the effects of this observance among ourselves have been such as we could desire; but if ever it is introduced into our great towns, much evil will come of it.[34] It is a very merciful provision, if we may thus speak of error overruled for good, that there should be so much opposition to it as there is at present. People say that the Holy Communion obscures the doctrine of Gospel grace; that in obeying Christ's command we are forgetting His atonement; that in coming for His benefits, we tend to deny His all-sufficient merits. Can any imputation be more preposterous and wild, however estimable the persons may be who cast it? Certainly none. But still I say this strange apprehension is doing us service. I am not at all sorry for it, and the clamour that follows upon it; for it hinders a great evil, it represses a luxuriant, rank, unhealthy vegetation in our religious habits.

Many a man, and especially many a woman, may abandon themselves to the real delight, as it will prove, of passing hours in repeating the Psalms, or in saying Litanies and Hymns, and in frequenting those Cathedrals and Churches where the old Catholic ideas are especially impressed upon their minds; and they will find, in the words of Scripture, that our Lord's "Name is like ointment poured forth," [Cant. i. 3.] and His "fruit is sweet to their taste." [Cant. ii. 3.] Yet like the Prophet's roll, though "in the mouth sweet as honey"—nay, almost literally so in a strange way—yet as soon as they have eaten it, it will be bitter, if they have forgotten that "before honour is humility," sowing in tears before reaping in joy, pain before pleasure, duty before privilege. Nothing

---

[34] Of course it must not be forgotten, that for the revival of the practice altogether we are indebted to clergymen in great towns, as in London and Leeds, whose instances cannot be supposed to come under the remark in the text.

lasts, nothing keeps incorrupt and pure, which comes of mere feeling; feelings die like spring-flowers, and are fit only to be cast into the oven. Persons thus circumstanced will find their religion fail them in time; a revulsion of mind will ensue. They will feel a violent distaste for what pleased them before, a sickness and weariness of mind; or even an enmity towards it; or a great disappointment; or a confusion and perplexity and despondence. They have learned to think religion easier than it is, themselves better than they are; they have drunk their good wine instead of keeping it; and this is the consequence. I need not enter, however, into the full consequences of this incaution; they are very various and sometimes very awful. I am but calling attention to the fact. And then the persons in question will be ashamed or afraid to confide to others what their state is, or will not have the opportunity; and all this the more, because affectionate, sensitive, delicate, retired persons are perhaps more open than others to the danger I have been describing.

The most awful consequences of this untrue kind of devotion, which would have all the glories of the Gospel without its austerities, of course are those into which the dreadful heretics fell who are alluded to in the text; and of which it is well not to speak. Yet it must not be forgotten that even in these latter times, though not in our own Church, and not certainly among persons of high or refined minds, even immoralities have been the ultimate consequents of religious enthusiasm. But one need not dwell upon extreme results, in order to be impressed with the danger to which our Church is at present exposed. What indeed but evil can come of living like the world, eating and drinking, marrying and giving in marriage, faring sumptuously, dressing in purple and fine linen, and increasing in goods, and yet affecting to be the children of Apostles, and using the devotion of Saints?

Christianity, considered as a moral system, is made up of two elements, beauty and severity; whenever either is indulged to the loss or disparagement of the other, evil ensues. In heathen times, Greek and Barbarian in some sense divided these two between them; the latter were the slaves of dreary and cruel superstitions, and the former abandoned themselves to a joyous polytheism. And so, again, in these latter times, the two chief forms of heresy into which opposition to primitive truth has developed, were remarkable, at least in their origin three hundred years ago, and at times since, the one for an unrefined and self-indulgent religiousness, the other for a stern, dark, cruel spirit, very unamiable, yet still inspiring more respect than the other.

Even the Jews, to whom this earth was especially given, and who might be supposed to be at liberty without offence to satiate themselves in its gifts, were not allowed to enjoy it without restraint. Even the paschal lamb, their great typical feast, was eaten "with bitter herbs." [Exod. xii. 8.] And, as time went on, the Prophets were given, who were more or less moulded after the pattern of Elijah, in "suffering affliction and in patience," and were typical of the one great Prophet of the Church who was to come. Much more are Christians bound to recollect, and to rejoice, that "the brother of low degree" is to be "exalted," and "the rich" to be "made low," and that the Apostles whose steps we are to follow (as we this day are especially reminded[35]) hungered and thirsted, and were naked, and were buffeted, and had no certain dwelling-place, and were accounted the filth of the world and the offscouring of all things.

Let us thus enter upon the rich and happy months which lie before us, when the earth puts forth all her excellence, and robes herself in her bright garments, and scatters her most precious gifts. Thus let us hallow Rogation Sunday, which is today,—suitably to the Church's intention which has made three days of abstinence attend upon it, by way of warning us that we must not enjoy our Father's temporal blessings without reserve. "He visiteth the earth and blesseth it; He maketh it very plenteous . . . He provideth for the earth; He watereth her furrows. He crowneth the year with His goodness, and His clouds drop fatness." [Ps. lxv. 9–12.]

And we acknowledge His bountifulness, we commemorate His providence, we enter upon His gifts, by abstaining from them. As the Israelites brought the first fruits of their land in a basket [Deut. xxvi. 1–11.] and left it in the priest's hand before the altar of the Lord their God, so do we in another way, but in the same spirit, begin our thankful use of God's blessings by a prudent delay and a lowly prayer. We deprecate wrath, we entreat mercy; as Job sacrificed for his sons, so we for ourselves. We remind ourselves that though "every creature of God is good," we ourselves, God's creatures, are the one exception to that rule; that though His gifts are holy and innocent, our hearts are frail and wayward; that they are good in the sending, yet dangerous in the taking—good in the use, but harmful in the enjoyment. As before meat, day by day, we say a grace and then begin, so now do we ask a blessing on the whole year by pausing ere we enter upon it.

This is to feed ourselves *with* fear. Thus let us proceed in the use of all our privileges, and all will be benefits. Let us not keep festivals without keeping vigils; let us not keep Eastertide without observing Lent; let us not approach the Sunday feast without keeping the Friday abstinence; let us not adorn churches without studying personal simplicity and austereness; let us not cultivate the accomplishments of taste and literature without the corrective of personal discomfort; let us not attempt to advance the power of the Church, to enthrone her rulers, to rear her palaces, and to ennoble her name,

---

[35] This sermon was preached on May 1st, the Feast of St. Philip and St. James.

without recollecting that she must be mortified within while she is in honour in the world, and must wear the Baptist's hair-shirt and leathern girdle under the purple ephod and the jewelled breastplate.

And lastly, let us beware, on the other hand, of dishonouring and rudely rejecting God's gifts, out of gloominess or sternness; let us beware of fearing without feasting. "Every creature of God is good, and nothing to be refused." Let us beware, though it must be a sad perversion of mind which admits of it,—let us beware of afflicting ourselves for sin, without first coming to the Gospel for strength to do so. And let us not so plunge ourselves in the sense of our offences, as not withal to take delight in the contemplation of our privileges. Let us rejoice while we mourn. Let us look up to our Lord and Saviour the more we shrink from the sight of ourselves; let us have the more faith and love the more we exercise repentance. Let us, in our penitence, not substitute the Law *for* the Gospel, but add the Law *to* the Gospel. Those who do despite to baptismal grace fall under the Law; but they do not fall *from* the Gospel, if they are repentant; they fall under the Law without the Gospel, if they continue in sin; they receive the Law with the Gospel, if they return. The Law which once introduced the Gospel, in such cases becomes its instrument. They fall indeed under bondage, but they have the power of Christ's grace to enable them to bear it.

And in like manner, as they must not defraud themselves of Christian privileges, neither need they give up God's temporal blessings. All the beauty of nature, the kind influences of the seasons, the gifts of sun and moon, and the fruits of the earth, the advantages of civilized life, and the presence of friends and intimates; all these good things are but one extended and wonderful type of God's benefits in the Gospel. Those who aim at perfection will not reject the gift, but add a corrective; they will add the bitter herbs to the fatted calf and the music and dancing; they will not refuse the flowers of earth, but they will toil in plucking up the weeds. Or if they refrain from one temporal blessing, it will be to reserve another; for this is one great mercy of God, that while He allows us a discretionary use of His temporal gifts, He allows a discretionary abstinence also; and He almost enjoins upon us the use of some, lest we should forget that this earth is His creation, and not of the evil one. I am not denying that there are certain individuals raised up from time to time to a still more self-denying life, and who have a corresponding measure of divine consolations. As some men are Apostles, others Confessors and Martyrs, as Missionaries in heathen countries may be called to give up all for Christ; so there are doubtless those, living in peaceable times and among their brethren, who acknowledge a call to give up every thing whatever for the sake of the Gospel, and in order to be perfect; and to become as homeless and as shelterless, and as resourceless and as solitary, as the holy Baptist in the wilderness: but extraordinary cases are not for our imitation, and it is as great a fault to act without a call as to refuse to act upon one.

May God give us grace to walk thus humbly, thus soberly, thus without censoriousness in this day of confusion; enjoying His blessings, yet taking them with fear and trembling; and disciplining ourselves without gloom, yet not judging or slandering those who are more rigid or less secular than ourselves!

Christian Nobleness[†]

"I will not leave you comfortless: I will come to you.
Yet a little while, and the world seeth Me no more; but ye see Me."
John xiv. 18, 19

WHEN OUR SAVIOUR was leaving His disciples, He told them that He would soon return to them, that their sorrow might be turned into joy. He was going away, yet they were to see Him, though the world saw Him not; for they were to be blessed with the presence of Him who was equal to Him and one with Him, and would unite them to Him, the Third Person in the Eternal Trinity, God the Holy Ghost.

He said that He was going away, and yet was coming again; for the Holy Ghost came, and His coming was really the coming of Christ. Christ said that it was to be but a short interval between His departure and His return; and such it was, ten days. He went on Holy Thursday; He returns on the day of Pentecost.

But, though our Lord and Saviour sent His Holy Spirit to be with us on His going away, still there was a difference between the Spirit's office, and that which He Himself graciously fulfilled towards His disciples in the days of His flesh; for their wants were not the same as before. Christ, while He was with them, had no occasion to console them under affliction, to stand by them in trial as their Paraclete; for trial and affliction did not visit them while He was with them; but, on the other hand, the Holy Spirit especially came to give them joy in tribulation. Again, He came to teach them fully, what our Lord had but in part revealed; and hence too it followed, that the consolation which the Spirit vouchsafed differed from that which they had received from Christ, just as the encouragements and rewards bestowed upon children, are far other than those which soothe and stimulate grown men in arduous duties. And there were, moreover, other circumstances, much to be dwelt upon, which altered the state of the Apostles' feelings and ideas, after their Lord had died and risen again, and which made them need a consolation different from that which His bodily presence gave them. There is no reason for supposing that, while He was with them, they apprehended the awful truth, that He is very God in our nature. "I am among you," He said, "as He that serveth." But on

---

[†] *Sermons on Subjects of the Day* (1843), Sermon 11, preached on Whitsuntide in 1831.

His resurrection He revealed the mystery. St. Thomas adored Him in the words, "My Lord and my God;" and He forthwith withdrew Himself from them, not living in their sight as heretofore, and soon ascending into heaven. It is plain, that, after such a revelation, the Apostles could not have returned to their easy converse with Him, even had He offered it. What had been, could not be again; their state of childhood, ere "their eyes were opened and they knew Him." Of necessity then, since they could not endure to see God and live, did He "vanish out of their sight." And if, according to His promise, He was to come to them again, it must be after a new manner, and with a higher consolation.

Accordingly, when the Spirit of Christ descended at the promised season, "He bowed the heavens and came down, and it was dark under His feet." He came invisibly, and invisibly hath He dwelt in the Church ever since. He does not manifest His glory to mortal sense. We do not hear the whisperings of His still small voice, nor do our hearts burn within us in token of His Presence. The truth is, we Christians know too much concerning Him to endure the open manifestation of His greatness. It is in mercy that He hides Himself from those who would be overcome by the sensible touch of the Almighty Hand. Still it is plain that, after all, in spite of this considerate regard for our frailness, His visitation cannot but be awful anyhow, to creatures who know what we know, and are what we are. This cannot be avoided; the very secrecy of His coming has its solemnity: is it not fearful to wait for Him, appalling to receive Him, a burden to have held communion with Him? and though we joy, as well we may, yet we cannot joy with the light hearts of children, who live by sight, but with the thoughtful gladness of grown men, who are anxious, who feel difficulties, who look out for dangers, who, in St. John's words, know both that "the whole world lieth in wickedness," and "that the Son of God is come, and hath given us an understanding that we may know Him that is true," [John v. 19, 20.] and discover His real majesty and power.

And hence, as we might expect, the Apostles' fellowship with Christ through the Spirit, after His ascension, was very different from their fellowship with Him on earth. Though they waited continually on Him for His peace, "not as the world giveth," and continually received it; yet, the history shows us, they feared the gift while they rejoiced in it. Consider, too, our Saviour's own most overpowering words, to be fulfilled in the coming of the Comforter,—"Whosoever speaketh a word against the Son of man, it shall be forgiven Him: but whosoever speaketh against the Holy Ghost, it shall not be forgiven him." Does not this Scripture imply thus much, whatever else it implies,— that our ascended Saviour, who is on God's right hand, and sends down from thence God's Spirit, is to be feared greatly, even amid His gracious consolations? Hence St. Paul says, "Work out your own salvation with fear and trembling " and again, "Grieve not the Holy Spirit of God;" and again, "Know ye not that ye are the temple of God, and that the Spirit of God dwelleth in you? If any man defile the temple of God, him shall God destroy." [Matt. xii. 32. Phil. ii. 12. Eph. iv. 30. 1 Cor. iii. 16, 17.]

This great truth is impressed upon the whole course of that sacred fellowship with Christ, which the Church provides for her children; in proportion as it is more high and gracious than that first intercourse, which the Apostles enjoyed, so is it also more awful. When He had once ascended, henceforth for unstudied speech there were solemn rites; for familiar attendance there were mysterious ministerings; for questioning at will there was silent obedience; for sitting at table there was bowing in adoration; for eating and drinking there was fasting and watching. He who had taken his Lord and rebuked Him, dared not speak to Him after His resurrection, when He saw and knew Him. He who had lain in His bosom at supper, fell at His feet as dead. Such was the vision of the glorified Saviour of man, returning to His redeemed in the power of the Spirit, with a Presence more pervading because more intimate, and more real because more hidden. And as the manner of His coming was new, so was His gift. It was peace, but a new peace, "not as the world giveth;" not the exultation of the young, light-hearted, and simple, easily created, easily lost: but a serious, sober, lasting comfort, full of reverence, deep in contemplation.

And hence the keener, the more rapturous are the feelings of the Christian, the more ardent his aspirations, the more glorious his visions; so much the graver, the more subdued, the more serene must be his worship and his confession. Who was so intoxicated with divine love as St. John? who so overcharged with the Spirit? yet what language can be calmer than when He says, "Behold what manner of love the Father hath bestowed upon us, that we should be called the sons of God! . . . When He shall appear, we shall be like Him, for we shall see Him as He is"? [1 John iii. 1, 2.] And who was possessed with a more burning zeal than St. Paul? yet observe his injunction to the spiritually-gifted Corinthians—"Let all things be done unto edifying; the spirits of the prophets are subject to the prophets; for God is not the author of confusion, but of peace . . . Let all things be done decently and in order." [1 Cor. xiv. 26, 32, 33, 40.] And in like manner, in anticipation of Gospel perfection, we read of the impressive gravity and saintly bearing of Samuel and his prophetic company, when Saul came to Ramah; while Saul's extravagance when he came within the Divine Influence, prefigures to us the wayward and unpeaceful behaviour of heretical sects in every age, who, in spite of whatever tokens they may bear of the presence of a good spirit among them, yet, whether they preach or pray, are full of tumult and violence, and cause wild alarm or fierce ecstasy, and even strange affections of body, convulsions and cries, in their converts or hearers.

But if gravity and sobriety were seen even in that time, when the heirs of promise were under age, as children submitted to a schoolmaster, and when holy David "danced before the Lord with all his might, leaping and dancing before the Lord;" [2 Sam. vi. 14, 16.] much more is the temper of the Christian Church high and heavenly, noble, majestic, calm, and untroubled. For it is the state of heart imparted by the Divine Paraclete, who stands by us to strengthen us and raise our stature, and, as it were, to straighten our limbs, and to provide us with the wings of Angels, wherewith to mount heavenward;—by Him who takes possession of us, and dwells in us, and makes us His agents and instruments, nay, in a measure, His confidants and counsellors, till we "comprehend the breadth and length and depth and height, and know the love of Christ, which passeth knowledge, that we may be filled with all the fulness of God." [Eph. iii. 18, 19.] Religious men, knowing what great things have been done for them, cannot but grow greater in mind in consequence. We know how power and responsibility change men in matters of this world. They become more serious, more vigilant, more circumspect, more practical, more decisive; they fear to commit mistakes, yet they dare more, because they have a consciousness of liberty and of power, and an opportunity for great successes. And thus the Christian, even in the way of nature, without speaking of the influence of heavenly grace upon him, cannot but change from the state of children to that of men, when he understands his own privileges. The more he knows and fears the gift committed to him, so much the more reverent is he towards himself, as being put in charge with it.

Consider the language in which our Lord and His Apostles describe the gift—"If a man love Me," says Christ, shortly after the text, "he will keep My words, and My Father will love him, and We will come unto him, and make Our abode with him." Again, in St. Paul's words, "Ye are the temple of the Living God; as God hath said, I will dwell in them and walk in them." Again, "Know ye not that your body is the temple of the Holy Ghost, which is in you, which ye have of God, and ye are not your own?" And St. John, "Whosoever shall confess that Jesus is the Son of God, God dwelleth in him, and he in God." [2 Cor. vi. 16. 1 Cor. vi. 19. 1 John iv. 15.] Is it not plain, that such a doctrine as is here declared will exceedingly raise the Christian above himself, and, without impairing—nay, even while increasing his humility, will make him feel all things of earth as little, and of small interest or account, and will preserve him from the agitations of mind which they naturally occasion?

Alas! I am not speaking of ourselves in this degenerate time, when we seem well nigh to have forfeited the Gospel gifts through our sins; but, without thinking of ourselves, surely it is not without its use to consider the high Gospel tone of thought in itself. He then, who believes that, in St. Paul's words, he is "joined to the Lord" as "one spirit," must necessarily prize his own blessed condition, and look down upon all things, even the greatest things here below. "Ye are of God, little children," says the beloved disciple, "and have overcome them; because greater is He that is in you than he that is in the world. They are of the world; . . . we are of God. He that knoweth God, heareth us; he that is not of God, heareth not us." [1 John iv. 6.] Here is the language of saints; and hence it is that St. Paul, as feeling the majesty of that new nature which is imparted to us, addresses himself in a form of indignation to those who forget it. "What!" he says, "what! know ye not that your body is the temple of the Holy Ghost?" As if he said, "Can you be so mean-spirited and base-minded as to dishonour yourselves in the devil's service? Should we not pity the man of birth, or station, or character, who degraded himself in the eyes of the world, who forfeited his honour, broke his word, or played the coward? And shall not we, from mere sense of propriety, be ashamed to defile our spiritual purity, the royal blood of the second Adam, with deeds of darkness? Let us leave it to the hosts of evil spirits, to the haters of Christ, to eat the dust of the earth all the days of their life. Cursed are they above all cattle, and above every beast of the field; grovelling shall they go, till they come to their end and perish. But for Christians, it is theirs to walk in the light, as children of the light, and to lift up their hearts, as looking out for Him who went away, that He might return to them again."

For the same reason Christians are called upon to think little of the ordinary objects which men pursue—wealth, luxury, distinction, popularity, and power. It was this negligence about the world which brought upon them in primitive times the reproach of being indolent. Their heathen enemies spoke truly; indolent and indifferent they were about temporal matters. If the goods of this world came in their way, they were not bound to decline them; nor would they forbid others in the religious use of them; but they thought them vanities, the toys of children, which serious men let drop. Nay, St. Paul betrays the same feeling as regards our temporal callings and states generally. After discoursing about them, suddenly he breaks off as if impatient of the multitude of words; "But this I Say, brethren," he exclaims, "the time is short."

Hence, too, the troubles of life gradually affect the Christian less and less, as his view of his own real blessedness, under the Dispensation of the Spirit, grows upon him; and even though persecuted, to take an extreme ease, he knows well that, through God's inward presence, he is greater than those who for the time have power over him, as Martyrs and Confessors have often shown.

And, in like manner, he will be calm and collected under all circumstances; he will make light of injuries, and forget them from mere contempt of them. He will be undaunted, as fearing God more than man; he will be firm in faith and consistent, as "seeing Him that is invisible;" not impatient, as one who has no self-will; not soon disappointed, who has no hopes; not anxious, who has no fears; nor dazzled, who has no ambition; nor open to bribes, who has no desires.

And now, further, let it be observed, on the other hand, that all this greatness of mind which I have been describing, which in other religious systems degenerates into pride, is in the Gospel compatible—nay, rather intimately connected—with the deepest humility. It is true, that, so great are the Christian privileges, there is serious danger lest common men should be puffed up by them; but this will be when persons take them to themselves who have no right to them. Did I not begin with saying, that the Dispensation of the Spirit is one of awe, of "reverence and godly fear"? Surely, then, they who pride themselves on the gift have forgotten the very elements of the Gospel of Christ. They have forgotten that the gift is not only "a savour of life unto life," but "of death unto death;" that it is possible to "do despite unto the Spirit of grace;" and that "it is impossible for those who were once enlightened, if they shall fall away, to renew them again unto repentance." [2 Cor. ii. 16. Heb. x. 29; vi. 4–6.] Again; if they do aught well, "what have they which they have not received?" and how know they but He, by whom their souls live, will withdraw that life—nay, will to a certainty withdraw it—if they take that glory to themselves which is His? Why was it that Herod was smitten by the Angel? O awful instance of the jealousy of God! "The people gave a shout, saying, It is the voice of a god, and not of a man; and immediately the Angel of the Lord smote him, because he gave not God the glory." [Acts xii. 22, 23.] He was smitten immediately: suddenly and utterly does our strength, and our holiness, and our blessedness, and our influence, depart from us, like a lamp that expires, or a weight that falls, as soon as we rest in them, and pride ourselves in them, instead of referring them to the Giver. God keep us in His mercy from this sin! St. Paul shows us how we should feel about God's gifts, and how to boast without pride, when He first says, "I laboured more abundantly than they all:" and then adds, "yet not I, but the grace of God which was with me." [1 Cor. xv. 10.]

Accordingly, the self-respect of the Christian is no personal and selfish feeling, but rather a principle of loyal devotion and reverence towards that Divine Master who condescends to visit him. He acts, not hastily, but under restraint and fearfully, as understanding that God's eye is over him, and God's hand upon him, and God's voice within him. He acts with the recollection that his Omniscient Guide is also his future Judge; and that while He moves him, He is also noting down in His book how he answers to His godly motions. He acts with a memory laden with past infirmity and sin, and a consciousness that he has much more to mourn over and repent of, in the years gone by, than to rejoice in. Yes, surely, he has many a secret wound to be healed; many a bruise to be tended; many a sore, like Lazarus; many a chronic infirmity; many a bad omen of perils to come. It is one thing, not to trust in the world; it is another thing to trust in one's self.

But, alas! I repeat it, how unreal in this age are such contemplations, when neither in ourselves nor in the Church around us have they a fulfilment! How is it fit to speak of thoughts and tempers which men of the day not only fail to cherish, but are eager to reprobate! Yet perchance what is lost upon the many, may gain a hearing with the few; what is lost today, may be recalled tomorrow; what is lost in fulness, may be retained in portions; what fails to convince, may excite misgivings; what fails with the heart, may create the wish. We must not grudge to speak, whether men will hear, or whether they will forbear; knowing that "he that observeth the wind shall not sow, and he that regardeth the clouds shall not reap." [Eccles. xi. 4.]

May we, one and all, set forward with this season, when the Spirit descended, that so we may grow in grace, and in the knowledge of our Lord and Saviour! Let those who have had seasons of seriousness, lengthen them into a life; and let those who have made good resolves in Lent, remember them in Eastertide; and let those who have hitherto lived religiously, learn devotion; and let those who have lived in good conscience, learn to live by faith; and let those who have made a good profession, aim at consistency; and let those who take pleasure in religious worship, aim at inward sanctity; and let those who have knowledge, learn to love; and let those who meditate, forget not mortification. Let not this sacred season leave us as it found us; let it leave us, not as children, but as heirs and as citizens of the kingdom of heaven. For forty days have we been hearing "the things pertaining to the kingdom of God." [Acts i. 3.] The time may come, when we shall desire to see one of the days of the Son of man, and see it not. Let us redeem the time while it is called today; "till we all come in the unity of the faith and of the knowledge of the Son of God, unto a perfect man, unto the measure of the stature of the fulness of Christ." [Eph. iv. 13.]

The Principle of Continuity between
the Jewish & Christian Churches[†]

"If ye be dead with Christ from the rudiments of the world,
why, as though living in the world, are ye subject to ordinances,
(Touch not, taste not, handle not, which all are to perish with the using;)
after the commandments and doctrines of men?"
Col. ii. 20–22

T HE WHOLE PASSAGE of which these words form part is often brought to show that any regard to outward religion is unchristian, and a mere remnant of Judaism. St. Paul just before seems to condemn, or at least to set aside, observance of meats and drinks, of holy days, of sabbaths, as being but a shadow of the good things which are given us in the Gospel, and perishable, or rather perished and dead ordinances, and of one family with those more dangerous and destructive superstitions which substituted Angels as the objects of our worship instead of the one Lord and Saviour. This, I say, is what is argued from this passage,—that the Gospel is quite contrary to the Law in this respect, that it has no ritual, no regimen, no ordinances; and that to submit to any such, is to do injury to the simplicity of the Christian religion.

Now, so far from this being true, I think even the contrary may be laid down; that the existence of a polity, a ceremonial, and a code of laws, under the Gospel, is the very point in which Christianity *agrees* with Judaism, and in consequence of which the Christian Church may be considered the continuation of the Jewish. And I think this very passage of St. Paul, which many consider to warrant them in the rejection of external religion, if it does not prove its obligation, as I consider it does, at least is quite consistent with it.

1. First, then, I observe, that certainly not all ordinances are done away under the Gospel, considering our Lord Himself instituted two Sacraments, and set up the Church as a city on a hill, and bade us hear her, and is frequent in laying down rules and directions as to what is to be done in indifferent matters. And further, St. Paul expressly says to the Corinthians, "I praise you, brethren, that ye remember me in all things, and keep the ordinances, as I delivered them to you;" [1 Cor. xi. 2.] and again, to the Thessalonians, "Breth-

---

[†] *Sermons on Subjects of the Day* (1843), Sermon 15, preached in 1842.

ren, stand fast, and hold the traditions which ye have been taught, whether by word or our epistle." [2 Thess. ii. 15.] And we read in the Acts of the Apostles, that St. Paul and his brethren, "as they went through the cities, delivered them the decrees," or (as the same word is translated in the text) the ordinances, "for to keep, that were ordained of the Apostles and elders which were at Jerusalem." [Acts xvi. 4.]

It is quite certain, then, that St. Paul did not mean to speak against all ritual ordinances and rules of discipline whatever, in the passage in which the text is found, because he himself enjoined and enforced certain such, at least on other occasions.

2. And in truth, a very little consideration will show, that the text does not at all speak against ordinances generally, but against those particular ordinances which did not come from Christ. Let it be observed, that the Apostle expressly adds, "after the commandments and doctrines *of men*." He does not forbid all ordinances, but mere human, unsanctioned, and therefore unchristian, ordinances. He does not say simply, "Why are ye subject to ordinances?" but "Why keep ye ordinances after the commandments of *men*?" Nor can this be treated as an accidental addition, because he uses the same language elsewhere. For instance, in the beginning of the chapter, "Beware, lest any man spoil you through philosophy and vain deceit, after the tradition *of men*, after the rudiments *of the world*, and not after Christ." The fault of the tradition was, that it came, not from Christ, but from man. And so, writing to the Galatians, "I certify you, brethren, that the Gospel which was preached of me is not *after man*; for I neither received it of man, neither was I taught it, but by the revelation of Jesus Christ." [Gal. i. 11, 12.] And accordingly, when he enjoins Christian ordinances, he is very particular, as indeed in the passage just quoted, to say that they, on the other hand, come from Christ; "Be ye followers of me, *even as* I also am of Christ: now I praise you, brethren, that ye remember me in all things, and keep the ordinances, as I delivered them to you." Again, "For I have received of the Lord that which also I delivered unto you." [1 Cor. xi. 1, 2, 23.] And those ordinances which he published in the course of his apostolic journey, from whom did they come? Hear the Apostles' own account of them: "It seemed good to the Holy Ghost and to us." [Acts xv. 28. Vide also 1 Thess. iv. 8.] Not to man merely, but to God; and therefore the ordinances put forth were not traditions of men, but traditions of God.

Our Saviour had made the same distinction in His own ministry. He had found fault with the Pharisees for their traditions; but why? because they were traditions of men, and such as obscured and resisted the tradition of God. "Why do ye," He says, "transgress the commandment *of God* by *your* tradition?" [Matt. xv. 3, 9.] and again, "In vain they do worship Me, teaching for doctrines the commandments of men." Again; "laying aside the commandment *of God*, ye hold the tradition *of men;*" [Mark vii. 8, 9, 13.] and again, "Full well ye reject the commandment *of God*, that ye may keep *your own* tradition;" and again, "making the word *of God* of none effect, through *your* tradition which *ye have delivered*." And then He adds, "Every plant which My Heavenly Father hath not planted, shall be rooted up." [Matt. xv. 13.]

3. Now let us turn back to the text, and the passage connected with it. Here, as elsewhere, the Apostle lays down the great principle, that every thing, to be done acceptably, must be done in Christ. "Other foundation can no man lay." [1 Cor. iii. 11.] Every plant, but the Cross, shall be rooted up; no fruit is good but what its branches bear. No person, no work of any kind will endure the judgment, but what comes of Christ, and is quickened by His Spirit. Every thing out of Him is dead. And as no virtue is real virtue, nor service true service, nor work good work, if He is not the life of it; so in like manner, no rite or ordinance is good, unless as grafted into Him and sanctified by Him. St. Paul does not speak against ordinances in themselves, but ordinances which are done beside or against Christ's grace and will. Such were those of the Pharisees which our Lord Himself denounced; such were those of the Galatians which St. Paul protested against; such were the ordinances of those Jews or Gnostics, or whoever they were, whom, in the passage connected with the text, he has in view. These teachers of error refused to take Christ as their Head,—"not holding the Head," he says; they would not believe that Christ was all-gracious, all-powerful; so the Apostle reminded them, "In Him dwelleth all the fulness of the Godhead bodily." Again," Ye are complete in Him which is the Head of all principality and power." Instead of remembering this, these false teachers made Angels their hope and their worship; "in a voluntary humility and worshipping of Angels."

And, in consequence, nothing they did, or said, or taught, or practised, was right. Their services, their rites, their ordinances were all reprobate. How does this show that there are no ordinances *in* Christ? why must ordinances in Christ be unacceptable, because they are unacceptable out of Christ? St. Paul says, "Let no man judge you in meat or in drink, or in respect of a holy day, or of the new moon, or of the Sabbath days." Why? Because these were not of the body. You see, then, there *is* a body; yes, but it is not the body of any angelic lord or teacher; it is not the body of Abraham, Isaac, and Jacob, though they are members of it; it is not the body of Moses, for Moses "was faithful in all his house," but "as a *servant*." It is Christ, who is Lord over His own house; it is Christ's, whose, and whose only, is the body. In Him only are we sanctified; in Him only are our works, our services, our ordinances sanctified; but in Him we *are* sanctified; in Him our works, our rites, our forms, our observances, are sanctified. We are wrong, not when we have works, rites, and observances, but when they are not in Him. All these make up the body of Christ:—first of all in the body are our persons; next our order and polity; then our rites and ceremonies; lastly, our professions and works. All are parts, each in its own way, of Christ's Body, in which is life; or in the words of the Apostle, from Him, as the Head, "all the body by joints and bands having nourishment ministered, and knit together, increaseth with the increase of God."

4. Nay, something more is yet to be said on this point. Not only do forms and ordinances remain under the Gospel equally as before; but, as is plain from the very chapter on which I am commenting, what was in use before is not so much superseded by the Gospel ordinances, as changed into them. What took place under the Law is a pattern, what was commanded is a rule, under the Gospel. The substance remains, the use, the meaning, the circumstances, the benefit is changed; grace is added, life is infused; "the body is of Christ;" but it is in great measure that same body which was in being before He came. The Gospel has not put aside, it has incorporated into itself, the revelations which went before it. It avails itself of the Old Testament, as a great gift to Christian as well as to Jew. It does not dispense with it, but it dispenses it. Persons sometimes urge that there is no code of duty in the New Testament, no ceremonial, no rules for Church polity. Certainly not; they are unnecessary; they are already given in the Old. Why should the Old Testament be retained in the Christian Church, but to be used? *There* are we to look for our forms, our rites, our polity; only illustrated, tempered, spiritualized, by the Gospel. The precepts remain; the observance of them is changed.

This, I say, is what many persons are slow to understand. They think the Old Testament must be supposed to be our rule directly and literally, or not at all; and since we cannot put ourselves under it absolutely and without explanation, they conclude that in no sense it is binding on us; but surely there is such a thing as the *application* of Scripture; this is no very difficult or strange idea. Surely we cannot make any practical use even of St. Paul's Epistles, without application. They are written to Ephesians or Colossians; we apply them to the case of Englishmen. They speak of customs, and circumstances, and fortunes, which do not belong to us; we cannot take them literally; we must adapt them to our own case; we must apply them to us. *We* are not in persecution, or in prison; we do not live in the south, nor under the Romans; nor have we been converted from heathenism; nor have we miraculous gifts; nor live we in a country of slaves; yet still we do not find it impossible to guide ourselves by inspired directions, addressed to those who were thus circumstanced. And in somewhat a like manner, the directions of the Old Testament, whether as to conduct, or ritual, or Church polity, may be our guides, though we are obliged to apply them. Scripture itself does this for us in some instances, and in some others we ourselves are accustomed to do so for ourselves; and we may do so in a number of others also in which we are slow to do it. For instance, the Law says, "Thou shalt love thy neighbour as thyself." [Lev. xix. 18.] Does the Gospel abrogate this command? of course not. What does it do with it? it explains and enlarges it. It answers the question, "*Who* is my neighbour?" [Luke x. 29.] The substance of the command is the same under Law and under Gospel; but the Gospel opens and elevates it. And so again the Ten Commandments belong to the Law, yet we read them still in the Communion Service, as binding upon ourselves; yet not in the mere letter; the Gospel has turned the letter into spirit. It has unfolded and diversified those sacred precepts which were given from the beginning.

To this, however, it may be answered, that what is true of the Moral Law is not true of the Ritual. That the Moral Law remains, that the rites and ceremonies are abrogated. They *are* abrogated, yet only in the letter; and not in such sense abrogated, but they are in their substance continued still. Let us recollect *why* they are abrogated, and we shall understand *in what sense.* They are abolished, because they were types, and because Christ, their Antitype, is come. True, *so far then* as they are types they are abolished; but not as they are religious services, and principles and elements of religious worship. That is, we must distinguish between the precept itself, and the particular fulfilment of it under the Jewish Law, that is, the Jewish rite. As the duty to love our neighbour continues still; but by our neighbours are no longer meant merely inhabitants of Palestine, nor our own countrymen, but all men; so also the duty remains of coming to God's house for His favours, of obeying His priests, of offering Him our sacrifices, though the particular forms in which these duties were fulfilled under the Law, being types of Christ, were abolished when Christ came. The Jewish temple, the Jewish priesthood, and the Jewish sacrifices, then, were abolished because they were but shadows, and "the body was of Christ;" but the precepts remain though the types disappear.

5. This, as I have already observed, is taught us in the chapter from which the text is taken, as is very plain. For instance, it tells us that the Sabbath is a shadow, and its observance not binding, since Christ is come, of whom is "the body." The Sabbath, according to St. Paul, is of the rudiments of this world, a carnal ordinance, and brings us into bondage. It had been a witness of the creation of heaven and earth, which was no longer needed. It was a memorial of past mercies to the Jews, which are surpassed in the Gospel. It was a type of the Gospel rest, which is now come. The type is fulfilled; the *whole* period of the Christian Church, from the day of Pentecost to the end of

all things, is one holy and spiritual Sabbath. Again, the whole life of each individual Christian, from his baptism to his death, is also an antitype of the Jewish Sabbath. The heaven on earth, which abides in the Christian Church and in the regenerate soul, this is that true spiritual rest which God promised of old time; in the words of Zacharias, "that we, being delivered out of the hands of our enemies, might serve Him without fear, in holiness and righteousness before Him all the days of our life." Yet, though this be so, shall we therefore say, that the Fourth Commandment is abrogated? surely not. The Sabbath indeed is abolished, but the commandment which enjoins it remains; it is fulfilled in another manner. The Sabbath, with other shadows of the Law, has flitted away; but "the word of God endureth for ever," and has a real and imperishable substance, issuing forth in ever fresh manifestations, fresh duties, fresh promises, as its older forms successively do their work and dissolve. The old fulfilment of this commandment, with its observance of the seventh day, its memorial of the creation, and of the deliverance from Egypt, its ceremonial inactivity, its preciseness and formality, is at an end; but the duty of keeping it, with new objects, and new acts of service, remains. It is observed still in substance, though not in the letter. And what is true of the institution of the Sabbath, is true also of other ritual precepts in the Old Testament; that they are typical, and, as such, fulfilled, is quite consistent with their ecclesiastical obligation, and their perpetual abidance.

The Sabbath then is one instance in point; though the Apostle implies that it has come to nought, yet it endures, though in a new manifestation. Another instance, suggested by the passage before us, is the rite of circumcision. This is altogether done away with in the Gospel; yet not so done away with, but it leaves behind it a representative. It is abolished as a type fulfilled, a type of Christian renewal; yet still there is such a rite as Christian circumcision, and it is called Baptism. This is what St. Paul expressly says in the chapter before us. "Ye are complete in Christ," he says, "which is the Head of all principality and power. In whom all ye are circumcised with the circumcision made without hands, in putting off the body of the sins of the flesh by the circumcision of Christ: buried with Him in baptism." Here he says, first, that the Colossians *had* received a circumcision, though not the Jewish; and then names what it is, "buried with Him in Baptism." Thus, though circumcision is abolished, Scripture has not left us without its substitute, lest the great and fundamental rule which circumcision implied, of entering God's service by a formal act of dedication, should be slighted. And on account of this correspondence between the two rites, we infer the duty of baptizing infants, because infants were circumcised, though there is no command to that effect in Scripture. Nor need there be, if, as I am here showing, the Law contains in it the ecclesiastical and ritual rules of the Gospel, only under a veil.

6. These two instances, of the Sabbath and of circumcision, are suggested by the very chapter of which I am speaking; but what is true of these, is true of many other parts of the Law, as in some particulars all will allow; and if in them, why not in others? No one will deny that the principle or spirit of the commandment concerning the Paschal feast is still fulfilled in our feast of Holy Communion. It is true, that the Paschal feast was a type of our Lord's atoning death, and therefore has come to an end, as being a type fulfilled; but it has not come to an end without leaving behind it a rite in its place, without reviving, as it were, in a new form; why? because the Jewish Church and the Christian Church are one; and the rules given to the Jewish are in some sort the ritual and the canons of the Christian, though not *as* Jewish rules; the form, the manner, the virtue being different, the substance the same.

I say, without looking for directions in the New Testament, we shall be able to see at once the reason of other institutions and usages, which have ever existed in the Christian Church, by merely referring to the Old. For instance, the three orders of the Jewish ministry, high-priest, priests, and Levites, are done away in Christ in their Jewish form; yet, let us suppose that the commandment on which they rested remains in force now, and needs not to be repeated in the New Testament, and we see it fulfilled in our three orders of bishops, priests, and deacons.

Again: we learn from the histories of Nadab and Abihu, of Korah, Dathan, and Abiram, and of Uzziah, that no one could intrude upon the priestly office, or rebel against the priest, without the most fearful responsibility. What was the rule of the Law is the rule of the Gospel, as St. Jude expressly teaches us; for he speaks of the opposers of Church authority in his day as "perishing in the gainsaying of Core;" nay, and St. Paul, who lays down the general principle, "No man taketh this honour unto himself, but he that is called of God, as was Aaron."

Again: under the Jewish law, the ministerial office was continued by a succession; it was not committed to men here and there, as it might be, but passed from father to son. The carnal form of this ordinance is now at an end, but the succession remains; spiritual sons succeed spiritual fathers. As under the Law, each preceding generation of priests begat the following, so each generation ordains the next, under the Gospel.

Again: the Jewish temple is abolished, because the True and Spiritual Temple, the Communion of Saints, has been established by Christ. Yet, though the type is at an end, the precept remains. Temples are to be built to God's honour under the Gospel, and to be consecrated, and to be treated as

His dwelling-places; and in other respects, as far as suitable, to be conformed to the model of that ancient building once commanded.

Once more: under the Law there were altars and sacrifices; these very altars, these very sacrifices, have come to nought, for they were a shadow of good things to come: but still Altars and Sacrifices endure, though with a different virtue, and a different purpose; they are part of that body which is of Christ. He has taken possession of them, and made them spiritual.

I will add, in corroboration, that as other Prophets, so especially Malachi, the last of them, in whom, as being the last, we might expect some clearer intimations of the destruction of ordinances on Christ's coming, if they were to be destroyed, when prophesying of Gospel times and speaking of the preparation necessary thereunto, builds up, instead of pulling down, the ritual system. For instance, "Even from the days of your fathers," he says, "ye are *gone away from Mine ordinances*, and have not kept them. Return unto Me, and I will return unto you, saith the Lord of Hosts." Again, as to the ordinance of tithes: "Bring ye all the tithes into the storehouse, that there may be meat in Mine House, and prove Me now herewith, saith the Lord of Hosts, if I will not open you the windows of heaven, and pour you out a blessing, that there shall not be room enough to receive it." And as to the priesthood, far from its abolition, Christ was but to purify and refine it. "He shall sit as a refiner and purifier of silver, and He shall *purify the sons of Levi*, and purge them as gold and silver." Nor was He to abolish sacrifice, for the Prophet proceeds, "He shall purge them as gold and silver, that they may offer unto the Lord an offering in righteousness." And what this offering was to be, the Prophet tells us, speaking of it as a rite of the Church in its universal or Catholic form. "From the rising of the sun even unto the going down of the same, My Name shall be great among the Gentiles; and in every place incense shall be offered unto My Name, and a pure offering;" [Mal. iii. 7, 10, 3; i. 11.] that is, the offering of fine flour or bread. What is thus instanced from Malachi might be drawn out from other Prophets also.

7. It seems, then, that making what allowance we will for the changes which were introduced by the Gospel, which in point of knowledge, grace, and influence upon the world, were incalculably great, and cannot be overrated, yet as regards the substantial form of religion, ecclesiastical order, ritual, polity, observance, the change was not considerable. Indeed, religion viewed as an institution, and that of a social nature, does not admit of any great variety. As all civil governments are one in their great characteristics, as all sciences proceed on common principles, else they would not be called by that one name, so in one sense religion, wherever found, is one thing, and one thing only. A true religion is a religion based on truth, and a false religion is a reli-

gion based on falsehood; but they would not be called by the same name, unless there were a substantial agreement between them. And if true and false religions are like each other, as to their bodily substance, much more are Judaism and Christianity alike, which are both from God; and, consequently, Catholic Christians must not be surprised, if on their submitting to Christianity *as* a religion, and not as a mere philosophy, or an opinion, or a sentiment, they are charged by those who do so treat it, with being Jews or even Pagans.

8. And what has just been said leads to another reflection. The Jews might quite as justly be charged with Paganism for their rites, as we with Judaism for ours; for ours are not so like the Jewish, as the Jewish were like those of the Pagans. This ought to be insisted on. It has been shown by learned men, that considerable portions of the Mosaic system were either taken from the heathen religions which surrounded it, or at least, from their likeness, must have had a common origin with them. In truth, Judaism was, in God's mercy, the correction, the restoration, of those degenerate and corrupt religions, just as Christianity is the development and spiritual perfection of the Jewish. Now, if it is a good argument against our priesthood, Christian sacrifices, Christian Sabbaths, and Christian sacraments, that they are like ordinances of the Jewish Law, which came from God, much more would it be an argument against that Law in Samuel's time or David's, as infidels have made it since, that in some chief portions of it, it is like the paganism of Egypt or Syria. And if it is a good argument against our Church system, that St. Paul denounces Judaism, surely it is not a worse argument against the Jewish system, that Moses denounces Paganism. If St. Paul says of Judaism, "Let no man judge you in meat or in drink;" or, "Ye observe days, and months, and times, and years," I suppose Moses says still more sternly of Paganism, "Ye shall overthrow their altars, and break their pillars, and burn their groves with fire." [Deut. xii. 3.] And if Moses adds the reason, as regards Paganism, viz. because they were dedicated to *false* gods; so does St. Paul give the reason, as regards Judaism, "which are a *shadow* of things to come." And as the ordinances of the Jewish Church were not paid to false gods, though they were ordinances like the Pagan; so those of the Christian are not a shadow, though they are ordinances like the Jewish. And since, supposing in the time of Samuel or of David, a reformer had arisen to set things to rights out of his own mind, he might have forcibly urged against all that he found established—rite, and ordinance, and government— that it was like heathenism, and that Moses, speaking from Almighty God, had denounced heathenism, and that, therefore, the existing system could not come from heaven,—and yet this in truth would have been a very bad argument, therefore, let us not be moved from our steadfastness by the arguments of innovators and heretics, who pretend that the Church system is a corrup-

347

tion, because it is like the Jewish, which St. Paul repudiates. For it is *not* Jewish *in spirit*, though it *is* Jewish in certain externals; nor was the Jewish system Pagan in spirit, though it was Pagan in externals. At one time, God dwelt in the Jewish ritual, though it was like the Pagan; and now He dwells in the Christian ritual, though it be like the Jewish. Forms are nothing without God's presence; but with His presence they are all things.

Thus then I answer the question, What is that substantial unity and identity of the Jewish and Christian Churches, since they so differ in their members, circumstances, and objects? Thus, too, I would answer that other question, How can the Jews be said to have rejected their Law, in rejecting the Gospel? The Gospel is but a development of the Law; and creeds and systems may at first sight be very far removed from certain known originals, and yet, after all, be but developments of them.

I conclude with one observation, viz. that a view of the Old Testament, such as I have been taking, makes it a book much more level to the comprehensions of the unlearned than the theories concerning it which have of late years prevailed. It is difficult to make an unlearned person understand, who comes to Scripture with reverence, that the commands of the Law are not binding on us now. To tell him that the Sabbath is a mere type, and that it does not concern him, and that it now means merely a life of religion, is too subtle an idea for him; but to tell him that the Fourth Commandment does bind him (though it bind not in the sense in which it bound the Jews), approves itself to him as natural and true. It is a refinement, again, in his judgment, to tell him that the Jewish temple was a mere type of the communion of saints, and is not a model for our cathedrals and churches. In like manner, he will easily understand, if he is so taught, that the other precepts of the Old Testament apply to us Christians; that what is said about holy rites, and holy days, and holy persons, has a literal sense now, though not the particular sense it had before Christ came. Thus we see how inconsistent is the false philosophy of modern religion. It professes to give the Bible to the poor that they may judge for themselves; yet it will not let them read it in a plain way, lest they read it like the saints of former ages—lest they become too catholic and primitive; but it interposes with its own officious note and comment, to fix upon it a strained figurative meaning.

Condition of the Members of
the Christian Empire[†]

"Lord, Thou hast heard the desire of the poor;
Thou preparest their heart, and Thine ear hearkeneth thereto;
to help the fatherless and poor unto their right,
that the man of the earth be no more exalted against them."
Ps. x. 19, 20

THE BOOK OF PSALMS has ever been one main portion of the devotions of the Christian Church, in public and in private, since that Church was. In the east and west, north and south, in quiet times, in troubled times, in the rise, and now in the decline, of the Kingdom of the Saints, the inspired words of the Prophets of Israel have been in the mouth of the children of grace. In consequence, it is natural to suppose that the Psalter has a Christian meaning. Since it has held its place at all times, it surely has a sense for all times. Since we especially use it, this surely must be because to us it is especially useful. Some free-thinkers have said, What is the book to us, relating, as it does, the history and expressing the feelings of a people who lived two or three thousand years ago? I grant it: if the book of Psalms be but a Jewish book, it is not a Christian book; but the question on which all turns is, whether the Psalms are the mere devotions of an extinct religion or no.

The very circumstance, then, that Christians use the Psalter, proves that they consider that it has a meaning over and above that Jewish meaning which lies on the surface of it. And when we consider how intimately it has been received into the Christian Church, how it is made the form of so great a portion of our devotions, how it enters into almost all our Services, equally with the Lord's Prayer—nay, it may be said, even more than the Lord's Prayer, because of its greater length and variety—it cannot be supposed that this Christian meaning contained in it is but occasional or faint; it must run through it; it must be strong, definite, and real; else why should Christians turn aside to use Jewish forms? They have ever acted as if no state of their minds but found its appropriate expression in the Psalms; no sentence in the Psalms but had its appropriate sense in their own mouths.

[†] *Sermons on Subjects of the Day* (1843), Sermon 18, preached in 1840.

349

Now as to a great portion of this sacred Book, we all know full well, and shall be able to reply at once, that it relates to our Lord and Saviour. Whatever is said in the first instance of David and his labours, trials, and sufferings in the cause of God, whatever is said of Solomon and his glory, and much beside which is more or less of a directly prophetic, and not of a mere typical character, is fulfilled in Christ. Much as we revere the memory of holy David, such reverence would not account for our commemorating him in preference to all saints, and him alone, in our daily devotions; but we know well, that in reading the 22nd, or the 69th, or the 109th Psalm, we are reading, not of David's trials, which are gone and over, but of the mediatory and expiatory work of him who ever liveth, a Priest for ever after the order of Melchizedek; and in like manner, when we read the 2nd, or the 45th, or the 72nd, we read of the triumph and exaltation, not of the monarchs of Israel, but of the same Lord and Saviour.

And further, much that does not on the surface bear tokens of a relation to the same great truths, and which we cannot absolutely pronounce to relate to them, doubtless may be interpreted of them by the pious mind for itself as it reads;—from its own intimate apprehension and continual contemplation of the details of the history of Christ. And in this way the book of Psalms may certainly be made to abound in edifying lessons, and to breathe of Christ. But, allowing this fully, still it is not a sufficient reason for using the devotions of the Jewish Church, that they admit of being turned to good account. Moreover, there are, after all, large portions of the Psalms which cannot be said to support such a sense at all, which do not carry it on and carry it out continuously, which give it forth but at intervals; and which, in consequence, if they are to be considered Christian devotions, would seem to require some other interpretation, more natural, obvious and uniform.

Great part of the Psalms, for instance, is employed in lamenting, entreating, hoping, about certain subjects; what is the Christian meaning of all this? I mean, what is a Christian to be thinking of when he uses the words?

Again, a Christian's devotion does and must consist, in great measure, in lamenting, entreating, hoping. What is the meaning then of making the Psalms the channel of his devotion, unless they do faithfully express that lamenting, intreating, and hoping, which a Christian exercises?

What, for instance, do we mean when we say, in the words of the text, "Lord, Thou hast heard the desire of the poor; Thou preparest their heart, and Thine ear hearkeneth thereto; to help the fatherless and poor unto their right, that the man of the earth be no more exalted against them"?

Either the Psalms are ever applicable to the state of the Christian Church, or one does not see why they have always formed so necessary a part of her devotions. And, as I have hinted, many persons feel this, and not understanding what is the present meaning of the Psalms, advocate their disuse.

Now it is obvious what a remarkable evidence is afforded us of the substantial agreement and the unity existing between the Christian and Jewish Church, by the continuation in the Christian of the Jewish devotions. For what is religion but worship? and whatever changes we make in the sense of its letter, these cannot be of a nature to reverse that letter; they can but enlarge the letter; they can but introduce a sense parallel to it; the substance of the ideas expressed by it must remain the same. This should be seriously thought of by those who disparage certain ordinances and customs as Jewish; such as reverence for sacred places, observance of holy days, adoption of a minute ceremonial, and the like; for if there be one thing more than another Jewish in our received form of religion, it is the use of the Psalter. If we may safely use the very same prayers and praises used by God's former people, it does not appear why we may not adopt ceremonies, not the same, but like those, which were divinely given to them; if the Psalter admits of a Christian and spiritual sense, it does not appear why rites and ceremonies may not be practised spiritually also.

But our business at present is to inquire *what* that sense is, in which we Christians are to use the Psalms in our devotions.

Now, if we bear in mind what Scripture teaches us concerning the Christian Church, as the Kingdom of heaven upon earth, if we consider what the Church is in office, and in circumstance, we shall, I think, see that the Psalms are no foreign tongue, but do speak the very language which is natural to her; that if Isaiah has given her picture, David has supplied her voice; that the two inspired writers harmonize with each other;—and again, with the four Evangelists, and our Lord's own account of the kingdom of the Saints, as recorded by them.

For what is this kingdom as I have already described it? a universal empire without earthly arms; temporal pretensions without temporal sanctions; a claim to rule without the power to enforce; a continual tendency to acquire with a continual exposure to be dispossessed; greatness of mind with weakness of body. What will be the fortunes of such an empire in the world? persecution; persecution is the token of the Church; persecution is the note of the Church, perhaps the most abiding note of all. The world is strong: men of the world have arms of the world; they have swords, they have armies, they have prisons, they have chains, they have wild passions. The Church has none of these, and yet it claims a right to rule, direct, rebuke, exhort, denounce, condemn. It claims the obedience of the powerful; it confronts the haughty; it places itself across the path of the wilful; it undertakes the defence of the poor;

it accepts the gifts of the world, and becomes involved in their stewardship; and yet it is at the mercy of these said powerful, haughty, and wilful men, to ill-treat and to spoil. Is not this too great a temptation for sinful nature to resist? Can it be otherwise, but that a kingdom which claims so much, which professes so much, yet can resist so little, which irritates the world's pride, which inflames its cupidity, which interferes with its purposes, which terrifies its conscience, yet does nothing in its defence but threaten; which deals with unseen ill and unseen good, whose only arms are what an unbelieving world calls priestcraft—is it not certain that such a kingdom will be the prey and sport of the world?

Moreover, the mustard-seed, small and vile though it be, was destined to spread and thrive; to thrive in spite of all the world's power. Here is a distinct provocation. What so irritating, so mortifying to the proud, who are conscious that they are in high place in the world, and have great worldly power or influence, the world's arms, the world's homage, as to find a despised doctrine "grow and multiply" in spite of them, and by means which they cannot investigate, by powers which they cannot analyze? Such was the nature of the Church's triumph over heathenism; and what the counter triumph of heathenism would be over the Church, was plain before the event. "It shall bruise thy head, and thou shalt bruise His heel." [Gen iii. 15.] The Church made progress, and the world persecuted. The Kingdom was set up, but it was set up in obloquy, ill-usage, suffering, in much weakness, in fear and trembling. It triumphed as a Church, it suffered in its members. Such, in its measure, has been its lot ever since. The age of Martyrs, indeed, is well nigh over; but scarce a Saint, but has been in his place and degree a Confessor. Hardly has any one done right without provoking the world to do him wrong. "All that will live godly in Christ Jesus shall suffer persecution," [2 Tim. iii. 12.] says St. Paul; and our Lord, "Blessed are ye, when men shall revile you, and persecute you, and shall say all manner of evil against you falsely, for My sake." [Matt. v. 11.]

But now to return to the Psalter. If the Church be what has been described; if it be great, and wide-spreading, yet ever open to attack; if it be ever strong, yet ever weak, weak in itself, strong in the Lord; ever persecuted, yet ever blessed and prospered; do you not see that the tenour of the book of Psalms does most exactly and minutely express what the feelings of the Church will be under such circumstances? The Church is holy, and the Church is defenceless. Now what is the Psalter, from beginning to end, but a supplication to God to rescue the poor and needy, and to justify the righteous? the very petitions which the Church has such urgent cause to offer.

It contains two main ideas; the defeat of God's enemies, yet the suffering of God's people. I will now quote passages from it at some length, in illustra-

352

tion and proof of what I have said; that is, not merely isolated texts, such as we all know to be prophetic, or to admit of a reference to the great events of the New Testament, but such prayers and aspirations as occur in course, and in a context which cannot be applied merely to our Lord's history; which need a sense if they are to be used by Christians, and which find a sufficient one in the view of the Gospel Church which I have been taking.

1. Now, on the one hand, when we sing the Psalms we triumph in the Church's exultation over the might of this world. "In Jewry is God known, His Name is great in Israel." [Ps. lxxvi.] What is meant by Israel, but the chosen people, even us Christians? The Psalm must say that God's Name is great in *us*; else, why read we the Psalms? Let us proceed. "At Salem is His tabernacle, and His dwelling in Sion. There brake He the arrows of the bow, the shield, the sword, and the battle. Thou art of more honour and might than the hills of the robbers." The earth is filled with robbery, plunder, violence, cruelty, except so far as it is Christian. All states of the world, all governments, except so far as they are Christian, except so far as they act upon Christian principles, are scarcely more than robbers and men of blood; and against these God exalts Himself; against these He is ever exalting Himself; against these at this very time is He rising, as in all times; against all states, all governments, all power of man which does not acknowledge Him, and bow before Him. And "the nation and kingdom that will not serve" Him, or rather, as the Prophet says, His Church, "shall perish." To proceed: "The proud are robbed, they have slept their sleep, and all the men whose hands were mighty have found nothing. At Thy rebuke, O God of Jacob, both the chariot and horse are fallen." Do we ask how this is fulfilled *now*? Have we not seen in our own time, or did not our fathers see a great anti-christian power in the world, exalting itself against religion, and especially against Christ's Church? and did it not seem sure of success? and yet has it not, after all its threats and triumphs, ceased to be, leaving nought behind it but the Egyptians upon the seashore, and a small dust and ashes, for its worshippers fondly to hang over? And this is but one instance of what takes place in every age, the triumph of the Church over the world. "Thou, even Thou art to be feared, and who may stand in Thy sight when Thou art angry? Thou didst cause Thy judgment to be heard from heaven; the earth trembled, and was still, when God arose to judgment, and to help all the meek upon earth." The meek of the earth; for it is pledged to them that they shall "inherit" it. "The fierceness of men shall turn to Thy praise, and the fierceness of them shalt Thou refrain . . . He shall refrain the spirit of princes, and is wonderful among the kings of the earth."

Again; the same triumph of God's Name in His chosen people over the mighty of the earth is spoken of in Psalm 93: "The floods are risen, O Lord, the floods have lift up their voice, the floods lift up their waves. The waves of the sea are mighty, and rage horribly; but yet the Lord who dwelleth on high is mightier."

Or again, in the 82nd, "God standeth in the congregation of princes; He is a Judge among gods," that is, among princes and rulers. "How long will ye give wrong judgment, and accept the persons of the ungodly? Defend the poor and fatherless; see that such as are in need and necessity have right. Deliver the outcast and poor; save them from the hand of the ungodly." Here the Church in her devotions speaks to the world, exhorting great men, and those who are rich in this world, to justice, impartiality, and mercy, and defending the poor, needy, and desolate—two of her special offices; but they will not listen: "they will not be learned, nor understand, but walk on still in darkness." Accordingly the Psalm ends, "Arise, O God, and judge *Thou* the earth; for *Thou* shalt take all heathen to Thine inheritance:" which is, in other words, calling on God to extend His kingdom into all lands.

Other notes of triumph at the sovereignty of the chosen people over the powers of the earth are such as the following:—"He shall subdue the people under us, and the nations under our feet . . . The princes of the people are joined unto the people of the God of Abraham." [Ps. xlvii. 3, 9.] Again, "Great is the Lord, and highly to be praised in the city of our God, even upon His holy hill. The hill of Sion is a fair place, and the joy of the whole earth . . . God is well known in her palaces as a sure refuge. For lo, the kings of the earth are gathered, and gone by together. They marvelled to see such things; they were astonished and suddenly cast down . . . Walk about Sion"—that is, the Church of Christ—"and go round about her, and tell the towers thereof. Mark well her bulwarks, set up her houses, that ye may tell them that come after." [Ps. xlviii. 1–12.] And again, "Jerusalem is built as a city that is at unity in itself . . . There are set thrones of judgment, the thrones of the house of David . . . O pray for the peace of Jerusalem: they shall prosper that love thee. Peace be within thy walls, and plenteousness within thy palaces." [Ps. cxxii. 3, 5, 7.] And again, "The Lord hath chosen Sion to be an habitation for Himself: He hath longed for her. This shall be My rest for ever; here will I dwell, for I have a delight therein." [Ps. cxxxii. 14–18.] Who or what is Sion? What do we mean when we read this Psalm, and say, "The Lord hath chosen Sion"? We mean the Church which He set up when He went away. The Psalm proceeds to speak of David—by whom, in like manner, is meant Christ: "As for His enemies, I shall clothe them with shame; but upon Himself shall His crown flourish."

2. So much on the one side. But now let us turn to the other aspect of the Christian Kingdom, which is much more frequently brought before us in

the Psalms, and to which I wish principally to draw attention: the suffering, troublous state which, in this world, naturally befalls an empire so large, so aggressive, so engrossing, so stately and commanding, yet so destitute of weapons of earth. It provokes persecution at all times, both from its claims and from its weakness.

(1.) Thus then we cry out to God against our enemies. "When the wicked, even mine enemies and my foes, came upon me to eat up my flesh, they stumbled and fell. Though an host of men were laid against me, yet shall not my heart be afraid; and though there rose up war against me, yet will I put my trust in Him . . . Teach me Thy way, O Lord, and lead me in the right way, because of mine enemies." [Ps. xxvii. 2, 3, 13.] Again, "O let not the foot of pride come against me, and let not the hand of the ungodly cast me down." [Ps. xxxvi. 11.] Again, "Strangers are risen up against me, and tyrants, which have not God before their eyes, seek after my soul." [Ps. liv. 3.] And again, "Mine enemies are daily in hand to swallow me up, for they be many that fight against me, O Thou Most Highest." [Ps. lvi. 2.] And again, "Hide me from the gathering together of the froward, and from the insurrection of wicked doers." [Ps. lxiv. 2.] Are the Psalms a dead letter, or are they spirit? Do we use them as a form, or as the voice of our hearts? If we have any meaning when we use them, surely we imply that the Church is always militant, always in warfare, never at ease, never well with the world, never shielded from its hatred, malice, and violence. And you will observe, that it is especially the proud and tyrannical who are her enemies. "Let not the foot of pride come against me." "Tyrants seek after my soul." "Princes also did sit and speak against me [Ps. cxix. 23, 46, 51, 69, 85.] . . . I will speak of Thy testimonies also even before kings [Ps. cxix. 46.] . . . The proud have had me exceedingly in derision; . . . the proud have imagined a lie against me; . . . the proud have digged pits for me . . . Princes have persecuted me without a cause." [Ps. cxix. 51, 69, 85, 161.]

(2.) Next, we lay before Almighty God our desolations. As, for instance, "Thou lettest us be eaten up like sheep, and hast scattered us among the heathen. Thou sellest Thy people for nought, and takest no money for them." [Ps. xliv. 12, 13.] "O God, wherefore art Thou absent from us so long? why is Thy wrath so hot against the sheep of Thy pasture? O think upon Thy congregation, whom Thou hast purchased and redeemed of old." [Ps. lxxiv. 1, 2.] For though the kingdom of the Saints extends and flourishes as a whole, yet it is open to reverses of any magnitude, schisms, defections, losses, in its separate parts.

(3.) And, further, we complain of our captivity. "Who shall give salvation unto Israel out of Sion? When the Lord turneth the captivity of His people, then shall Jacob rejoice, and Israel shall be glad." [Ps. xiv. 11.] "O that the salvation were given unto Israel out of Sion! O that the Lord would deliver His people out of captivity!" [Ps. liii. 7.] "Turn our captivity, O Lord, as the rivers in the south." [Ps. cxxvi. 5.]

(4.) Again, the Psalms say much concerning the poor and needy, and God's protecting them against bad men. "The Lord also will be a defence for the oppressed . . . The poor shall not alway be forgotten; the patient abiding of the meek shall not perish for ever. Up, Lord, and let not man have the upper hand." [Ps. ix. 9–19.] "The ungodly for his own lust doth persecute the poor . . . The poor committeth himself unto Thee, for Thou art the helper of the friendless." [Ps. x. 2, 16.] And in the text, "Lord, Thou hast heard the desire of the poor; . . . to help the fatherless and poor unto their right, that the man of the earth be no more exalted against them." "They smite down Thy people, O Lord, and trouble Thine heritage; . . . the Lord will not fail His people, neither will He forsake His inheritance." [Ps. xciv. 5, 14.] "Our soul is filled with the scornful reproof of the wealthy, and with the despitefulness of the proud." [Ps. cxxiii. 4.] Now consider the state of Christendom during many centuries, when tribes of fierce barbarians poured over its face, or settled in its territory; or when tyrannical kings and nobles oppressed its people, or rose against its rulers and pastors; or when power, whether barbarian or constituted, broke in upon its sacred retirements, ill-treated their holy or studious inmates, destroyed the work or scattered the fruits of years of tranquil diligence; and say whether the Psalter is not just the book which all those variously tried, equally helpless multitudes would choose, as more fitting than any other to express their sorrows and their faith, their prayers and their hopes?

(5.) Once more, the Psalms speak especially of the righteous being in trouble, plead for them, and wait for their deliverance. "The righteous cry, and the Lord heareth them." [Ps. xxxiv. 17.] "Fret not thyself because of the ungodly, neither be thou envious against the evil doers . . . The righteous shall inherit the land, and dwell therein for ever." [Ps. xxxvii. 1, 30.] "I was grieved at the wicked; I do also see the ungodly in such prosperity . . . O how suddenly do they consume, perish, and come to a fearful end!" [Ps. lxxiii. 3, 18.] "The righteous shall flourish like a palm-tree, and shall spread abroad like a cedar in Libanus." [Ps. xcii. 11.] "Do well, O Lord, unto those that are good and true of heart." [Ps. cxxv. 4.] Now, is it not just the peculiarity of the Christian Church, not only that it is slandered, scorned, ill-used by the world, but that all this happens to it *because* it is holy,—for its righteousness' sake?

Thus, on the whole, we see that in the Psalms a very wonderful provision is made by anticipation for the wants of the Christian Church. It is just the book of devotions needed by it, as it ever has been used; supposing it to be so

356

great and so weak, so vast a kingdom, but not of this world, as the Prophets and the Evangelists describe it to be.

Now here, of course, it is obvious to make this objection—*we* are *not* in persecution; for us to use the language of the Psalms is unreal. Christians in our own happy country have every thing their own way. The profession of the Gospel is an honour, the rejection of it a disgrace. Either, then, we are not a part of the Kingdom of Heaven, or that Kingdom is not what Gospels, Prophecies, and Psalms describe it to be. But many answers may be made to this objection.

1. First, it is not necessary that all parts of the Church should be in persecution at once, either to fulfil the Scripture statements, or to justify the use of the Psalms. It suffers in its different portions at different times. We have had our trials before now; and other portions of the Church are now under similar, or rather worse, afflictions. Of course, if we are members of the *one* body of Christ, we must feel for the rest, in whatever part of the world they are, when they are persecuted, and must remember them in our prayers. Nor does it avail to say that we differ from them in faith: what is that to the purpose in a question of love? Either Christianity is shut up in Britain, or not: if it is, Christ has no longer a Catholic Church, and then, certainly, the prophecies are not now fulfilled to us; or it does exist in other lands, and then we are bound to sympathize in the troubles which Christians there undergo for the name of Christ.

2. But, again, in spite of her prosperity for the moment, even in this country, the Church of Christ is in peril, as is obvious. Can we number the tens and hundreds of thousands who shrink from our Church as if antichristian, or who hate her for being Christian, and wish her downfall? Is there no battle between the Church and the world in this country? and no malevolence, no scorn, no unbelief, no calumny; no prospect, or, at least, materials of open persecution, though persecution, through God's mercy, as yet be away? Consider our great towns, and reflect what a scourge in God's anger they might be upon our many sins, unless He were most merciful.

3. But, further, if we are not altogether in a position to use the words of the Psalter, if we are too happy and secure, in too great abundance and too much honour, to be able to use them naturally, is it not possible that so far we really do lack a note of the Church? is there not a fear lest the world be friends with us, because we are friends with the world? This is no new or strange occurrence in the history of the Gospel. It is not peculiar to our age or country; it is the great disease of the Church in all ages. Whatever corruptions of doctrine there have been at particular times and places, no corruption has been so great as this practical corruption, which has existed in its measure in all times

and places—the serving God for the sake of mammon; the loving religion from the love of the world. And as to ourselves, I fear, it is no declamatory statement to say, that there never was an age in which it existed more largely, never an age in which the Church contained so many untrue members; that is, so many persons who profess themselves her members, when they know little or nothing about the real meaning of membership, and remain within her pale for some reasons short of religious and right ones. For instance, to put one question on the subject,—How many supporters of Christ's holy Catholic Church do you think would be left among us, if her cause were found to be, not the cause of order, as it happens to be now, but the cause of disorder, as it was when Christ came and his Apostles preached? It was the cry of the Jews of Thessalonica against St. Paul and St. Silas, "These that have turned the world upside down, are come hither also." [Acts xvii. 6.] Is it not as plain as the day, that the mass of persons who support the Church in her legal privileges, do so, not so much because they care for the Kingdom of the Saints, as because they think that the downfall of our civil institutions is involved in her downfall? I do not say that they have no love for the Church, but they have a greater love for worldly prosperity. They have just so much more love for the world than for the Church, as would lead them, were the peace of the world and the welfare of the Church at variance with each other, to side with the world against the Church. As it is, they see that the influence of the Gospel is on the side of good order; that it tends to make men contented and obedient subjects; that it keeps the lower orders from outbreaks; that it makes a firm stand against rebellion, sedition, conspiracy, riot, and fanaticism; that it is the best guarantee for the security of private property. It *does* all these benefits; they *are* benefits; and we may rightly be thankful for them. But numbers of professing Churchmen consider them *the* special benefits of Christ's Kingdom, caring little for the unseen and spiritual blessings which are its true and proper gifts. Look round upon our political parties, our literature, our science, our periodical publications: is it not too plain to need a word of proof, that religion is in the main honoured because it tends to make this life happier, and is expedient for the preservation of our persons, property, advantages, and position in the world? Can a greater stigma be placed upon any doctrine in the judgment of the community than that it is anti-social, or that it is irksome, gloomy, or inconvenient?

No wonder, then, while we are in the midst of this serious corruption, that the words of inspired Psalmists, which have been the solace of the Church in every age, do not seem real to us. Let us but put off the love of the world, and follow the precepts of our Lord and His Apostles, and then see in a little while *where* we should all find ourselves, and what would be the condition of the Church.

Meanwhile, whether we will believe it or no, the truth remains, that the strength of the Church, as heretofore, does not lie in earthly law, or human countenance, or civil station, but in her proper gifts; in those great gifts which our Lord pronounced to be beatitudes. Blessed are the poor in spirit, the mourners, the meek, the thirsters after righteousness, the merciful, the pure in heart, the peacemakers, the persecuted.

Feasting in Captivity[†]

"The fast of the fourth month, and the fast of the fifth,
and the fast of the seventh, and the fast of the tenth,
shall be to the house of Judah joy and gladness, and cheerful feasts;
therefore love the truth and peace."
Zech. viii, 19

W HEN we reflect upon the present state of the Holy Church throughout the world, so different from that which was promised to her in prophecy, the doubt is apt to suggest itself to us, whether it is right to rejoice when there is so much to mourn over and to fear. Is it right to keep holiday, when the Spouse of Christ is in bondage, and the iron almost enters into her soul? We know what prophecy promises us, a holy Church set upon a hill; an imperial Church, far-spreading among the nations, loving truth and peace, binding together all hearts in charity, and uttering the words of God from inspired lips; a Kingdom of Heaven upon earth, that is at unity within itself, peace within its walls and plenteousness within its palaces; "a glorious Church, not having spot or wrinkle or any such thing, but holy and without blemish." And, alas! what do we see? We see the Kingdom of God to all appearance broken into fragments—authority in abeyance—separate portions in insurrection—brother armed against brother—truth, a matter not of faith but of controversy. And looking at our own portion of the heavenly heritage, we see heresies of the most deadly character around us and within us; we see error stalking abroad in the light of day and over the length of the land unrebuked—nay, invading high places; while the maintainers of Christian truth are afraid to speak, lest it should offend those to whom it is a duty to defer. We see discipline utterly thrown down, the sacraments and ordinances of grace open to those who cannot come without profaning them and getting harm from them. Works of penance almost unthought of; the world and the Church mixed together; and those who discern and mourn over all this looked upon with aversion, because they will not prophesy smooth things and speak peace where there is no peace. On us have fallen the times described by the Psalmist when he laments, "Thou hast broken the covenant of Thy servant,

---

[†] *Sermons on Subjects of the Day* (1843), Sermon 25, preached on Thursday, Sept. 22, 1842, the anniversary of the consecration of the chapel in which the service was held.

360

and cast his crown to the ground. Thou hast overthrown all his hedges and broken down his strongholds . . . Thou hast put out his glory and cast his throne down to the ground. The days of his youth hast Thou shortened, and covered him with dishonour." The days of age have come on us, "the evil days" "when thou shalt say, I have no pleasure in them;" [Eccles. xii. 1.] the days when the Bridegroom has been taken away, and when men should fast;— how then in the day of our fast can we find pleasure and keep festival?

What profit is the full gathering and the concourse of men, when all the families of Israel that remain should rather mourn, "every family apart and their wives apart"? Music is for the merry; Darius put away his instruments of music when the Prophet was lost to him. The father of the family had music and dancing, and killed the fatted calf, when the wanderer came home. Tobit in captivity attempted to eat the bread of joyfulness on the feast of Pentecost, and was suddenly reduced to "eat his meat in heaviness," remembering the prophecy of Amos, as he said, "Your feasts shall be turned into mourning, and all your mirth into lamentation." Flowers are for the innocent and gay; how suit they with the dark prison and the fretting chain? Harmony in form and colour, the high arch and the rich window, what have these in common with the fallen and the polluted? Beauty for ashes, the oil of joy for mourning, the garment of praise for the spirit of heaviness,—these surely should be reserved for the year of Jubilee, and when the season of redemption draweth near. This is what may be said, not without plausibility.

Nay, not said plausibly but felt acutely; so acutely felt, as to hinder the mind from taking part in the rejoicing to which it is invited. When men discern duly the forlorn state in which the Spouse of Christ at present lies, how can they have the heart to rejoice? "The ark and Israel and Judah abide in tents," said Uriah, "and the servants of my lord are encamped in the open fields; shall I then go into mine house to eat and to drink? . . . as thou livest, and as thy soul liveth, I will not do this thing." The desponding soul falls back when it makes the effort; it is not equal to the ceremonial which comes natural to light hearts, and at best but coldly obeys what they anticipate without being bidden. What is to be done with this dull, dispirited, wearied, forlorn, foreboding heart of ours? "By the waters of Babylon we sat down and wept, when we remembered thee, O Sion. As for our harps, we hanged them up upon the trees that are therein. For they that led us away captive required of us then a song, and melody in our heaviness,—Sing us one of the songs of Sion. How shall we sing the Lord's song in a strange land?"

Yet, since there is some danger of over-sensitiveness in this matter, it may be useful here to make some remarks upon it.

This then must be ever kept in mind, when such thoughts arise within us, that cheerfulness and lightness of heart are not only privileges, but duties. Cheerfulness is a great Christian duty. Whatever be our circumstances, within or without, though "without be fightings and within be fears," yet the Apostle's words are express, "Rejoice in the Lord *always*." That sorrow, that solicitude, that fear, that repentance, is not Christian which has not its portion of Christian joy; for "God is greater than our hearts," and no evil, past or future, within or without, is equal to this saying, that Christ has died and reconciled the world unto Himself. We are ever in His Presence, be we cast down, or be we exalted; and "in His Presence is the fulness of joy." "Let the brother of low degree rejoice in that he is exalted, but the rich in that he is made low." [James i. 9, 10.] "He that is called in the Lord, being a servant, is the Lord's freeman; likewise also he that is called, being free, is Christ's servant." [1 Cor. vii. 22.] Whether we eat or drink, or whatever we do, to His glory must we do all, and if to His glory, to our great joy; for His service is perfect freedom: and what are the very Angels in heaven but His ministers? Nothing is evil but separation from Him; while we are allowed to visit His Temple, we cannot but "enter into His gates with gladness and thanksgiving, and into His courts with praise." "Is any," then, "among us afflicted? let him pray; is any merry? let him sing psalms."

Such even was the conduct of the devout Israelites, who had no promise such as we have, of a continual Divine Presence, which is our spiritual life,—which is the life of our very sorrow, if it be godly, the life of our repentance, our fear, our self-chastisement; and in which we must rejoice, because through it we repent, are in fear, and afflict ourselves. Even Jews, we see, attempted to rejoice in captivity, though it was prophesied against them, "I will turn your feasts into mourning, and all your songs into lamentation;" [Amos viii. 10.] whereas the very reverse is graciously assured in the text to the Gospel Church, that her times of humiliation should be times of rejoicing. "The fast of the fourth month, and the fast of the fifth, and the fast of the seventh, and the fast of the tenth, shall be to the house of Judah joy and gladness and cheerful feasts; therefore love the truth and peace."

What did Hezekiah and Josiah in those mournful times when wrath hung over the chosen people? In the Paschal Feast held by the former king, he prayed, "The good Lord pardon every one that prepareth his heart to seek God, the Lord God of his fathers, though he be not cleansed according to the purification of the sanctuary." And the children of Israel kept the feast seven days with great sadness, and the Levites and priests praised the Lord with loud instruments, and Hezekiah spake comfortably to the Levites,—so that "there was great joy in Jerusalem; for since the time of Solomon . . . there was not the like in Jerusalem." And of Josiah's passover it is said, "for there was no passover like to that kept in Israel, from the days of Samuel the Prophet."

Again, what could be more miserable and forlorn than the state of the Jews when they returned from captivity? yet, in spite of the ruins among which they dwelt, God *had* shown them mercy, and thereby given them hope; He had begun to be gracious to them, and though they had no heart for the work of rebuilding the Temple, when so many things were against them, and the new fabric would for certain be so poor and unworthy at the best, yet it was their duty to look to the future and rejoice. "Thus speaketh the Lord of hosts, saying, This people say, The time is not come, the time that the Lord's house should be built." [Haggai i. 2.] And He added for their encouragement, "According to the word that I covenanted with you when ye came out of Egypt, so My Spirit *remaineth* among you: fear ye not." [Haggai ii. 5.] And still more appositely, as we read elsewhere, "Nehemiah and Ezra the priest the scribe, and the Levites that taught the people, said unto all the people, This day is holy unto the Lord your God; mourn not, nor weep. For all the people wept, when they heard the words of the Law. Then he said unto them, Go your way, eat the fat, and drink the sweet, and send portions unto them for whom nothing is prepared: for this day is holy unto our Lord; neither be ye sorry, for the joy of the Lord is your strength." [Neh. viii. 9, 10.] The sacred narrative proceeds; "So the Levites stilled all the people, saying, Hold your peace, for the day is holy; neither be ye grieved. And all the people went their way to eat, and to drink, and to send portions, and to make great mirth, because they had understood the words that were declared unto them." And after this they proceeded to keep the feast of tabernacles, with "olive branches and pine branches, and myrtle branches, and palm branches, and branches of thick trees, to make booths, as it is written . . . And all the congregation of them that were come again out of the captivity made booths, and sat under the booths; for since the days of Joshua the son of Nun, unto that day, had not the children of Israel done so. And there was very great gladness."

We have a still more remarkable and solemn instance of the duty of keeping festival and rejoicing even in the darkest day, in our Lord's own history. If there was a season in which gloom was allowable, it was on the days and hours before His Passion: but He who came to bring joy on earth and not sorrow; who came eating and drinking, because He was the true Bread from heaven; who changed the water into wine at a marriage feast, and fed the hungry thousands in the wilderness; even in that awful time when His spirit fainted within Him, when, as He testified, His "soul was troubled," and He was led to cry, "Father, save Me from this hour," and more solemnly and secretly, "If it be possible, let this cup pass from Me;" He, our great Exemplar, kept the feast—nay, anticipated it, as if though He Himself was to be the very Paschal Lamb, still He was not thereby excused from sharing in the typical rite. "With desire" did He "desire to eat that passover" with His disciples before He suffered. And a few days before it, He took part in a public and (as it were) triumphant pageant, as though the bitterness of death had been already passed. He came to Bethany, where He had raised Lazarus; and there they made Him a supper; and Mary took the precious ointment and poured it on His head, and anointed His feet, and the house was filled with the fragrance. And next the people took branches of palm-trees, and went forth to meet Him, and strewed their garments in the way, and cried, "Hosanna, Blessed is the King of Israel, that cometh in the Name of the Lord!"

To rejoice, then, and to keep festival, is a Christian duty, under all circumstances. Indeed, is not this plain, by considering the obligation, yet the nature, of that chief Gospel Ordinance which we celebrate today? There is an ordinance which we are bound to observe always till the Lord come: is it an ordinance of humiliation and self-abasement, or is it a feast? The Holy Eucharist is a Feast; we cannot help feasting, we cannot elude our destiny of joy and thanksgiving, if we would be Christians.

As I have already remarked, the same rule is to be observed even in the instance of personal penitence, which is on no account to be separated from the duty of Christian cheerfulness. Penitents are as little at liberty to release themselves from Christian joy as from Christian love; love alone can make repentance available; and where there is love, there joy must be present also. The true penance is not to put away God's blessings, but to add chastisements. As Adam did not lose the flowers of Eden on his fall, but thorns and thistles sprung up around them; and he still had bread, but was forced to eat it in the sweat of his face; and as the Israelites ate their Paschal lamb with bitter herbs; so in like manner we show our repentance, not in rejecting what God gives, but in adding what sin deserves.

And I will add, that there is much which is expedient as well as dutiful in this simple adherence to the plain formularies of Christian devotion and practice, even under circumstances unsuitable to them. For if these observances are inconsistent with our actual state, they will force themselves upon our minds as a mockery, and thus suggest to us of what we ought to be, and make us discontented with what we are. Our Lord gives us a pattern of this in His very Prayer, in which we ask that our trespasses may be forgiven, *as* we forgive them that trespass against us; words which are quite out of place, or rather words which will do us harm, if we are not what Christians should be in spirit, but remember injuries and cherish malice. And thus, in like manner, when we profess to hold the Apostolic faith, *yet* take up with modern notions of Gospel truth, what is this but a great inconsistency?—yet a profitable one withal, if through God's grace the profession of what is ancient at length overcomes our attachment to what is novel and unauthorized. And, again, what can be more incongruous than for the run of Christians of this age to call themselves Catholics? yet their calling themselves so may be the first step to their becoming so. And how little fitted are we to discharge ecclesiastical censures, or to enforce ecclesiastical discipline, or to live by rule! yet, by attempting to do so, we may learn our wants, and seek the supply of them. And how unlike are the best among us to the Saints and Martyrs of old time; to St. Cyprian, or St. Basil, or St. Ambrose, or St. Leo! and what an utter mockery it is to couple their names with modern names, and to compare their words with our words, as is sometimes done! yet, if true love be the tie that binds us to them, since they most certainly cannot move towards us, we through God's mercy perchance may be drawn to them. And in like manner, poor and mean and unworthy as may be our attempts at a ceremonial on days such as this, yet we trust He will accept it, as He did her offering, who did "what she could," and will vouchsafe to bless it and to make it a means of teaching us a deeper reverence and a more constraining love, and will draw us on into the very bosom of Catholic sanctity and the very heart of Catholic affection, by observances and usages which in themselves are little worth, and excite the jeer or the criticism of the worldly or the profane. In a word, if we claim to *be* the Church, let us act *like* the Church, and we shall *become* the Church. Here, as in other matters, to doubt is to fail, and to go forward is to succeed.

One danger there is,—that of our attempting one of these aspects or constituent portions of the Christian character while we neglect the other. To attempt Apostolical Christianity at all, we must attempt it all. It is a whole, and cannot be divided; and to attempt one aspect of it only, is to attempt something else which looks like it, instead of it. "All is not gold that glitters," as the proverb goes; and all is not Catholic and Apostolic which affects what is high and beautiful, and speaks to the imagination. Religion has two sides, a severe side, and a beautiful; and we shall be sure to swerve from the narrow way which leads to life, if we indulge ourselves in what is beautiful, while we put aside what is severe.

I have a hope, my brethren, that we are not committing this fault; for to be aware of the danger is one special preservative against it, in the case of those who wish to do what is right. Had we no other memento of the duty of combining strictness of life with our attention to external religion, this very day would remind us of it, occurring as it does in so close a connexion with the Ember-week. We commemorate the dedication of this Chapel to God's service, either, as in this year, in the *midst* of the fast, or, as on other years, just *after* it. If, in the words of the text, our fasts issue in cheerful feasts, still this is only saying, in other words, that our feasts spring out of fasts.

And there are other reasons why we should be preserved (through God's mercy) from the temptation of indulging in (what may be called) the luxuries of religious worship; still there is great cause to fear that others are not equally out of danger. It were well, if others had more of that despondency and trouble of mind about the state of the Church, which I described when I began; it might preserve them from a very hurtful excess. Too many men at this time are for raising a high superstructure ere they have laid a deep foundation. They shrink from sowing in tears, though they would fain reap in joy. The austere doctrines of the Gospel they turn from them, like him who said, "Be it far from Thee, Lord: this shall not be unto Thee;" [Matt. xvi. 22.]—they stumble at the doctrine of post-baptismal sin; and what part of their creed can be profitable to them, if this is neglected? They are slow to admit that our times are like those of backsliding Israel, or treacherous Judah; and how can they attempt to mend them, if they see them not as God sees them? They scoff at the ascetic life of the Saints as an extravagance or corruption; or they slur over their austerities, as if they were an accident of their religion peculiar to *their* times; and they would live like the world, yet worship like the Angels. These things being so, misgivings of mind arise of necessity about the present growing attention, which is seen on all sides of us, to church architecture and church decoration; not as if all this were not right in itself, but lest we should be too fast about it; lest it be disjoined in the case of the multitude from real seriousness, from deep repentance, from strict conscientiousness, from inward sanctity, from godly fear and awe. There are other things to be done first. However, we can but leave the issue to God's Providence; and pray Him, who seems at present engaged in a great work among us, to overrule all our mistakes to His glory, and to the welfare of the Catholic Church, and to our salvation.

Let us recollect this for our own profit; that, if it is our ambition to follow the Christians of the first ages, as they followed the Apostles, and the Apostles followed Christ, they had the discomfort of this world without its compensating gifts. No high cathedrals, no decorated altars, no white-robed priests, no choirs for sacred psalmody, nothing of the order, majesty, and beauty of devotional services had they; but they *had* trials, afflictions, solitariness, contempt, ill-usage. They were "in weariness and painfulness, in watchings often, in hunger and thirst, in fastings often, in cold and nakedness." If we have only the enjoyment and none of the pain, and they only the pain and none of the enjoyment, in what does our Christianity resemble theirs? what are the tokens of identity between us? why do we not call theirs one religion and ours another? What points in common are there between the easy religion of this day, and the religion of St. Athanasius, or St. Chrysostom? How do the two agree, except that the name of Christianity is given to both of them?

O may we be wiser than to be satisfied with an untrue profession and a mere shadow of the Gospel! May God raise our hearts on high to seek first His kingdom and His righteousness, that all other things may he added to us! My brethren, let what is inward be chief with you, and what is outward be subordinate! Think nothing preferable to a knowledge of yourselves, true repentance, a resolve to live to God, to die to the world, deep humility, hatred of sin, and of yourselves as you are sinners, a clear and habitual view of the coming judgment. Let this be first; and secondly, labour for the unity of the Church; let the peace of Jerusalem and the edification of the body of Christ be an object of prayer, close upon that of your own personal salvation. Pray that a Divine Influence may touch the hearts of men, and that in spite of themselves, while they wonder at themselves, not to say while others wonder at them, they may confess and preach those Catholic truths which at present they scorn or revile; that so at length the language of the prophecy from which the text is taken, and which has been read in the course of the Service, may be fulfilled to us; "I am returned unto Zion, and will dwell in the midst of Jerusalem," and "the seed shall be prosperous, the vine shall give her fruit, and the ground shall give her increase, and the heavens shall give their dew;" and "many people and strong nations shall come to seek the Lord of Hosts in Jerusalem, and to pray before the Lord."

Integrity of Catholic Doctrine[†]

THE CATHOLIC DOCTRINES . . . are members of one family, and suggestive, or correlative, or confirmatory, or illustrative of each other. In other words, one furnishes evidence to another, and all to each of them; if this is proved, that becomes probable; if this and that are both probable, but for different reasons, each adds to the other its own probability. The Incarnation is the antecedent of the doctrine of Mediation, and the archetype both of the Sacramental principle, and of the merits of Saints. From the doctrine of Mediation follow the Atonement, the Mass, the merits of Martyrs and Saints, their invocation and *cultus*. From the Sacramental principle come the Sacraments properly so called, the unity of the Church, and the Holy See as its type and centre; the authority of Councils; the sanctity of rites; the veneration of holy places, shrines, images, vessels, furniture, and vestments. Of the Sacraments, Baptism is developed into Confirmation on the one hand; into Penance, Purgatory, and Indulgences on the other; and the Eucharist into the Real Presence, adoration of the Host, Resurrection of the body, and the virtue of Relics. Again, the doctrine of the Sacraments leads to the doctrine of Justification; Justification to that of Original Sin; Original Sin to the merit of Celibacy. Nor do these separate developments stand independent of each other, but by cross relations they are connected, and grow together while they grow from one. The Mass and Real Presence are parts of one; the veneration of Saints and their Relics are parts of one; their intercessory power, and the Purgatorial State, and, again, the Mass and that State are correlative; Celibacy is the characteristic mark of Monachism and of the Priesthood. You must accept the whole, or reject the whole; reduction does but enfeeble, and amputation mutilate. It is trifling to receive all but something which is as integral as any other portion; and, on the other hand, it is a solemn thing to receive any part, for, before you know where you are, you may be carried on by a stern logical necessity to accept the whole.

[†] Excerpt from *Essay on the Development of Christian Doctrine* (1845), Part 1, chapter 2, section 3. The selection, as well as its title, is from William Samuel Lilly's *Characteristics*.

Devotion to the Blessed Virgin[†]

I T HAS BEEN anxiously asked, whether the honours paid to St. Mary, which have grown out of devotion to her Almighty Lord and Son, do not, in fact, tend to weaken that devotion; and whether, from the nature of the case, it is possible so to exalt a creature without withdrawing the heart from the Creator. . . . I would here observe that the question is one of fact, not of presumption or conjecture. The abstract lawfulness of the honours paid to St. Mary, and their distinction in theory from the incommunicable worship paid to God, are points which have already been dwelt upon; but here the question turns upon their practicability or expedience, which must be determined by the fact whether they are practicable, and whether they have been found to be expedient.

1.

Here I observe, first, that, to those who admit the authority of the Fathers of Ephesus, the question is in no slight degree answered by their sanction of the [*Theotokos*] or "Mother of God," as a title of St. Mary, and as given in order to protect the doctrine of the Incarnation, and to preserve the faith of Catholics from a specious Humanitarianism. And if we take a survey at least of Europe, we shall find that it is not those religious communions which are characterized by devotion towards the Blessed Virgin that have ceased to adore her Eternal Son, but those very bodies, (when allowed by the law,) which have renounced devotion to her. The regard for His glory, which was professed in that keen jealousy of her exaltation, has not been supported by the event. They who were accused of worshipping a creature in His stead, still worship Him; their accusers, who hoped to worship Him so purely, they, wherever obstacles to the development of their principles have been removed, have ceased to worship Him altogether.

2.

Next, it must be observed, that the tone of the devotion paid to the Blessed Mary is altogether distinct from that which is paid to her Eternal Son, and to the Holy Trinity, as we must certainly allow on inspection of the Catholic

---

[†] Excerpt from *Essay on the Development of Christian Doctrine* (1845), Part 2, chapter 11, section 2. For further texts on Our Lady, see below, p. 395 and p. 438.

services. The supreme and true worship paid to the Almighty is severe, profound, awful, as well as tender, confiding, and dutiful. Christ is addressed as true God, while He is true Man; as our Creator and Judge, while He is most loving, gentle, and gracious. On the other hand, towards St. Mary the language employed is affectionate and ardent, as towards a mere child of Adam; though subdued, as coming from her sinful kindred. How different, for instance, is the tone of the *Dies Iræ* from that of the *Stabat Mater*. In the "Tristis et afflicta Mater Unigeniti," in the "Virgo virginum præclara Mihi jam non sis amara, Pœnas mecum divide," in the "Fac me verè tecum flere," we have an expression of the feelings with which we regard one who is a creature and a mere human being; but in the "Rex tremendæ majestatis qui salvandos salvas gratis, salva me Fons pietatis," the "Ne me perdas illâ die," the "Juste judex ultionis, donum fac remissionis," the "Oro supplex et acclinis, cor contritum quasi cinis," the "Pie Jesu Domine, dona eis requiem," we hear the voice of the creature raised in hope and love, yet in deep awe to his Creator, Infinite Benefactor, and Judge.

Or again, how distinct is the language of the Breviary Services on the Festival of Pentecost, or of the Holy Trinity, from the language of the Services for the Assumption! How indescribably majestic, solemn, and soothing is the "Veni Creator Spiritus," the "Altissimi donum Dei, Fons vivus, ignis, charitas," or the "Vera et una Trinitas, una et summa Deitas, sancta et una Unitas," the "Spes nostra, salus nostra, honor noster, O beata Trinitas," the "Charitas Pater, gratia Filius, communicatio Spiritus Sanctus, O beata Trinitas;" "Libera nos, salva nos, vivifica nos, O beata Trinitas!" How fond, on the contrary, how full of sympathy and affection, how stirring and animating, in the Office for the Assumption, is the "Virgo prudentissima, quo pregrederis, quasi aurora valde rutilans? filia Sion, tota formosa et suavis es, pulcra ut luna, electa ut sol;" the "Sicut dies verni circumdabant eam flores rosarum, et lilia convallium;" the "Maria Virgo assumpta est ad æthereum thalamum in quo Rex regum stellato sedet solio;" and the "Gaudent Angeli, laudantes benedicunt Dominum." And so again, the Antiphon, the "Ad te clamamus exules filii Hevæ, ad te suspiramus gementes et flentes in hac lacrymarum valle," and "Eia ergo, advocata nostra, illos tuos misericordes oculos ad nos converte," and "O clemens, O pia, O dulcis Virgo Maria." Or the Hymn, "Ave Maria stella, Dei Mater alma," and "Virgo singularis, inter omnes mitis, nos culpis solutos, mites fac et castos."

3.

Nor does it avail to object that, in this contrast of devotional exercises, the human will supplant the Divine, from the infirmity of our nature; for, I repeat, the question is one of fact, whether it has done so. And next it must be asked, whether the character of much of the Protestant devotion towards our Lord has been that of adoration at all; and not rather such as we pay to an excellent human being, that is, no higher devotion than that which Catholics pay to St. Mary, differing from it, however, in often being familiar, rude, and earthly. Carnal minds will ever create a carnal worship for themselves; and to forbid them the service of the Saints will have no tendency to teach them the worship of God.

Moreover, it must be observed, what is very important, that great and constant as is the devotion which the Catholic pays to the Blessed Mary, it has a special province, and has far more connexion with the public services and the festive aspect of Christianity, and with certain extraordinary offices which she holds, than with what is strictly personal and primary in religion.

Two instances will serve in illustration of this, and they are but samples of many others.[36]

4.

(1.) For example, St. Ignatius' Spiritual Exercises are among the most approved methods of devotion in the modern Catholic Church; they proceed from one of the most celebrated of her Saints, and have the praise of Popes, and of the most eminent masters of the spiritual life. A Bull of Paul the Third's "approves, praises, and sanctions all and everything contained in them;" indulgences are granted to the performance of them by the same Pope, by Alexander the Seventh, and by Benedict the Fourteenth. St. Carlo Borromeo declared that he learned more from them than from all other books together; St. Francis de Sales calls them "a holy method of reformation," and they are the model on which all the extraordinary devotions of religious men or bodies, and the course of missions, are conducted. If there is a document which is the authoritative exponent of the inward communion of the members of the modern Catholic Church with their God and Saviour, it is this work.

The Exercises are directed to the removal of obstacles in the way of the soul's receiving and profiting by the gifts of God. They undertake to effect this in three ways; by removing all objects of this world, and, as it were, bringing the soul "into the solitude where God may speak to its heart;" next, by setting before it the ultimate end of man, and its own deviations from it, the beauty

---

[36] *E.g.* the *De Imitatione*, the *Introduction à la Vie Dévote*, the *Spiritual Combat*, the *Anima Divota*, the *Paradisus Animæ*, the *Regula Cleri*, the *Garden of the Soul*, &c., &c. Also, the Roman Catechism, drawn up expressly for Parish instruction, a book in which, out of nearly 600 pages, scarcely half-a-dozen make mention of the Blessed Virgin, though without any disparagement thereby, or thought of disparagement, of her special prerogatives.

of holiness, and the pattern of Christ; and, lastly, by giving rules for its correction. They consist of a course of prayers, meditations, self-examinations, and the like, which in its complete extent lasts thirty days; and these are divided into three stages,—the *Via Purgativa*, in which sin is the main subject of consideration; the *Via Illuminativa*, which is devoted to the contemplation of our Lord's passion, involving the process of the determination of our calling; and the *Via Unitiva*, in which we proceed to the contemplation of our Lord's resurrection and ascension.

5.

No more need be added in order to introduce the remark for which I have referred to these Exercises; viz. that in a work so highly sanctioned, so widely received, so intimately bearing upon the most sacred points of personal religion, very slight mention occurs of devotion to the Blessed Virgin, Mother of God. There is one mention of her in the rule given for the first Prelude or preparation, in which the person meditating is directed to consider as before him a church, or other place with Christ in it, St. Mary, and whatever else is suitable to the subject of meditation. Another is in the third Exercise, in which one of the three addresses is made to our Lady, Christ's Mother, requesting earnestly "her intercession with her Son;" to which is to be added the Ave Mary. In the beginning of the Second Week there is a form of offering ourselves to God in the presence of "His infinite goodness," and with the witness of His "glorious Virgin Mother Mary, and the whole host of heaven." At the end of the Meditation upon the Angel Gabriel's mission to St. Mary, there is an address to each Divine Person, to "the Word Incarnate and to His Mother." In the Meditation upon the Two Standards, there is an address prescribed to St. Mary to implore grace from her Son through her, with an Ave Mary after it.

In the beginning of the Third Week one address is prescribed to Christ; or three, if devotion incites, to Mother, Son, and Father. In the description given of three different modes of prayer we are told, if we would imitate the Blessed Mary, we must recommend ourselves to her, as having power with her Son, and presently the Ave Mary, *Salve Regina*, and other forms are prescribed, as is usual after all prayers. And this is pretty much the whole of the devotion, if it may so be called, which is recommended towards St. Mary in the course of so many apparently as a hundred and fifty Meditations, and those chiefly on the events in our Lord's earthly history as recorded in Scripture. It would seem then that whatever be the influence of the doctrines connected with the Blessed Virgin and the Saints in the Catholic Church, at least they do not impede or obscure the freest exercise and the fullest manifestation of the devotional feelings towards God and Christ.

6

(2.) The other instance which I give in illustration is of a different kind, but is suitable to mention. About forty little books have come into my possession which are in circulation among the laity at Rome, and answer to the smaller publications of the Christian Knowledge Society among ourselves. They have been taken almost at hazard from a number of such works, and are of various lengths; some running to as many as two or three hundred pages, others consisting of scarce a dozen. They may be divided into three classes:—a third part consists of books on practical subjects; another third is upon the Incarnation and Passion; and of the rest, a portion is upon the Sacraments, especially the Holy Eucharist, with two or three for the use of Missions, but the greater part is about the Blessed Virgin.

As to the class on practical subjects, they are on such as the following: "La Consolazione degl' Infermi;" "Pensieri di una donna sul vestire moderno;" "L'Inferno Aperto; "Il Purgatorio Aperto;" St. Alphonso Liguori's " Massime eterne;" other Maxims by St. Francis de Sales for every day in the year; "Pratica per ben confessarsi e communicarsi;" and the like.

The titles of the second class on the Incarnation and Passion are such as "Gesu dalla Croce al cuore del peccatore;" "Novena del Ss. Natale di G. C.;" "Associazione pel culto perpetuo del divin cuore;" "Compendio della Passione."

In the third are "Il Mese Eucaristico," "Il divoto di Maria," Feasts of the Blessed Virgin, &c.

7

These books in all three divisions are, as even the titles of some of them show, in great measure made up of Meditations; such are the "Breve e pie Meditazioni" of P. Crasset; the "Meditazioni per ciascun giorno del mese sulla Passione;" the "Meditazioni per l'ora Eucaristica." Now of these it may be said generally, that in the body of the Meditation St. Mary is hardly mentioned at all. For instance, in the Meditations on the Passion, a book used for distribution, through two hundred and seventy-seven pages St. Mary is not once named. In the Prayers for Mass which are added, she is introduced, at the Confiteor, thus, "I pray the Virgin, the Angels, the Apostles, and all the Saints of heaven to intercede," &c.; and in the Preparation for Penance, she is once addressed, after our Lord, as the Refuge of sinners, with the Saints and Guardian Angel; and at the end of the Exercise there is a similar prayer of four lines for the intercession of St. Mary, Angels and Saints of heaven. In the Exercise for Communion, in a prayer to our Lord, "my only and infinite good, my treasure, my life, my paradise, my all," the merits of the Saints are mentioned, "especially of St. Mary." She is also mentioned with Angels and Saints at the termination.

In a collection of "Spiritual Lauds" for Missions, of thirty-six Hymns, we find as many as eleven addressed to St. Mary, or relating to her, among which are translations of the *Ave Maris Stella*, and the *Stabat Mater*, and the *Salve Regina*; and one is on "the sinner's reliance on Mary." Five, however, which are upon Repentance, are entirely engaged upon the subjects of our Lord and sin, with the exception of an address to St. Mary at the end of two of them. Seven others, upon sin, the Crucifixion, and the Four Last Things, do not mention the Blessed Virgin's name.

To the Manual for the Perpetual Adoration of the Divine Heart of Jesus there is appended one chapter on the Immaculate Conception.

8.

One of the most important of these books is the French *Pensez-y bien*, which seems a favourite, since there are two translations of it, one of them being the fifteenth edition; and it is used for distribution in Missions. In these reflections there is scarcely a word said of St. Mary. At the end there is a Method of reciting the Crown of the Seven Dolours of the Virgin Mary, which contains seven prayers to her, and the *Stabat Mater*.

One of the longest in the whole collection is a tract consisting principally of Meditations on the Holy Communion; under the title of the "Eucharistic Month," as already mentioned. In these "Preparations," "Aspirations," &c., St. Mary is but once mentioned, and that in a prayer addressed to our Lord. "O my sweetest Brother," it says with an allusion to the Canticles, "who, being made Man for my salvation, hast sucked the milk from the virginal breast of her, who is my Mother by grace," &c. In a small "Instruction" given to children on their first Communion, there are the following questions and answers: "Is our Lady in the Host? No. Are the Angels and the Saints? No. Why not? Because they have no place there."

9.

Now coming to those in the third class, which directly relate to the Blessed Mary, such as "Esercizio ad Onore dell' addolorato cuore di Maria," "Novena di Preparazione alla festa dell' Assunzione," "Li Quindici Misteri del Santo Rosario," the principal is Father Segneri's "Il divoto di Maria," which requires a distinct notice. It is far from the intention of these remarks to deny the high place which the Holy Virgin holds in the devotion of Catholics; I am but bringing evidence of its not interfering with that incommunicable and awful relation which exists between the creature and the Creator; and, if the foregoing instances show, as far as they go, that that relation is preserved inviolate in such honours as are paid to St. Mary, so will this treatise throw light upon the *rationale* by which the distinction is preserved between the worship of God and the honour of an exalted creature, and that in singular accordance with the remarks made in the foregoing Section.

10.

This work of Segneri is written against persons who continue in sins under pretence of their devotion to St. Mary, and in consequence he is led to draw out the idea which good Catholics have of her. The idea is this, that she is absolutely the first of created beings. Thus the treatise says, that "God might have easily made a more beautiful firmament, and a greener earth, but it was not possible to make a higher Mother than the Virgin Mary; and in her formation there has been conferred on mere creatures all the glory of which they are capable, remaining mere creatures," p. 34. And as containing all created perfection, she has all those attributes, which, as was noticed above, the Arians and other heretics applied to our Lord, and which the Church denied of Him as infinitely below His Supreme Majesty. Thus she is "the created Idea in the making of the world," p. 20; "which, as being a more exact copy of the Incarnate Idea than was elsewhere to be found, was used as the original of the rest of the creation," p. 21. To her are applied the words, "Ego primogenita prodivi ex ore Altissimi," because she was predestinated in the Eternal Mind coevally with the Incarnation of her Divine Son. But to Him alone the title of Wisdom Incarnate is reserved, p. 25. Again, Christ is the First-born by nature; the Virgin in a less sublime order, viz. that of adoption. Again, if omnipotence is ascribed to her, it is a participated omnipotence (as she and all Saints have a participated sonship, divinity, glory, holiness, and worship), and is explained by the words, "Quod Deus imperio, tu prece, Virgo, potes."

11.

Again, a special office is assigned to the Blessed Virgin, that is, special as compared with all other Saints; but it is marked off with the utmost precision from that assigned to our Lord. Thus she is said to have been made "the arbitress of every *effect* coming from God's mercy." Because she is the Mother of God, the salvation of mankind is said to be given to her prayers "*de congruo*, but *de condigno* it is due only to the blood of the Redeemer," p. 113. Merit is ascribed to Christ, and prayer to St. Mary, p. 162. The whole may be expressed in the words, "*Unica* spes mea Jesus, et post Jesum Virgo Maria. Amen."

Again, a distinct *cultus* is assigned to Mary, but the reason of it is said to be the transcendent dignity of her Son. "A particular *cultus* is due to the Virgin beyond comparison greater than that given to any other Saint, because her dignity belongs to another order, namely to one which in some sense belongs to the order of the Hypostatic Union itself, and is necessarily connected with it," p. 41. And "Her being the Mother of God is the source of all the extraordinary honours due to Mary," p. 35.

It is remarkable that the "Monstra te esse Matrem" is explained, p. 158, as "Show thyself to be *our* Mother;" an interpretation which I think I have found elsewhere in these Tracts, and also in a book commonly used in religious houses, called the "Journal of Meditations," and elsewhere.[37]

It must be kept in mind that my object here is not to prove the dogmatic accuracy of what these popular publications teach concerning the prerogatives of the Blessed Virgin, but to show that that teaching is not such as to obscure the divine glory of her Son. We must ask for clearer evidence before we are able to admit so grave a charge . . .

---

[37] Vid. *Via Media*, vol. ii. pp. 121–2.

The Church as Poet[†]

HE [JOHN KEBLE] did that for the Church of England which none but a poet could do: he made it poetical. It is sometimes asked whether poets are not more commonly found external to the Church than among her children; and it would not surprise us to find the question answered in the affirmative. Poetry is the refuge of those who have not the Catholic Church to flee to and repose upon, for the Church herself is the most sacred and august of poets. Poetry, as Mr. Keble lays it down in his University Lectures on the subject, is a method of relieving the over-burdened mind; it is a channel through which emotion finds expression, and that a safe, regulated expression.

Now what is the Catholic Church, viewed in her human aspect, but a discipline of the affections and passions? What are her ordinances and practices but the regulated expression of keen, or deep, or turbid feeling, and thus a "cleansing," as Aristotle would word it, of the sick soul? She is the poet of her children; full of music to soothe the sad and control the wayward,—wonderful in story for the imagination of the romantic; rich in symbol and imagery, so that gentle and delicate feelings, which will not bear words, may in silence intimate their presence or commune with themselves. Her very being is poetry; every psalm, every petition, every collect, every versicle, the cross, the mitre, the thurible, is a fulfilment of some dream of childhood, or aspiration of youth. Such poets as are born under her shadow, she takes into her service; she sets them to write hymns, or to compose chants, or to embellish shrines, or to determine ceremonies, or to marshal processions; nay, she can even make schoolmen of them, as she made St. Thomas, till logic becomes poetical.

Now the author of the Christian Year found the Anglican system all but destitute of this divine element, which is an essential property of Catholicism;—a ritual dashed upon the ground, trodden on, and broken piecemeal;—prayers, clipped, pieced, torn, shuffled about at pleasure, until the meaning of the composition perished, and offices which had been poetry were no longer even good prose;—antiphons, hymns, benedictions, invocations, shovelled away;—Scripture lessons turned into chapters;—heaviness, feebleness, unwieldiness, where the Catholic rites had had the lightness and airiness

---

[†] From *Essays Critical & Historical*, Volume 2 (1846). The title given to this excerpt is editorial, as is the paragraphing.

of a spirit;—vestments chucked off, lights quenched, jewels stolen, the pomp and circumstances of worship annihilated; a dreariness which could be felt, and which seemed the token of an incipient Socinianism, forcing itself upon the eye, the ear, the nostrils of the worshipper; a smell of dust and damp, not of incense; a sound of ministers preaching Catholic prayers, and parish clerks droning out Catholic canticles; the royal arms for the crucifix; huge ugly boxes of wood, sacred to preachers, frowning on the congregation in the place of the mysterious altar; and long cathedral aisles unused, railed off, like the tombs (as they were,) of what had been and was not; and for orthodoxy, a frigid, unelastic, inconsistent, dull, helpless dogmatic, which could give no just account of itself, yet was intolerant of all teaching which contained a doctrine more or a doctrine less, and resented every attempt to give it a meaning,—such was the religion of which this gifted author was,—not the judge and denouncer, (a deep spirit of reverence hindered it,)—but the renovator, as far as it has been renovated.

Clear as was his perception of the degeneracy of his times, he attributed nothing of it to his Church, over which he threw the poetry of his own mind and the memory of better days.

The Omnipotence of God
the Reason for Faith & Hope[†]

O UR LORD commanded the winds and the sea, and the men who saw it marvelled saying, What manner of man is this, for the winds and the sea obey him? It was a miracle. It showed our Lord's power over nature. And therefore they wondered, because they could not understand, and rightly, how any man could have power over nature, unless that power was given him by God. Nature goes on her own way and we cannot alter it. Man cannot alter it, he can only use it. Matter, for instance, falls downward, earth, stone, iron all fall to the earth when left to themselves. Again, left to themselves, they cannot move *except* by falling. They never move except they are pulled or pushed forward. Water again never stands in a heap or a mass, but flows out on all sides as far as it can. Fire again always burns, or tends to burn. The wind blows to and fro, without any discoverable rule or law, and we cannot tell how it will blow tomorrow by seeing how it blows today. We see all these things. They have their own way; we cannot alter them. All we attempt to do is to use them; we take them as we find them and we use them. We don't attempt to change the nature of fire, earth, air or water, but we observe what the nature of each is, and we try to turn it to account. We turn steam to account, and use it in carriages and ships; we turn fire to account and use it in a thousand ways. We use the things of nature, we submit to the laws of nature, and we avail ourselves of them; but we do not command nature. We do not attempt to alter it, but we merely direct it to our own purposes. Far different was it with our Lord: He used indeed the winds and the water; (He used the water when He got into a boat, and used the wind when He suffered the sail to be spread over Him). He used, but more than this, He commanded, the winds and the waves—He had power to rebuke, to change, to undo the course of nature, as well as to make use of it. He was above nature. He had power over nature. This is what made the men marvel. Experienced seamen can make use of the winds and the waves to get to the shore. Nay, even in a storm they know how to avail themselves of them, they have their rules what to do, and they are on the look out, taking advantage of everything that happens. But our

---

[†] From the nine sermons published as *Faith and Prejudice* (New York: Sheed & Ward, 1956), Sermon 1, preached on the Fourth Sunday after Epiphany, 30th January 1848.

Lord did not condescend to do this. He did not instruct them how to manage their sails, nor how to steer the vessel, but He addressed Himself directly to winds and waves, and stopped them, making them do that which was against their nature.

So again, when Lazarus was ill, our Lord might have gone to him, and have recommended the fitting medicine, and the treatment which would cure him. He did nothing of the kind—He let him die—so much so that St. Martha said when He at length came, "Lord, if Thou hadst been here, my brother had not died" (John 11). But our Lord had a reason. He wished to show His power over nature. He wished to triumph over death. So, instead of hindering Lazarus from dying by the art of medicine, He triumphed over death by a miracle.

No one has power over nature but He who made it. None can work a miracle but God. When miracles are wrought it is a proof that God is present. And therefore it is that, whenever God visits the earth, He works miracles. It is the claim He makes upon our attention. He thereby reminds us that He is the Creator. He who did, alone can undo. He who made, alone can destroy. He who gave nature its laws, alone can change those laws. He who made fire to burn, food to nourish, water to flow, iron to sink, He alone can make fire harmless, food needless, water firm and solid, iron light, and therefore whether He sent forth the Prophets or the Apostles, Moses, Josue, Samuel, or Elias, He always sent them with miracles, to show His presence with His servants. Then all things began to change their nature; the Egyptians were tormented with strange plagues, the waters stood in a heap for the Chosen people to pass over, they were fed with manna in the desert, the sun and the moon stood still—because God was there.

This then was what made the men marvel, when our Lord stilled the storm upon the sea. It was a proof to them that God was there, though they saw Him not. Nay, God was there and they saw Him—for Christ was God—but whether they learned this high and sacred truth or not from the miracle, so far they understood that God really was there. His hand was there, His power was there, and therefore they feared. You have read in books, I dare say, stories of great men who come in disguise, and at length are known by their voice, or by some deed, which betrays them. Their voices, or their words, or their manner, or their exploit, is their token—it is a sort of handwriting. And so when God walks the earth, He gives us means of knowing that He does so, though He is a hidden God, and does not display His glory openly. Power over nature is the token He gives us that He, the Creator of Nature, is in the midst of us.

And therefore God is called almighty—this is His distinguishing attribute. Man is powerful only by means of nature. He uses nature as his instrument, but God has no need of nature, in order to accomplish His will, but works His great work, sometimes by means of nature, and sometimes without nature, as it please Him.

And you will observe this attribute of God is the only one mentioned in the Creed. "I believe in God, the Father almighty." It is not said "I believe in God the Father All merciful, or All holy, or All wise," though all these attributes are His also, but "I believe in God the Father *Almighty.*" Why is this? It is plain why—because this attribute is the reason *why* we *believe.* Faith is the beginning of religion, and therefore the almightiness of God is made the beginning and first of His attributes, and just the attribute which ought to be mentioned in the Creed. We should not be able to believe in Him, did we not know that He is almighty. Nothing is too hard to believe of Him to whom nothing is too hard to do. You may recollect that when it was prophesied to Abraham that the old Sarah his wife should have a son, Sarah laughed. Why did she laugh? Because she did not bear sufficiently in mind that God is almighty. Therefore the Lord said to her, "Is anything *hard* for God?" (Gen. 18). And in like manner our Lord in the Gospel of this day, when He commanded the winds and the sea, said "Why are ye fearful, O ye of little *faith*?" If they had had a firm perception of His almightiness, they would have been sure that He could bring them out of danger. But when they saw Him asleep in the boat, they could not believe that they were safe, not understanding that He, awake or asleep, was almighty.

This thought is very important to us at this day, because it will be a means of sustaining our faith. Why do you believe all the strange and marvellous acts recorded in Scripture? Because God is almighty and can do them. Why do you believe that a Virgin conceived and bore a Son? Because it is God's act, and He can do anything. As the Angel Gabriel said to the Blessed Virgin, "No word is impossible with God." On the other hand, when holy Zacharias was told by the Angel that the old Elizabeth, his wife, should conceive, he said, "Whence shall I know this?" and he was punished at once for disbelieving. Why do you believe that our Lord rose from the dead? Why, that He redeemed us all with His precious blood? Why, that He washes away our sins in Baptism? Why do you believe in the power and grace which attends the other sacraments? Why do you believe in the resurrection of our bodies? You believe it because nothing is too hard for God—because however wonderful a thing may be, He can do it. Why do you believe in the virtue of holy relics? Why do you believe that the Saints hear your prayers? Because nothing is too hard for the Lord.

This especially applies to the great miracle of the Altar. Why do you believe that the Priest changes the bread into the body of Christ? Because God is almighty and nothing is too hard for Him. And moreover you know, as I have said, that miracles are the signs and tokens of God's presence. If then He is present in the Catholic Church, it is *natural* to expect that He will work some miracles, and if He did no miracle, we might be almost tempted to believe that He had left His Church.

When you assist at the holy sacrifice of the Altar and bow down at the elevation, and whenever you make an act of faith in God, steadily contemplating all that He has done for us in the Gospel, recollect God is almighty, and it will enable you to be bolder and more determined in making it. Say, I believe this and that, because God is almighty—I do not worship a creature: I am not the servant of a God of restricted power. But since God can *do* everything, I can *believe* everything. There is nothing too much for Him to do, and nothing too hard for me to believe. I will enlarge my heart. I will go forward in a generous way. "Open thy mouth wide," says God to me, "and I will fill it." Well, I do open my mouth, I desire to be fed with His words. I desire to live and to thrive by every word which He speaks. I desire to say with the prophet, "Speak, Lord, for thy servant heareth." I will not grudge, I will not doubt, because I believe that which takes away all doubting. All acts of divine power do but fall under, and are but instances of, that universal attribute on which I believe, omnipotence. If God can do all things, He can do this. He can do much more than this. Wonderful as this or that may be to our narrow minds, still if we knew all, we should see that this, whatever it is, was but one thing out of many. This is what our Lord signified to holy Nathanael. Nathanael, struck with something which our Lord said, cried out, "Rabbi, Thou art the Son of God, Thou art the King of Israel." He made answer "Believest thou on this account? thou shalt see a greater thing than this." There is no end of God's power; it is inexhaustible. Let there be no end to our faith. Let us not be startled at what we are called on to believe; let us still be on the look out. Some people are slow to believe the miracles ascribed to the Saints. Now we know that such miracles are not part of the *faith*; they have no place in the Creed. And some are reported on better evidence than others. Some may be true, and others not so certainly true. Others again may be true but not miracles. But still why should they be *surprised* to hear of miracles? Are they beyond the power of God, and is not God present with the Saints, and has He not wrought miracles of old? Are miracles a new thing? There is no reason to be surprised, on the contrary; because in the Sacrifice of the Mass He works daily the most wonderful of miracles at the word of the priest. If then He does daily a miracle greater than any that can be named, why should we be surprised to hear reports of His doing other and lesser miracles now and then?

The Gospel of the day then sets before us the duty of *faith*, and rests it upon God's almightiness or omnipotence, as it is called. Nothing is too hard for Him, and we believe what the Church tells us of His deeds and providences, because He can do whatsoever He will. But there is another grace which the Gospel teaches us, and that is *hope* or *trust*. You observe that when the storm came, the disciples were in great *distress*. They thought some great calamity was coming on them. Therefore Christ said to them, "Why are ye *fearful*?" Hope and fear are contrary to each other; they feared because they did not hope. To hope is, not only to believe in God, but to believe and be certain that He loves us and means well to us; and therefore it is a great Christian grace. For faith without hope is not certain to bring us to Christ. The devils believe and tremble (James 2). They believe, but they do not come to Christ— because they do not hope, but despair. They despair of getting any good from Him. Rather they know that they shall get nothing but evil, so they keep away. You recollect the man possessed of the devil said: "What have we to do with Thee, Jesus the Son of God—art Thou come hither to torment us before the time?" (Matt. 8). The coming of Christ was no comfort to them, the contrary: they shrank from Him. They knew He meant them not good, but punishment. But to men He meant good, and it is by knowing and feeling this that men are brought to Him. They will not come to God till they are sure of this. They must believe that He is not only almighty, but all merciful also. Faith is founded on the knowledge that God is almighty, hope is founded on the knowledge that God is all merciful. And the presence of our Lord and Saviour Jesus Christ excites us to hope quite as much as to faith, because His very name Jesus means Saviour, and because He was so loving, meek, and bountiful when He was on earth.

He said to the disciples when the storm arose, "Why are ye *fearful*?" That is, you ought to hope, you ought to trust, you ought to repose your heart on Me. I am not only almighty, but I am all merciful. I have come on earth because I am most loving to you. Why am I here, why am I in human flesh, why have I these hands which I stretch out to you, why have I these eyes from which the tears of pity flow, except that I wish you well, that I wish to save you? The storm cannot hurt you if *I* am with you. Can you be better placed than under my protection? Do you doubt My power or My will, do you think Me *negligent* of you that I sleep in the ship, and *unable* to help you except I am awake? Wherefore do you doubt? Wherefore do you fear? Have I been so long with you, and you do not yet trust Me, and cannot remain in peace and quiet by My side?"

And so, my Brethren, He says to us now. All of us who live in this mortal life, have our troubles. You have your troubles, but when you are in trouble, and the waves seem to mount high, and to be soon to overwhelm you, make an act of faith, an act of hope, in your God and Saviour. He calls you to Him who has His mouth and His hands full of blessings for you. He says: "Come unto Me, all that labour and are laden, and I will refresh you" (Matt. 11). "All ye that thirst," He cries out by His prophet, "come ye to the waters, and ye that have no money, haste ye, buy, and eat." Never let the thought come into your mind that God is a hard master, a severe master. It is true the day will come when He will come as a just Judge, but now is the time of mercy. Improve it and make the most of the time of grace. "Behold now is the acceptable time, behold now is the day of salvation." This is the day of hope, this is the day of work, this is the day of activity. "The night cometh when no man can work," but we are children of the light and of the day, and therefore despondency, coldness of heart, fear, sluggishness are sins in us. Temptations indeed come on you to murmur, but resist them, drive them aside, pray God to help you with His mighty grace. He allows no temptation to befall us which He does not give us grace to surmount. Do not let your hope give way, but "lift up the languid hands and the relaxed knees" (Heb. 12). "Lose not your confidence, which hath a great reward" (Heb. 10). Seek His face who ever dwells in real and bodily presence in His Church. Do at least as much as what the disciples did. They had but little faith, they feared, they had not any great confidence and peace, but at least they did not keep away from Christ. They did not sit still sullenly, but they came to Him. Alas, our very best state is not higher than the Apostles' worst state. Our Lord blamed them as having *little* faith, because they cried out to Him. I wish we Christians of this day did as much as this. I wish we went as far as to cry out to Him in alarm. I wish we had only as much faith and hope as that which Christ thought so little in His first disciples. At least imitate the apostles in their weakness, if you can't imitate them in their strength. If you can't act as saints, at least act as Christians. Do not keep from Him, but, when you are in trouble, come to Him day by day asking Him earnestly and perseveringly for those favours which He alone can give. And as He on this occasion spoken of in the Gospel, blamed indeed the disciples, but did for them what they asked, so, (we will trust in His great mercy), though He discerns much infirmity in you which ought not to be there, yet He will deign to rebuke the winds and the sea, and say "Peace, be still," and there will be a great calm.

May this be your happy lot, my dear Brethren, and may the blessing of God Almighty, the Father, &c.

The Catholic Church at Worship[†]

"WE HAVE no life or poetry in the Church of England; the Catholic Church alone is beautiful. You would see what I mean if you went into a foreign cathedral, or even into one of the Catholic churches in our large towns. The celebrant, deacon and subdeacon, acolytes with lights, the incense, and the chanting—all combine to one end, one act of worship. You feel it *is* really a worshipping; every sense, eyes, ears, smell, are made to know that worship is going on. The laity on the floor saying their beads, or making their acts; the choir singing out the *Kyrie*; and the priest and his assistants bowing low, and saying the *Confiteor* to each other. This is worship, and it is far above reason."

(Part 1, chapter 7)

❧

BATEMAN was startled, but recovered himself; "Heaven forbid," he said, "that I should treat these things lightly, or interfere with you unduly. I know, my dear friend, what a serious fellow you are; but do tell me, just tell me, how can you justify the Mass, as it is performed abroad; how can it be called a 'reasonable service,' when all parties conspire to gabble it over as if it mattered not a jot who attended to it, or even understood it? Speak, man, speak," he added, gently shaking him by the shoulder.

"These are such difficult questions," answered Willis; "must I speak? Such difficult questions," he continued, rising into a more animated manner, and kindling as he went on; "I mean, people view them so differently: it is so difficult to convey to one person the idea of another. The idea of worship is different in the Catholic Church from the idea of it in your Church; for, in truth, the *religions* are different. Don't deceive yourself, my dear Bateman," he said tenderly, "it is not that ours is your religion carried a little farther,—a little too far, as you would say. No, they differ in kind, not in degree; ours is one religion, yours another. And when the time comes, and come it will, for you, alien as you are now, to submit yourself to the gracious yoke of Christ, then, my dearest Bateman, it will be *faith* which will enable you to bear the ways

† Excerpts from the novel *Loss and Gain*, published in 1848. The title given to this excerpt is ours.

and usages of Catholics, which else might perhaps startle you. Else, the habits of years, the associations in your mind of a certain outward behaviour with real inward acts of devotion, might embarrass you, when you had to conform yourself to other habits, and to create for yourself other associations. But this faith, of which I speak, the great gift of God, will enable you in that day to overcome yourself, and to submit, as your judgment, your will, your reason, your affections, so your tastes and likings, to the rule and usage of the Church. Ah, that faith should be necessary in such a matter, and that what is so natural and becoming under the circumstances, should have need of an explanation! I declare, to me," he said, and he clasped his hands on his knees, and looked forward as if soliloquising,—"to me nothing is so consoling, so piercing, so thrilling, so overcoming, as the Mass, said as it is among us. I could attend Masses for ever and not be tired. It is not a mere form of words,—it is a great action, the greatest action that can be on earth. It is, not the invocation merely, but, if I dare use the word, the evocation of the Eternal. He becomes present on the altar in flesh and blood, before whom angels bow and devils tremble. This is that awful event which is the scope, and is the interpretation, of every part of the solemnity. Words are necessary, but as means, not as ends; they are not mere addresses to the throne of grace, they are instruments of what is far higher, of consecration, of sacrifice. They hurry on as if impatient to fulfil their mission. Quickly they go, the whole is quick; for they are all parts of one integral action. Quickly they go; for they are awful words of sacrifice, they are a work too great to delay upon; as when it was said in the beginning: 'What thou doest, do quickly'. Quickly they pass; for the Lord Jesus goes with them, as He passed along the lake in the days of His flesh, quickly calling first one and then another. Quickly they pass; because as the lightning which shineth from one part of heaven unto the other, so is the coming of the Son of Man. Quickly they pass; for they are as the words of Moses, when the Lord came down in the cloud, calling on the Name of the Lord as He passed by, 'the Lord, the Lord God, merciful and gracious, long-suffering, and abundant in goodness and truth'. And as Moses on the mountain, so we too 'make haste and bow our heads to the earth, and adore'. So we, all around, each in his place, look out for the great Advent, 'waiting for the moving of the water'. Each in his place, with his own heart, with his own wants, with his own thoughts, with his own intention, with his own prayers, separate but concordant, watching what is going on, watching its progress, uniting in its consummation;—not painfully and hopelessly following a hard form of prayer from beginning to end, but, like a concert of musical instruments, each different, but concurring in a sweet harmony, we take our part with God's priest, supporting him, yet guided by him. There are little children there, and old men, and simple labourers, and students in seminaries, priests preparing for Mass, priests making their thanksgiving; there are innocent maidens, and there are penitent sinners; but out of these many minds rises one eucharistic hymn, and the great Action is the measure and scope of it. And oh, my dear Bateman," he added, turning to him, "you ask me whether this is not a formal, unreasonable service—it is wonderful!" he cried, rising up, "quite wonderful. When will these dear good people be enlightened? *O Sapientia, fortiter suaviterque disponens omnia, O Adonai, O Clavis David et Exspectatio gentium, veni ad salvandum nos, Domine Deus noster.*"

Now, at least, there was no mistaking Willis. Bateman stared, and was almost frightened at a burst of enthusiasm which he had been far from expecting. "Why, Willis," he said, "it is not true, then, after all, what we heard, that you were somewhat dubious, shaky, in your adherence to Romanism? I'm sure I beg your pardon; I would not for the world have annoyed you, had I known the truth."

Willis's face still glowed, and he looked as youthful and radiant as he had been two years before. There was nothing ungentle in his impetuosity; a smile, almost a laugh, was on his face, as if he was half ashamed of his own warmth; but this took nothing from its evident sincerity. He seized Bateman's two hands before the latter knew where he was, lifted him up out of his seat, and, raising his own mouth close to his ear, said, in a low voice, "I would to God, that not only thou, but also all who hear me this day, were both in little and in much such as I am, except these chains". Then, reminding him it had grown late, and bidding him good-night, he left the room with Charles.

(Part II, chapter 20)

৵

"THIS will never do," said Charles, as he closed the door, and ran upstairs; "here is a day wasted, worse than wasted, wasted partly on strangers, partly on friends; and it's hard to say in which case a more thorough waste. I ought to have gone to the Convent at once." The thought flashed into his mind, and he stood over the fire dwelling on it. "Yes," he said, "I will delay no longer. How does time go? I declare it's past four o'clock." He then thought again: "I'll get over my dinner, and then at once betake myself to my good Passionists."

To the coffee-house then he went, and, as it was some way off, it is not wonderful that it was near six before he arrived at the Convent. It was a plain brick building; money had not been so abundant as to overflow upon the exterior, after the expense of the interior had been provided for. And it was incomplete; a large church had been enclosed, but it was scarcely more than a shell—altars, indeed, had been set up, but, for the rest, it had little more than good proportions, a broad sanctuary, a serviceable organ, and an effective choir. There was a range of buildings adjacent, capable of holding about half-a-dozen fathers; but the size of the church required a larger establishment. By this time, doubtless, things are different, but we are looking back at the first efforts of the English Congregation, when it had scarcely ceased to struggle for life, and when friends and members were but beginning to flow in.

It was indeed but ten years, at that time, since the severest of modern rules had been introduced into England. Two centuries after the memorable era when St. Philip and St. Ignatius, making light of those bodily austerities of which they were personally so great masters, preached mortification of will and reason as more necessary for a civilised age—in the lukewarm and self-indulgent eighteenth century, Father Paul of the Cross was divinely moved to found a Congregation in some respects more ascetic than the primitive hermits and the orders of the middle age. It was not fast, or silence, or poverty which distinguished it, though here too it is not wanting in strictness; but in the cell of its venerable founder, on the Celian Hill, hangs an iron discipline or scourge, studded with nails, which is a memorial, not only of his own self-inflicted sufferings, but of those of his Italian family. The object of those sufferings was as remarkable as their intensity; penance, indeed, is in one respect the end of all self-chastisement, but in the instance of the Passionists the use of the scourge was specially directed to the benefit of their neighbour. They applied the pain to the benefit of the holy souls in Purgatory, or they underwent it to rouse a careless audience. On their missions, when their words seemed uttered in vain, they have been known suddenly to undo their habit, and to scourge themselves with sharp knives or razors, crying out to the horrified people, that they would not show mercy to their flesh till they whom they were addressing took pity on their own perishing souls. Nor was it to their own countrymen alone that this self-consuming charity extended; how it so happened does not appear; perhaps a certain momento close to their house was the earthly cause; but so it was, that for many years the heart of Father Paul was expanded towards a northern nation, with which, humanly speaking, he had nothing to do. Over against St. John and St. Paul, the home of the Passionists on the Celian, rises the old church and monastery of San Gregorio, the womb, as it may be called, of English Christianity. There had lived that great Saint, who is named our Apostle, who was afterwards called to the chair of St. Peter; and thence went forth, in and after his pontificate, Augustine, Paulinus, Justus, and the other Saints by whom our barbarous ancestors were converted. Their names, which are now written up upon the pillars of the portico, would almost seem to have issued forth, and crossed over, and confronted the venerable Paul; for, strange to say, the thought of England came into his ordinary prayers; and in his last years, after a vision during Mass, as if he had been Augustine or Mellitus, he talked of his "Sons" in England.

It was strange enough that even one Italian in the heart of Rome should at that time have ambitious thoughts of making novices or converts in this country; but, after the venerable Founder's death, his special interest in our distant isle showed itself in another member of his institute. On the Apennines, near Viterbo, there dwelt a shepherd-boy, in the first years of this century, whose mind had early been drawn heavenward; and, one day, as he prayed before an image of the Madonna, he felt a vivid intimation that he was destined to preach the Gospel under the northern sky. There appeared no means by which a Roman peasant should be turned into a missionary; nor did the prospect open, when this youth found himself, first a lay-brother, then a Father, in the Congregation of the Passion. Yet, though no external means appeared, the inward impression did not fade; on the contrary, it became more definite, and in process of time, instead of the dim north, England was engraven on his heart. And, strange to say, as years went on, without his seeking, for he was simply under obedience, our peasant found himself at length upon the very shore of the stormy northern sea, whence Cæsar of old looked out for a new world to conquer: yet that he should cross the strait was still as little likely as before. However, it was as likely as that he should ever have got so near it; and he used to eye the restless, godless, waves, and wonder with himself whether the day would ever come when he should be carried over them. And come it did, not however by any determination of his own, but by the same Providence which thirty years before had given him the anticipation of it.

At the time of our narrative, Father Domenico de Matre Dei had become familiar with England; he had had many anxieties here, first from want of funds, then still more from want of men. Year passed after year, and, whether fear of the severity of the rule—though that was groundless, for it had been mitigated for England—or the claim of other religious bodies was the cause, his community did not increase, and he was tempted to despond. But every work has its season; and now for some time past that difficulty had been gradually lessening; various zealous men, some of noble birth, others of extensive acquirements, had entered the Congregation; and our friend Willis, who at this time had received the priesthood, was not the last of these accessions, though domiciled at a distance from London. And now the reader knows much more about the Passionists than did Reding at the time that he made his way to their monastery.

The church door came first, and, as it was open, he entered it. It apparently was filling for service. When he got inside, the person who immediately preceded him dipped his finger into a vessel of water which stood at the entrance, and offered it to Charles. Charles ignorant what it meant, and awkward from his consciousness of it, did nothing but slink aside, and look for some place of refuge; but the whole space was open, and there seemed no corner to retreat into. Every one, however, seemed about his own business; no one minded him and so far he felt at his ease. He stood near the door, and began to look about him. A profusion of candles was lighting at the High Altar, which stood in the centre of a semicircular apse. There were side-altars— perhaps half-a-dozen; most of them without lights, but, even here, solitary worshippers might be seen. Over one was a large old Crucifix with a lamp, and this had a succession of visitors. They came each for five minutes, said some prayers which were attached in a glazed frame to the rail, and passed away. At another, which was in a chapel at the farther end of one of the aisles, six long candles were burning, and over it was an image. On looking attentively, Charles made out at last that it was an image of Our Lady, and the Child held out a rosary. Here a congregation had already assembled, or rather was in the middle of some service, to him unknown. It was rapid, alternate, and monotonous; and, as it seemed interminable, Reding turned his eyes elsewhere. They fell first on one, then on another confessional, round each of which was a little crowd, kneeling, waiting every one his own turn for presenting himself for the sacrament—the men on the one side, the women on the other. At the lower end of the church were about three ranges of moveable benches with backs and kneelers; the rest of the large space was open, and filled with chairs. The growing object of attention at present was the High Altar; and each person, as he entered, took a chair, and, kneeling down behind it, began his prayers. At length the church got very full; rich and poor were mixed together—artisans, well-dressed youths, Irish labourers, mothers with two or three children—the only division being that of men from women. A set of boys and children, mixed with some old crones, had got possession of the altar-rail, and were hugging it with restless motions, as if in expectation.

Though Reding had continued standing, no one would have noticed him; but he saw the time was come for him to kneel, and accordingly he moved into a corner seat on the bench nearest him. He had hardly done so, when a procession with lights passed from the sacristy to the altar; something went on which he did not understand, and then suddenly began what, by the *Miserere* and *Ora pro nobis*, he perceived to be a litany; a hymn followed. Reding thought he never had been present at worship before, so absorbed was the attention, so intense was the devotion of the congregation. What particularly struck him was, that whereas in the Church of England the clergyman or the organ was everything and the people nothing, except so far as the clerk is their representative, here it was just reversed. The priest hardly spoke, or at least audibly; but the whole congregation was as though one vast instrument or Panharmonicon, moving all together, and what was most remarkable, as if self-moved. They did not seem to require any one to prompt or direct them, though in the Litany the choir took the alternate parts. The words were Latin, but every one seemed to understand them thoroughly, and to be offering up his prayers to the Blessed Trinity, and the Incarnate Saviour, and the great Mother of God, and the glorified Saints, with hearts full in proportion to the energy of the sounds they uttered. There was a little boy near him, and a poor woman, singing at the pitch of their voices. There was no mistaking it; Reding said to himself, "This *is* a popular religion". He looked round at the building; it was, as we have said, very plain, and bore the marks of being unfinished; but the Living Temple which was manifested in it needed no curious carving or rich marble to complete it, "for the glory of God had enlightened it, and the Lamb was the lamp thereof". "How wonderful," said Charles to himself, "that people call this worship formal and external; it seems to possess all classes, young and old, polished and vulgar, men and women indiscriminately; it is the working of one Spirit in all, making many one."

While he was thus thinking, a change came over the worship. A priest, or at least an assistant, had mounted for a moment above the altar, and removed a chalice or vessel which stood there; he could not see distinctly. A cloud of incense was rising on high; the people suddenly all bowed low; what could it mean? the truth flashed on him, fearfully yet sweetly; it was the Blessed Sacrament—it was the Lord Incarnate who was on the altar, who had come to visit and to bless His people. It was the Great Presence, which makes a Catholic Church different from every other place in the world; which makes it, as no other place can be, holy. The Breviary offices were by this time not unknown to Reding; and as he threw himself on the pavement, in sudden self-abasement and joy, some words of those great Antiphons came into his mouth, from which Willis had formerly quoted: "O Adonai, et Dux domûs Israel, qui Moysi in rubo apparuisti; O Emmanuel, Exspectatio Gentium et Salvator earum, veni ad salvandum nos, Domine Deus noster".

The function did not last very long after this; Reding, on looking up, found the congregation rapidly diminishing, and the lights in course of extinction. He saw he must be quick in his motions. He made his way to a lay-brother who was waiting till the doors could be closed, and begged to be conducted to the Superior. The lay-brother feared he might be busy at the moment, but conducted him through the sacristy to a small neat room, where, being left to himself, he had time to collect his thoughts. At length the Superior appeared; he was a man past the middle age, and had a grave yet familiar manner. Charles's feelings were indescribable, but all pleasurable. His heart beat, not with fear or anxiety, but with the thrill of delight with which he realised that he was beneath the shadow of a Catholic community, and face to face with one of its priests. His trouble went in a moment, and he could have laughed for joy. He could hardly keep his countenance, and almost feared to be taken for a fool. He presented the card of his railroad companion. The good Father smiled when he saw the name, nor did the few words which were written with pencil on the card diminish his satisfaction. Charles and he soon came to an understanding; he found himself already known in the community by means of Willis; and it was arranged that he should take up his lodgings with his new friends forthwith, and remain there as long as it suited him. He was to prepare for confession at once; and it was hoped that on the following Sunday he might be received into Catholic communion. After that, he was, at a convenient interval, to present himself to the Bishop, from whom he would seek the sacrament of confirmation. Not much time was necessary for removing his luggage from his lodgings; and in the course of an hour from the time of his interview with the Father Superior, he was sitting by himself, with pen and paper and his books, and with a cheerful fire, in a small cell of his new home.

(Part III, chapter 10)

Men, not Angels, the Priests of the Gospel[†]

WHEN CHRIST, the great Prophet, the great Preacher, the great Missionary, came into the world, He came in a way the most holy, the most august, the most glorious. Though He came in humiliation, though He came to suffer, though He was born in a stable, though He was laid in a manger, yet He issued from the womb of an Immaculate Mother, and His infant form shone with heavenly light. Sanctity marked every lineament of His character and every circumstance of His mission. Gabriel announced His incarnation; a Virgin conceived, a Virgin bore, a Virgin suckled Him; His foster-father was the pure and saintly Joseph; Angels proclaimed His birth; a luminous star spread the news among the heathen; the austere Baptist went before His face; and a crowd of shriven penitents, clad in white garments and radiant with grace, followed Him wherever He went. As the sun in heaven shines through the clouds, and is reflected in the landscape, so the eternal Sun of justice, when He rose upon the earth, turned night into day, and in His brightness made all things bright.

He came and He went; and, seeing that He came to introduce a new and final Dispensation into the world, He left behind Him preachers, teachers, and missionaries, in His stead. Well then, my brethren, you will say, since on His coming all about Him was so glorious, such as He was, such must His servants be, such His representatives, His ministers, in His absence; as He was without sin, they too must be without sin; as He was the Son of God, they must surely be Angels. Angels, you will say, must be appointed to this high office, Angels alone are fit to preach the birth, the sufferings, the death of God. They might indeed have to hide their brightness, as He before them, their Lord and Master, had put on a disguise; they might come, as they came under the Old Covenant, in the garb of men; but still men they could not be, if they were to be preachers of the everlasting Gospel, and dispensers of its divine mysteries. If they were to sacrifice, as He had sacrificed; to continue, repeat, apply, the very Sacrifice which He had offered; to take into their hands that very Victim which was He Himself; to bind and to loose, to bless and to ban, to receive the confessions of His people, and to give them absolution for their sins; to teach them the way of truth, and to guide them along the way of

---

[†] From *Discourses to Mixed Congregations* (1849), Discourse 3.

peace; who was sufficient for these things but an inhabitant of those blessed realms of which the Lord is the never-failing Light?

And yet, my brethren, so it is, He has sent forth for the ministry of reconciliation, not Angels, but men; He has sent forth your brethren to you, not beings of some unknown nature and some strange blood, but of your own bone and your own flesh, to preach to you. "Ye men of Galilee, why stand ye gazing up into heaven?" Here is the royal style and tone in which Angels speak to men, even though these men be Apostles; it is the tone of those who, having never sinned, speak from their lofty eminence to those who have. But such is not the tone of those whom Christ has sent; for it is your brethren whom He has appointed, and none else,—sons of Adam, sons of your nature, the same by nature, differing only in grace,—men, like you, exposed to temptations, to the same temptations, to the same warfare within and without; with the same three deadly enemies—the world, the flesh, and the devil; with the same human, the same wayward heart: differing only as the power of God has changed and rules it. So it is; we are not Angels from Heaven that speak to you, but men, whom grace, and grace alone, has made to differ from you. Listen to the Apostle:—When the barbarous Lycaonians, seeing his miracle, would have sacrificed to him and St. Barnabas, as to gods, he rushed in among them, crying out, "O men, why do ye this? we also are mortals, men like unto you;" or, as the words run more forcibly in the original Greek, "We are of like passions with you". And again to the Corinthians he writes, "We preach not ourselves, but Jesus Christ our Lord; and ourselves your servants through Jesus. God, who commanded the light to shine out of darkness, He hath shined in our hearts, to give the light of the knowledge of the glory of God in the face of Christ Jesus: *but* we hold this treasure *in earthen vessels.*" And further, he says of himself most wonderfully, that, "lest he should be exalted by the greatness of the revelations," there was given him "an angel of Satan" in his flesh "to buffet him". Such are your Ministers, your Preachers, your Priests, O my brethren; not Angels, not Saints, not sinless, but those who would have lived and died in sin except for God's grace, and who, though through God's mercy they be in training for the fellowship of Saints hereafter, yet at present are in the midst of infirmity and temptation, and have no hope, except from the unmerited grace of God, of persevering unto the end.

What a strange, what a striking anomaly is this! All is perfect, all is heavenly, all is glorious, in the Dispensation which Christ has vouchsafed us, except the persons of His Ministers. He dwells on our altars Himself, the Most Holy, the Most High, in light inaccessible, and Angels fall down before Him there; and out of visible substances and forms He chooses what is choicest to represent and to hold Him. The finest wheat-flour, and the purest wine, are taken as His outward symbols; the most sacred and majestic words minister to the sacrificial rite; altar and sanctuary are adorned decently or splendidly, as our means allow; and the Priests perform their office in befitting vestments, lifting up chaste hearts and holy hands; yet those very Priests, so set apart, so consecrated, they, with their girdle of celibacy and their maniple of sorrow, are sons of Adam, sons of sinners, of a fallen nature, which they have not put off, though it be renewed through grace, so that it is almost the definition of a Priest that he has sins of his own to offer for. "Every high Priest," says the Apostle, "taken from among men, is appointed for men, in the things that appertain unto God, that he may offer gifts and sacrifices for sins; who can condole with those who are in ignorance and error, because he also himself is compassed with infirmity. And therefore he ought, as for the people, so also for himself, to offer for sins." And hence in the Mass, when he offers up the Host before consecration, he says, *Suscipe, Sancte Pater, Omnipotens, æterne Deus*, "Accept, Holy Father, Almighty, Everlasting God, this immaculate Host, which I, Thine unworthy servant, offer to Thee, my Living and True God, for *mine* innumerable sins, offences, and negligences, *and* for all who stand around, and for all faithful Christians, living and dead".

Most strange is this in itself, my brethren, but not strange, when you consider it is the appointment of an all-merciful God; not strange in Him, because the Apostle gives the reason of it in the passage I have quoted. The priests of the New Law are men, in order that they may "condole with those who are in ignorance and error, because they too are compassed with infirmity". Had Angels been your Priests, my brethren, they could not have condoled with you, sympathised with you, have had compassion on you, felt tenderly for you, and made allowances for you, as we can; they could not have been your patterns and guides, and have led you on from your old selves into a new life, as they can who come from the midst of you, who have been led on themselves as you are to be led, who know well your difficulties, who have had experience, at least of your temptations, who know the strength of the flesh and the wiles of the devil, even though they have baffled them, who are already disposed to take your part, and be indulgent towards you, and can advise you most practically, and warn you most seasonably and prudently. Therefore did He send you men to be the ministers of reconciliation and intercession; as He Himself, though He could not sin, yet even He, by becoming man, took on Him, as far as was possible to God, man's burden of infirmity and trial in His own person. He could not be a sinner, but He could be a man, and He took to Himself a man's heart that we might entrust our hearts to Him, and "was tempted in all things, like as we are, yet without sin".

Ponder this truth well, my brethren, and let it be your comfort. Among the Preachers, among the Priests of the Gospel, there have been Apostles, there have been Martyrs, there have been Doctors;—Saints in plenty among them; yet out of them all, high as has been their sanctity, varied their graces, awful their gifts, there has not been one who did not begin with the old Adam; not one of them who was not hewn out of the same rock as the most obdurate of reprobates; not one of them who was not fashioned unto honour out of the same clay which has been the material of the most polluted and vile of sinners; not one who was not by nature brother of those poor souls who have now commenced an eternal fellowship with the devil, and are lost in hell. Grace has vanquished nature; that is the whole history of the Saints. Salutary thought for those who are tempted to pride themselves in what they do, and what they are; wonderful news for those who sorrowfully recognise in their hearts the vast difference that exists between them and the Saints; and joyful news, when men hate sin, and wish to escape from its miserable yoke, yet are tempted to think it impossible!

Come, my brethren, let us look at this truth more narrowly, and lay it to heart. First consider, that, since Adam fell, none of his seed but has been conceived in sin; none, save one. One exception there has been,—who is that one? not our Lord Jesus, for He was not conceived of man, but of the Holy Ghost; not our Lord, but I mean His Virgin Mother, who, though conceived and born of human parents, as others, yet was rescued by anticipation from the common condition of mankind, and never was partaker in fact of Adam's transgression. She was conceived in the way of nature, she was conceived as others are; but grace interfered and was beforehand with sin; grace filled her soul from the first moment of her existence, so that the evil one breathed not on her, nor stained the work of God. *Tota pulchra es, Maria; et macula originalis non est in te.* "Thou art all fair, O Mary, and the stain original is not in thee." But putting aside the Most Blessed Mother of God, every one else, the most glorious Saint, and the most black and odious of sinners, I mean, the soul which, in the event, became the most glorious, and the soul which became the most devilish, were both born in one and the same original sin, both were children of wrath, both were unable to attain heaven by their natural powers, both had the prospect of meriting for themselves hell.

They were both born in sin; they both lay in sin; and the soul, which afterwards became a Saint, would have continued in sin, would have sinned wilfully, and would have been lost, but for the visitings of an unmerited supernatural influence upon it, which did for it what it could not do for itself. The poor infant, destined to be an heir of glory, lay feeble, sickly, fretful, wayward, and miserable; the child of sorrow; without hope, and without heavenly aid.

So it lay for many a long and weary day ere it was born; and when at length it opened its eyes and saw the light, it shrank back, and wept aloud that it had seen it. But God heard its cry from heaven in this valley of tears, and He began that course of mercies towards it which led it from earth to heaven. He sent His Priest to administer to it the first sacrament, and to baptise it with His grace. Then a great change took place in it, for, instead of its being any more the thrall of Satan it forthwith became a child of God; and had it died that minute, and before it came to the age of reason, it would have been carried to heaven without delay by Angels, and been admitted into the presence of God.

But it did not die; it came to the age of reason, and, oh, shall we dare to say, though in some blessed cases it may be said, shall we dare to say, that it did not misuse the great talent which had been given to it, profane the grace which dwelt in it, and fall into mortal sin? In some instances, praised be God! we dare affirm it; such seems to have been the case with my own dear father, St. Philip, who surely kept his baptismal robe unsullied from the day he was clad in it, never lost his state of grace, from the day he was put into it, and proceeded from strength to strength, and from merit to merit, and from glory to glory, through the whole course of his long life, till at the age of eighty he was summoned to his account, and went joyfully to meet it, and was carried across purgatory, without any scorching of its flames, straight to heaven.

Such certainly have sometimes been the dealings of God's grace with the souls of His elect; but more commonly, as if more intimately to associate them with their brethren, and to make the fulness of His favours to them a ground of hope and an encouragement to the penitent sinner, those who have ended in being miracles of sanctity, and heroes in the Church, have passed a time in wilful disobedience, have thrown themselves out of the light of God's countenance, have been led captive by this or that sin, by this or that religious error, till at length they were in various ways recovered, slowly or suddenly, and regained the state of grace, or rather a much higher state, than that which they had forfeited. Such was the blessed Magdalen, who had lived a life of shame; so much so, that even to be touched by her was, according to the religious judgment of her day, a pollution. Happy in this world's goods, young and passionate, she had given her heart to the creature, before the grace of God prevailed with her. Then she cut off her long hair, and put aside her gay apparel, and became so utterly what she had not been, that, had you known her before and after, you had said it was two persons you had seen, not one; for there was no trace of the sinner in the penitent, except the affectionate heart, now set on heaven and Christ; no trace besides, no memory of that glittering and seductive apparition, in the modest form, the serene countenance, the composed gait, and the gentle voice of her who in the garden sought and found her Risen Saviour. Such, too, was he who from a publican became an Apostle and an Evangelist; one who for filthy lucre scrupled not to enter the service of the heathen Romans, and to oppress his own people. Nor were the rest of the Apostles made of better clay than the other sons of Adam; they were by nature animal, carnal, ignorant; left to themselves, they would, like the brutes, have grovelled on the earth, and gazed upon the earth, and fed on the earth, had not the grace of God taken possession of them, and set them on their feet, and raised their faces heavenward. And such was the learned Pharisee, who came to Jesus by night, well satisfied with his station, jealous of his reputation, confident in his reason; but the time at length came, when, even though disciples fled, he remained to anoint the abandoned corpse of Him, whom when living he had been ashamed to own. You see it was the grace of God that triumphed in Magdalen, in Matthew, and in Nicodemus; heavenly grace came down upon corrupt nature; it subdued impurity in the youthful woman, covetousness in the publican, fear of man in the Pharisee.

Let me speak of another celebrated conquest of God's grace in an after age, and you will see how it pleases Him to make a Confessor, a Saint and Doctor of His Church, out of sin and heresy both together. It was not enough that the Father of the Western Schools, the author of a thousand works, the triumphant controversialist, the especial champion of grace, should have been once a poor slave of the flesh, but he was the victim of a perverted intellect also. He, who of all others, was to extol the grace of God, was left more than others to experience the helplessness of nature. The great St Augustine (I am not speaking of the holy missionary of the same name, who came to England and converted our pagan forefathers, and became the first Archbishop of Canterbury, but of the great African Bishop, two centuries before him)— Augustine, I say, not being in earnest about his soul, not asking himself the question, how was sin to be washed away, but rather being desirous, while youth and strength lasted, to enjoy the flesh and the world, ambitious and sensual, judged of truth and falsehood by his private judgment and his private fancy; despised the Catholic Church because it spoke so much of faith and subjection, thought to make his own reason the measure of all things, and accordingly joined a far-spread sect, which affected to be philosophical and enlightened, to take large views of things, and to correct the vulgar, that is the Catholic notions of God and Christ, of sin, and of the way to heaven. In this sect of his he remained for some years; yet what he was taught there did not satisfy him. It pleased him for a time, and then he found he had been eating as if food what had no nourishment in it; he became hungry and thirsty after something more substantial, he knew not what; he despised himself for being a slave to the flesh, and he found his religion did not help him to overcome it; thus he understood that he had not gained the truth, and he cried out, "O, who will tell me where to seek it, and who will bring me into it?"

Why did he not join the Catholic Church at once? I have told you why; he saw that truth was nowhere else; but he was not sure it was there. He thought there was something mean, narrow, irrational, in her system of doctrine; he lacked the gift of faith. Then a great conflict began within him,—the conflict of nature with grace; of nature and her children, the flesh and false reason, against conscience and the pleadings of the Divine Spirit, leading him to better things. Though he was still in a state of perdition, yet God was visiting him, and giving him the first fruits of those influences which were in the event to bring him out of it. Time went on; and looking at him, as his Guardian Angel might look at him, you would have said that, in spite of much perverseness, and many a successful struggle against his Almighty Adversary, in spite of his still being, as before, in a state of wrath, nevertheless grace was making way in his soul,—he was advancing towards the Church. He did not know it himself, he could not recognise it himself; but an eager interest in him, and then a joy, was springing up in heaven among the Angels of God. At last he came within the range of a great Saint in a foreign country; and, though he pretended not to acknowledge him, his attention was arrested by him, and he could not help coming to sacred places to look at him again and again. He began to watch him and speculate about him, and wondered with himself whether he was happy. He found himself frequently in Church, listening to the holy preacher, and he once asked his advice how to find what he was seeking. And now a final conflict came on him with the flesh: it was hard, very hard, to part with the indulgences of years, it was hard to part and never to meet again. O, sin was so sweet, how could he bid it farewell? how could he tear himself away from its embrace, and betake himself to that lonely and dreary way which led heavenwards? But God's grace was sweeter far, and it convinced him while it won him; it convinced his reason, and prevailed;—and he who without it would have lived and died a child of Satan, became, under its wonder-working power, an oracle of sanctity and truth.

And do you not think, my brethren, that he was better fitted than another to persuade his brethren as he had been persuaded, and to preach the holy doctrine which he had despised? Not that sin is better than obedience, or the sinner than the just; but that God in His mercy makes use of sin against itself, that He turns past sin into a present benefit, that, while He washes away its guilt and subdues its power, He leaves it in the penitent in such sense as enables him, from his knowledge of its devices, to assault it more vigorously, and strike at it more truly, when it meets him in other men; that, while our

Lord, by His omnipotent grace, can make the soul as clean as if it had never been unclean, He leaves it in possession of a tenderness and compassion for other sinners, an experience how to deal with them, greater than if it had never sinned; and again that, in those rare and special instances, of one of which I have been speaking, He holds up to us, for our instruction and our comfort, what He can do, even for the most guilty, if they sincerely come to Him for a pardon and a cure. There is no limit to be put to the bounty and power of God's grace; and that we feel sorrow for our sins, and supplicate His mercy, is a sort of present pledge to us in our hearts, that He will grant us the good gifts we are seeking. He can do what He will with the soul of man. He is infinitely more powerful than the foul spirit to whom the sinner has sold himself, and can cast him out.

O my dear brethren, though your conscience witnesses against you, He can disburden it; whether you have sinned less or whether you have sinned more, He can make you as clean in His sight and as acceptable to Him as if you had never gone from Him. Gradually will He destroy your sinful habits, and at once will He restore you to His favour. Such is the power of the Sacrament of Penance, that, be your load of guilt heavier or be it lighter, it removes it, whatever it is. It is as easy to Him to wash out the many sins as the few. Do you recollect in the Old Testament the history of the cure of Naaman the Syrian, by the prophet Eliseus? He had that dreadful, incurable disease called the leprosy, which was a white crust upon the skin, making the whole person hideous, and typifying the hideousness of sin. The prophet bade him bathe in the river Jordan, and the disease disappeared; "his flesh," says the inspired writer, was "restored to him as the flesh of a little child". Here, then, we have a representation not only of what sin is, but of what God's grace is. It can undo the past, it can realise the hopeless. No sinner, ever so odious, but may become a Saint; no Saint, ever so exalted, but has been, or might have been, a sinner. Grace overcomes nature, and grace only overcomes it. Take that holy child, the blessed St. Agnes, who, at the age of thirteen, resolved to die rather than deny the faith, and stood enveloped in an atmosphere of purity, and diffused around her a heavenly influence, in the very home of evil spirits into which the heathen brought her; or consider the angelical Aloysius, of whom it hardly is left upon record that he committed even a venial sin; or St. Agatha, St. Juliana, St. Rose, St. Casimir, or St. Stanislas, to whom the very notion of any unbecoming imagination had been as death; well, there is not one of these seraphic souls but might have been a degraded, loathsome leper, except for God's grace, an outcast from his kind; not one but might, or rather would, have lived the life of a brute creature, and died the death of a reprobate, and

400

lain down in hell eternally in the devil's arms, had not God put a new heart and a new spirit within him, and made him what he could not make himself.

All good men are not Saints, my brethren—all converted souls do not become Saints. I will not promise, that, if you turn to God, you will reach that height of sanctity which the Saints have reached:—true; still, I am showing you that even the Saints are by nature no better than you; and so (much more) that the Priests, who have the charge of the faithful, whatever be their sanctity, are by nature no better than those whom they have to convert, whom they have to reform. It is God's special mercy towards you that we by nature are no other than you; it is His consideration and compassion for you that He has made us, who are your brethren, His legates and ministers of reconciliation.

This is what the world cannot understand; not that it does not apprehend clearly enough that we are by nature of like passions with itself; but what it is so blind, so narrow-minded as not to comprehend, is, that, being so like itself by nature, we may be made so different by grace. Men of the world, my brethren, know the power of nature; they know not, experience not, believe not, the power of God's grace; and since they are not themselves acquainted with any power that can overcome nature, they think that none exists, and therefore, consistently, they believe that every one, Priest or not, remains to the end such as nature made him, and they will not believe it possible that any one can lead a supernatural life. Now, not Priest only, but every one who is in the grace of God, leads a supernatural life, more or less supernatural, according to his calling, and the measure of the gifts given him, and his faithfulness to them. This they know not, and admit not; and when they hear of the life which a Priest must lead by his profession from youth to age, they will not credit that he is what he professes to be. They know nothing of the presence of God, the merits of Christ, the intercession of the Blessed Virgin; the virtue of recurring prayers, of frequent confession, of daily Masses; they are strangers to the transforming power of the Most Holy Sacrament, the Bread of Angels; they do not contemplate the efficacy of salutary rules, of holy companions, of long-enduring habit, of ready spontaneous vigilance, of abhorrence of sin and indignation at the tempter, to secure the soul from evil. They only know that when the tempter once has actually penetrated into the heart, he is irresistible; they only know that when the soul has exposed and surrendered itself to his malice, there is (so to speak) a necessity of sinning. They only know that when God has abandoned it, and good Angels are withdrawn, and all safeguards, and protections, and preventives are neglected, that then (which is their own case), when the victory is all but gained already, it is sure to be gained altogether. They themselves have ever, in their best estate, been all but beaten by the Evil One before they began to fight; this is the only state they have experienced: they know this, and they know nothing else. They have never stood on vantage ground; they have never been within the walls of the strong city, about which the enemy prowls in vain, into which he cannot penetrate, and outside of which the faithful soul will be too wise to venture. They judge, I say, by their experience, and will not believe what they never knew.

If there be those here present, my dear brethren, who will not believe that grace is effectual within the Church, because it does little outside of it, to them I do not speak: I speak to those who do not narrow their belief to their experience; I speak to those who admit that grace can make human nature what it is not; and such persons, I think, will feel it, not a cause of jealousy and suspicion, but a great gain, a great mercy, that those are sent to preach to them, to receive their confessions, and to advise them, who can sympathise with their sins, even though they have not known them. Not a temptation, my brethren, can befall you, but what befalls all those who share your nature, though you may have yielded to it, and they may not have yielded. They can understand you, they can anticipate you, they can interpret you, though they have not kept pace with you in your course. They will be tender to you, they will "instruct you in the spirit of meekness," as the Apostle says, "considering themselves lest they also be tempted". Come then unto us, all ye that labour and are heavy laden, and ye shall find rest to your souls; come unto us, who now stand to you in Christ's stead, and who speak in Christ's name; for we too, like you, have been saved by Christ's all-saving blood. We too, like you, should be lost sinners, unless Christ had had mercy on us, unless His grace had cleansed us, unless His Church had received us, unless His saints had interceded for us. Be ye saved, as we have been saved; "come, listen, all ye that fear God, and we will tell you what He hath done for our souls". Listen to our testimony; behold our joy of heart, and increase it by partaking in it yourselves. Choose that good part which we have chosen; join ye yourselves to our company; it will never repent you, take our word for it, who have a right to speak, it will never repent you to have sought pardon and peace from the Catholic Church, which alone has grace, which alone has power, which alone has Saints; it will never repent you, though you go through trouble, though you have to give up much for her sake. It will never repent you, to have passed from the shadows of sense and time, and the deceptions of human feeling and false reason, to the glorious liberty of the sons of God.

And O, my brethren, when you have taken the great step, and stand in your blessed lot, as sinners reconciled to the Father you have offended (for I will anticipate, what I surely trust will be fulfilled as regards many of you), O then forget not those who have been the ministers of your reconciliation; and as they now pray you to make your peace with God, so do you, when recon-

402

ciled, pray for them, that they may gain the great gift of perseverance, that they may continue to stand in the grace in which they trust they stand now, even till the hour of death, lest, perchance, after they have preached to others, they themselves become reprobate.

Growth of the Cultus of Mary [†]

O NE WORD MORE, and I have done; I have shown you how full of
meaning are the truths themselves which the Church teaches concerning the Most Blessed Virgin, and now consider how full of
meaning also has been the Church's dispensation of them.

You will find, that, in this respect, as in Mary's prerogatives themselves,
there is the same careful reference to the glory of Him who gave them to her.
You know, when first He went out to preach, she kept apart from Him; she
interfered not with His work; and, even when He was gone up on high, yet
she, a woman, went not out to preach or teach, she seated not herself in the
Apostolic chair, she took no part in the Priest's office; she did but humbly seek
her Son in the daily Mass of those, who, though her ministers in heaven, were
her superiors in the Church on earth. Nor, when she and they had left this
lower scene, and she was a Queen upon her Son's right hand, not even then
did she ask of Him to publish her name to the ends of the world, or to hold
her up to the world's gaze, but she remained waiting for the time when her
own glory should be necessary for His. He indeed had been from the very first
proclaimed by Holy Church, and enthroned in His temple, for He was God;
ill had it beseemed the living Oracle of Truth to have withholden from the
faithful the very object of their adoration; but it was otherwise with Mary. It
became her, as a creature, a mother, and a woman, to stand aside and make
way for the Creator, to minister to her Son, and to win her way into the
world's homage by sweet and gracious persuasion. So when His name was dishonoured, then it was that she did Him service; when Emmanuel was denied,
then the Mother of God (as it were) came forward; when heretics said that
God was not incarnate, then was the time for her own honours. And then,
when as much as this had been accomplished, she had done with strife; she
fought not for herself. No fierce controversy, no persecuted confessors, no he-
resiarch, no anathema, marks the history of her manifestation; as she had increased day by day in grace and merit, while the world knew not of it, so has
she raised herself aloft silently, and has grown into her place in the Church by
a tranquil influence and a natural process. It was as some fair tree, stretching

---

[†] Excerpt from *Discourses to Mixed Congregations* (1849), Discourse 17, "The Glories of Mary
for the Sake of Her Son." The selection, as well as its title, is from William Samuel Lilly's *Characteristics.*

forth her fruitful branches and her fragrant leaves, and overshadowing the territory of the Saints. And thus the Antiphon speaks of her: "Let thy dwelling be in Jacob, and thine inheritance in Israel, and *strike thy roots* in My elect". Again, "And so in Sion was I established, and in the holy city I likewise rested, and in Jerusalem was my power. And I *took root* in an honourable people, and in the glorious company of the Saints was I *detained*. I was exalted like a cedar in Lebanus, and as a cypress in Mount Sion; I have stretched out My branches as the terebinth, and My branches are of honour and grace." Thus was she reared without hands, and gained a modest victory, and exerts a gentle sway, which she has not claimed. When dispute arose about her among her children, she hushed it; when objections were urged against her, she waived her claims and waited; till now, in this very day, should God so will, she will win at length her most radiant crown, and, without opposing voice, and amid the jubilation of the whole Church, she will be hailed as immaculate in her conception.

Such art thou, Holy Mother, in the creed and in the worship of the Church, the defence of many truths, the grace and smiling light of every devotion. In thee, O Mary, is fulfilled, as we can bear it, an original purpose of the Most High. He once had meant to come on earth in heavenly glory, but we sinned; and then He could not safely visit us, except with a shrouded radiance and a bedimmed majesty, for He was God. So He came Himself in weakness, not in power; and He sent thee, a creature, in His stead, with a creature's comeliness and lustre suited to our state. And now thy very face and form, dear Mother, speak to us of the Eternal; not like earthly beauty, dangerous to look upon, but like the morning star, which is thy emblem, bright and musical, breathing purity, telling of heaven, and infusing peace. O harbinger of day! O hope of the pilgrim! lead us still as thou hast led; in the dark night, across the bleak wilderness, guide us on to our Lord Jesus, guide us home.

> Maria, mater gratiæ,
> Dulcis parens clementiæ,
> Tu nos ab hoste protégé
> Et mortis horâ suscipe.

Usages & Ordinances the Outward Shape
of an Inward Reality[†]

A PROTESTANT wanders into one of our chapels; he sees a priest kneeling and bowing and throwing up a thurible, and boys in cottas going in and out, and a whole choir and people singing amain all the time, and he has nothing to suggest to him what it is all about; and he calls it mummery, and he walks out again. And would it not indeed be so, my brethren, if this were all? But will he think it mummery when he learns and seriously apprehends the fact, that, according to the belief of a Catholic, the Word Incarnate, the Second Person of the Eternal Trinity, is there bodily present,—hidden, indeed, from our senses, but in no other way withheld from us? He may reject what we believe; he will not wonder at what we do. And so, again, open the Missal, read the minute directions given for the celebration of Mass,—what are the fit dispositions under which the Priest prepares for it, how he is to arrange his every action, movement, gesture, utterance, during the course of it, and what is to be done in case of a variety of supposable accidents. What a mockery would all this be, if the rite meant nothing! But if it be a fact that God the Son is there offered up in human flesh and blood by the hands of man, why, it is plain that no rite whatever, however anxious and elaborate, is equal to the depth of the overwhelming thoughts which are borne in upon the mind by such an action. Thus the usages and ordinances of the Church do not exist for their own sake; they do not stand of themselves; they are not sufficient for themselves; they do not fight against the State their own battle; they are not appointed as ultimate ends; but they are dependent on an inward substance; they protect a mystery; they defend a dogma; they represent an idea; they preach good tidings; they are the channels of grace. They are the outward shape of an inward reality or fact, which no Catholic doubts, which is assumed as a first principle, which is not an inference of reason, but the object of a spiritual sense.

Herein is the strength of the Church; herein she differs from all Protestant mockeries of her. She professes to be built upon facts, not opinions;

[†] Excerpt from *Certain Difficulties Felt by Anglicans in Catholic Teaching* (1850), Volume 1, Lecture 7, "The Providential Course of the Movement of 1833 Not in the Direction of a Sect." The title is taken from within the text.

on objective truths, not on variable sentiments; on immemorial testimony, not on private judgment; on convictions or perceptions, not on conclusions. None else but she can make this profession. She makes high claims against the temporal power, but she has that within her which justifies her. She merely acts out what she says she is. She does no more than she reasonably should do. If God has given her a specific work, no wonder she is not under the superintendence of the civil magistrate in doing it. If her Clergy be Priests, if they can forgive sins, and bring the Son of God upon her altars, it is obvious they cannot, considered as such, hold of the State. If they were not Priests, the sooner they were put under a minister of public instruction, and the Episcopate abolished, the better. But she has not disturbed the world for nothing. Her precision and peremptoriness, all that is laid to her charge as intolerance and exclusiveness, her claim entirely to understand and to be able to deal with her own deposit and her own functions; her claim to reveal the unknown and to communicate the invisible, is, in the eye of reason (so far from being an objection to her coming from above), the very tenure of her high mission,—just what would be sure to characterise her if she had received such a mission. She cannot be conceived without her message and her gifts. She is the organ and oracle, and nothing else, of a supernatural doctrine, which is independent of individuals, given to her once for all, coming down from the first ages, and so deeply and intimately embosomed in her, that it cannot be clean torn out of her, even if you should try; which gradually and majestically comes forth into dogmatic shape, as time goes on and need requires, still by no private judgment, but at the will of its Giver, and by the infallible elaboration of the whole body;—and which is simply necessary for the salvation of every one of us. It is not a philosophy, or literature, cognisable and attainable at once by those who cast their eyes that way; but it is a sacred deposit and tradition, a mystery or secret, as Scripture calls it, sufficient to arrest and occupy the whole intellect, and unlike anything else; and hence requiring, from the nature of the case, organs special to itself, made for the purpose, whether for entering into its fulness, or carrying it out in deed.

Prejudice the Life of the Protestant View[†]

T HE PREJUDICED Man travels, and then everything he sees in Catholic countries only serves to make him more thankful that his notions are so true; and the more he sees of Popery, the more abominable he feels it to be. If there is any sin, any evil in a foreign population, though it be found among Protestants also, still Popery is clearly the cause of it. If great cities are the schools of vice, it is owing to Popery. If Sunday is profaned, if there is a Carnival, it is the fault of the Catholic Church. Then, there are no private homes, as in England, families live on staircases; see what it is to belong to a Popish country. Why do the Roman labourers wheel their barrows so slow on the Forum? why do the Lazzaroni of Naples lie so listlessly on the beach? why, but because they are under the *malaria* of a false religion. Rage, as is well-known, is in the Roman like a falling sickness, almost as if his will had no part in it, and he had no responsibility; see what it is to be a Papist. Bloodletting is as frequent and as much a matter of course in the South, as hair-cutting in England; it is a trick borrowed from the convents, when they wish to tame down refractory spirits.

The Prejudiced Man gets up at an English hour, has his breakfast at his leisure, and then saunters into some of the churches of the place; he is scandalized to have proof of what he has so often heard, the infrequency of communions among Catholics. Again and again, in the course of his tour, has he entered them, and never by any chance did he see a solitary communicant:— hundreds, perhaps, having communicated in those very churches, according to their custom, before he was out of his bedroom. But what scandalizes him most, is that even bishops and priests, nay, the Pope himself does not communicate at the great festivals of the Church. He was at a great ceremonial, a High Mass, on Lady Day, at the Minerva; not one Cardinal communicated; Pope and Cardinals, and every Priest present but the celebrant, having communicated, of course, each in his own Mass, and in his own chapel or church early in the morning. Then the churches are so dirty; faded splendour, tawdriness, squalidness are the fashion of the day;—thanks to the Protestants and Infidels, who, in almost every country where Catholicism is found, have stolen the revenues by which they were kept decent. He walks about and looks at the monuments, what is this? the figure of a woman: who can it be? His Protestant

---

[†] Excerpt from *Lectures on the Present Position of Catholics in England* (1851), Lecture 6.

cicerone at his elbow, who perhaps has been chosen by his good father or guardian to protect him on his travels from a Catholic taint, whispers that it is Pope Joan, and he notes it down in his pocket-book accordingly. I am alluding to an accident, which in its substance befell a most excellent person, for whom I had and have a great esteem, whom I am sure I would not willingly offend, and who will not be hurt at this cursory mention of an unintentional mistake. He was positive he had seen Pope Joan in Rome,—I think, in St. Peter's; nay, he saw the inscription on the monument, beginning with the words, "Joannæ Papissæ." It was so remarkable a fact, and formed so plausible an argument against the inviolateness of the chair of St. Peter, that it was thought worth inquiring into. I do not remember who it was that the female, thus elevated by his imagination, turned into in the process of investigation, whether into the Countess Matilda, or Queen Christina, or the figure of Religion in the vestibule of St. Peter's; but certainly into no lady who had any claim on the occupation of the Ecumenical See.

This puts me in mind of another occurrence, of which the publications of the day have recently been full. A lady of high literary reputation deposed that Denon and other French savans had given her the information that, in the days of the Republic or Consulate, they had examined St. Peter's chair in the Vatican Basilica, and had found that it unquestionably had come from the East, long after the age of the Apostle, for it had inscribed upon it the celebrated confession of Islamism, "There is one God, and Mahomet is his prophet." Her prejudices sharpened her memory, and she was positive in her testimony. Inquiry was made, and it turned out that the chair of which she had spoken was at Venice, not at Rome; that it had been brought thither by the Crusaders from the East, and therefore might well bear upon it the Mahometan inscription; and that tradition gave it the reputation of being, by no means the Roman, but the Antiochene Chair of the Apostle. In this, as in other mistakes, there was no deliberate intention to deceive; it was an ordinary result of an ordinary degree of prejudice. The voucher of the story was so firmly convinced, I suppose, of the "childish absurdity and falsehood of all the traditions of the Romish Church," that she thought it unnecessary to take pains to be very accurate, whether in her hearing or her memory.

Our Prejudiced Man might travel half his life up and down Catholic Europe, and only be confirmed in his contempt and hatred of its religion. In every place there are many worlds, quite distinct from each other: there are good men and bad, and the good form one body, the bad another. Two young men, as is well known, may pass through their course at a Protestant University, and come away with opposite reports of the state of the place: the one will have seen all the bad, the other all the good; one will say it is a sober, well-conducted place, the other will maintain that it is the home of every vice. The Prejudiced Man takes care to mix only in such society as will confirm his views; he courts the society of Protestants and unbelievers, and of bad Catholics, who shelter their own vice under the imputations they cast on others, and whose lives are a disgrace to the Church prior to their testimony. His servants, couriers, *laquais de place*, and acquaintance, are all of his own way of thinking, and find it for their interest to flatter and confirm it. He carries England with him abroad; and, though he has ascended mountains and traversed cities, knows scarcely more of Europe than when he set out.

But perhaps he does not leave England at all; he never has been abroad; it is all the same; he can scrape together quite as good evidence against Catholicism at home. One day he pays a visit to some Catholic chapel, or he casually finds the door open, and walks in. He enters and gazes about him, with a mixed feeling of wonder, expectation and disgust; and according to circumstances, this or that feeling predominates, and shows itself in his bearing and his countenance. In one man it is curiosity; in another, scorn; in another, conscious superiority; in another, abhorrence; over all of their faces, however, there is a sort of uncomfortable feeling, as if they were in the cave of Trophonius or in a Mesmerist's lecture-room. One and all seem to believe that something strange and dreadful may happen any moment; and they crowd up together, if some great ceremony is going on, tiptoeing and staring, and making strange faces, like the gargoyles or screen ornaments of the church itself. Every sound of the bell, every movement of the candles, every change in the grouping of the sacred ministers and the assistants, puts their hands and limbs in motion, to see what is coming next; our own poor alleviation, in thinking of them, lying in this,—that they are really ignorant of what is going on, and miss, even with their bodily eyes, the distinctive parts of the rite. What is our ground of comfort, however, will be their ground of accusation against us; for they are sure to go away and report that our worship consists of crossings, bowings, genuflections, incensings, locomotions, and revolvings, all about nothing.

In this matter, my Brothers, as I have already said, the plain truth is the keenest of satires; and therefore, instead of using any words of my own, I shall put before you a Protestant's account of a Benediction of the Blessed Sacrament, which he went to see in the Chapel of the Fathers of the Oratory in London. I quote his words from a publication of an important body, the British Reformation Society, established in the year 1827, and supported, I believe, by a number of eminent persons, noblemen, gentlemen, and ministers of various denominations. The periodical I speak of is called "*The British Protestant, or Journal of the Religious Principles of the Reformation.*" It would seem to be one of the Society's accredited publications, as it has its device upon the title-page. In the 62nd Number of this work, being the Number for February, 1850, we are presented with "Extracts from the Journal of a Protestant Scripture Reader." This gentleman, among his missionary visits to various parts of London, dropt in, it seems, on Tuesday, January 8th, to the Roman Catholic Chapel in King William Street; which, he commences his narrative by telling us, for "the large roses of every colour, and laurel," "was more like the flower-shops in the grand row of Covent Garden than a place of worship." Well, he had a right to his opinion here as much as another; and I do not mean to molest him in it. Nor shall I say anything of his account of the Sermon, which was upon one of the January Saints, and which he blames for not having in it the name of Jesus, or one word of Scripture from beginning to end; not dreaming that a Rite was to follow, in which we not only bow before the Name, but worship the real and substantial presence of our exalted Lord.

I need hardly observe to you, my Brothers, that the Benediction of the Blessed Sacrament is one of the simplest rites of the Church. The priests enter and kneel down; one of them unlocks the Tabernacle, takes out the Blessed Sacrament, inserts it upright in a Monstrance of precious metal, and sets it in a conspicuous place above the altar, in the midst of lights, for all to see. The people then begin to sing; meanwhile the Priest twice offers incense to the King of heaven, before whom he is kneeling. Then he takes the Monstrance in his hands, and turning to the people, blesses them with the Most Holy, in the form of a cross, while the bell is sounded by one of the attendants to call attention to the ceremony. It is our Lord's solemn benediction of His people, as when He lifted up His hands over the children, or when He blessed His chosen ones when He ascended up from Mount Olivet. As sons might come before a parent before going to bed at night, so, once or twice a week the great Catholic family comes before the Eternal Father, after the bustle or toil of the day, and He smiles upon them, and sheds upon them the light of His countenance. It is a full accomplishment of what the Priest invoked upon the Israelites, "The Lord bless thee and keep thee; the Lord show His face to thee and have mercy on thee; the Lord turn His countenance to thee and give thee peace." Can there be a more touching rite, even in the judgment of those who do not believe in it? How many a man, not a Catholic, is moved, on seeing it, to say "Oh, that I did but believe it!" when he sees the Priest take up the Fount of Mercy, and the people bent low in adoration! It is one of the most beautiful, natural, and soothing actions of the Church—not so, however, in the judgment of our young Protestant Scripture Reader, to whom I now return.

This Protestant Scripture Reader then, as he calls himself, enters the chapel, thinking, of course, he knows all about everything. He is the measure of everything, or at least of everything Popish. Popery he knows perfectly well, in substance, in spirit, in drift, in results; and he can interpret all the details when they come before him at once, by this previous, or what a theologian might term "infused," knowledge. He knows, and has known from a child, that Popery is a system of imposture, nay, such brazen imposture, that it is a marvel, or rather miracle, that any one can be caught by it—a miracle, that is, of Satan: for without an evil influence it is quite impossible any single soul could believe what the Protestant Scripture Reader would call so "transparent a fraud." As a Scripture Reader he knows well the text, Second of Thessalonians, chapter two, verse eleven, "He shall send them strong delusion that they should believe a lie," and he applies it to the scene before him. He knows that it is the one business of the Priest to take in the people, and he knows that the people are so inconceivably brutish that nothing is too gross or absurd a trick to take them in withal. If the Priest were to put up a scarecrow, they, like the silly birds, would run away as if it were a man; and he has only to handle his balls or cards, and flourish them about, and they take him for a god. Indeed, we all know, he gives out he *is* a god, and can do what he pleases, for it is sin to doubt it. It is most wonderful, certainly, as to this Popery, that in spite of the Parliament all in a bustle, passing laws, as if against typhus or cholera, yet there it is, and spread it will; however, Satan is the father of lies; that is sufficient. With this great principle, I say, clearly impressed upon his mind, he walks into the chapel, knowing well he shall find some juggling there; accordingly, he is not at all surprised at the scene which passes before him. He looks on at his ease, and draws up his own account of it, all the time that the Catholic people are bowing and singing, and the Priest incensing; and his account runs thus:—

After the sermon, he tells us (I am quoting the very words of his Journal), "another young priest came in with a long wand in his hand, and an extinguisher on the top of it, and a small candle, and he began to light others." "*Another* young priest:" he thinks we are born priests; "priest" is a sort of race, or animal, or production, as oxen or sheep may be, and there are young priests and old priests, and black priests and white priests, and perhaps men priests and women priests; and so in came this "other young priest" with a wand. "With a wand:" he evidently thinks there is something religious about this lighter and extinguisher; it is a conjuror's wand; you will, I think, see presently I am borne out in saying this. He proceeds: "The next part of the play was four priests coming to the altar" (it is as I said; everything is a priest), "four priests and Gordon in the middle:" this is a mistake, and an unwarrantable and rude use of the name of one of the Fathers of the London Oratory, my dear brother and friend, the Reverend Philip Gordon—for it was not he, and he was not a priest; accordingly, I should leave the name out, except that it adds a good deal to the effect of the whole. "One of them," he proceeds, "took from a small cupboard on the altar," that is, from the tabernacle, "a gold star;" this is the *head* of the Monstrance, in which is placed the Blessed Sacrament, and screwed it on to a candlestick," that is, the *foot* of the Monstrance, "and placed it on the top of the altar, under the form of a beehive, supported by four pillars," that is, under the canopy. He calls the head of the Monstrance a star, because it consists of a circle surrounded by rays; and he seems to think it in some way connected with the season of the year, the Epiphany, when the Star appeared to the Wise Men.

"The Star," he proceeds, "glittered like diamonds, for it had a round lamp in the middle of it;" I suppose he means the glass covering the Blessed Sacrament, which reflected the light, and you will see clearly, as he goes on, that he actually thinks the whole congregation was worshipping this star and lamp. "This Star glittered like diamonds, for it had a round lamp in the middle of it; when placed under the beehive, the four priests began to burn incense, waving a large thing like a lanthorn" (the thurible) "towards the Star, and bowing themselves to kiss the foot of the altar before the Star." Now observe, my Brothers, I repeat, I am not blaming this person for not knowing a Catholic rite, which he had no means of knowing, but for thinking he knows it, when he does not know it, for coming into the chapel, with this most coxcombical idea in his head, that Popery is a piece of mummery, which any intelligent Protestant can see through, and therefore being not at all surprised, but thinking it very natural, when he finds four priests, a young priest with a wand, and a whole congregation, worshipping a gold star glittering like diamonds with a lamp in it. This is what I mean by *prejudice*.

Now you may really have a difficulty in believing that I have interpreted him rightly; so let me proceed. "The next piece acted was, one of them went to bring down the Star, and put it on the altar, while another put something like a white shawl round Gordon's shoulders." True; he means the veil which is put upon the Priest, before he turns round with the Blessed Sacrament in his hand. "Gordon next takes the Star, and, turning his face to the people, to raise up the Star, with part of the shawl round the candlestick, the other two priests, one on each side of him, drawing the shawl, it showed a real piece of magic art." Now what makes this so amusing to the Catholic is, that, as far as the priest's actions go, it is really so accurately described. It is the description of one who has his eyes about him, and makes the best of them, but who, as he goes on, is ever putting his own absurd comment on everything which occurs in succession. Now, observe, he spoke of "magic;" let us see what the magic is, and what becomes of the Star, the lamp, and the candlestick with the shawl round it.

"As Gordon raised the Star, with his back to all the lighted candles on the altar, he clearly showed the Popish deceit, for *in the candlestick there is a bell.*" Here is his first great failure of fact; he could not be looking at two places at once; he heard the bell, which the attendant was ringing at one side; he did not see it; where could it be? his ready genius, that is, the genius of his wonderful prejudice about us, told him at once where it was. It was a piece of priestcraft, and the bell was concealed inside the foot of the candlestick;— listen. "As Gordon raised the Star, with his back turned to all the lighted candles on the altar, he clearly showed the Popish deceit; for in the candlestick there is a bell, that rung three times of its own accord, to deceive the blind fools more; and the light through the shawl showed so many colours, as Father Gordon moved his body; the bell ringing they could not see, for the candlestick was covered with part of this magic shawl, and Gordon's finger at work underneath."

Such is his account of the rite of Benediction; he is so densely ignorant of us, and so supremely confident of his knowledge, that he ventures to put in print something like the following rubrical direction for its celebration:—

First, a young priest setteth up a golden, diamond-like star, with a lamp in it, sticking it on to the top of a candlestick, then he lighteth fifty candles by means of a wand with an extinguisher and wax candle upon it; then four priests bow, burn incense, and wave a lanthorn before the star; then one of the priests, hiding what he is at, by means of a great shawl about his hands and the foot of the candlestick, taketh up said candlestick, with the lamp and gold star glittering like diamonds, and beginneth secretly to tinkle with his finger a bell hid in its foot; whereupon the whole congregation marvelleth much, and worshippeth star, lamp and candlestick incontinently.

He ends with the following peroration:—"This the power of priests; they are the best play actors in this town. I should be glad to see this published, that I might take it to Father Gordon, to see if he could contradict a word of it." Rather, such is the power of prejudice, by good luck expressed in writing, and given to the world, as a specimen of what goes on, without being recorded, in so many hundred thousands of minds. The very confidence with which he appeals to the accuracy of his testimony only shows how prejudice can create or colour, where facts are harmless or natural. It is superior to facts, and lives in a world of its own.

Nor would it be at all to the purpose to object, that, had he known what the rite really meant, he would quite as much, or even more, have called it idolatry. The point is not what *he* would think of our rites, if he understood them exactly, for I am not supposing his judgment to be worth anything at all, or that we are not as likely to be right as an individual Scripture Reader; the question is not, what he would judge, but what he did think, and how he came to think it. His prejudice interpreted our actions.

6.

Alas, my Brothers, though we have laughed at the extravagance which shows itself in such instances of prejudice, it is in truth no matter for a jest. If I laugh, it is to hide the deep feelings of various kinds which it necessarily excites in the mind. I laugh at what is laughable in the displays of this wretched root of evil, in order to turn away my thoughts from its nature and effects, which are not laughable, but hateful and dangerous—dangerous to the Catholic, hateful to the Supreme Judge. When you see a beast of prey in his cage, you are led to laugh at its impotent fury, at its fretful motions and its sullen air and its grotesque expressions of impatience, disappointment, and malice, if it is baulked of its revenge. And, as to this Prejudice, Brothers of the Oratory, really in itself it is one of the direst, most piteous, most awful phenomena in the whole country; to see a noble, generous people the victims of a moral infirmity, which is now a fever, now an ague, now a falling sickness, now a frenzy, and now a St. Vitus's dance. Oh, if we could see as the angels see, thus should we speak of it, and in language far more solemn. I told you why in an earlier part of this Lecture;—not simply because the evil comes from beneath, as I believe it does; not only because it so falls upon the soul, and occupies it, that it is like a bad dream or nightmare, which is so hard to shake off;—but chiefly because it is one of the worst sins of which our poor nature is capable. Perhaps it is wrong to compare sin with sin, but I declare to you, the more I think of it, the more intimately does this prejudice seem to me to corrupt the soul, even beyond those sins which are commonly called most deadly, as the various forms of impurity or pride. And why? because, I repeat it, it argues so astonishing a want of mere natural charity or love of our kind. It is piercing enough to think what little faith there is in the country; but it is quite heartrending to witness so utter a deficiency in a mere natural virtue. Oh, is it possible, that so many, many men, and women too, good and kind otherwise, should take such delight in being quite sure that millions of men have the sign and seal of the Evil One upon them! Oh, is it conceivable that they can be considerate in all matters of this life, friendly in social intercourse, indulgent to the wayward, charitable to the poor and outcast, merciful towards criminals, nay, kind towards the inferior creation, towards their cows, and horses, and swine; yet, as regards us, who bear the same form, speak the same tongue, breathe the same air, and walk the same streets, ruthless, relentless, believing ill

415

of us, and wishing to believe it. I repeat it, they wish us to be what they believe us to be; what a portentous fact! They delight to look at us, and to believe that we are the veriest reptiles and vermin which belied the human form divine. It is a dear thought, which they cannot bear to lose. True, it may have been taught them from their youth, they never may have had means to unlearn it,—that is not the point; they have never *wished* better things of us, they have never *hoped* better things. They are tenacious of what they believe, they are impatient of being argued with, they are angry at being contradicted, they are disappointed when a point is cleared up; they had rather that *we* should be guilty than *they* mistaken; they have no wish at all we should not be blaspheming hypocrites, stupid idolaters, loathsome profligates, unprincipled rogues and bloodthirsty demons. They are kinder even to their dogs and their cats than to us. Is it not true? can it be denied? is it not portentous? does it not argue an incompleteness or hiatus in the very structure of their moral nature? has not something, in their case, dropped out of the list of natural qualities proper to man?

And hence it is, that, calm as may be the sky, and gentle the breeze, we cannot trust the morning: at any moment a furious tempest may be raised against us, and scatter calamity through our quiet homes, as long as the Prince of the power of the air retains this sovereignty. There is ever a predisposition in the political and social atmosphere to lour and thicken. We never are secure against the access of madness in that people, whose name and blood we share. Some accident,—a papal bull, worded as papal documents have been since the beginning of time, a sudden scandal among our priests or in our convents, or some bold and reckless falsehood, may raise all England against us. Such also was our condition in the first age of the Church: the chance of the hour brought the Pagan Romans upon us. A rash Christian tore down an Imperial manifesto from its place; the horrible Dioclesian persecution was the consequence. A crop failed, a foe appeared, it was all through the poor Christians. So speaks the Early Christian Apologist, the celebrated Tertullian, in his defence of us, about a hundred years after St. John's time. "They think the Christians," he says, "to be the cause of every public calamity, of every national ill. If the Tiber cometh up to the walls, if the Nile cometh not up to the fields, if the rain hath not fallen, if the earth hath been moved, if there be any famine, if any pestilence, *Christianos ad leonem*—to the lion with the Christians—is forthwith the cry." No limit could be put to the brutishness of the notions then entertained of us by the heathen. They believed we fed on children; they charged us with the most revolting forms of incest; they gave out that we worshipped beasts or monsters. "Now a new report of our God hath been lately set forth in this city," says the same Tertullian, "since a certain wretch put forth a picture with some such title as this,—The god of the Christians conceived of an ass. This was a creature with ass's ears, with a hoof on one foot, carrying a book and wearing a gown. We smiled both at the name and the figure." Not indeed the same, but parallel, are the tales told of us now. Scottish absurdities are gravely appropriated as precious truths. Our very persons, not merely our professions, are held in abhorrence; we are spit at by the malevolent, we are passed with a shudder of contemptuous pity by the better-natured; we are supposed to be defiled by some secret rites of blood by the ignorant. There is a mysterious pollution and repulsion about us, which makes those who feel its influence curious or anxious to investigate what it can be. We are regarded as something unclean, which a man would not touch, if he could help it; and our advances are met as would be those of some hideous baboon, or sloth, or rattle-snake, or toad, which strove to make itself agreeable.

Relics and Miracles[†]

I SUPPOSE there is nothing which prejudices us more in the minds of Protestants of all classes than our belief in miracles wrought by the relics and the prayers of the Saints. They inspect our churches, or they attend to our devotions, or they hear our sermons, or they open our books, or they read paragraphs in the newspapers, and it is one and the same story—relics and miracles. Such a belief, such a claim, they consider a self-evident absurdity; they are too indignant even to laugh; they toss the book from them in the fulness of anger and contempt, and they think it superfluous to make one remark in order to convict us of audacious imposture, and to fix upon us the brand of indelible shame. I shall show, then, that this strong feeling arises simply from their assumption of a First Principle, which ought to be proved, if they would be honest reasoners, before it is used to our disadvantage.

You observe, we are now upon a certain question of controversy, in which the argument is *not* directly about *fact* . . . We accuse our enemies of untruth in most cases; we do not accuse them, on the whole, of untruth here. I know it is very difficult for prejudice such as theirs to open its mouth at all without some misstatement or exaggeration; still, on the whole, they do bear true, not false witness, in the matter of miracles. We do certainly abound, we are exuberant, we overflow, with stories which cause our enemies, from no fault of ours, the keenest irritation, and kindle in them the most lively resentment against us. Certainly the Catholic Church, from east to west, from north to south, is, according to our conceptions, hung with miracles. The store of relics is inexhaustible; they are multiplied through all lands, and each particle of each has in it at least a dormant, perhaps an energetic virtue, of supernatural operation. At Rome there is the True Cross, the Crib of Bethlehem, and the Chair of St. Peter; portions of the Crown of Thorns are kept at Paris; the Holy Coat is shown at Trèves; the Winding-Sheet at Turin; at Monza, the iron crown is formed out of a Nail of the Cross; and another Nail is claimed for the Duomo of Milan; and pieces of our Lady's Habit are to be seen in the Escurial. The Agnus Dei, blessed medals, the scapular, the cord of St. Francis, all are the medium of divine manifestations and graces. Crucifixes have bowed

---

[†] Excerpt from *Lectures on the Present Position of Catholics in England* (1851), Lecture 7. The title is editorial.

the head to the suppliant, and Madonnas have bent their eyes upon assembled crowds. St. Januarius's blood liquefies periodically at Naples, and St. Winifred's well is the scene of wonders even in our unbelieving country. Women are marked with the sacred stigmata, blood has flowed on Fridays from their five wounds, and their heads are crowned with a circle of lacerations. Relics are ever touching the sick, the diseased, the wounded; sometimes with no result at all, at other times with marked and undeniable efficacy. Who has not heard of the abundant favours gained by the intercession of the Blessed Virgin, and of the marvellous consequences which have attended the invocation of St. Antony of Padua? These phenomena are sometimes reported of Saints in their lifetime, as well as after their death, especially if they were evangelists or martyrs. The wild beasts crouched before their victims in the Roman amphitheatre; the axe-man was unable to sever St. Cecilia's head from her body, and St. Peter elicited a spring of water for his jailor's baptism in the Mamertine. St. Francis Xavier turned salt water into fresh for five hundred travellers; St. Raymond was transported over the sea on his cloak; St. Andrew shone brightly in the dark; St. Scholastica gained by her prayers a pouring rain; St. Paul was fed by ravens; and St. Frances saw her guardian Angel. I need not continue the catalogue; here what one party urges, the other admits; they join issue over a fact; that fact is the claim of miracles on the part of the Catholic Church; it is the Protestants' charge, and it is our glory.

Observe, then, we affirm that the Supreme Being has wrought miracles on earth since the time of the Apostles. Protestants deny it. Why do we affirm? Why do they deny? We affirm it on a First Principle; they deny it on a First Principle; and on either side the First Principle is made to be decisive of the question . . . Both they and we start with the miracles of the Apostles, and then their First Principle, or presumption against our miracles, is, "What God did once, He is *not* likely to do again;" while our First Principle, or presumption for our miracles, is this: "What God did once, He *is* likely to do again." They say, "It cannot be supposed He will work *many* miracles;" we, "It cannot be supposed He will work *few*." . . . The two parties, you see, start with contradictory principles, and they determine the particular miracles, which are the subject of dispute, by their respective principles, without looking to such testimony as may be brought in their favour. They do not say, "St. Francis, or St. Antony, or St. Philip Neri, did no miracles, for the *evidence* for them is worth nothing," or "because what *looked* like a miracle was not a miracle;" no, but they say, "It is *impossible* they should have wrought miracles." Bring before the Protestant the largest mass of evidence and testimony in proof of the miraculous liquefaction of St. Januarius's blood at Naples, let him be urged by witnesses of the highest character, chemists of the first fame, circumstances the most favourable for the detection of imposture, coincidences and confirmations the most close, and minute, and indirect, he will not believe it; his First Principle *blocks* belief . . . He laughs at the very idea of miracles or supernatural acts, as occurring at this present day, . . . he laughs at the notion of evidence for them; one is just as likely as another, they are all false. Why? Because of his First Principle: there are no miracles since the Apostles.

II.

Now, on the other hand, let us take our own side of the question, and consider how we ourselves stand, relatively to the charge made against us. Catholics, then, hold the mystery of the Incarnation; and the Incarnation is the most stupendous event which ever can take place on earth; and after it, and henceforth, I do not see how we can scruple at any miracle on the mere ground of its being unlikely to happen. No miracle can be so great as that which took place in the Holy House at Nazareth; it is indefinitely more difficult to believe than all the miracles of the Breviary, of the Martyrology, of Saints' lives, of legends, of local traditions, put together; and there is the grossest inconsistency, on the very face of the matter, for any one so to strain out the gnat, and to swallow the camel, as to profess what is inconceivable, yet to protest against what is surely within the limits of intelligible hypothesis. If, through divine grace, we once are able to accept the solemn truth that the Supreme Being was born of a mortal woman, what is there to be imagined which can offend us on the ground of its marvellousness? Thus, you see, it happens that, though First Principles are commonly assumed, not proved, ours in this case admits, if not of proof, yet of recommendation, by means of that fundamental truth which Protestants profess as well as we. When we start with assuming that miracles are not unlikely, we are putting forth a position which lies imbedded, as it were, and involved in the great revealed fact of the Incarnation.

So much is plain on starting, but more is plain too. Miracles are not only not unlikely, they are positively likely, and for this simple reason, because, for the most part, when God begins, He goes on. We conceive that when He first did a miracle, He began a series; what He commenced, He continued; what has been, will be. Surely this is good and clear reasoning. To my own mind, certainly, it is incomparably more difficult to believe that the Divine Being should do one miracle and no more, than that He should do a thousand; that He should do one great miracle only, than that He should do a multitude of less besides. This beautiful world of nature, His own work, He broke its harmony, He broke through His own laws, which He had imposed on it; He worked out His purposes, not simply through it, but in violation of it. If He did this only in the lifetime of the Apostles; if He did it but once, eighteen hundred years ago and more, that isolated infringement looks as the mere infringement of a rule; if Divine Wisdom would not leave an infringement, an anomaly, a solecism, on His work, He might be expected to introduce a series of miracles, and turn the apparent exception into an additional law of His Providence. If the Divine Being does a thing once, He is, judging by human reason, likely to do it again. This surely is common sense . . . Suppose you yourselves were once to see a miracle, would you not feel that experience to be like passing a line? should you, in consequence of it, declare, "I never will believe another if I hear of one?" would it not, on the contrary, predispose you to listen to a new report? would you scoff at it, and call it priestcraft, for the reason that you had actually seen one with your own eyes? I think you would not; then, I ask, what is the difference of the argument, whether you have seen one or believe one? You believe the Apostolic miracles, therefore be inclined ,beforehand, to believe later ones. Thus you see, our First Principle, that miracles are not unlikely now, is not at all a strange one in the mouths of those who believe that the Supreme Being came miraculously into this world, miraculously united Himself to man's nature, passed a life of miracles, and then gave His Apostles a greater gift of miracles than He exercised Himself. So far on the principle itself; and now, in the next place, see what comes of it.

This comes of it,—that there are two systems going on in the world, one of nature, and one above nature; and two histories, one of common events, and one of miracles; and each system and each history has its own order. When I hear of the miracle of a Saint, my first feeling would be of the same kind as if it were a report of any natural exploit or event. Supposing, for instance, I heard a report of the death of some public man, it would not startle me, even if I did not at once credit it, for all men must die. Did I read of any great feat of valour, I should believe it, if imputed to Alexander or Coeur de Lion. Did I hear of any act of baseness, I should disbelieve it, if imputed to a friend whom I knew and loved. And so, in like manner, were a miracle reported to me as wrought by a member of Parliament, or a Bishop of the Establishment, or a Wesleyan preacher, I should repudiate the notion: were it referred to a Saint, or the relic of a Saint, or the intercession of a Saint, I should not be startled at it, though I might not at once believe it. And I certainly should be right in this conduct, supposing my First Principle be true. Miracles to the Catholic are facts of history and biography, and nothing else; and they are to be regarded and dealt with as other facts; and as natural facts, under circumstances, do not startle Protestants, so supernatural, under circumstances, do not startle the Catholic. They may or may not have taken place in particular cases; he may be unable to determine which; he may have no distinct evidence; he may suspend his judgment; but he will say, "It is very possible;" he never will say, "I cannot believe it."

III.

Such, then, is the answer I would make to those who would urge against us the multitude of miracles recorded in our Saints' Lives. We think them true in the sense in which Protestants think the details of English history true . . . If, indeed, miracles never can occur, then, indeed, impute the narratives to fraud; but, till you prove they are not likely, we shall consider the histories which have come down to us true on the whole, though in particular cases they may be exaggerated or unfounded. Where, indeed, they can certainly be proved to be false, there we shall be bound to do our best to get rid of them; but till that is clear, we shall be liberal enough to allow others to use their private judgment in their favour, as we use ours in their disparagement. For myself, lest I appear in any way to be shrinking from a determinate judgment on the claims of some of those miracles and relics, which Protestants are so startled at, and to be hiding particular questions in what is vague and general, I will avow distinctly, that, putting out of the question the hypothesis of unknown laws of nature (that is, of the professed miracle being not miraculous), I think it impossible to withstand the evidence which is brought for the liquefaction of the blood of St. Januarius at Naples, and for the motion of the eyes of the pictures of the Madonna in the Roman States. I see no reason to doubt the material of the Lombard crown at Monza; and I do not see why the Holy Coat at Trèves may not have been what it professes to be. I firmly believe that portions of the True Cross are at Rome, and elsewhere, that the Crib of Bethlehem is at Rome, and the bodies of St. Peter and St. Paul also. I believe that at Rome, too, lies St. Stephen, that St. Matthew lies at Salerno, and St. Andrew at Amalfi. I firmly believe that the relics of the Saints are doing innumerable miracles and graces daily, and that it needs only for a Catholic to show devotion to any Saint in order to receive special benefits from his intercession. I firmly believe that Saints in their lifetime have before now raised the dead to life, crossed the sea without vessels, multiplied grain and bread, cured incurable diseases, and superseded the operation of the laws of the universe in a multitude of ways. Many men, when they hear an educated man so speak, will at once impute the avowal to insanity, or to an idiosyncrasy, or to imbecility of mind, or to decrepitude of powers, or to fanaticism, or to hypocrisy. They have a right to say so, if they will; and we have a right to ask them why they do not say it of those who bow down before the Mystery of mysteries, the Divine Incarnation. If they do not believe this, they are not yet Protestants; if they do, let them grant that He who has done the greater may do the less.

Confession[†]

HOW MANY are the souls in distress, anxiety, or loneliness, whose one need is to find a being to whom they can pour out their feelings unheard by the world? Tell them out they must; they cannot tell them out to those whom they see every hour. They want to tell them and not to tell them; and they want to tell them out, yet be as if they be not told; they wish to tell them to one who is strong enough to bear them, yet not too strong to despise them; they wish to tell them to one who can at once advise and can sympathize with them; they wish to relieve themselves of a load, to gain a solace, to receive the assurance that there is one who thinks of them, and one to whom in thought they can recur, to whom they can betake themselves, if necessary, from time to time, while they are in the world. How many a Protestant's heart would leap at the news of such a benefit, putting aside all distinct ideas of a sacramental ordinance, or of a grant of pardon and the conveyance of grace! If there is a heavenly idea in the Catholic Church, looking at it simply as an idea, surely, next after the Blessed Sacrament, Confession is such. And such is it ever found in fact,—the very act of kneeling, the low and contrite voice, the sign of the cross hanging, so to say, over the head bowed low, and the words of peace and blessing. Oh, what a soothing charm is there, which the world can neither give nor take away! Oh, what piercing, heart-subduing tranquillity, provoking tears of joy, is poured almost substantially and physically upon the soul, the oil of gladness, as Scripture calls it, when the penitent at length rises, his God reconciled to him, his sins rolled away for ever! This is Confession as it is in fact; as those bear witness to it who know it by experience.

[†] Excerpt from *Lectures on the Present Position of Catholics in England* (1851), Lecture 8.

The Duties of a Preacher[†]

I T IS THE PREACHER'S duty to aim at imparting to others, not any fortui-
tous, unpremeditated benefit, but some *definite* spiritual good. It is here
that design and study find their place; the more exact and precise is the
subject which he treats, the more impressive and practical will he be; whereas
no one will carry off much from a discourse which is on the general subject of
virtue, or vaguely and feebly entertains the question of the desirableness of
attaining Heaven, or the rashness of incurring eternal ruin. As a distinct image
before the mind makes the preacher earnest, so it will give him something
which it is worth while to communicate to others. Mere sympathy, it is true, is
able, as I have said, to transfer an emotion or sentiment from mind to mind,
but it is not able to fix it there. He must aim at imprinting on the heart what
will never leave it, and this he cannot do unless he employ himself on some
definite subject, which he has to handle and weigh, and then, as it were, to
hand over from himself to others.

Hence it is that the Saints insist so expressly on the necessity of his addressing himself to the intellect of men, and of convincing as well as persuading. "Necesse est ut *doceat* et moveat," says St. Francis; and St. Antoninus still
more distinctly: "Debet prædicator clare loqui, *ut instruat intellectum* auditoris,
et doceat." Hence, moreover, in St. Ignatius's Exercises, the act of the intellect
precedes that of the affections. Father Lohner seems to me to be giving an instance in point when he tells us of a court-preacher, who delivered what would
be commonly considered eloquent sermons, and attracted no one; and next
took to simple explanations of the Mass and similar subjects, and then found
the church thronged. So necessary is it to have something to say, if we desire
any one to listen.

❧

In this respect the preacher differs from the minister of the sacraments, that he
comes to his hearers, in some sense or other, with antecedents.

Clad in his sacerdotal vestments, he sinks what is individual in himself
altogether, and is but the representative of Him from whom he derives his

---

[†] Excerpt from *The Idea of a University* (1852), Part 2, ch. 6: "University Preaching." The title is
editorial.

commission. His words, his tones, his actions, his presence, lose their personality; one bishop, one priest, is like another; they all chant the same notes, and observe the same genuflexions, as they give one peace and one blessing, as they offer one and the same sacrifice. The Mass must not be said without a Missal under the priest's eye; nor in any language but that in which it has come down to us from the early hierarchs of the Western Church.

But, when it is over, and the celebrant has resigned the vestments proper to it, then he resumes himself, and comes to us in the gifts and associations which attach to his person. He knows his sheep, and they know him; and it is this direct bearing of the teacher on the taught, of his mind upon their minds, and the mutual sympathy which exists between them, which is his strength and influence when he addresses them. They hang upon his lips as they cannot hang upon the pages of his book. Definiteness is the life of preaching. A definite hearer, not the whole world; a definite topic, not the whole evangelical tradition; and, in like manner, a definite speaker. Nothing that is anonymous will preach; nothing that is dead and gone; nothing even which is of yesterday, however religious in itself and useful. Thought and word are one in the Eternal Logos, and must not be separate in those who are His shadows on earth. They must issue fresh and fresh, as from the preacher's mouth, so from his breast, if they are to be "spirit and life" to the hearts of his hearers.

The Religion of the Pharisee,
the Religion of Mankind[†]

"O God, be merciful to me, a sinner."
Luke xviii. 13

THESE WORDS set before us what may be called the characteristic mark of the Christian Religion, as contrasted with the various forms of worship and schools of belief, which in early or in later times have spread over the earth. They are a confession of sin and a prayer for mercy. Not indeed that the notion of transgression and of forgiveness was introduced by Christianity, and is unknown beyond its pale; on the contrary, most observable it is, the symbols of guilt and pollution, and rites of deprecation and expiation, are more or less common to them all; but what is peculiar to our divine faith, as to Judaism before it, is this, that confession of sin enters into the idea of its highest saintliness, and that its pattern worshippers and the very heroes of its history are only, and can only be, and cherish in their hearts the everlasting memory that they are, and carry with them into heaven the rapturous avowal of their being, redeemed, restored transgressors. Such an avowal is not simply wrung from the lips of the neophyte, or of the lapsed; it is not the cry of the common run of men alone, who are buffeting with the surge of temptation in the wide world; it is the hymn of saints, it is the triumphant ode sounding from the heavenly harps of the Blessed before the Throne, who sing to their Divine Redeemer, "Thou wast slain, and hast redeemed us to God in Thy blood, out of every tribe, and tongue, and people, and nation."

And what is to the Saints above a theme of never-ending thankfulness, is, while they are yet on earth, the matter of their perpetual humiliation. Whatever be their advance in the spiritual life, they never rise from their knees, they never cease to beat their breasts, as if sin could possibly be strange to them while they were in the flesh. Even our Lord Himself, the very Son of God in human nature, and infinitely separate from sin,—even His Immaculate Mother, encompassed by His grace from the first beginnings of her existence, and without any part of the original stain,—even they, as descended from Adam,

---

[†] *Sermons Preached on Various Occasions* (1857), Sermon 2, preached on the Tenth Sunday after Pentecost, 1856, in the University Church, Dublin.

were subjected at least to death, the direct, emphatic punishment of sin. And much more, even the most favoured of that glorious company, whom He has washed clean in His Blood; they never forget what they were by birth; they confess, one and all, that they are children of Adam, and of the same nature as their brethren, and compassed with infirmities while in the flesh, whatever may be the grace given them and their own improvement of it. Others may look up to them, but they ever look up to God; others may speak of their merits, but they only speak of their defects. The young and unspotted, the aged and most mature, he who has sinned least, he who has repented most, the fresh innocent brow, and the hoary head, they unite in this one litany, "O God, be merciful to me, a sinner." So it was with St. Aloysius; so, on the other hand, was it with St. Ignatius; so was it with St. Rose, the youngest of the saints, who, as a child, submitted her tender frame to the most amazing penances; so was it with St. Philip Neri, one of the most aged, who, when some one praised him, cried out, "Begone! I am a devil, and not a saint;" and when going to communicate, would protest before his Lord, that he "was good for nothing, but to do evil." Such utter self-prostration, I say, is the very badge and token of the servant of Christ;—and this indeed is conveyed in His own words, when He says, "I am not come to call the just, but sinners;" and it is solemnly recognized and inculcated by Him, in the words which follow the text, "Every one that exalteth himself, shall be humbled, and he that humbleth himself, shall be exalted."

This, you see, my Brethren, is very different from that merely general acknowledgment of human guilt, and of the need of expiation, contained in those old and popular religions, which have before now occupied, or still occupy, the world. In them, guilt is an attribute of individuals, or of particular places, or of particular acts of nations, of bodies politic or their rulers, for whom, in consequence, purification is necessary. Or it is the purification of the worshipper, not so much personal as ritual, before he makes his offering, and an act of introduction to his religious service. All such practices indeed are remnants of true religion, and tokens and witnesses of it, useful both in themselves and in their import; but they do not rise to the explicitness and the fulness of the Christian doctrine. "There is not any man just." "All have sinned, and do need the glory of God." "Not by the works of justice, which we have done, but according to His mercy." The disciples of other worships and other philosophies thought and think, that the many indeed are bad, but the few are good. As their thoughts passed on from the ignorant and erring multitude to the select specimens of mankind, they left the notion of guilt behind, and they pictured for themselves an idea of truth and wisdom, perfect, indefectible, and self-sufficient. It was a sort of virtue without imperfection, which took pleasure in contemplating itself, which needed nothing, and which was, from its own internal excellence, sure of a reward. Their descriptions, their stories of good and religious men, are often beautiful, and admit of an instructive interpretation; but in themselves they have this great blot, that they make no mention of sin, and that they speak as if shame and humiliation were no properties of the virtuous. I will remind you, my Brethren, of a very beautiful story, which you have read in a writer of antiquity; and the more beautiful it is, the more it is fitted for my present purpose, for the defect in it will come out the more strongly by the very contrast, viz., the defect that, though in some sense it teaches piety, humility it does not teach. I say, when the Psalmist would describe the happy man, he says, "Blessed are they whose iniquities are forgiven, and whose sins are covered; blessed is the man to whom the Lord hath not imputed sin." Such is the blessedness of the Gospel; but what is the blessedness of the religions of the world? A celebrated Greek sage once paid a visit to a prosperous king of Lydia, who, after showing him all his greatness and his glory, asked him whom he considered to have the happiest lot, of all men whom he had known. On this, the philosopher, passing by the monarch himself, named a countryman of his own, as fulfilling his typical idea of human perfection. The most blessed of men, he said, was Tellus of Athens, for he lived in a flourishing city, and was prospered in his children, and in their families; and then at length when war ensued with a border state, he took his place in the battle, repelled the enemy, and died gloriously, being buried at the public expense where he fell, and receiving public honours. When the king asked who came next to him in Solon's judgment, the sage went on to name two brothers, conquerors at the games, who, when the oxen were not forthcoming, drew their mother, who was priestess, to the temple, to the great admiration of the assembled multitude; and who, on her praying for them the best of possible rewards, after sacrificing and feasting, lay down to sleep in the temple, and never rose again. No one can deny the beauty of these pictures; but it is for that reason I select them; they are the pictures of men who were not supposed to have any grave account to settle with heaven, who had easy duties, as they thought, and who fulfilled them.

Now perhaps you will ask me, my Brethren, whether this heathen idea of religion be not really higher than that which I have called pre-eminently Christian; for surely to obey in simple tranquillity and unsolicitous confidence, is the noblest conceivable state of the creature, and the most acceptable worship he can pay to the Creator. Doubtless it is the noblest and most acceptable worship; such has ever been the worship of the angels; such is the worship now of the spirits of the just made perfect; such will be the worship of the whole company of the glorified after the general resurrection. But we are engaged in considering the actual state of man, as found in this world; and I say, considering what he is, any standard of duty, which does not convict him of real and multiplied sins, and of incapacity to please God of his own strength, is untrue; and any rule of life, which leaves him contented with himself, without fear, without anxiety, without humiliation, is deceptive; it is the blind leading the blind: yet such, in one shape or other, is the religion of the whole earth, beyond the pale of the Church.

The natural conscience of man, if cultivated from within, if enlightened by those external aids which in varying degrees are given him in every place and time, would teach him much of his duty to God and man, and would lead him on, by the guidance both of Providence and grace, into the fulness of religious knowledge; but, generally speaking, he is contented that it should tell him very little, and he makes no efforts to gain any juster views than he has at first, of his relations to the world around him and to his Creator. Thus he apprehends part, and part only, of the moral law; has scarcely any idea at all of sanctity; and, instead of tracing actions to their source, which is the motive, and judging them thereby, he measures them for the most part by their effects and their outward aspect. Such is the way with the multitude of men everywhere and at all times; they do not see the Image of Almighty God before them, and ask themselves what He wishes: if once they did this, they would begin to see how much He requires, and they would earnestly come to Him, both to be pardoned for what they do wrong, and for the power to do better. And, for the same reason that they do not please Him, they succeed in pleasing themselves. For that contracted, defective range of duties, which falls so short of God's law, is just what they can fulfil; or rather they choose it, and keep to it, *because* they can fulfil it. Hence, they become both self-satisfied and self-sufficient;—they think they know just what they ought to do, and that they do it all; and in consequence they are very well content with themselves, and rate their merit very high, and have no fear at all of any future scrutiny into their conduct, which may befall them, though their religion mainly lies in certain outward observances, and not a great number even of them.

So it was with the Pharisee in this day's gospel. He looked upon himself with great complacency, for the very reason that the standard was so low, and the range so narrow, which he assigned to his duties towards God and man. He used, or misused, the traditions in which he had been brought up, to the purpose of persuading himself that perfection lay in merely answering the demands of society. He professed, indeed, to pay thanks to God, but he hardly apprehended the existence of any direct duties on his part towards his Maker. He thought he did all that God required, if he satisfied public opinion. To be religious, in the Pharisee's sense, was to keep the peace towards others, to take his share in the burdens of the poor, to abstain from gross vice, and to set a good example. His alms and fastings were not done in penance, but because the world asked for them; penance would have implied the consciousness of sin; whereas it was only Publicans, and such as they, who had anything to be forgiven. And these indeed were the outcasts of society, and despicable; but no account lay against men of well-regulated minds such as his: men who were well-behaved, decorous, consistent, and respectable. He thanked God he was a Pharisee, and not a penitent.

Such was the Jew in our Lord's day; and such the heathen was, and had been. Alas! I do not mean to affirm that it was common for the poor heathen to observe even any religious rule at all; but I am speaking of the few and of the better sort: and these, I say, commonly took up with a religion like the Pharisee's, more beautiful perhaps and more poetical, but not at all deeper or truer than his. They did not indeed fast, or give alms, or observe the ordinances of Judaism; they threw over their meagre observances a philosophical garb, and embellished them with the refinements of a cultivated intellect; still their notion of moral and religious duty was as shallow as that of the Pharisee, and the sense of sin, the habit of self-abasement, and the desire of contrition, just as absent from their minds as from his. They framed a code of morals which they could without trouble obey; and then they were content with it and with themselves. Virtue, according to Xenophon, one of the best principled and most religious of their writers, and one who had seen a great deal of the world, and had the opportunity of bringing together in one the highest thoughts of many schools and countries,—virtue, according to him, consists mainly in command of the appetites and passions, and in serving others in order that they may serve us. He says, in the well known Fable, called the choice of Hercules, that Vice has no real enjoyment even of those pleasures which it aims at; that it eats before it is hungry, and drinks before it is thirsty, and slumbers before it is wearied. It never hears, he says, that sweetest of voices, its own praise; it never sees that greatest luxury among sights, its own good deeds. It enfeebles the bodily frame of the young, and the intellect of the old. Virtue, on the other hand, rewards young men with the praise of their elders, and it rewards the aged with the reverence of youth; it supplies them pleasant memories and present peace; it secures the favour of heaven, the love of friends, a country's thanks, and, when death comes, an everlasting renown. In all such descriptions, virtue is something external; it is not concerned with motives or intentions; it is occupied in deeds which bear upon society, and which gain the praise of men; it has little to do with conscience and the Lord of conscience; and knows nothing of shame, humiliation, and penance. It is in substance the Pharisee's religion, though it be more graceful and more interesting.

Now this age is as removed in distance, as in character, from that of the Greek philosopher; yet who will say that the religion which it acts upon is very different from the religion of the heathen? Of course I understand well, that it might know, and that it will say, a great many things foreign and contrary to heathenism. I am well aware that the theology of this age is very different from what it was two thousand years ago. I know men profess a great deal, and boast that they are Christians, and speak of Christianity as being a religion of the heart; but, when we put aside words and professions, and try to discover what their religion is, we shall find, I fear, that the great mass of men in fact get rid of all religion that is inward; that they lay no stress on acts of faith, hope, and charity, on simplicity of intention, purity of motive, or mortification of the thoughts; that they confine themselves to two or three virtues, superficially practised; that they know not the words contrition, penance, and pardon; and that they think and argue that, after all, if a man does his duty in the world, according to his vocation, he cannot fail to go to heaven, however little he may do besides, nay, however much, in other matters, he may do that is undeniably unlawful. Thus a soldier's duty is loyalty, obedience, and valour, and he may let other matters take their chance; a trader's duty is honesty; an artisan's duty is industry and contentment; of a gentleman are required veracity, courteousness, and self-respect; of a public man, high-principled ambition; of a woman, the domestic virtues; of a minister of religion, decorum, benevolence, and some activity. Now, all these are instances of mere Pharisaical excellence; because there is no apprehension of Almighty God, no insight into His claims on us, no sense of the creature's shortcomings, no self-condemnation, confession, and deprecation, nothing of those deep and sacred feelings which ever characterize the religion of a Christian, and more and more, not less and less, as he mounts up from mere ordinary obedience to the perfection of a saint.

And such, I say, is the religion of the natural man in every age and place;—often very beautiful on the surface, but worthless in God's sight; good, as far as it goes, but worthless and hopeless, because it does not go further, because it is based on self-sufficiency, and results in self-satisfaction. I grant, it may be beautiful to look at, as in the instance of the young ruler whom our Lord looked at and loved, yet sent away sad; it may have all the delicacy, the amiableness, the tenderness, the religious sentiment, the kindness, which is actually seen in many a father of a family, many a mother, many a daughter, in the length and breadth of these kingdoms, in a refined and polished age like this; but still it is rejected by the heart-searching God, because all such persons walk by their own light, not by the True Light of men, because self is their supreme teacher, and because they pace round and round in the small circle of their own thoughts and of their own judgments, careless to know what God says to them, and fearless of being condemned by Him, if only they stand approved in their own sight. And thus they incur the force of those terrible words, spoken not to a Jewish Ruler, nor to a heathen philosopher, but to a fallen Christian community, to the Christian Pharisees of Laodicea,— "Because thou sayest I am rich, and made wealthy, and have need of nothing; and knowest not that thou art wretched, and miserable, and poor, and blind, and naked; I counsel thee to buy of Me gold fire-tried, that thou mayest be made rich, and be clothed in white garments, that thy shame may not appear, and anoint thine eyes with eye-salve, that thou mayest see. Such as I love, I rebuke and chastise; be zealous, therefore, and do penance."

Yes, my Brethren, it is the ignorance of our understanding, it is our spiritual blindness, it is our banishment from the presence of Him who is the source and the standard of all Truth, which is the cause of this meagre, heartless religion of which men are commonly so proud. Had we any proper insight into things as they are, had we any real apprehension of God as He is, of ourselves as we are, we should never dare to serve Him without fear, or to rejoice unto Him without trembling. And it is the removal of this veil which is spread between our eyes and heaven, it is the pouring in upon the soul of the illuminating grace of the New Covenant, which makes the religion of the Christian so different from that of the various human rites and philosophies, which are spread over the earth. The Catholic saints alone confess sin, because the Catholic saints alone see God. That awful Creator Spirit, of whom the Epistle of this day speaks so much, He it is who brings into religion the true devotion, the true worship, and changes the self-satisfied Pharisee into the broken-hearted, self-abased Publican. It is the sight of God, revealed to the eye of faith, that makes us hideous to ourselves, from the contrast which we find ourselves to present to that great God at whom we look. It is the vision of Him in His infinite gloriousness, the All-holy, the All-beautiful, the All-perfect, which makes us sink into the earth with self-contempt and self-abhorrence. We are contented with ourselves till we contemplate Him. Why is it, I say, that the moral code of the world is so precise and well-defined? Why is the worship of reason so calm? Why was the religion of classic heathenism so joyous? Why is the framework of civilized society all so graceful and so correct? Why, on the other hand, is there so much of emotion, so much of conflicting and alternating feeling, so much that is high, so much that is abased, in the devotion of Christianity? It is because the Christian, and the Christian alone, has a revelation of God; it is because he has upon his mind, in his heart, on his conscience, the idea of one who is Self-dependent, who is from Everlasting, who is Incommunicable. He knows that One alone is holy, and that His own creatures are so frail in comparison of Him, that they would dwindle and melt away in His presence, did He not uphold them by His power. He knows that there is One whose greatness and whose blessedness are not affected, the centre of whose stability is not moved, by the presence or the absence of the whole creation with its innumerable beings and portions; whom nothing can touch, nothing can increase or diminish; who was as mighty before He made the worlds as since, and as serene and blissful since He made them as before. He knows that there is just One Being, in whose hand lies his own happiness, his own sanctity, his own life, and hope, and salvation. He knows that there is One to whom he owes every thing, and against whom he can have no plea or remedy. All things are nothing before Him; the highest beings do but worship Him the more; the holiest beings are such, only because they have a greater portion of Him.

Ah! what has he to pride in now, when he looks back upon himself? Where has fled all that comeliness which heretofore he thought embellished him? What is he but some vile reptile, which ought to shrink aside out of the light of day? This was the feeling of St. Peter, when he first gained a glimpse of the greatness of his Master, and cried out, almost beside himself, "Depart from me, for I am a sinful man, O Lord!" It was the feeling of holy Job, though he had served God for so many years, and had been so perfected in virtue, when the Almighty answered him from the whirlwind: "With the hearing of the ear I have heard Thee," he said; "but now my eye seeth Thee; therefore I reprove myself, and do penance in dust and ashes." So was it with Isaias, when he saw the vision of the Seraphim, and said, "Woe is me . . . I am a man of unclean lips, and I dwell in the midst of a people that hath unclean lips, and I have seen with my eyes the King, the Lord of Hosts." So was it with Daniel, when, even at the sight of an Angel, sent from God, "there remained no strength in him, but the appearance of his countenance was changed in him, and he fainted away, and retained no strength." This then, my Brethren, is the reason why every son of man, whatever be his degree of holiness, whether a returning prodigal or a matured saint, says with the Publican, "O God, be merciful to me;" it is because created natures, high and low, are all on a level in the sight and in comparison of the Creator, and so all of them have one speech, and one only, whether it be the thief on the cross, Magdalen at the feast, or St. Paul before his martyrdom:—not that one of them may not have, what another has not, but that one and all have nothing but what comes from Him, and are as nothing before Him, who is all in all.

For us, my dear Brethren, whose duties lie in this seat of learning and science, may we never be carried away by any undue fondness for any human branch of study, so as to be forgetful that our true wisdom, and nobility, and strength, consist in the knowledge of Almighty God. Nature and man are our studies, but God is higher than all. It is easy to lose Him in His works. It is easy to become over-attached to our own pursuit, to substitute it for religion, and to make it the fuel of pride. Our secular attainments will avail us nothing, if they be not subordinate to religion. The knowledge of the sun, moon, and stars, of the earth and its three kingdoms, of the classics, or of history, will never bring us to heaven. We may "thank God," that we are not as the illiterate and the dull; and those whom we despise, if they do but know how to ask mercy of Him, know what is very much more to the purpose of getting to heaven, than all our letters and all our science. Let this be the spirit in which we end our session. Let us thank Him for all that He has done for us, for what He is doing by us; but let nothing that we know or that we can do, keep us from a personal, individual adoption of the great Apostle's words, "Christ Jesus came into this world to save sinners, of whom I am the chief."

Intimate, Immediate Dependence[†]

T HE ENERGETIC, direct apprehension of an unseen Lord and Saviour has not been peculiar to Prophets and Apostles; it has been the habit of His Holy Church, and of her children, down to this day. Age passes after age, and she varies her discipline, and she adds to her devotions, and all with the one purpose of fixing her own and their gaze more fully upon the person of her unseen Lord. She has adoringly surveyed Him, feature by feature, and has paid a separate homage to Him in every one. She has made us honour His Five Wounds, His Precious Blood, and His Sacred Heart. She has bid us meditate on His infancy, and the acts of His ministry; His agony, His scourging, and His crucifixion. She has sent us on pilgrimage to His birthplace and His sepulchre, and the mount of His ascension. She has sought out, and placed before us, the memorials of His life and death; His crib and holy house, His holy tunic, the handkerchief of St. Veronica, the cross and its nails, His winding-sheet, and the napkin for His head.

And so, again, if the Church has exalted Mary or Joseph, it has been with a view to the glory of His sacred humanity. If Mary is proclaimed as immaculate, it illustrates the doctrine of her Maternity. If she is called the Mother of God, it is to remind Him that, though He is out of sight, He, nevertheless, is our possession, for He is of the race of man. If she is painted with Him in her arms, it is because we will not suffer the Object of our love to cease to be human, because He is also divine. If she is the Mater Dolorosa, it is because she stands by His cross. If she is Maria Desolata, it is because His dead body is on her lap. If, again, she is the Coronata, the crown is set upon her head by His dear hand. And, in like manner, if we are devout to Joseph, it is as to His foster-father; and if he is the saint of happy death, it is because he dies in the hands of Jesus and Mary.

And what the Church urges on us down to this day, saints and holy men down to this day have exemplified. Is it necessary to refer to the lives of the Holy Virgins, who were and are His very spouses, wedded to Him by a mystical marriage, and in many instances visited here by the earnests of that ineffable celestial benediction which is in heaven their everlasting portion? The mar-

---

[†] Excerpt from *Sermons Preached on Various Occasions* (1857), Sermon 3, "Waiting for Christ," preached on the Twenty-Seventh Sunday after Pentecost, 1856, in the University Church, Dublin. The title is taken from within the selection.

tyrs, the confessors of the Church, bishops, evangelists, doctors, preachers, monks, hermits, ascetical teachers,—have they not, one and all, as their histories show, lived on the very name of Jesus, as food, as medicine, as fragrance, as light, as life from the dead?—as one of them says, "in aure dulce canticum, in ore mel mirificum, in corde nectar coelicum."

Nor is it necessary to be a saint thus to feel: this intimate, immediate dependence on Emmanuel, God with us, has been in all ages the characteristic, almost the definition, of a Christian. It is the ordinary feeling of Catholic populations; it is the elementary feeling of every one who has but a common hope of heaven. I recollect, years ago, hearing an acquaintance, not a Catholic, speak of a work of devotion, written as Catholics usually write, with wonder and perplexity, because (he said) the author wrote as if he had "a sort of personal attachment to our Lord"; "it was as if he had seen Him, known Him, lived with Him, instead of merely professing and believing the great doctrine of the Atonement." It is this same phenomenon which strikes those who are not Catholics, when they enter our churches. They themselves are accustomed to do religious acts simply as a duty; they are serious at prayer time, and behave with decency, because it is a duty. But you know, my brethren, mere duty, a sense of propriety, and good behaviour, these are not the ruling principles present in the minds of our worshippers. Wherefore, on the contrary, those spontaneous postures of devotion? why those unstudied gestures? why those abstracted countenances? why that heedlessness of the presence of others? why that absence of the shame-facedness which is so sovereign among professors of other creeds? The spectator sees the effect; he cannot understand the cause of it. *Why* is this simple earnestness of worship? *we* have no difficulty in answering. It is because the Incarnate Saviour is present in the tabernacle; and then, when suddenly the hitherto silent church is, as it were, illuminated with the full piercing burst of voices from the whole congregation, it is because He now has gone up upon His throne over the altar, there to be adored. It is the visible Sign of the Son of Man, which thrills through the congregation, and makes them overflow with jubilation.

Order, the Witness and Instrument of Unity[†]

"And He sent them to preach the kingdom of God, and to heal the sick. And He said to them: Take nothing for your journey, neither staff, nor scrip, nor bread, nor money; neither have two coats; and whatever house you shall enter into, abide there, and depart not from thence."   Luke ix. 2–4

THESE WORDS, taken from the Gospel which has just now found a place in the sacred solemnity in which we are at present engaged, may be called the ceremonial, with which the preachers of the New Law were ordered to go forward for the execution of their charitable work. In this point of view, as in other respects, they are remarkable words, as intimating to us how utterly contrary it is to the character and spirit of the Divine Appointments to do anything without order and prescription. If an occasion could be supposed on which external forms might have been dispensed with, surely it was then, when the Disciples were to be wanderers on the face of the earth, to be whirled about as leaves by the rude blast, and to be accounted fortunate if they managed in their mission to secure themselves from torture and death. Yet even on that their first entrance into the regions of darkness and sin, ere the faithful had grown into an extended, and were formed into an organized body, ere they had secured vigour and weight sufficient to act upon the world, even in the Church's initiatory and provisional state, we find her furnished by her Divine Founder with canons and decrees for the first simple movements and actions of her ministers. Even in those rudimental efforts, the Apostle's rule is to be verified: "Non est dissentionis Deus sed pacis." He is not a God of confusion, of discordance, of accidental, random, private courses in the execution of His will, but of determinate, regulated, prescribed action. It might have seemed a matter of indifference how the Disciples addressed themselves to their missionary work; but no, they were to go forth "in pace, et in nomine Domini": their very dress, their carriage, and their journeying, were anticipated for them, and were to be of one kind, not of another.

All the works of God are founded on unity, for they are founded on Himself, who is the most awfully simple and transcendent of possible unities.

[†] *Sermons Preached on Various Occasions* (1857), Sermon 11, preached Nov. 9, 1853, in St. Chad's, in the first Diocesan Synod of Birmingham.

He is emphatically One; and whereas He is also multiform in His attributes and His acts, as they present themselves to our minds, it follows that order and harmony must be of His very essence. To be many and distinct in His attributes, yet, after all, to be but one,—to be sanctity, justice, truth, love, power, wisdom, to be at once each of these as fully as if He were nothing but it, as if the rest were not,—this implies in the Divine Nature an infinitely sovereign and utterly incomprehensible order, which is an attribute as wonderful as any, and the result of all the others. He is an infinite law, as well as an infinite power, wisdom, and love. Moreover, the very idea of order implies the idea of the subordinate. If order exists in the Divine Attributes, they must have relations one to another, and though each is perfect in itself, it must act so as not to impair the perfection of the rest, and must seem to yield to the rest on particular occasions. Thus God's power, indeed, is infinite, but it is still subordinate to His wisdom and His justice; His justice, again, is infinite, but it, too, is subordinate to His love; and His love, in turn, is infinite, but it is subordinate to His incommunicable sanctity. There is an understanding between attribute and attribute, so that one does not interfere with the other, for each is supreme in its own sphere; and thus an infinitude of infinities, acting each in its own order, are combined together in the infinitely simple unity of God.

Such is the unity, and consequent harmony and beauty of the Divine Nature, even when viewed in the lights which are supplied to us by the traditions of the human race and the investigations of the human intellect. But, wonderful as is that order and harmony, considered only in the way of nature, much more wonderful is it in the mysteries of Revelation. There we are introduced to the ineffable, the adorable, the most gracious dogma of a Trinity in Unity, which is what I may call the triumph of Unity over difficulties, which, to our limited faculties, seem like impossibilities and contradictions. How strong, how severe, how infinitely indivisible, must be that Unity of God, which is not compromised by the truth of His being Three! How surpassing is that Unity of substance which remains untroubled and secure, though it is occupied and possessed wholly and unreservedly, not only by the Father, but also by the Son; not only by Father and Son, but by the Holy Ghost also! And, moreover, as there is a subordination, as I have said, of attribute to attribute, without any detriment to the infinitude of each of them individually, and this is the glory of the God of Nature; so also does an order, and, as I may say, a subordination exist between Person and Person, and this is the incommunicable glory of the God of Grace. Father, Son, and Holy Ghost, are all equal to Each Other in their Divinity, else They would not Each be the One God. Yet, true as it is, that not one of the Divine Persons is less infinite, less eternal, less all-sufficient, than the Other Two, it is true also that, in the history of the Everlasting mystery, the Father comes first in order, as the Fountain-head of Divinity; the Son second, as being the Offspring of the First; and the Holy Ghost third, as proceeding from the Father and the Son. And for this reason it would appear that the Second and Third Persons hold certain offices, such as that of mission, which are fitting only in Them. Hence it was fitting that the Son should be incarnate, and not the Father; and fitting that the Holy Ghost should be the energizing life, both of the animate and rational creation, rather than the Father or the Son.

Nay, further than this still: so dear to Almighty God is that principle of order and of law, which is a characteristic of His glorious Essence, that, when He would reveal Himself to man, He even placed Himself under the conditions of an additional law, which did not belong to His nature, but was the mere creation of His will. He limited, as I may say, the range of His omnipotence by the obligation of His promise. Considered in Himself, He is, of course, in no respect a debtor to His creatures, nor answerable to them; there was no justice that could exist between them and Him; they could not profit Him; nor claim anything of Him; they were, in our Lord's words, but "servi inutiles"; yet the Almighty, after wonderfully calling into existence the rational creation, has more wonderfully placed it on a level with Himself. He has invested it with rights and titles. He has given it a power of meriting, and a ground for encountering and influencing His own determinations and acts. Henceforth, not only are His creatures bound but He also. "Dimitte Me," He said to Moses, on his pleading for Israel; "Let Me go," "Set Me free," "Do not stand in the way of My will," "Dimitte Me ut irascatur furor meus contra eos," "that My wrath may be kindled against them." He was restrained in the exercise of His attribute of justice by the necessity of faithfulness to His word; but what I remark is, that unless the notion of law, and of subjection to it, were elementary to the idea of the Divine Being, He never would have previously placed Himself in what (as in this instance) may be called a state of restraint. He voluntarily made promises and put Himself under engagements, from it being of His very nature to love order, and rule, and subordination for their own sake.

Such being the teaching, both of nature and of grace, concerning the Almighty, it is not surprising that, whereas in all things our blessedness lies in being like Him, in this respect especially His pattern should be our duty and our good. The God of order has set up all creation upon unity, and therefore upon law. Time was when philosophists contended that all things went on at random; that the phenomena of the material world were the result of the blind dance of everlasting atoms, and that the beauty on the face of nature was no earnest or evidence of the existence of any systematic plan of which it was the result. Such a fancy is now simply despised and abandoned even by those who do not recognize the Divine Creator in His works. Even those who have no eyes to see the Omniscient and the Omnipotent, now ridicule and repudiate the idea of chance and hazard in the course of physical nature: for the further their investigations are carried into the material framework of the universe, the more certain is the existence, the more encompassing is the range, of order and of law. There is no unrestrained, no lawless freedom in the physical world,—after the pattern of its Maker. It is not, indeed, good as He is good, even in its own degree; for it is full of fault and imperfection, and might be better than it is. It is not wise as He is wise; rather it has no intelligence at all lodged in it. It is not stable as He is stable; but, on the contrary, it is ever in motion and ever on the change. But one attribute it has of God, without exception or defect, and that is the attribute of order. Here it is as perfect in its finite degree and after its kind, it is as simply the manifestation of harmony and of law, as the infinite Creator Himself.

And so of the rational creation also, both in heaven and upon earth. The Angels have their hierarchy above; distributed into nine orders, they hymn the praises, and they fulfil the will, of the Omnipotent. And here below the history of mankind is founded upon the existence of society, and before and without formed political bodies there is no course of events to record. While men remain as savages, there is nothing to tell of them; nor is this all;—but the more accurately the history of the world can be investigated and put into shape, the more does it evidently appear to advance upon fixed laws, both as regards time and place, though, of course, without interfering with the responsibility of the individual.

But amongst all the instances of unity, of harmony, and of law, which the Creator has given us after His own image, the most remarkable is that which He set up when He came upon earth, the most perfect is that which exists in His Church. In the awful music of her doctrines, in the deep wisdom of her precepts, in the majesty of her Hierarchy, in the beauty of her Ritual, in the dazzling lustre of her Saints, in the consistent march of her policy, and in the manifold richness of her long history,—in all of these we recognize the Hand of the God of order, luminously, illustriously displayed. In her whole and in her parts, in her diversified aspects, the one same image of law and of rule ever confronts us; as in those crystallized substances of the physical world, which, both in the mass and in the details, consist in a reiteration of one and the same structure.

My Brethren in the Sacred Ministry, you see to what conclusion I am conducting the train of thought which I have been pursuing. We, indeed, by virtue of that ministry, are at all times subjects and guardians of that

Sacramentum Unitatis, which the Holy Fathers have ever recognized as lodged in the Church of God. Such we are by our office under all circumstances;—but, if there be a time when we are pre-eminently witnesses of this great and eternal truth, it is not when we are performing one by one our daily duties, though even then we represent in our individual persons the unity of her teaching and of her rule;—nor is it even when we offer Mass amid our own people, though then, indeed, we formally unite and seal them all with the impress of the One God, the One Mediator, the One Sacrifice for sin once offered, and the One Faith,—but it is surely at those special and rare seasons, of which the present is one, when all ranks and orders of the elect household are brought together from all parts into one place, under the invocation of One Spirit, in the form of a visible Hierarchy, and as an image of the whole Catholic Church;—when the Bishop in his Cathedral and on his throne, the Clergy who share his counsels and his anxieties, the Pastors who are deputed from him to feed his flock in every place, the Regulars whom Christ's own Vicar has sent to minister to him in his incessant toils, the ecclesiastics of inferior rank, the students from the Seminary, and the faithful people in attendance, when all are thus brought together in the august form of Synod, and in the solemnity of its prescribed ceremonial: and still more, if more need be said, when such a meeting of the Church has the singular and most touching prerogative of being the first which has been held through a long three hundred years, and is the token of a change of times, and of a resurrection in this island, of the fair presence of Catholicism.

My Reverend Brethren, under such circumstances is it wonderful that my mind recurs to the history and the teaching of a great servant of God, of a primitive Bishop and Martyr, whose lot was cast in a day, which, as regards the particular subject before us, may be paralleled to our own? In the beginning of the New Dispensation, things were in that provisional state which I touched upon when I began;—not as if the dogma and the rule of the Church could be different at one time and at another, but "Hæc omnia operatur unus atque idem Spiritus, dividens singulis, prout vult"; "All these things one and the same Spirit worketh, dividing to every one according as He will." From the first, indeed, as ever, there was but one source of ecclesiastical jurisdiction; from the first, one Pastor Ordinarius of all the faithful; from the first, bishops had their thrones in the Church, of divine right; from the first, the hierarchy was determined; but not from the first were all these appointments observed with the exactness which they admitted and required. At first, twelve, and not one, were possessed of universal jurisdiction; at first, bishops and priests, though ever separate in their office, were not always separate in their work and their position; at first, those who were called to follow the evangelical counsels,

441

observed them, not in community, nor in solitude, but in the bosom of their families. In these, and many other ways, the visible Church, though set up from the first in its substance, was not from the first manifested in the fulness of operation and institution.

But, when the last Apostle had been taken to his throne above, and the oracle of inspiration was for ever closed, when the faithful were left to that ordinary government which was intended to supersede the special season of miraculous action, then arose before their eyes in its normal shape and its full proportions that majestic Temple, of which the plans had been drawn out from the first by our Lord Himself amid His elect Disciples. Then was it that the Hierarchy came out in visible glory, and sat down on their ordained seats in the congregation of the faithful. Then followed in due course the holy periodical assemblies, and the solemn rites of worship and the honour of sacred places, and the decoration of material structures; one appointment after another, realizing in act and deed the great idea which had been imparted to the Church since the day of Pentecost. Then, in a word, was it that the Church passed from what I may call the Apostolic Vicariate, to its true form of Diocesan Episcopacy, which whoso destroys, as a Pope and Doctor especially dear to English Catholics has intimated, is the forerunner of Antichrist.

And this change of government took place, not because persecution had ceased, not because the powers of the world gave leave, but because it seemed good to the Holy Ghost, for the welfare of the faithful, at that very time to bind together, in every part of the Church, ruler and subjects, into a closer and more loving unity. And so, as a beginning and in encouragement of the good work, the same Divine Providence at that very time sent her a glorious martyr, St. Ignatius of Antioch, to be her prophet and doctor,—as in regard to the doctrine of the Incarnation, as in regard to the "science of the saints," so preeminently as regards the structure and the sacramental power of the Ecclesiastical Hierarchy. Welcome and cheering did his words sound in the ears of those early Christians, as they were wafted to them while he travelled along to martyrdom. Suitably and seasonably do they speak to us at present, who are now assisting in the same ecclesiastical revolution which was in progress then. Appositely, surely, and without apology, I may now quote some portion of them, as a fit comment on the ceremonial of these days.

"Jesus Christ," he says to the Ephesians, "our true Life, is the Mind of the Father; and so the Bishops, appointed even to the utmost bounds of the earth, are after the mind of Jesus Christ. Wherefore it will become you to concur in the mind of your Bishop, as also ye do. For your famous Presbytery, worthy of God, is knit as closely to its Bishop as the strings to a harp. Therefore by your unanimity and harmonious love, Jesus Christ is sung; and each of you taketh part in the chorus. Wherefore, it is profitable for you to live in blameless unity, that so ye may always have fellowship with God. Let no man deceive himself; if he be not within the Altar, he faileth of the bread of God. For, if the prayer of one or two be of such force, as we are told, how much more that of the Bishop and the whole Church? He therefore that does not join himself to the congregation, is proud, and has already condemned himself. Let us take heed, then, not to set ourselves against the Bishop, that we may be subject to God. And the more any one seeth his Bishop keep silence, the more let him reverence him; for whomsoever the Master of the house sends to be over His own household, we ought to receive him, even as we would Him that sent him. It is plain, therefore, that we ought to look to the Bishop, even as to the Lord Himself."

To the Magnesians: "Meet it is, that for the honour of Jesus Christ, the Bishop of us all,[38] who wills it, that ye should preserve an obedience that is without guile; since a man does not deceive the Bishop whom he sees, but he practises rather with the Bishop invisible, and so the question is not with flesh, but with God, who knows the secret heart."

To the Trallians: "He that is within the Altar is pure; but he that is without is not pure. That is, he that doeth anything without the Bishop and the Presbyters and Deacons, is not pure in his conscience."

To the Philadelphians: "Although some would have deceived me according to the flesh, yet the spirit is not deceived, being from God. For it knows both whence it comes, and whither it goes, and reproves the secret heart. I cried whilst I was among you, I spoke with a loud voice: Give ear to the Bishop and to the Presbytery and to the Deacons. And some suppose that I spake this, as knowing beforehand the separation of some. But He is my witness, for whose sake I am in bonds, that I knew nothing from any man. But the Spirit spake, saying in this wise: Do nothing without the Bishop; keep your bodies as the temples of God; love unity; flee division; be followers of Christ, as He of His Father."

May we all learn from the parting words of one, who warned us, as I may say, in the very agonies of martyrdom, to advance more and more in the spirit of obedience, in brotherly affection, in mutual forbearance and concession, in sympathy and compassion one for another. "In humilitate superiores sibi invicem arbitrantes," says the apostle, "non quæ sua sunt singuli considerantes, sed ea quæ aliorum. Supportantes invicem, et donantes vobismet ipsis, si quis adversus aliquem habet querelam," "In humility, esteeming others better than themselves: each one not considering the things that are his own, but those that are other men's; bearing with one another, and forgiving one another, if

---

[38] Parts of two sentences are put together here.—*JHN*

any have a complaint against another." The world looks upon us as a political, crafty, grasping set of men, like its own children. It recognizes, in the establishment of our Hierarchy, the work of an ambitious aspiration; and thinks us bound together by mere earthly bond, by selfishness, by expedience, by party spirit, by servile fear, and by ignorance. It knows nothing (how can it know?) of that hidden life, of that faith, that love, that spirit of adoration, which is our incorporating principle. It knows nothing of His Divine Presence, who, when He left the earth visibly, told us that we should still possess Him, though the world would not. It has no experience of the operations of grace, of the efficacy of the Sacraments, of the power of prayer, of the virtue of holy relics, of the communion of Saints, of the glorious intercession of the Mother of God, and of the care and tenderness of the Guardian Angel. It takes for granted, that what it sees, and just as much as it sees, is the whole of us. *We* know, my dear and Reverend Brethren, we know, we witness to each other, and to God, in calm and thankful confidence, that we have that which the world does not dream of. We know well, that in all these matters which, during the last several years, have brought the wrath of man upon us, in the establishment of the Hierarchy and the celebration of Synods, we have but been aiming to do God's will more perfectly. We know well, that we have acted as those who one day must give account for their gifts and their works before the awful judgment seat; and that what the world takes for ambition or craft, has been but an effusion of love.

You, my Lord and Father, are by these very changes,—by becoming the Bishop of an English Diocese, and no longer the Vicar of the Holy See, sent hither for the charge of the faithful,—you are circumscribing your power, and laying yourself under obligations which before you had not. Now no longer the mere representative of him who has the plenitude of jurisdiction, but as the shepherd of a flock you are bound to your clergy and people, you are knit into the body of the faithful whom you rule and whom you serve, by a more intimate tie, and a severer liability. Not only in will and in intention, but from your office and your position, henceforth you will be taking no measures by yourself, but with the counsel of others, as well as for their well-being. As the Eternal placed Himself under the conditions of a compact, when He would reveal Himself to sinful man, as He made Himself subject to the law of human nature when He took human flesh, so do the diocesan obligations which you have undertaken make you less free than you were before, and, from love to the souls of your priests and your people, do you rejoice in such captivity.

And still more is this true, my Reverend Brethren, of each of us, the Bishop's children and servants, each in his own place. We are no longer solitary labourers in our several spheres, cut off from our brethren, and at a distance from our head. We are, in a sense in which we were not before, members of a body. We are participating in a special way in the great Sacramentum Unitatis, and are bringing ourselves thereby nearer to the Divine Source of truth, purity, and charity, who is present when we are gathered together. We are met here to gain grace, and instruction, and consolation, and encouragement, from the One Eternal Bishop of the Church, whom our visible Father and Head represents. We are come, that that celestial order and peace, and that perfection of law, and that hierarchy of gifts and virtues, of which the Church is the manifestation, may also be set up and manifested, according to our measure, in our own persons. We come here to go back more able to govern ourselves, and to do God's will, and to preach His word, and to be a pattern to His people.

Yes! if there be on earth a visible image of heaven, it is in the Church collected together in one place; and we come here to drink, from that present source of grace, the strength, and health, and vigour needful for us on our journey thither. When even a fallen servant of God and his satellites entered the company of prophets under the Old Law, and saw them prophesying, and Samuel standing over them, the Spirit of God came upon the intruders, and they too began to prophesy. Again, under the New law, when even an unbeliever came into the assemblies of the infant Church (an Apostle is our warrant for saying it), he was overcome and transformed by the harmony of her worship. Her very presence and action was the sufficient note of her divinity. What, then, my Reverend Brethren, will not be the influence of her ceremonial on us, who, erring though we be as mortal men, still, as we trust, have the grace of God within us, are aiming after meekness, purity, charity, and detachment from the world, and are faithfully though imperfectly fulfilling the high commission severally given to us? May we not believe, through the mercy of Him who has chosen us, that we shall carry back with us a something which hitherto we had not?—a fuller and deeper view of the great dispensation of which we are the ministers, a clearer understanding of the beauty of God's House, a firmer faith in the solidity of that rock on which it stands, a closer devotion to Him who inhabits it, a more subdued, more peaceful, and more happy temper, to encounter the trials which meet us on our course, and which are appointed to lead us forward to heaven.

Transubstantiation[†]

P
EOPLE SAY that the doctrine of Transubstantiation is difficult to believe; I did not believe the doctrine till I was a Catholic. I had no difficulty in believing it, as soon as I believed that the Catholic Roman Church was the oracle of God, and that she had declared this doctrine to be part of the original revelation. It is difficult, impossible to imagine, I grant;—but how is it difficult to believe? Yet Macaulay thought it so difficult to believe that he had need of a believer in it, of talents as eminent as Sir Thomas More, before he could bring himself to conceive that the Catholics of an enlightened age could resist the overwhelming force of the argument against it. "Sir Thomas More," he says, "is one of the choice specimens of wisdom and virtue; and the doctrine of Transubstantiation is a kind of proof charge. A faith which stands that test, will stand any test." But, for myself, I cannot indeed prove it, I cannot tell *how* it is; but I say, "Why should not it be? What's to hinder it? What do I know of substance or matter? just as much as the greatest philosophers, and that is nothing at all." So much is this the case, that there is a rising school of philosophy now, which considers phenomena to constitute the whole of our knowledge in physics. The Catholic doctrine leaves phenomena alone. It does not say that the phenomena go; on the contrary, it says that they remain; nor does it say that the same phenomena are in several places at once. It deals with what no one on earth knows anything about, the material substances themselves. And, in like manner, of that majestic Article of the Anglican as well as of the Catholic Creed,—the doctrine of the Trinity in Unity. What do I know of the Essence of the Divine Being? I know that my abstract idea of three is simply incompatible with my idea of one; but when I come to the question of concrete fact, I have no means of proving that there is not a sense in which one and three can equally be predicated of the Incommunicable God.

[†] Excerpts from *Apologia Pro Vita Sua* (1865), chapter 5.

Devotional Freedom & Excess[†]

I BEGIN by making a distinction which will go far to remove good part of the difficulty of my undertaking, as it presents itself to ordinary inquirers,—the distinction between faith and devotion. I fully grant that devotion towards the blessed Virgin has increased among Catholics with the progress of centuries; I do not allow that the doctrine concerning her has undergone a growth, for I believe that it has been in substance one and the same from the beginning.

By "faith" I mean the Creed and assent to the Creed; by "devotion" I mean such religious honours as belong to the objects of our faith, and the payment of those honours. Faith and devotion are as distinct in fact, as they are in idea. We cannot, indeed, be devout without faith, but we may believe without feeling devotion. Of this phenomenon every one has experience both in himself and in others; and we bear witness to it as often as we speak of realizing a truth or not realizing it. It may be illustrated, with more or less exactness, by matters which come before us in the world. For instance, a great author, or public man, may be acknowledged as such for a course of years; yet there may be an increase, an ebb and flow, and a fashion, in his popularity. And if he takes a lasting place in the minds of his countrymen, he may gradually grow into it, or suddenly be raised to it. The idea of Shakespeare as a great poet, has existed from a very early date in public opinion; and there were at least individuals then who understood him as well, and honoured him as much, as the English people can honour him now; yet, I think, there is a national devotion to him in this day such as never has been before. This has happened, because, as education spreads in the country, there are more men able to enter into his poetical genius, and, among these, more capacity again for deeply and critically understanding him; and yet from the first, he has exerted a great insensible influence over the nation, as is seen in the circumstance that his phrases and sentences, more than can be numbered, have become almost proverbs among us. And so again in philosophy, and in the arts and sci-

---

[†] Excerpts from *A Letter Addressed to the Rev. E. B. Pusey, D.D., on Occasion of His Eirenicon* (1865), §3, The Belief of Catholics concerning the Blessed Virgin as distinct from their Devotion to her, and §5, Anglican Misconceptions and Catholic Excesses in Devotion to the Blessed Virgin; published in Volume 2 of *Certain Difficulties Felt by Anglicans in Catholic Teaching* (1900). The title here is editorial.

ences, great truths and principles have sometimes been known and acknowledged for a course of years; but, whether from feebleness of intellectual power in the recipients, or external circumstances of an accidental kind, they have not been turned to account. Thus the Chinese are said to have known of the properties of the magnet from time immemorial, and to have used it for land expeditions, yet not on the sea. Again, the ancients knew of the principle that water finds its own level, but seem to have made little application of their knowledge. And Aristotle was familiar with the principle of induction; yet it was left for Bacon to develop it into an experimental philosophy. Illustrations such as these, though not altogether apposite, serve to convey that distinction between faith and devotion on which I am insisting. It is like the distinction between objective and subjective truth. The sun in the spring-time will have to shine many days before he is able to melt the frost, open the soil, and bring out the leaves; yet he shines out from the first notwithstanding, though he makes his power felt but gradually. It is one and the same sun, though his influence day by day becomes greater; and so in the Catholic Church it is the one Virgin Mother, one and the same from first to last, and Catholics may have ever acknowledged her; and yet, in spite of that acknowledgment, their devotion to her may be scanty in one time and place, and overflowing in another.

This distinction is forcibly brought home to a convert, as a peculiarity of the Catholic Religion, on his first introduction to its worship. The faith is everywhere one and the same, but a large liberty is accorded to private judgment and inclination as regards matters of devotion. Any large church, with its collections and groups of people, will illustrate this. The fabric itself is dedicated to Almighty God, and that, under the invocation of the Blessed Virgin, or some particular Saint; or again, of some mystery belonging to the Divine Name or the Incarnation, or of some mystery associated with the Blessed Virgin. Perhaps there are seven altars or more in it, and these again have their several Saints. Then there is the Feast proper to the particular day; and during the celebration of Mass, of all the worshippers who crowd around the Priest, each has his own particular devotions, with which he follows the rite. No one interferes with his neighbour; agreeing, as it were, to differ, they pursue independently a common end, and by paths distinct, but converging, present themselves before God. Then there are confraternities attached to the Church,—of the Sacred Heart, or of the Precious Blood; associations of prayer for a good death, or for the repose of departed souls, or for the conversion of the heathen; devotions connected with the brown, blue, or red scapular;—not to speak of the great ordinary Ritual observed through the four seasons, or of the constant Presence of the Blessed Sacrament, or of its ever-recurring rite of

Benediction, and its extraordinary forty hours' Exposition. Or, again, look through such manuals of prayers as the *Raccolta*, and you at once will see both the number and the variety of devotions which are open to individual Catholics to choose from, according to their religious taste and prospect of personal edification.

Now these diversified modes of honouring God did not come to us in a day, or only from the Apostles; they are the accumulations of centuries; and, as in the course of years some of them spring up, so others decline and die. Some are local, in memory of some particular Saint, who happens to be the Evangelist, or Patron, or pride of the nation, or who lies entombed in the church or in the city where it is found; and these devotions, necessarily, cannot have an earlier date than the Saint's day of death or interment there. The first of these sacred observances, long before such national memories, were the devotions paid to the Apostles, then those which were paid to the Martyrs; yet there were Saints nearer to our Lord than either Martyrs or Apostles; but, as if these sacred persons were immersed and lost in the effulgence of His glory, and because they did not manifest themselves, when in the body, in external works separate from Him, it happened that for a long while they were less dwelt upon. However, in process of time, the Apostles, and then the Martyrs, exerted less influence than before over the popular mind, and the local Saints, new creations of God's power, took their place, or again, the Saints of some religious order here or there established. Then, as comparatively quiet times succeeded, the religious meditations of holy men and their secret intercourse with heaven gradually exerted an influence out of doors, and permeated the Christian populace, by the instrumentality of preaching and by the ceremonial of the Church. Hence at length those luminous stars rose in the ecclesiastical heavens, which were of more august dignity than any which had preceded them, and were late in rising, for the very reason that they were so specially glorious. Those names, I say, which at first sight might have been expected to enter soon into the devotions of the faithful, with better reason might have been looked for at a later date, and actually were late in their coming. St. Joseph furnishes the most striking instance of this remark; here is the clearest of instances of the distinction between doctrine and devotion. Who, from his prerogatives and the testimony on which they come to us, had a greater claim to receive an early recognition among the faithful than he? A Saint of Scripture, the foster-father of our Lord, he was an object of the universal and absolute faith of the Christian world from the first, yet the devotion to him is comparatively of late date. When once it began, men seemed surprised that it had not been thought of before; and now, they hold him next to the Blessed Virgin in their religious affection and veneration.

SUCH WAS the origin of that august *cultus* which has been paid to the Blessed Mary for so many centuries in the East and in the West. That in times and places it has fallen into abuse, that it has even become a superstition, I do not care to deny; for, as I have said above, the same process which brings to maturity carries on to decay, and things that do not admit of abuse have very little life in them. This of course does not excuse such excesses, or justify us in making light of them, when they occur. I have no intention of doing so as regards the particular instances which you bring against us, though but a few words will suffice for what I need say about them:—before doing so, however, I am obliged to make three or four introductory remarks in explanation.

1. I have almost anticipated my first remark already. It is this: that the height of our offending in our devotion to the Blessed Virgin would not look so great in your Volume as it does, had you not deliberately placed yourself on lower ground than your own feelings towards her would have spontaneously prompted you to take. I have no doubt you had some good reason for adopting this course, but I do not know it; what I do know is, that, for the Fathers' sake who so exalt her, you really do love and venerate her, though you do not evidence it in your book. I am glad then in this place to insist on a fact which will lead those among us, who know you not, to love you from their love of her, in spite of what you refuse to give her; and lead Anglicans, on the other hand, who do know you, to think better of us, who refuse her nothing, when they reflect that, if you come short of us, you do not actually go against us in your devotion to her.

2. As you revere the Fathers, so you revere the Greek Church; and here again we have a witness on our behalf, of which you must be aware as fully as we are, and of which you must really mean to give us the benefit. In proportion as the Greek ritual is known to the religious public, that knowledge will take off the edge of the surprise of Anglicans at the sight of our devotions to our Lady. It must weigh with them, when they discover that we can enlist on our side in this controversy those "seventy millions" (I think they do so consider them) of Orientals, who are separated from our communion. Is it not a very pregnant fact, that the Eastern Churches, so independent of us, so long separated from the West, so jealous for Antiquity, should even surpass us in their exaltation of the Blessed Virgin? That they go further than we do is sometimes denied, on the ground that the Western devotion towards her is brought out into system, and the Eastern is not; yet this only means really, that the Latins have more mental activity, more strength of intellect, less of routine, less of mechanical worship among them, than the Greeks. We are

450

able, better than they, to give an account of what we do; and we seem to be more extreme, merely because we are more definite. But, after all, what have the Latins done so bold, as that substitution of the name of Mary for the Name of Jesus at the end of the collects and petitions in the Breviary, nay, in the Ritual and Liturgy? Not merely in local or popular, and in semi-authorized devotions, which are the kind of sources that supply you with your matter of accusation against us, but in the formal prayers of the Greek Eucharistic Service, petitions are offered, not in "the name of Jesus Christ," but in that "of the Theotocos." Such a phenomenon, in such a quarter, I think ought to make Anglicans merciful towards those writers among ourselves, who have been excessive in singing the praises of the Deipara. To make a rule of substituting Mary with all Saints for Jesus in the public service, has more "Mariolatry" in it, than to alter the Te Deum to her honour in private devotion.[39]

3. And thus I am brought to a third remark, supplemental to your accusation of us. Two large views, as I have said above, are opened upon our devotional thoughts in Christianity; the one centering in the Son of Mary, the other in the Mother of Jesus. Neither need obscure the other; and in the Catholic Church, as a matter of fact, neither does. I wish you had either frankly allowed this in your Volume, or proved the contrary. I wish, when you report that "a certain proportion" of Catholics, "it has been ascertained by those who have inquired, do," in their devotions, "stop short in her," p. 107, that you had added your belief, that the case was far otherwise with the great bulk of Catholics. Might I not have expected such an avowal? May I not, without sensitiveness, be somewhat pained at the omission? From mere Protestants, indeed, I expect nothing better. They content themselves with saying that our devotions to our Lady *must necessarily* throw our Lord into the shade; and thereby they relieve themselves of a great deal of trouble. Then they catch at any stray fact which countenances or seems to countenance their prejudice. Now I say plainly, I never will defend or screen any one from your just rebuke, who, through false devotion to Mary, forgets Jesus. But I should like the fact to be proved first; I cannot hastily admit it. There is this broad fact the other way;—that, if we look through Europe, we shall find, on the whole, that just those nations and countries have lost their faith in the divinity of Christ, who have given up devotion to His Mother, and that those on the other hand, who had been foremost in her honour, have retained their orthodoxy. Contrast, for instance, the Calvinists with the Greeks, or France with the North of Germany, or the Protestant and Catholic communions in Ireland. As to England, it is scarcely doubtful what would be the state of its Established Church, if the Liturgy and

---

[39] Here, Newman sends the reader to a lengthy appendix, Note IV, "On the Teaching of the Greek Church about the Blessed Virgin."—*Ed.*

Articles were not an integral part of its Establishment; and, when men bring so grave a charge against us, as is implied in your Volume, they cannot be surprised if we in turn say hard things of Anglicanism.[40] In the Catholic Church Mary has shown herself, not the rival, but the minister of her Son; she has protected Him, as in His infancy, so in the whole history of the Religion. There is then a plain historical truth in Dr. Faber's words, which you quote to condemn, "Jesus is obscured, because Mary is kept in the background."

This truth, exemplified in history, might also be abundantly illustrated, did my space admit, from the lives and writings of holy men in modern times. Two of them, St. Alfonso Liguori and the Blessed Paul of the Cross, for all their notorious devotion to the Mother, have shown their supreme love of her Divine Son, in the names which they have given to their respective Congregations, viz. that "of the Redeemer," and that "of the Cross and Passion." However, I will do no more than refer to an apposite passage in the Italian translation of the work of a French Jesuit, Fr. Nepveu, "Christian Thoughts for every Day in the Year," which was recommended to the friend who went with me to Rome, by the same Jesuit Father there, with whom, as I have already said, I stood myself in such intimate relations; I believe it is a fair specimen of the teaching of our spiritual books.

"The love of Jesus Christ is the most sure pledge of our future happiness, and the most infallible token of our predestination. Mercy towards the poor, devotion to the Holy Virgin, are very sensible tokens of predestination; nevertheless they are not absolutely infallible; but one cannot have a sincere and constant love of Jesus Christ, without being predestinated . . . The destroying angel, which bereaved the houses of the Egyptians of their first-born, had respect to all the houses which were marked with the blood of the Lamb."

And it is also exemplified, as I verily believe, not only in formal and distinctive Confessions, not only in books intended for the educated class, but also in the personal religion of the Catholic populations. When strangers are so unfavourably impressed with us, because they see Images of our Lady in our

---

[40] I have spoken more on this subject in my *Essay on Development*, p. 488, "Nor does it avail to object, that, in this contrast of devotional exercises, the human is sure to supplant the Divine, from the infirmity of our nature; for, I repeat, the question is one of fact, whether it has done so. And next, it must be asked, *whether the character of Protestant devotion towards our Lord, has been that of worship at all*; and not rather such as we pay to an excellent human being . . . Carnal minds will ever create a carnal worship for themselves; and to forbid them the service of the saints, will have no tendency to teach them the worship of God. Moreover, . . . great and constant as is the devotion which the Catholic pays to St. Mary, it has a special province, and *has far more connexion with the public services and the festive aspect of Christianity*, and with certain extraordinary offices which she holds, *than with what is strictly personal and primary* in religion." Our late Cardinal, on my reception, singled out to me this last sentence, for the expression of his especial approbation.

churches, and crowds flocking about her, they forget that there is a Presence within the sacred walls, infinitely more awful, which claims and obtains from us a worship transcendently different from any devotion we pay to her. That devotion to her might indeed tend to idolatry, if it were encouraged in Protestant churches, where there is nothing higher than it to attract the worshipper: but all the images that a Catholic church ever contained, all the Crucifixes at its Altars brought together, do not so affect its frequenters, as the lamp which betokens the presence or absence there of the Blessed Sacrament. Is not this so certain, so notorious, that on some occasions it has been even brought as a charge against us, that we are irreverent in church, when what seemed to the objector to be irreverence was but the necessary change of feeling, which came over those who were in it, on their knowing that their Lord was no longer there, but away?

The Mass again conveys to us the same lesson of the sovereignty of the Incarnate Son; it is a return to Calvary, and Mary is scarcely named in it. Hostile visitors enter our churches on Sunday at midday, the time of the Anglican Service. They are surprised to see the High Mass perhaps poorly attended, and a body of worshippers leaving the music and the mixed multitude who may be lazily fulfilling their obligation, for the silent or the informal devotions which are offered at an Image of the blessed Virgin. They may be tempted, with one of your informants, to call such a temple, not a "Jesus church," but a "Mary church". But, if they understood our ways, they would know that we begin the day with our Lord and then go on to His Mother. It is early in the morning that religious persons go to Mass and Communion. The High Mass, on the other hand, is the festive celebration of the day, not the special devotional service; nor is there any reason why those who have been at low Mass already, should not at that hour proceed to ask the intercession of the Blessed Virgin for themselves and all that is dear to them.

Communion, again, which is given in the morning, is a solemn unequivocal act of faith in the Incarnate God, if any can be such; and the most gracious of admonitions, did we need one, of His sovereign and sole right to possess us. I knew a lady, who on her deathbed was visited by an excellent Protestant friend. The latter, with great tenderness for her soul's welfare, asked her whether her prayers to the Blessed Virgin did not, at that awful hour, lead to forgetfulness of her Saviour. "Forget Him?" she replied with surprise, "Why, He was just now here." She had been receiving Him in communion. When then, my dear Pusey, you read anything extravagant in praise of our Lady, is it not charitable to ask, even while you condemn it in itself, did the author write nothing else? Had he written on the Blessed Sacrament? had he given up "all for Jesus?" I recollect some lines, the happiest, I think, which that author wrote, which bring out strikingly the reciprocity, which I am dwelling on, of the respective devotions to Mother and Son:—

"But scornful men have coldly said
    Thy love was leading me from God;
And yet in this I did but tread
    The very path my Saviour trod.

"They know but little of thy worth
    Who speak these heartless words to me;
For what did Jesus love on earth
    One half so tenderly as thee?

"Get me the grace to love thee more;
    Jesus will give, if thou wilt plead;
And, Mother, when life's cares are o'er,
    Oh, I shall love thee then indeed.

"Jesus, when His three hours were run,
    bequeath'd thee from the Cross to me;
And oh! how can I love thy Son,
    Sweet Mother, if I love not thee."

4. Thus we are brought from the consideration of the sentiments themselves, of which you complain, to the persons who wrote, and the places where they wrote them. I wish you had been led, in this part of your work, to that sort of careful labour which you have employed in so masterly a way in your investigation of the circumstances of the definition of the Immaculate Conception. In the latter case you have catalogued the bishops who wrote to the Holy See, and analyzed their answers. Had you in like manner discriminated and located the Marian writers as you call them, and observed the times, places, and circumstances of their works, I think, they would not, when brought together, have had their present startling effect on the reader. As it is, they inflict a vague alarm upon the mind, as when one hears a noise, and does not know whence it comes and what it means. Some of your authors, I know are Saints; all, I suppose, are spiritual writers and holy men; but the majority are of no great celebrity, even if they have any kind of weight. Suarez has no business among them at all, for, when he says that no one is saved without the Blessed Virgin, he is speaking not of devotion to her, but of her intercession. The greatest name is St. Alfonso Liguori; but it never surprises me to read anything extraordinary in the devotions of a saint. Such men are on a level very different from our own, and we cannot understand them. I hold this to be an

454

important canon in the Lives of the Saints, according to the words of the Apostle, "The spiritual man judges all things, and he himself is judged of no one." But we may refrain from judging, without proceeding to imitate. I hope it is not disrespectful to so great a servant of God to say, that I never have read his Glories of Mary; but here I am speaking generally of all Saints, whether I know them or not;—and I say that they are beyond us, and that we must use them as patterns, not as copies. As to his practical directions, St. Alfonso wrote them for Neapolitans, whom he knew, and we do not know. Other writers whom you quote, as De Salazar, are too ruthlessly logical to be safe or pleasant guides in the delicate matters of devotion. As to De Montfort and Oswald, I never even met with their names, till I saw them in your book; the bulk of our laity, not to say of our clergy, perhaps know them little better than I do. Nor did I know till I learnt it from your Volume, that there were two Bernardines. St. Bernardine of Sienna, I knew of course, and knew too that he had a burning love for our Lord. But about the other, "Bernardine de Bustis," I was quite at fault. I find from the Protestant Cave, that he, as well as his namesake, made himself also conspicuous for his zeal for the Holy Name, which is much to the point here. "With such devotion was he carried away," says Cave, "for the bare Name of Jesus, (which, by a new device of Bernardine of Sienna, had lately begun to receive divine honours,) that he was urgent with Innocent VIII. to assign it a day and rite in the Calendar."

One thing, however, is clear about all these writers; that not one of them is an Englishman. I have gone through your book, and do not find one English name among the various authors to whom you refer, except of course the name of the author whose lines I have been quoting, and who, great as are his merits, cannot, for the reasons I have given in the opening of my Letter be considered a representative of English Catholic devotion. Whatever these writers may have said or not said, whatever they may have said harshly, and whatever capable of fair explanation, still they are foreigners; we are not answerable for their particular devotions; and as to themselves, I am glad to be able to quote the beautiful words which you use about them in your letter to the *Weekly Register* of November 25th last. "I do not presume," you say, "to prescribe to Italians or Spaniards, what they shall hold, or how they shall express their pious opinions; and least of all did I think of imputing to any of the writers whom I quoted that they took from our Lord any of the love which they gave to His Mother." In these last words too you have supplied one of the omissions in your Volume which I noticed above.

5. Now then we come to England itself, which after all, in the matter of devotion, alone concerns you and me; for though doctrine is one and the same everywhere, devotions, as I have already said, are matters of the particular time

and the particular country. I suppose we owe it to the national good sense, that English Catholics have been protected from the extravagances which are elsewhere to be found. And we owe it also to the wisdom and moderation of the Holy See, which, in giving us the pattern for our devotion, as well as the rule of our faith, has never indulged in those curiosities of thought which are both so attractive to undisciplined imaginations and so dangerous to grovelling hearts. In the case of our own common people I think such a forced style of devotion would be simply unintelligible; as to the educated, I doubt whether it can have more than an occasional or temporary influence. If the Catholic faith spreads in England, these peculiarities will not spread with it. There is a healthy devotion to the Blessed Mary, and there is an artificial; it is possible to love her as a Mother, to honour her as a Virgin, to seek her as a Patron, and to exalt her as a Queen, without any injury to solid piety and Christian good sense:—I cannot help calling this the English style. I wonder whether you find anything to displease you in the *Garden of the Soul,* the *Key of Heaven,* the *Vade Mecum,* the *Golden Manual,* or the *Crown of Jesus.* These are the books to which Anglicans ought to appeal, who would be fair to us in this matter. I do not observe anything in them which goes beyond the teaching of the Fathers, except so far as devotion goes beyond doctrine.

There is one collection of Devotions besides, of the highest authority, which has been introduced from abroad of late years. It consists of prayers of very various kinds which have been indulgenced by the Popes; and it commonly goes by the name of the *Raccolta.* As that word suggests, the language of many of the prayers is Italian, while others are in Latin. This circumstance is unfavourable to a translation, which, however skilful, must ever savour of the words and idioms of the original; but, passing over this necessary disadvantage, I consider there is hardly a clause in the goodsized volume in question which even the sensitiveness of English Catholicism would wish changed. Its anxious observance of doctrinal exactness is almost a fault. It seems afraid of using the words "give me," "make me," in its addresses to the Blessed Virgin, which are as natural to adopt in speaking to her, as in addressing a parent or friend. Surely we do not disparage Divine Providence when we say that we are indebted to our parents for our life, or when we ask their blessing; we do not show any atheistical leaning, because we say that a man's recovery must be left to nature, or that nature supplies brute animals with instincts. In like manner it seems to me a simple purism, to insist upon minute accuracy of expression in devotional and popular writings. However, the *Raccolta,* as coming from responsible authority, for the most part observes it. It commonly uses the phrases "gain for us by thy prayers," "obtain for us," "pray to Jesus for me," "speak for me, Mary," "carry thou our prayers," "ask for us grace;" "intercede for the people of God," and the like, marking thereby with great emphasis that she is nothing more than an Advocate, and not a source of mercy. Nor do I recollect in this book more than one or two ideas to which you would be likely to raise an objection. The strongest of these is found in the Novena before her Nativity, in which, *apropos* of her Birth, we pray that she "would come down again, and be reborn spiritually in our souls;"—but it will occur to you that St. Paul speaks of his wish to impart to his converts, "not only the gospel, but his own soul;" and writing to the Corinthians, he says he has "begotten them by the gospel," and to Philemon, that he had "begotten Onesimus, in his bonds;" whereas St. James, with greater accuracy of expression, says "of His own will hath God begotten us with the word of truth." Again, we find the petitioner saying to the Blessed Mary, "In thee I place all my hope;" but this is explained by another passage, "Thou art my best hope after Jesus." Again, we read elsewhere, "I would I had a greater love for thee, since to love thee is a great mark of predestination;" but the prayer goes on, "Thy Son deserves of us an immeasurable love; pray that I may have this grace, a great love for Jesus," and further on, "I covet no good of the earth, but to love my God alone."

Then again, as to the lessons which our Catholics receive, whether by catechising or instruction, you would find nothing in our received manuals to which you would not assent, I am quite sure. Again, as to preaching, a standard book was drawn up three centuries ago, to supply matter for the purpose to the parochial clergy. You incidentally mention, p. 153, that the comment of Cornelius à Lapide on Scripture is "a repertorium for sermons;" but I never heard of this work being so used, nor indeed can it, because of its size. The work provided for the purpose by the Church is the "Catechism of the Council of Trent," and nothing extreme about our Blessed Lady is propounded there. On the whole I am sanguine that you will come to the conclusion, that Anglicans may safely trust themselves to us English Catholics, as regards any devotions to the Blessed Virgin which might be required of them over and above the rule of the Council of Trent.

6. And, now at length coming to the statements, not English, but foreign, which offend you in works written in her honour, I will allow that I like some of those which you quote as little as you do. I will frankly say that, when I read them in your volume, they affected me with grief and almost anger; for they seemed to me to ascribe to the Blessed Virgin a power of "searching the reins and hearts," which is the attribute of God alone; and I said to myself, how can we any longer prove our Lord's divinity from Scripture, if those cardinal passages which invest Him with divine prerogatives, after all invest Him with nothing beyond what His Mother shares with Him? And how, again, is there anything of incommunicable greatness in His death and passion, if He

who was alone in the garden, alone upon the cross, alone in the resurrection, after all is not alone, but shared His solitary work with His Blessed Mother,—with her to whom, when He entered on His ministry, He said for our instruction, not as grudging her her proper glory, "Woman, what have I to do with thee?" And then again, if I hate those perverse sayings so much, how much more must she, in proportion to her love of Him? and how do we show our love for her, by wounding her in the very apple of her eye? This I felt and feel; but then on the other hand I have to observe that these strange words after all are but few in number, out of the many passages you cite; that most of them exemplify what I said above about the difficulty of determining the exact point where truth passes into error, and that they are allowable in one sense or connection, though false in another. Thus to say that prayer (and the Blessed Virgin's prayer) is omnipotent, is a harsh expression in every-day prose; but, if it is explained to mean that there is nothing which prayer may not obtain from God, it is nothing else than the very promise made us in Scripture. Again, to say that Mary is the centre of all being, sounds inflated and profane; yet after all it is only one way, and a natural way, of saying that the Creator and the creature met together, and became one in her womb; and as such, I have used the expression above. Again, it is at first sight a paradox to say that "Jesus is obscured, because Mary is kept in the background;" yet there is a sense, as I have shown above, in which it is a simple truth.

And so again certain statements may be true, under circumstances and in a particular time and place, which are abstractedly false; and hence it may be very unfair in a controversialist to interpret by an English or a modern rule, whatever may have been asserted by a foreign or medieval author. To say, for instance, dogmatically, that no one can be saved without personal devotion to the Blessed Virgin, would be an untenable proposition; yet it might be true of this man or that, or of this or that country at this or that date; and, if that very statement has ever been made by any writer of consideration (and this has to be ascertained), then perhaps it was made precisely under these exceptional circumstances. If an Italian preacher made it, I should feel no disposition to doubt him, at least if he spoke of Italian youths and Italian maidens.

Next I think you have not always made your quotations with that consideration and kindness which is your rule. At p. 106, you say, "It is commonly said that, if any Roman Catholic acknowledges that 'it is good and useful to pray to the saints,' he is not bound himself to do so. Were the above teaching true, it would be cruelty to say so; because, according to it, he would be forfeiting what is morally necessary to his salvation." But now, as to the fact, by whom is it said that to pray to our Lady and the Saints is necessary to salvation? The proposition of St. Alfonso is, that "God gives no grace except

458

through Mary;" that is through her intercession. But intercession is one thing, devotion is another. And Suarez says, "It is the universal sentiment that the intercession of Mary is not only useful, but also in a certain manner necessary;" but still it is the question of her intercession, not of our invocation of her, not of devotion to her. If it were so, no Protestant could be saved; if it were so, there would be grave reasons for doubting of the salvation of St. Chrysostom or St. Athanasius, or of the primitive Martyrs; nay, I should like to know whether St. Augustine, in all his voluminous writings, invokes her once. Our Lord died for those heathens who did not know Him; and His Mother intercedes for those Christians who do not know her; and she intercedes according to His will, and, when He wills to save a particular soul, she at once prays for it. I say, He wills indeed according to her prayer, but then she prays according to His will. Though then it is natural and prudent for those to have recourse to her, who from the Church's teaching know her power, yet it cannot be said that devotion to her is a *sine-quâ-non* of salvation. Some indeed of the authors, whom you quote, go farther; they do speak of devotion; but even then, they do not enunciate the general proposition which I have been disallowing. For instance, they say, "It is morally impossible for those to be saved who *neglect* the devotion to the Blessed Virgin;" but a simple omission is one thing, and neglect another. "It is impossible for any to be saved who *turns away* from her," yes; but to "turn away" is to offer some positive disrespect or insult towards her, and that with sufficient knowledge; and I certainly think it would be a very grave act, if in a Catholic country (and of such the writers were speaking, for they knew of no other), with Ave-Marias sounding in the air, and images of the Madonna in every street and road, a Catholic broke off or gave up a practice that was universal, and in which he was brought up, and deliberately put her name out of his thoughts.

7. Though, then, common sense may determine for us, that the line of prudence and propriety has been certainly passed in the instance of certain statements about the Blessed Virgin, it is often not easy to convict them of definite error logically; and in such cases authority, if it attempt to act, would be in the position which so often happens in our courts of law, when the commission of an offence is morally certain, but the government prosecutor cannot find legal evidence sufficient to insure conviction. I am not denying the right of sacred Congregations, at their will, to act peremptorily, and without assigning reasons for the judgment they pass upon writers; but, when they have found it inexpedient to take this severe course, perhaps it may happen from the circumstances of the case, that there is no other that they can take, even if they would. It is wiser then for the most part to leave these excesses to the gradual operation of public opinion, that is, to the opinion of educated

and sober Catholics; and this seems to me the healthiest way of putting them down. Yet in matter of fact I believe the Holy See has interfered from time to time, when devotion seemed running into superstition; and not so long ago. I recollect hearing in Gregory the XVI.'s time, of books about the Blessed Virgin, which had been suppressed by authority; and in particular of a pictorial representation of the Immaculate Conception which he had forbidden; and of measures taken against the shocking notion that the Blessed Mary is present in the Holy Eucharist, in the sense in which our Lord is present; but I have no means of verifying the information I then received.[41]

Nor have I time, any more than you have had, to ascertain how far great theologians have made protests against those various extravagances of which you so rightly complain. Passages, however, from three well-known Jesuit Fathers have opportunely come in my way, and in one of them is introduced in confirmation, the name of the great Gerson. They are Canisius, Petavius, and Raynaudus; and as they speak very appositely, and you do not seem to know them, I will here make some extracts from them:—

(1.) Canisius:—"We confess that in the *cultus* of Mary it has been, and is possible for corruptions to creep in; and we have a more than ordinary desire that the Pastors of the Church should be carefully vigilant here, and give no place to Satan, whose characteristic office it has ever been, while men sleep, to sow the cockle amid the Lord's wheat . . . For this purpose it is his wont gladly to avail himself of the aid of heretics, fanatics, and false Catholics, as may be seen in the instance of this *Marianus cultus*. This *cultus*, heretics, suborned by Satan, attack with hostility . . . Thus too, certain mad heads are so demented by Satan, as to embrace superstitions and idolatries instead of the true *cultus*, and neglect altogether the true measures whether in respect to God or to Mary. Such indeed were the Collyridians of old . . . Such that German herdsman a hundred years ago, who gave out publicly that he was a new prophet, and had had a vision of the Deipara, and told the people in her name to pay no more tributes and taxes to princes . . . Moreover, how many Catholics does one see who, by great and shocking negligence, have neither care nor regard for her *cultus*; but, given to profane and secular objects, scarce once a year raise their earthly minds to sing her praises or to venerate her."—*De Mariâ Deiparâ*, p. 518.

(2.) Father Petau says, when discussing the teaching of the Fathers about the Blessed Virgin (*de Incarn.* xiv. 8):—"I will venture to give this advice to all who would be devout and panegyrical towards the Holy Virgin, viz., not to exceed in their piety and devotion to her, but to be content with true and solid praises, and to cast aside what is otherwise. This kind of idolatry, lurking, as

---

[41] Here, Newman sends the reader to an appendix, Note V, "On a Scandalous Tenet Concerning the Blessed Virgin."—*Ed.*

St. Augustine says, nay implanted in human hearts, is greatly abhorrent from Theology, that is, from the gravity of heavenly wisdom, which never thinks or asserts anything, but what is measured by certain and accurate rules. What that rule should be, and what caution is to be used in our present subject, I will not determine of myself; but according to the mind of a most weighty and most learned theologian, John Gerson, who in one of his Epistles proposes certain canons, which he calls truths, by means of which are to be measured the assertions of theologians concerning the Incarnation . . . By these truly golden precepts Gerson brings within bounds the immoderate licence of praising the Blessed Virgin, and restrains it within the measure of sober and healthy piety. And from these it is evident that that sort of reasoning is frivolous and nugatory, in which so many indulge, in order to assign any sort of grace they please, however unusual, to the Blessed Virgin. For they argue thus; 'Whatever the Son of God could bestow for the glory of His Mother, that it became Him in fact to furnish;' or again, 'Whatever honours or ornaments He has poured out on other saints, those altogether hath He heaped upon His Mother;' whence they draw their chain of reasoning to their desired conclusion; a mode of argumentation which Gerson treats with contempt as captious and sophistical."

He adds, what of course we all should say, that, in thus speaking, he has no intention to curtail the liberty of pious persons in such meditations and conjectures, on the mysteries of faith, sacred histories, and the Scripture text, as are of the nature of comments, supplements, and the like.

(3.) Raynaud is an author, full of devotion, if any one is so, to the Blessed Virgin; yet in the work which he has composed in her honour (*Diptycha Mariana*), he says more than I can quote here, to the same purpose as Petau. I abridge some portions of his text:—"Let this be taken for granted, that no praises of ours can come up to the praises due to the Virgin Mother. But we must not make up for our inability to reach her true praise, by a supply of lying embellishment and false honours. For there are some whose affection for religious objects is so imprudent and lawless, that they transgress the due limits even towards the saints. This Origen has excellently observed upon in the case of the Baptist, for very many, instead of observing the measure of charity, considered whether he might not be the Christ," p. 9. . . . "St. Anselm, the first, or one of the first champions of the public celebration of the Blessed Virgin's Immaculate Conception, says, *de Excell. Virg.*, that the Church considers it indecent, that anything that admits of doubt should be said in her praise, when the things which are certainly true of her supply such large materials for laudation. It is right so to interpret St. Epiphanius also, when he says that human tongues should not pronounce anything lightly of the Deipara; and who is more justly to be charged with speaking lightly of the most Holy Mother of God, than he, who, as if what is certain and evident did not suffice for her full investiture, is wiser than the aged, and obtrudes on us the toadstools of his own mind, and devotions unheard of by those Holy Fathers who loved her best? Plainly, as St. Anselm says, that she is the Mother of God, this by itself exceeds every elevation which can be named or imagined, short of God. About so sublime a majesty we should not speak hastily from prurience of wit, or flimsy pretext of promoting piety; but with great maturity of thought; and whenever the maxims of the Church and the oracles of faith do not suffice, then not without the suffrages of the Doctors . . . Those who are subject to this prurience of innovation, do not perceive how broad is the difference between subjects of human science, and heavenly things. All novelty concerning the objects of our faith is to be put far away; except so far as by diligent investigation of God's Word, written and unwritten, and a well-founded inference from what is thence to be elicited, something is brought to light which though already indeed there, has not hitherto been recognized. The innovations which we condemn are those which rest neither on the written nor unwritten Word, nor on conclusions from it, nor on the judgment of ancient sages, nor sufficient basis of reason, but on the sole colour and pretext of doing more honour to the Deipara," p. 10.

In another portion of the same work, he speaks in particular of one of those imaginations to which you especially refer, and for which, without strict necessity (as it seems to me) you allege the authority of à Lapide.

"Nor is that honour of the Deipara to be offered, viz. that the elements of the body of Christ, which the Blessed Virgin supplied to it, remain perpetually unaltered in Christ, and thereby are found also in the Eucharist . . . This solicitude for the Virgin's glory must, I consider, be discarded; since, if rightly considered, it involves an injury towards Christ, and such honour the Virgin loveth not. And first, dismissing philosophical bagatelles about the animation of blood, milk, &c., who can endure the proposition that a good portion of the substance of Christ in the Eucharist should be worshipped with a *cultus* less than *latria*? viz. by the inferior *cultus* of *hyperdulia*? The preferable class of theologians contend that not even the humanity of Christ, is to be materially abstracted from the Word of God, and worshipped by itself; how then shall we introduce a *cultus* of the Deipara in Christ, which is inferior to the *cultus* proper to Him? How is this other than a casting down of the substance of Christ from His Royal Throne, and a degradation of it to some inferior sitting place? It is nothing to the purpose to refer to such Fathers, as say that the flesh of Christ is the flesh of Mary, for they speak of its origin. What will hinder, if this doctrine be admitted, our also admitting that there is something in Christ which is detestable? for, as the first elements of a body which were communicated by the Virgin to Christ, have (as these authors say) remained perpetually in Christ, so the same *materia*, at least in part, which belonged originally to the ancestors of Christ, came down to the Virgin from her father, unchanged, and taken from her grandfather, and so on. And thus, since it is not unlikely that some of these ancestors were reprobate, there would now be something actually in Christ, which had belonged to a reprobate, and worthy of detestation."—p. 237.

8. After such explanation, and with such authorities, to clear my path, I put away from me, as you would wish, without any hesitation, as matters in which my heart and reason have no part, (when taken in their literal and absolute sense, as any Protestant would naturally take them, and as the writers doubtless did not use them), such sentences, and phrases, as these:—that the mercy of Mary is infinite; that God has resigned into her hands His omnipotence; that it is safer to seek her than to seek her Son; that the Blessed Virgin is superior to God; that our Lord is subject to her command; that His present disposition towards sinners, as well as His Father's, is to reject them, while the Blessed Mary takes His place as an Advocate with Father and Son; that the Saints are more ready to intercede with Jesus than Jesus with the Father; that Mary is the only refuge of those with whom God is angry; that Mary alone can obtain a Protestant's conversion; that it would have sufficed for the salvation of men if our Lord had died, not in order to obey His Father, but to defer to the decree of His Mother; that she rivals our Lord in being God's daughter, not by adoption, but by a kind of nature; that Christ fulfilled the office of Saviour by imitating her virtues; that, as the Incarnate God bore the image of His Father, so He bore the image of His Mother; that redemption derived from Christ indeed its sufficiency, but from Mary its beauty and loveliness; that, as we are clothed with the merits of Christ, so we are clothed with the merits of Mary; that, as He is Priest, in a like sense is she Priestess; that His Body and Blood in the Eucharist are truly hers and appertain to her; that as He is present and received therein, so is she present and received therein; that Priests are ministers as of Christ, so of Mary; that elect souls are born of God and Mary; that the Holy Ghost brings into fruitfulness His action by her, producing in her and by her Jesus Christ in His members; that the kingdom of God in our souls, as our Lord speaks, is really the kingdom of Mary in the soul; that she and the Holy Ghost produce in the soul extraordinary things; and that when the Holy Ghost finds Mary in a soul He flies there.

Sentiments such as these I freely surrender to your animadversion; I never knew of them till I read your book, nor, as I think, do the vast majority of English Catholics know them. They seem to me like a bad dream. I could not have conceived them to be said. I know not to what authority to go for them,

463

to Scripture, or to the Fathers, or to the decrees of Councils, or to the consent of schools, or to the tradition of the faithful, or to the Holy See, or to Reason. They defy all the *loci theologici*. There is nothing of them in the Missal, in the Roman Catechism, in the Roman *Raccolta*, in the *Imitation of Christ*, in Gother, Challoner, Milner or Wiseman, as far as I am aware. They do but scare and confuse me. I should not be holier, more spiritual, more sure of perseverance, if I twisted my moral being into the reception of them; I should but be guilty of fulsome frigid flattery towards the most upright and noble of God's creatures, if I professed them,—and of stupid flattery too; for it would be like the compliment of painting up a young and beautiful princess with the brow of a Plato and the muscle of an Achilles. And I should expect her to tell one of her people in waiting to turn me off her service without warning. Whether thus to feel be the *scandalum parvulorum* in my case, or the *scandalum Pharisæorum*, I leave others to decide; but I will say plainly that I had rather believe (which is impossible) that there is no God at all, than that Mary is greater than God. I will have nothing to do with statements, which can only be explained, by being explained away. I do not, however, speak of these statements, as they are found in their authors, for I know nothing of the originals, and cannot believe that they have meant what you say; but I take them as they lie in your pages. Were any of them the sayings of Saints in ecstasy, I should know they had a good meaning; still I should not repeat them myself; but I am looking at them, not as spoken by the tongues of Angels, but according to that literal sense which they bear in the mouths of English men and English women. And, as spoken by man to man, in England, in the nineteenth century, I consider them calculated to prejudice inquirers, to frighten the unlearned, to unsettle consciences, to provoke blasphemy, and to work the loss of souls.

9. And now, after having said so much as this, bear with me, my dear Friend, if I end with an expostulation. Have you not been touching us on a very tender point in a very rude way? is it not the effect of what you have said to expose her to scorn and obloquy, who is dearer to us than any other creature? Have you even hinted that our love for her is anything else than an abuse? Have you thrown her one kind word yourself all through your book? I trust so, but I have not lighted upon one. And yet I know you love her well. Can you wonder, then,—can I complain much, much as I grieve,—that men should utterly misconceive of you, and are blind to the fact that you have put the whole argument between you and us on a new footing; and that, whereas it was said twenty-five years ago in the British Critic, "Till Rome ceases to be what practically she is, union is *impossible* between her and England," you declare on the contrary, "Union *is possible*, as soon as Italy and England, having

the same faith and the same centre of unity, are allowed to hold severally their own theological opinions"? They have not done you justice here; because in truth, the honour of our Lady is dearer to them than the conversion of England.

Take a parallel case, and consider how you would decide it yourself. Supposing an opponent of a doctrine for which you so earnestly contend, the eternity of punishment, instead of meeting you with direct arguments against it, heaped together a number of extravagant descriptions of the place, mode, and circumstances of its infliction, quoted Tertullian as a witness for the primitive Fathers, and the Covenanters and Ranters for these last centuries; brought passages from the Inferno of Dante, and from the Sermons of Wesley and Whitfield; nay, supposing he confined himself to the chapter on the subject in the work, which has the sanction of Jeremy Taylor, on "The State of Man," or to his Sermon on "The Foolish Exchange," or to particular passages in Leighton, South, Beveridge, and Barrow, would you think this a fair and becoming method of reasoning? and if he avowed that he should ever consider the Anglican Church committed to all these accessories of the doctrine, till its authorities formally denounced Beveridge, and Whitfield, and a hundred others, would you think this an equitable determination, or the procedure of a theologian?

So far concerning the Blessed Virgin; the chief but not the only subject of your Volume. And now, when I could wish to proceed,[42] she seems to stop all controversy, for the Feast of her Immaculate Conception is upon us; and close upon its Octave, which is kept with special solemnities in the Churches of this town, come the great Antiphons, the heralds of Christmas. That joyful season, joyful for all of us, while it centres in Him who then came on earth, also brings before us in peculiar prominence that Virgin Mother, who bore and nursed Him. Here she is not in the background, as at Easter-tide, but she brings Him to us in her arms. Two great Festivals, dedicated to her honour, tomorrow's and the Purification, mark out and keep the ground, and, like the towers of David, open the way to and fro, for the high holiday season of the Prince of Peace. And all along it her image is upon it, such as we see it in the typical representation of the Catacombs. May the sacred influences of this tide bring us all together in unity! May it destroy all bitterness on your side and ours! May it quench all jealous, sour, proud, fierce antagonism on our side; and dissipate all captious, carping, fastidious refinements of reasoning on yours! May that bright and gentle Lady, the Blessed Virgin Mary, overcome you with her sweetness, and revenge herself on her foes by interceding effectually for their conversion!

---

[42] The sequel to this letter never was written.

Christ, the Surpassing Fulfilment of Prophecies & Natural Religion[†]

8.

WHEN I IMPLIED that in some points of view Christianity has not answered the expectations of the old prophecies, of which it claims to be the fulfilment, I had in mind principally the contrast which is presented to us between the picture which they draw of the universality of the kingdom of the Messiah, and that partial development of it through the world, which is all the Christian Church can show; and again the contrast between the rest and peace which they said He was to introduce, and the Church's actual history,—the conflicts of opinion which have raged within its pale, the violent acts and unworthy lives of many of its rulers, and the moral degradation of great masses of its people. I do not profess to meet these difficulties here, except by saying that the failure of Christianity in one respect in corresponding to those prophecies cannot destroy the force of its correspondence to them in others; just as we may allow that the portrait of a friend is a faulty likeness to him, and yet be quite sure that it is his portrait. What I shall actually attempt to show here is this,—that Christianity was quite aware from the first of its own prospective future, so unlike the expectations which the prophets would excite concerning it, and that it meets the difficulty thence arising by anticipation, by giving us its own predictions of what it was to be in historical fact, predictions which are at once explanatory comments upon the Jewish Scriptures, and direct evidences of its own prescience.

I think it observable then, that, though our Lord claims to be the Messiah, He shows so little of conscious dependence on the old Scriptures, or of anxiety to fulfil them; as if it became Him, who was the Lord of the Prophets, to take His own course, and to leave their utterances to adjust themselves to Him as they could, and not to be careful to accommodate Himself to them. The evangelists do indeed show some such natural zeal in His behalf, and thereby illustrate what I notice in Him by the contrast. They betray an earnestness to trace in His Person and history the accomplishment of prophecy, as when they discern it in His return from Egypt, in His life at Nazareth, in the gentleness and tenderness of His mode of teaching, and in the various mi-

---

[†] From *An Essay in Aid of a Grammar of Assent* (1870), Part II, ch. 10, §2. The title is editorial.

nute occurrences of His passion; but He Himself goes straight forward on His way, of course claiming to be the Messiah of the Prophets,[43] still not so much recurring to past prophecies, as uttering new ones, with an antithesis not unlike that which is so impressive in the Sermon on the Mount, when He first says, "It has been said by them of old time," and then adds, "But I say unto you." Another striking instance of this is seen in the Names under which He spoke of Himself, which have little or no foundation in anything which was said of Him beforehand in the Jewish Scriptures. They speak of Him as Ruler, Prophet, King, Hope of Israel, Offspring of Judah, and Messiah; and His Evangelists and Disciples call Him Master, Lord, Prophet, Son of David, King of Israel, King of the Jews, and Messiah or Christ; but He Himself, though, I repeat, He acknowledges these titles as His own, especially that of the Christ, chooses as His special designations these two, Son of God and Son of Man, the latter of which is only once given Him in the Old Scriptures, and by which He corrects any narrow Judaic interpretation of them; while the former was never distinctly used of Him before He came, and seems first to have been announced to the world by the Angel Gabriel and St. John the Baptist. In those two Names, Son of God and Son of Man, declaratory of the two natures of Emmanuel, He separates Himself from the Jewish Dispensation, in which He was born, and inaugurates the New Covenant.

This is not an accident, and I shall now give some instances of it, that is, of what I may call the independent autocratic view which He takes of His own religion, into which the old Judaism was melting, and of the prophetic insight into its spirit and its future which that view involves. In quoting His own sayings from the Evangelists for this purpose, I assume (of which there is no reasonable doubt) that they wrote before any historical events had happened of a nature to cause them unconsciously to modify or to colour the language which their Master used.

1. First, then, the fact has been often insisted on as a bold conception, unheard of before, and worthy of divine origin, that He should even project a universal religion, and that to be effected by what may be called a propagandist movement from one centre. Hitherto it had been the received notion in the world, that each nation had its own gods. The Romans legislated upon that basis, and the Jews had held it from the first, holding of course also, that all gods but their own God were idols and demons. It is true that the Jews ought to have been taught by their prophecies what was in store for the world

---

[43] He appeals to the prophecies in evidence of His Divine mission, in addressing the people of Nazareth (Luke iv. 18), St. John's disciples (Matt. xi. 5), and the Pharisees (Matt. xxi. 42, and John v. 39), but not in details. The appeal to details He reserves for His disciples. *Vide* Matt. xi. 10; xxvi. 24, 31, 54: Luke xxii. 37; xxiv. 27, 46.

and for them, and that their first dispersion through the Empire centuries before Christ came, and the proselytes which they collected around them in every place, were a kind of comment on the prophecies larger than their own; but we see what was, in fact, when our Lord came, their expectation from those prophecies, in the passages which I have quoted above from the Roman historians of His day. But He from the first resisted those plausible, but mistaken interpretations of Scripture. In His cradle indeed He had been recognized by the Eastern Sages as their king; the Angel announced that He was to reign over the house of Jacob; Nathanael, too, owned Him as the Messiah with a regal title; but He, on entering upon His work, interpreted these anticipations in His own way, and that not the way of Theudas and Judas of Galilee, who took the sword, and collected soldiers about them,—nor the way of the Tempter, who offered Him "all the kingdoms of the world." In the words of the Evangelists, He began, not to fight, but "to preach;" and further, to "preach the kingdom of heaven," saying, "The time is accomplished, and the kingdom of God is at hand; repent, and believe the Gospel." This is the significant title, "the kingdom of heaven,"—the more significant, when explained by the attendant precept of repentance and faith,—on which He founds the polity which He was establishing from first to last. One of His last sayings before He suffered was, "My kingdom is not of this world." And His last words, before He left the earth, when His disciples asked him about His kingdom, were that they, preachers as they were, and not soldiers, should "be His witnesses to the end of the earth," should "preach to all nations, beginning with Jerusalem," should "go into the world and preach the Gospel to every creature," should "go and make disciples of all nations till the consummation of all things."

The last Evangelist of the four is equally precise in recording the initial purpose with which our Lord began His ministry, viz. to create an empire, not by force, but by persuasion. "Light is come into the world: every one that doth evil, hateth the light, but he that doth truth, cometh to the light." "Lift up your eyes, and see the countries, for they are white already to harvest." "No man can come to Me, except the Father, who hath sent Me, draw him." "And I, if I be lifted up from the earth, will draw all things to Myself."

Thus, while the Jews, relying on their Scriptures with great appearance of reason, looked for a deliverer who should conquer with the sword, we find that Christianity, from the first, not by an afterthought upon trial and experience, but as a fundamental truth, magisterially set right that mistake, transfiguring the old prophecies, and bringing to light, as St. Paul might say, "the mystery which had been hidden from ages and generations, but now was made manifest in His saints, the glory of this mystery among the Gentiles, which is

Christ in you," not simply over you, but in you, by faith and love, "the hope of glory."

2. I have partly anticipated my next remark, which relates to the means by which the Christian enterprise was to be carried into effect. That preaching was to have a share in the victories of the Messiah was plain from Prophet and Psalmist; but then Charlemagne preached, and Mahomet preached, with an army to back them. The same Psalm which speaks of those "who preach good tidings," speaks also of their King's "foot being dipped in the blood of His enemies;" but what is so grandly original in Christianity is, that on its broad field of conflict its preachers were to be simply unarmed, and to suffer, but to prevail. If we were not so familiar with our Lord's words, I think they would astonish us. "Behold, I send you as sheep in the midst of wolves." This was to be their normal state, and so it was; and all the promises and directions given to them imply it. "Blessed are they that suffer persecution;" "blessed are ye when they revile you;" "the meek shall inherit the earth;" "resist not evil;" "you shall be hated of all men for My Name's sake;" "a man's enemies shall be they of his own household;" "he that shall persevere to the end, he shall he saved." What sort of encouragement was this for men who were to go about an immense work? Do men in this way send out their soldiers to battle, or their sons to India or Australia? The King of Israel hated Micaiah, because he always "prophesied of him evil." "So persecuted they the Prophets that were before you," says our Lord. Yes, and the Prophets failed; they were persecuted and they lost the battle. "Take, my brethren," says St. James, "for an example of suffering evil, of labour and patience, the Prophets, who spake in the Name of the Lord." They were "racked, mocked, stoned, cut asunder, they wandered about,—of whom the world was not worthy," says St. Paul. What an argument to encourage them to aim at success by suffering, to put before them the precedent of those who suffered and who failed!

Yet the first preachers, our Lord's immediate disciples, saw no difficulty in a prospect to human eyes so appalling, so hopeless. How connatural this strange, unreasoning, reckless courage was with their regenerate state is shown most signally in St. Paul, as having been a convert of later vocation. He was no personal associate of our Lord's, yet how faithfully he echoes back our Lord's language! His instrument of conversion is "the foolishness of preaching;" "the weak things of the earth confound the strong;" "we hunger and thirst, and are naked, and are buffeted, and have no home;" "we are reviled and bless, we are persecuted, and blasphemed, and are made the refuse of this world, and the offscouring of all things." Such is the intimate comprehension, on the part of one who had never seen our Lord on earth, and knew little from His original disciples of the genius of His teaching;—and considering that the prophecies, upon which he had lived from his birth, for the most part bear on their surface a contrary doctrine, and that the Jews of that day did commonly understand them in that contrary sense, we cannot deny that Christianity, in tracing out the method by which it was to prevail in the future, took its own, independent line, and, in assigning from the first a rule and a history to its propagation, a rule and a history which have been carried out to this day, rescues itself from the charge of but partially fulfilling those Jewish prophecies, by the assumption of a prophetical character of its own.

3. Now we come to a third point, in which the Divine Master explains, and in a certain sense corrects, the prophecies of the Old Covenant, by a more exact interpretation of them from Himself. I have granted that they seemed to say that His coming would issue in a period of peace and religiousness. "Behold," says the Prophet, "a king shall reign in justice, and princes shall rule in judgment. The fool shall no more be called prince, neither shall the deceitful be called great. The wolf shall dwell with the lamb, and the leopard lie down with the kid. They shall not hurt nor kill in all My holy mountain, for the earth is filled with the knowledge of the Lord, as the covering waters of the sea."

These words seem to predict a reversal of the consequences of the fall, and that reversal has not yet been granted to us, it is true; but let us consider how distinctly Christianity warns us against any such anticipation. While it is so forcibly laid down in the Gospels that the history of the kingdom of heaven begins in suffering and sanctity, it is as plainly said that it results in unfaithfulness and sin; that is to say, that, though there are at all times many holy, many religious men in it, and though sanctity, as at the beginning, is ever the life and the substance and the germinal seed of the Divine Kingdom, yet there will ever be many too, there will be more, who by their lives are a scandal and injury to it, not a defence. This again is an astonishing announcement, and the more so when viewed in contrast with the precepts delivered by our Lord in His Sermon on the Mount, and His description to the Apostles of their weapons and their warfare. So perplexing to Christians was the fact when fulfilled, as it was in no long time on a large scale, that three of the early heresies more or less originated in obstinate, unchristian refusal to readmit to the privileges of the Gospel those who had fallen into sin. Yet our Lord's words are express: He tells us that "Many are called, few are chosen;" in the parable of the Marriage Feast, the servants who are sent out gather together "all that they found, both bad and good;" the foolish virgins "had no oil in their vessels;" amid the good seed an enemy sows seed that is noxious or worthless; and "the kingdom is like to a net which gathered together all kind of fishes;" and "at the end of the world the Angels shall go forth, and shall separate the wicked from among the just."

Moreover, He not only speaks of His religion as destined to possess a wide temporal power, such, that, as in the case of the Babylonian, "the birds of the air should dwell in its branches," but He opens on us the prospect of ambition and rivalry in its leading members, when He warns His disciples against desiring the first places in His kingdom; nay, of grosser sins, in His description of the Ruler, who "began to strike his fellow-servants, and to eat and drink and be drunken,"—passages which have an awful significance, considering what kind of men have before now been His chosen representatives, and have sat in the chair of His Apostles.

If then it be objected that Christianity does not, as the old prophets seem to promise, abolish sin and irreligion within its pale, we may answer, not only that it did not engage to do so, but that actually in a prophetical spirit it warned its followers against the expectation of its so doing.

9.

According to our Lord's announcements before the event, Christianity was to prevail and to become a great empire, and to fill the earth; but it was to accomplish this destiny, not as other victorious powers had done, and as the Jews expected, by force of arms or by other means of this world, but by the novel expedient of sanctity and suffering. If some aspiring party of this day, the great Orleans family, or a branch of the Hohenzollern, wishing to found a kingdom, were to profess, as their only weapon, the practice of virtue, they would not startle us more than it startled a Jew eighteen hundred years ago, to be told that his glorious Messiah was not to fight, like Joshua or David, but simply to preach. It is indeed a thought so strange, both in its prediction and in its fulfilment, as urgently to suggest to us that some Divine Power went with him who conceived and proclaimed it. This is what I have been saying;— now I wish to consider the fact, which was predicted, in itself, without reference to its being the subject whether of a prediction or of a fulfilment: that is, the history of the rise and establishment of Christianity; and to enquire whether it is a history that admits of being resolved, by any philosophical ingenuity, into the ordinary operation of moral, social, or political causes.

As is well known, various writers have attempted to assign human causes in explanation of the phenomenon: Gibbon has especially mentioned five, viz. the zeal of Christians, inherited from the Jews, their doctrine of a future state, their claim to miraculous power, their virtues, and their ecclesiastical organization. Let us briefly consider them.

He thinks these five causes, when combined, will fairly account for the event; but he has not thought of accounting for their combination. If they are ever so available for his purpose, still that availableness arises out of their coincidence, and out of what does that coincidence arise? Until this is explained, nothing is explained, and the question had better have been let alone. These presumed causes are quite distinct from each other, and, I say, the wonder is, what made them come together. How came a multitude of Gentiles to be influenced with Jewish zeal? How came zealots to submit to a strict, ecclesiastical *régime*? What connexion has a secular *régime* with the immortality of the soul? Why should immortality, a philosophical doctrine, lead to belief in miracles, which is a superstition of the vulgar? What tendency had miracles and magic to make men austerely virtuous? Lastly, what power was there in a code of virtue, as calm and enlightened as that of Antoninus, to generate a zeal as fierce as that of Maccabæus? Wonderful events before now have apparently been nothing but coincidences, certainly; but they do not become less wonderful by cataloguing their constituent causes, unless we also show how these came to be constituent.

However, this by the way; the real question is this,—are these historical characteristics of Christianity, also in matter of fact, historical causes of Christianity? Has Gibbon given proof that they are? Has he brought evidence of their operation, or does he simply conjecture in his private judgment that they operated? Whether they were adapted to accomplish a certain work, is a matter of opinion; whether they did accomplish it is a question of fact. He ought to adduce instances of their efficiency before he has a right to say that they are efficient. And the second question is, what is this effect, of which they are to be considered as causes? It is no other than this, the conversion of bodies of men to the Christian faith. Let us keep this in view. We have to determine whether these five characteristics of Christianity were efficient causes of bodies of men becoming Christians? I think they neither did effect such conversions, nor were adapted to do so, and for these reasons:—

1. For first, as to zeal, by which Gibbon means party spirit, or *esprit de corps*; this doubtless is a motive principle when men are already members of a body, but does it operate in bringing them into it? The Jews were born in Judaism, they had a long and glorious history, and would naturally feel and show *esprit de corps*; but how did party spirit tend to transplant Jew or Gentile out of his own place into a new society, and that a society which as yet scarcely was formed in a society? Zeal, certainly, may be felt for a cause, or for a person; on this point I shall speak presently; but Gibbon's idea of Christian zeal is nothing better than the old wine of Judaism decanted into new Christian bottles, and would be too flat a stimulant, even if it admitted of such a transference, to

be taken as a cause of conversion to Christianity without definite evidence in proof of the fact. Christians had zeal for Christianity after they were converted, not before.

2. Next, as to the doctrine of a future state. Gibbon seems to mean by this doctrine the fear of hell; now certainly in this day there are persons converted from sin to a religious life, by vivid descriptions of the future punishment of the wicked; but then it must be recollected that such persons already believe in the doctrine thus urged upon them. On the contrary, give some Tract upon hell-fire to one of the wild boys in a large town, who has had no education, who has no faith; and instead of being startled by it, he will laugh at it as something frightfully ridiculous. The belief in Styx and Tartarus was dying out of the world at the time that Christianity came in, as the parallel belief now seems to be dying out in all classes of our own society. The doctrine of eternal punishment does only anger the multitude of men in our large towns now, and make them blaspheme; why should it have had any other effect on the heathen population in the age when our Lord came? Yet it was among those populations, that He and His made their way from the first. As to the hope of eternal life, that doubtless, as well as the fear of hell, was a most operative doctrine in the case of men who had been actually converted, of Christians brought before the magistrate, or writhing under torture, but the thought of eternal glory does not keep bad men from a bad life now, and why should it convert them then from their pleasant sins, to a heavy, mortified, joyless existence, to a life of ill-usage, fright, contempt, and desolation.

3. That the claim to miracles should have any wide influence in favour of Christianity among heathen populations, who had plenty of portents of their own, is an opinion in curious contrast with the objection against Christianity which has provoked an answer from Paley, viz. that "Christian miracles are not recited or appealed to, by early Christian writers themselves, so fully or so frequently as might have been expected." Paley solves the difficulty as far as it is a fact, by observing, as I have suggested, that "it was their lot to contend with magical agency, against which the mere production of these facts was not sufficient for the convincing of their adversaries:" "I do not know," he continues, "whether they themselves thought it quite decisive of the controversy." A claim to miraculous power on the part of Christians, which was so unfrequent as to become now an objection to the fact of their possessing it, can hardly have been a principal cause of their success.

4. And how is it possible to imagine with Gibbon that what he calls the "sober and domestic virtues" of Christians, their "aversion to the luxury of the age," their "chastity, temperance, and economy," that these dull qualities were persuasives of a nature to win and melt the hard heathen heart, in spite too of

the dreary prospect of the *barathrum*, the amphitheatre, and the stake? Did the Christian morality by its severe beauty make a convert of Gibbon himself? On the contrary, he bitterly says, "It was not in this world that the primitive Christians were desirous of making themselves either agreeable or useful." "The virtue of the primitive Christians, like that of the first Romans, was very frequently guarded by poverty and ignorance." "Their gloomy and austere aspect, their abhorrence of the common business and pleasures of life, and their frequent predictions of impending calamities, inspired the Pagans with the apprehension of some danger which would arise from the new sect." Here we have not only Gibbon hating the moral and social bearing, but his heathen also. How then were those heathen overcome by the amiableness of that which they viewed with such disgust? We have here plain proof that the Christian character repelled the heathen; where is the evidence that it converted them?

5. Lastly, as to the ecclesiastical organization, this, doubtless, as time went on, was a special characteristic of the new religion; but how could it directly contribute to its extension? Of course it gave it strength, but it did not give it life. We are not born of bones and muscles. It is one thing to make conquests, another to consolidate an empire. It was before Constantine that Christians made their great conquests. Rules are for settled times, not for time of war. So much is this contrast felt in the Catholic Church now, that, as is well known, in heathen countries and in countries which have thrown off her yoke, she suspends her diocesan administration and her Canon Law, and puts her children under the extraordinary, extra-legal jurisdiction of Propaganda.

This is what I am led to say on Gibbon's Five Causes. I do not deny that they might have operated now and then; Simon Magus came to Christianity in order to learn the craft of miracles, and Peregrinus from love of influence and power; but Christianity made its way, not by individual, but by broad, wholesale conversions, and the question is, how they originated?

It is very remarkable that it should not have occurred to a man of Gibbon's sagacity to inquire, what account the Christians themselves gave of the matter. Would it not have been worth while for him to have let conjecture alone, and to have looked for facts instead? Why did he not try the hypothesis of faith, hope, and charity? Did he never hear of repentance towards God, and faith in Christ? Did he not recollect the many words of Apostles, Bishops, Apologists, Martyrs, all forming one testimony? No; such thoughts are close upon him, and close upon the truth; but he cannot sympathize with them, he cannot believe in them, he cannot even enter into them, *because* he needs the due formation for such an exercise of mind. Let us see whether the facts of the case do not come out clear and unequivocal, if we will but have the patience to endure them.

A Deliverer of the human race through the Jewish nation had been promised from time immemorial. The day came when He was to appear, and He was eagerly expected; moreover, One actually did make His appearance at that date in Palestine, and claimed to be He. He left the earth without apparently doing much for the object of His coming. But when He was gone, His disciples took upon themselves to go forth to preach to all parts of the earth with the object of preaching *Him*, and collecting converts *in His Name*. After a little while they are found wonderfully to have succeeded. Large bodies of men in various places are to be seen, professing to be His disciples, owning Him as their King, and continually swelling in number and penetrating into the populations of the Roman Empire; at length they convert the Empire itself. All this is historical fact. Now, we want to know the farther historical fact, viz. the cause of their conversion; in other words, what were the topics of that preaching which was so effective? If we believe what is told us by the preachers and their converts, the answer is plain. They "preached Christ;" they called on men to believe, hope, and place their affections, in that Deliverer who had come and gone; and the moral instrument by which they persuaded them to do so, was a description of the life, character, mission, and power of that Deliverer, a promise of His invisible Presence and Protection here, and of the Vision and Fruition of Him hereafter. From first to last to Christians, as to Abraham, He Himself is the centre and fulness of the dispensation. They, as Abraham, "see His day, and are glad."

A temporal sovereign makes himself felt by means of his subordinate administrators, who bring his power and will to bear upon every individual of his subjects who personally know him not; the universal Deliverer, long expected, when He came, He too, instead of making and securing subjects by a visible graciousness or majesty, departs;—*but* is found, through His preachers, to have imprinted the Image or idea of Himself in the minds of His subjects individually; and that Image, apprehended and worshipped in individual minds, becomes a principle of association, and a real bond of those subjects one with another, who are thus united to the body by being united to that Image; and moreover that Image, which is their moral life, when they have been already converted, is also the original instrument of their conversion. It is the Image of Him who fulfils the one great need of human nature, the Healer of its wounds, the Physician of the soul, this Image it is which both creates faith, and then rewards it.

When we recognize this central Image as the vivifying idea both of the Christian body and of individuals in it, then, certainly, we are able to take into account at least two of Gibbon's causes, as having, in connexion with that idea, some influence both in making converts and in strengthening them to persevere. It was the Thought of Christ, not a corporate body or a doctrine, which inspired that zeal which the historian so poorly comprehends; and it was the Thought of Christ which gave a life to the promise of that eternity, which without Him would be, in any soul, nothing short of an intolerable burden.

Now a mental vision such as this, perhaps will be called cloudy, fanciful, unintelligible; that is, in other words, miraculous. I think it is so. How, without the Hand of God, could a new idea, one and the same, enter at once into myriads of men, women, and children of all ranks, especially the lower, and have power to wean them from their indulgences and sins, and to nerve them against the most cruel tortures, and to last in vigour as a sustaining influence for seven or eight generations, till it founded an extended polity, broke the obstinacy of the strongest and wisest government which the world has ever seen, and forced its way from its first caves and catacombs to the fulness of imperial power?

In considering this subject, I shall confine myself to the proof, as far as my limits allow, of two points,—first, that this Thought or Image of Christ was the principle of conversion and of fellowship; and next, that among the lower classes, who had no power, influence, reputation, or education, lay its principal success.[44]

As to the vivifying idea, this is St. Paul's account of it: "I make known to you the gospel which I preached to you, which also you have received, and wherein you stand; by which also you are saved. For I delivered to you first of all that which I also received, how that Christ died for our sins according to the Scriptures," &c., &c. "I am the least of the Apostles; but, whether I or they, so we preached, and so you believed." "It has pleased God by the foolishness of preaching to save them that believe." "We preach Christ crucified." "I determined to know nothing among you, but Jesus Christ, and Him crucified." "Your life is hid with Christ in God. When Christ, who is your life, shall appear, then you also shall appear with Him in glory." "I live, but now not I, but Christ liveth in me."

St. Peter, who has been accounted the master of a separate school, says the same: "Jesus Christ, whom you have not seen, yet love; in whom you now believe, and shall rejoice."

And St. John, who is sometimes accounted a third master in Christianity: "It hath not yet appeared what we shall be; but we know that, when He

---

[44] Had my limits allowed it, I ought, as a third subject, to have described the existing system of impure idolatry, and the wonderful phenomenon of such multitudes, who had been slaves to it, escaping from it by the power of Christianity,—under the guidance of the great work ("On the Gentile and the Jew") of Dr. Döllinger.

shall appear, we shall be like to Him, because we shall see Him as He is."

That their disciples followed them in this sovereign devotion to an Invisible Lord, will appear as I proceed.

And next, as to the worldly position and character of his disciples, our Lord, in the well-known passage, returns thanks to His Heavenly Father, "because," He says, "Thou hast hid these things"—the mysteries of His kingdom—"from the wise and prudent, and hast revealed them to little ones." And, in accordance with this announcement, St. Paul says that "not many wise men according to the flesh, not many mighty, not many noble," became Christians. He, indeed, is one of those few; so were others his contemporaries, and, as time went on, the number of these exceptions increased, so that converts were found, not a few, in the high places of the Empire, and in the schools of philosophy and learning; but still the rule held, that the great mass of Christians were to be found in those classes which were of no account in the world, whether on the score of rank or of education.

We all know this was the case with our Lord and His Apostles. It seems almost irreverent to speak of their temporal employments, when we are so simply accustomed to consider them in their spiritual associations; but it is profitable to remind ourselves that our Lord Himself was a sort of smith, and made ploughs and cattle-yokes. Four Apostles were fishermen, one a petty tax collector, two husbandmen, and another is said to have been a market gardener.[45] When Peter and John were brought before the Council, they are spoken of as being, in a secular point of view, "illiterate men, and of the lower sort," and thus they are spoken of in a later age by the Fathers.

That their converts were of the same rank as themselves, is reported, in their favour or to their discredit, by friends and enemies, for four centuries. "If a man be educated," says Celsus in mockery, "let him keep clear of us Christians; we want no men of wisdom, no men of sense. We account all such as evil. No; but, if there be one who is inexperienced, or stupid, or untaught, or a fool, let him come with good heart." "They are weavers," he says elsewhere, "shoemakers, fullers, illiterate, clowns." "Fools, low-born fellows," says Trypho. "The greater part of you," says Cæcilius, "are worn with want, cold, toil, and famine; men collected from the lowest dregs of the people; ignorant, credulous women;" "unpolished, boors, illiterate, ignorant even of the sordid arts of life; they do not understand even civil matters, how can they understand divine?" "They have left their tongs, mallets, and anvils, to preach about the things of heaven," says Libanius. "They deceive women, servants, and

---

[45] On the subjects which follow, *vide* Lami, *De Eruditione Apostolorum*; Mamachius, *Origines Christ.*; Ruinart, *Act. Mart.*; Lardner, *Credibility*, &c.; Fleury, *Eccles. Hist.*; Kortholt, *Calumn. Pagan.*; and *De Morib. Christ.*

slaves," says Julian. The author of Philopatris speaks of them as "poor creatures, blocks, withered old fellows, men of downcast and pale visages." As to their religion, it had the reputation popularly, according to various Fathers, of being an anile superstition, the discovery of old women, a joke, a madness, an infatuation, an absurdity, a fanaticism.

The Fathers themselves confirm these statements, so far as they relate to the insignificance and ignorance of their brethren. Athenagoras speaks of the virtue of their "ignorant men, mechanics, and old women." "They are gathered," says St. Jerome, "not from the Academy or Lyceum, but from the low populace." "They are whitesmiths, servants, farm-labourers, woodmen, men of sordid trades, beggars," says Theodoret. "We are engaged in the farm, in the market, at the baths, wine-shops, stables, and fairs; as seamen, as soldiers, as peasants, as dealers," says Tertullian. How came such men to be converted? and, being converted, how came such men to overturn the world? Yet they went forth from the first, "conquering and to conquer."

The first manifestation of their formidable numbers is made just about the time when St. Peter and St. Paul suffered martyrdom, and was the cause of a terrible persecution. We have the account of it in Tacitus. "Nero," he says, "to put an end to the common talk [that Rome had been set on fire by his order], imputed it to others, visiting with a refinement of punishment those detestable criminals who went by the name of Christians. The author of that denomination was Christus, who had been executed in Tiberius's time by the procurator, Pontius Pilate. The pestilent superstition, checked for a while, burst out again, not only throughout Judea, the first seat of the evil, but even throughout Rome, the centre both of confluence and outbreak of all that is atrocious and disgraceful from every quarter. First were arrested those who made no secret of their sect; and by this clue a vast multitude of others, convicted not so much of firing the city, as of hatred to the human race. Mockery was added to death; clad in skins of beasts, they were torn to pieces by dogs; they were nailed up to crosses; they were made inflammable, so that, when day failed, they might serve as lights. Hence, guilty as they were, and deserving of exemplary punishment, they excited compassion, as being destroyed, not for the public welfare, but from the cruelty of one man."

The two Apostles suffered, and a silence follows of a whole generation. At the end of thirty or forty years, Pliny, the friend of Trajan, as well as of Tacitus, is sent as that Emperor's Proprætor into Bithynia, and is startled and perplexed by the number, influence, and pertinacity of the Christians whom he finds there, and in the neighbouring province of Pontus. He has the opportunity of being far more fair to them than his friend the historian. He writes to

Trajan to know how he ought to deal with them, and I will quote some portions of his letter.

He says he does not know how to proceed with them, as their religion has not received toleration from the state. He never was present at any trial of them; he doubted whether the children among them, as well as grown people, ought to be accounted as culprits; whether recantation would set matters right, or whether they incurred punishment all the same; whether they were to be punished, merely because Christians, even though no definite crime was proved against them. His way had been to examine them, and put questions to them; if they confessed the charge, he gave them one or two chances, threatening them with punishment; then, if they persisted, he gave orders for their execution. "For," he argues, "I felt no doubt that, whatever might be the character of their opinions, stubborn and inflexible obstinacy deserved punishment. Others there were of a like infatuation, whom, being citizens, I sent to Rome."

Some satisfied him; they repeated after him an invocation to the gods, and offered wine and incense to the Emperor's image, and in addition, cursed the name of Christ. "Accordingly," he says, "I let them go; for I am told nothing can compel a real Christian to do any of these things." There were others, too, who sacrificed; who had been Christians, some of them for as many as twenty years.

Then he is curious to know something more definite about them. "This, the informers told me, was the whole of their crime or mistake, that they were accustomed to assemble on a stated day before dawn, and to say together a hymn to Christ as a god, and to bind themselves by an oath [sacramento] (not to any crime, but on the contrary) to keep from theft, robbery, adultery, breach of promise, and making free with deposits. After this they used to separate, and then to meet again for a meal, which was social and harmless. However, they left even that off, after my Edict against their meeting."

This information led him to put to the torture two maid-servants, "who were called ministers," in order to find out what was true, what was false in it; but he says he could make out nothing, except a depraved and excessive superstition. This is what led him to consult the Emperor, "especially because of the number who were implicated in it; for these are, or are likely to be, many, of all ages, nay, of both sexes. For the contagion of this superstition has spread, not only in the cities, but about the villages and the open country." He adds that already there was some improvement. "The almost forsaken temples begin to be filled again, and the sacred solemnities after a long intermission are revived. Victims, too, are again on sale, purchasers having been most rare to find."

The salient points in this account are these, that, at the end of one generation from the Apostles, nay, almost in the lifetime of St. John, Christians had so widely spread in a large district of Asia, as nearly to suppress the Pagan religions there; that they were people of exemplary lives; that they had a name for invincible fidelity to their religion; that no threats or sufferings could make them deny it; and that their only tangible characteristic was the worship of our Lord.

This was at the beginning of the second century; not a great many years after, we have another account of the Christian body, from an anonymous Greek Christian, in a letter to a friend whom he was anxious to convert. It is far too long to quote, and difficult to compress; but a few sentences will show how strikingly it agrees with the account of the heathen Pliny, especially in two points,—first, in the numbers of the Christians, secondly, on devotion to our Lord as the vivifying principle of their association.

"Christians," says the writer, "differ not from other men in country, or speech, or customs. They do not live in cities of their own, or speak in any peculiar dialect, or adopt any strange modes of living. They inhabit their native countries, but as sojourners; they take their part in all burdens, as if citizens, and in all sufferings, as if they were strangers. In foreign countries they recognize a home, and in every home they see a foreign country. They marry like other men, but do not disown their children. They obey the established laws, but they go beyond them in the tenor of their lives. They love all men, and are persecuted by all; they are not known, and they are condemned; they are poor, and make many rich; they are dishonoured, yet in dishonour they are glorified; they are slandered, and they are cleared; they are called names, and they bless. By the Jews they are assailed as aliens, by the Greeks they are persecuted, nor can they who hate them say why.

"Christians are in the world, as the soul in the body. The soul pervades the limbs of the body, and Christians the cities of the world. The flesh hates the soul, and wars against it, though suffering no wrong from it; and the world hates Christians. The soul loves the flesh that hates it, and Christians love their enemies. Their tradition is not an earthly invention, nor is it a mortal thought which they so carefully guard, nor a dispensation of human mysteries which is committed to their charge; but God Himself, the Omnipotent and Invisible Creator, has from heaven established among men His Truth and His Word, the Holy and Incomprehensible, and has deeply fixed the same in their hearts; not, as might be expected, sending any servant, angel, or prince, or administrator of things earthly or heavenly, but the very Artificer and Demiurge of the Universe. Him God hath sent to man, not to inflict terror, but in clemency and gentleness, as a King sending a King who was His Son; He sent Him as

God to men, to save them. He hated not, nor rejected us, nor remembered our guilt, but showed Himself long-suffering, and, in His own words, bore our sins. He gave His own Son as a ransom for us, the just for the unjust. For what other thing, except His Righteousness, could cover our guilt? In whom was it possible for us, lawless sinners, to find justification, save in the Son of God alone? O sweet interchange! O heavenly workmanship past finding out! O benefits exceeding expectation! Sending, then, a Saviour, who is able to save those who of themselves are incapable of salvation, He has willed that we should regard Him as our Guardian, Father, Teacher, Counsellor, Physician; our Mind, Light, Honour, Glory, Strength, and Life."[46]

The writing from which I have been quoting is of the early part of the second century. Twenty or thirty years after it St. Justin Martyr speaks as strongly of the spread of the new Religion: "There is not any one race of men," he says, "barbarian or Greek, nay, of those who live in waggons, or who are Nomads, or Shepherds in tents, among whom prayers and eucharists are not offered to the Father and Maker of the Universe, through the name of the crucified Jesus.

Towards the end of the century, Clement:—"The word of our Master did not remain in Judea, as philosophy remained in Greece, but has been poured out over the whole world, persuading Greeks and Barbarians alike, race by race, village by village, every city, whole houses, and hearers one by one, nay, not a few of the philosophers themselves."

And Tertullian, at the very close of it, could in his *Apologia* even proceed to threaten the Roman Government:—"We are a people of yesterday," he says; "and yet we have filled every place belonging to you, cities, islands, castles, towns, assemblies, your very camp, your tribes, companies, palaces, senate, forum. We leave you your temples only. We can count your armies, and our numbers in a single province will be greater. In what war with you should we not be sufficient and ready, even though unequal in numbers, who so willingly are put to death, if it were not in this Religion of ours more lawful to be slain than to slay?"

Once more, let us hear the great Origen, in the early part of the next century:—"In all Greece and in all barbarous races within our world, there are tens of thousands who have left their national laws and customary gods for the law of Moses and the word of Jesus Christ; though to adhere to that law is to incur the hatred of idolaters, and the risk of death besides to have embraced that word. And considering how, in so few years, in spite of the attacks made on us, to the loss of life or property, and with no great store of teachers, the preaching of that word has found its way into every part of the world, so that

---

[46] *Ep. ad Diognet.*

Greek and barbarians, wise and unwise, adhere to the religion of Jesus, doubt-less it is a work greater than any work of man."

We need no proof to assure us that this steady and rapid growth of Christianity was a phenomenon which startled its contemporaries, as much as it excites the curiosity of philosophic historians now; and they too had their own ways then of accounting for it, different indeed from Gibbon's, but quite as pertinent, though less elaborate. These were principally two, both leading them to persecute it,—the obstinacy of the Christians and their magical pow-ers, of which the former was the explanation adopted by educated minds, and the latter chiefly by the populace.

As to the former, from first to last, men in power magisterially reprobate the senseless obstinacy of the members of the new sect, as their characteristic offence. Pliny, as we have seen, found it to be their only fault, but one suffi-cient to merit capital punishment. The Emperor Marcus seems to consider obstinacy the ultimate motive-cause to which their unnatural conduct was traceable. After speaking of the soul, as "ready, if it must now be separated from the body, to be extinguished, or dissolved, or to remain with it;" he adds, "but the readiness must come of its own judgment, not from simple perverse-ness, as in the case of Christians, but with considerateness, with gravity, and without theatrical effect, so as to be persuasive." And Diocletian, in his Edict of persecution, professes it to be his "earnest aim to punish the depraved per-sistence of those most wicked men."

As to the latter charge, their founder, it was said, had gained a knowledge of magic in Egypt, and had left behind him in his sacred books the secrets of the art. Suetonius himself speaks of them as "men of a magical superstition;" and Celsus accuses them of "incantations in the name of demons." The officer who had custody of St. Perpetua, feared her escape from prison "by magical incantations." When St. Tiburtius had walked barefoot on hot coals, his judge cried out that Christ had taught him magic. St. Anastasia was thrown into prison as dealing in poisons; the populace called out against St. Agnes, "Away with the witch! away with the sorceress!" When St. Bonosus and St. Maximili-an bore the burning pitch without shrinking, Jews and heathen cried out, "Those wizards and sorcerers!" "What new delusion," says the magistrate con-cerning St. Romanus, in the Hymn of Prudentius, "has brought in these soph-ists who deny the worship of the Gods? how doth this chief sorcerer mock us, skilled by his Thessalian charm to laugh at punishment?"[47]

It is indeed difficult to enter into the feelings of irritation and fear, of contempt and amazement, which were excited, whether in the town populace or in the magistrates, in the presence of conduct so novel, so unvarying, so

---

[47] *Essay on Development of Doctrine*, ch. iv. § 1.

absolutely beyond their comprehension. The very young and the very old, the child, the youth in the heyday of his passions, the sober man of middle age, maidens and mothers of families, boors and slaves as well as philosophers and nobles, solitary confessors and companies of men and women,—all these were seen equally to defy the powers of darkness to do their worst. In this strange encounter it became a point of honour with the Roman to break the determination of his victim, and it was the triumph of faith when his most savage expedients for that purpose were found to be in vain. The martyrs shrank from suffering like other men, but such natural shrinking was incommensurable with apostasy. No intensity of torture had any means of affecting what was a mental conviction; and the sovereign Thought in which they had lived was their adequate support and consolation in their death. To them the prospect of wounds and loss of limbs was not more terrible than it is to the combatant of this world. They faced the implements of torture as the soldier takes his post before the enemy's battery. They cheered and ran forward to meet his attack, and as it were dared him, if he would, to destroy the numbers who kept closing up the foremost rank, as their comrades who had filled it fell. And when Rome at last found she had to deal with a host of Scævolas, then the proudest of earthly sovereignties, arrayed in the completeness of her material resources, humbled herself before a power which was founded on a mere sense of the unseen.

In the colloquy of the aged Ignatius, the disciple of the Apostles, with the Emperor Trajan, we have a sort of type of what went on for three, or rather four centuries. He was sent all the way from Antioch to Rome to be devoured by the beasts in the amphitheatre. As he travelled, he wrote letters to various Christian Churches, and among others to his Roman brethren, among whom he was to suffer. Let us see whether, as I have said, the Image of that Divine King, who had been promised from the beginning, was not the living principle of his obstinate resolve. The old man is almost fierce in his determination to be martyred. "May those beasts," he says to his brethren, "be my gain, which are in readiness for me! I will provoke and coax them to devour me quickly, and not to be afraid of me, as they are of some whom they will not touch. Should they be unwilling, I will compel them. Bear with me; I know what is my gain. Now I begin to be a disciple. Of nothing of things visible or invisible am I ambitious, save to gain Christ. Whether it is fire or the cross, the assault of wild beasts, the wrenching of my bones, the crunching of my limbs, the crushing of my whole body, let the tortures of the devil all assail me, if I do but gain Christ Jesus." Elsewhere in the same Epistle he says, "I write to you, still alive, but longing to die. My Love is crucified! I have no taste for perishable food. I long for God's Bread, heavenly Bread, Bread of life, which is Flesh of Jesus Christ, the Son of God. I long for God's draught, His Blood, which is Love without corruption, and Life for evermore." It is said that, when he came into the presence of Trajan, the latter cried out, "Who are you, poor devil, who are so eager to transgress our rules?" "That is no name," he answered, "for Theophorus." "Who is Theophorus?" asked the Emperor. "He who bears Christ in his breast." In the Apostle's words, already cited, he had "Christ in him, the hope of glory." All this may be called enthusiasm; but enthusiasm affords a much more adequate explanation of the confessorship of an old man, than do Gibbon's five reasons.

Instances of the same ardent spirit, and of the living faith on which it was founded, are to be found wherever we open the *Acta Martyrum*. In the outbreak at Smyrna, in the middle of the second century, amid tortures which even moved the heathen bystanders to compassion, the sufferers were conspicuous for their serene calmness. "They made it evident to us all," says the Epistle of the Church, "that in the midst of those sufferings they were absent from the body, or rather, that the Lord stood by them, and walked in the midst of them."

At that time Polycarp, the familiar friend of St. John, and a contemporary of Ignatius, suffered in his extreme old age. When, before his sentence, the Proconsul bade him "swear by the fortunes of Cæsar, and have done with Christ," his answer betrayed that intimate devotion to the self-same Idea, which had been the inward life of Ignatius. "Eighty and six years," he answered, "have I been His servant, and He has never wronged me, but ever has preserved me; and how can I blaspheme my King and my Saviour?" When they would have fastened him to the stake, he said, "Let alone; He who gives me to bear the fire, will give me also to stand firm upon the pyre without your nails."

Christians felt it as an acceptable service to Him who loved them, to confess with courage and to suffer with dignity. In this chivalrous spirit, as it may be called, they met the words and deeds of their persecutors, as the children of men return bitterness for bitterness, and blow for blow. "What soldier," says Minucius, with a reference to the invisible Presence of our Lord, "does not challenge danger more daringly under the eye of his commander?" In that same outbreak at Smyrna, when the Proconsul urged the young Germanicus to have mercy on himself and on his youth, to the astonishment of the populace he provoked a wild beast to fall upon him. In like manner, St. Justin tells us of Lucius, who, when he saw a Christian sent off to suffer, at once remonstrated sharply with the judge, and was sent off to execution with him; and then another presented himself, and was sent off also. When the Christians were thrown into prison, in the fierce persecution at Lyons, Vettius

Epagathus, a youth of distinction who had given himself to an ascetic life, could not bear the sight of the sufferings of his brethren, and asked leave to plead their cause. The only answer he got was to be sent off the first to die. What the contemporary account sees in his conduct is, not that he was zealous for his brethren, though zealous he was, nor that he believed in miracles, though he doubtless did believe; but that he "was a gracious disciple of Christ, following the Lamb whithersoever He went."

In that memorable persecution, when Blandina, a slave, was seized for confessorship, her mistress and her fellow-Christians dreaded lest, from her delicate make, she should give way under the torments; but she even tired out her tormentors. It was a refreshment and relief to her to cry out amid her pains, "I am a Christian." They remanded her to prison, and then brought her out for fresh suffering a second day and a third. On the last day she saw a boy of fifteen brought into the amphitheatre for death; she feared for him, as others had feared for her; but he too went through his trial generously, and went to God before her. Her last sufferings were to be placed in the notorious red-hot chair, and then to be exposed in a net to a wild bull; they finished by cutting her throat. Sanctus, too, when the burning plates of brass were placed on his limbs, all through his torments did but say, "I am a Christian," and stood erect and firm, "bathed and strengthened," say his brethren who write the account, "in the heavenly well of living water which flows from the breast of Christ," or, as they say elsewhere of all the martyrs, "refreshed with the joy of martyrdom, the hope of blessedness, love towards Christ, and the spirit of God the Father." How clearly do we see all through this narrative what it was which nerved them for the combat! If they love their brethren, it is in the fellowship of their Lord; if they look for heaven, it is because He is the Light of it.

Epipodius, a youth of gentle nurture, when struck by the Prefect on the mouth, while blood flowed from it, cried out, "I confess that Jesus Christ is God, together with the Father and the Holy Ghost." Symphorian, of Autun, also a youth, and of noble birth, when told to adore an idol, answered, "Give me leave and I will hammer it to pieces." When Leonidas, the father of the young Origen, was in prison for his faith, the boy, then seventeen, burned to share his martyrdom, and his mother had to hide his clothes to prevent him from executing his purpose. Afterwards he attended the confessors in prison, stood by them at the tribunal, and gave them the kiss of peace when they were led out to suffer, and this, in spite of being several times apprehended and put upon the rack. Also in Alexandria, the beautiful slave, Potamiæna, when about to be stripped in order to be thrown into the cauldron of hot pitch, said to the Prefect, "I pray you rather let me be dipped down slowly into it with my clothes on, and you shall see with what patience I am gifted by Him of whom you are ignorant, Jesus Christ." When the populace in the same city had beaten out the aged Apollonia's teeth, and lit a fire to burn her, unless she would blaspheme, she leaped into the fire herself, and so gained her crown. When Sixtus, Bishop of Rome, was led to martyrdom, his deacon, Laurence, followed him weeping and complaining, "O my father, whither goest thou without thy son?" And when his own turn came, three days afterwards, and he was put upon the gridiron, after a while he said to the Prefect, "Turn me; this side is done." Whence came this tremendous spirit, scaring, nay, offending, the fastidious criticism of our delicate days? Does Gibbon think to sound the depths of the eternal ocean with the tape and measuring-rod of his merely literary philosophy?

When Barulas, a child of seven years old, was scourged to blood for repeating his catechism before the heathen judge—viz. "There is but one God, and Jesus Christ is true God"—his mother encouraged him to persevere, chiding him for asking for some drink. At Merida, a girl of noble family, of the age of twelve, presented herself before the tribunal, and overturned the idols. She was scourged and burned with torches; she neither shed a tear, nor showed other signs of suffering. When the fire reached her face, she opened her mouth to receive it, and was suffocated. At Cæsarea, a girl, under eighteen, went boldly to ask the prayers of some Christians who were in chains before the Prætorium. She was seized at once, and her sides torn open with the iron rakes, preserving the while a bright and joyous countenance. Peter, Dorotheus, Gorgonius, were boys of the imperial bedchamber; they were highly in favour with their masters, and were Christians. They too suffered dreadful torments, dying under them, without a shadow of wavering. Call such conduct madness, if you will, or magic: but do not mock us by ascribing it in such mere children to simple desire of immortality, or to any ecclesiastical organization.

When the persecution raged in Asia, a vast multitude of Christians presented themselves before the Proconsul, challenging him to proceed against them. "Poor wretches!" half in contempt and half in affright, he answered, "if you must die, cannot you find ropes or precipices for the purpose?" At Utica, a hundred and fifty Christians of both sexes and all ages were martyrs in one company. They are said to have been told to burn incense to an idol, or they should be thrown into a pit of burning lime; they without hesitation leapt into it. In Egypt a hundred and twenty confessors, after having sustained the loss of eyes or of feet, endured to linger out their lives in the mines of Palestine and Cilicia. In the last persecution, according to the testimony of the grave Eusebius, a contemporary, the slaughter of men, women, and children, went on by twenties, sixties, hundreds, till the instruments of execution were worn out, and the executioners could kill no more. Yet he tells us, as an eye-witness, that, as soon as any Christians were condemned, others ran from all parts, and surrounded the tribunals, confessing the faith, and joyfully receiving their condemnation, and singing songs of thanksgiving and triumph to the last.

Thus was the Roman power overcome. Thus did the Seed of Abraham, and the Expectation of the Gentiles, the meek Son of man, "take to Himself His great power and reign" in the hearts of His people, in the public theatre of the world. The mode in which the primeval prophecy was fulfilled is as marvellous, as the prophecy itself is clear and bold.

"So may all Thy enemies perish, O Lord; but let them that love Thee shine, as the sun shineth in his rising!"

I will add the memorable words of the two great Apologists of the period:—

"Your cruelty," says Tertullian, "though each act be more refined than the last, doth profit you nothing. To our sect it is rather an inducement. We grow up in greater numbers, as often as you cut us down. The blood of the martyrs is their seed for the harvest."

Origen even uses the language of prophecy. To the objection of Celsus that Christianity from its principles would, if let alone, open the whole empire to the irruption of the barbarians, and the utter ruin of civiliz1tion, he replies, "If all Romans are such as we, then too the barbarians will draw near to the Word of God, and will become the most observant of the Law. And every worship shall come to nought, and that of the Christians alone obtain the mastery, for the Word is continually gaining possession of more and more souls."

One additional remark:—It was fitting that those mixed unlettered multitudes, who for three centuries had suffered and triumphed by virtue of the inward Vision of their Divine Lord, should be selected, as we know they were, in the fourth, to be the special champions of His Divinity and the victorious foes of its impugners, at a time when the civil power, which had found them too strong for its arms, attempted, by means of a portentous heresy in the high places of the Church, to rob them of that Truth which had all along been the principle of their strength.

10.

I have been forestalling all along the thought with which I shall close these considerations on the subject of Christianity; and necessarily forestalling it, because it properly comes first, though the course which my argument has taken has not allowed me to introduce it in its natural place. Revelation begins where Natural Religion fails. The Religion of Nature is a mere inchoation, and needs a complement,—it can have but one complement, and that very complement is Christianity.

Natural Religion is based upon the sense of sin; it recognizes the disease, but it cannot find, it does but look out for the remedy. That remedy, both for guilt and for moral impotence, is found in the central doctrine of Revelation, the Mediation of Christ. I need not go into a subject so familiar to all men in a Christian country.

Thus it is that Christianity is the fulfilment of the promise made to Abraham, and of the Mosaic revelations; this is how it has been able from the first to occupy the world and gain a hold on every class of human society to which its preachers reached; this is why the Roman power and the multitude of religions which it embraced could not stand against it; this is the secret of its sustained energy, and its never-flagging martyrdoms; this is how at present it is so mysteriously potent, in spite of the new and fearful adversaries which beset its path. It has with it that gift of staunching and healing the one deep wound of human nature, which avails more for its success than a full encyclopedia of scientific knowledge and a whole library of controversy, and therefore it must last while human nature lasts. It is a living truth which never can grow old.

Some persons speak of it as if it were a thing of history, with only indirect bearings upon modern times; I cannot allow that it is a mere historical religion. Certainly it has its foundations in past and glorious memories, but its power is in the present. It is no dreary matter of antiquarianism; we do not contemplate it in conclusions drawn from dumb documents and dead events, but by faith exercised in ever-living objects, and by the appropriation and use of ever-recurring gifts.

Our communion with it is in the unseen, not in the obsolete. At this very day its rites and ordinances are continually eliciting the active interposition of that Omnipotence in which the Religion long ago began. First and above all is the Holy Mass, in which He who once died for us upon the Cross, brings back and perpetuates, by His literal presence in it, that one and the same sacrifice which cannot be repeated. Next, there is the actual entrance of Himself, soul and body, and divinity, into the soul and body of every worshipper who comes to Him for the gift, a privilege more intimate than if we lived with Him during His long-past sojourn upon earth. And then, moreover, there is His personal abidance in our churches, raising earthly service into a foretaste of heaven. Such is the profession of Christianity, and, I repeat, its very divination of our needs is in itself a proof that it is really the supply of them.

Upon the doctrines which I have mentioned as central truths, others, as we all know, follow, which rule our personal conduct and course of life, and our social and civil relations. The promised Deliverer, the Expectation of the nations, has not done his work by halves. He has given us Saints and Angels for our protection. He has taught us how by our prayers and services to benefit our departed friends, and to keep up a memorial of ourselves when we are gone. He has created a visible hierarchy and a succession of sacraments, to be the channels of His mercies, and the Crucifix secures the thought of Him in every house and chamber. In all these ways He brings Himself before us. I am not here speaking of His gifts as gifts, but as memorials; not as what Christians know they convey, but in their visible character; and I say, that, as human nature itself is still in life and action as much as ever it was, so He too lives, to our imaginations, by His visible symbols, as if He were on earth, with a practical efficacy which even unbelievers cannot deny, so as to be the corrective of that nature, and its strength day by day,—and that this power of perpetuating His Image, being altogether singular and special, and the prerogative of Him and Him alone, is a grand evidence how well He fulfils to this day that Sovereign Mission which, from the first beginning of the world's history, has been in prophecy assigned to Him.

I cannot better illustrate this argument than by recurring to a deep thought on the subject of Christianity, which has before now attracted the notice of philosophers and preachers,[48] as coming from the wonderful man who swayed the destinies of Europe in the first years of this century. It was an argument not unnatural in one who had that special passion for human glory, which has been the incentive of so many heroic careers and of so many mighty revolutions in the history of the world. In the solitude of his imprisonment, and in the view of death, he seems to have expressed himself to the following effect:—

"I have been accustomed to put before me the examples of Alexander and Cæsar, with the hope of rivalling their exploits, and living in the minds of men for ever. Yet, after all, in what sense does Cæsar, in what sense does Alexander live? Who knows or cares anything about them? At best, nothing but their names is known; for who among the multitude of men, who hear or who utter their names, really knows anything about their lives or their deeds, or attaches to those names any definite idea? Nay, even their names do but flit up and down the world like ghosts, mentioned only on particular occasions, or from accidental associations. Their chief home is the schoolroom; they have a foremost place in boys' grammars and exercise books; they are splendid examples for themes; they form writing-copies. So low is heroic Alexander fallen, so low is imperial Cæsar, 'ut pueris placeat et declamatio fiat.'

"But, on the contrary" (he is reported to have continued), "there is just One Name in the whole world that lives; it is the Name of One who passed

[48] Fr. Lacordaire and M. Nicolas.

His years in obscurity, and who died a malefactor's death. Eighteen hundred years have gone since that time, but still it has its hold upon the human mind. It has possessed the world, and it maintains possession. Amid the most varied nations, under the most diversified circumstances, in the most cultivated, in the rudest races and intellects, in all classes of society, the Owner of that great Name reigns. High and low, rich and poor, acknowledge Him. Millions of souls are conversing with Him, are venturing on His word, are looking for His Presence. Palaces, sumptuous, innumerable, are raised to His honour; His image, as in the hour of His deepest humiliation, is triumphantly displayed in the proud city, in the open country, in the corners of streets, on the tops of mountains. It sanctifies the ancestral hall, the closet, and the bedchamber; it is the subject for the exercise of the highest genius in the imitative arts. It is worn next the heart in life; it is held before the failing eyes in death. Here, then, is One who is *not* a mere name, who is not a mere fiction, who is a reality. He is dead and gone, but still He lives,—lives as a living, energetic thought of successive generations, as the awful motive-power of a thousand great events. He has done without effort what others with life-long struggles have not done. Can He be less than Divine? Who is He but the Creator Himself; who is sovereign over His own works, towards whom our eyes and hearts turn instinctively, because He is our Father and our God?"[49]

Here I end my specimens, among the many which might be given, of the arguments adducible for Christianity. I have dwelt upon them, in order to show how I would apply the principles of this Essay to the proof of its divine origin. Christianity is addressed, both as regards its evidences and its contents, to minds which are in the normal condition of human nature, as believing in God and in a future judgment. Such minds it addresses both through the intellect and through the imagination; creating a certitude of its truth by arguments too various for direct enumeration, too personal and deep for words, too powerful and concurrent for refutation. Nor need reason come first and faith second (though this is the logical order), but one and the same teaching is in different aspects both object and proof, and elicits one complex act both of inference and of assent. It speaks to us one by one, and it is received by us one by one, as the counterpart, so to say, of ourselves, and is real as we are real.

In the sacred words of its Divine Author and Object concerning Himself, "I am the Good Shepherd, and I know Mine, and Mine know Me. My sheep hear My voice, and I know them, and they follow Me. And I give them everlasting life, and they shall never perish; and no man shall pluck them out of My hand."

---

[49] *Occas. Serm.*, pp. 49–51.

Difficulties in the Scripture Proof of Rites, Ceremonies, and Customs[†]

T HOSE WHO commonly urge the objection which is now to be considered, viz., the want of adequate Scripture evidence for the Church creed, have, I feel sure, no right to make it; that is, *they* are *inconsistent* in making it; inasmuch as they cannot consistently find fault with a person who believes more than they do, unless they cease to believe just so much as they do believe. They ought, on their own principles, to doubt or disown much which happily they do not doubt or disown. This then is the direct, appropriate, polemical answer to them, or (as it is called) *an argumentum ad hominem.* "Look at home, and say, if you can, *why* you believe this or that, which you do believe: whatever reasons you give for your own belief in one point, this or that article, of your Creed, those parallel reasons we can give for our belief in the articles of our Creed. If you are reasonable in believing the one, we are reasonable in believing the other. Either we are reasonable, or you are not so. You ought not to stand where you are; you ought to go further one way or the other." Now it is plain that if this be a sound argument against our assailants, it is a most convincing one; and it is obviously very hard and very unfair if we are to be deprived of the use of it. And yet a cautious mind will ever use it with anxiety; not that it is not most effective, but because it may be (as it were) too effective: it may drive the parties in question the wrong way, and make things worse instead of better. It only undertakes to show that they are inconsistent in their present opinions; and from this inconsistency it is plain they can escape, by going further either one way or the other—by adding to their creed, or by giving it up altogether. It is then what is familiarly called a kill-or-cure remedy. Certainly it is better to be inconsistent, than to be consistently wrong—to hold some truth amid error, than to hold nothing but error—to believe than to doubt. Yet when I show a man that he is inconsistent, I make him decide whether of the two he loves better, the portion of truth or the portion of error, which he already holds. If he loves the truth better, he will abandon the error; if the error, he will abandon the truth. And this is a fearful and anxious trial to put him under, and one cannot but feel loth to

---

[†] Excerpt from *Discussions and Arguments* (1872), Part III, Lecture 1. Difficulties in the Scripture Proof of the Catholic Creed. The title here is editorial.

have recourse to it. One feels that perhaps it may be better to keep silence, and to let him, in shallowness and presumption, assail one's own position with impunity, than to retort, however justly, his weapons on himself;—better for oneself to seem a bigot, than to make him a scoffer.

Thus, for instance, a person who denies the Apostolical Succession of the Ministry, because it is not clearly taught in Scripture, ought, I conceive, if consistent, to deny the divinity of the Holy Ghost, which is nowhere literally stated in Scripture. Yet there is something so dreadful in his denying the latter, that one may often feel afraid to show him his inconsistency; lest, rather than admit the Apostolical Succession, he should consent to deny that the Holy Ghost is God. This is one of the great delicacies of disputing on the subject before us: yet, all things considered, I think, it only avails for the cautious use, not the abandonment, of the argument in question. For it is our plain duty to preach and defend the truth in a straightforward way. Those who are to stumble must stumble, rather than the heirs of grace should not hear. While we offend and alienate one man, we secure another; if we drive one man further the wrong way, we drive another further the right way. The cause of truth, the heavenly company of saints, gains on the whole more in one way than in the other. A wavering or shallow mind does perhaps as much harm to others as a mind that is consistent in error, nay, is in no very much better state itself; for if it has not developed into systematic scepticism, merely because it has not had the temptation, its present conscientiousness is not worth much. Whereas he who is at present obeying God under imperfect knowledge has a claim on His Ministers for their doing all in their power towards his obtaining further knowledge. He who admits the doctrine of the Holy Trinity, in spite of feeling its difficulties, whether in itself or in its proof,—who submits to the indirectness of the Scripture evidence as regards that particular doctrine,—has a right to be told those other doctrines, such as the Apostolical Succession, which are as certainly declared in Scripture, yet not more directly and prominently, and which will be as welcome to him, when known, because they are in Scripture, as those which he already knows. It is therefore our duty to do our part, and leave the event to God, begging Him to bless, yet aware that, whenever He visits, He divides.

In saying this, I by no means would imply that the only argument in behalf of our believing more than the generality of men believe at present, is, that else we ought in consistency to believe less—far from it indeed; but this argument is the one that comes first, and is the most obvious and the most striking. Nor do I mean to say—far from it also—that all on whom it is urged, *will* in fact go one way or the other; the many will remain pretty much where education and habit have placed them, and at least they will not confess that they are affected by any new argument at all. But of course when one speaks of anxiety about the effect of a certain argument, one speaks of cases in which it will have effect, not of those in which it will not. Where it *has* effect, I say, that effect may be for good *or* for evil, and that is an anxious thing.

1.

Now then, first, let me state the objection itself, which is to be considered. It may be thrown into one or other of the following forms: that "if Scripture laid such stress, as we do, upon the ordinances of Baptism, Holy Eucharist, Church Union, Ministerial Power, Apostolical Succession, Absolution, and other rites and ceremonies,—upon external, or what is sometimes called formal religion,—it would not in its general tenor make such merely indirect mention of them;—that it would speak of them as plainly and frequently as we always speak of them now; whereas every one must allow that there is next to nothing on the surface of Scripture about them, and very little even under the surface of a satisfactory character." Descending into particulars, we shall have it granted us, perhaps, that Baptism is often mentioned in the Epistles, and its spiritual benefits; but "its peculiarity as the *one plenary* remission of sin," it will be urged, "is not insisted on with such frequency and earnestness as might be expected—chiefly in one or two passages of one Epistle, and there obscurely" (in Heb. vi. and x.) Again, "the doctrine of Absolution is made to rest on but one or two texts (in Matt. xvi. and John xx.), with little or no practical exemplification of it in the Epistles, where it was to be expected. Why," it may be asked, "are not the Apostles continually urging their converts to rid themselves of sin after Baptism, as best they can, by penance, confession, absolution, satisfaction? Again, why are Christ's ministers nowhere called Priests? or, at most, in one or two obscure passages (as in Rom. xv. 16)? Why is not the Lord's Supper expressly said to be a Sacrifice? why is the Lord's Table called an Altar but once or twice (Matt. v. and Heb. xiii.), even granting these passages refer to it? why is consecration of the elements expressly mentioned only in one passage (1 Cor. x.) in addition to our Lord's original institution of them? why is there but once or twice express mention made at all of the Holy Eucharist, all through the Apostolic Epistles, and what there is said, said chiefly in one Epistle? why is there so little said about Ordination? about the appointment of a Succession of Ministers? about the visible Church (as in 1 Tim. iii. 15)? why but one or two passages on the duty of fasting?"

"In short, is not (it may be asked) the state of the evidence for all these doctrines just this—a few striking texts at most, scattered up and down the inspired Volume, or one or two particular passages of one particular Epistle, or a number of texts which may mean, but need not mean, what they are said by

493

Churchmen to mean, which say something looking like what is needed, but with little strength and point, inadequately and unsatisfactorily? Why then are we thus to be put off? why is our earnest desire of getting at the truth to be trifled with? is it conceivable that, if these doctrines were from God, He would not tell us plainly? why does He make us to doubt? why does 'He keep us in suspense?' [John x. 24.]—it is impossible He should do so. Let us, then, have none of these expedients, these makeshift arguments, this patchwork system, these surmises and conjectures, and here a little and there a little, but give us some broad, trustworthy, masterly view of doctrine, give us some plain intelligible interpretation of the sacred Volume, such as will approve itself to all educated minds, as being really gained from the text, and not from previous notions which are merely brought to Scripture, and which seek to find a sanction in it. Such a broad comprehensive view of Holy Scripture is most assuredly fatal to the Church doctrines." "But this (it will be urged) is not all; there are texts in the New Testament actually inconsistent with the Church system of teaching. For example, what can be stronger against the sanctity of particular places, nay of any institutions, persons, or rites at all, than our Lord's declaration, that 'God is a Spirit, and they that worship Him, must worship Him in spirit and in truth'? or against the Eucharistic Sacrifice, than St. Paul's contrast in Heb. x. between the Jewish sacrifices and the one Christian Atonement? or can Baptism really have the gifts which are attributed to it in the Catholic or Church system, considering how St. Paul says, that all rites are done away, and that faith is all in all?"

Such is the sort of objection which it is proposed now to consider.

2.

My first answer to it is grounded on the *argumentum ad hominem* of which I have already spoken. That is, I shall show that, if the objection proves anything, it proves too much for the purposes of those who use it; that it leads to conclusions beyond those to which they would confine it; and if it tells for them, it tells for those whom they would not hesitate to consider heretical or unbelieving.

Now the argument in question proves too much, first, in this way, that it shows that external religion is not only not important or necessary, but not allowable. If, for instance, when our Saviour said, "Woman, believe Me, the hour cometh, when ye shall neither in this mountain, nor yet at Jerusalem, worship the Father . . . The hour cometh, and now is, when the true worshippers shall worship the Father in spirit and in truth: for the Father seeketh such to worship Him. God is a Spirit, and they that worship Him must worship Him in spirit and in truth," [John iv. 21–24.]—if He means that the external local worship of the Jews was so to be abolished, that no external local worship should again be enjoined, that the Gospel worship was but mental, stripped of everything material or sensible, and offered in that simple spirit and truth which exists in heaven, if so, it is plain that all external religion is not only not imperative under the Gospel, but forbidden. This text, if it avails for any thing against Sacraments and Ordinances, avails entirely; it cuts them away root and branch. It says, not that they are unimportant, but that they are not to be. It does not leave them at our option. Any interpretation which gives an opening to their existing, gives so far an opening to their being important. If the command to worship in spirit and truth is consistent with the permission to worship through certain rites, it is consistent with the duty to worship through them. Why are *we* to have a greater freedom, if I may so speak, than God Himself? why are *we* to choose what rites we please to worship in, and not He choose them?—as if spirituality consisted, not in doing without rites altogether, (a notion which at least is intelligible,) but in our forestalling our Lord and Master in the choice of them. Let us take the text to mean that there shall be no external worship at all, if we will (we shall be wrong, but we shall speak fairly and intelligibly); but, if there may be times, places, ministers, ordinances of worship, although the text speaks of worshipping in spirit and in truth, then, what is there in it to negative the notion of God's having chosen those times, places, ministers, and ordinances, so that if *we* attempt to choose, we shall be committing the very fault of the Jews, who were ever setting up golden calves, planting groves, or consecrating ministers, without authority from God?

And what has been observed of this text, holds good of all arguments drawn, whether from the silence of Scripture about, or its supposed positive statements against, the rites and ordinances of the Church. If obscurity of texts, for instance, about the grace of the Eucharist, be taken as a proof that no great benefit is therein given, it is an argument against there being any benefit. On the other hand, when certain passages are once interpreted to refer to it, the emphatic language used in those passages shows that the benefit is not small. We cannot say that the subject is unimportant, without saying that it is not mentioned at all. Either no gift is given in the Eucharist, or a great gift. If only the sixth chapter of St. John, for instance, does allude to it, it shows it is not merely an edifying rite, but an awful communication beyond words. Again, if the phrase, "the communication of the Body of Christ," used by St. Paul, means any gift, it means a great one. You may say, if you will, that it does not mean any gift at all, but means only a representation or figure of the communication; this I call explaining away, but still it is intelligible; but I do not see how, if it is to be taken literally as a real *communication* of something, it can be other than a communication of *His Body*. Again, though the Lord's

Table be but twice called an Altar in Scripture, yet, granting that it *is* meant in those passages, it is there spoken of so solemnly, that it matters not though it be nowhere else spoken of. "We have an Altar, whereof they have no right to eat which serve the tabernacle." We do not know of the existence of the Ordinance except in the knowledge of its importance; and in corroboration and explanation of this matter of fact, let it be well observed that St. Paul expressly declares that the Jewish rites are *not* to be practised because they are *not* important.

This is one way in which this argument proves too much; so that they who for the sake of decency or edification, or from an imaginative turn of mind, delight in Ordinances, yet think they may make them for themselves, in that those ordinances bring no special blessing with them, such men contradict the Gospel as plainly as those who attribute a mystical virtue to them,—nay more so; for if any truth is clear, it is, that such ordinances as are without virtue are abolished by the Gospel, this being St. Paul's very argument against the use of the Jewish rites.

3.

Now as to the other point of view in which the argument in question proves too much for the purpose of those who use it:—If it be a good argument against the truth of the Apostolical Succession and similar doctrines, that so little is said about them in Scripture, this is quite as good an argument against nearly all the doctrines which are held by any one who is called a Christian in any sense of the word; as a few instances will show.

(1.) First, as to Ordinances and Precepts. There is not a single text in the Bible enjoining infant baptism: the Scripture warrant on which we baptize infants consists of inferences carefully made from various texts. How is it that St. Paul does not in his Epistles remind parents of so great a duty, if it is a duty?

Again, there is not a single text telling us to keep holy the first day of the week, and that *instead* of the seventh. God hallowed the seventh day, yet we now observe the first. Why do we do this? Our Scripture warrant for doing so is such as this: "*since* the Apostles met on the first day of the week, *therefore* the first day is to be hallowed; and *since* St. Paul says the Sabbath is abolished, *therefore* the seventh day (which is the Sabbath) is not to be hallowed:"—these are true inferences, but very indirect surely. The duty is not on the surface of Scripture. We might infer,—though incorrectly, still we might infer,—that St. Paul meant that the command in the second chapter of Genesis was repealed, and that now there is no sacred day at all in the seven, though meetings for prayer on Sunday are right and proper. There is nothing on the surface of Scripture to prove that the sacredness conferred in the beginning on the seventh day now by transference attaches to the first.

Again, there is scarcely a text enjoining our going to Church for joint worship. St. Paul happens in one place of his Epistle to the Hebrews, to warn us against forgetting to assemble together for prayer. Our Saviour says that where two or three are gathered together, He is in the midst of them; yet this alludes in the first instance not to public worship, but to Church Councils and censures, quite a distinct subject. And in the Acts and Epistles we meet with instances or precepts in favour of joint worship; yet there is nothing express to show that it is necessary for all times,—nothing more express than there is to show that in 1 Cor. vii. St. Paul meant that an unmarried state is better at all times,—nothing which does not need collecting and inferring with minute carefulness from Scripture. The first disciples did pray together, and so in like manner the first disciples did not marry. St. Paul tells those who were in a state of distress to pray together so much the more *as they see the day approaching*—and he says that celibacy is "good *for the present distress*." The same remarks might be applied to the question of community of goods. On the other hand, our Lord did not use social prayer: even when with His disciples He prayed by Himself; and His directions in Matt. vi. about *private* prayer, with the silence which He observes about *public*, might be as plausibly adduced as an argument against public, as the same kind of silence in Scripture concerning turning to the east, or making the sign of the Cross, or concerning commemorations for the dead in Christ, accompanied with its warnings against formality and ceremonial abuses, is now commonly urged as an argument against these latter usages.

Again:—there is no text in the New Testament which enjoins us to "establish" Religion (as the phrase is), or to make it national, and to give the Church certain honour and power; whereas our Lord's words, "My kingdom is not of this world" (John xviii. 36), may be interpreted to discountenance such a proceeding. We consider that it is right to establish the Church on the ground of mere deductions, though of course true ones, from the sacred text; such as St. Paul's using his rights as a Roman citizen.

There is no text which allows us to take oaths. The words of our Lord and St. James look plainly the other way. Why then do we take them? We *infer* that it is allowable to do so, from finding that St. Paul uses such expressions as "I call God for a record upon my soul"—"The things which I write unto you, behold, before God, I lie not" (2 Cor. i. 23; Gal. i. 20); these we *argue*, and rightly, are equivalent to an oath, and a precedent for us.

Again, considering God has said, "Whoso sheddeth man's blood, by man shall his blood be shed," it seems a very singular power which we give to the Civil Magistrate to take away life. It ought to rest, one might suppose, on some very clear permission given in Scripture. Now, on what does it rest? on one or two words of an Apostle casually introduced into Scripture, as far as anything is casual,—on St. Paul's saying in a parenthesis, "he (the magistrate) beareth not the *sword* in vain;" and he is speaking of a *heathen* magistrate, *not* of Christian.

Once more:—On how many texts does the prohibition of polygamy depend, if we set about counting them?

(2.) So much for ordinances and practices: next, consider how Doctrine will stand, if the said rule of interpretation is to hold.

If the Eucharist is never distinctly called a Sacrifice, or Christian Ministers never called Priests, still, let me ask (as I have already done), is the Holy Ghost ever expressly called God in Scripture? Nowhere; we infer it from what is said then; we compare parallel passages.

If the words Altar, Absolution, or Succession, are not in Scripture (supposing it), neither is the word Trinity.

Again: how do we know that the New Testament is inspired? does it anywhere declare this of itself? nowhere; *how*, then, do we know it? we infer it from the circumstance that the very office of the Apostles who wrote it was to publish the Christian Revelation, and from the Old Testament being said by St. Paul to be inspired.

Again: whence do Protestants derive their common notion, that every one may gain his knowledge of revealed truth from Scripture for himself?

Again: consider whether the doctrine of the Atonement may not be explained away by those who explain away the doctrine of the Eucharist: if the expressions used concerning the latter are merely figurative, so may be those used of the former.

Again: on how many texts does the doctrine of Original Sin rest, that is, the doctrine that we are individually born under God's displeasure, in consequence of the sin of Adam? on one or two.

Again: how do we prove the doctrine of justification by faith only? it is nowhere declared in Scripture. St. Paul does but speak of justification by faith, not by faith only, and St. James actually denies that it is by faith only. Yet we think right to infer, that there is a correct sense in which it is by faith only; though an Apostle has in so many words said just the contrary. Is any of the special Church doctrines about the power of Absolution, the Christian Priesthood, or the danger of sin after Baptism, so disadvantageously circumstanced in point of evidence as this, "articulus," as Luther called it, "stantis ut cadentis ecclesiæ"?

On the whole, then, I ask, on how many special or palmary texts do any of the doctrines or rites which we hold depend? what doctrines or rites would be left to us, if we demanded the clearest and fullest evidence, before we believed anything? what would the Gospel consist of? would there be any Revelation at all left? Some all-important doctrines indeed at first sight certainly would remain in the New Testament, such as the divinity of Christ, the unity of God, the supremacy of divine grace, our election in Christ, the resurrection of the body, and eternal life or death to the righteous or sinners; but little besides. Shall we give up the divinity of the Holy Ghost, original sin, the Atonement, the inspiration of the New Testament, united worship, the Sacraments, and Infant Baptism? Let us do so. Well:—I will venture to say, that then we shall go on to find difficulties as regards those other doctrines, as the divinity of Christ, which at first sight seem to be in Scripture certainly; they are only *more* clearly there than the others, not so clearly stated as to be secured from specious objections. We shall have difficulties about the *meaning* of the word "everlasting," as applied to punishment, about the *compatibility* of divine grace with free-will, about the *possibility* of the resurrection of the body, and about the *sense* in which Christ is God. The inquirer who rejects a doctrine which has but one text in its favour, on the ground that if it were important it would have more, may, even in a case when a doctrine is mentioned often, always find occasion to wonder that still it is not mentioned in this or that particular place, where it might be expected. When he is pressed with such a text as St. Thomas's confession, "My Lord and my God," he will ask, But why did our Lord say but seven days before to St. Mary Magdalen, "I ascend to My Father and your Father, to My God and your God"? When he is pressed with St. Peter's confession, "Lord, Thou knowest all things,—Thou knowest that I love Thee," he will ask, "But why does Christ say of Himself, that He does not know the last day, but only the Father?" Indeed, I may truly say, the more arguments there are for a certain doctrine found in Scripture, the more objections will be found against it; so that, on the whole, after all, the Scripture evidence, even for the divinity of Christ, will be found in fact as little able to satisfy the cautious reasoner, when he is fairly engaged to discuss it, as that for Infant Baptism, great as is the difference of strength in the evidence for the one and for the other. And the history of these last centuries bears out this remark.

I conclude, then, that there must be some fault somewhere in this specious argument; that it does not follow that a doctrine or rite is not divine, because it is not directly stated in Scripture; that there are some wise and unknown reasons for doctrines being, as we find them, not clearly stated there.

Doctrines Embodied in Rites[†]

THE DOCTRINES of the Church are after all not mere matters of opinion; they were not in early times mere ideas in the mind to which no one could appeal, each individual having his own, but they were external facts, quite as much as the books of Scripture;—how so? Because they were embodied in rites and ceremonies. A usage, custom, or monument, has the same kind of identity, is in the same sense common property, and admits of a common appeal, as a book. When a writer appeals to the custom of the Sign of the Cross, or the Baptism of infants, or the Sacrifice or the Consecration of the Eucharist, or Episcopal Ordination, he is not speaking of an opinion in his mind, but of something external to it, and is as trustworthy as when he says that the Acts of the Apostles is written by St. Luke. Now such usages are symbols of common, not individual opinions, and more or less involve the doctrines they symbolize. Is it not implied, for instance, in the fact of priests only consecrating the Eucharist, that it is a gift which others have not? in the Eucharist being offered to God, that it *is* an offering? in penance being exacted of offenders, that it is right to impose it? in children being exorcised, that they are by nature children of wrath, and inhabited by Satan? On the other hand, when the Fathers witness to the inspiration of Scripture, they are surely as much witnessing to a mere doctrine,—not to the book itself, but to an opinion,—as when they bear witness to the grace of Baptism.

[†] Excerpt from *Discussions and Arguments* (1872), Part III, Lecture 8, Difficulties of Jewish and of Christian Faith compared. The title here is editorial.

Meditations & Devotions[†]

☙

Twelve Meditations & Intercessions for Good Friday

(1) JESUS THE LAMB OF GOD

BEHOLD the Lamb of God, behold Him who taketh away the sins of the world. So spoke St. John Baptist, when he saw our Lord coming to him. And in so speaking, he did but appeal to that title under which our Lord was known from the beginning. Just Abel showed forth his faith in Him by offering of the firstlings of his flock. Abraham, in place of his son Isaac whom God spared, offered the like for a sacrifice. The Israelites were enjoined to sacrifice once a year, at Easter time, a lamb—one lamb for each family, a lamb without blemish—to be eaten whole, all but the blood, which was sprinkled, as their protection, about their house doors. The Prophet Isaias speaks of our Lord under the same image: "He shall be led as a sheep to the slaughter, and shall be dumb as a lamb before his shearers" (liii. 7); and all this because "He was wounded for our iniquities, He was bruised for our sins; . . . by His bruises we are healed" (liii. 5). And in like manner the Holy Evangelist St. John, in the visions of the Apocalypse, thus speaks of Him: "I saw, . . . (Apoc. v. 6), and behold a lamb standing as it were slain;" and then he saw all the blessed "fall down before the Lamb," . . . (verses 8, 9), and they sung a new canticle saying, "Thou wast slain, and hast redeemed us to God in Thy blood, out of every tribe and tongue and people and nation" (verse 9) . . . Worthy is the Lamb that was slain, to receive power, and divinity, and wisdom, and strength, and honour, and glory, and benediction" (verse 12).

This is Jesus Christ, who when darkness, sin, guilt and misery had overspread the earth, came down from Heaven, took our nature upon Him, and shed His precious blood upon the Cross for all men.

Let us pray for all pagan nations, that they may be converted.

O Lord Jesus Christ, O King of the whole world, O Hope and Expectation of all nations, O Thou who hast bought all men for Thy own at the price

---

[†] This precious volume of Newman's spiritual writings was edited by Rev. W.P. Neville and published in 1893.

of Thy most precious blood, look down in pity upon all races who are spread over the wide earth, and impart to them the knowledge of Thy truth. Remember, O Lord, Thy own most bitter sufferings of soul and body in Thy betrayal, Thy passion and Thy crucifixion, and have mercy upon their souls. Behold, O Lord, but a portion of mankind has heard of Thy Name—but a portion even professes to adore Thee—and yet thousands upon thousands in the East and the West, in the North and the South, hour after hour, as each hour comes, are dropping away from this life into eternity. Remember, O my dear Lord, and lay it to heart, that to the dishonour of Thy name, and to the triumph of Thine enemies, fresh victims are choking up the infernal pit, and are taking up their dwelling there for ever. Listen to the intercessions of Thy Saints, let Thy Mother plead with Thee, let not the prayers of Holy Church Thy Spouse be offered up in vain. Impute not to the poor heathen their many sins, but visit the earth quickly and give all men to know, to believe, and to serve Thee, in whom is our salvation, life and resurrection, who with the Father, etc.

(12) JESUS OUR DAILY SACRIFICE

O UR LORD not only offered Himself as a Sacrifice on the Cross, but He makes Himself a perpetual, a daily sacrifice, to the end of time. In the Holy Mass that One Sacrifice on the Cross once offered is renewed, continued, applied to our benefit. He seems to say, My Cross was raised up 1800 years ago, and only for a few hours—and very few of my servants were present there—but I intend to bring millions into my Church. For their sakes then I will perpetuate my Sacrifice, that each of them may be as though they had severally been present on Calvary. I will offer Myself up day by day to the Father, that every one of my followers may have the opportunity to offer his petitions to Him, sanctified and recommended by the all-meritorious virtue of my Passion. Thus I will be a Priest for ever, after the order of Melchisedech—My priests shall stand at the Altar—but not they, but I rather, will offer. I will not let them offer mere bread and wine, but I myself will be present upon the Altar instead, and I will offer up myself invisibly, while they perform the outward rite. And thus the Lamb that was slain once for all, though He is ascended on high, ever remains a victim from His miraculous presence in Holy Mass under the figure and appearance of mere earthly and visible symbols.

Let us pray for all who day by day have calls upon us.

My Lord Jesus Christ, Thou hast given me this great gift, that I am allowed, not only to pray for myself, but to intercede for others in Thy Holy Mass. Therefore, O Lord, I pray Thee to give all grace and blessing upon this town and every inhabitant of it—upon the Catholic Church in it, for our Bishop, and his clergy, and for all Catholic places of worship and their congregations. I pray Thee to bless and prosper all the good works and efforts of all priests, religious, and pious Catholics—I pray for all the sick, all the suffering, all the poor, all the oppressed—I pray for all prisoners—I pray for all evil doers. I pray for all ranks in the community—I pray for the Queen and Royal Family—for the Houses of Parliament—for the judges and magistrates—for all our soldiers—for all who defend us in ships—I pray for all who are in peril and danger. I pray for all who have benefited me, befriended me, or aided me. I pray for all who have asked my prayers—I pray for all whom I have forgotten. Bring us all after the troubles of this life into the haven of peace, and reunite us all together for ever, O my dear Lord, in Thy glorious heavenly kingdom.

❦

God with us

(2) JESUS THE HIDDEN GOD

Noli incredulus esse, sed fidelis.—Be not faithless, but believing.

I ADORE THEE, O my God, who art so awful, because Thou art hidden and unseen! I adore Thee, and I desire to live by faith in what I do not see; and considering what I am, a disinherited outcast, I think it has indeed gone well with me that I am allowed, O my unseen Lord and Saviour, to worship Thee anyhow. O my God, I know that it is sin that has separated between Thee and me. I know it is sin that has brought on me the penalty of ignorance. Adam, before he fell, was visited by Angels. Thy Saints, too, who keep close to Thee, see visions, and in many ways are brought into sensible perception of Thy presence. But to a sinner such as I am, what is left but to possess Thee without seeing Thee? Ah, should I not rejoice at having that most extreme mercy and favour of possessing Thee at all? It is sin that has reduced me to live by faith, as I must at best, and should I not rejoice in such a life, O Lord my God? I see and know, O my good Jesus, that the only way in which I can possibly approach Thee in this world is the way of faith, faith in what Thou hast told me, and I thankfully follow this only way which Thou hast given me.

2. O my God, Thou dost over-abound in mercy! To live by faith is my necessity, from my present state of being and from my sin; but Thou hast pronounced a blessing on it. Thou hast said that I am more blessed if I believe on Thee, than if I saw Thee. Give me to share that blessedness, give it to me in its fulness. Enable me to believe as if I saw; let me have Thee always before me as if Thou wert always bodily and sensibly present. Let me ever hold communion with Thee, my hidden, but my living God. Thou art in my innermost heart. Thou art the life of my life. Every breath I breathe, every thought of my

mind, every good desire of my heart, is from the presence within me of the unseen God. By nature and by grace Thou art in me. I see Thee not in the material world except dimly, but I recognise Thy voice in my own intimate consciousness. I turn round and say Rabboni. O be ever thus with me; and if I am tempted to leave *Thee*, do not Thou, O my God, leave *me*!

3. O my dear Saviour, would that I had any right to ask to be allowed to make reparation to Thee for all the unbelief of the world, and all the insults offered to Thy Name, Thy Word, Thy Church, and the Sacrament of Thy Love! But, alas, I have a long score of unbelief and ingratitude of my own to atone for. Thou art in the Sacrifice of the Mass, Thou art in the Tabernacle, verily and indeed, in flesh and blood; and the world not only disbelieves, but mocks at this gracious truth. Thou didst warn us long ago by Thyself and by Thy Apostles that Thou wouldest hide Thyself from the world. The prophecy is fulfilled more than ever now; but *I* know what the world knows not. O accept my homage, my praise, my adoration!—let me at least not be found wanting. I cannot help the sins of others—but one at least of those whom Thou hast redeemed shall turn round and with a loud voice glorify God. The more men scoff, the more will I believe in Thee, the good God, the good Jesus, the hidden Lord of life, who hast done me nothing else but good from the very first moment that I began to live.

❦

The Holy Sacrifice

(1) THE MASS

I ADORE THEE, O my Lord God, with the most profound awe for thy passion and crucifixion, in sacrifice for our sins. Thou didst' suffer incommunicable sufferings in Thy sinless soul. Thou wast exposed in Thy innocent body to ignominious torments, to mingled pain and shame. Thou wast stripped and fiercely scourged, Thy sacred body vibrating under the heavy flail as trees under the blast. Thou wast, when thus mangled, hung up upon the Cross, naked, a spectacle for all to see Thee quivering and dying. What does all this imply, O Mighty God! What a depth is here which we cannot fathom! My God, I know well, Thou couldst have saved us at Thy word, without Thyself suffering; but Thou didst choose to purchase us at the price of Thy Blood. I look on Thee, the Victim lifted up on Calvary, and I know and protest that that death of Thine was an expiation for the sins of the whole world. I believe and know, that Thou alone couldst have offered a meritorious atonement; for it was Thy Divine Nature which gave Thy sufferings worth. Rather then than I should perish according to my deserts, Thou wast nailed to the Tree and didst die.

2. Such a sacrifice was not to be forgotten. It was not to be—it could not be—a mere event in the world's history, which was to be done and over, and was to pass away except in its obscure, unrecognised effects. If that great deed was what we believe it to be, what we know it is, it must remain present, though past; it must be a standing fact for all times. Our own careful reflection upon it tells us this; and therefore, when we are told that Thou, O Lord, though Thou hast ascended to glory, hast renewed and perpetuated Thy sacrifice to the end of all things, not only is the news most touching and joyful, as testifying to so tender a Lord and Saviour, but it carries with it the full assent and sympathy of our reason. Though we neither could, nor would have dared, anticipate so wonderful a doctrine, yet we adore its very suitableness to Thy perfections, as well as its infinite compassionateness for us, now that we are told of it. Yes, my Lord, though Thou hast left the world, Thou art daily offered up in the Mass; and, though Thou canst not suffer pain and death, Thou dost still subject Thyself to indignity and restraint to carry out to the full Thy mercies towards us. Thou dost humble Thyself daily; for, being infinite, Thou couldst not end Thy humiliation while they existed for whom Thou didst submit to it. So Thou remainest a Priest for ever.

3. My Lord, I offer Thee myself in turn as a sacrifice of thanksgiving. Thou hast died for me, and I in turn make myself over to Thee. I am not my own. Thou hast bought me; I will by my own act and deed complete the purchase. My wish is to be separated from everything of this world; to cleanse myself simply from sin; to put away from me even what is innocent, if used for its own sake, and not for Thine. I put away reputation and honour, and influence, and power, for my praise and strength shall be in Thee. Enable me to carry out what I profess.

(2) Holy Communion

MY GOD, who can be inhabited by Thee, except the pure and holy? Sinners may come to Thee, but to whom shouldst Thou come except to the sanctified? My God, I adore Thee as the Holiest; and, when Thou didst come upon earth, Thou didst prepare a holy habitation for Thyself in the most chaste womb of the Blessed Virgin. Thou didst make a dwelling place special for Thyself. She did not receive Thee without first being prepared for Thee; for from the moment that she was at all, she was filled with Thy grace, so that she never knew sin. And so she went on increasing in grace and merit year after year, till the time came, when Thou didst send down the Archangel to signify to her Thy presence within her. So holy must be the dwelling place of the Highest. I adore and glorify Thee, O Lord my God, for Thy great holiness.

2. O my God, holiness becometh Thy House, and yet Thou dost make Thy abode in my breast. My Lord, my Saviour, to me Thou comest, hidden under the semblance of earthly things, yet in that very flesh and blood which Thou didst take from Mary. Thou, who didst first inhabit Mary's breast, dost come to me. My God, Thou seest me; I cannot see myself. Were I ever so good a judge about myself, ever so unbiassed, and with ever so correct a rule of judging, still, from my very nature, I cannot look at myself, and view myself truly and wholly. But Thou, as Thou comest to me, contemplatest me. When I say, *Domine, non sum dignus*—"Lord, I am not worthy"—Thou whom I am addressing, alone understandest in their fulness the words which I use. Thou seest how unworthy so great a sinner is to receive the One Holy God, whom the Seraphim adore with trembling. Thou seest, not only the stains and scars of past sins, but the mutilations, the deep cavities, the chronic disorders which they have left in my soul. Thou seest the innumerable living sins, though they be not mortal, living in their power and presence, their guilt, and their penalties, which clothe me. Thou seest all my bad habits, all my mean principles, all wayward lawless thoughts, my multitude of infirmities and miseries, yet Thou comest. Thou seest most perfectly how little I really feel what I am now saying, yet Thou comest. O my God, left to myself should I not perish under the awful splendour and the consuming fire of Thy Majesty. Enable me to bear Thee, lest I have to say with Peter, "Depart from me, for I am a sinful man, O Lord!"

3. My God, enable me to bear Thee, for Thou alone canst. Cleanse my heart and mind from all that is past. Wipe out clean all my recollections of evil. Rid me from all languor, sickliness, irritability, feebleness of soul. Give me a true perception of things unseen, and make me truly, practically, and in the details of life, prefer Thee to anything on earth, and the future world to the present. Give me courage, a true instinct determining between right and wrong, humility in all things, and a tender longing love of Thee.

(3) THE FOOD OF THE SOUL

Sitivit in Te anima mea.—For Thee my soul hath thirsted.

IN THEE, O Lord, all things live, and Thou dost give them their food. *Oculi omnium in Te sperant*—"the eyes of all hope in Thee." To the beasts of the field Thou givest meat and drink. They live on day by day, because Thou dost give them day by day to live. And, if Thou givest not, they feel their misery at once. Nature witnesses to this great truth, for they are visited at once with great agony, and they cry out and wildly wander about, seeking what they need. But, as to us Thy children, Thou feedest us with another food. Thou knowest, O my God, who madest us, that nothing can satisfy us but Thyself, and therefore Thou hast caused Thy own self to be meat and drink to us. O most adorable mystery! O most stupendous of mercies! Thou most Glorious, and Beautiful, and Strong, and Sweet, Thou didst know well that nothing else would support our immortal natures, our frail hearts, but Thyself; and so Thou didst take a human flesh and blood, that they, as being the flesh and blood of God, might be our life.

2. O what an awful thought! Thou dealest otherwise with others, but, as to me, the flesh and blood of God is my sole life. I shall perish without it; yet shall I not perish with it and by it? How can I raise myself to such an act as to feed upon God? O my God, I am in a strait—shall I go forward, or shall I go back? I will go forward: I will go to meet Thee. I will open my mouth, and receive Thy gift. I do so with great awe and fear, but what else can I do? to whom should I go but to Thee? Who can save me but Thou? Who can cleanse me but Thou? Who can make me overcome myself but Thou? Who can raise my body from the grave but Thou? Therefore I come to Thee in all these my necessities, in fear, but in faith.

3. My God, Thou art my life; if I leave Thee, I cannot but thirst. Lost spirits thirst in hell, because they have not God. They thirst, though they fain would have it otherwise, from the necessity of their original nature. But I, my God, wish to thirst for Thee with a better thirst. I wish to be clad in that new nature, which so longs for Thee from loving Thee, as to overcome in me the fear of coming to Thee. I come to Thee, O Lord, not only because I am unhappy without Thee, not only because I feel I need Thee, but because Thy grace draws me on to seek Thee for Thy own sake, because Thou art so glorious and beautiful. I come in great fear, but in greater love. O may I never lose, as years pass away, and the heart shuts up, and all things are a burden, let me never lose this youthful, eager, elastic love of Thee. Make Thy grace supply the failure of nature. Do the more for me, the less I can do for myself. The more I refuse to open my heart to Thee, so much the fuller and stronger be Thy supernatural visitings, and the more urgent and efficacious Thy presence in me.

※

The Sacred Heart

O SACRED HEART of Jesus, I adore Thee in the oneness of the Personality of the Second Person of the Holy Trinity. Whatever belongs to the Person of Jesus, belongs therefore to God, and is to be worshipped with that one and the same worship which we pay to Jesus. He did not take on Him His human nature, as something distinct and separate from Himself, but as simply, absolutely, eternally His, so as to be included by us in the very thought of Him. I worship Thee, O Heart of Jesus, as being Jesus Himself, as being that Eternal Word in human nature which He took wholly and lives in wholly, and therefore in Thee. Thou art the Heart of the Most High made man. In worshipping Thee, I worship my Incarnate God, Emmanuel. I worship Thee, as bearing a part in that Passion which is my life, for Thou didst burst and break, through agony, in the garden of Gethsemani, and Thy precious contents trickled out, through the veins and pores of the skin, upon the earth. And again, Thou hadst been drained all but dry upon the Cross; and then, after death, Thou wast pierced by the lance, and gavest out the small remains of that inestimable treasure, which is our redemption.

2. My God, my Saviour, I adore Thy Sacred Heart, for that heart is the seat and source of all Thy tenderest human affections for us sinners. It is the instrument and organ of Thy love. It did beat for us. It yearned over us. It ached for us, and for our salvation. It was on fire through zeal, that the glory of God might be manifested in and by us. It is the channel through which has come to us all Thy overflowing human affection, all Thy Divine Charity towards us. All Thy incomprehensible compassion for us, as God and Man, as our Creator and our Redeemer and Judge, has come to us, and comes, in one inseparably mingled stream, through that Sacred Heart. O most Sacred symbol and Sacrament of Love, divine and human, in its fulness, Thou didst save me by Thy divine strength, and Thy human affection, and then at length by that wonder-working blood, wherewith Thou didst overflow.

3. O most Sacred, most loving Heart of Jesus, Thou art concealed in the Holy Eucharist, and Thou beatest for us still. Now as then Thou savest, *Desiderio desideravi*—"With desire I have desired." I worship Thee then with all my best love and awe, with my fervent affection, with my most subdued, most resolved will. O my God, when Thou dost condescend to suffer me to receive Thee, to eat and drink Thee, and Thou for a while takest up Thy abode within me, O make my heart beat with Thy Heart. Purify it of all that is earthly, all that is proud and sensual, all that is hard and cruel, of all perversity, of all disorder, of all deadness. So fill it with Thee, that neither the events of the day nor the circumstances of the time may have power to ruffle it, but that in Thy love and Thy fear it may have peace.

Newman's private chapel at the Birmingham Oratory

Contents Listed by Source & Year of Publication

This list follows the order in which items appear in this volume, but arranges them under their source and year of publication. Where applicable, the feastday with which a sermon is connected has been listed in brackets. If a certain item has been given an editorial title in abstraction from its larger context, this title has been enclosed in braces.

Lectures on the Prophetical Office of the Church (1837)
Lecture 6. On the Abuse of Private Judgment

Preface to *Hymni Ecclesiæ*, Pars I: *E Breviario Parisiensi* (1838)
{On Ecclesiastical Hymns}

Lectures on the Doctrine of Justification (1838)
Lecture 9. Righteousness the Fruit of our Lord's Resurrection

Letter to the Margaret Professor of Divinity on Mr. R. H. Froude's Statements on the Holy Eucharist, in *Via Media,* vol. 2 (1838)
{Witnesses to the Christian Altar}

Parochial & Plain Sermons, volume 4 (1839)
Sermon 5. Reliance on Religious Observances
Sermon 16. Christ Hidden from the World [Christmas Day]
Sermon 18. The Gainsaying of Korah
Sermon 23. Keeping Fast and Festival [Easter Day]

Parochial & Plain Sermons, volume 5 (1840)
Sermon 1. Worship, a Preparation for Christ's Coming [Advent]
Sermon 2. Reverence, a Belief in God's Presence [Adv ent]
Sermon 12. The New Works of the Gospel [Epiphany]

Parochial & Plain Sermons, volume 6 (1842)
Sermon 7. The Cross of Christ the Measure of the World [Lent]
Sermon 19. The Gospel Palaces [Pentecost]
Sermon 20. The Visible Temple [Pentecost]
Sermon 21. Offerings for the Sanctuary [Pentecost]

Parochial & Plain Sermons, volume 7 (1842)
Sermon 6. The Season of Epiphany [Epiphany]
Sermon 11. Attendance on Holy Communion [Eastertide]
Sermon 12. The Gospel Feast
Sermon 13. Love of Religion, a New Nature
Sermon 18. Steadfastness in Old Paths

Oxford University Sermons (1843)
Sermon 9. Wilfulness, the Sin of Saul

Parochial & Plain Sermons, volume 8 (1843)
Sermon 1. Reverence in Worship
Sermon 6. Miracles no Remedy for Unbelief

Sermons on Subjects of the Day (1843)
Sermon 9. Indulgence in Religious Privileges [Rogation Sunday]
Sermon 11. Christian Nobleness
Sermon 15. Continuity between the Jewish & Christian Churches
Sermon 18. Condition of the Members of the Christian Empire
Sermon 25. Feasting in Captivity

Essay on the Development of Christian Doctrine (1845)
Part 1, chapter 2, section 3. {Integrity of Catholic Doctrine}
Part 2, chapter 11, section 2. {Devotion to the Blessed Virgin}

Essays Critical & Historical, Volume 2 (1846)
{The Church as Poet}

Faith and Prejudice (New York: Sheed & Ward, 1956)
Sermon 1. The Omnipotence of God the Reason for Faith & Hope
[Fourth Sunday after Epiphany, 1848]

Loss and Gain (1848)
{The Catholic Church at Worship}

Discourses to Mixed Congregations (1849)
Discourse 3. Men, not Angels, the Priests of the Gospel
Discourse 17. {Growth of the Cultus of Mary}

Certain Difficulties Felt by Anglicans in Catholic Teaching, Volume 1 (1850)
Usages & Ordinances Outward Shape of Inward Reality

Lectures on the Present Position of Catholics in England (1851)
Lecture 6. Prejudice the Life of the Protestant View
Lecture 7. {Relics and Miracles}
Lecture 8. {Confession}

The Idea of a University (1852)
Part 2, ch. 6. {The Duties of a Preacher}

Sermons Preached on Various Occasions (1857)
  Sermon 2. The Religion of the Pharisee, the Religion of Mankind
    [Tenth Sunday after Pentecost]
  Sermon 3. {The Religion of Catholics}
  Sermon 11. Order, the Witness and Instrument of Unity

Apologia Pro Vita Sua (1865)
  Chapter 5. {Transubstantiation}

A Letter Addressed to the Rev. E. B. Pusey, D.D., on Occasion of His Eirenicon
(1865); published in Volume 2 of *Certain Difficulties Felt by Anglicans in
Catholic Teaching* (1900).
  {Devotional Freedom & Excess}

An Essay in Aid of a Grammar of Assent (1870)
  Part II, ch. 10, §2. {Christ, the Surpassing Fulfilment of Prophecies
    and Natural Religion}

Discussions and Arguments (1872)
  Part III, Lecture 1. {Difficulties in the Scripture Proof of Rites,
    Ceremonies, and Customs}
  Part III, Lecture 8. {Doctrines Embodied in Rites}

Meditations & Devotions (1893)

❦

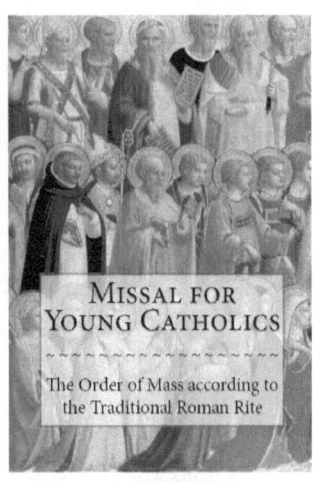

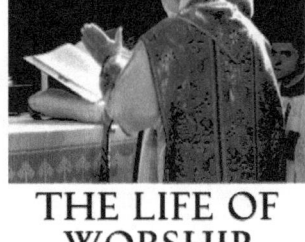
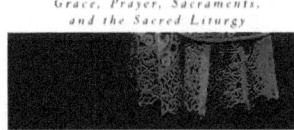

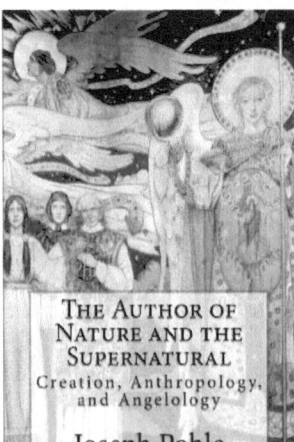
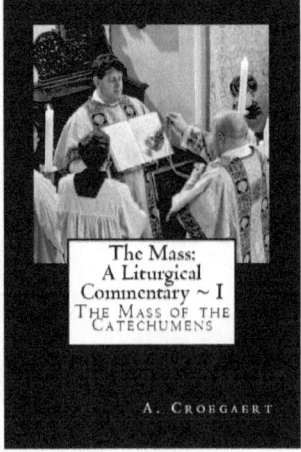
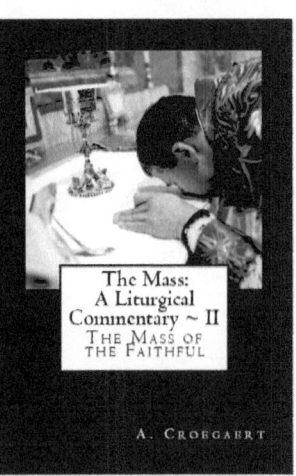

www.ingramcontent.com/pod-product-compliance
Lightning Source LLC
Chambersburg PA
CBHW021602120626
46545CB00001B/22